International Economic Law and the Challenges of the Free Zones

Global Trade Law Series

VOLUME 51

Series Editors

Introduction and Contents/Subjects

The *Global Trade Law Series* addresses key issues in international trade law. It covers a broad range of topics, including WTO dispute settlement, free trade agreements, investment law and arbitration, export control, and compliance with international trade obligations.

Objective & Readership

The volumes published in this series are aimed at offering high-quality analytical information and practical solutions, for practitioners, policy makers and academics.

Frequency of Publication

2-3 new volumes published each year.

The titles published in this series are listed at the end of this volume.

International Economic Law and the Challenges of the Free Zones

Edited by

Julien Chaisse
Jiaxiang Hu

Wolters Kluwer

Published by:
Kluwer Law International B.V.
PO Box 316
2400 AH Alphen aan den Rijn
The Netherlands
E-mail: international-sales@wolterskluwer.com
Website: lrus.wolterskluwer.com

Sold and distributed in North, Central and South America by:
Wolters Kluwer Legal & Regulatory U.S.
7201 McKinney Circle
Frederick, MD 21704
United States of America
Email: customer.service@wolterskluwer.com

Sold and distributed in all other countries by:
Air Business Subscriptions
Rockwood House
Haywards Heath
West Sussex
RH16 3DH
United Kingdom
Email: international-customerservice@wolterskluwer.com

ISBN 978-94-035-0893-1

e-Book: ISBN 978-94-035-0900-6
web-PDF: ISBN 978-94-035-0903-7

Editors

Mr Julien Chaisse is Professor at The Chinese University of Hong Kong (CUHK), Faculty of Law and Advisory Board member, Asian Academy of International Law (AAIL). Dr. Chaisse is an award-winning scholar of international law with a special focus on the regulation and development of economic globalization. His teaching and research include international trade/investment law, international taxation, law of natural resources, and Internet law. Prior to joining CUHK in 2009, Dr Chaisse was a senior research fellow at the World Trade Institute (Switzerland). He also held an appointment as lecturer at elite school Sciences Po Aix (France) and served as a diplomat at the Embassy of France in New Delhi (India). Dr Chaisse held the appointment of Director of the Centre for Financial Regulation and Economic Development at CUHK Law from 2013 to 2017, and has established forward-looking legal projects and events in Hong Kong, including the series of 'Asia FDI Forum', which has become the most prominent conference on foreign investment law and economics in Asia. Since September 2017, he is the Director of the Law Faculty Research Postgraduates Programme (PhD and MPhil). Dr Chaisse has published numerous well-regarded and widely-cited books and articles, such as 'China's International Investment Strategy', Oxford University Press (2019); 'The Regulation of Global Water Services Market', Cambridge University Press (2017); 'International Economic Law and Governance', Oxford University Press (2016); 'Shareholder Protection Reloaded', Stanford Journal of International Law (2016); 'Navigating the Expanding Universe of International Treaties on Foreign Investment', Journal of International Economic Law (2015); 'Maintaining the WTO's Supremacy in the International Trade Order', Journal of International Economic Law (2013); and 'Promises and Pitfalls of the European Union Policy on Foreign Investment', Journal of International Economic Law (2012). In recognition of his outstanding academic performance, Dr Chaisse received the University's Research Excellence Award 2012, Vice-Chancellor's Exemplary Teaching Award 2015, and the Vice-Chancellor's Young Researcher Award 2017. In addition to his professorship, Dr. Chaisse is a well-experienced arbitrator and a leading consultant to international organizations, governments, multinational law firms, and private investors.

Jiaxiang HU is professor of international economic law and director of the Asian Law Center, KuGuan Law School of Shanghai Jiao Tong University, China. He earned a BA degree and an MA degree from Hangzhou University, the MPhil degree in law from Zhejiang University and the PhD degree in law from the University of Edinburg. He is also a visiting scholar of International Economic Law Institute of Georgetown University, the East Asian Studies Center of Harvard University and the Asian Law Institute of National University of Singapore. Professor Hu has been awarded the honors for his excellent teachings from the Ministry of Education, Shanghai Municipality and Shanghai Jiao Tong University. He is the author of seven books and nearly a hundred articles published in those prestigious journals like JIEL. His recent publications include *Regional Cooperation and Free Trade Agreements in Asia* (Brill Publisher 2014), *Finance, Rule of Law and Development in Asia: Perspectives from Singapore, Hong Kong and Mainland China* (Brill Publisher 2016), *From Imitation to Innovation: Legal Education in Asia* (Brill Publisher 2017). Currently, he is also the team leader of several national research programmes including *A Comparative Study on the Regulations of GM Food by Law and Policies in Different Countries* and *The Construction of the Legal Framework of the Free Trade Area of the Asia-Pacific*. Professor HU is teaching International Economic Law to the undergraduates and World Trade Organization (WTO) Law to the postgraduates. His research interests include Public International Law, International Economic Law and WTO Law.

Contributors

Ms Olga Boltenko is a chairperson of the ICC Hong Kong Commercial Law and Practice Committee and a partner in the Hong Kong office of Fangda Partners. She specializes in international trade, investment protection, and investment arbitration. She acted as legal counsel in investor-state disputes under the auspices of the Permanent Court of Arbitration and as tribunal secretary in dozens of commercial disputes, both ad hoc and institutional (including Singapore International Arbitration Centre (SIAC), International Chamber of Commerce (ICC), Hong Kong International Arbitration Center (HKIAC), Arbitration Institute of the Stockholm Chamber of Commerce (SCC)), in a wide array of industries including oil and gas, infrastructure, construction, telecommunications and pharmaceuticals. She is listed as arbitrator on the Hong Kong International Arbitration Centre (HKIAC) list of arbitrators, and on the arbitrator panels of CIETAC, SIAC, and AIAC. She teaches international arbitration at The University of Hong Kong, and investment law at the Royal University for Law and Economics in Phnom Penh.

Mr Guilherme Vargas Castilhos is a Brazilian researcher and practitioner lawyer specialized in international law, namely the legal aspects concerning foreign investment between China and Latin America. He is an SJD candidate at the Shanghai Jiao Tong University (China), LLM at the University of Macau (Macau SAR, China) and holder of bachelor's degree in Law from the Federal University of Pelotas (Brazil). As a certified and enrolled member of the Brazilian Bar Association (*Ordem dos Advogados do Brasil*) and an external legal analyst for the Consulate General of Brazil in Shanghai, he participated in projects involving the incorporation and maintenance of foreign invested companies in Latin America and China. Currently living in Shanghai, and with more than four years residing in China, Mr Guilherme has experience and acquaintance to many aspects of Chinese culture and legal system.

Mr Michael Castle-Miller is an attorney who has helped advise governments throughout Africa, Asia, the Middle East, and Latin America on economic development, trade and investment, public-sector reform, business regulatory environment, urban planning, and post-conflict transition. As CEO of Politas Consulting, he primarily assists clients with special economic zone (SEZ) legal and institutional frameworks, as well as investment climate improvement, infrastructure finance arrangements, PPPs, and social and environmental safeguards. Michael is also the founder and Executive Director of Refugee Cities, an NGO dedicated to creating special-status settlements in which displaced people could legally work, thereby providing for their families and contributing to the economic and social development of their hosts and homelands. Prior to his current work, Michael worked on urban law and development projects for the World Bank Legal Vice Presidency in the Private Sector, Infrastructure, and Finance Unit. Before that, he worked for the Public International Law and Policy Group, where he helped the governments of South Sudan, Georgia, and Yemen on matters ranging from trade agreements to anti-corruption measures and minority representation. Michael graduated with a JD, summa cum laude, Order of the Coif, from American University, Washington College of Law and an MA in International Politics from American University, School of International Service. His publications in legal journals cover the political economy of international trade and investment, comparative local government, 'Charter Cities', US immigration law, and expropriation jurisprudence. Michael is a member of the Bar of the State of New York in good standing.

Ms Susan Finder is a scholar of China's judicial system (in comparative perspective). Her current research concentrates on Supreme People's Court (SPC) and Chinese judicial reforms, much of which is published on her blog, the SPC Monitor (最高人民法院观察). The blog is widely cited in books, academic journals, PhD theses, and government reports. This is Susan's second career in academia, and she comes to STL after twenty years in China-related practice at Freshfields Bruckhaus Deringer (and other firms), in legal publishing, and (briefly) as a securities regulator. In her first academic career (at what is now the City University of Hong Kong) she published the first comprehensive study of the operations of the SPC. Professor Finder received her undergraduate degree from Yale College, her Juris Doctor degree from Harvard Law School, and a Master of Laws degree from Columbia Law School. She was a visiting scholar at Peking University Law School as well. Professor Finder regularly is invited to make presentations and publish in mainland China and abroad. She has spoken at conferences sponsored by the SPC, Chinese Academy of Social Sciences, and Chinese University of Political Science and Law, among other institutions. She has spoken at some of the leading American law schools (including Columbia Law School, New York University, and the University of Pennsylvania), in all three Hong Kong law schools, as well as elsewhere in the world.

Ms Ting Han is a PhD candidate at The Graduate Institute, Geneva. Ting earlier was a Visiting Fellow at Melbourne Law School. She works in the field of international economic law, specializing in foreign investment law and policy.

Associate Professor Jie (Jeanne) Huang's teaching and research interests are in private international law, e-commerce law, international investment law, international litigation and arbitration, and underwater cultural heritage protection. She has published four books and authored more than thirty articles in law journals, such as

Journal of International Economic Law and Journal of Private International Law. Twelve of her articles are indexed by SSCI. As a chief investigator, she has received funding from China National Social Science Fund (equivalent to ARC), China Ministry of Education, the China Law Society, Shanghai Philosophy and Social Science Fund, and Shanghai Government Development and Research Center Fund. Before moving to the University of Sydney, she held academic positions at University of New South Wales Faculty of Law in Australia and Shanghai University of International Business and Economics School of Law (SUIBE Law) in China. She served as Associate Dean at SUIBE Law. She was awarded Pujiang Rencai (Pujiang Scholar) in 2011 and Shuguang Xuezhe (Dawn Scholar) in 2013 by Shanghai Education Committee. She was a Foreign Research Fellow at the Max Planck Institute for Comparative and International Private Law in Hamburg, Germany, and also had research experience at The Hague Academy of International Law, and the Academy of International Arbitration Law, Paris, France. She is a member of the Chartered Institute of Arbitrators. She also serves as an Arbitrator at the Hong Kong International Arbitration Center, Shanghai International Economic and Trade Arbitration Commission (Shanghai International Arbitration Center) and Xi'an Arbitration Commission. She has been interviewed for Chinese law and related dispute resolution by Jiefang Daily (解放日报), Wenhui Daily (文汇报), and ABC News Australia.

Ms Hongzhen Jiang is currently an Associate professor and Vice Dean of KoGuan School of Law, Shanghai Jiao Tong University. She obtained her PhD in Law from Zhejiang University (2007). Professor Jiang was once a visiting scholar at Cambridge Law School (2009–2010). She has published more than ten books (including book chapters) and thirty academic articles. The representative work includes 'Principle of Proportionality: as a Judicial Review Standard to Regulatory Alternatives' (Law Press, 2010); 'Legislative policies for the dominant tasks of e-government push in the Chinese context' (Information Development, Vol. 32, No. 4 [2015], pp. 247–250). Her academic interests include administrative law and regulatory analysis, E-government and E-rulemaking, judicial review under administrative litigation system.

Ms Avantika Kapoor is a Senior Researcher at Indian Council for Research on International Economic Relations (ICRIER). Her areas of interest include international trade and policy, and food safety policies. She has worked on survey-based studies for Indian government departments, including the Directorate General of Commercial Intelligence and Statistics under the Ministry of Commerce and Industry, and for international governments such as the European Commission. At ICRIER, she has worked for organizations such as the Amway India Enterprises Private Limited and PepsiCo India, and has contributed to the Working Paper Series and popular media articles. Under these projects, she contributed to sampling framework designing for pan-India survey, questionnaire designing and she also did field visit for pilot survey. She analysed the survey data and wrote the corresponding reports. Avantika has completed her M.Sc. in Economics from University of Warwick, England and a BA (Hons) in Economics from University of Delhi.

Mr Francisco José B.S. Leandro received a PhD in political science-international relations from the Catholic University of Portugal in 2010 and in 2011 an Advanced Diploma in International Law from the Istituto per gli Studi di Politica Internazionale jointly with the Institute of International Humanitarian Law (Italy). From 2005 to 2008, he was appointed as the Portuguese Representative to the Council of Europe - Committee of Experts for the Development of Human Rights' Group on Human Rights of Members of the Armed Forces (DH-DEV-FA). In 2014 and 2017, he was awarded the Institute of European Studies in Macau (IEEM) Academic Research Grant, which is a major component of the Asia-Europe Comparative Studies Research Project. From 2016 to 2017, he joined a post-doctoral research programme at University of Macau on state monopolies in China - One belt one road studies. From 2014 to 2018, he was the Coordinator of the Institute of Social and Legal Studies, Faculty of Humanities at the University of Saint Joseph, Macau, China. Currently, he is Associate Professor and Assistant-Dean at the Institute for Research on Portuguese-Speaking Countries at the City University of Macau, China. His most recent book, published in 2018, is titled Steps of Greatness: The Geopolitics of OBOR.

Mr Graham Mather is the Chairman of the World Free Zone Convention (WFZC). Since 2001 WFZC has built up an unparalleled network of partners, sponsors and speakers who have contributed to Free Zones trainings and events held worldwide. Graham Mather also advises hedge funds on EU issues, serves on the Competition Appeal Tribunal, and was a Conservative Member of the European Parliament. He has also been General Director of the Institute of Economic Affairs and Head of the Institute of Directors Policy Unit. He was an open scholar of New College, Oxford and Visiting Fellow of Nuffield College.

Mr Andrew D. Mitchell is Professor at Melbourne Law School, Australian Research Council Future Fellow, Director of the Global Economic Law Network, a member of the Indicative List of Panelists to hear WTO disputes, and a member of the Energy Charter Roster of Panelists. He has previously practiced law with Allens Arthur Robinson (now Allens Linklaters) and consults for States, international organizations and the private sector. Andrew has taught law in Australia, Canada, Singapore, and the US and is the recipient of four major grants from the Australian Research Council and the Australian National Preventive Health Agency. He has published over 130 academic books and journal articles and is a Series Editor of the Oxford University Press International Economic Law Series, an Editorial Board Member of the Journal of International Economic Law and a General Editor of the Journal of International Dispute Settlement. He has law degrees from Melbourne, Harvard and Cambridge and is a Barrister and Solicitor of the Supreme Court of Victoria.

Ms Arpita Mukherjee is a Professor at ICRIER. She has several years of experience in policy-oriented research, working closely with the government in India and policymakers in the EU, US, ASEAN and in East Asian countries. She has conducted studies for international organizations such as ADB, ADBI, ASEAN Secretariat, FCO (UK), Italian

Trade Commission, Konrad-Adenauer Stiftung, Organisation for Economic Co-operation and Development, Taipei Economic and Cultural Centre, UNCTAD and the WTO and Indian industry associations such as NASSCOM, FICCI, IBA, IDSA and EICI. Her research is a key contributor to India's negotiating strategies in the WTO and bilateral agreements. She has authored chapters in joint study group reports set up by Indian government and has led research teams contributing to India's domestic policy reforms in areas such as logistics, retail and SEZs. Her research interest includes trade and domestic reforms; WTO; bilateral/regional agreements; retail; infrastructure; FDI; SEZs; economic corridors and production networks; and migration. Dr Mukherjee has a PhD in Economics from the University of Portsmouth, UK. She has published widely and presented her research in various international and national forums.

Ms Caroline Nicholas is a Senior Legal Officer with the International Trade Law Division of the United Nations Office of Legal Affairs (the UNCITRAL Secretariat). She has served as Secretary to its Working Group on Procurement and Infrastructure Development, which drafted the UNCITRAL Model Law on Public Procurement (issued in 2011), an accompanying Guide to Enactment (2012), and other UNCITRAL documents in the field. As Secretary to this and other UNCITRAL Working Groups, she provides legal and policy advice and works in partnership with other international bodies engaged in public procurement policy activities. She advises on public procurement reform and its role in supporting international trade and development and the rule of law and provides regular technical assistance to national governments in all regions. She also serves as a Chairman of a UN Performance Appraisal Rebuttal Panel and undertakes voluntary policy advice and conflict resolution roles within the UN Secretariat. She previously advised on international war damage claims at the UN Compensation Commission, was a UN internal investigator, and has practiced law in the City of London and Hong Kong. Caroline is a Solicitor of the Supreme Court of England and Wales and of the Supreme Court of Hong Kong, an Associate of the Chartered Institute of Arbitrators, and the Chairman of the Board of Governors of the Vienna International School. She is a member of the Editorial Board of the Public Procurement Law Review and a regular contributor to it and other journals. She is married with three children and speaks four languages fluently.

Ms Kehinde Olaoye holds a Bachelor of Laws (LLB) Degree from the University of Ibadan, Nigeria. She is qualified to practice law in Nigeria and also holds a master's degree in Transnational law from King's College London. She is currently pursuing a PhD at the CUHK with a focus on international economic law. Ms Olaoye is particularly interested in sustainable development and economic development in Africa.

Mr Stephen Kim Park is an Associate Professor of Business Law and the Satell Fellow in Corporate Social Responsibility at the University of Connecticut School of Business. His research is in the areas of international financial regulation, international trade law, corporate social responsibility and accountability, and corporate compliance. At the University of Connecticut, he is the inaugural Director of the Business and Human Rights Initiative and Co-Director of the Corporate and Regulatory Compliance Graduate

Certificate Programme. He holds a J.D. from Harvard Law School, a M.A.L.D. in International Affairs from The Fletcher School at Tufts University, and a BA in Ethics, Politics, & Economics from Yale University.

Mr Marc Proksch has Master's Degrees from the Free University of Amsterdam in political science, international relations and from the London School of Economics in international political economy. After working in the private sector in the UK as a research analyst at a management consultancy, he joined the United Nations in 1990 in the Economic and Social Commission for Asia and the Pacific (ESCAP) in Bangkok. From 2000 until 2010, Proksch worked in ESCAP's Trade Policy Section of the Trade and Investment Division. Proksch is currently Chief of the Business and Development Section in the Trade and Investment Division and manages the work of the section in the areas of development of SMEs, promotion and facilitation of investment for development, and the promotion of responsible business practices.

Mr Prabhash Ranjan graduated as a lawyer from University of Delhi in 2003. Thereafter, he went for higher studies to SOAS, University College, London. Later, he received his PhD from King's College, London. He worked as a consultant to Oxfam, taught at NUJS, Kolkata and NLU, Jodhpur and presently he is an Assistant Professor at South Asian University.

Mr Sherzod Shadikhodjaev is a Professor at the KDI School of Public Policy and Management, Sejong City, Republic of Korea. He obtained his LLB (with honours) from the University of World Economy and Diplomacy (Uzbekistan), and LLM and PhD in Law from Korea University. Previously, he worked for Korea Institute for International Economic Policy as a research fellow. He has done extensive academic and policy research in international economic law. He is the author of the books 'Industrial Policy and the World Trade Organization: Between Legal Constraints and Flexibilities' (Cambridge University Press, 2018) and 'Retaliation in the WTO Dispute Settlement System' (Kluwer Law International, 2009). His articles were published in leading journals, such as American Journal of International Law, Chinese Journal of International Law, Journal of International Economic Law, World Trade Review, Journal of World Trade and others.

Mr Alessandro Spano holds a PhD in European and Chinese law at King's College London (KCL), an MA in Advanced European Studies at the College of Europe, Natolin and a degree in law at Paris X Nanterre. Dr Spano is currently a Senior Research Associate at the Dickson Poon School of Law at KCL where he conducts research in the areas of EU law, international trade law and Chinese law. At King's, Dr Spano is one of the co-ordinators of the *'Jean Monnet Network LAwTTIP – Legal Ambiguities withstanding TTIP'* which intends to promote a large-scale legal reflection of both the ongoing negotiations on the Transatlantic Trade Investment Partnership (TTIP) and its possible implications for the EU legal order. Since 2012, Dr Spano has also been a Research Associate at the Centre for Commercial Law at University College London (UCL). At UCL, Dr Spano lectures, as a Module Convenor, EU law, public International law and the course *'Law and Governance in Contemporary China'*. From 2009 to 2012, Dr Spano was awarded with the European Commission's EU-China Science and Technology Fellowship Programme. In this respect, he conducted research in academic institutions in mainland China and Hong Kong in the areas of WTO law, competition law and Chinese law. From 2009 to 2011, he was Research Fellow at the School of Law of the Tsinghua University of Beijing.

Mr Matthias Vanhullebusch (PhD, School of Oriental and African Studies, University of London; LLM (Adv.), Leiden) is Chenxing Associate Professor and Executive Director of the Asian Law Center at the KoGuan Law School of the Shanghai Jiao Tong University since 2012. He has an expertise in international law with a regional focus on the Middle East and Asia. He is the Senior Managing Editor of the Asian Journal of Law and Society (Cambridge University Press), Series Editor of Brill's Asian Law Series (Brill/Nijhoff) and the Routledge Studies on Asia in the World (Taylor & Francis), Associate Editor of the Asian Yearbook of Human Rights and Humanitarian Law (Brill/Nijhoff) and Managing Editor of Brill's Encyclopedia of Public International Law in Asia (Brill/Nijhoff). He is the Rapporteur of the International Law Association's Study Group on Asian State Practice of Domestic Implementation of International Law. He is a Visiting Professor on various training programmes organised by the International Committee of the Red Cross across Asia. His latest monographs include: War and Law in the Islamic World (Brill/Nijhoff, 2015) and Global Governance, Conflict and China (Brill/Nijhoff, 2018).

Mr Haonan Zhong is a PhD candidate majoring in legal theory at KoGuan School of Law, Shanghai Jiao Tong University. He acquired his bachelor's degree of law and master's degree in constitutional and administrative law in 2014 and 2017 in Southwest University of Political Science and Law. His research fields include political and legal philosophy, sociological theory of law and constitutional and administrative law. From June to August in 2012, he practiced in Dongguan Intermediate People's Court as the court clerk. From March to June in 2016, he practiced in Kunming Yingdian Law Office as a paralegal. From June 2017 to the present, he has been serving as a Research Assistant in KoGuan School of Law, Shanghai Jiao Tong University. He has been involved in several research projects including List of Government Power of Chongqing sponsored by the Legal Affairs Office of Chongqing in 2014, The Research of the Regulation of Zhang Jiang National Innovation Model Area sponsored by the Legislation Research Institute of Shanghai in 2017, Judicial Influences of Justices' Cognitive Style sponsored by the Ministry of Justice from 2017 to 2018, the Index System of University Management by Law sponsored by Shanghai Education Evaluation Institute from 2017 to 2018, and The Legal Regulation of Artificial Intelligence System Security sponsored by the Shanghai Science and Technology Council in 2019.

Summary of Contents

Table of Contents

Foreword

Special economic zones have existed for centuries. The free cities and free ports of the Hanseatic League encapsulated the concept as long ago as the sixteenth century. More recently the focus has shifted to Asia and today it is China which is in the vanguard of the development and elaboration of the concept, with its rich opportunities to promote investment and economic growth and bringing with it important questions of law and policy.

In 1980, I was asked to join a Working Party set up by Mrs Thatcher's Government, under the auspices of Her Majesty's Treasury to investigate the potential launch of Freeports in the United Kingdom. Subsequently, a number of Freeports were introduced and alongside them a series of Enterprise Zones. The Freeports were designed to provide streamlined customs and other procedures to attract trade and investment; the Enterprise Zones offered fiscal incentives including the reduction of business rates and other taxes to try to revive depressed areas affected by structural and industrial change.

At the time, international understanding of the potential of SEZs was very limited and academic literature on them scarce. Some Special Zones shone as beacons where imaginative Governments, such as the Irish Government with the establishment of the Shannon Airport Free Zone, had made use of the concept. In Latin American, the Maquiladoras in Mexico had shown that a measure of deregulation could foster economic activity and innovation. In pockets elsewhere around the world, Free Trade Zones were beginning to be more visible. But Zones were relatively thin on the ground and academic literature including legal and economic analyses was very limited.

The publication of this important volume shows how much has changed over the last four decades. We can analyse it in various dimensions.

First, there has been a secular growth in the number and significance of SEZs. They have grown in the Middle East with Dubai probably the flagship. They have flourished in Asia, where programmes exist in many economies but perhaps most notably in India and in China. The Zone programme in India is a flexible, bottom up one designed to capture entrepreneurial surges and it has created several hundred Zones of varying scales. Politically it has encountered challenge from adjoining areas and traditional interests.

It is in China that the major advance in the deployment and development of Economic Zones has occurred, and this volume rightly devotes considerable attention to the legal, economic and public policy dimensions of China's Free Trade Zones initiative.

The policy choice has been to use pilot Free Trade Zones to help design the future development of China's economy using lessons from approaches and experiments tested in the Zones. China has also innovated in developing legal regimes and arbitration systems better suited to the needs of international investors and the challenges of Zone operation than her traditional legal code.

A somewhat similar trend can be traced internationally as Economic Zones have become a more permanent feature of the world trade scene. Originally, they were viewed with some suspicion by the international organizations. A suspicion that they may attempt to undercut wage levels or employment conditions elsewhere in a national economy led the International Labour Organization to show a close interest. Such work suggested, however, that far from undercutting pay and reducing working standards, a typical Zone showed best practice in good working conditions and the attraction of well-rewarded talent.

It was therefore, significant that the next wave of interest by the international bodies came from the World Bank, which over the years has now actively assisted in the establishment of Zone programmes around the world. It has produced valuable material analysing the reasons behind the success of the contribution of Economic Zones.

A third dimension has been the treatment of Economic Zones under World Trade Organization rules. Especially because many early Zones were focused on export processing activity in entrepots dealing with traditional cargos there was nervousness as to whether the incentives available in Zones could count as export subsidies prohibited under WTO rules. In practice the issue has been much less significant: complaints have been few and countries have tended to adopt a policy of live-and-let-live, recognising that in their different forms most economies will seek to incentivize inward investment and to produce measures that attract foreign direct investment. These may include fiscal and other incentives.

The great exception to this approach, of course, has been in the European Union (EU) where custom rules and state aid requirements – the latter increasingly used to define low taxes as a form of subsidization – have meant that the scope for new Zones has been extremely limited and the Zone programmes which existed in joining Member States have been wound down to comply with EU rules.

This volume is of assistance to the future development of Economic Zones around the world. It offers analysis of this dynamic phenomenon across legal, economic, investment, regulatory and policy matrices. Its careful examination of theory and practice and its comprehensive approach to developing best practice and the lessons from case studies will reward all interested in this ever-more important area of law and economics.

Graham Mather
CBE, Chairman, World Free Zone Convention
London, January 2019

CHAPTER 1

International Economic Law and the Challenges of Economic Zones: An Introduction

Julien Chaisse & Jiaxiang Hu

This book is about the phenomenon and challenges of special economic zones (SEZs) which are a major aspect of many countries' economic policy. The book provides a comprehensive analysis of the phenomenon, across many continents and jurisdictions, and a finer understanding of the complex interactions between SEZs and international economic law and policy. The book is a major contribution to the literature on SEZs also because it involves a number of leading experts to comment on the main problems confronting the actors of the SEZs world such as governments, companies, international organizations, and businessmen.

§1.01 AN OVERVIEW OF THE LAW AND POLICY

SEZs are free zones, at the scale of a port, a district or a city, functioning as economic and fiscal enclaves. In particular, they have been a tool for the establishment of capitalist enterprises in countries with controlled economies, and more particularly in Chinese coastal cities in the early 1980s.[1] One of the most famous examples, because of its success, is that of the city of Shenzhen, on the Pearl River Delta.[2]

Many are the reasons why governments decide to implement an SEZ in their own countries. The most common one is to boost the economic development of a specific

1. *See* Abdul Rahoof TK, P. G. Arul, "An Evaluation of Special Economic Zones (SEZs) Performance Post SEZs Act 2005", (2016) 4(2) Universal Journal of Industrial and Business Management 44.
2. *See* Meng Guangwen, The Theory and Practice of Free Economic Zones: A Case Study of Tianjin, People's Republic of China (doctoral thesis, Ruprecht-Karls University of Heidelberg, Germany, 2003); Edward Graham, Do Export Processing Zones Attract FDI and Its Benefits? The Experience from China, International Economics and Economic Policy. (Springer-Verlag 2004).

region of a nation by offering incentives to domestic and foreign companies such as the non-applicability of certain taxes and duties on production, income or on imported goods that enter the zone and are destined to the industrial activity.[3] SEZs can be of many types, including Free trade zones (FTZs), Export processing zones (EPZs), Free Economic Zones (FEZs), Industrial Parks (IP), Free Ports (FP) and so on.[4]

SEZs can also be transnational. For instance, an SEZ will see the light of day shortly between the regions of Sikasso in Mali, Korogho in Ivory Coast and Bobo-Dioulasso in Burkina Faso.[5] The aim is to boost cross-border economic activity by offering companies in the region advantageous terms. Transforming borders into growth engines is the ambition of Mali, Burkina Faso and Côte d'Ivoire. In other words, companies that want to invest in the Korogho, Sikasso and Bobo-Dioulasso border areas will be offered benefits. For the moment, the three countries have set the framework of the SEZ and should in the coming months define the precise modality. It will probably be tax benefits and financial incentives, and probably also projects common to all three countries, public projects or public-private partnership. These three countries that belong to the UEMOA area already apply the free movement of people and goods, but cross-border trade still has a strong potential for development, says a senior Ivorian official. Agriculture, mining, but also processing industries and services could benefit greatly from increased integration.

In any case, an SEZ is by definition a site designed to massively attract private investment.[6] It is governed by a specific legal regime and offers fiscal, administrative and customs incentives as well as viable infrastructures for the companies that settle there.[7] As a general rule, SEZs are created on the initiative of either the government or private developers.

This book shows that the establishment of SEZs does not systematically reinforce entrepreneurship but contributes to it by promoting the implementation of reforms that make the environment favorable for productive investments. The establishment of SEZs should therefore be accompanied by mechanisms to strengthen human capital, ensure technological development and improve the business climate, among others. The economic policies put in place should not be articulated around the zone but should take into account their particularity while remaining specific to the entire

3. Jürgen Basedow (2016), "Boosting the Economy—Special Economic Zone or Nationwide Deregulation?", Max Planck Private Law Research Paper 17/3, 4. *See also* Hyung-Gon Jeong and Douglas Zhihua Zeng (2016), "Promoting Dynamic & Innovative Growth in Asia: The Case of Special Economic Zones and Business Hub", Korea Institute for International Economic Policy Research Paper Policy Analysis-16-01.
4. *See* Connie Carter and Andrew Harding (2010), Special Economic Zones in Asian Market Economies, Routledge.
5. Africa: Launch of A Special Economic Zone Between Burkina Faso, Côte D'ivoire and Mali, Building Africa Future News, May 14, 2018 (available at https://www.cac-international.com/africa-launch-of-a-special-economic-zone-between-burkina-faso-cote-divoire-and-mali/?lang=en).
6. *See* Dhingra, Tarun., Singh, Tripti. and Sinha, Ambalika., "Location Strategy for Competitiveness of Special Economic Zones: A Generic Framework for India" (2009) 19(4) Competitiveness Review: An International Business Journal pp. 272–289.
7. *See* Lotta Moberg (2017), The Political Economy of Special Economic Zones: Concentrating Economic Development, Routledge 124.

economy. Thus, if the establishment of an SEZ requires the removal of certain regulatory barriers, it should be possible to identify all that would constitute barriers to the entire economy and provide appropriate solutions. If the establishment of an SEZ requires the establishment of a favorable framework to promote access to bank financing, for example, any policy aimed at achieving this objective should not be limited to companies located in the area but should be extended to all businesses in the economy.

Another very important point is the geographical location. An SEZ should not be articulated around the development of a locality or a region but should rather be part of a logic of setting up an economic lung capable of punctuating and stimulating the activity. All in all, in order to effectively take advantage of the SEZ's capacity to generate employment and boost structural transformation (which is essential for the sustainability of growth), the authorities should, in addition, integrate this tool into their development strategy, put in place mechanisms to strengthen the resilience of the economy to international conjecture, rely on local actors (entrepreneurs) to identify the reforms to be undertaken to make the business environment supportive and to support technology innovation and development.

SEZs raise also many concerns that go beyond their mere efficiency and sustainability. For the International Monetary Fund (IMF), the fears relate mainly to the impacts of the establishment of SEZs on tax revenues.[8] Since SEZs are intended to provide a competitive environment for business and investment, companies placed under this regime will benefit from a number of administrative, financial and tax benefits. At first glance, reduced taxation can only have positive effects on investments. But recent studies have shown that tax incentives are not very effective in attracting investment to developing countries where the investment climate is facing much more acute and urgent challenges. Given there are fears that there will be no new investors, but that it is rather those who are already there who are moving to SEZs to take advantage of the benefits offered by this regime, which would imply loss of tax revenue. In addition to the tax advantages, the possibility of selling both on the local market and export is another benefit that can lead existing companies to want to benefit from the SEZ scheme at all costs.

§1.02 THE CHINESE SCENARIO

The most famous SEZs are those created in the People's Republic of China (PRC, hereinafter "China") under the government of Deng Xiaoping in 1980, especially the one near Hong Kong, nicknamed "The Miracle of Shenzhen." While many countries have created SEZs, China has been the most successful in this process, due to a significant regulatory gap between its SEZs and the rest of the country. SEZs of China

8. IMF (2015) Options for Low Income Countries' Effective and Efficient Use of Tax Incentives for Investment A Report to the G-20 Development Working Group by the IMF, OECD, Un And World Bank (available at https://www.imf.org/external/np/g20/pdf/101515.pdf).

differ from each other by their dimensions and their purpose.[9] Some are designated geographical areas, where policies and measures particularly support specific economic functions. Others consist of zones of free trade, industrial parks, technological innovation parks or customs zones that facilitate experimentation and innovation in a wide range of business sectors.

In fact, China has a long history of SEZs.[10] This experience dates back to the early 1980s, when the country introduced the market economy in a number of areas, including Shenzhen. A few years later, open coastal cities were created, such as Zhangzhou, to encourage economic growth by taking advantage of the geographic location of these cities and the liberalization of the national economy. At the end of the 1980s, building on this experience, central and provincial governments established high-tech development zones to capitalize on global capital, technology and talent. In the 1990s, as a result of economic growth and changes in this country, other areas were created, including the China-Singapore business park, and the existing SEZs were modernized for the purpose. Since the beginning of the twenty-first century, many regional areas have been established to stimulate and anchor regional development.

Various management models have been implemented: (a) administrative management, with management functions provided by administrative bodies set up by the State; (b) an administrative council, with management by state-appointed committees, or (c) joint management by SEZ partners and by state-run administrative bodies. SEZs have made a significant contribution to China's development. They have made it possible to experiment with market-oriented reforms and act as a catalyst for the efficient allocation of national and international resources. They also deepened the openness of the Chinese economy by attracting capital, technology, and technical and managerial know-how from abroad, which fostered China's industrial development and increased integration in the global economy.

§1.03 THE WORLDWIDE DEVELOPMENT OF SEZs

In India, the SEZ are free zones created by the Indian central government from 1965. The first was created in Kandla, Gujarat: this EPZ was the first free zone of Asia.[11] The first EPZ specialized in the production of high value-added products (jewelry, electronics) and skilled labor, unlike the SEZs of other countries. Acceleration is taking place from the 2005 SEZ Act, which allows private actors and industrial development agencies from the states of the Indian Union to create their SEZs. To attract foreign investment, these areas enjoy significant tax benefits and better infrastructure (electricity, transport). Their productions, mainly for export, are experiencing very strong

9. *See* Wei Shen, "A Tale of Three Zones—Promises and Pitfalls of Three Financial Experimental Zones in China" (2014) 131 Banking Law Journal 399.
10. *See* Daqing Yao and John Whalley, "The China (Shanghai) Pilot Free Trade Zone: Background, Developments and Preliminary Assessment of Initial Impacts" (2016) 39 The World Economy 15.
11. *See* Kasturi Bhagat, "Implementation of Labor Laws Inside SEZs in India: A Perfect Example of Economic Development Versus Social Security", (April 2015) 5(2) The IUP Law Review p. 32.

growth.[12] They constitute extraterritorial enclaves: ground (available), taxation (lightened), bureaucracy (lightened), infrastructures (improved), of all sizes, in one or several industrial sectors, with various actors: private (ex: Nokia, Flexotronic, Mahindra, Reliance) or public (federal state, federated state or even Singapore). The reports are often conflicting between the national policy favorable to the SEZ, and the interest of the local populations who consider themselves the victims of the expropriation of their lands.

South-East Asia is also a major area in the development of SEZs.[13] By the end of 2015, regional integration finally became part of the ASEAN Economic Community. It is the culmination of an international movement that began in 1967 when Indonesia, Malaysia, the Philippines, Singapore and Thailand formed the Association of the Southeast Asian Nation (ASEAN) and demonstrated a remarkable foreknowledge to plan a united future. The rationale that regional integration was needed to enhance development opportunities; face new challenges and threats; increase bargaining power and reduce dependence on global economies; to strengthen the international competitiveness of the region; and to prevent member countries from tackling various problems as a group. The establishment of SEZs in ASEAN border areas is a development strategy designed to take advantage of the geographical situation of the country; preparation of its commercial channels with neighboring countries; the current model of border trade; opportunities arising from economic development in neighboring countries; investment requests in border areas; and in general; opportunities arising from the ACS. The special zones are expected to help to strengthen the ASEAN countries' competitiveness in trade and investment in border areas. For instance, Thailand has begun to seriously pursue the SEZ policy in 2014, with the main objectives of attracting investment from local and foreign investors, distributing wealth to the provinces, reducing inequalities, improving the quality of life, to solve security problems in border regions like the illegal immigration and agricultural products and narcotics entering Thailand from neighboring countries. A National Committee for the Development of SEZs is the main mechanism for implementing the SEZ Plan. The Prime Minister is the chair of the committee and its members include representatives of the relevant government agencies and the private sector. The Office of the National Council for Economic and Social Development is the secretariat of the committee, and six sub-committees examine areas to be designated as SEZs, as well as projects and measures to support their development.

Beyond Asia, SEZs have also appeared in Africa. Africa's current economic performance is not systematically accompanied by a change in its economic structure

12. *See* Aradhna Aggarwal (2007) Impact of Special Economic Zones on Employment, Poverty and Human Development, Indian Council for Research on International Economic Relations Working Paper No. 194. *See also* Krishna Chaitanya Vadlamannati and Haider Ali Khan (2017), "Race to the Top or Race to the Bottom? Competing for Investment Proposals in Special Economic Zones? Evidence from Indian States, 1998–2009", in Jason Miklian and Åshild Kolås (Eds.) "Invisible India: Hidden Risks Within an Emerging Superpower": Routledge, 19.
13. *See* e.g., Peter G. Warr and Jayant Menon (2016), "Cambodia's Special Economic Zones", Asian Development Bank Economics Working Paper Series No. 459, 2.

and, to a lesser extent, social conditions, including access to employment.[14] In fact, growth figures published for Africa are driven by private consumption and natural resource exploitation. To sustain these performances, job creation and structural transformation constitute a considerable challenge for African countries' development strategies. The complexity of this process will require state action. These strategies therefore incorporate policies aimed at generating employment and sustainably consolidating the country's economic performance. One of its strategies is the establishment of SEZs.

SEZs being now a global phenomenon, they also pose a number of challenges confronting researchers, policy-makers and international organizations. This book identifies and discusses specifically the international challenges raised by SEZs. The contributions in this book are grouped around specific themes. In Part I, the contributions address the development of SEZs throughout the world. In Part II, the authors explore the interactions between international trade law and policy and SEZs. In Part III, the discussion covers the growing interactions between international investment law and arbitration and SEZs.

[A] Part I—Economic Zones: Development, Players, and Contribution

Part I contains contributions that analyze the regulatory, economic and political foundations of SEZ. It looks at the drivers and determinants of SEZs throughout the work considering some key examples across countries. This Part also considers the changing drivers and determinants of SEZs which are reflected in the ongoing regulatory changes of SEZs.

In Chapter 2, Marc Proksch provides a thorough analysis of the success factors and required policies for SEZs. Marc Proksch explains that experiences with SEZs have demonstrated that they have been relatively successful in terms of economic impact depending on their specific purpose in some countries but not in others. Empirical studies tend to focus on the economic impact of government-run zones rather than private sector-run zones. Studies that have focused on the social and environmental impact of SEZs usually found a negative impact, but failed to address the economic impacts which may have been positive. Studies have also generally failed to compare the impact of incentives in SEZs compared to the impact of incentives in sectors operating outside the zones.

In Chapter 3, Alessandro Spano focuses on investment, regional development and compliance with internal market rules in EU free zones. EU free zones consist of geographic areas where state authorities may decide to introduce a series of ad hoc incentives for companies conducting their business activities in the region. As a result, these areas have often become "growth poles" for the concerned regions and, ultimately, for the whole country. Incentives may assume various forms including exemptions on customs arrangements and, in particular, tax incentives. However,

14. *See* Watson, P. (2001) "Export Processing Zones: Has Africa Missed the Boat?" Not yet! World Bank Africa Region Working Paper Series No. 17. Washington DC.

national tax measures are subject to careful scrutiny by the European Commission to verify their compliance with EU State aid rules and, ultimately, common market. In its essence, the approach of the European Commission to State aid policy seems to be functional to the common market's principles. On the one side, such an approach confers upon the European Commission enough flexibility to tackle tax measures with potentially harmful effects on competition. However, on the other side, it may affect legal certainty in relation to the notion of aid and, reducing the tax sovereignty of Member States. Within this context, this chapter discusses the regulatory challenges related to EU free zones to avoid competition distortions within the common market with particular focus on the implementation of tax incentives offered in these areas by Member States. The analysis also attempts to study if existing EU legal and policy instruments have been successful in connecting the different levels of national and European governance in a satisfactory manner, and in ensuring effectiveness and transparency in the regulation of EU free zones.

In Chapter 4, Guilherme V. Castilhos turns to another continent and reviews the SEZ in the Brazilian Amazon Rain Forest. The Brazilian Amazon Region is home to the State of Amazonas, where in the middle of the jungle, cities and urban centers emerged with a total population of around 4 million people. It was taking this region and these people into consideration that the Brazilian government decided to implement its first SEZ in the city of Manaus, capital of the State of Amazonas. Created as a free trade area to develop the Western Amazon, the Manaus Free Trade Zone (MFTZ) became a center of intense commercial and industrial activity, notably due to domestic and foreign investments performed in the district during the late seventies until the present days. This chapter will first present a historical background and explanation of the MFTZ alongside the economic history of the Amazon Region, as well as an accounting on the reasons for the choice of its peculiar location as well as its main characteristics and its use as an instrument for the region's development. Going further, in the next section of this research, the goal is to identify and elucidate the negative and positive impacts of the MFTZ for the development and economy of the Amazonian Region and its society. After the analysis of its effects, this study will present a section indicating new policies and models that can be adopted by the MFTZ administrative authorities in order to better generate its desired objectives, in light of the new multilateral economy of the twenty-first century. The final section will show a compendium of the topics stressed and a closure for this research.

In Chapter 5, Arpita Mukherjee turns to Asia and looks at India's experience with the SEZs. The objective of this chapter is to examine India's SEZ policy and the country's experience with SEZs. It identifies the challenges faced by SEZs and makes policy recommendations on how their performance can be improved to drive India's economic growth and development. The chapter is based on secondary data analysis and a primary survey. The chapter shows that India has been less successful than countries such as China in attracting investment in the manufacturing sector in SEZs and a number of SEZs have failed to become operational. This is primarily due to certain gaps in the SEZ policy and its linkages with other polices of the government. Given this scenario, the book suggests policy measures such as: (a) better coordination between government agencies, (b) providing more non-fiscal incentives to SEZs, (c) designing the right fiscal incentives that are compliant with World Trade Organization's (WTO's) Subsidies and Countervailing Measures Agreement, (d) using SEZs as a test-bed for reforms, (e) improving inside-zone infrastructure and outside-zone connectivity, and (f) ensuring that the SEZ policy is consistent with the country's trade policy, which can help make SEZ policies successful.

In Chapter 6, Hongzhen Jiang and Haonan Zhong look at the practice of the ongoing reform of administrative approval system in Shanghai Free Trade Pilot Zone (SFTPZ), and, critically examine the issue of licenses and permits reform. The reform of administrative approval system is a key issue concerned with the market access. Form the SFTPZ, the practice of negative list has been adopted not only in other eleven free trade pilot zones, but also extended nationwide despite in two different lists. This article has introduced the most recent development of SEZs in China and pointed out the difference between the current free trade pilot zones and the previous SEZs, the former focusing on the streamlining of administrative approval while the later providing more preferential treatment including tax reduction. The authors may add a little more to the article on the impact of the reform of administrative approval on the free trade pilot zones and even on the development of China's economy.

In Chapter 7, Matthias Vanhullebusch explains how to mitigate inequality in the development of SEZs in Asia. The development of SEZs in Asia has attracted foreign investments and ensured spectacular economic growth at the (sub-)national level. While their competitiveness has initially been marked by deregulation, their integration into the global value chains as well as international financial markets has triggered a number of international regulatory agendas and perspectives to ensure their sustainable development. Respect for the international rule of law would improve urban governance, corporate responsibility and even promote the role of civil society in mitigating the various socio-economic and environmental risks that have accompanied the fast development of Asian SEZs. Tackling labor protection/migration, adequate/affordable housing as well as environmental pollution has become a common concern amongst those share- and stakeholders. The ever-widening socio-economic gap between groups within societies, however, is immune to such legal engineering and experiments and has opened the floor for religious, ethnic, ethical, nationalist and anti-globalist discourses to justify and/or contest inevitable inequality.

In Chapter 8, Francisco José Leandro further extends the reflection on SEZs by considering the case of Economic Corridors, Transit Routes and SEZs in the context of the Belt and Road Initiative (B&RI). More specifically, Francisco José Leandro explores the linkages between Economic Corridors, Transit Routes and SEZs using the Budapest-Belgrade-Skopje-Piraeus (BBSP) as a case study. This chapter maps out "one belt, one road" (OBOR) also known as the B&RI involves different types of infrastructure to advance economic and trade flows. B&RI is an access strategy, which aims to establish a network of global reach, shortening distances between markets and production centers. Moreover, this is an access strategy that uses key infrastructure to develop interconnectivity as it emphasizes the importance of connecting routes, and establishment of synergies between the different legs of the "land belt" (the economic corridors) vis-á-vis the complementary sailing options of the "maritime road" (the sea lines of communication). In this line of reasoning, we concluded that the SEZs and other similar arrangements are, from a geopolitical perspective, "exceptional interface-gateways" between economic agents, using economic and transit routes to promote and facilitate flows of economic exchange. This chapter analyzes the B&RI and its connectivity elements, presenting the BBSP fast transit route as a case study, operating as link between two major economic corridors and a vital maritime sailing route. Therefore, in our vision, the BBSP performs a complementary function, dissimilar from the economic corridors, but even though, it maximizes the true potential of B&RI in Western and Central Europe. The BBSP is particularly decisive for landlocked economies, such as Hungary and Serbia that are not located in the main axis of the six land economic corridors, and it stands as a "golden" brick in the larger wall of the cooperation between China and Central and Eastern European Countries. All in all, the B&RI connectivity elements, such as SEZs (and similar arrangements), economic corridors, fast transit routes, economic development axes, and China's Special Administrative Regions are paired instruments of global reach, requiring minimal levels of economic integration and recognized standards of legal compatibility. Finally, this chapter adopts a geopolitical perspective, grounded in geo-economics and using comparative qualitative data and case-study methodology.

[B] Part II—International Trade Law and Policy and SEZs

Part II extends the reflection on SEZs by looking at the interactions between international trade and policy and SEZs.[15] It is important as SEZs have the objective to increase trade and export which in turns has ramifications on labor and capital allocation within each country.

In Chapter 9, Stephen provides a lucid and compelling analysis of SEZs and the Perpetual Pluralism of Global Trade and Labor Migration. While agreements to lower barriers to cross-border trade are enforced by global legal rules and institutions, national governments indisputably control and limit cross-border labor migration. However, the relationship between trade and labor migration in international law is anything but clear-cut and simple—rather, it is ad hoc, decentralized, and pluralistic. To analyze the relationship between trade and labor migration, this chapter focuses on the use of SEZs, which enable countries to selectively open borders to higher-skilled foreign workers while maximizing economic returns and minimizing socio-political costs. This chapter includes an illustrative case study, the Panamá Pacífico SEZ at the intersection of the Panama Canal and the Pacific Ocean. While advantageous to individual countries, this chapter argues that the pluralistic status quo hinders comprehensive initiatives to harmonize the liberalization of trade and labor and promote freedom of movement in international labor markets.

In Chapter 10, Michael Castle-Miller turns to the Law and Policy of Refugee Cities and considers the case of SEZs for Migrants. Migration is quickly becoming one of the

15. *See* Stephen Creskoof and Peter Walkenhorst (2009), "Implications of WTO Disciplines for Special Economic Zones in Developing Countries" World Bank Policy Research Working Paper, 8 https://elibrary.worldbank.org/doi/abs/10.1596/1813-9450-4892 accessed November 12, 2018.

most pressing issues of our time. Conflict, persecution, natural disasters, and economic inequality are driving people from their homes in record numbers. Meanwhile, traditional responses to mass migration are becoming increasingly inadequate. Recognizing this, some countries are exploring pragmatic pathways toward integrating migrants into economies. The SEZ concept offers one potential path forward. SEZs are designated areas designed to promote development through a distinct policy and administrative framework. They can serve as vehicles for initiating beneficial policies when political obstacles stand in the way of nationwide reform. Refugee cities would be a type of SEZ designed to facilitate migrant integration. They would be special-status jurisdictions in which displaced people — who would otherwise be barred from working — can be employed, start businesses, access finance, and rebuild their lives. Applying principles from SEZs, refugee cities could help countries benefit from migrants' presence in a politically realistic manner. They could also deliver high-quality infrastructure, foreign direct investment, and improvements to the business environment. Refugee cities would also serve as a pathway for countries to come into closer alignment with international law. Under the Convention and Protocol Relating to the Status of Refugees ("Refugee Convention" and "1967 Protocol," respectively), refugees are entitled to relatively strong rights regarding property, employment, and entrepreneurship. However, most countries' domestic legislation falls well short of these rights. This article explores these gaps to show how refugee cities could fill them by creating designated areas in which refugee rights are respected and the policy benefits of migrant integration are achieved. It covers the background of the global migration situation, the evolution and role of SEZs in the world, the refugee-cities concept and its policy benefits, and the international and domestic law pertaining to refugees, including a special focus on Turkey.

In Chapter 11, Sherzod Shadikhodjaev begins the analysis of SEZs under the WTO's Scrutiny. Despite their name, SEZs are not treated in the WTO in a "special" way. This book examines WTO accession, transparency and case law materials to identify specific trade issues associated with SEZs. The accession instruments of thirty-six members contain SEZ-related commitments regarding acceptance of WTO-applicability, treatment of zone-located firms, withdrawal of fiscal preferences for SEZ products entering home markets and notifications. Questions raised in the transparency procedures range from notifiability of SEZs to the specifics of national SEZ policies and WTO-consistency of SEZ measures. It is remarkable that unlike the past practice, SEZ-related measures have recently been targeted in WTO disputes. Since most of the issues addressed in different WTO forums have concerned SEZ incentives, it is suggested that the host governments, as a minimum, provide incentives in a transparent and non-discriminatory way without any localization, exportation or other overly burdensome requirements.

In Chapter 12, Andrew D. Mitchell and Ting Han focus on China's FTZs and their WTO Compatibility, in particular the Case Study of China (Shanghai) Free Trade Pilot Zone. In 2013, China established its first FTZ in Shanghai as a testing ground for further economic reform. Followed by the Shanghai FTZ, China has successively established eleven FTZs nationwide. Different from China's SEZs in the 1970s, the FTZs function as higher-level platforms for more advanced and comprehensive trade liberalizaion. This chapter introduces China's FTZs through a case study of the Shanghai FTZ and by examining its further market accessions and investment policies against specific WTO agreements, including the Agreement on Subsidies and Countervailing Measures, the Agreement on Trade-Related Investment Measures and the General Agreement on Tariff and Trade. This chapter demonstrates the new traits and development of China's economic zones.

In Chapter 13, Jie (Jeanne) Huang scrutinizes the recent Developments of Institutional Arbitration in China. Since the enactment of China Arbitration Law in 1994, institutional arbitration has dominated China's arbitration market. The recent developments of institutional arbitration in China is featured with three keywords: specialization, digitalization and internationalization. Many of important developments took place in China's FTZs and generated positive national-wide impacts. This chapter analyzes the recent developments of institutional arbitration in China and asks whether these developments would bring more use of Chinese arbitration institutions in the "OBOR" contexts.

In Chapter 14, Susan Finder looks at How the Supreme People's Court serves national strategy and "makes law." This analysis shows that the ability of the Chinese courts to have greater international credibility and influence is linked to having some basic legal infrastructure that better meets the expectations of international litigants (and its domestic ones as well). This legal infrastructure relates to both substantive and procedural rules. The highly knowledgeable members of the Fourth Civil Division of the SPC are likely acutely aware of these issues. On the procedural side, those include a large number of formalistic requirements creating obstacles for a foreign litigant, lack of discovery procedures, difficulties for a Chinese court to apply the governing law selected by the parties, as well as an absence of institutions needed to make the concerns of litigants known. For these reasons, the newly established China International Commercial Law relaxes some of these formalistic requirements. The performance indicator's driving decision making in Chinese courts often leads Chinese judges to ignore the express intent of contracting parties and declare that foreign law cannot be ascertained. A better method of requiring litigating parties to disclose evidence closer to international standards may apparently lead to fewer cases tried in the Chinese courts. A court system, particularly in the FTZs, that operates according to more international standards, particularly procedurally, would better strengthen the international credibility of the Chinese courts.

[C] Part III—International Investment Law and Policy and SEZs

In Part III, the book turns to the interactions between SEZs and international investment law and arbitration. Investor-state dispute settlement (ISDS) is designed to protect investors from rich countries for their activities in developing countries, against the risk of expropriation and arbitrary decisions by government's disrespect of the rule of law or failing justice. For years, this device was used very little and only three cases of prosecution had been identified in 1995. But this legal innovation, has gradually spread well beyond the original framework and there are a number of cases which involve SEZs. In Part III, the book provides a series of case studies which shed light on the role of investment arbitration (and this investment law and policy) to regulate SEZs.

In Chapter 15, Caroline Nicholas provides a detailed review of the work conducted by United Nations Commission on International Trade Law (UNCITRAL) to reform ISDS. UNCITRAL's work on ISDS reform is therefore proceeding at a measured pace, for the reasons set out above. The Working Group has noted that the concerns identified for future consideration do not presuppose any conclusion on the desirability of reform to address those concerns, and that desirability will be considered as it continues its work. It has emphasized that the government-led approach mandated by the Commission had been supported by the provision of information by States and observer organizations alike. The Commission will review the reports of the thirty-fourth and thirty-fifth sessions of the Working Group at the annual plenary session of the Commission from June 25 to July 13, 2018, in New York. It is anticipated, in light of the constructive manner in which the Working Group has proceeded, supported by awareness- and fund-raising efforts described above, that the Commission will agree that the Commission's instructions on how the Working Group is to undertake its work are being followed, and that the Working Group will contribute to establishing a "harmonized legal framework for a fair and efficient settlement of international investment disputes, increase[d] transparency and accountability and ... good governance."

In Chapter 16, Kehinde Olaoye analyzes the *Goetz v. the Republic of Burundi I&II* awards with the objective to explain how foreign investors challenge "free-zone regimes." *Goetz v. Burundi* is the first publicly known investor-state dispute arbitration award resulting from a dispute over the grant of SEZ status to a foreign investor. Although this decision has been analyzed in investment law scholarship, governance of SEZs through foreign investment norms has not been sufficiently explored. This chapter thus contributes to existing literature by examining SEZ governance against the foreground of the Goetz disputes. In view of China's FDI driven multiplication of SEZs in Asia and the rest of the world, this chapter is an important contribution, providing useful insights for investors, host states and policy makers.

In Chapter 17, Olga Boltenko continues the discussion of the interactions between ISDS and SEZs by looking at investment protection in China's SEZs in light of the *Lee Jong Baek* award. China's economic miracle in the last several decades is premised to a large extent on the establishment and operation of multiple SEZs. With that level of concentration of FDI in SEZs, the scope of international law protection afforded to foreign investors in SEZ becomes of crucial importance, in particular when it comes to investor risk analysis and the associated costs of foreign investment. China's multiple investment protection treaties and free trade agreement afford varying levels of investment protection to foreign investors. These treaties apply to SEZs as well. The latest investor-State case law suggests that SEZs public solicitation of foreign investment and open investor incentives may serve as basis for investors' claims against China if the foreign investment in SEZ is expropriated or if the SEZs' administration breach the investors' legitimate expectations through adverse regulation or other measures. It is likely that the acts of SEZs' administration that negatively impact foreign investors may engage China's international law liability. On the Lee Jong Baek authority, foreign investors are not defenceless in China's SEZs. If anything, foreign investors have easier access to international investment protection in SEZs, in particular against breaches of their legitimate expectation and indirect expropriation, because the investment incentives offered by SEZs tend to be public and specific. In other words, while there is no risk-free investment, SEZs are no more a "trap" than any other territory or economic unit in China.

In Chapter 18, Prabhash Ranjan completes the review of SEZs-related investment disputes in the difficult context of the Arab Spring and the *Ampal-American and Others v. Egypt* award. The interface between a state's regulatory measures pertaining to the working of a SEZ and the state's international economic law obligations is an interesting area of study. In recent times, a number of states have faced claims before ISDS tribunals for regulations pertaining to SEZ. This chapter studies one such case brought by United States (US) investors against Egypt, challenging Egypt's regulatory measures pertaining to the functioning of their investment in an FEZ. The investment was provided a number of benefits such as lower taxes and duties by the Egyptian authorities. However, later the Egyptian authorities adopted a number of regulatory measures that revoked the benefits such as lower taxation that the foreign investment enjoyed as a free zone company. Subsequently, in view of the Arab Spring Revolution, investor's gas pipeline project was attacked thirteen times. The investor successfully challenged many of these regulatory measures and the acts and omissions of the state of Egypt under the US-Egypt BIT. The case has lessons for Egypt in terms of carefully adopting regulatory measures pertaining to free zones so as to avoid international liability under international investment law.

This book is the product of a conference, the Asia FDI Forum IV, held in Hong Kong on March 22–23, 2018, an event jointly sponsored by the CUHK Law Faculty, KuGuan Law School of Shanghai Jiao Tong University, and the Columbia University Centre for Sustainable Investment (CCSI). Launched by Julien Chaisse in 2015, the series of Asia FDI Forum offers a multi-stakeholder platform anchored in Hong Kong for participants from academia, government, the private section and civil society to discuss regional investment trends, highlight specific characteristics of investment treaties and policies, analyze Asia relationship with other nations of the world and explore the several legal policy implications of the emergence of new actors, issues and norms which determine the future of Asia FDI. The Asia FDI Forum is established to offer an avenue for expert discussion based on academic research and policy-based presentations mostly related to legal development but also supreme economics and politics on FDI in Asia. The theme of SEZs, which was at the core of the Asia FDI Forum IV, also is at the core of the academic collaboration engaged by Professor Jiaxiang Hu and Professor Julien Chaisse.

This book has benefited immensely from contributions from many sources, both at the institutional as well as at the individual level. We are delighted at the final result and would sincerely like to express our gratitude to all who have contributed to this project in one way or the other. We also want to express our gratitude to the many colleagues who supported us in this endeavor, including Cristian Rodriguez Chiffelle and Aditi Sara Verghese (World Economic Forum), Anna Joubin-Bret (Director

UNCITRAL), Jacopo Dettoni (Deputy Editor, FDI Intelligence), Yousuf Mohamed Al-Jaida (Chief Executive Officer and Board Member, Qatar Financial Centre Authority), James Lockett (Vice President, Head of Trade Facilitation and Market Access, Huawei Technologies), Professor Tomoko Ishikawa (University of Nagoya), Li Ka-Yin (Consultant, AnJie Law Firm, Beijing), Professor Rodolphe Desbordes, (SKEMA Business School, Paris), Professor Manjiao Chi (Xiamen University, Xiamen). We are also sincerely thankful to Kluwer Law International for processing this work with efficiency for publication.

CHAPTER 2

Success Factors and Required Policies for SEZs

Marc Proksch

§2.01 INTRODUCTION

Special economic zones (SEZs) take on many different forms but share some common characteristics.[1] SEZs can be defined as 'demarcated geographic areas contained within a country's national boundaries where the rules of business are different from those that prevail in the national territory'.[2] The different rules principally deal with investment conditions, international trade and customs duties, taxation, and the regulatory framework, including incentives not available outside the zone. In particular, the rules and regulations prevailing in SEZs are more liberal than in the rest of the country. However, there is no uniform definition and different countries use different definitions. Common characteristics include a demarcated area with special (more liberal) regulatory frameworks with a specialized decentralized governance structure and containing more developed infrastructural facilities.

1. This chapter was prepared by Marc Proksch, Chief, Investment and Enterprise Development Section of the Trade, Investment and Innovation Division of the United Nations Economic and Social Commission for Asia and the Pacific as an adapted version of Chapter V, section C of the ESCAP Handbook on Policies, Promotion and Facilitation of Foreign Direct Investment for Sustainable Development in Asia and the Pacific (2017), http://www.unescap.org/sites/default/files/FDI%20Handbook-low.pdf.
2. Foreign Investment Advisory Service (FIAS). *Special economic zones: performance, lessons learned, and implications for zone development* (Washington, D.C.: World Bank. 2008). http://documents.worldbank.org/curated/en/343901468330977533/pdf/458690WP0Box331s0April200801PUBLIC1.pdf; Farole, Thomas. *Special economic zones in Africa: comparing performance and learning from global experiences* (Washington, D.C.: World Bank. 2011). http://dx.doi.org/10.1596/978-0-8213-8638-5.

In practice, the category 'SEZ' covers a broad range of more specific zone types, including Free Trade Zones (FTZ), Export Processing Zones (EPZ), Free Zones (FZ), Industrial Estates, Free Ports, Urban Enterprise Zones and others. There are many variations on the theme. FTZs around the world are called by a number of different names, depending on the country in which they are located and the particular type of zone. In the United States, they are referred to as foreign-trade zones. Those in developing countries producing specifically for export are typically called EPZs. They are also called SEZs in China, industrial FZs or export FZs in Ireland, Qualifying Industrial Zones in Jordan and Egypt, FZs in the United Arab Emirates, maquiladoras in Mexico, duty free EPZs or free export zones in the Republic of Korea, EPZs in the Philippines, investment promotion zones in Sri Lanka and foreign trade zones in India.[3] FTZs are a specific type of restricted access (e.g., fenced-in) industrial park housing concentrations of production facilities and related infrastructure. They are typically located at or near sea, air, or land ports. FTZs have become a substantial part of the structure underpinning the global supply chain. United Nations Industrial Development Organization (UNIDO) refers to the more generic term 'economic zones' comprising of industrial parks, SEZs, eco-industrial parks, technology parks and innovation districts.[4] Chen uses the term 'free economic zone' and points out that such zones can also be cross-border cross-national and include international growth zones and growth triangles.[5] However, at the other extreme a single SEZ can contain multiple 'specific' zones within its boundaries. The most prominent examples of this layered approach are Subic Bay Freeport Zone in the Philippines, the Aqaba SEZ Authority in Jordan, Sri City Multi-product SEZ and Mundra SEZ in India.

SEZs are set up for various purposes, often to experiment with economic reform, create employment, and provide superior infrastructure in a smaller area. SEZs are often set up as a pilot project for wider economic reform and almost always involve the attraction of foreign direct investment (FDI) though in many cases SEZs are open to domestic companies (suppliers) also.

SEZs have played an important role in the expansion of global value chains. While rules differ among individual countries, zones typically operate outside the country's boundaries for customs purposes even though they are geographically located inside the country. As a result, the supply chain of products may be scattered among zones all over the world without concern for tariffs, quotas, and detailed customs procedures, until they finally exit the zone system in the country where the

3. Creskoff, Stephen & Peter Walkenhorst. *Implications of WTO disciplines for special economic zones in developing countries*. World Bank Policy Research Working Paper No. 4892. (Washington, D.C. 2009). http://papers.ssrn.com/sol3/papers.cfm?abstract_id = 1410477.
4. United Nations Industrial Development Organization. *Economic zones in the ASEAN: industrial parks, special economic zones, eco-industrial parks, innovation districts as strategies for industrial competitiveness*. (UNIDO Country Office in Viet Nam 2015). http://www.unido.org/fileadmin/user_media_upgrade/Worldwide/Offices/ASIA_and_PACIFIC/UCO_Viet_Nam_Working_Doc.pdf.
5. Chen, Xiangming. *The evolution of free economic zones and the recent development of cross-national growth zones*. 19 International Journal of Urban and Regional Research 593–621 (2009). doi 10.1111/j.1468-2427.1995.tb00530.x.

final product is produced. At that time only, they are subject to tariffs, quotas and full customs procedures.[6]

Bolle and Williams provide a useful description of FTZs and note that such zones around the world are similar in the way they function to facilitate trade but differ in terms of size, economic development purposes, physical characteristics, government incentives, and the final dispensation of their products: 'They may represent large shares of the country's manufacturing employment and occupy huge geographic areas, as in China; or they may be small enclaves housing a few businesses.[7] In developing countries with little infrastructure, they may be self-sufficient city-like industrial complexes with housing, restaurants and banking, as well as production and/or transport facilities. In developed countries, that have extensive infrastructure and modern facilities, they are more narrowly limited to providing production and/or transport facilities. [...]. All zones typically include streamlined customs procedures and exemption or deferral of tariffs and quotas on stored inventories. Those in developing countries are more likely to have additional incentives such as subsidies, more flexible labour market regulations, and additional tax exemptions. While developing countries typically produce for export, they increasingly consume ("import") substantial shares of products made in their free trade zones as they develop.'

Following the Chinese success, SEZs have been established with various success rates in several countries, including Bangladesh, Brazil, Cambodia, India, Islamic Republic of Iran, Jordan, Kazakhstan, Pakistan, the Philippines, Poland, Republic of Korea, Russian Federation, Ukraine, United Arab Emirates, Cambodia, and the Democratic People's Republic of Korea.

For the purpose of attracting FDI, two specific forms of zones can be distinguished: (1) the EPZ or FZ, which focuses on manufacturing for export; and (2) the large-scale SEZ, which usually combines residential and multi-use commercial and industrial activity.[8] The former represents a traditional model which has been used widely throughout the developing world, for instance in Bangladesh, Cambodia, Philippines and Thailand for almost four decades. The latter represents a more recent form of economic zone, originating in the 1980s in China and gaining in popularity in recent years.

The institutional arrangement for SEZs typically involves a developer (investor), operator, and regulator (zone authority) and owner (government or private sector). The institutional structure can vary from fully public (government operator, government developer, government regulator) to fully private (private operator, private developer, public regulator). In many cases, public sector operators and developers act

6. Bolle, Mary Jane & Brock R. Williams. *U.S. foreign-trade zones: background and issues for Congress*. Congressional Research Service. CRS Report no. 7-5700 (2013). http://fas.org/sgp/crs/misc/R42686.pdf.
7. Bolle, Mary Jane & Brock R. Williams. *U.S. foreign-trade zones: background and issues for Congress*. Congressional Research Service. CRS Report no. 7-5700. (2013). http://fas.org/sgp/crs/misc/R42686.pdf.
8. Farole, Thomas & Gokhan Akinci (eds). *Special economic zones: progress, emerging challenges and future directions* (Washington, D.C.: World Bank Group. 2011). https://openknowledge.worldbank.org/handle/10986/2341.

as quasi-government agencies in that they have a pseudo-corporate institutional structure and have budgetary autonomy. SEZs are often developed under a public-private partnership arrangement, in which the public sector provides some level of support (provision of off-site infrastructure, equity investment, soft loans, bond issues, etc.) to enable a private sector developer to obtain a reasonable rate of return on the project (typically 10–20% depending on risk levels).[9]

The Foreign Investment Advisory Services (FIAS) of the World Bank notes that the majority of SEZs in developing and transitional economies are private sector developed and operated.[10] It lists the following models for public-private partnerships:

- Public provision of off-site infrastructure and facilities (utilities connections, roads) as an incentive for private funding of on-site infrastructure and facilities.
- Assembly of land parcels with secure title and development rights by the government for lease to private zone development groups, development of better land use/ownership laws and regulations and adoption of enforceable zoning and land use plans.
- Build-operate-transfer and build-own-operate approaches to on-site and off-site zone infrastructure and facilities, with government guarantees and/or financial support.
- Contracting private management for government-owned zones or lease of government zone assets by a private operator (beneficial ownership).

Equity-shifting arrangements whereby a private contract manager of a government zone can exercise a purchase option once pre-defined performance levels have been reached.

[A] Have SEZs Been Successful?

Experiences with SEZs have demonstrated that they have been relatively successful in terms of economic impact depending on their specific purpose in some countries but not in others. Empirical studies tend to focus on the economic impact of government-run zones rather than private sector run zones. Studies that have focused on the social and environmental impact of SEZs usually found a negative impact, but they failed to address the economic impacts which may have been positive.[11] Studies have also generally failed to compare the impact of incentives in SEZs compared to the impact of

9. http://www.internationaldevelopmentgroup.com/practice-areas/public-private-partnerships-special-economic-zones.
10. Foreign Investment Advisory Service (FIAS). *Special economic zones: performance, lessons learned, and implications for zone development*. (Washington, D.C.: World Bank. 2008). http://documents.worldbank.org/curated/en/343901468330977533/pdf/458690WP0Box331s0April200801PUBLIC1.pdf.
11. Foreign Investment Advisory Service (FIAS). *Special economic zones: performance, lessons learned, and implications for zone development*. (Washington, D.C.: World Bank. 2008). http://documents.worldbank.org/curated/en/343901468330977533/pdf/458690WP0Box331s0April200801PUBLIC1.pdf.

incentives in sectors operating outside the zones. In any case, in order to appropriately ssess impact, there is a need to define what constitutes zone benefits and costs. FIAS and Farole and Akinci distinguish both static and dynamic economic benefits:[12]

- Direct employment creation and income generation.
- Export growth and export diversification.
- Foreign exchange earnings.
- FDI attraction (and the benefits of FDI).
- Contribution to government revenues.

The dynamic benefits are long-term and much harder to measure, but are potentially far more important and are directly linked to the expected benefits of FDI and include:

- Indirect employment creation (including through backward linkages between transnational corporations (TNCs) and domestic companies which are located either inside or outside the zone).
- Skills upgrading.
- Female employment.
- Technology transfer.
- 'Demonstration effect' arising from the application of 'best practices'.

FIAS further notes that regional development zone development also entails a range of financial and economic costs, including salaries of government workers in the zone authority and other operating expenses; infrastructure development outlays; import duties and charges lost; and taxes foregone from firms relocating from the domestic customs territory to the zone.[13] Clearly, the costs to government are higher for government-developed, operated and managed SEZs. The costs also tend to be higher for SEZs that have been developed without a proper cost-benefit analysis with reference to their selected location and stated purpose and SEZs that have been developed and operated by government entities and/or officials that do not have the required competence, skills or resources. With broad-based political commitments and a conducive policy environment SEZs have clearly had a positive impact on economic variables such as employment generation, exports and FDI as China's and Bangladesh's SEZs have demonstrated. However, these benefits have to be assessed against the costs, including social and environmental costs.

12. Foreign Investment Advisory Service (FIAS). *Special economic zones: performance, lessons learned, and implications for zone development*. (Washington, D.C.: World Bank. 2008). http://documents.worldbank.org/curated/en/343901468330977533/pdf/458690WP0Box331s0April200801PUBLIC1.pdf; Farole, Thomas & Gokhan Akinci (eds). *Special economic zones: progress, emerging challenges and future directions*. (Washington, D.C.: World Bank Group. 2011). https://openknowledge.worldbank.org/handle/10986/2341.
13. Foreign Investment Advisory Service (FIAS). *Special economic zones: performance, lessons learned, and implications for zone development*. (Washington, D.C.: World Bank. 2008). http://documents.worldbank.org/curated/en/343901468330977533/pdf/458690WP0Box331s0April200801PUBLIC1.pdf.

The costs of SEZs clearly go beyond economic costs only and include social and environmental costs. Many SEZs have been accused of undermining labour and environmental standards as incentives for foreign investors seeking pollution havens. Often, land grabbing has displaced farmers who have received little compensation. SEZs often lead to negative impacts on the environment through unsustainable water use, air pollution and factory effluents. For instance, UNIDO reports that 'although industrial parks in Vietnam have positively contributed to Vietnam's rapid economic transformation, they have also widely contributed to Vietnam's environmental degradation.[14] Around one-third of all industrial zones in Vietnam do not have a centralized waste water treatment or sewage system. Additionally, industrial zones consume lots of energy due to inefficient production methods. Most companies in industrial zones have not adopted strict environmental standards and release toxic emissions such as dust, SO_2, NOx, GHG, UP-POP contributing to the air quality degradation.' In order to fast track approvals for investors in SEZs, a proper environmental impact assessment is often done away with. FIAS comprehensively discusses the economic, social and environmental impacts of SEZs.[15] In order to make SEZs contribute to sustainable development, these issues need to be addressed through a proper policy and regulatory package.

The empirical evidence of the actual impact is mixed and hampered by considerable statistical challenges. Farole and Akinci cite evidence of the successful contribution of SEZs to static economic benefits (in particular employment) in Bangladesh, China, Republic of Korea, Taiwan Province of China and Vietnam but notes that the cheap labour advantage of SEZs is being eroded by more sophisticated determinants of FDI such as higher skills, technology and the need for better infrastructure in sectors other than labour-intensive industries (which are, in any case, subject to a high level of automation).[16] In addition, as members of the World Trade Organization (WTO), countries may need to review the structure of export incentives and subsidies in order to make it compatible with the WTO regime (in particular the ban on specific subsidies which are contingent on export performance). Similarly, performance requirements may run afoul with the WTO Agreement on Trade-Related Investment Measures (TRIMS).

Aggarwal and others note that that the role SEZs have played in export performance and productive diversification in Bangladesh, India and Sri Lanka varied across

14. United Nations Industrial Development Organization. *Economic zones in the ASEAN: industrial parks, special economic zones, eco-industrial parks, innovation districts as strategies for industrial competitiveness*. (UNIDO Country Office in Viet Nam. 2015) http://www.unido.org/fileadmin/user_media_upgrade/Worldwide/Offices/ASIA_and_PACIFIC/UCO_Viet_Nam_Working_Doc.pdf.
15. Foreign Investment Advisory Service (FIAS). *Special economic zones: performance, lessons learned, and implications for zone development*. (Washington, D.C.: World Bank. 2008). http://documents.worldbank.org/curated/en/343901468330977533/pdf/458690WP0Box331s0April200801PUBLIC1.pdf.
16. Farole, Thomas & Gokhan Akinci (eds). *Special economic zones: progress, emerging challenges and future directions*. (Washington, D.C.: World Bank Group. 2011). https://openknowledge.worldbank.org/handle/10986/2341.

sectors and products.[17] In particular, they note that 'some of the sectors in Bangladesh, India, and Sri Lanka in which substantial exports from SEZs can be observed were already outward-oriented before SEZs were set up'. They do find evidence of the contribution of SEZs in these countries to product and export diversification and growth.

SEZs have been relatively successful in ASEAN countries, in particular in Malaysia and the Philippines. For instance, in 2012, Clark SEZ in the Philippines contributed to USD 4 billion export revenue and employment for 70,000 workers while economic zones in Vietnam contribute to 40% of the country's total exports.[18] A study on Malaysia's SEZs, which played an important role in boosting the country's production and exports of electronics, found that the EPZs have been a success when it comes to direct effects, but that the indirect effects are still relatively limited and concentrated to certain areas, such as Penang.[19]

A UNIDO study reports that there are more than 1,000 economic zones in ASEAN (most are industrial parks) including over eighty SEZs.[20] The study also notes that ASEAN countries compete fiercely in attracting FDI in SEZs through generous incentives. It is difficult to measure the impact of SEZs in ASEAN as management structures and compilation of statistics differ widely among the individual countries. For instance, Malaysia and Indonesia have no government body in charge of economic zones, while Thailand and Vietnam have government bodies, i.e., the Industrial Estate Authority of Thailand in Thailand and Department of Economic Zones at the Ministry of Planning and Investment in Vietnam, respectively. These bodies are in charge of monitoring and promoting economic zones in their respective countries. SEZs also play an important role in the drive of Cambodia and Vietnam to achieve middle income status through industrialization though there are serious social and environmental concerns as noted above. Myanmar is the latest country to jump on the SEZ bandwagon. In particular, the country's development of the Dawei SEZ in Myanmar has been plagued by numerous delays, sustainability concerns, cost overruns, lack of rule of law and proper governance.

17. Aggarwal, Aradhna et al. *Special economic zones and economic diversification: some evidence from South Asia*. In *Breaking into new markets: emerging lessons for export diversification*. (Richard Newfarmer et al. eds., Washington, D.C. World Bank. 2009) chapter 13. http://citeseerx.ist.psu.edu/viewdoc/download?doi=10.1.1.457.488&rep=rep1&type=pdf#page=249.
18. United Nations Industrial Development Organization. *Economic zones in the ASEAN: industrial parks, special economic zones, eco-industrial parks, innovation districts as strategies for industrial competitiveness*. (UNIDO Country Office in Viet Nam. 2015). http://www.unido.org/fileadmin/user_media_upgrade/Worldwide/Offices/ASIA_and_PACIFIC/UCO_Viet_Nam_Working_Doc.pdf.
19. Furby, Mats. *Evaluating the Malaysian export processing zones with special focus on the electronic industry* (Master thesis. School of Economics and Management. Lund University. 2005). http://econwpa.repec.org/eps/it/papers/0510/0510004.pdf.
20. United Nations Industrial Development Organization. *Economic zones in the ASEAN: industrial parks, special economic zones, eco-industrial parks, innovation districts as strategies for industrial competitiveness*. (UNIDO Country Office in Viet Nam. 2015). http://www.unido.org/fileadmin/user_media_upgrade/Worldwide/Offices/ASIA_and_PACIFIC/UCO_Viet_Nam_Working_Doc.pdf.

Based on several decades of experience with SEZs, FIAS cites the most common obstacles to their success:[21]

- poor site locations, entailing heavy capital expenditures;
- uncompetitive policies – reliance on tax holidays, rigid performance requirements, poor labour policies and practices;
- uncompetitive fiscal incentives;
- poor zone development practices – inappropriately designed or over-designed facilities, inadequate maintenance and promotion practices;
- subsidized rent and other services;
- cumbersome regulations and procedures and restrictive controls on zone activity;
- inadequate administrative structures or too many bodies involved in zone administration; weak administrative bodies;
- lack of coordination between private developers and governments in infrastructure provision;
- exclusion of merchandise processed in zones from entry under bilateral and regional trade agreements.

Some other reasons why SEZs have failed to increase economic development include poor strategic planning, corruption, lack of finance and mismatch of comparative advantages. The failure to create an attractive investment environment has also been one of the factors.[22]

There is a lack of systematic data-driven analysis on the performance of economic zones around the world which hampers evidence-based policy making.[23] In this regard, the opportunity costs of developing SEZs can be significant, i.e., could the resources be used for more socially-desirable policies instead, such as education and health? Or could the same development objectives be achieved more efficiently through other modalities than SEZs? And to what extent are SEZs trying to compensate for the lack of nation-wide economic reforms? Another obstacle is the lack of a proper demand assessment. SEZ developments should be demand-driven and respond to market requirements which often require a feasibility study.

In the end, the experiences with SEZs have been mixed. There is ample evidence that they have been relatively successful in East Asia in terms of employment

21. Foreign Investment Advisory Service (FIAS), *Special economic zones: performance, lessons learned, and implications for zone development*. (Washington, D.C.: World Bank. 2008).
22. International Finance Corporation (IFC). 'Assessing private sector contributions to job creation and poverty reduction' (2013). http://www1.ifc.org/wps/wcm/connect/0fe6e2804e2c0a8f8d3bad7a9dd66321/IFC_FULL + JOB + STUDY + REPORT_JAN2013_FINAL.pdf?MOD = AJPERES; Farole, Thomas. *Special economic zones in Africa: comparing performance and learning from global experiences*. (Washington, D.C.: World Bank. 2011) http://dx.doi.org/10.1596/978-0-8213-8638-5.
23. Farole, Thomas. *Special economic zones in Africa: comparing performance and learning from global experiences*. (Washington, D.C.: World Bank. 2011). http://dx.doi.org/10.1596/978-0-8213-8638-5.

generation, technology transfer and industrial restructuring, mostly through the attraction of FDI. As FIAS (2008) notes:

> In Malaysia and the Philippines, there has been significant industrial upgrading in the electronics sector located mainly within zones. The Philippine Economic Zone Authority has documented the substantial rise in skill levels in the Philippine eco-zones, with decreases in the proportion of the production workforce in electronics industries in favour of more skill-intensive design and research activities. The software technology parks in India, for example, were critical to the expansion and upgrading of ICT activities, not just in terms of routine data entry and software coding operations, but also in much more complex software development, content development, and multimedia operations.

The next sub-section seeks to summarize the success factors for SEZs and policy recommendations for successful SEZ development, operation and management.

[B] Success Factors and Policy Recommendations for SEZ Development, Operation and Management

Based on the previous analysis, the following key success factors for effective SEZs can be identified:

- They meet FDI determinants/investor requirements.
- They have a clear purpose and objective.
- They are well integrated in national development strategies.
- They have good governance and competent management.
- There is private sector participation in SEZ development and management.
- They are governed by proper regulation and incentive structure (including a specific SEZ Law).
- They have excellent infrastructure and logistics, including multi-modal connectivity, superior to the rest of the country.
- They have been developed on the basis of proper land and resource use planning and rights/zoning.
- There are developed on the basis of international demand for products and services produced in SEZs.
- They have access to suitably skilled labour.
- They are actually competitive with other locations for investors.
- They have proper linkages with the domestic economy outside the SEZs and allow domestic enterprises, including SMEs to operate within the zones.
- They enjoy flexibility and incorporate industry/cluster formation.
- They are environmentally and socially sustainable, as determined by appropriate feasibility studies undertaken before their development.

§2.02 CONCLUSION

Based on best practices and the available literature the following observations and recommendations regarding SEZs as a modality to attract FDI and stimulate economic growth can be made:[24]

(1) As the global economy is changing and the United States and Europe are losing their position as the drivers of global demand, the establishment of traditional SEZs/EPZs focusing on assembly activities may not be as successful a strategy as in the past. Unless countries have significant labour cost advantages or can offer a large domestic market, they need more sophisticated strategies to attract investment.

(2) SEZs need to be competitive and prevent 'enclave' syndrome. In particular, the focus of SEZs needs to shift from attracting labour-intensive to innovation-driven investment. The traditional concept of SEZs/EPZs is losing competitive relevance in the wake of global supply chain consolidation, weaknesses in traditional export markets, global regulation (WTO) and the loss of low labour costs as a competitive advantage. Higher value-added, technology- and service-driven zones are more important (ICT, biotech, etc.).

(3) New SEZs should focus on wielding stronger physical, strategic and financial links with the local economy. The provision of excellent infrastructure, reliable power and skilled labour is much more important than incentives. SEZs should have a fully operational single window for all investment approvals and facilitation. Attractive on-site residential facilities (schools, shopping, R&R) should be available. In short, SEZs need to create a more attractive investment environment than in the rest of the country.

(4) SEZs should be located in strategic locations, i.e., close to population and urban centres with sophisticated infrastructure (ports, railroads, roads, etc.). SEZs could be developed as part of dry ports as well in inland areas.

(5) SEZ regimes should be flexible, allowing a range of commercial as well as manufacturing activities. Ideally, modern SEZs should become part of national and subnational innovation systems, with focus on R&D, compliance with international standards and availability of certification agencies, and training of SEZ personnel.

---

24. Engman, Michael et al. *Export processing zones: past and future role in trade and investment*. OECD Trade Policy Working Paper No. 53. (2007). http://search.oecd.org/officialdocuments/displaydocumentpdf/?doclanguage=en&cote=td/tc/wp(2006)39/final; Farole, Thomas & Gokhan Akinci (eds). *Special economic zones: progress, emerging challenges and future directions*. (Washington, D.C.: World Bank Group 2011). https://openknowledge.worldbank.org/handle/10986/2341; Foreign Investment Advisory Service (FIAS), *Special economic zones: performance, lessons learned, and implications for zone development*. (Washington, D.C.: World Bank. 2008). http://documents.worldbank.org/curated/en/343901468330977533/pdf/458690WP0Box331s0April200801PUBLIC1.pdf.

(6) Incentives can be provided through regulatory and administrative incentives and facilitation rather than fiscal incentives; business development services (including facilities for R&D and skills development) are more important than tax incentives. Incentives should be performance based.
(7) Zones should not replace efforts to implement trade and investment reform in the whole country. They can be used as a testing ground to see what reforms could work on an economy-wide basis. The success of the economic zone is determined by the extent it can create linkages with the local economy.[25]
(8) Domestic (SME) suppliers need the required capacity to meet prevailing industry standards. SMEs in the zone or supplying companies that are resident in the zone may also need access to incentives such as duty-free imports and tax privileges. The clustering effects may be so strong that foreign investors are willing to invest in the area even if the policy environment or location is less attractive.[26]
(9) Services industry and FDI in services are becoming increasingly important. However, there is no explicit need to have SEZs to develop services.
(10) Legal restrictions for domestic investment in SEZs need to be lifted while labour markets need to be flexible: seamless movement of labour between the zones and rest of the economy. There should be no discrimination between foreign and local companies in treatment. Zones should preferably have a multi-market orientation, not just for export.
(11) Logistics costs are sometimes higher than manufacturing costs. SEZs need to address logistics, i.e., location and multi-modal transportation links as well as proximity to distribution channels and sales support are important.
(12) SEZs need to be aligned with changing competitiveness as a result of FTAs, in particular mega-regionals such as the ASEAN Economic Community, Comprehensive and Progress Agreement for Trans-Pacific Partnership and Regional Comprehensive Economic Partnership.
(13) SEZs should provide necessary infrastructure and common services. However, they do not address the need for investment facilitation and cutting red tape. In addition, skilled labour supply is another prerequisite which does not automatically come with SEZs. SEZs can only be effective with a proper and competent management structure.
(14) SEZs need independent regulatory bodies backed up by law. The regulatory authority may be different from the development agency.
(15) The private sector should take the lead in development and management; public-private partnerships for infrastructure development and financing work best under proper management and regulatory structures.

25. Organisation for Economic Co-operation and Development (OECD) (2010). *Designing economic zones for effective investment promotion. Presentation.* http://www.oecd.org/mena/investment/44866506.pdf.
26. Yehoue, Etienne B, *Clusters as a driving engine for FDI*, 26 Economic Modelling 934–945 (2009). Elsevier. http://www.sciencedirect.com/science/article/pii/S0264999309000467.

(16) Zone authorities should have sufficient autonomy, particularly over staffing, budgets, spending, and policymaking. An independent board should oversee the operations of the zone authority. The board should comprise of key government ministers and private sector representatives and report to the highest level of government. Ideally, private sector representatives should constitute the majority of board membership to ensure flexibility, results-orientation, and customer-focus.

(17) Zone designation criteria are helpful in fulfilling zone objectives. Such criteria address requirements for area, space and site allocations, locations, usage of facilities, residents, type of business and investors, sewage and waste water disposal, wages and labour conditions, public utilities, time indications for development, etc.

(18) Zones should be managed on a cost recovery basis and should be customer focused. Cost recovery basis is enhanced by limiting subsidies and charging fees that are based on market prices.

(19) Proper coordination mechanisms among government agencies involved in policy making, investment, trade, zone development, land development, labour, finance and customs, etc.) should be established. Proper coordination between national and local government is also necessary.

(20) Environmental and social sustainability is essential for SEZs but often lacking. Full transparency is required in construction, bidding and operations. Involvement of local communities in the establishment of zones and land purchases, relocation and determining compensation strategies is also required.

(21) SEZs need to comply with international standards and rules, i.e., prevailing FTAs and WTO (e.g., TRIMS, SCM Agreement), ILO (on labour standards).

(22) SEZs should be demand-led. The information contained in the feasibility study should be used in master planning and development phasing and: (a) should be based on 'real-world' financial and economic-impact analyses; (b) ensure that public investments in infrastructure are economically efficient; (c) analyse potential market appetite and demand (both 'pent-up' and existing) for investment in manufacturing and commercial sectors bearing in mind the improved business environment offered by an SEZ regime.

Hence, the purpose of demand assessment is to: identify the main target sectors for investment at SEZs; determine investors' critical investment drivers and constraints; Estimate investor demand for serviced land (m^2), pre-built facility space (m^2), and utility services in two twenty-year scenarios: a base case – likely scenario and an aggressive case – best-case scenario.

CHAPTER 3

Investment, Regional Development and Compliance with Internal Market Rules in EU Free Zones: Challenges Ahead

Alessandro Spano

§3.01 INTRODUCTION

European Union (EU) free zones consist of geographic areas where state authorities may decide to introduce a series of ad hoc incentives for companies conducting their business activities in the region. As a result, these zones have often become 'growth poles' for the concerned regions and, ultimately, for the whole country. Incentives may assume various forms including exemptions on customs arrangements and, in particular, tax incentives. However, special tax regimes available in free zones are subject to the careful scrutiny of the European Commission (EC) to verify their compliance with EU State aid rules and, ultimately, with common market principles. Within this context, this chapter discusses the regulatory challenges related to EU free zones to avoid competition distortions within the common market with particular focus on the issue of tax incentives offered by Member States in these zones. The analysis also attempts to study if existing EU legal and policy instruments have been successful in connecting the different levels of national and European governance in a satisfactory manner, and in ensuring effectiveness and transparency in the regulation of free zones in the EU. The Chapter is divided in three parts. In discussing the rationale and some key aspects of free zones in the EU, the first part of the Chapter examines the relationship of tax incentives in free zones with EU State aid rules. The second part of the Chapter discusses how the concept of State aid in relation to direct tax measures has been interpreted by the EC and by the EU courts. It appears that EU State aid policy is functional to the achievement of the goals of the common market. On the one side, such an approach allows EU institutions to target a wide range of national tax measures with potentially harmful effects on competition. However, on the other side, by affecting the fiscal autonomy of Member States, it raises tensions between national fiscal policy and EU state aid policy. The final part of this Chapter discusses the past and current approaches of EU institutions towards special tax regimes available in free zones. The study will also consider the importance of transparency and effective supervision in the use of tax incentives by businesses operating in these zones to preserve the unity of the common market. Ultimately, the analysis aims to highlight recent trends and regulatory challenges in relation to the functioning of economic zones in the EU and the role played by international economic law within this context.

[A] EU Free Zones: Regional Development, Tax Incentives and State Aid Policy

In the EU, 'free zones' are defined as '*enclosed areas within the customs territory of the Union where non-Union goods can be introduced free of import duty, other charges (i.e. taxes) and commercial policy measures*'.[1] However, the enactment of more liberal trade measures in these free zones is not a goal in itself but it aims to promote the economic and social development of the concerned region or industry.[2] For this purpose, in addition to exemptions on customs arrangements to attract investors in the region, many other incentives are usually implemented by State authorities in free zones including tax exemptions, simplified administrative procedures, streamlined customs administration and the provision of infrastructure.[3] In the EU, free zones including special economic zones (SEZs) are present in the territory of many Member States. Some examples include the Shannon free zone established in Ireland in 1959; the Madeira free zone established in Portugal in 1980; and fourteen SEZs operating in Poland.[4]

As a general rule, Member States are free to designate parts of the customs territory as free zones, but these zones must be communicated to the EC for prior approval. Thus, the establishment of a free zone in the EU requires careful planning by

1. European Commission, *Taxation and Custom Union – Free Zones*, https://ec.europa.eu/taxation_customs/business/customs-procedures/what-is-importation/free-zones_en#.

   The European Commission further clarifies that these non-Union goods 'may, following the period in the free zones, be released for free circulation (subject to payment of import duty and other charges), or be placed under another special procedure (e.g. inward processing, temporary admission or end-use procedures – under the conditions laid down for these procedures) or re-exported. Union goods may also be entered into or stored, moved, used, processed or consumed in free zones. Such goods may afterwards be exported or brought into other parts of the customs territory of the Union.' Ibid.
2. Willemijn de Jong, *Establishing Free Zones for regional development*, Library of the European Parliament, Briefing (12 March 2013), http://www.europarl.europa.eu/RegData/bibliotheque/briefing/2013/130481/LDM_BRI(2013)130481_REV1_EN.pdf.
3. *Ibid.*, at p. 2. Free zones generally fall into the following categories: '*free trade zones (pure re-export of traded goods), export processing zones (export of goods with value added), special economic zones (multi-sectoral approaches to economic activity within the zone), and industrial zones (specific economic activities hosted in the zone).*' *Ibid.*, at p. 1.
4. A list of free zones in the Member States and the competent customs authorities is https://ec.europa.eu/taxation_customs/sites/taxation/files/resources/documents/customs/procedural_aspects/imports/free_zones/list_freezones.pdf.

national policy makers since one of the most critical aspects in this area is the obligation to comply with the EU legal framework. The reasons behind the decision to create free zones are multiple and, although these zones do not represent an answer to all possible regional problems, they may be successful in improving the economic and social conditions in Member States' underdeveloped regions. Indicators of the success of free economic zones entail, *inter alia*, a higher level of productivity, an increased employment rate and more disposable income for the local population in the concerned region. However, the implementation of special rules and policies in free zones is subject to a series of restrictions and to the continuous regulatory supervision of EU institutions. Although poverty reduction is still a priority in various European regions, at European level, there is no consensus about what interventions and policies are more successful to tackle this issue in the long term.[5]

Furthermore, the sui generis system of governance and regulatory framework of the EU entail additional challenges in relation to the type, number and duration of free zones in Member States. From a substantive point of view, the interconnection between EU and national legal sources cannot be ignored. This mainly refers to the system of primary and secondary legal sources provided in the EU Treaty and their relationship with national law on the basis of the well-known doctrines of direct effect and supremacy of EU law.[6] From a procedural perspective, the EU's judicial architecture, as currently conceived, is vertically integrated. Judicial functions are shared between the EU and the national level. Accordingly, both EU courts and national judicial bodies are required in their respective jurisdictions to ensure the harmonious interpretation and application of the EU legal principles across Member States.[7] This is the reason why in the EU, legal and economic relations among Member States are specifically regulated. It follows that this common legal framework and, more in general, the EU law making process itself limit the (economic) sovereignty of Member States, at least, in certain areas. [8]

To complicate matters further, if compared to the situation in other jurisdictions, in the EU, transparency issues related to the existence and the functioning of free zones touch upon the constitutional foundation of the EU system itself. It is worth noting that the limits of EU competences are governed by the principle of conferral and their use is governed by the principles of subsidiarity and proportionality.[9] Under the principle of conferral, EU institutions can act only within the limits of the competences conferred upon them by Member States in the Treaties to attain the objectives set out therein.

5. This issue refers, *inter alia*, to the implementation of the European Structural and Investment Funds. *See*, for instance, European Commission, *Strategic report 2017 on the implementation of European Structural and Investment Funds*, COM(2017) 755 final. http://ec.europa.eu/regional_policy/en/information/publications/reports/2017/strategic-report-2017-on-the implementation-of-european-structural-and-investment-funds.
6. For a general discussion, *see inter alia*, Paul Craig & Gráinne de Búrca, *EU Law – Text, Cases, and Materials* (sixth edition, OUP, 2015); and Damian Chalmers et al., *European Union Law Text and Materials* (third edition, CUP, 2014).
7. *Ibid.*
8. *Ibid.*
9. Article 5(1) TEU. Treaty of Lisbon amending the Treaty on European Union and the Treaty establishing the European Community [2007] OJ C306/01.

Competences not conferred upon them in the Treaties remain with the Member States.[10]

At the same time, the EU Treaty expressly states that: '*pursuant to the principle of sincere cooperation, the Union and the Member States shall, in full mutual respect, assist each other in carrying out tasks which flow from the Treaties.*'[11] This obligation is twofold. On the one side, Member States are required to take any appropriate measure, whether general or particular, to ensure the fulfilment of the obligations arising out of the EU Treaty or resulting from the acts of EU institutions (i.e., positive obligation). On the other side, Member States must facilitate the achievement of EU tasks and refrain from any measure which could jeopardise the attainment of the EU objectives (i.e., negative obligation).[12] From an institutional viewpoint, the EC is the guardian of the Treaties, and, in this role, it must ensure and verify the compliance of Member States' legislation with EU law in selected fields.[13] Free zones, however, are special areas which are in essence granted a series of exemptions from the normal EU law regime. Accordingly, the special legal status of these areas implies additional regulatory efforts for the EC to avoid the emergence of asymmetries and imbalances in the common market. Within this context, transparency becomes crucial. Free zones generally operate as specific entities within a larger administration, and, thus, roles and prerogatives need to be clearly distributed. This is not always an easy task to achieve and, the risk is that free economic zones may be perceived '*as reducing trade in competing normal jurisdictions, whereas, on the other hand, local constituencies could perceive enquires to be intrusive*'.[14] Furthermore, an additional risk is that free economic zones not only attract legitimate business but they may also offer opportunities for the perpetration of illegal activities. Finally, when it comes to financial services and tax incentives, these zones may be perceived to function like offshore jurisdictions.[15] In this regard, the lack of transparency in the functioning and supervision of free zones has the potential to undermine the credibility and, in turn, the stability of the EU system of governance that, in its essence, depends on the respect of mutual obligations by all Members States and where exceptions to this common system of rules must be justified on the basis of objective criteria.

Beyond more favourable customs arrangements, exemptions and incentives in free zones may assume various forms. However, in recent years, particular attention from EU institutions has focused on tax schemes and incentives granted by Member

10. Article 5(2) TEU.
11. Article 4(3) TEU.
12. *Ibid.* For general discussion, *see* Craig and de Búrca, *supra*, footnote 6.
13. With reference to the relevant legal basis in the Lisbon Treaty, *see* Article 17 TEU, and Articles 234, 244 to 250, 290 and 291TFEU.
14. de Jong, *supra*, footnote 2, at p. 6.
15. For instance, this issue was recently the subject of a heated debate in the case of the FTZ of Madeira which was labelled by the European Green Party as a '*tax haven*' in the EU. *See* Maximilian Zierer et al., *Madeira – A Tax Haven Approved by the European Commission* (BR Data and BR Recherce, 2017), http://web.br.de/madeira/english/.

States in these areas.[16] Tax incentives available in free zones are meant to make a particular region more attractive for potential investors but, at the same time, they may distort competition and, consequently, affect the accomplishment of the EU common market. This is the reason why, in the EU, national tax incentives are subject to EU State aid rules. For instance, once the key features of a free zone have been designed, national authorities will need to notify the EC to assess compliance with State aid legislation under the EU Treaty.[17] In its *'Guidelines on regional state aid for 2014–2020'*, the EC expressly recognises that regional State aid is a key instrument to promote regional development in many Member States.[18] On the basis of Article 107(3)(a) and (c) TFEU, the EC may consider compatible with the internal market State aid to promote the economic development of disadvantaged areas in the EU.[19] Furthermore, in the Guidelines, the EC lists under what conditions regional aid may be considered compatible with the internal market and establishes the criteria for identifying the areas that fulfil the conditions laid down in Article 107(3)(a) and (c) of the Treaty.[20] However, while the primary objective of State aid control in the field of regional aid is to allow aid for regional development, at the same time, the EC aims at establishing *'a level playing field between Member States, in particular by preventing subsidy races that may occur when they try to attract or retain businesses in disadvantaged areas of the Union, and to limit the effects of regional aid on trade and competition to the minimum necessary'*.[21] Member States enjoy a high degree of autonomy in the formulation of their fiscal policy but tax incentives are closely related to State aid, and, consequently, they are not automatically valid under EU law. Relevant legal and economic arguments can still be raised by State authorities to justify the existence of tax incentives in free zones since the principles governing the EU State aid regime can be overweight, under certain circumstances, by legitimate national interests. However, although no absolute prohibition exists against tax incentives, the actual content, functioning and duration of these measures always depends on a preliminary assessment of the EC in the process of granting exemptions. In this regard, the EU legal framework reflects the attempt of EU policy makers to balance the multiple objectives and policies of the EU with the ones of Member States. However, although the EU Treaty emphasises the respect of the

16. For a general discussion on types of tax incentives available in free zones, *see* Chang Woon Nam & Doina Radulescu, *Types of Tax Concessions for Attracting Foreign Direct Investment in Free Economic Zones*, CESifo Working paper No. 1175, 1-21 (2004).
17. *See* Articles 107–109 TFEU. It is worth noting that, as a general rule, all measures consisting of State aid must be notified by Member States to the European Commission for approval unless they fall under the scope of the *de minimis* Regulation or the General Block Exemption Regulation. Furthermore, the European Commission has the duty to order recovery of State aid which requires Member States to seek a refund from the recipients. For a general discussion on the State aid legal regime in the EU, *see* Andrea Biondi et al., *The Law of State Aid in the European Union* (OUP, 2004).
18. European Commission, *Guidelines on regional state aid for 2014–2020,* [2013] OJ C209/1. https://eur-lex.europa.eu/LexUriServ/LexUriServ.do?uri=OJ:C:2013:209:0001:0045:EN:PDF.
19. *Ibid.*, point 1.
20. *Ibid.*, point 2.
21. *Ibid.*, point 3.

essential functions of Member States by EU institutions,[22] the expansion of the reach of EU action has progressively increased tensions and frictions between different levels of governance in the EU.

[B] The Application of EU State Aid Rules to Direct Tax Measures

The qualification of a public measure as State aid precedes the assessment of its compatibility with Treaty rules and the analysis of its potentially positive effects on the market. For instance, Biondi notes that Article 107 TFEU (the main Treaty provision in the area of State aid) does not provide a list of prohibited measures.[23] The Article simply reads that: '*any aid granted by a Member State or through State resources in any form whatsoever which distorts or threatens to distort competition by favouring certain undertakings or the production of certain goods shall, in so far as it affects trade between Member States, be incompatible with the internal market.*'[24] It follows that the notion of State aid is extremely broad and, consequently, it allows a flexible interpretation by the EU institutions.[25] Furthermore, in its case law, the CJEU clarified that the classification as aid requires that all the conditions set out in Article 107 TFEU should be fulfilled. In Altmark, the Court held: '*First, there must be an intervention by the State or through State resources. Second, the intervention must be liable to affect trade between Member States. Third, it must confer an advantage on the recipient. Fourth, it must distort or threaten to distort competition.*'[26] Thus, if a public measure satisfies all these four conditions, it is classified as aid and it is automatically incompatible with the common market, unless the exceptions listed in Article 107 (2) or (3) are applicable in the concrete case. In sum, the definition of State aid as provided in the EU Treaty and as developed in the jurisprudence of the CJEU includes any direct intervention by a Member State or every intervention where a transfer of public resources is present.[27] Moving to the issue of State aid in the forms of tax measures, it is worth noting that EU rules on State aid target all public measures even in cases where no explicit provision

22. Article 4(2) TEU reads: '*The Union shall respect the equality of Member States before the Treaties as well as their national identities, inherent in their fundamental structures, political and constitutional, inclusive of regional and local self-government. It shall respect their essential State functions [...].*'
23. Andrea Biondi, *Gli aiuti di Stato*, in *La concorrenza, Trattato di diritto privato dell' UE* 447–488 (Aldo Frignani & Roberto Pardolesi eds, Giappichelli 2006). For general discussion, *see also* Biondi et al., *supra*, footnote 17.
24. Article 107(1) TFEU.
25. Jan Alex Winter, *Redefining the Notion of State Aid in Article 87(1) of the EC Treaty*, 41 Common Market Law Review 475–504 (2004).
26. Case C-280/00 *Altmark Trans GmbH, Regierungspräsidium Magdeburg v. Nahverkerge-sellschaft Altmark GmbH* [2003] ECR I-7747, para. 75.
27. Alice Pisapia, *The Role of EU State Aid Policy in Enhancing the Development of the Industrial Sector* (Economic Trends & Economic Policy, 135, 45–65, 51, 2015). For a discussion on the notion of State aid as interpreted by EU courts in recent years *see* Andrea Biondi, *State Aid is Falling down, Falling down: An Analysis of the Case Law on the Notion of Aid*, 50(6) Common Market Law Review 1719–1743 (2013); and Andrea Biondi & Oana Andreea Stefan, *The Notice on the Notion of State Aid: Every Light Has Its Shadow*, in *The Modernisation of EU State Aid Control – Evolution and Perspectives of the EU Rules on State Aids and Services of General Economic Interest* (Nascimbene eds, Springer, 2017).

is provided in the EU Treaty. Accordingly, State aid rules also apply in the area of direct taxation, although, no general competence to regulate national tax measures exists at EU level. In this regard, in its case law, the CJEU pointed out that, in the exercise of their reserved powers, Member States can derogate from the obligation imposed on them by the EU Treaties only on the conditions laid down in the Treaties themselves.[28] Furthermore, in the event of a unilateral action or measure implemented by a State in derogation of the provisions of the Treaty, an intervention by the EU institutions as soon as possible meets a fundamental requirement for the proper functioning of the common market.[29] The EU Treaty does not contain an express definition of the concept of subsidy or aid. A subsidy is generally defined as a payment made in support of an enterprise (or a group of enterprises) other than the payment by the purchaser or consumer for the goods or services. An aid is a similar concept but, here, emphasis is placed on its purpose and it seems especially devised for a particular objective which cannot usually be achieved without outside help.[30] Furthermore, in its early case law on State aid, the CJEU pointed out that: *'the concept of aid is nevertheless wider than that of a subsidy because it embraces not only positive benefits, such as subsidies themselves, but also interventions which, in various forms, mitigate the charges which are normally included in the budget of an undertaking and which, without, therefore, being subsidies in the strict meaning of the word, are similar in character and have the same effect'*.[31] Thus, the scope of EU rules on State aid is much wider than that of World Trade Organization (WTO) rules on subsidies. For instance, under WTO rules, the default principle is that subsidies are normally legal, while under EU rules subsidies are normally illegal. Moreover, WTO rules consider as subsidies only financial contributions, whereas the EU regime prohibits any form of assistance, whether financial or not.[32] As a result, the possibility of intervention by the EU Member States is considerably reduced if compared to that of public authorities in other jurisdictions. In this regard, when formulating and implementing national fiscal and social policies, EU Member States need to consider compliance with a substantially more stringent set of rules. The idea that national fiscal measures may be caught by the prohibition of State aid rules emerged at an early stage of the jurisprudence of the CJEU in this area. However, it was noted that until the mid-1990s, the EC essentially overlooked the application of State aid rules in the forms of direct fiscal measures implemented by Member States. Then, in just a few years the approach of the EC on direct taxation radically changed.[33]

The turning point was perhaps in 1997 when the Council of Ministers (Ecofin) passed a resolution on a Code of Conduct for business taxation to implement a

28. *See*, for instance, Joined Cases 6/69 and 11/69 *Commission v. France* [1969] ECR 523; Case 173/73 *Italy v. Commission* [1974] ECR 709.
29. *See Commission v. France* [1969], para. 30.
30. *See* Case 30/59 *Steenkolenmijnen v. High Authority* [1961] ECR 1, para. 1.
31. *Ibid.*, para. 13.
32. For general discussion, *see* Luca Rubini, *The Definition of Subsidy and State Aid – WTO and EC Law in Comparative Perspective* (OUP, 2009).
33. Phedon Nicolaides, *Fiscal State Aid in the EU: The Limits of Tax Autonomy*, 27(3) World Competition 365–396, 365 (2004).

coordinated action at EU level to deal with harmful tax competition.[34] Linked with this intervention, the EC issued a notice on the application of State aid rules addressing measure related to direct business taxation.[35] The aim of the Code of Conduct was to improve transparency in the tax area by means of a system of information exchanges between Member States and of assessment of any tax measures that may fall under its scope. On its part, the EC sought to use State aid policy as a means to fight against harmful tax competition.[36] In this regard, Nicolaides notes that: '*It is now firmly recognised that State aid rules apply to tax measures, that Member States, despite their tax autonomy, have to comply with those rules and that the Commission can exercise its normal powers in assessing whether national tax measures contain elements of State aid.*'[37] In various occasions, the CJEU made clear that Article 107 TFEU aims to prevent trade between Member States from being affected by benefits granted by public authorities that, in various forms, distort or threaten to distort competition by favouring certain undertakings (or the production of certain goods). Accordingly, the Court held that Article 107 TFEU '*does not distinguish between the measures of State intervention concerned by reference to their causes or aims but defines them in relation to their effects*'.[38] Thus, the key implication for Member States is that the alleged fiscal nature or social aim of a national measure is not sufficient to shield them from the application of State aid rules.[39] The second aspect to be considered is the selective nature of the fiscal measure in question. General fiscal measures do not fall under the scope of State aid rules, only selective measures do. The reason for this distinction is not only textual. As de Cecco notes: '*other provisions in the Treaty that address distortions of competition stemming from legislative or regulatory measures have as their object distortions arising from differences in the legislation and regulations of different Member States (Articles 116 and 117 TFEU, in particular), rather than regulatory and legislative differences within Member States.*'[40] It follows that the EU Treaty sets a clear division of roles between Article 107 TFEU and other Treaty provisions dealing with approximation and harmonisation.[41] This division, however,

34. Conclusions of the ECOFIN Council Meeting Concerning Taxation Policy [1998] OJ C 2/1. It is also worth noting that the Code of Conduct was an instrument of soft law and, as such, it did not create legal obligations for the Member States.
35. European Commission, *Notice on the Application of the State Aid Rules to Measures Relating to Direct Business Taxation*, OJ C 384 (1998).
36. Between 2001 and 2003, the European Commission initiated fifteen investigations on national tax measures in twelve Member States. In the end, all measures were found to fall within the prohibition of Article 107(1) TFEU. *See* European Commission, *Report on the implementation of the Commission notice on the application of the state aid rules to measures relating to direct business taxation*, C(2004) 434 (Brussels, 2004). For a general discussion on the matter and on the outcome of the relevant legal proceedings before the EU Courts, *see* Nicolaides, *supra*, footnote 33, at p. 366.
37. Nicolaides, *supra*, footnote 33, at p. 366.
38. *See*, *Italy v. Commission* [1974], para. 13. *See also* Case C-241/94 *France v. Commission (Kimberly Clark)* [1996] ECR I-4551.
39. *Ibid.*
40. Francesco de Cecco, *State Aid and Self-Government: Regional Taxation and the Shifting Spaces of Constitutional Autonomy*, in *From Single Market to Economic Union: Essays in Memory of John A. Usher* 221–239, 223 (Niamh Nic Shuibhne & Laurence W Gormley (eds), OUP, 2012).
41. *Ibid.*

generates a series of controversies and tensions between the EU and the national level in the application of State aid rules on fiscal measures. The evolutionary nature of the process of European integration also as a result of the expansion of EU competences and the continuous formulation of EU policies by the EU institutions in multiple areas blur this distinction when considering concrete cases. In its essence, the approach of the EC to State aid policy seems to be functional to the common market's principles.[42] On the one side, such a functional approach confers upon the EC enough flexibility to tackle tax measures with potentially harmful effects on competition. However, on the other side, it partly affects legal certainty in relation to the definition of aid and, consequently, the possibility for national authorities to implement national tax measures which remain compatible with EU State aid rules over the time.[43]

When looking at the EC's practice and the case law of the EU Courts in this area, the interpretation of the concept of selectivity in relation to tax measures leaves a series of open questions. Statistics show that, in recent years, tax measures have become one of the preferred State aid tools used by Member States.[44] Furthermore, fiscal measures have progressively become more complex and sophisticated. In this regard, it was noted that: '*Although perhaps a speculation, it is highly likely that one of the main reasons (even though certainly not the only one) for such a burst of creative fiscal advantages is that State aid taxation cases allow for a broader margin of defence for Member States, and the more complicated the tax mechanisms used, the broader the margin of defence.*'[45] Thus, the progressive widening of the notion of aid by the EC may partly be interpreted as a response to Member States' action. Whether some commentators, such as Quigley, consider that, in doing so, the EC '*has caused unnecessary confusion in relation to such matters as economic sovereignty, regional autonomy, free movement of capital, and the status of tax relief for investments*'.[46] Merola notes that the EC '*simply reacted to circumventing practices of Member States*'.[47] However, a general consensus exists that the EC practice confirms that although Member States remain free to decide on the fiscal policy that they consider the most appropriate, nonetheless they must exercise their competence in accordance with EU law. In particular, Member States must not introduce or maintain legislation which entails incompatible State aid contrary to the fundamental freedoms.[48] Tax schemes implemented by State authorities, whether general or specific, serve multiple purposes and, in doing this, they reflect the complexity and the needs of the national political and social system. As said, in

42. For an insightful discussion on the underlying philosophy of State aid control in the EU, *see* Andrea Biondi, *The Rationale of State Aid Control: A Return to Orthodoxy*, 12 Cambridge Yearbook of European Legal Studies 35–52 (2010).
43. *Ibid.*
44. *See* European Commission, *Notice on the notion of State aid as referred to in Article 107(1) of the Treaty on the Functioning of the European Union*, OJ C 262, 19 (Brussels, 2016). For discussion on this point, *see* Massimo Merola, *The Rebus of Selectivity in Fiscal Aid: A Nonconformist View on and Beyond Case Law*, 39(4) World Competition 533–566, 533 (2016).
45. *Ibid.*, 533–534.
46. *See* Biondi et al., Eeckhout, *supra*, footnote 17, at p. 207.
47. Merola, *supra*, footnote 44, at p. 534.
48. This is further confirmed by EU case law. *See*, *inter alia*, Case C-182/08, *Glaxo Wellcome GmbH & Co. KG v. Finanzamt München II*, [2009] ECR I-8591, para. 34 and case law cited.

principle, general tax measures are excluded from the application of State aid rules.[49] However, it seems that, over the years, the EC has tried to broaden the scope of application of the provisions on State aid to target also those tax measures having a general nature and aimed to foster State competition as opposed to tax measures simply affecting competition between undertakings.[50] It is suggested that a clear example of this trend refers to the above-mentioned Notice of the EC on the application of State aid rules to direct business taxation where the expansion of the concept of aid was considered as a necessary step to tackle tax measures with harmful effects on competition in the common market. Nevertheless, the expansion of the concept of aid has progressively started to raise tensions between national fiscal policies and EU state aid policy.[51] In this regard, the debate has focused on the desirability of introducing a rule of reason in the application of EU rules State aid law, but EU case law confirms that *'the definition of State aid is an objective exercise'*.[52] As seen, the CJEU held that Article 107 TFEU defines measures of State intervention in relation to their effects and, thus, the social character of a tax measure is not sufficient to exclude it from being categorised as State aid.[53] The decision to implement a certain tax measure by national authorities is essentially the result of a series of policy considerations. Furthermore, fiscal autonomy represents perhaps one of the key aspects of the political autonomy of any State. However, under the EU State aid regime, *'measures may not escape the prohibition of State aid on the basis of policy considerations, as these come into play once the question as to the existence of a State aid is answered affirmatively'*.[54] Accordingly, since the assessment of a national fiscal measure in light of its policy objectives is exercised by the EC, governance in tax matters in the EU is transferred in a significant manner at supranational level.

[C] Past and Current Approaches to Free Zones in the EU: Challenges Ahead

The analysis conducted so far shows that since the late 1990s the EC started to consider the control of State aid in the forms of tax measures, as pivotal for the proper functioning of the common market. The reasons behind this mutated attitude are mainly related to the advancement of the process of market integration in the EU.

49. However, the CJEU held that, at times, general tax measures may encompass some selective elements. *See, inter alia*, Case C-75/97 *Belgium v. Commission* [1999] ECR I-3671, paras 26–31; Case T-55/99 *CETM v. Commission* [2000] ECR II-3207, para. 39; Case C-143/99 *Adria- Wien Pipeline GmbH, Wietersdorfer & Peggauer Zementwerke GmbH v. Finanzlandesdirektion fur Karnten* [2001] ECR I-8365, para. 48.
50. Merola, *supra*, footnote 44, at p. 537.
51. *See* Biondi et al., Eeckhout, *supra*, footnote 17, at p. 207. For a general discussion on this point *see also*, Merola, *supra*, footnote 44, 533–534 and 537.
52. de Cecco, *supra*, footnote 40, at p. 223. For discussion, *see also* Andreas Bartosch, *Is there a Need for a Rule of Reason In European State Aid Law?*, 47(3) CMLRev 729–752 (2010); and Kelyn Bacon, *European Union Law of State Aid* 19 (third Edition, OUP, 2017). With reference to EU case law, *see* Case C-241/94 *France v. Commission* [1996] ECR I-4551, paras 19 and 20; Case T-52/94 *Ladbroke Racing Ltd v. Commission* [1998] ECR II-1, para. 52.
53. *Italy v. Commission* [1974] ECR 709, para. 13.
54. de Cecco, *supra*, footnote 40, at p. 223.

However, an aspect that has perhaps been partly overlooked by academic literature so far is that the emergence of a more stringent approach in relation to the enforcement of State aid rules on tax measures by the EC during this period was also depending on the challenges deriving from the envisaged EU enlargement process which culminated in the two rounds of accession of central and eastern European (CEE) countries in 2004 and 2007.[55] These countries came a long way to achieve the goal of EU membership. The accession process was particularly long and tortuous since their political and economic systems went through a process of drastic transformation. During the early 1990s, CEE countries moved from authoritarian governments and centrally planned economies to democracy and market-oriented economies. However, reshaping the constitutional and economic architecture of the state had an impact on the pace and effectiveness of compliance with the EU requirements for accession since this also demanded to initiate a process of specific reforms for certain areas of the national economy such as existing SEZs.[56] Granting accession to the EU to CEE countries, without first expecting the (full) compliance of their legal systems with EU rules, could seriously undermine, *inter alia*, the implementation of State aid policy among existing Member States and, in turn, affect the smooth functioning of the common market. As Kislowska notes: '*In light of these conclusions, it is clear why this area of EU policy [State aid] has become especially controversial during the organization's enlargement process and why the organization strived so hard to ensure that there existed uniformity in the legislation of each new Member State and the EU body of law called the "acquis communautaire".*'[57] Since the Treaty of Rome in 1957, the founding fathers of the European project considered State aid rules as complementary to other competition provisions on undertakings and, in turn, all set of competition rules as complementary to the goals pursued by the fundamental freedoms. Thus, in the EU, State aid policy is an essential components of competition policy, and both should be read in light of the establishment of the common market.[58] In sum, competition appears to serve the ultimate purpose of market integration. Since State aid legislation in CEE countries significantly differed from the EU one, adjustments in this area were necessary for the successful outcome of the accession process. For instance, in the case of Poland (the largest country in the area), among the many fields of the economy undergoing substantial changes to meet the EU requirements for accession, '*State aid proved to be*

---

55. These include: Czech Republic, Estonia, Hungary, Latvia, Lithuania, Poland, Slovak Republic and Slovenia in 2004; and Bulgaria and Romania in 2007. Cyprus and Malta also joined the EU in 2004.
56. For discussion, *see* Iraj Hashi et al., *The Comparative Analysis of State Aid and Government Policy in Poland, Hungary and the Czech Republic*, Center for Social and Economic Research, Warsaw, Poland (2004), http://www.case-research.eu/sites/default/files/18.%20The%20Comparative%20Analysis%20of%20State_0.pdf. *See also* Marcin Sowa, *State Aid and Government Policy in Poland, 1994–2002* (CASE, Warsaw, 2003); and Jens Hölscher et al., *State Aid in the New EU Member States*, 55(4) Journal of Common Market Studies 779–797 (2017).
57. Monika G. Kislowska, *The Future of Special Economic Zones in the Aftermath of Poland's Accession to the European Union*, 5(1) Journal of International Business and Law 174–202, 181 (2006).
58. For general discussion, *see* Juan Jorge Piernas López, *The Concept of State Aid Under EU Law: From Internal Market to Competition and Beyond* (OUP, 2015). *See also* Biondi et al., *supra*, footnote 17.

one of the most complicated to adjust.'[59] In countries like Poland, the presence of an extensive system of SEZs counting for a substantial part of national State aid policy created additional difficulties on the path of compliance with the *'acquis communautaire'*. More specifically, State aid in the form of fiscal measures operating in these SEZs were viewed by the EU institutions as a severe barrier to the maintenance of fair competition in the common market in case of accession. Accordingly, during the years preceding the EU's membership, the original architecture and functioning of these SEZs witnessed structural reforms.[60] However, after being aligned with EU requirements, SEZs in Poland and other CCE countries appear to have positively contributed not only to the development of the concerned areas but also to that of the national economy as a whole. In this regard, SEZs proved to be successful in fostering the competitiveness of the enterprises working within them, attracting direct investment, increasing exports and reducing unemployment.[61] The example of Poland and the general discussion on SEZs in CEE countries may help to better understand the past and current approach of EU institutions towards the functioning of free zones and, in particular, towards the use of tax incentives in these areas. Although, EU institutions have often voiced serious concerns about the potential harmful effects of specific fiscal measures available in free economic zones on the common market, at the same time, they have recognised their potential contribution to regional development. However, it appears evident that the approximation of the special fiscal regime available in free zones with EU State aid rules remains a dynamic process. In this regard, in an enlarged EU which has seen its objectives and competences expanded by the Lisbon Treaty, the EC faces now a series of unprecedented challenges in the enforcement of State aid policy. It seems that, more than ever before in the history of European integration, State aid policy has become an instrument of market governance. One of the main reasons why the EC has progressively adopted a more stringent approach in the assessment of tax measures under State aid rules, is that, in its effort to gradually reduce the level of State provided by Member States, it perceived the special regime available in free zones as a further obstacle to the unity of the common market. These policy considerations from the EC, however, have often clashed with opposite policy considerations from the Member States. For instance, it was noted that although the EC is very critical towards State aid granted in free zones in the form of tax incentives, this type of measures seems to be the most advantageous from the point of view of a Member State's budget. This is because if compared to direct subsidies which are granted regardless the positive outcome of the investment, in case of tax reliefs, investors are granted exemptions only when the investment has been made, production has started and income has been generated.[62]

Furthermore, it is worth noting that not all types of State aid measures have the same harmful effect on competition. Tax incentives available in free zones fall into the scope of regional aid which is not as harmful as sectoral aid for competition in the

59. Kislowska, *supra*, footnote 57, at p. 174.
60. *Ibid.*
61. *Ibid.*
62. Kislowska, *supra*, footnote 57, at p. 194.

common market.[63] However, while most of the arguments raised by Member States to justify tax incentives in free zones are based on (national) policy considerations, as seen, EU case law shows that the definition of state aid remains an '*objective exercise*'[64]

One final aspect to be considered to explain the EC critical attitude towards the use of tax measures in free zones refers to the transparency and effectiveness of supervision of business activities operating in these areas. Tax reliefs granted by State authorities to investors in free zones must be constantly monitored and, are subject to an audit process. Furthermore, due to the special features of free zones the relevant supervisory authorities are conferred with more extensive inspections powers than those available to monitor businesses operating in other parts of the country. In case of State aid, for instance, Member States are required to report to the EC all business activities in free zones. However, it appears that it is common practice that auditing and reporting are done by local authorities themselves often without any further controls by national authorities.[65] This is a complex issue because, on the one side, the existence of opaque supervisory procedures may increase the perception that business operations in free zones have a harmful effect on competition and on the common market, but, on the other side, local authorities could consider more intrusive system of inspections operated by national authorities as a threat to their political autonomy.[66] The rationale for the establishment of free zones is to support the economic and social development of poor regions. However, it is suggested that, at times, free zones are not really functioning where most needed but rather in those regions where local authorities are able to exercise political leverage at national level.[67] For instance, supervision and transparencies issues in the functioning of free zones have recently emerged in relation to the free zone of Madeira.[68] The Madeira's free zone was established in 1980 when Portugal was not a member of the European Community (the predecessor of the EU) yet. In 1986, the country entered the EU and, one year later, the EC approved Madeira's special tax regime for the first time.[69] However, in 2000, the EC found that while the amount of aid granted in the form of tax exemptions amounted to more than EUR 1 billion per year, the approximately 4,000 companies operating in Madeira's Free Trade Zone (FTZ) had employed no more than 1,000 people. In this regard, it concluded that the public measures granted in the form of state aid failed to provide

63. For an insightful discussion on recent case law on regional tax autonomy and on the concept of geographic selectivity, *see* de Cecco, *supra*, footnote 40.
64. *Ibid.*, at p. 223.
65. de Jong, *supra*, footnote 2, at p. 5.
66. *Ibid.*
67. Kislowska, *supra*, footnote 57, at p. 200.
68. The free zone of Madeira consists of four areas: (1) International Shipping Register, (2) Industrial Free Trade Zone, (3) Financial Services Centre, and (4) International Services Centre. For an insightful discussion on the complex evolution of the Madeira Free Zone, *see* Fernando Brás et al., '*The Madeira Free Zone and Its Standpoint Within the European Union*', 3 EC Tax Review 122 (2004).
69. Zierer, *supra*, footnote 15, Since the special tax regime (corporate tax rate was set at 0%) was only applicable to business registered at the International Services Center of Madeira, tax incentives were considered as State aid and, consequently, the European Commission's approval was necessary.

any effective contribution to regional development.[70] Then, an investigation from the EC followed to check the complaisance of Madeira's tax regime with EU State aid rules but, two years later, the procedure was concluded with no significant result.[71] More recently, the situation in Madeira started to raise serious concerns among other EU institutional actors. For instance, pressure on the EC to rethink its policy towards the Madeira's FTZ has come from members of the European Parliament.[72] In 2017, the European Green Party released a report, *'Madeira – a Tax Haven Approved by the European Commission'*, explaining that instead of attracting investors and creating jobs for the development of the local economy, the special tax measures available in the free zone had only benefited multinationals and wealthy individuals, while other Member States had been losing billions of tax revenues.[73] In this regard, it was reported that the EC started to think about the issuance of stricter guidelines for tax incentives in free zones with the objective to more strictly regulate SEZs.[74] The guiding principle of the EC's proposal seems to be that tax incentives in free zones should be granted in ways which are commensurate with the existence of a real economic activity.[75] Furthermore, the proposed guidelines would list a series of situations and criteria that, if present in free zones with tax incentives, should trigger the 'scrutiny' by the EU Code of Conduct Group for Business Taxation.[76] The EC's proposal, however, sparked criticism from some members of the European Parliament who considered the criteria in the proposed guidelines, especially the one referring to links with the presence of a (genuine) economic activity in the concerned area, as insufficient to effectively deal with the improper use of tax incentives in free zones.[77] In sum, it appears that the discussion on the functioning and supervision of EU free zones with their special tax regimes lies at the heart of the process of European integration in an enlarged Union and reveals the many challenges deriving from the EU multi-level system of market governance as emerged post-Lisbon.

70. *Ibid.*
71. *Ibid.* Since that time the EU-Commission keeps on approving the tax scheme, e.g., in 2002, 2007, 2013, 2014 and 2015. The only change: Companies nowadays have to pay 5% business tax and – in order to benefit from the preferential tax rate – create a certain number of new jobs, depending on their profits. *Ibid.*
72. *Ibid.* It was also reported that together with representatives from other Member States, they proposed to put the Madeira's free zone on the agenda of European Parliament's Panama Papers committee of inquiry. However, the European Commission had already approved the Madeira Free Trade Zone until 2027. *Ibid.*
73. *Ibid.*
74. Joe Kirwin, *EU Sets Sights on Tax Privileges in Special Economic Zones* (Bloomberg Law News, 2017), https://www.bna.com/eu-sets-sights-n57982086492/. It was further noted that.
75. It was reported that in its proposal, the European Commission listed a series of situations which, if allowed in free zones with tax incentives, should trigger the 'scrutiny' by the EU Code of Conduct Group for Business Taxation. *Ibid.*
76. *Ibid.*
77. It was further noted that: '*The issue of the tax privileges allowed in EU member state economic zones has taken on more importance as the EU draws up its tax haven blacklist. Critics within the EU and outside the EU claim the bloc is using double standards by taking a tough line on countries and tax jurisdictions beyond its borders compared to those within.*' *Ibid.*

§3.02 CONCLUSION

Tax incentives offered in free zones by states authorities may distort competition among the Member States and, consequently, they need to comply with EU State aid rules. In the EU, the EC enjoys the exclusive authority to review these tax measures to assess whether they are compatible with the EU legal framework. However, national fiscal policy and political autonomy are closely linked. The implementation of tax schemes by State authorities depends on a series of policy considerations related to the political, economic and social context and priorities at national level. Yet, under the EU State aid regime, tax measures cannot escape the prohibition of State aid on the basis of national policy considerations since these may only be taken into account at supranational level after a tax measure has already been found incompatible with EU State rules by the EC. This situation helps to explain the existing tensions between the Member States and the EU in relation to special tax regimes available in free zones.

Furthermore, if compared to the situation in other jurisdictions around the world, in the EU, transparency issues related to the functioning of free zones assume a constitutional significance. The lack of transparency in the functioning and supervision of free zones with their tax incentives undermine the stability of the EU multi-level system of governance which is based on the respect of mutual obligations by all Members States. This is a very sensitive issue as this situation may lead to major ruptures in the EU institutional dialogue and, ultimately, in the process of European integration. However, despite EU State aid policy has progressively become a powerful instrument of governance in the hands of the EC in light of the achievement of common market goals in an enlarged Union, it is still not clear, if existing EU legal and policy instruments are adequate to connect the different levels of regional, national and European governance and ensuring effectiveness and transparency in the regulation of free zones in the EU. In conclusion, although recent trends show the growing awareness of policy makers globally about the role of free zones in promoting economic growth, the mixed results in different countries demonstrate the necessity to consider that '*economic law does not exist in a constitutional vacuum*'[78], but it should be carefully tailored to meet the regulatory challenges related to a country's specific context.

78. de Cecco, *supra*, footnote 40, at p. 239.

CHAPTER 4

A Special Economic Zone in the Brazilian Amazon Rain Forest: Progress and Hazards of the Manaus Free Trade Zone

Guilherme Vargas Castilhos

§4.01 INTRODUCTION

Many are the reasons why governments decide to implement a special economic zone (SEZ) in their countries. In Brazil, the choice of state authorities was to establish such framework in the vast and sparsely inhabited region of the Amazon Rainforest in the northwest of the country. Currently, the importance of the Amazon Rainforest is a consolidated fact among scientists, governments and civil societies of not just Brazil, but all around the globe. Comprising of more than 60% of all forests of its kind, the Amazon is the largest rainforest in the world. It is home to the most abundant and diverse biological repository in the world, encompassing various species of birds, insects, plants and other biological structures, of which many are still not cataloged by the scientific community. The sumptuous flora embodies an extensive assortment of trees, such as mahogany, Amazonian Cedar, myrtle, laurel, palm, and acacia, as well as rosewood, Brazil nut, and rubber tree. On its fauna, major animals such as jaguar, manatee, tapir, spiders, red deer, capybara, scorpions, several kinds of rodents, centipedes, millipedes and various types of monkeys.[1] In addition, of all the rainforests in the world, the Amazon is the only one that is still mainly preserved, both in terms of its size and biodiversity.

The Brazilian Amazon region is also home to the State of Amazonas, where in the middle of the jungle, cities and urban centers emerged with a total population of

1. Encyclopaedia Britannica, *Amazon Rainforest*, https://www.britannica.com/place/Amazon-Rainforest, accessed October 25, 2018.

around 4 million people. It was taking this region and these people into consideration that the Brazilian government decided to implement its first special economic zone (SEZ) in the city of Manaus, capital of the State of Amazonas. Created as a free trade area to develop the Western Amazon, the Manaus Free Trade Zone (MFTZ) became a center of intense commercial and industrial activity, notably due to domestic and foreign investments performed in the district during the late seventies until the present days.[2]

Likewise, a Free Trade Zone of such peculiarities arouses many repercussions in the economic and social life of the region. This impact range goes from the enactment of special legislations of economic nature, migration movements, social changes, to the relation with environmental standards of the Amazon. This vast scope of factors influenced by the MFTZ deserves an important scrutiny from scholars and interested researchers on the topic.

In this sense, this chapter will first present a historical background and explanation of the MFTZ alongside the economic history of the Amazon region, as well as an accounting on the reasons for the choice of its peculiar location as well as its main characteristics and its use as an instrument for the region's development. Going further, in the next section of this research, the goal is to identify and elucidate the negative and positive impacts of the MFTZ for the development and economy of the Amazonian Region and its society. After the analysis of its effects, this study will present a section indicating new policies and models that can be adopted by the MFTZ administrative authorities in order to better generate its desired objectives, in light of the new multilateral economy of the twenty-first century. The final section will show a compendium of the topics stressed and a closure for this research.

§4.02 THE SPECIAL ECONOMIC ZONE IN THE MIDDLE OF THE AMAZON RAIN FOREST

[A] A Historical Account of the MFTZ

Since the start of the colonial period with the Portuguese arrival in Brazil, the Amazon Rainforest was one of the most hostile environments for the development of economic activities and life as a society. The immense and densely forested landscape with and exuberant wildlife that is both beautiful and rich in biological diversity but can many times be fatal in human encounters, the extreme humid weather and the distance from the main economic and social centers in the Brazilian coast contributed to this inhospitable feature of the Amazon region.

The economic experience of the Brazilian Amazon starts in the seventeenth century with the removal of elements from the forest such as cinnamon, cocoa beans, vanilla, guarana, Brazil nuts, pepper, achiote and so on. These spices were extracted by

2. SUFRAMA, *Manaus Free Trade Zone*, http://www.suframa.gov.br/invest/en-zona-franca-de-manaus.cfm, accessed October 29, 2018.

Native Americans under the supervision of Portuguese officials and were intended for export.[3]

With the Brazilian independence in 1822, the further development of economic activities and occupation of the Amazon was of immense relevance for the defense and integration of the Brazilian territory. The embodiment of this policy became a reality with the extraction of latex for the production of rubber, an economic phase that became known as the "The Rubber Cycle" and whose pinnacle was during the mid-nineteenth and beginning of twentieth centuries when the international market was booming due to the soaring necessities of the industrial revolution and the product was exclusive to the Amazon basin.[4] The relevance of latex in the Brazilian exports grew exponentially during this period, from 10% of all exports in 1890; 20% in 1900 and in 1910 even competing with coffee, while the latter was 41% of the Brazilian exports, latex reached the level of 40%.[5] The boom was such that the city of Manaus, capital of the State of Amazonas rapidly developed, with an increase in its population and commerce, the construction of buildings with European architecture and was even called "The Paris of the Tropics", due to the luxurious lifestyle of latex entrepreneurs.[6]

Sadly, this period got to an end when Henry Wickham, a British citizen smuggled more than 70,000 seeds of Rubber Tree to the Royal Botanic Gardens of London, where they were germinated and later cultivated in the British Colonies of Malaysia and Sri Lanka. The Asian production, which was cheaper and more efficient, resulted in the doom of the "Rubber Cycle" and the collapse of the Amazon region's economy.[7]

Therewith, a stage of detachment from the rest of the country occurred. The Amazon region was neglected from the Brazilian federal government in terms of policies for its economic progress and could not reproduce the development index that the southeast portion of the country was experiencing. In this sense, Barbosa (2013) explains:

> While economic stagnation remained in the Amazon, after the rubber cycle, the social and economic difficulties in which the populations of this region of Brazil lived were not perceived with the same magnitude by the populations of other Brazilian regions. Thus, the development did not exist in the Amazon and this region geographically distant from the large producers and consumers centers in Brazil and the world did not experience any economic policy administered by the Federal and state governments capable of generating jobs and income to resume at least economic growth and subsequently the development.[8] (Translated by the Author)

3. Cardoso, A. *Especiarias na Amazônia Portuguesa: Circulação Vegetal e Comércio Atlântico no Final da Monarquia Hispânica*. 21 Revista Tempo 1, 3 (2015).
4. Mendonça, M. *O Processo de Decisão Política e a Zona Franca de Manaus*. 1, 35 (Ph.D Thesis. Fundação Getúlio Vargas. São Paulo, Brazil, 2013).
5. Fausto, B. *História do Brasil*. 8 Fundação de Desenvolvimento da Educação 239 (1995).
6. Ramm, B. BBC, *The Beautiful Theatre in the Heart of the Amazon Rainforest*, http://www.bbc.com/culture/story/20170316-the-beautiful-theatre-in-the-heart-of-the-amazon-rainforest, accessed October 27, 2018.
7. Pennington, D. *Manaus e Liverpool: Uma Ponte Marítima Centenária—Anos Finais do Império/Meados Do Século XX*. 1 Editora da Universidade Federal do Amazonas 124 (2009).
8. Barbosa, E. *Zona Franca de Manaus: Política Bra sileira de Desenvolvimento Socioeconômico Regional*. 184 Observatorio de la Economía Latinoamericana 1, 5 (2013).

It was in this context, the second half of the nineteenth century, with the Law n. 3,173 of June 6, 1957 that the initial structures that would lead to the MFTZ were created.[9] Initially, the zone was denominated as a "Free Port" intended to serve as a customs warehouse of imported goods heading to neighboring countries such as Bolivia and Peru who could use the zone to perform their exports.[10]

Ten years later, the Decree-Law n. 288 of February 28, 1967 was put into force, in order to provide additional regulation to the existent structure and thus, creating the MFTZ, reformulating its operational model and amending certain points of the 1957 law. For the first time, tax benefits for the establishment of an industrial, commercial and agricultural center in the Amazon were established. The tax benefits were mainly adopted with the goal of reducing local disadvantages and to allow conditions for the development of the region. The law expressly defines these principles, the Article 1 of Decree-Law n. 288 states:

> The Manaus Free Trade Zone is a free import and export trade area where special fiscal incentives apply, set up with the objective of creating in the Amazon Region an industrial, commercial and agricultural center under economic conditions that allow its development, given local factors and the great distance separating it from its markets.[11] (Translated by the Author)

At that time, Brazil was going through a military dictatorship who considered the Amazon as a strategic parcel of the country's territory. Therefore, the creation of the Manaus Free Zone was also justified by the military dictatorship as a necessity for occupying a depopulated region in order to protect it from potential foreign intervention. In order to achieve this purpose, it was necessary to create in the region beneficial conditions of livelihood and infrastructure that would attract domestic and foreign investment as well as labor force.[12]

Other factors influenced the decision of the Brazilian government to establish the MFTZ. During the 1960s, the economic policy context of the country was of Import Substitution Industrialization (ISI). This economic and trade policy preaches that homemade products, in the largest possible extent, should replace imports. Therefore, creating the MFTZ was an opportunity for foreign companies to produce their goods in the Brazilian soil.

The 1960s were also a period of decentralization of industries, where many transnational businesses from industrialized nations were moving part of their production scale to other continents. At the same time, there were host countries with political and legal settings that offered a reduction in production costs and an amplification of the access to their consumer market. With the MFTZ, it was a chance for Brazil to

9. Brasil. Law n. 3,173 of June 6, 1957. *Creates a Free Trade Zone in the city of Manaus and Provides Additional Regulation*. Official version in Portuguese available from http://www.planalto.gov.br/ccivil_03/LEIS/1950-1969/L3173.htm, accessed October 14, 2018.
10. Nascimento, I. *Suframa: Agência dos Agentes*. 4 Revista dos Estudos Amazônicos 1, 9 (2004).
11. Brasil, Decree-Law n. 288 of February 28, 1967. *Amends the provisions of Law n. 3173 of 6 June 1957 and regulates the Manaus Free Trade Zone*. Official version in Portuguese available from: http://www.planalto.gov.br/ccivil_03/Decreto-Lei/Del0288.htm, accessed October 15, 2018.
12. Seráfico, J. Seráfico, M. *A zona Franca e o Capitalismo*. 19(54) Estudos Avançados 99, 99 (2005).

create these political and legal conditions, including Latin America in the decentralization trend of the time.[13]

Moreover, the United Nations also recommended the adoption of these models to increase the export and production capacity of developing countries. Tiefenbrun (2015) explains:

> The developing countries neglected to focus on free trade zones until the late 1960s, after the United Nations' Economic and Social Council adopted a resolution at the 1506th plenary meeting on August 4, 1967 suggesting that one of the fundamental means of export expansion was the improvement of ports, Customs, and trade zone facilities in developing countries.[14]

Since its establishment in 1967 until the present days, the MFTZ accompanied distinct phases of the political and economic history of Brazil. Major policy changes adopted by the federal government were reflected in the warehouses located in the Amazon jungle. Therewith, it is possible to identify four diverse stages in the production activities realized in the MFTZ.

The first stage comprises the years from 1967 to 1975, when the industrial policy of Brazil was encouraging the formation of a more expressive and consolidated domestic market and the operation of Import Substitution Industrialization schemes. At this stage, the MFTZ had predominance of the commercial activity, without limits on the import of foreign components and products, with only few restrictions being made to goods such as arms and ammunition, tobacco, alcoholic beverages and cars. Furthermore, the production was based on Completely Knocked Down and Semi Knocked Down model, where semi-disassembled inputs would be imported to the zone to be finished and later sold in the domestic market.[15] Since in the MFTZ it was possible to import several products whose imports were constrained in the rest of the country, a huge domestic tourism took place during this stage. Many Brazilians would travel to Manaus in order to purchase products, mostly electronics that could not be found in the stores of other states. In the mid-1970s, the Federal Government even started to limit the quantity of goods that could be purchased and attached a baggage quota for visitors who would leave the zone.

The second stage ranged from 1975 to 1990, where the economic policy of the country was characterized by the adoption of measures fostering the national industry of primary products. So, with the issuance of Decree-Law n. 1,435 of December 16, 1975, for the application of tax exemptions it was required for industries in the MFTZ to apply a minimum quantity of national inputs in their products, so they could be later commercialized in other localities of the Brazilian territory.[16] In addition, annual

13. *Ibid.*, at 105.
14. Tiefenbrun, S. *U.S. Foreign Trade Zones and Chinese Free Trade Zones: A Comparative Analysis.* 14 Journal of International Business and Law 1, 7 (2015).
15. SUFRAMA, *Modelo Zona Franca—História*, http://www.suframa.gov.br/zfm_historia.cfm, accessed October 29, 2018.
16. Brasil, Decree Law n. 1,435 of December 16, 1975. *Changes the text of Article 7 of Decree-Law n. 288 of 28 January 1967 and provides additional regulation.* Article 1. Official Version in Portuguese available from: http://www.planalto.gov.br/ccivil_03/decreto-lei/Del1435.htm, accessed October 29, 2018.

import quotas were implemented, imposing a cap on the amount of foreign inputs to be used in an annual production. In this phase, the commercial aspect of the zone still is relevant, serving as center for Brazilians looking for technological products at a more competitive price.

Moving on, the third stage was short lived, from 1991 to 1996, however with significant alterations in the production model and the Brazilian economy as a whole. In 1985, the military dictatorship was over. After a transition period of four years, the first democratically elected president in more than thirty years, Mr. Fernando Collor de Mello, was appointed. His economic policy was defined by an open market strategy towards international trade and foreign investment. The import tax was reduced in the whole country. With this, the MFTZ lost the relevance of its commercial aspect, once it ceased to have exclusivity of imported products and inputs as a comparative advantage. It was also during this phase that the companies located in the MFTZ initiated a vast process of industrial modernization, focusing in the automation of its production, and the increase of the quality and productivity. As a result, in the end of 1996, the revenues of the zone reached the amount of USD 13.2 billion, a record for the decade.[17]

The fourth stage encompass the period from 1996 to 2002, where the country's industrial policy was marked by actions to adapt the country to the globalized economy of the time. In this phase, the increase of the zone's exports were at the core of the implemented policies. So far, the majority of product sales made by industries from the MFTZ were destined to the domestic market, so there was a need to stimulate external sales of the zone. The outcome of this movement was that export levels went from little more than USD 140 million in 1996 to USD 2 billion in 2005.[18]

[B] Main Benefits and Current Characteristics

Like in the majority of Free Trade Zones and SEZ around the world, the MFTZ offers benefits to companies who establish themselves in its constraints, seeking to attract foreign and domestic investments. These benefits aim to reduce local negative circumstances and stimulate regional development. Following this model, land in the MFTZ is sold at a cost lower than the average price for the region with facilities containing a complete infrastructure on sanitation, energy and communications services.[19]

The main advantage is the granting of tax incentives governed mostly by federal and state laws. First, an 88% reduction on the Import Duties *(Imposto de Importação)* relating to raw materials, intermediate products, secondary and packing materials, components and other inputs of foreign origin used in the manufacture of products for

17. SUFRAMA, *supra* note 16.
18. *Ibid.*
19. Miranda, R. *Zona Franca de Manaus: Desafios e Vulnerabilidades*. 126 Textos para Discussão, Núcleo de estudos e Pesquisas do Senado Federal 4, 4 (2013).

the consumption in other parts of Brazil.[20] Second, a total exemption on the Industrialized Products Tax *(Imposto sobre Produtos Industrializados)* for the products produced in zone, destined for sale in other Brazilian regions.[21] Third, a 75% reduction on the Income Tax *(Imposto de Renda)* applicable to legal persons.[22] Finally, the suspension of the contribution to the Social Security Financing *(Contribuição para Financiamento da Seguridade Social—COFINS)* and the contribution to the Social Integration Program *(Programas de Integração Social—PIS)*.[23]

Also, the state of Amazonas, where the MFTZ is located, offers a credit that varies from 55% to 100% on the Tax on Circulation of Goods and Services (*Imposto sobre Circulação de Mercadorias e Serviços*) if a company can approve an investment project that effectively offers contributions to the economic and social life of the Amazonas' state. Among those improvements are: the promotion of activities connected with tourism, education, the increase in the amount of Brazilian imports, relevant level of job creation and others.[24]

Besides these, there are also tax benefits in the township level. The municipality of Manaus offers an exemption for ten years of the Municipal Property Tax (*Imposto Predial e Territorial Urbano*) applicable to natural and legal persons owning properties in the urban district of the city of Manaus. Moreover, there are also exemptions of the Service Taxes of Garbage Collection, Public Cleaning, Road and Land Conservation. For the application of these privileges, it is necessary for companies operating in the MFTZ to generate a minimum of five hundred direct jobs.[25]

The duration of the MFTZ is guaranteed, at least until the second half of the twenty-first century. The Constitutional Amendment 83 of August 5, 2014 extended the special tax incentives of the zone by the year 2073.[26] Taking into account that this is the fourth time in history that an extension of the MFTZ model occurs, it is very likely that the mentioned time limit will, once again, be broaden in a near future.

20. Brasil, Decree-Law n. 288 of February 28, 1967, *supra* note 12, Article 3, para. 1.
21. Brasil, Law 8,032 of April 12, 1990, *Provides for the Exemption or Reduction of Import Taxes, and Provides Additional Regulation*, Article 4, Official version in Portuguese available from: http://www.planalto.gov.br/ccivil_03/LEIS/L8032.htm, accessed October 30, 2018.
22. Brasil, Ministry of National Integrity, Ministry Ordinance 283 of July 4, 2013. Article 1. Portuguese Version available from: https://www.legisweb.com.br/legislacao/?id=256154, accessed October 29, 2018.
23. Brasil, Law 10,865 of April 30, 2004. *Provides on the Contribution to the Social Security Financing and the formation of public server heritage and the contribution to the Social Security Programs on the importation of goods and services and provides other measures.* Official version in Portuguese available from: http://www.planalto.gov.br/ccivil_03/_Ato2004-2006/2004/Lei/L10.865compilado.htm, accessed October 30, 2018. Article 14, para. 1, Article 14-A.
24. SUFRAMA, *Incentivos fiscais do Estado do Amazonas à Indústria*, http://www.suframa.gov.br/zfm_incentivos_estado.cfm, accessed October 29, 2018.
25. Brasil, City of Manaus, Ordinary Law 427 of January 12, 1998, *It grants tax incentives, for ten years, to industrial companies that are installed in the area of the Manaus free zone*, Portuguese version available from: https://www.legisweb.com.br/legislacao/?id=175820, accessed October 29, 2018.
26. Brasil, Constitutional Amendment 83 of August 5, 2014, *Adds the Article 92 to the Act of the Transitional constitutional provisions-ADCT*, Official version in Portuguese available from: https://www.planalto.gov.br/ccivil_03/Constituicao/Emendas/Emc/emc83.htm, accessed October 30, 2018.

On the management of the zone, the Decree-Law n. 288 in its Article 10, also created the administration organ of the zone, the MFTZ Superintendence *(Superintendência da Zona Franca de Manaus)*, known as SUFRAMA.[27] The organ, is a public administration agency member of the Ministry of Development, Industry and Foreign Trade. One of its main goals is to administrate and regulate the tax advantages awarded to the enterprises established in the MFTZ. Therefore, it acts as an agency stimulating investments for the area. It also has the function to promote development strategies for the western Amazon region of Brazil.

Another benefit brought by the Decree-Law was the expansion of the zone's territory that in the present days consists of a range of 10,000 kilometers with an industrial, commercial and agricultural center. Also, the complex has an equipped port to receive goods and ship the production. On these facets of the MFTZ, Pena (2013) explains:

> The main feature of the Manaus Free Trade Zone is the fact that it is made up of three economic centers: commercial, industrial and agricultural. The commercial center was created in the 1980s and had a larger activity when the Brazilian economy was still closed to the foreign market. The industrial center on the other hand, is the main activity in the region, responsible for the majority of the jobs created and the capital that influx in the region. The agricultural pole in turn, operates mainly in agro industrial activity as well as in other links, such as wood trading, fish farming, among others.[28] (Translated by the Author)

In the present days, the zone has more than 600 companies, domestic and foreigners, with an extensive concentration of major industries, in sectors like electronics, watches, bicycles, computers, toys, motorcycles and others. Relevant international companies are established in the MFTZ, such as: Nokia do Brasil Tecnologia Ltda, Pepsi Cola Industrial Da Amazônia Ltda, Philips Do Brasil Ltda, Samsung Eletrônica da Amazônia Ltda, Sony Brasil Ltda and others.[29]

§4.03 THE IMPACT OF THE MANUS FREE TRADE ZONE: ACHIEVEMENTS AND DRAWBACKS

Throughout the decades, the MFTZ caused economic and social repercussions in the economy and social life of the Brazilian Amazon region. As expected, these results are dubious, sometimes having positive effects to the region and its population, while in other moments having backlashed and being prejudicial to the ultimate desired goals. This section will explore and comment on these results.

One of the first factors the establishment of the zone brought to the region was the increase of its population, with a great number of immigrants from other regions of

27. Brasil, Decree-Law n. 288 of February 28, 1967, *supra* note 12, Article 10.
28. Pena, R. Zona Franca de Manaus; *Brasil Escola*, http://www.brasilescola.com/brasil/zona-franca-manaus.htm, accessed October 17, 2018.
29. Brasil, Ministry of Development, Industry and Foreign Trade. *Manaus Free Trade Zone: Meeting with ChineseTaipei Delegation* (2013), http://investimentos.mdic.gov.br/public/arquivo/arq1383326303.pdf, accessed October 18, 2018.

Brazil drifting to the city of Manaus in search for jobs in industries of the zone itself and better opportunities correlated with it. The concentration of new industries in the zone caused an urban boom in the city, which saw its population jump from 300,000 in the 1970s to more than 2 million inhabitants in 2015, according to the Brazilian Institute of Geography and Statistics.[30]

This process of urban conglomeration, which resulted from the migration of people from the neighboring states of the State of Amazonas and from the Brazilian Northeast region, contributed to a downside on the urban planning of the city. Parts of the capital grew in a disorderly way, with irregular land occupations that demands basic utilities such as sanitation, water distribution and energy.[31] Currently, the city of Manaus is the most populous in the northern region of Brazil. On the other hand, the strategy set by the Brazilian government in the 1960s, of fostering the settlement of people to the Amazon region to guarantee its security and the Brazilian presence proved to be successful. Data obtained from the Brazilian Institute of Geography and Statistics demonstrate that in the 1970s the total population of the State of Amazonas was of 950,000 people. Fast-forward five decades and in 2010, the population of the state already reached the figure of 3.5 million people, an increase of more than 268%.[32] In total, the Amazon region spreads out crossing the territory of seven countries: Brazil, Peru, Colombia, Venezuela, Ecuador, Bolivia and Guyana. From the number of residents of the Amazon Basin per country, Brazil holds for 49% of the amazon inhabitants.[33]

Concerning the economy of the Amazon, the MFTZ contributed for the relative positive results of the state where it is located. In 2015, the Gross Domestic Product (GDP) of the State of Manaus was approximate of USD 21,585 billion.[34] This places the state in the 15th position of the Brazilian states with higher economy. Although this fact does not seem impressive on the first sight, it is remarkable taking into account that is a state with only 1.9% of the Brazilian population.[35] In terms of regional comparison, the GDP of the State of Manaus is higher than the other four states of the northern region combined. In 2017, the revenues of the MFTZ alone were of USD 2,564 billion.[36] The most profitable industry sectors of the zone are the electronics, computing,

30. Instituto Brasileiro de Geografia e Estatística (IBGE). *Censo 2010*. http://www.censo2010.ibge.gov.br/sinopse/index.php?dados=6&uf=00, accessed October 22, 2018.
31. United Nations Environment Programme, Projeto Geo Cidades, *Relatório Ambiental Urbano Integrado Informe GEO Manaus*, 17, 21 (2002) http://apps.unep.org/repository/free-keywords/environmental-assessment?page=38, accessed October 30, 2018.
32. IBGE, *Portal Manaus*, https://cidades.ibge.gov.br/brasil/am accessed October 30, 2018.
33. United Nations, Food and Agriculture Organization, *Amazon Basin*, http://www.fao.org/nr/water/aquastat/basins/amazon/index.stm, accessed October 30, 2018.
34. IBGE, *Contas Regionais do Brasil—Manaus*, https://www.ibge.gov.br/estatisticas-novoportal/economicas/contas-nacionais/9054-contas-regionais-do-brasil.html, accessed October 30, 2018.
35. Bessa, I. G1: Globo, *Número de habitantes do AM chega a 4 milhões em 2016, aponta IBGE*, http://g1.globo.com/am/amazonas/noticia/2016/08/numero-de-habitantes-do-am-chega-4-milhoes-em-2016-aponta-ibge.html, accessed October 30, 2018.
36. SUFRAMA, *Indicadores Econômicos do Modelo Zona Franca de Manaus*, p. 2, http://site.suframa.gov.br/assuntos/modelo-zona-franca-de-manaus/apresentacao-resumo-indicadores, accessed October 27, 2018.

motorbikes and chemical components. These four sectors combined represented 74.65% of the total revenues of companies located in the zone.[37]

A criticism to these facts is the consensus that the MFTZ, during the more than half a century of its existence, has become the only economic alternative of the Western Amazon, whose economy is concentrated in the capital city of Manaus. As an illustration of this fact, the already mentioned total GDP of the State of Amazonas in 2015 was of USD 21,585 billion. From this, USD 2,409 billion were from the revenues of industries located in the Zone.[38] This was such, that in 2013 the European Union (EU) abdicated mentioning the MFTZ in a request for the establishment of a panel in the World Trade Organization against allegedly unfair advantages Brazil was granting to its automotive industry. At that time, the EU considered that some of the tax incentives of the MFTZ were in breach of the GATS agreement. However, after a visit to the zone and recognition of its development model to the Amazon, the issue was removed from the question's list.[39]

Despite all, the lack of diversity in the economic activities of the region indicates that the full development aspirations from the 1960s are yet to be obtained, once the productive capacity of the Amazon region cannot be totally dependent from artificial advantages subsidized by the state.

Moreover, another downturn on the economic gains produced by the MFTZ are the relative low salaries paid to the employees of such industries in comparison with other regions of the country. The significant tax advantages and positive revenues do not reflect on higher salaries. A demonstration of this circumstance, comes on analysing data from the year of 2011 where the total salaries paid by companies in the MFTZ, including wages, social charges and benefits, did not reach BRL 4.5 billion in 2011, despite the industries having a total turnover of almost BRL 70 billion in that year. Between 2006 and 2011, the portion destined to the payment of salaries did not reach an average of 6% of revenues.[40]

The combination of considerable subsidies to the production, payment of low salaries in sectors with a, relatively, high productivity implies that the current model has an effect supporting income inequality in the region. In an ideal scheme, part of the resources obtained through subsidies and tax exemptions should be used to qualify and boost service providers and human resources in general, which would reduce inequality in the region and ultimately contribute to its proper development.

In terms of development of the region, an analysis on official indexations also points out the fact that it is still not appropriate according to the goals set in the foundation of the MFTZ. The last report published by the United Nations Development Programme (UNDP) in 2010 comparing the Human Development Index (HDI) of the Brazilian states, indicates that the State of Amazonas has an HDI level of 0,674, which is still considered as low according to international standards and occupies the

37. *Ibid.*, at 6.
38. *Ibid.*, at 2.
39. Amazonas Sustainable Foundation (FAS), *EU withdraws questioning Zona Franca de Manaus in Brazil against contecioso*, http://fas-amazonas.org/2014/10/uniao-europeia-retira-zona-franca-de-manaus-de-contencioso-sobre-o-brasil/?lang=en, accessed March 15, 2019.
40. Miranda, R., *supra* note 20, at 13.

eighteenth position among all Brazilian states.[41] This becomes more apparent if the discrepancy with other states is taken into account. Southern Brazilian states have better results, such as the States of São Paulo with 0,783 and Santa Catarina with 0,774. Comparing this data globally, the State of Amazonas has a lower HDI than countries such as Gabon (0,684) and Turkmenistan (0,688).[42] However, if we consider only the city of Manaus, it is realized that the capital of the state showed continuous improvements in indicators since 2000, rising from 1,545th position among all Brazilian cities, with an average HDI of 0,601 to 850th place in the ranking, in 2010 with an index of 0,737, which is considered by the UNDP as a high level of human development.[43] This shows that the benefits of the zone are constrained to the city where it is located and not to the State of Amazonas and Amazon region as whole.

The MFTZ has other peculiar aspects that makes it an exclusive experience in the world. Initially, is important to highlight its unique nature of being "Domestic Market Oriented" that differs it from other SEZ. Brazil is considered the first country to create a free zone model different from the more notorious ones of the United States of America and China. The MFTZ offers a full and favored access to the domestic market, while in the United States, and mostly in China, the model focus in the insertion of the country in the world, increase of exports, access to the international market, technology and new forms of production.[44]

This strategy also reflected in the choice of location for the establishment of the zone. Unlike its counterparts that established SEZ near the shore and seaports, Brazil installed the Free Trade Zone in the Amazon region, with its serious logistical obstacles, distant from the major internal consumer markets and away from the maritime coast. This exceptional location, in a continental area with a frail road connection system, that the majority of transport lines take place by air and waterways, which raises, besides costs, the level of criticism about the capacity of the model to really become an exporter pole. In this sense, date from the SUFRAMA's indicators show that in 2010 exports reached the amount of USD 1 billion while the total input of the zone was of USD 3,511.[45] Therewith, only 2.5% of the production of that year was destined for the international market.

These factors also point the difference of the MFTZ and its real contribution to the development of the Amazon region, notably if compared to the Chinese involvement with SEZ, considered by many experts as one of the most successful and complete implementations of the system. Many are the determinants in the Chinese model that indicate a discrepancy with the one adopted by Brazil. In China in the beginning of the SEZ implementation, the model was established in locations closer to the ocean, in

41. United Nations Development Programme, Brazil: *Ranking IDHM Unidades da Federação 2010*, http://www.br.undp.org/content/brazil/pt/home/idh0/rankings/idhm-uf-2010.html, accessed October 30, 2018.
42. United Nations Development Programme, *Ranking IDH Global 2014*, http://www.br.undp.org/content/brazil/pt/home/idh0/rankings/idh-global.html, accessed October 30, 2018.
43. United Nations Development Programme, *Ranking IDHM Municípios 2010*, http://www.br.undp.org/content/brazil/pt/home/idh0/rankings/idhm-municipios-2010.html, accessed October 30, 2018.
44. Miranda, R., *supra* note 20, at 19.
45. SUFRAMA, *supra* note 37, at 12.

areas with proper infrastructure and conveniently adjacent to more dynamic economic centers of the country and international markets. If in 1967, the Brazilian government had the same mindset as China in 1980s, the MFTZ would have been arranged along the coast of the southeast or southern states, where investors would find favorable port and airport infrastructure and abundant supply of skilled labor. Another option could have been the northeast coast, where, despite the worst quality infrastructure, the location would facilitate trade with important markets such the United States, Mexico and the European Union.

Moreover, the SEZ in China were created to test development models that, if satisfactory, could be disseminated throughout the country. In Brazil, the main goal was the development of Manaus and the State of Amazon, considering the peculiarities of the region, in particular the difficulty of access but not a development design that, if successful, should be copied in other regions of the country. As an illustration, in 2014 there were already six SEZ in China (and a diverse number of other models such as Free Trade Zones, open coastal cities and so on) corresponding for 45% of the total foreign direct investment in China, and 60% of the country's exports.[46]

As in China the companies operating on SEZ are oriented to the external market, they were focused on the acquisition of different technology methods and competitive conditions. The effects of the Chinese model are perceived in the international community on the increase of patent registrations performed by Chinese companies. According to a report of the World Intellectual Property Organization, in 2017 China was the second country in number of applications through the Patent Cooperation Treaty with 48,882 requests and an increase of 13.4% if compared with 2016.[47]

Even though in that year the United States were still in first place of applications combined, on individual terms a Chinese company, Huawei Technologies, was the major sole applicant in the world with 4,024 requests. Coincidentally, the company was formed and is headquartered in Shenzhen, in the Chinese southern Province of Guangdong, a city that in the 1970s was predominantly a fishing village with 30,000 inhabitants. Currently the city has an estimate population of 15 million people and is a new technological center of the world, a world-class hub.[48] How this substantial growth and development occurred in an approximate forty years range? Shenzhen is the site of the first SEZ of China established in 1980. This answer reveals on the intentions of this research on pointing out some of the drawbacks of the model adopted by Brazil. As an illustration on the benefits for the development of the region provided by the Chinese model, the GDP per capita of Shenzhen grew a spectacular range of 24,569% between 1978 and 2014.[49] This is a far higher growth and development than

46. World Bank, *Investing in Africa Forum China's Special Economic Zones*, p. 2, https://www.worldbank.org/content/dam/Worldbank/Event/Africa/Investing%20in%20Africa%20Forum/2015/investing-in-africa-forum-chinas-special-economic-zone.pdf, accessed October 29, 2018.
47. World Intellectual Property Organization, *Who filed the most PCT patent Applications in 2017?*, http://www.wipo.int/export/sites/www/ipstats/en/docs/infographic_pct_2017.pdf, accessed October 30, 2018.
48. Holmes, F., Forbes, *China's New Special Economic Zone Evokes Memories of Shenzhen*, https://www.forbes.com/sites/greatspeculations/2017/04/21/chinas-new-special-economic-zone-evokes-memories-of-shenzhen/#8e2802976f23, accessed October 30, 2018.
49. *Ibid.*

the one supplied by the MFTZ to its home region. This outcome is exactly what it is expected from a SEZ. In this sense, Vanhullebusch and Shen (2015) explain:

> Setting up economic development zones offers substantial benefits. Technologically, these zones can produce more manufacturing-specific human capital, and laborers can be better trained in more experienced manufacturing skills. The other advantage is that intermediate industrial inputs are developed and that manufacturing and service entities are clustered together, which creates a demand for specialized skills, know-how and experience.[50]

However, companies located in the MFTZ have a wide and favored access to the domestic market, with persistent incentives, which does not favor the search for competitiveness and increase of technological capacity and, ultimately, autonomy in relation to the concession of these incentives. This is an indication that the current model of the MFTZ is fragile, once it is fully dependent of government subsidies to maintain its competitive advantage.

The vulnerability of the zone is also demonstrated on how the stages of production are distributed among the city of Manaus and other cities in the south and southeast of the country, and even abroad. In cities like São Paulo and in foreign offices, are located the activities of research and development of products, the production of certain components with greater added value and complexity, the design of new products, decisions and the strategic planning of the companies installed in the zone. However, in Manaus there are activities of small value added, like assembly and final packaging of products. Since the exercises carried out abroad and in São Paulo have a great capacity for aggregating value to the product, the relevance of Manaus is restricted to the availability of lower labor costs, as already demonstrated in this research, and to the low cost on imports of inputs through the granting of tax benefits. Therefore, it is possible to affirm that following the current model, the MFTZ resembles a major assembly line, where inputs are brought to the country with tax incentives and put together into the final product, similar to the "Maquiladoras" factories, in Mexico close to the border with the United States of America.[51] Besides, there is the inclination to believe that foreign companies decide to establish themselves in the zone in order to secure a facilitated access to the Brazilian market, once an assembly line for the international market can be easily operated in other regions with even cheaper labor costs such as Mexico and Asia. In this scenario, becomes important for the zone to diversify its model and production scale in order to comprehensively reach the desired goals of fostering the development and quality of life in the Amazon region and inserting itself in the routes of international trade.

50. Vanhullebusch, M., Shen, W., *Where Is the Alchemy? The Experiment of the Shanghai Free Trade Zone in Freeing the Foreign Investment Regime in China*. 16(2) European Business Organization Law Review 321, 336 (2015).

51. "A maquiladora in Mexico is a factory that operates under preferential tariff programs established and administered by the United States and Mexico. Materials, assembly components, and production equipment used in maquiladoras are allowed to enter Mexico duty-free. Products made can be exported into the U.S. at lower tariffs than those from other countries." Manufacturing in Mexico, *Maquiladora in Mexico* http://manufacturinginmexico.org/maquiladora-in-mexico/, accessed October 27, 2018.

§4.04 FUTURE PERSPECTIVES

Despite the setbacks exposed in the previous section, the MFTZ partially achieved a set of the targets it was destined to accomplish. For the continuity of the zone and seeking the improvement of its effectiveness towards the development of the Amazon region and economy, it becomes necessary for shifts in its production patterns to be performed, seeking new options for economic expansion and sustainability.

Therefore, efforts should be directed in two main strands that may be crucial for achieving these goals and enhance the MFTZ and its repercussions. These strands are investments in education and research centers seeking for the increase of science and technology and projects fostering the use of local inputs and raw materials. By doing these, the zone can reach a level of effective production that will walk side by side with other top manufacturing hubs in the world such as the Chinese SEZ. Moreover, by using local resources it will make use of one of its exclusive features compared to other economic centers in the globe, which is the direct access to the vast and diversified assets the Amazonian rain forest has to offer.

In this sense, there are already efforts being made by the Brazilian government to materialize these innovations. It is clear that Brazilian authorities are seeking to expand the technological competitiveness of the industries of Manaus. The initial action was the creation of the Science, Technology and Innovation Center of the Manaus Industrial Complex, known as CT-PIM. The center is located in Manaus and is maintained by the SUFRAMA, with resources obtained from collection of fees from companies located in the MFTZ.[52] As stated by the government, the installation of the CT-PIM has as its main motivations: to increase the competitiveness of the industries in the MFTZ; reduce the zone's deficit on international trade and increase exports; evaluate the opportunity for production with local components, stimulate the formation of professionals and researchers in science and technology.[53] Despite these objectives, the search for international cooperation is also in the agenda of the CT-PIM. Therewith, since its inception the center already has partnerships with other centers of excellence around the world. For research on electronics and micro technology, it has a partnership with the IMEC (Interuniversity Microelectronics Center) from Belgium. Moreover, also on micro biotechnology and reliability engineering it maintains cooperation with the Fraunhofer Institute for Reliability and Microintegration IZM from Germany, considered one of the largest research centers in the world. Furthermore, it also has partnerships with the Leti Minatec center from France, specializing in micro biotechnology and mechanical-microelectronic systems and the Superior School of Technology of Viseu, Portugal, specialist in furniture production and industrial design.[54]

52. Menezes, E. Anais da 61ª Reunião Anual da SBPC: Manaus, AM: Julho/2009, Mesa-Redonda: A Pesquisa Científica e a Indústria, *Ações da Suframa no fortalecimento do Sistema Regional de Educação, Ciência, Tecnologia e Inovação*, p. 9, http://www.sbpcnet.org.br/livro/61ra/mesas_redondas/MR_ElildeMenezes.pdf, accessed October 30, 2018.
53. SUFRAMA, *Linhas Estratégicas CT-Pim*, http://www.suframa.gov.br/suframa_linhas_estrategicas_ct-pim.cfm, accesssed October 30, 2018.
54. SUFRAMA Invest, *CT-PIM*, http://www.suframa.gov.br/invest/zona-franca-de-manaus-ct-pim.cfm, accessed October 30, 2018.

The companies located in the MFTZ also contribute with 2.5% of their annual revenues to the Amazonas State University.[55] The university has more than twenty thousand students and offers programs on key areas for the zone such as logistics, biotechnology, industrial automation, mechatronic engineering, production engineering and so on.[56] It is expected that these centers can provide with the innovation necessary to increase the economy and development of the region with the use of local talents and human resources.

In addition, there were initiatives for the creation of a bio-industry hub in the Amazon that culminated with the establishment of the Amazon Biotechnology Center, known as CBA. The center is also located in Manaus and kept by SUFRAMA with resources prevenient from the MFTZ. The center currently offers support to industries of transformation and industrialization of natural products in its most diverse applications ranging from pharmaceuticals, cosmetics and bio insecticides for agriculture, food industry, dyes, flavors, essential oils, among others.[57] Another goal is to contribute with the regional development by integrating the local population and communities, generating employment and income from biotechnological innovation.

The physical facilities of the CBA comprise of a 12,000 square kilometers built area and have twenty-five laboratories including molecular biology and microbiology, nuclear magnetic resonance, pharmacodynamics, pharmacological safety, toxicology, tissue culture, natural products, chromatography, plant tissues, among others. Apart from the laboratories, the center has a Pilot plant for industrial processes, a technological-based business incubator, a vivarium, an extract production center and a show room.[58]

Promoting the knowledge of the Amazonian biodiversity, associating it with technologies that can provide for its economic exploitation is one of the key topics for the CBA and development of the Amazon region. Especially if it is taken into consideration, the fact that the Amazon rainforest contains at least 10% of the biodiversity known in the world.[59] The economic gains from materials and inputs may come from the research of the Amazonian flora and fauna are tremendous. An estimation of monetary value is troublesome to calculate, but areas with a high biodiversity contain more biological resources and thus, are more valuable from an economic point of view.[60] This shows the unique advantage that the MFTZ has in comparison with other SEZ in the world. So far, the finest example of an economy

55. Costa, D. O Globo, *Zona Franca de Manaus faz 50 anos, com incentivo centenário*, https://oglobo.globo.com/economia/zona-franca-de-manaus-faz-50-anos-com-incentivo-centenario-21013725, accessed October 30, 2018.
56. Universidade do Estado do Amazonas, *Cursos UEA*, http://cursos3.uea.edu.br/, accessed October 30, 2018.
57. SUFRAMA, *CBA*, http://www.suframa.gov.br/publicacoes/site_cba/index.htm, accessed October 30, 2018.
58. ARAÚJO, I. C. de. Centro de Biotecnologia da Amazônia—CBA e o Desenvolvimento Sustentável da Amazônia. 1 T&C Amazônia 30, 33 (2003).
59. WWF, *About the Amazon*, http://wwf.panda.org/knowledge_hub/where_we_work/amazon/about_the_amazon/, accessed October 30, 2018.
60. Centro de Sensoriamento Remoto, Universidade Federal de Minas Gerais. *Economic Valuation of Changes in the Amazon Rainforest Area* 4 (2016), https://csr.ufmg.br/amazones/wp-content/uploads/2017/05/Report_Biodiversity.pdf, accessed October 30, 2018.

arising from the Amazonian biodiversity is the considerable amount of cosmetic industries utilizing sustainable and other raw materials from the region that has emerged in the last decades.[61] Seemingly, with further research on the biodiversity of the Amazon, the potential of new, competitive and exclusive products to arise is immeasurable, and so is the sustainable economic development it can create.

Despite the difficulties challenging the proper development of the Amazon region, it is clear that the potential and assets to achieve the objectives originally delineated by the Brazilian government exist, are abundant and are being conducted in the Amazon Basin. It is expected that with the increase research on science and technology in the region, the MFTZ model may shift from an economy based on tax incentives, to a production pattern galvanized by singular features and advantages that only the Amazon Rain Forest can offer.

§4.05 CONCLUSION

Since the arrival of the Europeans to South America in the sixteenth century, the Amazon basin was a belligerent habitat for the proper development of economic activities and prosperous societies. The difficulties come from different factors, such as natural circumstances like the densely forested landscape, diseases deteriorated from the extreme hot and humid tropical weather as well as the long distance between the Amazon Rainforest to the major centers of Brazil located in the south and southeast coast of the country. There were some economic booms in the region during the seventeenth and nineteenth centuries, however those were primarily based on extractivism of natural and raw materials from the forest, with the most evident and predominant input of this nature being latex for the production of rubber.

With the end of the "Rubber Cycle", the greatest period of economic exuberance that the region had experienced so far, the Amazon remained without getting attention from the Brazilian government in terms of policies that could foster its economic growth and development. After some decades, this factor changed in 1967 with the enactment of laws creating the MFTZ in the city of Manaus, capital of the State of Amazonas. The premise of the model was, and still is, to offer tax incentives for companies who decided to establish and produce inside the zone. The main tax incentives are on the import tax for inputs utilized by the industries of the zone on the manufacturing of its products, a total exemption on the Industrialized Products Tax and a reduction on the Income Tax applicable to legal persons.

The MFTZ was established with these features with the objective of reducing local disadvantages that would make the region unattractive for investments of industrial nature. Besides, it would provide an opportunity for the region to develop itself, increasing its social conditions, quality of life and ultimately attracting workers from other regions of the country that would help occupy a scarcely populated region. Inserting more people to live on the region, was a fundamental strategy of the Brazilian

61. World Bank, *Fostering "Sustainable" Cosmetics from the Amazon a Private Sector Partnership to Conserve the Rainforest*, p. 2, http://documents.worldbank.org/curated/en/689701468770146508/pdf/312220PAPER0EN1ustainable0cosmetics.pdf, accessed October 30, 2018.

government to secure and protect the Amazon from an eventual foreign intervention, believed to be possible during the Cold War framework.

The MFTZ indeed caused an increase on the population of the city that saw its population grow more than six times the number during the 1970s and its currently the biggest urban conglomeration of the northern region of the country. The zone also contributed for the growth of the region's GDP that increased to substantial amounts during the following decades. An illustration of this is that the GDP of the State of Manaus is higher than the other four states of the northern region combined.

Despite this positive factor, criticism is made because the economy of the state is concentrated on the capital city and totally depended of the MFTZ. Besides, the economic exuberance experienced by the city of Manaus and the State of Amazonas does not reflect in a development of the region and increase of its quality of life. The HDI level of the Amazon region is still low if compared to other regions in Brazil.

An interesting factor is that the MFTZ has some peculiar features that distinguish it from other similar experiences across the globe. First, it was established oriented to the domestic market, unlike the majority of other SEZ around the world that are focused on exports and the international market. Going further, the choice of location is also unique since Brazil installed the Free Trade Zone in the Amazon region, with its logistical obstructions, distant from the major internal consumer markets and away from the maritime coast. While the international practice, especially the Chinese example, tended to create SEZ close to the sea cost, maritime ports and most developed cities. Moreover, if comparing the MFTZ with the Chinese SEZ it is realized that the latter was far more successful on contributing with the growth and development of the region it is situated in and to its habitants.

For the continuation of the MFTZ and more properly results on its goals of fostering the development, not just economically, but socially of the Amazon region it is advisable for changes in its model. Namely the investment in education and research centers seeking for the increase of science and technology and projects fostering the use of local inputs and raw materials. Steps towards this direction were already taken with the inauguration of the Center of Science, Technology and Innovation of the Industrial Pole of Manaus (CT-PIM) was launched. Furthermore, in order to create a bio-industry hub in the Amazon, the Biotechnology Center of the Amazon was created. These two organizations have an important role to play in the further development of the region's economy and the MFTZ itself. On utilizing these methods, the zone can increase the effectiveness of its production, with modern and more advanced technological machinery. Finally, by using local resources it will make use of one of its best advantages and features compared to other economic centers in the globe, which is the direct access to the vast and precious assets that the biodiversity of the Amazonian rain forest has to offer.

CHAPTER 5

India's Experience with the SEZs: Status, Concerns and Way Forward

Arpita Mukherjee & Avantika Kapoor

§5.01 INTRODUCTION

Special economic zones (SEZs) are industrial enclaves within a country that primarily focus on exports. They can cover a range of free zones such as Free Trade Zones, Export Processing Zones (EPZs), and industrial parks, among others. The major reasons why governments create SEZs include: (a) to promote exports and competitiveness, and (b) to attract foreign direct investment (FDI), technology, and global best practices. SEZs were initially developed to promote growth of manufacturing and exports through a cluster-based approach, which would lead to economies of scale. However, with growth in services trade, SEZs have enabled countries such as India and Philippines to export services such as information technology and information technology enabled services (IT/ITeS). SEZs have also been used as test-bed for reforms in countries such as China. In developing countries such as India, where it is difficult for the government to provide the state-of-the-art infrastructure throughout the country, it is expected that SEZs will provide such infrastructure, and thereby help attract global companies to invest in the country. (Palit and Bhattacharjee, 2008).

To attract private and foreign investment, countries offer a range of fiscal and non-fiscal incentives to the SEZs that are often not available to the rest of the country. Fiscal incentives include tax or duty reductions and/or exemptions, and subsidies. These can include direct tax benefits such as income tax holidays for a certain period of time, and indirect tax benefits such as service tax or value added tax exemptions. Non-fiscal incentives are in the form of single-window clearances for setting up of units, government support in acquisition of contiguous land, training for employees and simplified procedures for custom clearances. The incentives may be given to both developers and units in these zones (Mukherjee and Bhardwaj, 2016).

Some of the incentives given to the SEZs can be prohibited or actionable under the World Trade Organization (WTO) Agreement on Subsidies and Countervailing Measures (SCM Agreement). Therefore, developed countries such as the United States of America (US) and the European Union have moved away from the concept of providing fiscal incentives to 'special zones'. However, a number of Asian countries including India, China, Philippines and Republic of Korea continue to promote SEZs and provide them with various fiscal and non-fiscal incentives. Some of them have carefully designed the incentives to make them non-actionable under the WTO's SCM Agreement. In these countries, SEZs are also an important policy instrument for linking the domestic companies with global value chains (Ramizo, 2014).

India was one of the first Asian countries to have a Central Government owned and managed EPZ in Kandla (Gujarat) as early as 1965. To promote exports, bring in private investment in world class infrastructure, create employment opportunities, and bring in global best practices in zone management, India came up with the SEZ Act in 2005, followed by the SEZ Rules in the year 2006. The Government was of the view that an Act followed by the Rules will ensure predictable business environment and operational certainty for businesses.

Given this background, the objective of this paper is to: (a) examine India's SEZ policy and experience with SEZs, (b) identify the issues that SEZs are facing in India, and (c) make policy recommendations on how their performance can be improved to drive India's economic growth and development. The paper is based on secondary data and information analysis, and face-to-face interviews with fifty units, ten SEZ developers, and ten policymakers and sector experts.

The layout of the paper is as follows. The next section – section §5.03 – analyses the evolution of SEZs and the SEZ policy in India, section §5.04 looks at the issues SEZs have faced in India, and section §5.05 makes policy recommendations to improve the performance of SEZs with the right policy intervention.

§5.02 EVOLUTION OF SEZs IN INDIA

India was a closed economy prior to the 1990s, with high tariffs on imported raw materials, licenses required for establishing presence, and foreign investment restrictions. This was a phase of 'import substitution' industrialization, but it also adversely impacted exports (*see* Aggarwal, 2004; Tantri, 2010). To promote exports, India's first EPZ was set up in Kandla, Gujarat, in 1965 and by the year 1989, the country had seven EPZs that were owned and managed by the Central Government, with Department of Commerce under the Ministry of Commerce and Industry as the nodal agency.

The EPZs were given certain fiscal incentives and other benefits to attract foreign investment, technology, and upgrade labour and management skills apart from promoting exports. However, studies and Government committee reports (for details, *see* Aggarwal, 2004; Kaul Committee, 1978; Tandon Committee, 1980) show that the zones have not been successful in achieving the desired objectives as the policies were rigid and the package of incentives given were not attractive. Further, there was no single window facility within the zone, and there were infrastructural bottlenecks.

While these reports criticised the zones, some (such as the Tandon Committee, 1980) also recommended creation of more zones. Based on those recommendations, the Government decided to establish more zones and in total seven zones were created between 1965 and 1989.

In early 1990s, India initiated a series of reforms and liberalization after the country faced a serious balance of payment crisis. Some key features of the liberalization included removal of quantitative restrictions, reduction of tariffs, allowing FDI, and streamlining the approval process. A key feature of the liberalization process was to attract private and foreign investment in the development of infrastructure including industrial clusters. This somewhat made the EPZ model – where the Central Government owned and managed the EPZs – less attractive. At the same time, the Foreign Trade Policy[1] of the Ministry of Commerce and Industry was modified in 1994 to enable state governments, autonomous agencies, and the private sector to develop EPZs, and accordingly the first private EPZ was set up in Surat in Gujarat under the 1994 policy.

In the late 1990s, a high-level delegation led by the then Minister of Commerce and Industry, Mr Murasoli Maran, visited China, and influenced by China's experiences in developing SEZs, the Minister of Commerce and Industry decided to have an SEZ policy (Tantri, 2010). The Export Import (EXIM) Policy (1997–2002)[2] introduced a new scheme from 1 April 2000 for establishment of the SEZs in different parts of the country. The SEZ Policy was announced in the year 2000. The Policy had many new features to distinguish existing EPZs and export-oriented units (EOUs) from SEZs, and envisaged setting up of SEZs in the public, private and joint sectors or by state governments. The existing EPZs were converted into SEZs. The state governments and private sector set up eleven new SEZs during 2000–2005. There were no formal legislations during this period and incentives were given under the Foreign Trade Policy of the Ministry of Commerce and Industry.

To instil confidence in investors and signal the Government's commitment to a stable SEZ policy regime, the Parliament passed the SEZs Act in May 2005. The objective of the SEZ Act is:

> generation of additional economic activity, promotion of exports of goods and services, promotion of investment from domestic and foreign sources, creation of employment opportunities and development of infrastructure facilities and maintenance of sovereignty and integrity of India, and security of the state and friendly relations with foreign states. [SEZ Act 2005 pp. 8]

This was followed by the SEZ Rules, which came into effect on 10 February 2006, to help the effective operationalization and implementation of SEZs.

1. India's Foreign Trade Policy, also known as Export Import Policy (EXIM), aims at developing export potential, improving export performance, encouraging foreign trade, and creating favorable balance of payments position. Foreign Trade Policy is prepared and announced by the Ministry of Commerce and Industry. It is a set of guidelines and instructions established by the Directorate General of Foreign Trade in matters related to the import and export of goods in India. The Government of India notifies the Policy for a period of five years under section 5 of the Foreign Trade (Development and Regulation Act), 1992.
2. Directorate General of Foreign Trade, Ministry of Commerce. *See* http://dgftcom.nic.in/exim/2000/pol/indexpol.htm (accessed on 7 March 2018).

The SEZ Division of Department of Commerce (under the Ministry of Commerce and Industry) is the nodal agency for SEZs in India. For administrative purposes, the country is divided into seven zones and each zone is headed by a Development Commissioner (DC), who is appointed by the Ministry of Commerce and Industry. An inter-ministerial body with representative from state government, known as Board of Approval, was set up to promote and ensure orderly development of the SEZs. Its role encompasses granting, rejecting, and modifying proposals for the establishment of SEZs, as well as approval of authorized operations, approval to units and developers for foreign collaboration or FDI, etc.[3]

To understand the governance structure of SEZs, one needs to look at the governance structure as is laid by the Indian Constitution. India follows a quasi-federal governance structure - with division of responsibilities between the Central Government and state governments. There are three lists - the Union List, the State List and the Concurrent List - which allocate the legislative powers between the Union/Central Government and state governments. The Union List includes items which are of national importance such as railways, major ports, national highways, import and exports, among others, which are under the jurisdiction of Central Government, and the State List includes items such as land, which are under the jurisdiction of state governments. The state governments have jurisdiction over items such as water supply, state highways, and inland waterways, while the Concurrent List contains items of joint jurisdiction by the Central and state governments. These include labour and electricity, among others. Unlike countries such as China, the Indian SEZs do not have complete autonomy, and different ministries and departments of both Central and state governments play a key role in governance of the zones. Some of the Central and state government ministries and departments which are involved in giving clearances are given in Figure 5.1. While in principal, the process should have been a single window clearance through the DC's office, studies have shown that this is not the case. For example, although DCs have been given the power of Labour Commissioners under the SEZ Act of 2005, some state government still pay a key role and are not willing to give the power to the DCs (Tantri, 2010).

3. SEZ Act (2005) section 9(2).

Figure 5.1 Select Central and State Government Ministries / Departments for SEZ Clearance

Central Government Ministries/Departments

- Department of Commerce (nodal body)
- Ministry of Finance - Revenue Department, Customs
- Department of Industrial Policy and Promotion (DIPP) - FDI
- Department of Environment and Forests
- Directorate General of Foreign Trade (DGFT)
- Ministry of Micro, Small and Medium Enterprises (MSME)
- Ministry of Home Affairs

State Government Ministries/ Departments

- State Industrial Development Corporation
- Finance Department
- Forest and Environment Department
- Electricity Board
- Labour and Employment Department
- Town and Country Planning Department
- Irrigation Department

Source: Compiled from various Ministries' websites.

Approach of state governments towards SEZs vary and has changed over time. Some states such as Gujarat, Haryana, Tamil Nadu, Maharashtra and Punjab have come up with their own SEZ Acts. Others such as Andhra Pradesh are yet to come up with an SEZ Act. The state of West Bengal came up with SEZ Act in 2003 (Government of West Bengal, 2003), which was later scrapped by the new political party which won the state elections (PTI, 2014).

The SEZ policy in India is not static but evolving. Certain changes have been made through amendments and notifications which include procedural relaxations, operational flexibility, withdrawal of tax incentives, etc. Some of these have benefited the industry, while others such as withdrawal of tax incentives have adversely impacted the industry. For example, from 1 April 2012, the Government of India removed the exemption from Minimum Alternate Tax (MAT) and Dividend Distribution Tax (DDT), which the SEZs earlier enjoyed. Minimum Alternate Tax is a form of income tax levied on companies. The rationale behind the imposition of MAT is to bring 'zero tax' companies into the tax net. Under the SEZ Act, 2005, there was no sunset date for MAT exemption for SEZ developers and units, which implied that they may enjoy such exemption for an indefinite period. In the Union Budget 2011-12, it was announced that the MAT exemption will be withdrawn, and subsequently the Finance Act of 2011 imposed MAT from 1 April 2012 retrospectively on SEZ developers and units from 1 April 2005. The sudden imposition of MAT on SEZs and that too retrospectively, without any changes in the SEZ Act of 2005, has faced significant criticism from various stakeholders including developers, units and experts (for details *see* Sharma et al., 2014; Mukherjee and Bhardwaj, 2016). While tax incentives cannot be for an indefinite period, most studies argued against the sudden decision to withdraw it retrospectively.

More recently, India introduced the Goods and Services Tax (GST) in July 2017, through which multitude of taxes have now been subsumed into one single tax, which is expected to not only give a boost to the economy, but to also bring about transparency and create a self-disciplined tax ecosystem. All SEZs notified under the SEZ Act, 2005 are covered in the definition under the GST Act, 2017. Under the GST regime, registration rules have mandated SEZs to take separate registration, since they are considered as separate business verticals. This will result in increased compliance and record maintenance in sectors having multiple SEZ units. While all export of goods and services, and supplies of goods and services made to an SEZ are chargeable to Integrated GST (IGST), these supplies shall be treated as zero-rated supplies under GST. Further, any procurement (of raw material, goods or services) made by an SEZ from outside India for its authorised operations have been exempted from IGST. Most SEZ developers and units have welcomed the exemption they are given from paying GST on goods imported by them (PTI, 2017).

[A] The Process of Setting up an SEZ

According to the SEZ Act of 2005, SEZs can be established by the Central Government, state government, jointly in a public-private partnership format, or by the private sector to manufacture goods or render services. The stages of setting up an SEZ are given in Figure 5.2.

Figure 5.2 The Process of Setting up an SEZ

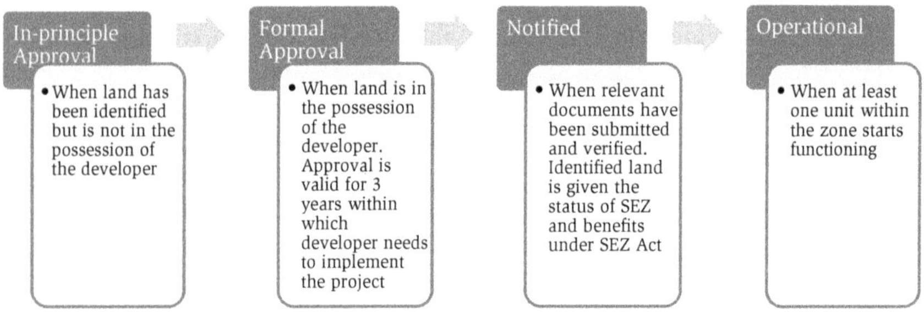

Source: Compiled by the authors.

India has promoted different types of SEZs including single-product, single-services SEZs, multi-product SEZs, and multi-services SEZs. There are specified land area criteria for setting up of SEZs of different types. The SEZ Act 2005 states that 50% of the area should be earmarked as processing area where units and Free Trade & Warehousing Zones (FTWZs) are located, and the remaining area should be designated as non-processing area which can include commercial and social infrastructure such as residential complexes, educational institutions and hospitals. However, since developers were facing problems in aggregating large tracks of land, the SEZ Amendment Rules were brought about on 13 September 2013, to relax the land criteria and help the developers to acquire land (*see* Appendix 1 for details). Yet, developers have been facing issues in India in aggregating large acres of continuous land, which is discussed later. Further, the policy requires that acquiring land preference should be given for acquisition of waste and barren land, followed by single crop land and double crop land necessary to meet the contiguity requirements. It also mentions that as far as possible, SEZs may be located outside an urban agglomeration/municipal limit, and sufficient land and water resources for the population envisaged in the SEZs should be available. The SEZ policy does not favour acquisition of cultivable land, and cultivable land can be considered only if adequate quantum of other land is not available.

[B] Incentives Given to SEZs

SEZs in India get both fiscal and non-fiscal incentives. The examples of fiscal incentives given by Central Government to developers and units at the development and profit-making stages are given in Figure 5.3.

Figure 5.3 Fiscal Incentives Given to SEZ by the Central Government

	DEVELOPERS	UNITS
Development/ Operation Stage	**Exempted From** • Customs Duty • Sales Tax • Service Tax • Stamp Duty and Registration Fees • Stamp Duty on Mortgages • Electricity Duty (on capital goods, consumables, component and spares)	**Exempted From** • Customs Duty • Sales Tax • Service Tax • Stamp Duty and Registration Fees • Stamp Duty on Mortgages • Electricity Duty (on capital goods, consumables, component and spares)
Profit Stage	**Income Tax:** Deduction of 100% Income tax for 10 consecutive years out of first 15 years since the SEZ was notified	**Income Tax:** Exemption on export profits as follows:- • 100% for the first 5 years • 50% for the next 5 years • 50% of profits ploughed back for the next 5 years

Source: SEZ India, Ministry of Commerce and Industry.

To avail such benefits, there is a mandatory requirement that companies located in SEZs have to be net foreign exchange earners in five years. This requirement makes export linked incentives given to units in SEZs non-compliant and prohibitory under the WTO's SCM Agreement. The WTO rules contain some 'Special and Differential Treatment' for developing countries and least developed countries (LDCs), which India earlier enjoyed. Specifically, Article 27.2 of the SCM Agreement exempts LDCs and developing countries with per capita income of less than USD 1,000 from the prohibition of export subsidies. The list of these countries is given in Annex VII of the SCM Agreement.[4] According to the WTO rules of 1995, the threshold was calculated in terms of current prices. However, concerns were raised that a country may cross the per capita income threshold of USD 1,000 merely by having inflation. Hence, in the Doha Round of negotiations, the WTO has adopted an alternate methodology that calculates the threshold in constant 1990 US dollars. Moreover, to graduate, a country must reach or cross the USD 1,000 threshold (measured in terms of constant 1990 US dollars) for three consecutive years. Based on this criteria and notification issued by the Committee on Subsidies and Countervailing Measures dated 11 July 2017 (G/SCM/110/Add.14), India can no longer qualify for the 'Special and Differential Treatment', which it earlier received as a developing country. Hence, the export linked incentives given to Indian SEZs can now be prohibited under the WTO. A survey conducted by the authors in the year 2015 for the SEZ Division of the Department of Commerce covering 144 SEZ units and forty-six SEZ developers of operational SEZs found that 70% of the total respondents (units and developers) rated the importance of fiscal incentives as 'very important' and therefore, withdrawal of any incentives given to SEZ units have to be examined in this context. In the year 2018, the US has challenged India's export subsidy programme in the WTO including subsidies given to SEZs, stating that it is inconsistent with the WTO's SCM Agreement. The two countries (India and the US) will have consultations on the issue in April 2018. However, since the subsidy given to SEZs are under the category of prohibited subsidy, experts opined that India should have a relook at subsides given to SEZs and reorient them to make them WTO-compliant (Ranade, 2018).

SEZs were proposed to receive exemption from state sales tax and other levies as extended by the respective state governments.[5] Prior to the implementation of the GST, many states initiated the process of granting indirect tax benefits to SEZs. However, the levels and extent/quantum, as well as the legal framework for granting these benefits, varied across states.

In terms of non-fiscal incentives, SEZs were proposed to receive single window clearance for Central and state level approvals. However, this has not happened (Mukherjee et al., 2016). Some state governments have been more proactive than others in supporting SEZs; they have helped companies in acquiring land, developing the SEZs, providing administrative assistance, etc. However, non-fiscal incentives enjoyed by Indian SEZ developers and units are far less than those offered by countries

4. The Annex VII countries are Bolivia, Cameroon, Congo, Côte d'Ivoire, Dominican Republic, Egypt, Ghana, Guatemala, Guyana, India, Indonesia, Kenya, Morocco, Nicaragua, Nigeria, Pakistan, Philippines, Senegal, Sri Lanka and Zimbabwe.

5. Source: https://www.ibef.org/download/SEZs-Role-in-Indian-Manufacturing-Growth.pdf (accessed on 7 March 2018).

such as Republic of Korea, China, Philippines and Bangladesh (Tantri, 2010). For example, in the Philippines, the Philippine Economic Zone Authority (PEZA) registered economic zone enterprises can employ non-resident foreign nationals in supervisory, technical or advisory positions. PEZA helps in the visa processing, and foreign nationals in a PEZA-registered enterprise are given special non-immigrant visas with multiple entry privileges. To encourage foreign investment and improve living conditions for foreign nationals, the Republic of Korea allows the establishment of foreign educational institutes (schools and universities) and foreign hospitals in Free Economic Zones. Such facilities are not available in India (Tantri, 2010).

[C] Current Status of SEZs in India

SEZs began developing at a fast pace in India from the year 2006, when the SEZ Rules came into effect. Initially, there were a fairly large number of proposals as private investors were highly motivated by the framework. By June 2007, there were 303 formal approvals and 161 in-principle approvals. By September 2014, there were 564 formal approvals, 406 notified SEZs, and 192 operational SEZs.[6] As on 7 February 2018, in addition to seven Central Government SEZs and eleven State/Private Sector SEZs set up prior to the enactment of the SEZ Act, 2005, formal approvals have been given to 423 proposals, 357 SEZs have been notified, and 221 SEZs are operational.[7] The number of formal approvals has reduced in three years because some projects have been cancelled at the planning stage due to various reasons such as developers being unable to get contiguous land. A number of notified SEZs have not become operational as they have not been able to attract a single unit.

The SEZ policy is a pan-India policy but data shows that the SEZs are not spread uniformly across India. Top five states with notified SEZs account for almost 63% of the total notified SEZs in the country, and top five states with operational SEZs account for 65% of total operational SEZs in the country (*see* Figure 5.4). SEZs are highly concentrated in the southern states, and there are no SEZs in the north-eastern states of India, which are gateways to the Association of Southeast Asian Nations (ASEAN) countries.

6. Source: SEZ India, Ministry of Commerce and Industry.
7. Source: Rajya Sabha (Upper House of the Parliament of India). Unstarred Question No. 492. http://rajyasabha.nic.in/rsnew/question/introduction.asp (accessed on 23 February 2018).

Figure 5.4 Distribution of Approved SEZs by Major States (as on 16 February 2017)

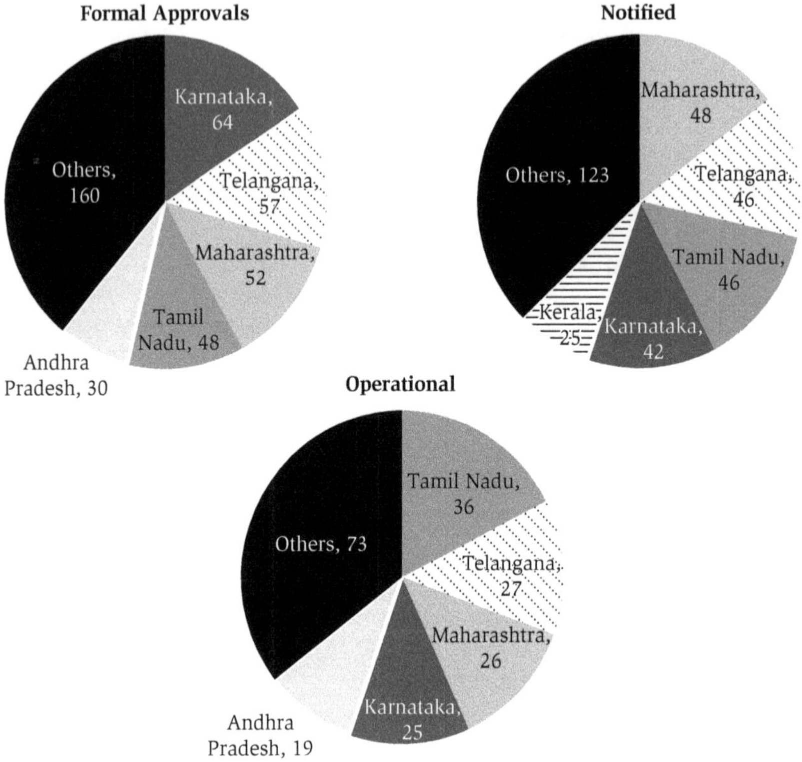

Source: <http://sezindia.nic.in/upload/uploadfiles/files/4Sector-wise%20distribution-SEZ.pdf> accessed on 1 March 2018.

In terms of products and sectors, as of 16 February 2017, India had twenty-three operational multi-product SEZs (including two port based multi-product SEZs) and two operational multi-services SEZs. The maximum number of approved and operational SEZs is in the IT/ITeS, electronic hardware, and telecom equipment sector. However, the data for the biotechnology sector shows that while twenty-two SEZs had formal approvals and fifteen were notified, only two were operational (*see* Table 5.1).

India has been experimenting with different types of SEZs; there are three operational FTWZs and two operational handicraft and carpets SEZs. Thus, SEZs are spread across both high technology and labour-intensive sectors. Overall, India has been more successful in services-based SEZs rather than using SEZs as a tool to develop manufacturing capabilities, especially high value and high technology-oriented manufacturing.

Table 5.1 Distribution of Approved SEZs by Major Sectors (as on 16 February 2017)

Sector	*Formal Approval*	*Notified*	*Operational*
IT/ITES/Electronic Hardware/Telecom equipment	263	211	117
Biotechnology	22	15	2
Pharmaceuticals/ chemicals	16	16	12
Engineering	14	14	13
Textiles/Apparel/Wool	7	6	7
Others	58	12	30
Total (excluding multi-product, multi-services, and port-based multi-product SEZs)	**380**	**274**	**181**

Source: http://sezindia.nic.in/upload/uploadfiles/files/3StatewiseDistribution-SEZ.pdf (accessed on 1 March 2018).

§5.03 PERFORMANCE OF SEZs

A number of studies, including government sponsored studies, have tried to provide data and information on performance of SEZs (e.g., *see* Lakshmanan, 2009; Mathiraj and Devi, 2015; Khurud, 2013; Kumar and Kumar, 2017; TK and Arul, 2016). Most of these studies have pointed out that the performance of SEZs in India can be measured against the objectives for which it was created which includes: (a) exports of goods and services, (b) promotion of investment from domestic and foreign sources, (c) creation of employment opportunities, and (d) development of infrastructure facilities. Figure 5.5 and Table 5.2 show that although overall exports have increased over the years, the rise in exports from SEZs is not large and shows a fluctuating trend. Detailed sector-wise data on exports from SEZs is not available in the public domain. The available data shows that IT/ITeS exports accounts for the majority of the SEZ exports. According to the Export Promotion Council for EOUs & SEZs (EPCES), during the period April-December 2017, the major sectors that have recorded the highest growth in exports include non-conventional energy (82%), trading and services (24%), computer/electronic software (18%), engineering (17%), electronics and hardware (15%), plastics and rubber (14%), and handicrafts (13%) (The Dollar Business Bureau, 2018).

Figure 5.5 Exports from SEZs vis-á-vis Total Exports (in USD Billion)

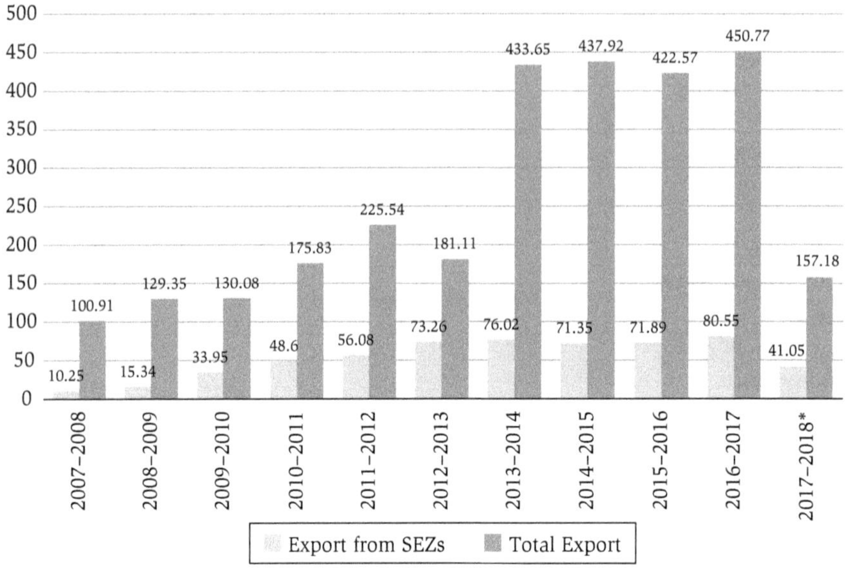

Source: EPCES Factsheet, Rajya Sabha (Upper House of the Parliament of India) Unstarred Question Numbers 1762, 492, 971, and 3693 (available at http://rajyasabha.nic.in/rsnew/question/introduction.asp (accessed on 23 February 2018)).

*The data is calculated for April-March every year. The data for 2017–2018 is from April 2017 to September 2017, which explains the low values.

Table 5.2 SEZ Exports Compared to Total Exports

Years	*SEZs Exports (USD Billion)*	*Percentage Increase in SEZ Exports*	*Total Exports (USD Billion)*	*Percentage Increase in Total Exports*	*Share of SEZs Exports in Total Exports (in Percentage)*
2007–2008	10.25	–	100.91	–	10.16
2008–2009	15.34	50	129.35	28.18	11.86
2009–2010	33.95	121	130.08	0.56	26.11
2010–2011	48.60	43.11	175.83	35.17	27.64
2011–2012	56.08	15.39	225.54	28.27	24.86
2012–2013	73.26	31	181.11	-19.70	40.45
2013–2014	76.02	4	433.65	139	17.53

Years	*SEZs Exports (USD Billion)*	*Percentage Increase in SEZ Exports*	*Total Exports (USD Billion)*	*Percentage Increase in Total Exports*	*Share of SEZs Exports in Total Exports (in Percentage)*
2014–2015	71.35	-0.06	437.92	0.98	16.29
2015–2016	71.89	0.11	422.57	-3.51	17.01
2016–2017	80.55	12.05	450.77	6.67	17.87

Source: Compiled from EPCES Factsheet, Rajya Sabha (Upper House of the Parliament of India) Unstarred Question Numbers 1762, 492, 971, and 3693 (available at http://rajyasabha.nic.in/rsnew/question/introduction.asp (accessed on 23 February, 2018)), and Kumar and Kumar (2017).

Data for employment in SEZs shows that cumulative employment has increased steadily in the past decade (*see* Figure 5.6).

Figure 5.6 Employment in SEZs (In Cumulative Numbers)

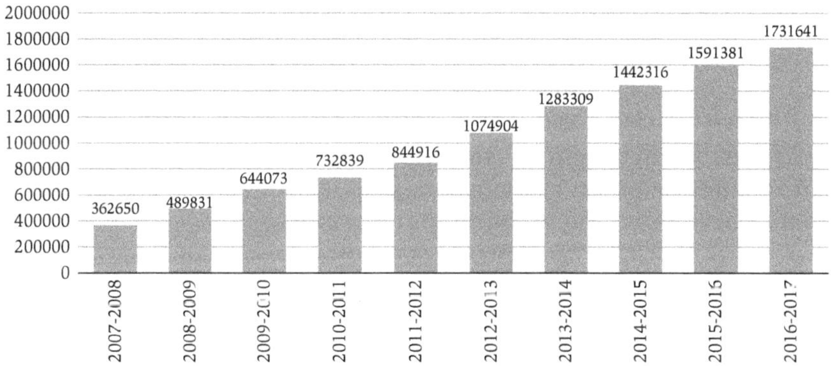

Source: EPCES Factsheet, Rajya Sabha (Upper House of the Parliament of India) Unstarred Question Numbers 1762, 492, 971, and 3693 (available at http://rajyasabha.nic.in/rsnew/question/introduction.asp (accessed on 23 February 2018)).

Investment in the SEZs has increased, although not exponentially (*see* Figure 5.7). There is no data on foreign versus domestic investment in SEZs. Indian software multinationals such as Tata Consultancy Services Limited, Infosys Limited, and Wipro Limited have invested in multiple SEZs.

Figure 5.7 Cumulative Investment in SEZs (in USD Billion)

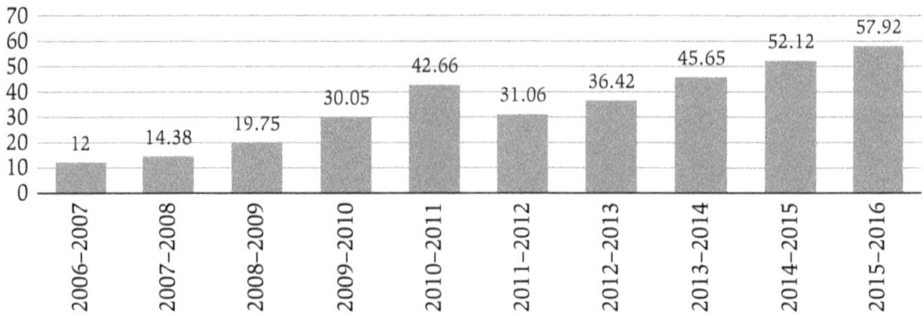

Source: EPCES Factsheet, Rajya Sabha (Upper House of the Parliament of India) Unstarred Question Numbers 1762, 492, 971, and 3693 (available at http://rajyasabha.nic.in/rsnew/question/introduction.asp (accessed on 23 February 2018)).

Some Indian corporates have made substantial investments in SEZs and allied infrastructure. For example, the Adani Group developed the Adani Ports and Special Economic Zone Limited in Gujarat. The other example is that of Sri City's SEZ, which is part of an integrated business city with multi-product SEZ, located in the state of Andhra Pradesh, and apart from the SEZs, it also has a FTWZ, a Domestic Tariff Zone (DTZ), and an Electronics Manufacturing Cluster. Over 150 companies from twenty-seven countries have set up their facilities within Sri City[8] but most of them are located in the Domestic Tariff Area (DTA).[9] This is because: (a) incentives given to companies in DTA are sometimes higher than incentives given to SEZs, (b) the SEZ policy changes frequently and incentives can be prohibited and/or actionable under the WTO, and (c) companies located in India would like to cater to the large domestic market along with exports (for details *see* Mukherjee et al., 2016).

The location of SEZs in a few states, the difficulties faced by SEZ developers in getting contiguous land and in attracting units to their SEZs, approvals given to SEZ developers without evaluating their past projects, the substantial revenue foregone through tax benefits without commensuration growth in exports, and inability of the SEZs to make India a manufacturing hub and attract foreign investment in manufacturing have prompted some experts to believe that the Indian SEZ experience has not be very successful (*see* Lakshmanan, 2009; Kumar and Kumar, 2017). However, SEZs, along with the policy on Software Technology Parks,[10] did help India in becoming a

8. For details *see* http://www.sricity.in/why-sri-city/ (accessed on 7 March 2018).
9. Domestic Tariff Area (DTA) or Domestic Tariff Zone (DTZ) means an area within India that is outside the SEZs. An SEZ unit can sell goods and services manufactured in the DTA on payment of Customs duties or Excise Duties, as required.
10. For the promotion of software exports from the country, the Software Technology Parks of India (STPI) was set up in 1991 as an Autonomous Society under the Department of Electronics and Information Technology (under the Ministry of Electronics and Information Technology). The services rendered by STPI for the software exporting community have been statutory services, data communications servers, incubation facilities, training and value-added services. For details, *see* https://www.stpi.in/11019 (accessed on 7 March 2018).

major exporter of IT/ITeS services, and India is among the top ten WTO member countries in exports of services. The country has a positive trade balance in services and much of it can be attributed to software companies located in SEZs. Given this, it is important to identify the issues faced by SEZ developers and units, and make policy recommendations.

§5.04 ISSUES FACED BY SEZs IN INDIA

The authors conducted face-to-face interactions with fifty units, ten SEZ developers, and ten policymakers and sector experts to understand the challenges SEZs faced in India. The discussions highlighted that there are certain loopholes in the policy itself and in the institutional framework governing SEZs in India. For example, the objective of developing an SEZ under the SEZ Act is generic and does not distinguish an SEZ from other forms of industrial clusters. Therefore, what the policy aims to deliver is not clear, and there is often confusion between SEZs and other forms of industrial clusters. Moreover, there is no vision document regarding SEZs, which highlights what the long-term objectives and goals of setting up SEZs are. Often, approvals are given to companies which have not completed the previous projects. In some states, the state governments have not accepted the Central Government SEZ regulations and have not facilitated the clearance process. The single window process is not working efficiently, and SEZ developers and units have to go to different state government departments to get clearances.

Globally, SEZs gain certain subsidies and fiscal incentives and in India, the SEZ Act offers direct and indirect tax benefits. However, given the large number of SEZs which require the subsidies, they may not receive them quickly in a given fiscal year. In terms of tax benefits, the income tax holiday given to the SEZs is uniform for all SEZs, without taking into account the fact that different SEZs have different sizes, types of units, break-even periods, and needs for investment in infrastructure. For example, a large, multi-sector, manufacturing SEZ requires more investment and a longer time to break-even, and therefore needs incentives tailor-made for their needs, compared to a single sector SEZs in IT/ITeS sector. Further, the export-linked subsidies given to units under the SEZ Act are actionable under the WTO's SCM Agreement, which makes SEZs unattractive. If the SEZs offer subsidies that are actionable under the SCM Agreement, they can face countervailing duties. Certain countries have taken measures to avoid that. For example, Thailand has removed mandatory export requirement conditions under its zone legislation, and Vietnam changed its policy from the use of tax-based incentives to offering better services in the zones. The survey found that for foreign investors, Indian SEZs are not as attractive as SEZs is countries such as Thailand, China and Vietnam as the incentive package in India is not WTO-compliant.

In several cases, incentives given to units located outside SEZs (in DTAs) and to developers through other policies and schemes are easier to get than the incentives given under the SEZ policy. For example, under the Ministry of Food Processing Industries' Mega Food Park Scheme, a capital grant of 50% of the eligible project cost (maximum up to approximately USD 8 million) is provided in a phased manner in four instalments.[11] This incentive is considered better by some developers. In the apparel and textile sector, the Ministry of Textiles' Scheme for Integrated Textile Parks (which was launched in 2005) provides a grant worth 40% of the project cost to create state-of-the-art infrastructure facilities for setting up textile units. This grant is also provided in a phased manner consisting of four instalments.[12] Such grants are provided outright upon the conception of the project (in a phased manner), unlike in the case of SEZs. Thus, SEZs in India have not been successful in attracting apparel industry, unlike countries such as Bangladesh which has attracted foreign investment from countries such as the Republic of Korea. Moreover, the units in the DTA in India are eligible for export incentives under the Foreign Trade Policy, some of which are better than what is given to units in SEZs.

Unlike some countries, SEZ incentives in India are not linked to scale upgradation, use of clean technology and green resources, and investment in research and development (R&D). For example, Dubai has SEZs which pioneer 'green prints' to help metropolitan cities accommodate rapid urbanization, and reduce energy, water and waste.[13] Moreover, the UAE government also provides incentives to SEZs for conducting research in the areas of energy and sustainability, and adopting clean technology. In China, SEZs have played an important role in bringing new technologies and they have been successful in increasing the export of technological goods by having fast track patents (Zeng, 2011). However, in India, there are limited innovations and R&D in the SEZs.

While regulations have to evolve, the SEZ policy has changed frequently resulting in uncertain operating environment. For example, the sudden and retrospective withdrawal of the MAT and DDT exemptions from the SEZs has adversely affected the developers and investor sentiments, and faced severe criticism. The SEZ developers argued that while a country has the right to change its direct tax regime, there should be predictability in the tax policy, and changes should not be made randomly so that it does not adversely impact investor sentiments. MAT should not have been imposed retrospectively. Several SEZs became less attractive with the withdrawal of MAT and DDT exemptions, due to which a number of developers sought to get their zones de-notified and approvals cancelled. For example, in 2007, Reliance Industries Limited (RIL) was permitted to convert its existing refinery at Jamnagar (Gujarat) into an SEZ. This entitled the company to get various tax exemptions, including automatic duty-free import of crude oil and duty-free imports of equipment to expand or upgrade the refinery (Times News Network, 2007). However, in 2013, after the MAT and DDT exemptions were withdrawn, RIL sought to partly de-notify the SEZ.

Several countries have used SEZs as a test-bed for reforms. For example, China used SEZs to test market-based reforms and policies, and to test land and tax-related policies. This enabled China to implement land and labour reforms, and also attract FDI especially in sensitive sectors such as retail in a phased manner. Once a policy

11. Source: http://mofpi.nic.in/Schemes/mega-food-parks (accessed on 13 March 2018).
12. Source: http://texmin.nic.in/sites/default/files/sitp%20new%20park%20guidelines.pdf (accessed on 13 March 2018).
13. Source: http://www.masdar.ae/ (accessed on 13 March 2018).

succeeded in an SEZ, it was implemented in the whole country. India has not used SEZs to try out reforms or liberalization policies. India is one of the few emerging markets which continue to have FDI restrictions or rigid conditions across a number of services sectors. Further, the labour laws are rigid and companies do face problems in hiring and firing employees.

There is a serious shortage of data on SEZs, based on which government can take informed decisions. For example, there is no comprehensive data on domestic and foreign investment in SEZs. Moreover, the data collated and collected in not presented in correct format that enables analysis. For example, the IT/ITeS sector is clubbed with telecommunication equipment, while aviation, aerospace, animation and gaming, and copper sectors are all clubbed together.[14] Further, there are issues with the presentation of data in the Department of Commerce website. For example, sector-wise data is uploaded under state-wise distribution and vice versa. The paucity of data and its incorrect presentation have made it difficult to conduct detailed performance analysis.

A major problem for SEZs is acquiring large acreage of contiguous land for developing a proposed SEZ. In India, land acquisition is a political issue because it has led to displacement of farmers without adequate compensation, and that has led to political protests, which has in the past stalled projects (e.g., *see* Levien, 2013; Mukherjee et al., 2016). The SEZ developers have faced issues in acquiring large acres of contiguous and vacant land, which is mandated in the Act. In many cases, the developers may get the required acres of land, but it may not be contiguous. Even with the support of state government, such projects can fail. For example, the Reliance Haryana SEZ project (Reliance Haryana SEZ Limited) was approved in 2006 over two districts in the state of Haryana (Gurugram and Jhajjar). There were large-scale protests by farmers over land acquisition for the SEZ, and moreover, Reliance Ventures Limited (RVL) was unable to acquire contiguous land to meet the minimum holding requirements. This led to delays, subsequent to which RVL walked out of the joint venture with the Haryana state government (Saini, 2015). India enacted the Right to Fair Compensation and Transparency in Land Acquisition, Rehabilitation and Resettlement Act, 2013[15] which covers fair compensation for land acquisition for SEZs. However, private players have raised concern about the high compensation for land acquisition as per the Act, which makes projects non-viable. The interviews with SEZ developers also found that in India, there are delays in land allotment, lack of maintenance of proper land ownership records, and confusion in land valuation.

As per the World Bank's 'Ease of Doing Business 2018' index, which uses indicators such as registering land, regulations for entering the industry, getting electricity, trading across borders, and dealing with permits to rank countries, India was ranked 100,[16] which was an improvement of thirty places from the previous year,

14. Source: http://sezindia.nic.in/upload/uploadfiles/files/3StatewiseDistribution-SEZ.pdf (accessed on 8 March 2018).
15. Source: http://lawmin.nic.in/ld/P-ACT/2013/The%20Right%20to%20Fair%20Compensation%20and%20Transparency%20in%20Land%20Acquisition,%20Rehabilitation%20and%20Resettlement%20Act,%202013.pdf (accessed on 1 March 2018).
16. Source: http://www.doingbusiness.org/data/exploreeconomies/india (accessed on 5 March 2018).

but still lower compared to countries such as Republic of Korea (4), Malaysia (24), Thailand (26), Vietnam (68) and China (78). The survey found that there is a lack of fast track and single window clearances even for SEZs, and SEZ developers and units face delays in obtaining permits and clearances such as environment clearance. The power supply is erratic and the cost of power is much higher than in competing countries such as China, which increases cost of production. Firms in SEZs have to invest in power back-up systems.

India has a high corporate tax rate (25% for smaller companies and over 30% for larger companies), compared to countries such as Cambodia (20%), Thailand (20%) and Vietnam (20%)[17] which along with other cesses makes it an unattractive destination for investment destination.

India has signed Free Trade Agreements (FTAs)/comprehensive trade agreements with ASEAN and its member countries, Republic of Korea, Japan, Sri Lanka, etc., through which there have been zero duty or duty reduction on imported products. Due to this, a product exported from a SEZ in India to DTA in India faces a high autonomous tariff compared to imported products from FTA partner countries. Thus, SEZ units in India are at a disadvantage compared to SEZ units located in countries with which India has signed FTAs.

The success of an SEZ depends on access to global markets and this in turn requires efficient logistics networks and outside zone connectivity. The logistics cost in India is around 14% of the GDP, compared to less than 8% by other developing countries.[18] Location, infrastructure and logistics network are key factors to enable success of SEZs, and in case of India, these are some of the reasons for the failure of SEZs to attract units, especially those located in remote areas.

§5.05 THE WAY FORWARD

This paper discusses India's experiences with the SEZ policy. The paper highlights that unlike many ASEAN countries and China, India has not been successful in using the SEZs to promote manufacturing growth, attract foreign investment, and move into high value manufacturing. However, SEZs have been successful in promoting exports of services such as IT/ITeS services. Although India continues to have FDI restrictions in a number of services sectors such as the legal, architecture and accountancy services, SEZs have not been used as a test-bed of reforms.

The discussions with developers and units show that SEZs will be successful in India if the Department of Commerce design 'smart subsides' that are not actionable in the WTO. For example, with increased servicification of manufacturing, services used by SEZ units can be subsidised. Second, the government may or may not support the SEZ policy, but if it does, the incentives given to SEZs cannot be lower than that is offered to companies located in DTA. Third, government can use SEZs as a test-bed of

17. Source: https://home.kpmg.com/xx/en/home/services/tax/tax-tools-and-resources/tax-rates-online/corporate-tax-rates-table.html (accessed on 13 March 2018).
18. Source: http://www.assocham.org/downloads/?filename=1455984479.pdf (accessed on 5 March 2018).

reforms and provide certain benefits to SEZs including relaxed FDI conditions and requirements, single window clearances, fast track visa, etc., which makes SEZs attractive to domestic and foreign companies. The government needs to focus more on non-fiscal incentives and ease of doing business. This will require greater collaboration between the Central and state governments.

Fourth, there is need to collect, collate and analyse data on SEZ performance which will enable the government to understand the issues, and support the policy. Fifth, approved SEZs have to be carefully monitored and no new approvals should be given unless the existing SEZs are fully utilised. It is important for the government to create few good quality SEZs rather than approving a large number of SEZs which fail to become operational. The government should also carefully monitor the land uses in SEZ and allied connectivity. Ideally, SEZs should be located in the proposed dedicated freight corridors and be well-connected to ports and airports.

Sixth, the SEZ policy should not change frequently, and industry consultation and research should be done before making policy changes. Seventh, if benefits have to be phased out, they should be phased out over time and not retrospectively.

Eight, corporate tax in India has to be lowered to at least 25% or else India will not be able to attract industry which will move to competing ASEAN countries.

Ninth, The SEZ policy cannot be delinked with overall trade policy. For SEZs to be successful, India needs to lower the tariffs and remove the barriers to export from domestic SEZs to DTA. Units in SEZs should be treated at par with units from countries with whom India has signed trade agreements, and has lowered tariffs and duties.

Tenth, it is important for the government to ensure that zones not only have state-of-the-art inside zone infrastructure, but also access to good quality outside zone infrastructure and logistics connectivity. The logistics costs have to be reduced and delays in transit have to be addressed through streamlining of processing and use of technology. Within zones, efforts have to be made to provide basic utilities such as electricity at competitive rates. It is important to ensure consistent quality 24x7 power supply.

To conclude, the government needs to create a long-term plan and/or vision document about its strategies with respect to SEZs which offers operational certainty to businesses. It is important for policymakers to understand that in a competitive global world, industry will locate in places where there is ease of doing business and a large market. If units in SEZs are not able to access the large Indian market, they will not find the scheme attractive. Policies need to focus on making units in SEZs globally competitive by supporting them in adoption of technology and best management practices, and by reducing their operational and logistics costs. If that is done, SEZs will become an engine of growth and development, and will attract investment.

Appendix 1: Minimum Land Requirement for SEZs (Before and After Amendment to SEZ Rules 2013)

Type of SEZ	*Minimum Land Requirements for SEZs*			
	For Normal Areas (in Hectares)		*Area for Special States/Union Territories[a] (in Hectares)*	
	Before Sept. 2013	*After Sept. 2013*	*Before Sept. 2013*	*After Sept. 2013*
Multi-product SEZ	1,000	500	200	100
Multi-services SEZ	100	50	50	25
Sector-specific SEZ/Port/Airport	100	50	50	25
Gems and jewellery	10	10	10	10
Biotech and non-conventional energy (including solar energy equipment/cell, but excluding SEZs for non-conventional energy production and manufacturing)	10	10	10	10
FTWZ	40	40[b]	40	25
IT/ITeS SEZ	10	No minimum land requirement	10	No minimum land requirement
Electronics Hardware and Software	10	10	10	10
Agro-based food processing		10		10

Source: Mukherjee et al. (2016).

[a]Assam, Meghalaya, Nagaland, Arunachal Pradesh, Mizoram, Manipur, Tripura, Himachal Pradesh, Uttarakhand, Sikkim, Jammu and Kashmir, Goa or a Union Territory.

[b]In an SEZ having area less than 500 hectares, FTWZs may be permitted with no minimum area requirement but subject to the condition that the maximum area of the FTWZ shall not exceed 20% of the processing area.

CHAPTER 6

The Practice of the Reform of Administrative Approval System in Shanghai Free Trade Zone: Taking the Licenses and Permits Reform as a Breakthrough Point

Hongzhen Jiang & Haonan Zhong

§6.01 INTRODUCTION

In 2001, the State Council issued the "*Implementation Opinions on the Reform of the Administrative Approval System*" as the symbol that the reform of China's administrative approval system started officially. In 2004, "*Administrative Licensing Law*" was enacted, announcing that the reform of the administrative approval system has entered into a new stage of legalization. After the effort of more than ten years, China has made remarkable achievements in reducing approval items, optimizing the approval process, and promoting the legalization of approval. The openness of the market has been continuously improved, the economic vitality has been significantly enhanced, the resources allocation has become more reasonable, and the approval operation has been further standardized.

However, at the same time, the structural problems inherent in the former reform strategies have gradually emerged. First, in the relation between government, market and society, the traditional administrative mode which is dominated by the government has not been fundamentally changed. In the reform, it was mainly reflected in the fact that though many approval items are cancelled, their significance was still insufficient. Many core projects that involve market access, resource allocation, and large rent-seeking space have not yet been properly cleaned up, and some projects which were repealed have been retained by transformations, which led to a huge gap between public's feelings about the effect of the reform and the official statistical data.[1] Second, the unreasonable institutional setup and power allocation of the current government has become an institutional obstacle of administrative approval reform. The problem of overlapping functions among departments, and their unclear power and responsibilities, are magnified in the administrative approval process. This has resulted in a series of approval items that overlap or presuppose each other and even have logical contradictions, which greatly reduces the efficiency of approval.[2] Third, in the relationship between the central and local government, the local government lacks the necessary autonomy for the approval system reform. Since the Administrative License Law has centralized the main administrative approvals while a great deal of previous local approval items were cancelled, local governments lack necessary reformatory power for the centrally delegating licensing items thus cannot adjust them to local actual situations. The provisions originally set up to restrict local governments to set redundant licenses have become an institutional obstacle to the streamline administration and institute decentralization.[3] Finally, in the aspect of the legalization of the reform, because of the hysteresis quality of legislation, the reforms are often promoted solely by the policies of the State Council. The legitimacy of concrete measures and the institutional vacuum resulted from the reforms have become prominent contradictions in the reform process. All these conditions manifest that China's current reform of the administrative approval system has entered a critical stage. Only by seeking institutional innovation based on the reflection of past policies can the reform be further deepened.

Taking Permit and License reform as a breakthrough point, Shanghai Free Trade Zone (SFTZ) has successively implemented measures such as "Business Licenses Before Government Permits" and "Separating Permits from Business License", and adopting a "negative list" management mode, which finally changed its holistic market access arrangement. In addition, the aforementioned measures in the SFTZ have also produced spillover effects. The three stages that from the "leadership in command" in 2013 to the "advance side by side" that radiated Guangdong, Tianjin, and Fujian, and to the "geese sprinting" in Liaoning, Zhejiang, Henan, Hubei, Sichuan, Shaanxi and Chongqing provinces in 2017, was hailed as the realization of the new strategic mode of the "1 + 3 + 7" model of the free trade zone (FTZ). In this process, the SFTZ is the "leader" and "first mover" in the construction of the entire FTZ system. Summarizing the successful experience of the SFTZ is of great significance in resolving the difficulties of China's current approval system reform.

1. Wang Kewen, *The Reform of China's Administrative Approval System and Its Legal Regulations*, Chinese Journal of Law, No. 2 (2014).
2. Zhang Dingan, *Problems Analysis and Breakthrough Strategy of the Administrative Approval System Reform in Its Critical Stage*, Chinese Public Administration, No. 9 (2002).
3. Li Jun, *The Local Innovation and Difficulty Overcoming of Administrative Approval Reform*, Social Sciences in Guangdong, No. 4 (2015).

§6.02 THE OPTIMIZATION OF ADMINISTRATIVE APPROVAL PROCESS: FROM "GOVERNMENT PERMITS BEFORE BUSINESS LICENSES" TO "BUSINESS LICENSES BEFORE GOVERNMENT PERMITS"

[A] The Disadvantages of "Government Permits Before Business Licenses" Approval Mode

The permit and license system in industrial and commercial registration, that is business license and permit, is two basic institutions by which the state regulates the qualification of commercial entities and their business activities. Business license and business permit respectively correspond to the subject and business qualifications of enterprises. According to the legal logic of "obtaining subject qualification before business qualification", enterprises should have obtained a business license first and then obtain a business permit. The standards of the latter are accordingly higher than that of the former.

However, for a long time, China has been implementing the "Government Permits Before Business Licenses" approval mode, artificially inverting the institutional logic of industrial and commercial registration thus setting many unreasonable obstacles for the market access obtaining license before permit. In practice, due to the large number of pre-approval items and the over strict licensing conditions, the mode of "obtaining license before permit" first objectively caused the threshold for the establishment of commercial subjects which fall into the area requiring pre-approvals to be too high, exacerbating unlicensed business activities. Second, during the process of approval of business qualifications, an enterprise cannot engage in activities such as raising funds, leasing business premises, and hiring staff as a company because it has not obtained a business permit. Therefore, it is difficult to meet the requirements of the approval department for operating conditions so the company would be trapped into an endless loop in which the business licenses and permits are the conditions of each other. For example, when a new-type enterprise applies for an industrial and commercial business permit, the Trade and Industry Bureau shall require the environmental impact assessment documents be provided based on the "*Regulations on the Environmental Protection of Construction Projects*"; when the enterprise applies for an environmental assessment to the Environmental Protection Agency, it is required to provide the documents of item recordation according to the "*Regulation of the recordation of enterprise investment project*"; and when the enterprise turn to project recordation procedures, the National Development and Reform Commission requires the industrial and commercial business permit.[4] Third, the over-high threshold of the establishment of enterprises also makes administrative activities after the approval become formalistic. Many departments hold the idea of "replace supervision with approval" or even "lesser approval lesser supervision." They simply focus on the prior review of the company's establishment but ignore the interim and ex post supervision of the substantial business operations or equate it with the penalization the unlicensed

4. Luo Haiying, *Conflict and Its Resolution on the Standards of Administrative Approval*, Chinese Journal of Law, No. 2 (2014).

business, which makes the supervision activities increasingly out of step with the need of market. Finally, as for the determination of legal liability, an enterprise loses its legal capacity after its business license was revoked. At this time, there was considerable controversy over the subject of the illegal responsibilities and the nature of the conduct of paying off debt.

[B] From "Government Permits Before Business Licenses" to "Business Licenses Before Government Permits"

In view of these problems, the SFTZ has implemented reform measures—from "Government Permits Before Business Licenses" to "Government Permits Before Business Licenses", which is of great significance for optimizing the authority structure of approval of permits. The "*Notice of the State Administration for Industry and Commerce on Issuing the Several Opinions of the State Administration for Industry and Commerce on Supporting the Construction of China (Shanghai) Pilot Free Trade Zone*" explicitly stipulates "Unless any law, administrative regulation, or decision of the State Council requires any prior licensing in enterprise registration, a registration system of 'Business Licenses Before Government Permits' shall be implemented in SHFTZ on a trial basis." Continuing the path of the "*the Plan for Institutional Reform and Functional Transformation of the State Council*" in 2013, the registration system is divided into three categories in the FTA: First, companies in the FTA can engage in general production after applying for registration to the industrial and commercial department and obtain a business license; second, if a business project involves a prepositioned-permissive item of enterprise registration, after obtaining a permit or an approval document, it can apply for a business license to the industrial and commercial department; thirdly, if it applies for engaging in other licensed business project, it shall be engaged in business activities after it obtains a business license or approval documents. In 2014, the "*Report of the State Council on Deepening the Reform of the Administrative Approval System and Accelerate the Transition of the Government's Functions*" further proposed that "the industrial and commercial registration system should be reformed and market access should be widened. Transform 126 pre-approvals for industrial and commercial registration to post-approval, accounting for about three-fifths of the pre-approvals before reforms." It not only clarifies the reform of administrative approval system as the breakthrough of the transformation of government's function, but also treats the permit and license reform and the alteration of prepositioned permissive items in industrial and commercial registration as an important window of administrative approval system.

With the practice of the SFTZ system,[5] the State Council issued the "*Decision on A Group of Administrative Approval Items to Be Cancelled or Adjusted and Other*

5. In regards to the establishment of the Shanghai Free Trade Zone, on August 22, 2013, the China (Shanghai) Free Trade Pilot Zone was approved to establish; on August 30 of the same year, the Standing Committee of the National People's Congress passed "*Decision on Authorizing the State Council to Temporarily Adjust the Relevant Administrative Approval Items Prescribed in Laws in China (Shanghai) Pilot Free Trade Zone*" (hereinafter referred to as the "*authorizing decision*");

Matters" many times with the Order No. 5 [2014] of the State Council,[6] No. 27 [2014] of the State Council,[7] No. 50 [2014] of the State Council,[8] and No. 11 [2015] of the State Council.[9] A batch of administrative approval items and other matters. After each decision, not only a large number of administrative approval items were cancelled, but also many pre-approvals of business registration were changed to post-approvals.[10]

[C] The Institutional Significance of "Business Licenses Before Government Permits" Reform

The approval mode of "Business Licenses Before Government Permits" can effectively solve the problems in the process of "Government Permits Before Business Licenses." First of all, business permits are no longer required as the preconditions of applying business license, companies can thus obtain business licenses more easily and then engage in general production and business activities such as loans, equipment and raw materials purchasing, and premises leasing. Therefore, the threshold for enterprises to engage in general business activities is greatly lowered, and a large number of competent business entities will no longer be excluded from the market because of administrative approval.

Second, after recovering the institutional logic of the license approval, business licenses and permits no longer presuppose each other, and the endless loop that occurred when companies applied for licenses disappeared.

Third, the "Business Licenses Before Government Permits" helps clarify the scope of each department's respective powers and responsibilities and resolve the deep

---

on September 18th of the same year, the "*The Framework Plan for China (Shanghai) Pilot Free Trade Zone*" (hereinafter referred to as the "*Framework Plan*") was issued. On September 29, 2013, China (Shanghai) Free Trade Pilot Zone was formally established. The "authorizing decision" passed by the Standing Committee of the National People's Congress came into effect on October 1, 2013.

6. Issued on January 28, 2014. Sixty-four administrative approval items and eighteen sub-items were cancelled and decentralized in total, and it was also proposed to cancel and decentralize six administrative approval items set in accordance with relevant laws.
7. Issued on July 22, 2014. Thirty-one administrative pre-approval items, including Public places hygiene licenses, establishment of entertainment venues, Internet access services, were transformed into post-approval items.
8. Issued on October 23, 2014. Fifty-eight administrative approval items were cancelled and decentralized in total. Sixty-seven occupational qualifications and certification items and nineteen commendation items were cancelled. Eighty-two pre-approval items for industrial and commercial registration were transformed into or determined as post-approval items.
9. Issued on February 24. Ninety administrative approval items were cancelled and decentralized in total. Sixty-seven occupational qualifications and certification items and ten commendation items were cancelled. Twenty-one pre-approvals items for industrial and commercial registration were transformed into as post-approval items, while thirty-four items for industrial and commercial registration were maintained.
10. In addition to cancelling and adjusting the administrative approval items by way of publishing orders, the State Council also directly decided to cancel and deregulate relevant approval items at government's executive meetings. For example, the State Council Executive Meeting decided to cancel and deregulate seventy-five approval items on September 25, 2013. On January 8, 2014, the State Council executive meeting decided the three measures to deepen the reform of the administrative approval system.

problems of administrative department setup and function distribution among them. According to the principle of "the one who permits takes charge" the specialized supervision has been achieved—the industrial and commercial administration are responsible for investigating and panelizing business activities without licenses, and the approval departments for those without permits, avoiding the chaos that the previous scope of supervision of the industrial and commercial administration overlaps with other functional departments due to pre-approval.

At last, the "Business Licenses Before Government Permits" mode ensures that the company's subject qualification be separated from business qualification. When an enterprise is revoked a license for violation of the law, it loses not its subject qualification but the business qualification, so still has the ability to take on administrative and civil liabilities, which makes the previous dispute over the qualification of the responsible subject no longer exist.

§6.03 THE REDUCTION OF APPROVAL ITEMS: FROM "BUSINESS LICENSES BEFORE GOVERNMENT PERMITS" TO "REDUCTION OF GOVERNMENT PERMITS AFTER BUSINESS LICENSE"

[A] The Leftover Problems of "Business Licenses Before Government Permits" Reform

Although the reform from the "Government Permits Before Business Licenses" to "Business Licenses Before Government Permits" have provided convenience for companies to engage in general business activities, it is still difficult for them to operate if they do not obtain certain permits from administrative departments. In addition, the reform of "Government Permits Before Business Licenses" merely postponed the permits which according to laws and regulations should have been postponed but not in practice, thus to a large extent is a correction under old institution framework and did not change the existing approval system arrangement. This means that those lawful but unreasonable pre-permits cannot be cancelled through the "Business Licenses Before Government Permits" reform, and there are still much obstacles for enterprises to enter markets.

Therefore, the "Separation of Business Licenses and Government Permits" resulted from "Business Licenses Before Government Permits" is far from the end of the reform, while the latter's fundamental purpose is to realize the "Reduction of Government Permits after Business License" through separating them, that is to promote the reduction of approval items though the optimization of the approval process. Nevertheless, by decoupling of business license from permits, the "Business Licenses Before Government Permits" reform exposes those inefficient and redundant approval items, which reversely propels the reform of approval items. To some extent, the institutional practice of the SFTZ itself is the result forced in the context that the global economic and trade structure is being reformed and the problems of domestic regulatory patterns has accumulated for a long time. The market economy model is constrained by the administrative approval system, which hinder the reform of the administrative management system and the release of market vitality. The license and permit reform in the business registration thus relates to and affects the approval system reform of deeper level.[11]

[B] The Implementation of "Separation of Business Licenses and Government Permits" Reform

On December 22, 2015, the State Council passed the "*the Framework Plan for the Implementation of the Pilot Program on the Reform of 'Separation of Business Licenses and Government Permits' in Shanghai Municipality*" and carried out a pilot program of "Separation of Business Licenses and Government Permits" in the Pudong New Area: by reforming approval methods and strengthening comprehensive supervision to further improve market access, the handling of business certification become more convenient and efficient. In affirming besides that "Effective ways and measures for strengthening interim and ex post regulation shall be further explored, and the comprehensive regulatory system shall be established, so as to effectively enhance the joint regulatory abilities and improve the regulatory efficiency", the "Separation of Business Licenses and Government Permits" mode divides the approval system reforms involving the management of enterprises into four levels: (1) The administrative approval of the business activities concerning which enterprises can make independent decisions shall be cancelled and change to recordation administration; (2) Where the approval of any administrative licenses cannot be cancelled temporarily, the approval ways shall be simplified and the notification and commitment system shall be implemented. (3) For the administrative licensing items which are not appropriate to be subject to the notification and commitment system, the work process shall be simplified, and the affair-handling procedures shall be disclosed, so as to improve the transparency and predictability of approval. (4) In the specific fields which involve national security and public security, among others, the market access administration shall be further intensified, and risk prevention shall be strengthened. "*The specific item list of the Pilot Program on the Reform of 'Separation of Business Licenses and Government Permits' in Shanghai Municipality*" as its appendix clarifies the implement departments and reform method. The reform method falls into two categories, the former contains "complete reduction" and "transform permits into recordation", while the latter includes "full implementation of notification and commitment system", "improve the transparency and predictability" and "intensify market access administration." *See* particularly in Table 6.1.

11. For the administrative approval system reform, *see* Wang Kewen, *The Reform of China's Administrative Approval System and Its Legal Regulations*, Chinese Journal of Law, No. 2 (2014).

Table 6.1 The List of Approval Reform Type in the Pilot Program on the "Separation of Business Licenses and Government Permits"

	Categories	*Conditions*	*The Number of Items*	*Examples*
Cancel the approvals	Completely cancel the approvals	Enterprises can make independent decisions shall be cancelled and change to recordation administration	10	The approval of the formation of compact disc-recordable production enterprises
	transform permits into recordation	In order to obtain better conduct industry guidance and develop industry policies and maintain public interests, governments shall conduct recordation administration of administrative licensing items.	6	The approval of processing trade contracts
Maintain the approval	full implementation of notification and commitment system	Where the approval of any administrative licensing items cannot be cancelled temporarily, but the relevant acts that do not meet the approval conditions can be corrected through the interim and ex post regulation and will not cause serious consequences, such administrative licensing items shall be subject to the notification and commitment system. The administrative approval authorities shall develop the letters of notification and commitment, and provide applicants with model texts, and	26	Motor vehicle maintenance operation license

Categories	*Conditions*	*The Number of Items*	*Examples*
	inform enterprises of the approval conditions and the materials required to be submitted at one time; and enterprises may handle the relevant administrative licensing items on the spot immediately after they make a commitment that the relevant acts comply with the approval conditions and submit the relevant materials.		
improve the transparency and predictability	For the administrative licensing items the approval of which cannot be cancelled temporarily and which are not appropriate to be subject to the notification and commitment system, the work process shall be simplified; the affair-handling procedures shall be disclosed; standardization administration and online handling shall be promoted; and approval standards and the time limits for handling shall be specified, so as to minimize the discretion of approval, and achieve the openness and transparency of the handling process and the predictability of the handling results.	41	the approval of the formation of accounting firms and their branches

Categories	Conditions	The Number of Items	Examples
intensify market access administration	As for the administrative licensing items directly related to national security, public security, ecological environmental protection, and other specific activities directly concerning personal health, and life and property safety, among others, the risk control and market access administration shall be strengthened in accordance with the internationally accepted rules	33	he approval of formation of operational Internet cultural entities

Source: Compiled bu the author from The State Council The People's Republic of China Official website: http://english.gov.cn/

After the successful practice of the "Separation of Business Licenses and Government Permits" reform in the SFTZ for more than one year, its measures began to have widespread spillover effects. In September 2017, the "*Opinions of the State Council on Advancing the Pilot Program of the Reform of 'Separating Certificates from Business License' in a Larger Scope*",[12] on the basis of in-depth summary of the experience of the pilot program of the reform of "separating license from permits" in Pudong New Area Shanghai, reproduces and promotes the mature practice in the pilot program of reform in Shanghai, advance the reform of "separating business license from permits" and "integrating licenses into one" in an overall manner, and comprehensively sort out and handle various enterprise-related license and permit items by category in ten pilot free trade zones—Tianjin, Liaoning, Zhejiang, Fujian, Henan, Hubei, Guangdong, Chongqing, Sichuan and Shaanxi. Various certificates and licenses falling into the categories of information collection, entry publication and administration for reference upon the reform of "separating business license from permits" shall be further integrated into the business license to realize "integration of permits into one and one code for one business license." Items which the market mechanism is capable of effectively adjusting, or which enterprises are able to manage alone, or enterprise-related certificate and license items of which the originally set objective may be accomplished by

12. No. 45 [2017] of the State Council.

interim and ex post regulation, shall be gradually cancelled or changed to recordation administration.

In October 2017, the "*the Framework Plan for the Deepening Implementation of the Pilot Program on the Reform of 'Separation of Business Licenses and Government Permits' in Pudong New Area*"[13] was enacted as the symbol that the "Separation of Business Licenses and Government Permits" reform in the SFTZ entered into the second stage. The scope of the approval items covered by the reform has been further expanded. The "Framework" proposes to continue to deepen the reform of 116 pilot items that stipulated in the State Council's official reply in 2015, treating notification and commitment system as the main method of deepening reform, and to include all seventy-six items enrolled in the scope of the reform study in 2015 into the reform scope, actively seek the support of the relevant state ministries and commissions. Support, cancel as much approval items as possible, transform those which cannot be cancelled into recordation or notification and commitment. At the same time, reforms should be promoted under the requirement of complete coverage.

[C] The Upgrade of Supervision Mode Promoted by "Separation of Business Licenses and Government Permits" Reform

The "Separation of Business Licenses and Government Permits" reform has also promoted the upgrade of methods while simultaneously interconnected the reform of approval items. With a large number of approval items cancelled, transferred to recordation or maintained with conditions, the previous phenomenon of "emphasize approval while neglect supervision" or even "replacing supervision with approval" has also been fundamentally reversed. Although the "Separation of Business Licenses and Government Permits" reform has largely eliminated the restrictions on market access for enterprises, it has not reduced the administrative department's duty to supervise business operations. Instead, it has imposed higher requirements on its management ability. The administrative departments should shift from focusing on prior approval to on interim and ex post supervision; from passively approve business qualifications of enterprises on applications to actively carry out regulatory activities on business conduct, and not just investigate and penalize unpermitted and unlicensed operations in the past. In addition, the transferring of the supervision focus from the prior to the interim and ex post also requires the combination of administrative management with informational means, such as establishing video surveillance and informational recording system for production processes in risk-prone industries such as food and drug production, elevators, safety production, and construction project to realize the dynamic traceability supervision of whole process; to realize cross-departmental information sharing and work linkage, and to establish a multi-departmental joint disciplinary mechanism.

13. Letter No. 222 [2015] of the State Council.

§6.04 THE PROMOTION OF LIST MANAGEMENT MODE TO ADMINISTRATIVE APPROVAL SYSTEM

[A] Transform from "Positive List" to "Negative List" Mode

The list management mode was originally applied to the access restrictions of the industries for foreign investment. Prior to the establishment of the SFTZ, China's industries permitting foreign investment were regulated according to "*the Catalogue of Industries for Guiding Foreign Investment*" in which foreign investment industries falls into three categories—encouraged industries, restricted industries and prohibited industries. Since the *Catalogue* contains both approved and prohibited items, whether it is a "positive list" or a "negative list", in other words whether the unlisted items are permitted or forbidden, has long been controversial.[14] On the whole, because the number of restricted and prohibited investment areas in the catalog is quite large, and the process of foreign investment requires examinations and approvals at all levels, this mode sets a high threshold for foreign investment, which greatly affects the degree of opening of the Chinese market.

In contrast, in 2013 according to the "*China (Shanghai) Pilot Free Trade Pilot Area Special Administrative Measures for Foreign Investment Access (Negative List)*", the SFTZ pioneered the adoption of "pre-establishment national treatment with a negative list" management mode. It means that foreign investments would not be subject to any restrictions in other industrial areas except for those that are explicitly enumerated in the list, so enjoy the equal national treatment as domestic enterprises.

[B] The Application Scope of the Negative List Extending from Foreign Investment to Market Access

After the negative list's successful practice in the field of foreign investment for two years, the "*Opinions on the Implementation of the Negative List System on Market Access*"[15] issued by the State Council in 2015 further made the negative list mode generate spillover effects that apply to all domestic and foreign market subject. The "*Opinions*" clearly stipulated that the negative list included negative list of market access and that of foreign investment, thus break the restriction that the negative list management mode was initially only applied to foreign investment, and further extended the scope of application to all market subjects. The former applies to domestic and foreign investors and implements it to all market entities, while the latter applies exclusively to foreign investors. The negative list of market access also includes the type of prohibition and restriction, which is applicable to various types of market subjects, such as voluntary initial investment, expanding investment, merger and acquisition investment and other investment business behaviors as well as market entry behaviors. With regard to the prohibitive access items, market subjects may not

14. Gong Bohua, *The Legal Principle of "All is Permissible Unless Prohibited" and the "Negative List" Mode in Shanghai Free Trade Zone*, Oriental law, No. 6 (2013).
15. No. 55 [2014] of the State Council.

enter, and the administrative organs shall not approve such applications and shall not deal with relevant formalities. With regard to restricted access items, either market subject file an application, and the administrative agency shall make a decision on whether to permit the access according to laws and regulations, or market subjects enter in accordance with the access conditions and requirements stipulated by the government. For the industries, fields, and businesses which are not enumerated in the negative list of market access, all types of market subjects have legal and equal access to them.

The transformation and upgrade of the list mode is not only a change of the way how the items are enumerated and of the scope of application, but also a substantial promotion of reducing administrative approval items. As manifested in Table 6.2, although the negative list of the 2013 version basically duplicated the prohibitive and restrictive industries in "*the Catalogue of Industries for Guiding Foreign Investment*", after three revisions in 2014, 2015 and 2017, the number of special management measures has been reduced from the initial 190 to 95. At the same time the number of major catalogs has also been reduced from 89 to 40, the scale of which is nearly half of what it was before.

Table 6.2 Previous Negative List Revisions[16]

Items / **Years**	2013	2014	2015	2017
Catalogue	18	16	15	15
Major Catalogue	89	78	50	40
Medium Catalogue	419	386		
Special Management Measures	190	139	122	95

Source: Compiled by the author from various public sources including The State Council The People's Republic of China Official website: http://english.gov.cn/

[C] The Significance of Negative List for Rule of Law

The change from a positive list to a negative list seems to be merely a difference in the way of enumerating approval items, while in fact, it reflects the profound changes in the administrative management mode. The principle adopted by "positive list" to restrain the freedom of subjects is "all is prohibited unless permissible." By positively enumerating the activities that are permitted to be carried out, the scope of freedom is clearly define. The guiding ideas behind it are that government are bound to dominate and control market activities, which is the relic of planned economy. The attitude

16. Chen Yanhe & Wang Jiang, *The Analysis of Innovative Achievements and Problems in Shanghai Free Trade Zone*, 18 Journal of Shanghai Business School, No. 6 (2017).

towards them is vigilant and suppressive. The "negative list" instead follows the rule of law thinking of the socialist market economy and adopts the principle of "all is permissible unless prohibited" on the activities of market subjects. What is clearly listed is no longer the scope of freedom of citizens, but the boundaries of the exercise of public power. This has greatly improved the transparency and openness of administrative approval items and processes. In this way, the negative list fulfills the institutional function of restricting power.[17]

In addition, the change from positive list to negative list is also a reflection of the transformation of government functions and "streamlining administration and delegating powers." As mentioned above, China's administrative approval system reform has long been dominated by the government alone so lacks the participation of market and society. It is often trapped in the cycle that "loose policies cause chaos then tight supervision cause stagnation", whose root lies in that the government's paternalistic control of the market did not provide space for the latter's self-governance. In the negative list mode, by contrast, the market was given more freedom and its ability to self-regulate economic activities was stimulated. Accordingly, the government was freed from the heavy burden of administrative approvals and focused on the interim and ex post supervision of economic activities, by which a two-way collaborative governance pattern between government and market is formed.[18] The role of the government has changed from the leader of economic activities to the guardian and participant of market order.

§6.05 THE PRACTICAL PROBLEMS IN THE REFORM OF ADMINISTRATIVE APPROVAL SYSTEM

After the effort of more than five years, the reform of administrative approval system in SFTZ, represented by the "Separation of Business Licenses and Government Permits" and negative list, has made outstanding progress in optimizing process and reducing approval items. Its overall reform direction deserves affirmation. However, as various measures of reform are still in the exploration and adjustment stage, some deficiencies are inevitable in practice, which are mainly reflected in the following three aspects:

[A] The Implementation of Policies Needs to Be Improved

Although the "Separation of Business Licenses and Government Permits" reform reduced plenty of administrative approval items through five ways, these policies were intentionally derogated in the process of implementation, which undermined their effect. Taking the "transform permits into recordation" as an example, the original intention of the policy is that enterprises can engage in corresponding business

17. Wang Liming, *Negative List: A New Kind of Way to Govern a State*, Development, No. 1 (2015).
18. Yu Shaoru, *Negative List Mode and Administrative Approval System Reform*, Journal of Harbin Institute of Technology (Social Sciences Edition), No. 2 (2016).

activities after registering the items in competent authorities, and do not need to be substantively examined and permitted. However, such as the establishment of profitable chess room, the competent authorities still conduct site visits before recordation in practice, and only after confirming that the applicants meet corresponding conditions do they issue a so-called recordation certificate permitting the applicants to engage in business activities, which makes recordation no different from permits. For another example, after the permit of cleanup, collection, transportation and disposal services for municipal solid waste was changed into recordation, the competent departments still require the enterprises to provide administrative agreements signed with the government to engage in relevant activities during the recordation, thereby deliberately increasing the threshold of market access. In addition, in the course of implementing policies, there are cases where the law enforcement agencies restrictively interpret the statute to the disadvantage of market subjects. For example, though the business permits of small restaurants of 50 square meters and below has been transformed into recordation, the question of how to define small restaurant is still controversial. The Food and Drug Administration interpreted it as containing only steamed bun stores, wonton stores and drink stores, which greatly reduces the policies' scope of application.[19]

[B] The System of Interim and Ex Post Supervision Require to Be Perfect

As discussed above, the reform of the administrative approval system has greatly lowered the threshold of market access for enterprises by optimizing process and the reducing approval items, but it also requires the transformation of the regulatory model of the administrative department—from focusing on prior review to focusing on interim and ex post supervision. At present in the SFTZ, there is still a certain gap between the supervision system of and the ideal standard.

First of all, the competence, responsibilities, and coordination mechanism for the departments which take charge of interim and ex post supervision still lack institutional top-level design. Although in respect of the respective responsibilities of departments, the State Council has stipulated the principle of "the one who approves supervises and the one who takes charge supervises" in *"Opinions on Strengthening the Interim and Ex Post Supervision after the Reform of Business Licenses Before Government Permits"*, there are still numerous uncertainties when it comes to specific approval items.

First, as for "the department which approves supervises", in practice because the legal competence and law enforcement force of approval departments are limited, it is usual that the approval and the ex post supervisory departments are separated. For example, the tobacco retailing is approved by Tobacco Monopoly Bureau, while the supervision power for unlicensed business activities belongs to Industrial and Commercial Bureau. However, the demarcation of the supervision competence of approval

19. Shen Xiaoping et al., *The Problems and Thinking in Pudong's "Separation of Business Licenses and Government Permits"*, Pudong Development, No. 2 (2017).

and non-approval departments in the interim and ex post supervision is not clearly defined by laws and regulations.

Second, as for "the one who takes charge supervises", former competent and supervisory departments of an industry are separated in the past. The former is mainly in charge of matters such as industrial planning and propaganda but not engage in supervision. Now reforms impose supervisory duties on the competent departments, while its status in the regulatory system as well as the demarcation of competence of competent and other regulatory departments have yet to be refined.

Third, the mechanism for multi-department cooperative supervision requires perfection. Taking joint discipline as an example, the *Opinions* stipulate that investigations of violations of laws and regulations shall be led by approval departments, competent departments of an industry or industry and commerce departments. However, the questions such as how each department joint together, what duties does each department has and whether they have the corresponding legal competence to perform the duties are not clearly stipulated. As a result, it often happens that departments cannot cooperate well and even shuffle the responsibilities to each other.

In the second place, the law enforcement force of the supervisory departments is insufficient and their supervisory mode needs to be upgraded. At present, the interim and ex post supervision in SFTZ is led by government. However, with market access thresholds lowered, a large number of enterprises entered into the FTZ, which caused the existing law enforcement forces of the regulatory agencies unable to meet practical needs. According to statistics, at the time of zone expansion in 2015, there has been more than 80,000 enterprises of various types in the SFTZ, and the regulatory matters include investment, trade, finance, land planning, construction, afforestation, environmental protection, labor and personnel, intellectual property, culture, health, statistics, customs, quarantine, industry and commerce, quality inspection, public security, taxation, etc., a total of eighteen items.[20]

Compared with loads of such scale, the law enforcement forces of the supervisory departments limited by their administrative establishment is becoming more and more overstretched.[21] In the investigation, it was also found that many competent departments undertook too many functions but lacked sufficient law enforcement forces or had none at all, so were unable to perform their supervisory duties. Therefore, there was a phenomenon that "no personnel, no supervision." It manifests that the government's unilaterally-dominated mode of supervision is no longer able to cope with the market conditions in the FTZ, thus it is necessary to introduce industry associations, enterprises, and the general public to form a new pattern of social co-governance in which the government, the market, and the public collaborate.

Finally, the depth of information sharing is insufficient. With the focus of administrative supervision shifted from ex ante to interim and ex post, the static

20. Jiang Shuoliang & Liu Kai, *The Innovation of Interim and Ex Post Supervision System in Shanghai Free Trade Zone: Establish the Large Supervisory Pattern of Quaternity*, Foreign Economics & Management, No. 8 (2015).
21. Chen Zili, *The Study on the Practice, Difficulties and Development Approach of Interim and Ex Post Supervision in Shanghai Free Trade Zone: Take Pudong New Zone as an Example*, Journal of Anhui Administration Institute, No. 6 (2016).

supervision of "replace supervision with approval" needs to be transformed into dynamic supervision over the whole process of business operations. In this regard, the in-depth sharing of regulatory information helps to break down information barriers among departments and achieve the seamless connection between the approval and supervisory departments, and supervisory departments between each other.

However, at present, the SFTZ is confronted with the "three-cross difficulties" -"difficult to cross 'bar and block'[22] to integrate resources, difficult to cross departments to share information, and difficult to cross area to cooperate", which to some extent affects the effectiveness of ex post supervision. For example, the safety supervision department revealed that only one of the nine existing systems is district-level system, while others are systems of national bureaus and the municipal bureaus. The inconsistence of the levels of the systems makes sharing information difficult. In addition, poor horizontal information transfer between departments is another reason for supervisory chaos. Taking the "double-notification" platform as an example, the permit-issuing department revealed that it cannot find applicants according to the information delivered by license-issuing departments during ex ante services. Furthermore, the information is only delivered to approval departments, while other departments which also owe supervisory duties have no access to necessary information.[23]

[C] The Quality of Negative List Is Yet to Be Enhanced

First, though many items have been incorporated in the negative list, the overall openness is still limited. The negative list of 2013 version basically followed the contents of "*the Catalogue of Industries for Guiding Foreign Investment*", that is absorbed the restricted and prohibited items of the latter. Therefore, the actual market openness did not expand due to the introduction of the negative list mode.[24]

After the negative list reform of the 2014 and 2015 versions, special management measures have been reduced from the initial 190 to 122. "Although the degree of opening is increasing, there are still problems in the 2015 version negative list, such as too wide restriction field, insufficient service industry openness and insufficient compliance with international standards, etc."[25] Comparing with the negative list of 2015, the 2017 version has reduced twenty-seven items and has made breakthroughs in opening up the market of manufacturing, service and financial industries.

Second, the formulation of restricted items is too general so its transparency needs to be increased. For one thing, some items in the negative list merely enumerate the objects, but do not specify the specific restrictive or prohibitive measures, such as

22. "Government Services Cloud Platform in Pudong district Shanghai: Solve the 'Three-Cross Difficulties' of Information Sharing in Free Trade Zone Time" in People's Daily, http://sh.people.com.cn/n2/2016/1008/c377889-29102367.html.
23. Shen Xiaoping et al., *The Problems and Thinking in Pudong's "Separation of Business Licenses and Government Permits" Reform*, Pudong Development, No. 2 (2017).
24. Gong Bohua, *The Legal Analysis of "Negative List" Mode of Access to Foreign Investment in China (Shang Hai) Free Trade Zone*, in World Trade Organization Focus, No. 6 (2013).
25. Hu Jiaxiang, *The Summary and Outlook of the Three-Year Achievements in Shanghai Free Trade Zone*, Oriental Law, No. 1 (2017).

"exploration and exploitation of graphite" and "smelting and rolling of non-ferrous metal, as well as smelting and processing of radioactive minerals." For another thing, although some items are included in the negative list, their expressions have the meaning of a "positive list", that is "an act is prohibited if it is not clearly authorized by law." For example, "medical institutions", "market surveys", "the smelting and separation of rare earth" are all "subject to joint venture and cooperation." This is tantamount to a positive list of activities that companies are allowed to engage in. Moreover, the formulations of some restrictive measures are ambiguous thus easily constitute hidden barriers. For example, "the educational activities and course materials shall abide by the corresponding laws and regulations of China and the relevant provisions", but no specific restrictions have been clarified, which impairs the predictability of the list.[26]

§6.06 CONCLUSION

Taking the licenses and permits reform as breakthrough point, the administrative examination and approval system reform in the SFTZ first changed the "Government Permits Before Business Licensess" to "Business Licenses Before Government Permits", and then promote the "Reduction of Government Permits after Business License" with "Separation of Business Licenses and Government Permits": force the substantial reduction of approval items by the formal optimization of process, at the same time propel the supervision mode transforming from the "replace supervision with approval" to focusing on interim and ex post overall supervision. In addition, the FTZ has also introduced the "negative list" management mode, which further improves the transparency and predictability of administrative approval system. After the list items reduced several times, the market has been increasingly open.

Although in practice the SFTZ still has many problems with respect to policy implementation, interim and ex post supervision and the quality of negative lists, the overall direction and approach of the reform deserves recognition, which is a significant reference for the administrative approval of other FTZs and even the entire country.

26. Shen Haiping, *The Legal Status of Negative List in Shanghai Free Trade Zone and Its Adjustment*, Oriental Law, No. 5 (2014).

CHAPTER 7

Mitigating Inequality in the Development of SEZs in Asia: Risks, Rules and Recipes

Matthias Vanhullebusch

§7.01 INTRODUCTION

Since the end of last century, the proliferation of special economic zones (SEZs) has skyrocketed.[1] Asia alone houses one quarter of all SEZs worldwide.[2] The SEZs have opened up the economies of Asian nations for foreign direct investment that, in turn, has been responsible for transforming those economies into the world's manufacturing bases. As a result, Asia's earlier SEZs, including those in Mainland China, South Korea and Taiwan, have generated spectacular economic growth and those economic experiments have set the tone for the establishment of more zones within the respective national jurisdictions. Many other Asian developing countries have followed in their pursuit to upgrade their national economies and to integrate them into the global value chains, service industries and financial markets. Moreover, such interconnectivity in the realm of trade, service and capital has been made possible through the supply of skilled – in particular for tertiary industries, including IT, R&D and banking – as well as cheap labour forces – in the manufacturing sectors – that have migrated domestically and internationally alike within and/or the vicinity of the SEZs. In this respect, Asia's SEZs have pooled much of 85 % of all export processing workers globally.[3] Regionally,

1. *Special Economic Zones: Not So Special*, The Economist (London, 2015).
2. Asian Development Bank, *Asian Economic Integration Report 2015*, 114 (Asian Development Bank 2015). The latest report of the Asian Development Bank (2017), however, on Asian Economic Integration deals with matters of financial interconnectivity alone. *See* Asian Development Bank, *Asian Economic Integration Report 2017: The Era of Financial Interconnectedness – How Can Asia Strengthen Financial Resilience* (Asian Development Bank 2017).
3. Asian Development Bank, *Asian Economic Integration Report 2015*, 110 (Asian Development Bank 2015).

there are still sharp differences amongst countries regarding the added values generated by the export of services.[4]

The concentration of valued added to exports of goods and services that has contributed significantly to the gross national product of Asian nations has not only created disproportionate development levels countrywise, on the one hand. It has also caused new forms of exclusive wealth creation within the hands of a global yet locally embedded elite within the SEZs, on the other hand.[5] The Gini-coefficient or the Inequality-adjusted Human Development Index in most Asian countries shows proof of an ever-widening gap between the rich and the poor.[6] At least on the national level, on the one hand, such socio-economic gaps and exclusion could have been mitigated if more economic bridges were built between the SEZs and their hinterland. As a result, foreign investment within the zones could reduce a differentiated picture on the levels of economic development within the country in question. Under such circumstances, the economic benefits of the SEZs could trickle down and remain embedded within the national economies via a comprehensive nationwide foreign investment regime. Within the SEZs, on the other hand, the perception of being destitute is much more prevalent than merely being it.[7] Both feelings and conditions are not the mere outcome of personal life choices but are also the (unwarranted) product of rapid unsustainable economic growth across Asian countries.

In this respect, there are other socio-economic as well as regulatory forces at work. The initial benefits to establish SEZs through deregulation, tax exemptions, subsidies, etc. have created a race to the bottom whose costs are born not only with the respective bounded territories but also beyond.[8] Those include but are not limited to social exclusion of local unskilled workers and internal and external migrant workers, lack of social security and protection against exploitation at work, speculation in the real estate market, expropriation, gentrification, displacement as well as pollution and environmental degradation. As the tentacles of the SEZs are spreading more 'inland'

4. Asian Development Bank, *Asian Economic Integration Report 2015*, 110 (Asian Development Bank 2015). India accounts 23% of its export to its service industry (in particular in its IT sector) that constitutes 51% of its value added whereas China and Korea only 14% of its export or 35% value added to its exports.
5. Jana M. Kleibert, *Exclusive Development(s): Special Economic Zones and Enclave Urbanism in the Philippines*, Critical Sociology (2017), doi/10.1177/0896920517698538?cookieSet = 1; *see also* Thomas Pikkety, *Capital in the Twenty-First Century* (Harvard University Press 2014) for a US-EU perspective on social consequences of income inequality and the limits of unrestricted accumulation of capital.
6. United Nations Development Programme (UNDP), *Human Development Indices and Indicators: 2018 Statistical Update* 30–33 (UNDP 2018), Table 3.
7. Keith Payne, *The Broken Ladder: How Inequality Affects the Way We Think, Live, and Die* (Penguin Books 2017). Conversely, the affluent members of society are also coping with their anxieties linked to their wealthy status. *See* Rachel Sherman, *Uneasy Street: The Anxieties of Affluence* (Princeton University Press 2017).
8. H. Jeffrey Leonard, *Confronting Industrial Pollution in Rapidly Industrializing Countries: Myths, Pitfalls, and Opportunities*, 12 Ecology Law Quarterly 779, 781 (1985); Richard P. Appelbaum, *Giant Transnational Contractors in East Asia: Emergent Trends in Global Supply Chains*, 12 Competition & Change 69 (2008); Raphael Kaplinsky & Masuma Farooki, *Global Value Chains, the Crisis, and the Shift of Markets from North to South*, in *Global Value Chains in a Post-Crisis World: A Development Perspective* 125–153 (Olivier Cattaneo and others eds, The World Bank 2010).

and tightening their grip, those various socio-economic and environmental problems and challenges will too. The socio-economic status of people living in the SEZs and its vicinity determine the degree of vulnerability to cope with those problems.[9] One's place on the socio-economic ladder, origin (local or migrant), nationality as well as set of skills and educational background (or absence thereof) shall affect to what extent one can face, resist or survive those over-arching socio-economic and regulatory forces as well as the opportunities and problems which they engender.[10]

The nexus between law within those emerging economies in Asia and their long-term development trajectory has been one of the responses to render their development sustainable in socio-economic and environmental terms alike.[11] This would require a number of legal reforms within the SEZs and nationwide which goes beyond the traditional forms of policy approaches.[12] Those legal reforms must take into account the development and application of substantive norms regulating socio-economic and environmental impacts of economic growth and foreign direct investment, on the one hand, as well as capacity-building enhancing modes of governance, accountability and responsiveness on behalf of governments and (inter)national businesses, on the other hand. Regarding the former, human rights discourses have informed how rights and duties amongst the different share- and stakeholders within the SEZs and beyond should be apportioned.[13] Depending on the different rights-bearers, including workers, women, children, migrants, etc., different claims to protect their livelihood pursuant to international human rights norms (treaties and customs) can be addressed before and against local, regional and national regulators as well as corporations domestically and international alike. Regarding the latter, international standards developed by the United Nations (UN), World Bank and the Organisation of Economic Cooperation and Development (OECD) have sought to align the realisation of and respect for those substantive human rights norms and the rule of law with

9. Nick Brooks et al., *The Determinants of Vulnerability and Adaptive Capacity at the National Level and the Implications for Adaptation*, 15 Global Environmental Change 151 (2004); Richard W. Wilkinson & Kater E. Pickett, *Income Inequality and Population Health: A Review and Explanation of the Evidence*, 62 Social Science & Medicine 1768 (2006); Yung-Jaan Lee, *Social Vulnerability Indicators as a Sustainable Planning Tool*, 44 Environmental Impact Assessment Review 31 (2013); *see also* Bingqin Li, *Floating Population or Urban Citizens? Status, Social Provision and Circumstances of Rural-Urban Migrants in China*, 40 Social Policy & Administration 174 (2006).
10. Arjan de Haan, *Livelihoods and Poverty: The Role of Migration: A Critical Review of the Migration Literature*, 36 Journal of Development Studies 1 (1999); Nitya Rao, *Migration, Education and Socio-Economic Mobility*, 40 Compare: A Journal of Comparative and International Education 137 (2010).
11. David M. Trubek & Alvaro Santos (eds), *The New Law and Economic Development: A Critical Appraisal* (Cambridge University Press 2006); Kevin E. Davis & Michael J. Trebilcock, *The Relationship Between Law and Development: Optimists Versus Skeptics*, 56 American Journal of Comparative Law 895 (2010); Yong-Shik Lee, *General Theory of Law and Development*, 50 Cornell International Law Journal 415 (2017).
12. Peter Muchlinski, *SEZs: A Policy Tool in Search of a New Agenda*, in *Special Economic Zones in Asian Market Economies* 15–37 (Connie Carter & Andrew eds, Routledge 2010).
13. Yemi Osinbajo & Olukonyisola Ajayi, *Human Rights and Economic Development in Developing Countries*, 28 The International Lawyer 727 (1994).

corporate social responsibility[14] as well as with good governance and state institutions.[15] Moreover, from the liberal perspective, the relationship between the realisation of those socio-economic rights and the rule of law could gradually contribute to the development of civil-political rights and transform authoritarian regimes towards liberal democracies.[16]

Law, however, has not only been instrumental to pursue sustainable economic development or even democratic rule. It has also caused market distortions, unfair competition and social inequalities within the SEZs and beyond. Furthermore, deregulated markets have disrupted the social fabric and cohesion that once reigned with traditional societies.[17] Law and development perspectives have not fully accounted for those disadvantages nor have they explained the tremendous economic growth of numerous Asian countries – China in particular – and the alleged absence of the rule of law in its initial phases of opening up to the world.[18] In this regard, the right to development invoked by developing countries has served as a justification to postpone legal reforms that would undermine their positioning within a competitive global market space for goods, services and capital – at least in the beginning.[19] Furthermore, developing countries have continued to resist international regulatory agendas that seek to curtail their competitiveness by imposing strict social and environmental standards in the realm of international and regional trade negotiations.[20] While international standards in this realm may, arguably, contribute to sustainable economic development at the macro-economic level, within the minds and hearts of peoples deprived from the fruits of economic growth, such regulatory approach has failed to provide remedies.

Regardless of the democratic or authoritarian nature of governments of Asian countries, incumbent political authorities have sought to mitigate social instability that could undermine the continued economic growth as well as their leadership locally and nationwide.[21] Within democratic systems, opposition parties, instead, have tried to

14. UN Guiding Principles on Business and Human Rights, UNHRC Doc. 17/4 (16 June 2011); OECD, *OECD Guidelines for Multinational Enterprises* (OECD Publishing 2011).
15. World Bank, *Development and Human Rights: The Role of the World Bank* (World Bank 1998); D. Acemoglu & J. Robinson, *The Role of Institutions in Growth and Development* (Commission on Growth and Development Working Papers. No. 10) (World Bank 2008).
16. *China and the West: Not the Partner You Were Looking For*, The Economist (Hong Kong 2018).
17. David Beetham, *Market Economy and the Democratic Polity*, 4 Democratization 76 (1997); Seizaburo Sato, *Democracy and Market Economy*, 7 Asia-Pacific Review 2 (2000).
18. Nevertheless, some scholars have sought to refine the existing law and economic development approaches based on a non-Western praxis, especially when examining China's peculiar economic growth trajectory and the (non-)use of domestic law to that effect. *See* Guangdong Xu, *Is China an Anomaly for the 'Law Matters' Hypothesis*, 1 Asian Journal of Law and Society 339 (2014); Weitseng Chen (ed), *The Beijing Consensus: How China Has Changed Western Ideas of Law and Economic Development* (Cambridge University Press 2017).
19. UN GA Res. 41/128, UN Doc. A/RES/41/128 (4 December 1986).
20. Matthias Vanhullebusch, *Searching for Human Rights: Free Trade Agreements in Asia*, in *Regional Cooperation and Free Trade Agreements in Asia* 226 (Jiaxiang Hu & Matthias Vanhullebusch eds, Brill/Nijhoff 2014).
21. Ulrich Beck, *Risk Society: Towards a New Modernity* (Sage Publications 1992); Robert J. Sampson, *Urban Sustainability in an Age of Enduring Inequalities: Advancing Theory and Ecometrics for the 21st-Century City*, 114 Proceedings of the National Academy of Sciences of the United States of America 8957 (2017).

challenge the parties in power when exploiting the grievances of people that have disproportionately borne the social and environmental costs that have accompanied economic growth and uneven wealth creation. Each side has made recourse to so-called transcendental recipes that would justify, alleviate or contest the socio-economic inequalities of peoples that could not be redressed by the proper implementation of the rule of law even by properly functioning and accountable governmental agencies and businesses. Religious and ethical frameworks have been deployed to make inequality more acceptable based on God's volition and/or one's assigned place within a harmonious society, on the one hand. Communist, nationalist, anti-globalist/nativist discourses have been invoked to challenge inequality domestically and internationally alike and to pursue a nation's own (protectionist) economic trajectory independently from other global market forces, on the other hand – thus compromising the very prospects of interconnectivity through SEZs in the first place.[22]

Certainly, those socio-economic and environmental challenges are not unique to SEZs alone. Yet, SEZs have been pioneers in economic development, urban planning and management as well as in legal engineering and practicing the rule of law in some Asian countries. Since they are at the forefront of all those socio-economic and regulatory agendas which have repercussions beyond their own economic and regulatory space, their trajectory is under permanent scrutiny in those domains and their progress constitutes a benchmark against which future SEZs could be planned in other parts of the country in question. This paper is challenging that the implementation of the rule of law – within the economic, social and environmental realm – is the only means to ensure long-term prosperity and well-being in the SEZ for its citizens and beyond. It argues that addressing the psychology of inequality – that inevitably accompanies economic progress within Asian SEZs and constitutes a potential source for social instability undermining economic objectives – also resides in the acknowledgement of the human desire for recognition in particular of those marginalised voices in the spur towards globalisation within the SEZs and beyond regardless whether this is taking place within a democratic or authoritarian regime. Without such contextualisation, without such acknowledgment, international economic law through its various branches as well as international human rights and environmental law will lack its binding force in the end. The SEZs are equally at the forefront to take this in account if their experience is intended to be successfully extended nationally and internationally alike.

This chapter firstly addresses a number of causes of socio-economic instability within the SEZs in Asia that can potentially jeopardise the economic and political system of the bounded areas as well as for the entire country and region. It will focus on three aspects where such risks are occurring, namely in respect of people, land and the environment. Second, this chapter is exploring a number of regulatory approaches that seek to mitigate those socio-economic risks in order to ensure sustainable economic development and political stability in the interest of the country in question but also for the sake the regional and global economy. It looks at matters of good

22. *Globalisation's Losers: The Right Way to Help Declining Places – Time for Fresh Thinking about the Changing Economics of Geography*, The Economist (London, 2017).

governance and corporate responsibility to that effect and the role of civil society in those regulatory agendas. Finally, this chapter examines how two distinctive patterns of political behaviour are responding to the failure of the rule of law to close the socio-economic gaps and, thus, in its promise to mitigate socio-economic shocks within Asian societies. Based on different sources, they are either justifying present and evolving forms of socio-economic inequality and vindicating socio-economic justice at home or in the world at large.

§7.02 RISK SOCIETY AND SEZs IN ASIA

[A] People

The relationship between the means of production, i.e., capital and labour, within the SEZs in Asia (and beyond) has always been a tense one from the beginning onwards, i.e., from their establishment, to their development and operation. The SEZs aim to attract overseas and domestic (human) capital.[23] The tension not only resides between those who own capital or knowledge/skills or those who do not, this division manifests itself particularly between local and external actors. In this respect, the initial absence of local capital as well as skilled labour necessitates the import and/or migration of domestic and foreign corporations/persons who have those means of production to sustain the initial investment costs, support the knowledge transfer and ensure continued economic growth. The SEZs are becoming successful when ensuring capital gains and an alignment of demand and supply of labour and capital. A disconnect between those market dynamics can and has become a source of frustration on behalf of investors as well as unskilled workers within and outside the SEZs.[24] While the former may have lost money, the latter have nothing to lose and should be the biggest concern to local and national authorities if their socio-economic conditions are not alleviated. Instead, they may engage on an individual basis to criminal activities or fall into hands of (trans-)national/local crime networks (including counterfeiting, concealment, drug/arms trafficking, prostitution, etc.). When not properly policed, those non-traditional security threats may become more endemic and permanent causing a deterrent effect upon investors as well as skilled workers that would undermine the establishment and existence of SEZs and thus the global value chains.[25]

Developing nations in Asia, however, have been lacking properly functioning social security systems to mitigate the effects of such potential socio-economic instability. Furthermore, as developing countries they are not obliged, in accordance with international treaty law, to grant such socio-economic rights to non-nationals, in

---

23. John H. Dunning, *Global Capitalism, FDI and Competitiveness* (Edward Elgar 2002); Stephen Kim Park, *Special Economic Zones and the Perpetual Pluralism of Global Trade and Labor Migration*, 47 Georgetown Journal of International Law 1379 (2016).
24. Jamie Cross, *Neoliberalism as Unexceptional: Economic Zones and the Everyday Precariousness of Working Life in South India*, 30 Critique of Anthropology 355, 361 (2010).
25. Björn Hettne, *Development and Security: Origins and Future*, 41 Security Dialogue 31, 43 (2010).

particular migrant workers.[26] Without proper budgets to train the local workforce which triggered the supply of external workers (domestic and international alike) in the first place, education has remained one of the weakest workings of Asia's developing countries in the global value chains. Nonetheless, the governments of emerging economies like that of China have invested increasingly into their research and development[27] as well as their corporations[28] - state-owned and private alike - have purchased overseas companies with strong innovation backgrounds in order to narrow down the technology gap.[29] Yet, in the meanwhile, as those economies are transforming their economic models from manufacturing to innovation and service-oriented industries, other measures have been taken to cope with socio-economic tensions between local and external as well as skilled and unskilled workers which (local/national) governments - given their developmental status and budget - cannot afford.[30]

First, restrictions are imposed to cap (legal) migration domestically and internationally alike.[31] If there are real labour shortages, those measures can trigger illegal forms of migration that not only jeopardise labour and social protection of the migrant workers but also antagonise their relationship with the local workers in particular and the local population in general. Second, limitations are put in place regarding social welfare benefits that are enjoyed by local citizens thus leaving those domestic and overseas workers deprived from healthcare, educational opportunities, access to the public housing, etc.[32] Third, long-term residence could also be circumscribed by limited forms of citizenship rights yet those can be fully denied by national governments.[33] Those precarious conditions tied to the (illegal) migrant status can become a source of further exploitation on behalf of employers who take advantage of the

26. Article 2(3), 1966 International Covenant on Economic, Social and Cultural Rights. Conversely, states can sign up to the 1990 International Convention on the Protection of the Rights of All Migrant Workers and Members of Their Families to extend human rights protection to migrant workers and their family members.
27. Soumitra Dutta et al., *The Global Innovation Index 2018: Energizing the World with Innovation* 9 (Cornell University, INSEAD and WIPO 2018).
28. Some have argued that the profitability of foreign companies can be enhanced by localisation - internally and externally alike. In particular, the productivity of local staff members can be improved through delegation and sufficient internal training programmes provided by the foreign company. *See* Seung Ho Park et al., *Scaling the Tail: Managing Profitable Growth in Emerging Markets* 123-124 (Palgrave Macmillan 2015).
29. Jose Ramon Perea & Matthew Stephenson, *Outward FDI from Developing Countries*, in *Global Investment Competitiveness Report 2017/2018: Foreign Investor Perspectives and Policy Implications* 101, 102 (World Bank ed., World Bank 2018).
30. C. Upadhya, *Employment and Exclusion, and 'Merit' in the Indian IT Industry*, 42 Economic and Political Weekly 1863 (2007).
31. Conversely, deportation laws are administered to remove (illegal) migrant workers. *See* Charanpal S. Bal, *Dealing with Deportability: Deportation Laws and the Political Personhood of Temporary Migrant Workers in Singapore*, 2 Asian of Law and Society 267 (2015).
32. World Health Organisation, *Our Cities, Our Health, Our Future: Acting on Social Determinants for Health Equity in Urban Settings* 6 (WHO 2011); Qiqi Fu & Paola Pasquali, *Legal Instrumentalism in China: The Case of Hukou Legislation in Beijing and Shenzhen*, in *East Asia's Renewed Respect for the Rule of Law in the 21st Century: The Future of Legal and Judicial Landscapes in East Asia* 261 (Setsuo Miyazawa and others eds, Brill/Nijhoff 2015).
33. Wui Ling, *Migrant Workers as Citizens Within the ASEAN Landscape: International Law and the Singapore Experiment*, 8 Chinese Journal of International Law 205, 208 (2009).

migrant workers that would be willing to work for lower wages.[34] The working conditions have also put the safety of workers at risk.[35] Domestic and overseas migrants are also divorced from their families nor have they time or money to raise their own families.[36]

The lack of social protection as evidenced in the treatment of migrant workers on behalf of governmental authorities and employers has further exposed their vulnerability in their quest for a better life and human dignity as their home and host nations are rising economically. This leaves particularly migrant rural populations without a proper educational background behind with deep frustration which need to be ventilated in order to preserve social, economic and political stability for the sake of the SEZs, nation, state, region and the world at large.[37] The absence and ineffectiveness, however, of formal procedures in developing nations to channel unfair treatment have repeatedly led to labour strikes, popular protests and riots harming the economic activities as well as political stability.[38] Such development of a rights consciousness could contribute to the peaceful resolution of socio-economic conflicts yet the lack of the rule of law and formal institutions may lead to often disproportionate violent actions and responses.[39]

[B] Property

The SEZs in Asia are particularly prone to the divergent socio-economic statuses amongst its inhabitants and have increasingly constituted potential sources of social instability that inevitably accompanied the rapid urbanisation in Asian developing countries.[40] Unsurprisingly, the socio-economic inequalities between various groups within societies, (non-)migrant workers, employees and (urban) elite alike, are intimately connected to territorial dimensions. In this regard, many of the destitute

34. Samuel Chung-him Yip, *The Status of Undocumented Migrant Workers and Their Legally Enforceable Rights in Hong Kong*, 1 Hong Kong Journal of Legal Studies 59 (2007); Bingqin Li & Mark Duda, *Employers as Landlords for Rural-to-Urban Migrants in Chinese Cities*, 22 Environment and Urbanization 13 (2010).
35. John A. Hall, *Human Rights and the Garment Industry in Contemporary Cambodia*, 36 Stanford Journal of International Law 119 (2000).
36. Mary Romero, *Reflections on Globalized Care Chains and Migrant Women Workers*, Critical Sociology 1 (2018); Youyenn Teo, *Whose Family Matters? Work-Care-Migration Regimes and Class Inequalities in Singapore*, Critical Sociology 1 (2018).
37. Zhikai Wang, *China's Labour Shortage and Migrant Workers' Lack of Social Security*, 153 International Labour Review 649 (2014); *Internal Migrants: The Bitter Generation – Angry Young City Folk with Rural Backgrounds Threaten Social Stability*, The Economist (Beijing & Guangzhou, 2018).
38. Linda Wong, *Chinese Migrant Workers: Rights Attainment Deficits, Rights Consciousness and Personal Strategies*, 208 China Quarterly 870 (2011).
39. Sarah Biddulph & Sean Cooney, *Regulation of Trade Unions in the People's Republic of China*, 19 Melbourne University Law Review 253, 261 (1993); Jaclyn L. Neo, *Riots and Rights: Law and Exclusion in Singapore's Migrant Worker Regime*, 2 Asian Journal of Law and Society 137 (2015); Dina M. Siddiqi, *Starving for Justice: Bangladeshi Garment Workers in a 'Post-Rana Plaza' World*, 87 International Labor and Working-Class History 165 (2015).
40. Ramin Keivani, *A Review of the Main Challenges to Urban Sustainability*, 1 International Journal of Urban Sustainable Development 5, 7 (2010).

members of society lacking basic amenities, including clean water, sanitation and adequate housing are slum dwellers. Although the percentage of people subject to those living conditions has declined over the years, their absolute number has gone up in line with the urbanisation trends - globally and in particular in South and East Asia.[41] The living conditions, however, have gradually improved. Yet, inadequate urban housing in Asia ranges between 61.6% in Bangladesh to 23% in Indonesia.[42]

In the pursuit of their right to development, the demands of the economic transformation of Asian nations are closely tied to the availability of limited urban space to accommodate economic activities and house its people.[43] In this respect, the reclamation of rural lands - voluntary and forcefully alike - has often been accompanied by popular protests on behalf of farmers - in particular in India.[44] The inclusion of their fertile agricultural land in the new urban agglomeration has redefined their status within the national and local labour market. Since they are no longer farming, they have become wage-labourers[45] or may in return become rentiers as property developers have exchanged their land for housing units/apartments. Under both circumstances, former farmers can become socially excluded within their new professions as well as in their new urban environments where they may not be accepted by new local residents. For those wage-labourers who were on the wrong side of the bargain, their commute from home to work within the same city may take a long time - causing economic inefficiency in addition to their personal hardship.

Those 'socio-spatial' injustices[46] are further reinforced by so-called speculative urbanism whereby the demand and supply of property - residential and business alike - have been responsible for steady increases of the prices on the real estate market.[47] Less wealthy migrant and local inhabitants are pushed out from more affluent neighbourhoods into far-away suburban areas, on the one hand, and newcomers - especially young skilled employees - do not necessarily have the financial means to ever purchase property within the speculative property markets of the SEZs, on the other hand. Regarding the members of the former, they are often forced to live in areas

41. UN Development Programme, *United Nations Millennium Goals Report 2014* (UNDP 2014). This was the latest report when the MDGs were concluded in 2015. From then onwards, the UN adopted the Sustainable Development Goals - to be realised by 2030.
42. UN Habitat, *The State of Asian and Pacific Cities 2015: Urban Transformations - Shifting from Quantity to Quality* 75 (UNESCAP and UN Habitat 2015) UN Habitat and the UN Economic and Social Commission for Asia and the Pacific are planning to launch their latest report on 'The Future of Asia and Pacific Cities' in the second half of 2019.
43. Y Hsing, *The Great Urban Transformation: The Politics of Land and Property in China* (Oxford University Press 2010).
44. Aradhna Aggarwal, *Social and Economic Impact of SEZs in India* 230–231 (Oxford University Press 2012); Michael Levien, *The Land Question: Special Economic Zones and the Political Economy of Dispossession in India*, 39 Journal of Peasant Studies 933 (2012).
45. Kalyan Sanyal, *Rethinking Capitalist Development: Primitive Accumulation, Governmentality, and Post-Colonial Capitalism* (Routledge 2007).
46. Neil Smith, *New Globalism, New Urbanism: Gentrification as Global Urban Strategy*, 34 Antipode 427 (2002); David Ley & Sin Yih Teo, *Gentrification in Hong Kong? Epistemology v. Ontology*, 38 International Journal of Urban and Regional Research 1286 (2014).
47. Michael Goldman, *Speculative Urbanism and the Making of the Next World City*, 35 International Journal of Urban and Regional Research 555 (2011); Anthony Fensom, *Asia Joins Global Mega-Cities in League of Their Own*, The Diplomat (2018).

which themselves are more vulnerable to external environmental conditions, including land-slides, flooding, etc. Regarding the latter group, given the middle-income trap in Asian nations, it will become an ever-problematic challenge to attract middle class people whose labour has become indispensable to the transformation of the economic models of Asian economies from manufacturing to service industries in particular in the evolution of the SEZs. Without their labour, such economic transition would be compromised.[48] While gentrification could improve the living quality and safety of the general public in downtown urban areas,[49] the exclusion of local and (un)skilled migrant workers in favour of the (new) urban elite could create far greater mobility and thus environmental problems affecting the economies within the SEZs and beyond.

[C] Pollution

The frustration regarding socio-economic inequality as translated in the strict separation of socio-economic classes within the SEZs in Asia has real consequences for the commute of workers from their home to working spaces. Those who have more means may use their own vehicles to get to work while other rely often on a deficient public and/or private transportation depleting their productivity and well-being. Given poor (sub-)urban planning, traffic congestion does not only immediately cause air and noise pollution, it equally has negative repercussions upon the economic activities within the urban areas, including the delay of delivery of goods and services.[50] Traffic alone is not only responsible for air pollution, manufacturing and energy (coal) industries have been the primary emitters of air and soil pollution (through acid rains). The long-term consequences of exposure to air pollution cause an increase of strokes (heart), lung cancer and other respiratory diseases. The air quality of 97% of big cities in low- and middle-income countries such as those in Asia do not meet the guidelines of the World Health Organisation (WHO).[51] The resulting costs for welfare are born predominantly by developing countries.[52] The transboundary nature of air pollution has further warranted an international and regional response to the matter of climate change.

In addition to (outdoor and indoor) air pollution, within the slums of Asia's big cities, water pollution has been the cause of other health problems including diarrheal and other infectious diseases thus affecting the personal health and those of one's family members. Market-oriented solutions, such as the provision of clean water supplies, have further depleted the economic resources of the most vulnerable

48. Francis E. Hutchinson & Sanchita Basu Das (eds), *Asia and the Middle-Income Trap* (Routledge 2016); Robert J. Shiller, *Why Do Cities Become Unaffordable*, Asia Times (2017).
49. Trevor Hogan et al., *Asian Urbanisms and the Privatization of Cities*, 29 Cities 59 (2012).
50. Sutapa Das, *Hidden Cost in Public Infrastructure Project: A Case Study of Kolkata East–West Metro*, in *Urbanization in Asia: Governance, Infrastructure and the Environment* 149 (Kala Seetharam Sridhar & Guanghua Wan eds, Springer 2014).
51. World Health Organisation, *WHO Global Ambient Air Quality Database (Update 2018)* http://www.who.int/airpollution/data/cities/en/ (accessed 22 May 2018).
52. World Bank and Institute for Health Metrics and Evaluation, *The Cost of Air Pollution: Strengthening the Economic Case for Action* (World Bank 2016).

populations including migrant workers.[53] It has further tested the vulnerability of those urban populations to external threats to their health, well-being and economic opportunities. It may further push them into vicious circles of poverty as well as violence thus undermining social and economic stability. Connected with the unbridled industrialisation of many emerging economies in Asia, is the contamination of the soil in particular in agricultural lands adjoining SEZs. As a result, the production of crops that have entered into the food chain has caused severe health risks to the animal as well as human populations of those countries. The rising demand of food within urban environments has increasingly put additional pressure on the food production where the use of chemical fertilisers and pesticides has increased the health hazards and food insecurity accordingly.[54] Needless to say that the socio-economic status of the citizens will once again determine whether or not they are able to pay for a safer (and imported) and more expensive diet.

§7.03 RULE OF LAW AND THE SEZs IN ASIA

In order to ensure social stability that in turn safeguards a sustainable economic growth trajectory envisaged by local and national governmental authorities within the SEZs and beyond, rule of law and good governance, from the law and development perspective, are prerequisites.[55] As a result, the governance of SEZs must seek to balance economic with social and environmental interests at home and overseas.[56] The latter is particularly important given the protection of migrant workers as well as the prevention of transboundary pollution. A duty to protect the rights of people and the environment is bestowed upon the territorial states where such SEZs are located.[57] This duty is the corollary to the various sets of socio-economic and environmental rights defined in international treaties, including the right to safe work and decent pay,[58] right to social security,[59] right to adequate living standards including health and housing,[60] right to a clean environment,[61] etc. Yet, not all nations accept the justiciability of socio-economic rights and may not have and/or deny formal procedures within their domestic codes to pursue such demands before courts.[62]

53. World Health Organisation, *Our Cities, Our Health, Our Future: Acting on Social Determinants for Health Equity in Urban Settings* 21, 26 (WHO 2011).
54. Emilie Cassou and others, *The Challenge of Agricultural Pollution: Evidence from China, Vietnam, and the Philippines* (World Bank 2018).
55. Lok Raj Baral, *The Relevance and Application of Human Rights to Development*, 3 Human Rights Quarterly 31 (1981).
56. Giok Ling Ooi, *Urbanization of Everything – Governance Challenges in Southeast Asia*, 8 Georgetown Journal of International Affairs 39, 40 (2007).
57. International Commission of Jurists, Special Economic Zones in Myanmar and the State Duty to Protect Human Rights (ICJ 2017).
58. Article 7, 1966 International Covenant of Economic, Social and Cultural Rights.
59. Article 9, 1966 International Covenant of Economic, Social and Cultural Rights.
60. Article 11, 1966 International Covenant of Economic, Social and Cultural Rights.
61. Article 3, 1992 UN Framework Convention on Climate Change.
62. Abul Hasnat Monjurul Kabir, *Development and Human Rights: Litigating the Right to Adequate Housing*, 3 Asia-Pacific Journal on Human Rights & Law 97 (2002); Malcolm Langford, *Social Rights Jurisprudence: Emerging Trends in International and Comparative Law* (Cambridge

The fulfilment of such duty is foremost reflected in the urban planning of governmental authorities seeking to prevent the erosion of human rights of the local and migrating residents as well as the (natural) environment. To that effect, labour laws as well as house- and safety regulations protect the workers' rights and their living conditions such as adequate and affordable housing. Environmental regulations govern the construction and operation of manufacturing sites and energy plants, the use of private and public vehicles on the SEZs' roads and seek to reduce the impact of air, water and soil pollution. Poly-centric city planning could also contribute to reducing traffic congestion and evenly spread economic activities and opportunities across the SEZs thus improving work-house commuting (preconditioned upon social housing measures in a speculative housing market) and avoiding segregation of socio-economic classes.[63] A correlation exists between the transformation of the initial manufacturing economic model to services-related industries and the upgrading of socio-economic and environmental rights protection within the SEZs and beyond.[64]

Third states, too, are concerned with such sustainable economic development of the SEZs. On the one hand, Asian nations that are pools of migration, such as Pakistan in South Asia or the Philippines in southeast Asia, are worried about the well-being of their nationals who work as migrants overseas. Their workers' rights and dignity should be respected in those countries where there is shortage of labour.[65] On the other hand, trading partners within the region and outside have sought to put human rights conditionalities upon the table when negotiating their bilateral and/or regional free trade agreements (FTA) in order to improve the working conditions as well as environmental standards of production of traded goods as well as in the delivery of cross-border services. In the long-term, those agreements aim to upgrade those socio-economic and environmental rights throughout the global value chains yet at same time have restricted access of those developing countries that cannot currently meet those criteria from participating in global and regional trade – thus, potentially denying further opportunities for economic growth and an increase of the living standards of their peoples within the SEZs and nationwide.[66]

University Press 2008); Luke Marsh, *The Strategic Use of Human Rights Treaties in Hong Kong's Cage-Home Crisis: No Way Out?*, 3 Asian Journal of Law and Society 159 (2016).

63. Junyi Zhang et al., *Comprehensive Travel Demand Analysis in Asian Developing Megacities*, in *Sustainable Transport Studies in Asia* 65 (Akimasa Fujiwara & Junyi Zhang eds, Springer 2013); Radhika Balakrishnan et al., *Rethinking Economic Policy for Social Justice: The Radical Potential of Human Rights* 12–28 (Routledge 2016).
64. Stephanie Barrientos et al., *Economic and Social Upgrading in Global Production Networks: A New Paradigm for a Changing World*, 150 International Labour Review 319 (2011).
65. Asian Development Bank, *Asian Economic Integration Report 2015*, 41 (Asian Development Bank 2015) The new Global Compact for Safe, Orderly and Regular Migration negotiated within the siege of the UN and adopted in December 2018 is the first comprehensive approach to deal with migration in all its aspects ranging from its benefits to its challenges not only in respect of individual migrants themselves but also for the communities in the host, transit and countries of origin.
66. Matthias Vanhullebusch, *Searching for Human Rights: Free Trade Agreements in Asia*, in *Regional Cooperation and Free Trade Agreements in Asia* 226 (Jiaxiang Hu & Matthias Vanhullebusch eds, Brill/Nijhoff 2014).

Voluntary resistance on behalf of Asian developing countries to the implementation of such rule-based governance is evidenced in multiple ways. First, corruption and bureaucratic mismanagement have undermined the realisation of such respect for human rights.[67] Second, the right to development discourse has favoured economic development above human rights protection by means of deregulation[68] and the creation of special exception regimes applicable within SEZs in order to make them more competitive.[69] Third, Asian countries have challenged the viability and desirability of a human rights discourse to achieve socio-economic and environmental justice. Economically and politically alike, the costs for Asian governments would be too high: the realisation of human rights would create social and political instability.[70] Indifference, however, to the psychology of inequality of destitute members of society regardless of the positive attempts to redress it – even through successful rule-based governance – that continues to persist would be a far greater threat to society as well as to the economic and the political system. Especially, when such frustrations were to be ventilated violently in densely populated areas.[71]

Under those circumstances, the realisation of human rights cannot rely on the commitments of states alone, corporations – domestic and international alike – are expected to pay due respect for social rights of workers and the environment too. The very nature of the SEZs to attract FDI has accelerated the process of transforming the economic activities of the SEZs and nationwide. In this regard, the privatisation of national industries[72] including those that deliver public services including healthcare, transportation, energy supply has, arguably, positively contributed to more efficient urban and environmental governance.[73] Moreover, victims of labour exploitation, property expropriation and evictions, pollution and environmental man-made disasters have been increasingly successful to seek remedies against (inter)national economic players and obtain compensation. Tort claims against prior violations of labour, property and environmental law have been raised either before judicial authorities in

67. James Thuo Gathii, *Defining the Relationship Between Human Rights and Corruption*, 31 University Pennsylvania Journal of International Law 125 (2009).
68. Richard Mitchell et al., *The Evolution of Labour Law in India: An Overview and Commentary on Regulatory Objectives and Development*, 1 Asian Journal of Law and Society 413, 426 (2014).
69. Shatadru Chakraborty, *Discrimination Against Workers under the Special Economic Zones Act, 2005: A Hindrance to India's Development*, 27 Singapore Law Review 179 (2009).
70. Michael C. Davis, *The Price of Rights: Constitutionalism and East Asian Economic Development*, 20 Human Rights Quarterly 303, 304 (1998).
71. Xiaogang Wu & Jinhua Cheng, *The Emerging New Middle Class and the Rule of Law in China*, 13 The China Review 43 (2013).
72. Ileana M. Porras, *The City and International Law: In Pursuit of Sustainable Development*, 36 Fordham Urban Law Journal 537, 539 (2009).
73. Benjamin J. Richardson, *Is East Asia Industrializing Too Quickly – Environmental Regulation in Its Special Economic Zones*, 22 UCLA Pacific Basin Law Journal 150 (2004); Benjamin J. Richardson, *Uneven Modernisation: Environmental Regulation in China's Special Economic Areas*, 12 Asia Pacific Law Review 126 (2004); Klaus Dieter Wolf & Nicole Deitelhoff, *Business and Human Rights: How Norm Violators Become Norm Entrepreneurs*, in *From Commitment to Compliance. The Persistent Power of Human Rights* 222 (Thomas Risse et al. eds, Cambridge University Press 2013).

the territorial state where those violations occurred or in third states where the multinational foreign corporations are located.[74]

Beyond matters of jurisdiction and admissibility of such cases, it is in the interest of corporations as well as their employees and the environment to preventively pursue accountability strategies for their past, present and future actions and activities – especially in nations where the rule of law is lacking in order to reduce social risks and frustrations that inevitably accompany their investments and to give further effect to the protection of human rights.[75] For such purposes, businesses have started regulating themselves and developed their own (non-binding) codes on corporate social responsibility.[76] Where state- and self-regulations are absent, guidance has been provided by the UN – in particular by virtue of the UN Guiding Principles on Business and Human Rights.[77] Under the framework to 'Protect, Respect and Remedy', businesses are preventing and addressing negative human rights impacts by virtue of their exercise of due diligence, on the one hand. Individual/communities are empowered by the (non-) judicial means at their disposals to give effect to their remedies against state and corporations alike, on the other hand.[78]

The participation of civil society in governing socio-economic and environmental challenges that accompany the fast-economic growth trajectory of Asian countries could further prevent poor urban planning affecting the public health and security. Such inclusiveness and participatory model within governmental decision-making at the level of the SEZs or nationwide promotes local ownership, accountability and mutual respect for the outcomes. The presence of (in)formal procedures and rules can assist in administering different claims.[79] The independence of civil society groups, however, must be guaranteed in order to hold the government and its officials accountable to the entire population – the present and future generations (especially in

---

74. Jamie Cassels, *The Uncertain Promise of Law: Lessons from Bhopal*, 29 Osgood Hall Law Journal 1 (1991); Kathy Walker, *'Gangster Capitalism' and Peasant Protest in China: The Last Twenty Years*, 33 Journal of Peasant Studies 1 (2006); Iman Prihandono, *Litigating Human Rights-Related Cases Against Transnational Corporations in Indonesia*, Lawasia Journal 133 (2012); S. M. Atia Naznin and Shawkat Alam, *Judicial Remedies for Forced Slum Evictions in Bangladesh: An Analysis of the Structural Injunction*, Asian Journal of Law and Society (Forthcoming).
75. Olivier De Schutter et al., *Foreign Direct Investment, Human Development and Human Rights: Framing the Issues*, 3 Human Rights and International Legal Discourse 137 (2009); Abdullah Al Faruque, *Mapping the Relationship Between Investment Protection and Human Rights*, 11 Journal of World Investment & Trade 539 (2010); Johanna Aleria P. Lorenzo, *Investment Promotion as Progressive Realization of Economic and Social Rights*, 16 Asia-Pacific Journal on Human Rights & Law 55 (2015).
76. T. Sagafi-Nejad, *The UN and Transnational Corporations: From Code of Conduct to Global Compact* (Indiana University Press 2008).
77. Guiding Principles on Business and Human Rights: Implementing the United Nations 'Protect, Respect and Remedy' Framework (Guiding Principles), UN Doc. HR/PUB/11/04 (2011). *See also* Giovanni Mantilla, *Emerging International Human Rights Norms for Transnational Corporations*, 15 Global Governance 279 (2009); John G. Ruggie, *Just Business: Multinational Corporations and Human Rights* (W.W. Norton 2013).
78. John G. Ruggie & John F. Sherman, *The Concept of 'Due Diligence' in the UN Guiding Principles on Business and Human Rights: A Reply to Jonathan Bonnitcha and Robert McCorquodale*, 28 European Journal of International Law 921, 923 (2017).
79. Marilyn Rice & Trevor Hancock, *Equity, Sustainability and Governance in Urban Settings*, 23 Global Health Promotion 94 (2015).

respect of environmental protection).[80] The trade unions that are defending the social well-being of workers and their legal rights will also hold corporations accountable for violations of labour law.[81] However, not all communities within complex multi-ethnic/religious societies are equally well-represented to voice their concerns and offer their grass-root input. Thus, conflicting arguments have to be managed well in order to reach a synthesis of views that can work in practice.

International solidarity with the socio-economic and environmental causes that are witnessed in Asian developing countries and their SEZs is also supported by overseas civil non-governmental organisations. More than ever has consumer behaviour been a policy and advocacy tool to steer production process elsewhere towards respect for the labour conditions of the workforce and (international) environmental production standards – in particular given the difficulties to enforce socio-economic/environmental rights in the short term through (non-)judicial means.[82] Consumer boycotts as well as individual and collective strikes may also generate negative repercussions upon the present economic activities of certain industries where there are serious labour and environmental costs as well as their suppliers. Potential losses of revenues may lead to job losses and more precarious conditions for those who have become unemployed – adding to the sources of socio-economic risks. Nonetheless, long-term solutions – such as fair-trade labelling – can be designed upon a participatory basis involving different share- and stakeholders, including businesses, employees, government and (inter)national civil society groups, seeking to improve the socio-economic well-being and environmental protection in compliance with the (evolving) rule of law.

§7.04 TRANSCENDENTAL RECIPES AND THE PSYCHOLOGY OF INEQUALITY IN THE SEZs IN ASIA

The pursuit of an open economic system through the establishment of SEZs and investment treaties pushing the boundaries of competition in its benefits and costs could ultimately deliver on the protection of human rights – civil-political and socio-economic alike.[83] The development and the role of legal reforms and institutions to guide those processes towards the protection of those human rights have become the lens through which economic progress within Asian developing countries has been evaluated on behalf of Western developed nations. In this regard, within the liberal law and development discourse, respect for the standards of the international rule of law has been the benchmark to measure progress in its civil-political and socio-economic

80. Larry Diamond, *Rethinking Civil Society: Towards Democratic Consolidation*, 5 Journal of Democracy 4 (1994).
81. Mary E. Gallagher, *Authoritarian Legality in China: Law, Workers, and the State* (Cambridge University Press 2017).
82. N. Craig Smith, *Morality and the Market: Consumer Pressure for Corporate Responsibility* (Routledge 1990); Monroe Friedman, *Consumer Boycotts: Effecting Change Through the Market Place and the Media* (Routledge 1999).
83. Jonathan Bonnitcha, *Investment Treaties and Transition from Authoritarian Rule*, 15 Journal of World Investment and Trade 965 (2014).

dimensions. In reality, regarding the latter, the distribution of socio-economic rights, however, has always been a challenge, namely to balance between macro-economic goals and the right to development in its collective dimension as well as individual concerns which are tied to the particular status of workers and employees within a given economy – SEZs and national alike. Regarding the former, the pursuit of a liberal democracy has equally faced similar challenges when aligning civil and political liberties with socio-economic progress.[84]

The financial and economic crisis in the West has more than ever challenged the democratic recipes to solve macro-economic problems. The technocratic budgetary responses to bail-out the banking systems and the austerity measures have seriously undermined the faith in the political elite to serve the general interests of their populations. The erosion of political middle field – which traditionally compromises between liberal economic and social policies – in the West coincides with the gradual disappearance of the middle classes. The alternative political responses are voiced at the extremities of the political spectre, i.e., from the far-left to the far-right, pulling the consensus parties into their grip – more successfully so on the far-right side. The rise of populist and anti-globalist political parties rejecting the coalition governments and political establishments has resulted in an immediate backlash on their government's trade and human rights strategies and agendas – domestic and internationally alike. Despite real socio-economic inequality in developed Western countries, they feed themselves from the psychology of inequality and seek culprits for the precarious socio-economic conditions of local populations within the unfair trade treaties as well as amongst migrant communities. Such nativism justifies further discrimination – thus undermining the realities of economic interdependence and opportunities for skilled workers to contribute to the economic growth of those nations in a peaceful, rational and tolerant manner – and fails to deliver on the improvement of the socio-economic injustices in real terms.[85]

Asian nations are not immune either to those populist as well as nationalist uprisings. Asia's general openness to trade and its integration into the global value chains make its economies particularly vulnerable to protectionist measures from Western developed countries reducing foreign direct investment and imposing tariffs on import of goods from Asian developing countries or even preventing the former to trade with latter.[86] As a response, counter-measures on behalf of Asian countries would risk undermining free trade at the global/regional level and thus affecting domestic growth and highlighting the internal differences on the domestic labour market as well as the ever-widening socio-economic gaps within those Asian nations and their SEZs.[87] Those divisions – also in the realm of migration and citizenship rules – are then

84. Samuel Moyn, *Not Enough: Human Rights in an Unequal World* (Harvard University Press 2018).
85. David H. Bennett, *The Party of Fear: From Nativist Movements to the New Right in American History* (University of North Carolina Press, 1988); Martin Schain et al. (eds), *Shadows Over Europe: The Development and Impact of the Extreme Right in Western Europe* 83 (Palgrave Macmillan 2002).
86. *See* 2018 United States-Mexico-Canada Agreement, Article 32:10 Non-Market Country FTA.
87. International Monetary Fund, *Regional Economic Outlook: Asia-Pacific* (IMF May 2018).

exploited for political gains by Asian nationalist parties.[88] The rise of nationalism in Asia is not the outcome of such macro-economic problems at home and abroad alone. Such economic protectionism is also closely intertwined with geopolitical tensions – in particular with the rise of China that is perceived as threatening the status quo in economic, political and strategic terms. As a self-fulling prophecy, economic protectionism depletes the national budget from economic investments that are partly directed towards increased military expenditures for defence – and potentially expansionist – purposes.[89] The latter military agendas are also often accompanied with foreign direct investment in those nations where the strategic choke points on Asia's sea lines of communication are situated.

In any event, the externalisation of the domestic socio-economic injustices that have accompanied the rapid economic growth and untapped economic potential within Asia shows similar patterns with the developments within Western countries – with the exception of the rise of the middle classes. The latter's perception of inequality is no longer viewed in socio-economic (except for those who are in the middle-income trap) yet in civil-political terms – at least from the liberal perspective which has found its expression in the (liberal) law and development discourse. Their demands for greater participation in the political processes that determine the individual and collective well-being of citizens within Asian developing countries have become a challenge to govern and manage those political aspirations and expectations – especially within authoritarian regimes. Granting civil-political rights for this ever-growing group within society will inevitably cause additional frustration on those people that are deprived from the same socio-economic opportunities and benefits within their nations in general and the SEZs in particular.

In traditional societies, however, socio-economic injustice as well as demands for socio-economic and civil-political rights are managed through societal relationships that have been developing over the centuries into a sophisticated framework where each member is assigned its own (fixed) place within that society. As a result, the goals of the collectivity transcend the demands of the individual members of society.[90] Within the economic realm, the achievement of GDP targets would align individual workers' demands with macro-economic objectives whose latter realisation, however, is not possible without individual labour. The expectations of workers whose labour is an indispensable mode of production to the capitalist economic growth model have been managed in different ways in Asia's developing economies, ranging from

88. Arianto Patunru & Sjamsu Rahardja, *Trade Protectionism in Indonesia: Bad Times and Bad Policy* (The Lowy Institute 2017); Barbara Grossman-Thompson & Dannah Dennis, *Citizenship in the Name of the Mother: Nationalism, Social Exclusion, and Gender in Contemporary Nepal*, 25 Positions: East Asia Cultures Critique 795 (2017).

89. Chris Ogden, *Hindu Nationalism and the Evolution of Contemporary Indian Security* (Oxford University Press 2014); Nakano Koichi, *Contemporary Political Dynamics of Japanese Nationalism*, 14 The Asia-Pacific Journal 1 (2016).

90. Roda Mushkat, *Contextualizing Environmental Human Rights: A Relativist Perspective*, 26 Pace Environmental Law Review 119, 137 (2009).

downgrading[91] to harmonising[92] them within the country's and SEZs' economic trajectory. Although those traditional forms of societal ordering appear to deviate from individual human rights entitlements, the right to development in its collective dimension has been the connecting factor to lay down the foundation for the future realisation of individual human rights as developing nations become more prosperous and capable to fulfil those human rights promises. In the meantime, the right to development prioritises the collective demands of nations and societies over the individual realisation of civil-political and socio-economic demands. It may temporarily avoid social instability and political insecurity and give more time to the political establishments and business communities to design more sustainable forms of economic growth that at least are experienced more broadly and positively by all members of society as well as those migrant workers contributing to their economic progress.

§7.05 CONCLUSION

Socio-economic inequality in Asia's SEZs in particular and Asian developing countries in general has real implications for domestic and migrant workers alike who are deprived of adequate housing, decent public transportation, education, safe food and a clean environment in their personal sphere, on the one hand, and from a proper salary, safe working conditions and social security in their professional sphere, on the other hand. They are inevitably tied to the rapid economic growth trajectory whose socio-economic and environmental costs have been borne disproportionately by the weaker members of society. While in collective terms, unprecedented growth numbers achieved in those SEZs and nationwide have boosted the confidence of Asian developing countries in their ability to integrate themselves in the global value chains of production, services and capital, they have yet to show further commitment to address socio-economic injustices by means of (non-)regulatory approaches. Not only to preserve sustainable development and economic growth nationally and globally alike, but to ensure domestic stability in the first place so that the members of their societies can become more resilient to the internal as well as external economic and political risks and shockwaves to which Asia's global economies are more than ever subjected.

Yet, from the perspective of liberal law and development discourses, respect for international economic law through its various branches as well as international human rights and environmental law as the precondition of sustainable economic growth has not been sufficiently met in the SEZs and by extension nationwide across Asia's emerging economies. Mitigating inequality and fostering economic prosperity in Asia, they argue, could be successfully pursued not only through the rule of law but exclusively within a democratic system. Conversely, within Western democracies, the

91. Jan Breman, *Outcast Labour in Asia: Circulation and Informalization of the Workforce at the Bottom of the Economy* (Oxford University Press 1999).
92. Eric Meyer, *Sois Riche et Tais-Toi! Portrait de la Chine d'Aujourd'hui* (Robert Laffont 2002); Chenyang Li, *The Confucian Philosophy of Harmony* 124 (Routledge 2015); Delia Lin and Sue Trevaskes, *Creating a Virtuous Leviathan: The Party, Law and Socialist Core Values*, 6 Asian Journal of Law and Society (2019, Forthcoming).

gap between the rich and the poor has been growing steadily and exponentially so ever since the global financial crisis giving rise to populist responses undermining the respect for their thick definition of rule of law at the same time. Such democratic idealism projected as a universal standard must reconnect itself with its inner values if were to survive in the face of counter-productive empirical realities challenging its faith on the ground. In other words, a liberal law and development discourse must acknowledge in the first place the primary human desire for recognition, so-called thymos, as political scientists and cognitive psychologists have identified decades ago.[93] It is the foundation upon which individualistic and communitarian societies – regardless of its democratic (procedural) properties – can be built and where all its (marginalised) members are – or at least have the impression that they are – recognised.

Without an acknowledgment of the human desire for recognition on behalf of those who govern – democratically elected or authoritarian alike, frustrations driven by the inevitable psychology of inequality experienced by some of its subjects may continue to undermine the social and political stability of the SEZs and the country and be further exploited along dichotomous lines ever dividing Asian and Western societies as whole. Democratic elections alone will not suffice to sustain socio-economic stability and long-term sustainable economic development. The acknowledgment of thymos is an intrinsic part of governing upon the basis of the (international) rule of law around the world and at all levels of jurisdiction. The challenge to preserve the law's normativity depends not only on the mere existence of norms laid down in the actual rules of international economic, human rights and environmental law and the values which underpin those normative frameworks, including free trade, humanity and accountability, it equally relies on the quality of the relationship between the governors and their subjects. The survival of a political system and its economic orders, including those of the SEZs in Asian countries – irrespective of the nature of such system, depends on the rule of law whose respect by and belief in it on behalf of all share- and stakeholders in society must be guaranteed – through the acknowledgment of thymos.

93. Francis Fukuyama, *The End of History: The Last Man Standing* (The Free Press 1998); Francis Fukuyama, *Identity: The Demand for Dignity and the Politics of Resentment* (Farrar 2018).

CHAPTER 8

Belt and Road Initiative: Economic Corridors, Transit Routes and SEZs – Exploring the Linkages Using the BBSP as a Case Study

Francisco José B.S. Leandro

§8.01 INTRODUCTION

The recent policy concerns of BREXIT, immigration, the Russian Federation and the current American administration, have diverted European Union (EU) public opinion away from the latest developments in global policy. Among them stands the 'belt and road' initiative (B&RI) launched by President Xi Jinping in 2013. The first Belt and Road Forum for International Cooperation, held in Beijing in May 2017, inaugurated a new era of infrastructural realizations, involving cooperation agreements with approximately seventy countries and international organizations. For the purpose of this chapter, B&RI will be discussed as an access strategy based on infrastructural connectivity, acknowledging the colossal efforts of China to strengthen its economic capacity based on regional integration, market-oriented reforms and policies such as 'going out' and 'coming in'. If the year 2001 marked the moment of economic change with the Chinese accession to the World Trade Organization (WTO), 2013 marked the beginning of a global access network facilitating economic and trade flows between markets and production centres, 2016 flagged the moment that the RMB become part of the (IMF/Special drawing rights), and 2017–2018 marks the call for effective international participation in this network.

Two initial ideas are worth mentioning. First, most geo-economic or geopolitical approaches addressing the B&RI assume the existence of a land belt composed of six economic corridors (the land belt) and a maritime road (the maritime silk road (MSR) – with different sailing options), without discussing their origin and rationale. We must be clear that the land belt and maritime road are natural extensions of the three Chinese domestic development and mobility axes (Figure 8.1), which connect peripheral economic hubs to China's economic heartland.

Figure 8.1 The Domestic Mobility Axes and the B&R Corridors

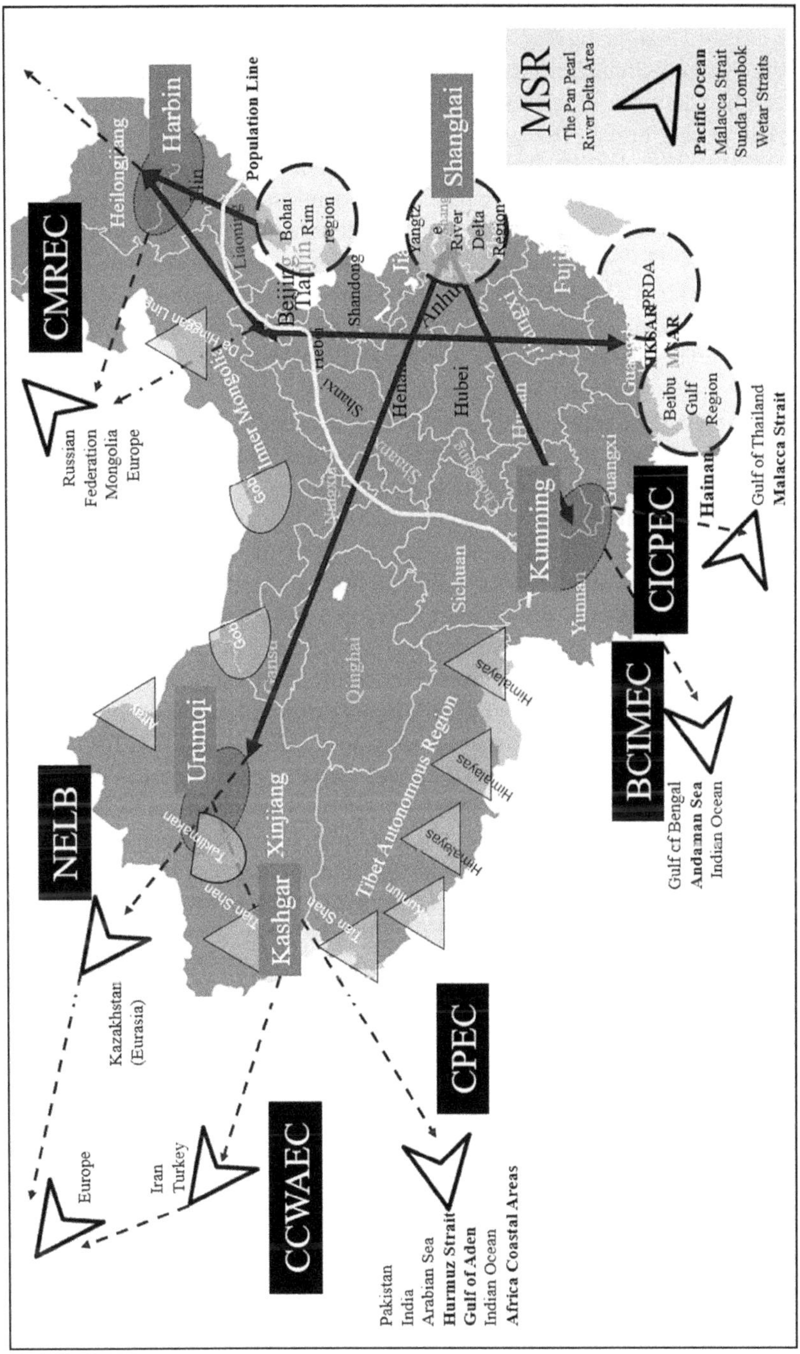

Source: Adapted from China-British Business Council, a role for UK companies in developing China's new initiative, 2015, page 18.

The three major development and mobility axes which make up a central mobility triangle are: (1) the Urumqi-Shanghai axis, with a deviation to the Kashgar area, (2) the Guangdong-Beijing-Harbin axis, with a deviation to the Dalian area, and (3) the Kunming-Shanghai axis. The three domestic development and mobility axes are the result of domestic geopolitical features such as climate, railway-highway networks, population distribution, the location of power production plants, centres of economic activity (the geographical distribution of industrial clusters in China and their industrial specialization), Chinese administrative organization, the west-east orientation of the main rivers, peripheral mountains and deserts, and physical distances between first-tier cities. The extension of these three domestic axes aims to overcome the insular geopolitical status of China (China is an island from the geopolitical point of view), inducing economic connectivity to Eurasia and to markets and production centres worldwide. The six land corridors and the maritime road are the natural extensions of the three major domestic development and mobility axes. They maximize economic flows between the Chinese heartland and suppliers and markets abroad. Alternatively, in other words, the six land corridors (the land belt) are the direct connecting instruments, liking different economic-legal-social orders, and the MSR is the complementary instrument reinforcing that connection. They are the connecting instruments advancing B&RI as a global reach initiative. Their organization can be outlined as follows: AXIS 1 – Linking China to Europe through Central Asia: The New Eurasian Land Bridge Economic Corridor (NELB); AXIS 1 – Linking China to the Middle East through Central Asia: China-Central Asia-West Asia Economic Corridor (CCWAEC); AXIS 1 – Linking China to southeast Asia, South Asia and the Indian Ocean: China-Pakistan Economic Corridor (CPEC); AXIS 2 – Linking China to Europe through Russia: The China-Mongolia-Russia Economic Corridor (CMREC); AXIS 3 – Linking China to Europe through the South China Sea and Indian Ocean: Bangladesh-China-India-Myanmar Economic Corridor (BCIMEC); AXIS 3 – Linking China to the South Pacific Ocean through the South China Sea: China-Indochina Peninsula Economic Corridor (CICPEC), and AXES 1, 2 and 3 – Linking coastal areas in China to the different route options offered by the MSR. In view of economic corridors with the Chinese heartland, bearing in mind that geopolitics reads the Chinese territory as an island, and acknowledging China's vital interests, B&RI is a smart strategy for establishing a cooperative network of flows with a regional rationale and a global scale. The three major domestic development and mobility axes are the strategic origin of the six well-known economic corridors: (1) the CMREC, connecting Tianjin and Dalian to the Baltic region, (2) the NELB that connects the Chinese heartland through Xingjian to Kazakhstan, Russia, Belorussia, Central Europe and the Northern Mediterranean Sea, (3) the China-Central Asia-West Economic Corridor that connects Urumqi, Kazakhstan, Kirghizstan, Tajikistan, Turkmenistan, Iran, Turkey, the Persian Gulf, the Mediterranean Sea and the Arabian Peninsula, (4) the CPEC, connecting Kashgar, Khunjerab Pass, Islamabad and Gwadar, (5) the BCIMEC, and (6) the CICPEC that connects Kunming, Nanning, Laos, Vietnam, Cambodia, Thailand, Malaysia and Singapore.

Second, Chinese regional economic integration calls for extended development and mobility axes. Precisely because the Chinese heartland is geographically isolated, and due to the existence of asymmetric development zones (the Tibet Autonomous

Region, the Xinjiang Uygur Autonomous Region and the Inner Mongolian Autonomous Region), the obvious solution for economic balance is to combine functional (Figure 8.3) regional integration with key development and mobility axes. The Bohai Rim Area, the Yangtze River Delta Area, the southeast Fujian Area, the Pan Pearl River Delta Area, the Great Pearl River Delta Area, the Beibu Gulf Area, the Chengdu-Chongqing Area, the Middle Yangtze Area, the Central Plains Area, the Guanzhong Area, the Hohhot-Baotou-Yinchuan Area, the Northern Slope of Tianshan Mountains Area and the Harbin-Changchun Area are examples of ongoing functional economic regional integration that also integrates the rationale of the three domestic development and mobility axes. The process of regional functional integration is based on the creation of regional infrastructural development plans with smart, non-competitive and complementary industrial and technological production. As an access strategy, the ultimate goal of the B&RI is to connect the Chinese economic heartland to key markets and production centres worldwide, and therefore diminish the natural isolation of China.

§8.02 B&R AS NETWORK OF GLOBAL REACH

B&RI is an attempt to establish a network of trade and economic flows with a global reach. The extended domestic development and mobility axes induce economic connectivity to China's neighbourhood and to Eurasia. The six land corridors are complemented by the one MSR with various route options. The function of this MSR is to link, mesh, complement, support and expand the land belt by developing three basic route options from seaports located in the Chinese coastal areas:[1] (1) to Malacca, the Indian Ocean and Europe-Africa; (2) to Indonesia-Australia and the South Pacific; and (3) to Pacific Ocean towards to the Arctic Ocean or the Panama Canal. According to the International Chamber of Shipping (2018),[2] around 90% of world trade is carried by the international shipping industry. Almost 40% of the global liquefied natural gas trade moves through the South China Sea,[3] more than 10% of world trade sails through the Red Sea basin,[4] 95% of EU Member States' trade (by volume) is transported by sea, and 20% of global trade passes through the Gulf of Aden.[5] China's ultimate strategy is to establish a global maritime trade network, interconnecting the land network, supported by maritime infrastructure, controlled through public and private Chinese investments. Recalling the strategic theories proposed by Rear Admiral Alfred Thayer Mahan, a global maritime trade network will naturally nurture an immense sea power.

The projected global network of trade and economic flows will be supported by a smart combination of land economic corridors (the land belt) and a maritime road with a global reach. The land belt will connect the Chinese heartland with key strategic regions in the Chinese periphery and with Eurasia, but it is the maritime road that will

1. The Chinese coastal areas discussed in this article are: Guangdong, Fujian, Zhejiang, Jiangsu, Shangdong, Hebei and Liaoning.
2. http://www.ics-shipping.org/shipping-facts/shipping-and-world-trade (accessed 10 October 2018).
3. https://www.eia.gov/todayinenergy/detail.php?id=33592 (accessed 10 October 2018).
4. http://www.arabnews.com/columns/news/879221 (accessed 25 March 2018).
5. http://eunavfor.eu/mschoa/ (accessed 25 March 2018).

give the initiative a global reach by establishing maritime sea lines of communication (SLOC) connecting the largest production and consumption regions of the world. In light of this, Matolcsy[6] recently observed: '[This New Silk Road] ... encompasses sixty-four countries, including China, two-thirds of the world's population, and currently only 40% of the global GDP ... This Silk Road will connect the participants constituting the new, twenty-first century phase of globalisation. It can already be seen that the network of the Silk Road consists of a northern, a middle and a southern branch ...

6. Governor, Central Bank of Hungary, http://www.geopolitika.hu/en/2017/03/20/hungary-a-key-state-on-the-silk-road/ (accessed 2 May 2018). Matolcsy, G, *Hungary – A Key State on the Silk Road* (Opening Presentation Delivered at the 54th Annual Meeting of Economists, 15 September 2016), http://www.geopolitika.hu/en/2017/03/20/hungary-a-key-state-on-the-silk-road/ (accessed 2 May 2018).

Figure 8.2 B&R a Network of Global Reach

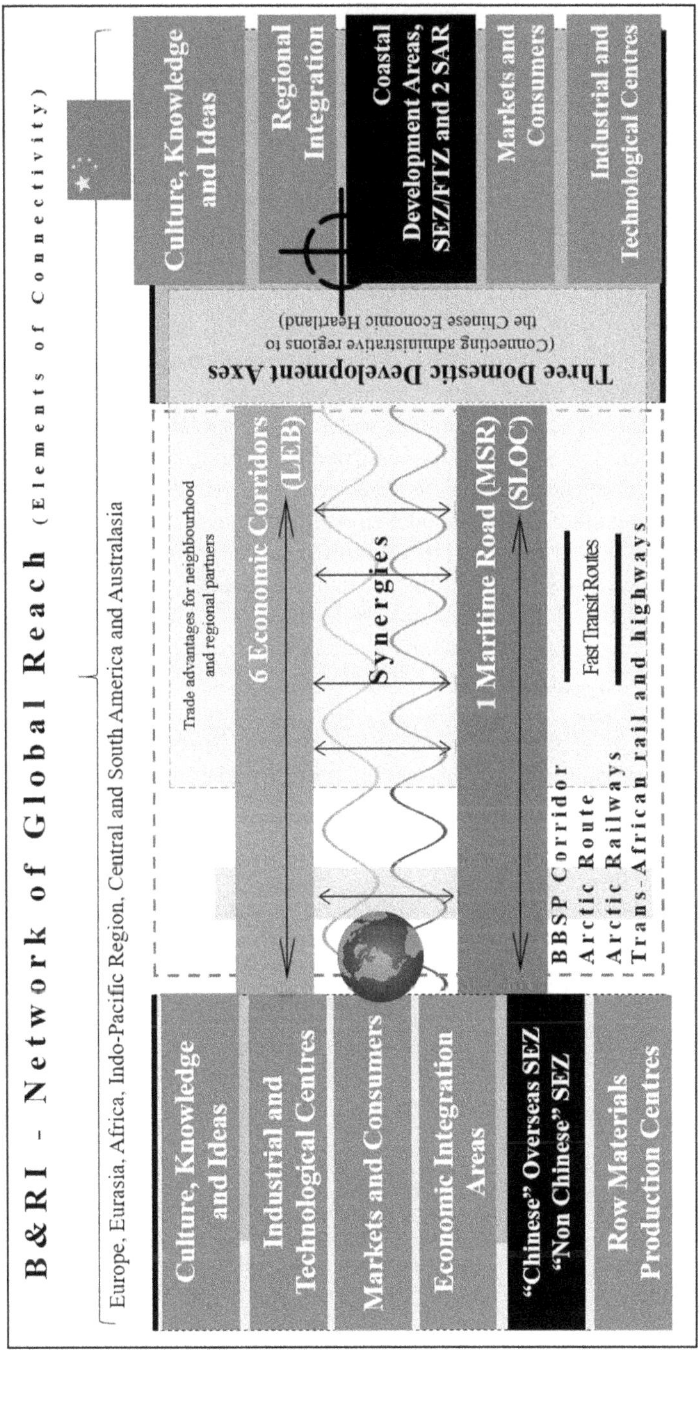

Source: Author.

There is a maritime Silk Road which is especially promising.' At this point, I would like to attempt to map out B&R as a global access initiative (Figure 8.2). In fact, B&RI plays three very important roles in terms of economic connectivity. The first is exercised domestically, by paving the way for a regional functional integration policy, which aims to maximize the potential of each Chinese administrative region and combine each administrative region with special economic zones (SEZs) inside and outside Chinese territory. The domestic development and mobility axes are the links between the domestic production centres and the domestic markets. Second, B&RI facilitates the reduction of distances between the Chinese economic heartland, industrial production centres, markets, different types of SEZs[7] in China and those located abroad, by extending the three domestic axes internationally. Third, the initiative combines different structural arrangements to maximize the potential of both the land belt and the MSR. Figure 8.2 maps B&RI, depicting the architecture of global access, the combination of domestic development and mobility axes, international economic and development corridors, SLOC, fast transit routes (FTR), special administrative zones, material and immaterial flows,[8] and the reduction of material and immaterial distances between industrial production and technological centres and markets. The SEZs, coastal development areas, free trade pilot zones, industrial-technological hubs, export processing zones (EPZs) and special administrative regions function as physical delimited interfaces, between the Chinese economic heartland, regional integration efforts and international economic and trade flows. They combine the essential characteristics of open markets in delimited areas, protecting the key political driving principle of centralized planning and redistribution. In other words, they are ad hoc connectivity-instruments, designed to facilitate the flows between different legal-economic-social orders, allowing for the preservation of the essence of the socialism model with Chinese characteristics and at the same time to project influence across the globe under the principle of free markets.

§8.03 WHAT IS AN SEZ?

The concept of SEZ encompasses analogous legal, economic and policy arrangements applied to a designated geographical area to advance an economic function. There are

7. According to Herlevi, A, *What's So Special about Special Economic Zones? China's National and Provincial-Level Development Zones* 13 (2016), http://web.isanet.org/Web/Conferences/AP%20Hong%20Kong%202016/Archive/3a83092a-cbfa-4526-85d7-3ca39931b3b4.pdf (accessed 14 March 2018), these are the types of SEZ in China: comprehensive SEZs; economic and technological development zones (ETDZs); high-tech industrial development zones (HIDZs); border economic cooperation zones; export-processing zones (EPZs); bonded zones; and 'pilot' free trade zones (PFTZs).
8. The sine waves (sinusoids) represent immaterial flows (soft infrastructure) such as cyber economy, information networks, media interplay, internet industries, national big data strategy, information security ....

several types of SEZ[9] with different management systems,[10] and more than sixty countries have implemented (or are implementing) them as economic assets.[11] SEZs perform a similar role to that of a vehicle's differential, but in relation to a certain economic-legal system. Differentials are gears which give a vehicle's wheels the permanent ability to adapt to the terrain, especially to curves and uneven rotational movements. SEZs are the result of set of political, economic and legal mechanisms which allow states to use them like 'differentials', to adapt their economic-legal systems to economic, trade and market circumstances. SEZs are intended to deal with national economic infrastructure difficulties, but they are not merely a domestic phenomenon; they also compete to attract foreign direct investment (FDI) and bilateral trade agreements. They are indeed a sort of geographically delimitated areas, with an exceptional combination of legal and economic regimes, provided with relevant infrastructures, collocated with public and private institutions, to encourage and facilitate the formation of networks of trade flows. SEZs are instruments of reducing trade barriers or bureaucratic obstacles. SEZs are more adaptable to ever-changing market conditions, with a higher degree of flexibility than the state economy as a whole. SEZ combine economic and legal regimes, with sustainable infrastructures and advanced specialized human capital. Hence, SEZs are not only about fiscal incentives, they are carefully selected geographic areas, different from the 'regular' national market, strategically collocated with transport facilities, in which ad hoc (good) governance and interconnected supporting institutions, transforms them into synergetic international gateways.

9. The World Bank Group, *Special Economic Zones Performance, Lessons Learned, and Implications for Zone Development* 3 (2008), http://documents.worldbank.org/curated/pt/343901468330977533/pdf/458690WP0Box331s0April200801PUBLIC1.pdf (accessed 2 February 2018) reported that the first 'modern zone' was established in Ireland in 1959. Since then, a variety of different zone setups have evolved that are subsumed under the SEZ concept, namely: free trade zones (FTZs; also known as commercial free zones) are fenced-in, duty-free areas, offering warehousing, storage, and distribution facilities for trade, transhipment, and re-export operations. EPZs are industrial estates aimed primarily at foreign markets. Hybrid EPZs are typically subdivided into a general zone open to all industries and a separate EPZ area is reserved for export-oriented, EPZ-registered enterprises. Enterprise zones are intended to revitalize distressed urban or rural areas through the provision of tax incentives and financial grants. Free ports typically encompass much larger areas. They accommodate all types of activities, including tourism and retail sales, permit on-site residence, and provide a broader set of incentives and benefits. Single factory EPZ schemes provide incentives to individual enterprises regardless of location; factories do not have to locate within a designated zone to receive incentives and privileges. Specialized zones include science/technology parks, petrochemical zones, logistics parks, airport-based zones, and so on.
10. According to the China Development Bank, *Experience Gained in the Development of China's Special Economic Zones* (2014), http://www.worldbank.org/content/dam/Worldbank/Event/Africa/Investing%20in%20Africa%20Forum/2015/investing-in-africa-forum-chinas-special-economic-zone.pdf (accessed 14 March 2018), various management models have been followed. These include (a) administrative management, with managerial functions performed by government-instituted administrative bodies; (b) administrative committee, with management by government-appointed committees; and (c) joint management by SEZ partners and government-instituted administrative bodies.
11. Namely, China, Thailand, Vietnam, Qatar (Qatar financial centre (QFC) operating as an SEZ and as an FTZ), South Korea, Philippines, Bangladesh, Myanmar, East-Timor, and Sri Lanka.

If we consider 'EPZs' a category of 'SEZ'[12], it is worth quoting Engman, Onodera, and Pinali, who stressed that EPZs … can provide an interim solution to countries with poor business environments where bridging deficiencies at a national level is not possible.[13] This type of policy – with resources and market incentives focused on a subset of the economy – may be less time-consuming and may require less political capital in the short term as it allows for continued protection of domestic industry. 'As an interim solution, EPZs should not be considered a substitute for general economic reform. While incentives may make up for certain deficiencies, governments should bear in mind that such incentives are made possible by taxing other parts of the economy, and thus should provide commensurate benefits to the economy.' Nevertheless, SEZs advance different and specific economic functions, such as attracting FDI, encouraging local entrepreneurship and joint ventures (as they incubate local ideas), spurring technical innovation, attracting and developing new industries (taxes incentives), reducing duplication, creating jobs, integrating learning, innovation and production, deepening and accelerating reforms, stimulating economic competitiveness, bringing together resources/expertise from government, private investors, industry and research institutions, cultivating market leaders, helping to build brands, promoting human capital, and facilitating experimentation and technology transfer.

Salah El-Rashidy asserted that SEZs are considered successful if they are able to bring about significant structural change in the economy or render long-term 'dynamic economic benefits' – coined by Thomas Farole to indicate the achievement of a significant level of diversification and openness, in addition to facilitating the transfer of knowledge.[14] The impact of a SEZ is largely dependent on the degree of integration in the domestic economy, in terms of backward and forward linkages, exchange of skilled labour and attracting domestic investments. It is precisely to facilitate the integration between the connectivity elements (such as SEZ) and the domestic market, that China has developed the three main domestic development axes. According to the China Development Bank, 'SEZs have contributed significantly to China's development. They have permitted experimentation with market-oriented reforms, and acted as a catalyst for efficient allocation of domestic and international resources. They have also deepened economic opening by attracting international capital, technology, and technical and managerial expertise that stimulated industrial development and China's

12. The largest and most comprehensive types of development zones are SEZs and ETDZs. While SEZs and ETDZs are technically development zones, they are large in scope and focus. Investors will not likely find specific services or tailored benefits to meet their needs. It is often more helpful to look at the following types of development zone such as HTIDZ, FTZ, EPZ, and bonded logistics zone, http://www.china-briefing.com/news/2011/10/05/understanding-development-zones-in-china.html (accessed 11 October 2018).
13. Engman, M et al., *Working Party of the Trade Committee – Export Processing Zones: Past and Future Role in Trade and Development*, 53 OECD Trade Policy Working Paper 6 (2017).
14. El-Rashidy, S, *The Role of China's Overseas Special Economic Zones in Economic Development*, 4 (PhD thesis, The American University in Cairo 2016), http://dar.aucegypt.edu/bitstream/handle/10526/4878/Thesis.Salah.El-Rashidy.Final.pdf?sequence=1 (accessed 12 September 2018).

greater integration into the global economy.'[15] SEZs in China have certainly made a substantial contribution to China's GDP and are the origin of most of China's exports.

15. China Development Bank, *Experience Gained in the Development of China's Special Economic Zones* (2014), http://www.worldbank.org/content/dam/Worldbank/Event/Africa/Investing%20in%20Africa%20Forum/2015/investing-in-africa-forum-chinas-special-economic-zone.pdf (accessed 14 March 2018).

Figure 8.3 B&RI and Its Domestic Elements of Connectivity

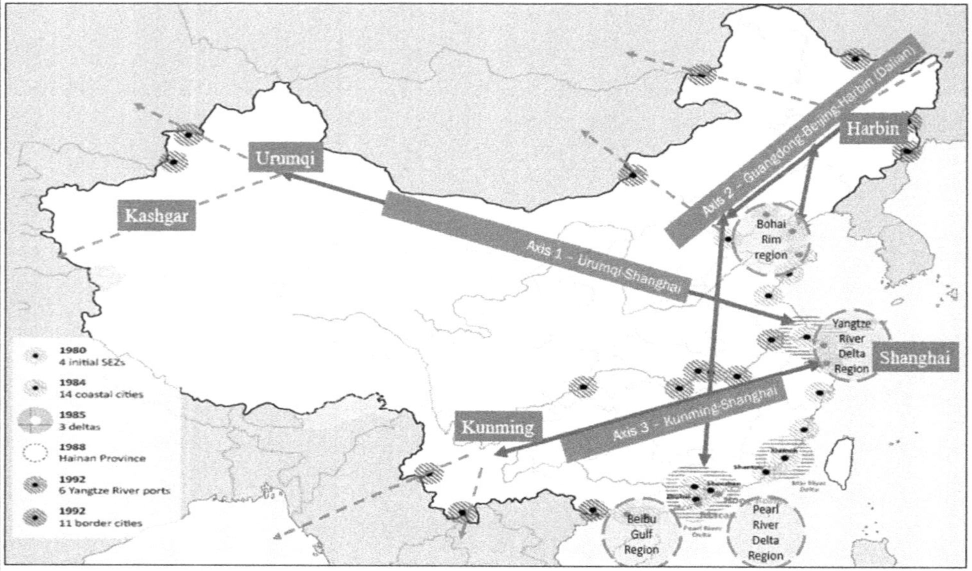

5 Sub Provincial Special Economic Zones (SEZ) (City)
Shenzhen - Guangdong
Zhuhai - Guangdong
Shantou - Guangdong
Xiamen - Fujian
Kashgar - Xinjiang

14 Coastal Development Areas
Dalian - Liaoning
Qinhuangdao - Hebei
Tianjin - Tanjin
Yantai - Shandong
Qingdao - Shandong
Lianyungang - Jiangsu
Nantong - Jiangsu
Shanghai - Shanghai
Ningbo - Zhejiang
Wenzhou - Zhejiang
Fuzhou - Fujian
Guangzhou - Guangdong
Zhanjiang - Guangdong
Beihai - Guangxi

PDRA - Experimental Free Trade Zones
EFTZ (Guangdong)
Hengqin district of Zhuhai (Financial Centre)
Nansha district in South of Guangzhou (Logistical Centre)
Qianhai district of Shenzhen (HK duty-free)
EFTZ
Shanghai (2013) (HK Synergies), Fujian (2014) (Taiwan Economy) and Tianjin (1984) (Bohai Region)

Source: Author adapted from G. Insausti and http://beyondplanb.eu/projects/projec_deng_xiaoping_s_sezs.html. (accessed 11 October 2018).

China has been developing domestic (since 1979) and overseas (since 1999)[16] SEZs, with varying degrees of success, as part of two intertwined policies – 'open door' and 'going out' – contributing to China's 'going global' objective. By combining two elements of analysis, the 'location' and the 'differential role', we consider SEZs a vital element of the B&RI. Indeed, SEZs are established as domestic and overseas interfaces between the Chinese economy and overseas trade and investment dynamics, using domestic axes, international economic land corridors, maritime roads and immaterial flows to maximize their potential. Engman, Onodera, and Pinali, concluded that 'choice of location is critical for zone type EPZs'.[17] That is why the strategic location of SEZs in China and abroad is a result of a careful geopolitical and geo-economic analysis, as part of an integrated network of flows. They were designed with relevant trade locations in mind, along with the need to involve the Chinese neighbourhood strategy as part of the regional strategy. They are an important part of the global access strategy, as facilitators of domestic and international flows. The majority of China's SEZs are in the eastern and southern coastal regions, in locations served by several seaports, river piers, airports, railways, highways and complementary communication infrastructure. But, there similar arrangements in border remote areas with double functional value (as Urumqi): To curb domestic inequalities and to maximize transnational infrastructural usage. Likewise, the selection of their location took into consideration the domestic mobility and development axes as well as the possibilities offered by the SLOC, which since 2013 have been transformed into the MSR. In other words,

16. According to El-Rashidy, S, *The Role of China's Overseas Special Economic Zones in Economic Development*, 42–43 (PhD thesis, The American University in Cairo 2016), http://dar.aucegypt.edu/bitstream/handle/10526/4878/Thesis.Salah.El-Rashidy.Final.pdf?sequence=1 (accessed 2 January 2018), in 1999 China and Egypt signed an agreement to set up an economic zone in Suez. Later, in 2003, similar arrangements were put in place between China and Zambia. According to Bräutigam, D, *Chinese Development Aid in Africa: What, Where, Why, and How Much?* in *Rising China: Global Challenges and Opportunities* (Jane Golley & Ligang Song eds, ANU Press 2011), they are found in Algeria (Chinese Jiangling Economic and Trade Cooperation Zone, 2007) and Egypt (Tianjin TEDA Suez Economic and Trade Cooperation Zone, 2007), Ethiopia (Eastern/Orient Industrial Park, Jiangsu Qiyaan Investment, 2006), Mauritius (Tianli (now JinFei) Economic and Trade Cooperation Zone, 2006), Niger (Guangdong Ogun Economic and Trade Cooperation Zone, 2006 and Lekki Free Trade Zone, 2007), Zambia (Chambishi Nonferrous Metal Mining Group Industrial Park, 2006), Cambodia (Taihu International Economic Cooperation Zone, Sihanouk, 2006), Indonesia (Chinese Guangxi Economic and Trade Cooperation Zone, 2007), South Korea (The Saemangeum Gunsan Free Economic Zone, 2007), Thailand (Luoyong Industrial Zone, 2006), Vietnam (Chinese (Shenzhen) Economic and Trade Cooperation Zone, 2007 and Longjiang Economic and Trade Cooperation Zone, 2007), Pakistan (Haier-Ruba Home Appliance Industrial Zone, 2006), Mexico (Ningbo Geely Industrial Economic and Trade Cooperation Zone, 2007), Venezuela (Lacua Tech and Industrial Trade Zone, 2007), and the Russian Federation (St. Peterburg Baltic Economic and Trade Cooperation Zone, 2006 and Ussuriysk Economic and Trade Cooperation Zone, 2006 and Tomsk Siberia Industrial and Trade Cooperation Zone, 2007). Deborah and Xiaoyang stated, 'In 2006, Beijing initiated an overseas trade and cooperation zone program, assisting Chinese companies to invest abroad while also building China's soft power through the transfer of a key component of China's development success. Little is known about the 19 zones approved so far under this program, or the impact they are likely to have on structural transformation and industrial development in their host countries.' Bräutigam, D & Tang, Xiaoyang, *African Shenzhen: China's Special Economic Zones in Africa*, 49(1) The Journal of Modern African Studies 27 (2011).
17. Engman, M. et al., *Working Party of the Trade Committee – Export Processing Zones: Past and Future Role in Trade and Development*, 53 OECD Trade Policy Working Paper 52 (2017).

they combine regional integration with the extension of domestic axes beyond national borders projecting Chinese influence according to key strategic directions.

§8.04 WHAT IS AN ECONOMIC DEVELOPMENT CORRIDOR?

To answer this question, we must consider the innovative work of Charles Kunaka et al. who observed that, 'A corridor has three main categories of intertwined dimensions: infrastructure, services, and institutions for coordinating corridor activities ... In its most common configuration, a trade and transport corridor has an international gateway (for example, ports, airports, or a land border) at one end and a large metropolitan area or production cluster at the other.[18] These gateways usually provide an intramodal or intermodal transfer ... Additional gateways (for instance, regional airports or domestic seaports serving coastal or inland waterway corridors) may be located at an intermediate point in the corridor. Gateways are included as part of a corridor because their capacity and quality of service can affect the cost of international movements.' According to Brunner, 'Economic corridors are not mere transport connections along with which people and goods move'; rather, these corridors 'connect economic agents along a defined geography. They provide connection between economic nodes or hubs, usually centred on urban landscapes, in which many economic resources and actors are concentrated.[19] They link the supply and demand sides of markets. Economic corridors are integral to the economic fabric and the economic actors surrounding [them]. Economic corridors [do not generate] significant economic benefits in isolation, but rather they have to be analyzed as part of integrated economic networks, such as global and regional value chains and production networks.' Economic development corridors are geographically co-located sets of mechanisms to facilitate interaction between economic agents. It is also important to understand that they do not exist in isolation but have a regional development role, 'comprehended only in terms of the network effects that they induce'. Brunner further demonstrated that there is 'no standard picture of what economic corridor development is and what it can achieve. What economic corridors can achieve for regional economic integration depends first on what characteristics the specific existing economic networks in which the economic corridors are embedded personify, and second on which characteristics corridor development are intended to introduce or strengthen. Corridor characteristics interact dynamically to create patterns of regional economic development.' Mulenga proposed two important aspects of the concept of economic corridors: corridor characteristics and the different stages of corridor transformation. According to Mulenga, the general characteristics of economic corridors are: 'A smaller, defined geographic space, usually the area straddling a central transport artery such as a road, a rail line, or a canal; Bilateral rather than multilateral initiatives

18. Kunaka, C & Carruthers, R, *Trade and Transport Corridor Management Toolkit,* 16 (World Bank 2014), doi: 10.1596 /978-1-4648-0143-3.
19. Brunner, H-P, *What Is Economic Corridor Development and What Can It Achieve in Asia's Subregions?* 117 Asian Developing Bank Working Paper Series on Regional Economic Integration 9 (2013).

focusing on strategic nodes, particularly border crossings between two countries, principally to promote a sense of ownership; An emphasis on physically planning the corridor and its surrounding area, to concentrate infrastructure development and maximize benefits; and strong public-private partnerships, which promote sustainability.'[20] Again, the concept of an economic corridor seems to be associated to the idea of co-location of access infrastructure (to promote mobility), and trade facilitation mechanisms. Mulenga elaborated on the four stages of the development of an economic corridor: (1) the physical development;[21] (2) the logistics development;[22] (3) the economic and social development;[23] and (4) the integration of crosscutting issues.[24] Once again we observe the centrality of infrastructure at the very beginning of the physical development. Brunner, discussing the evaluation of economic corridors, observed: 'A comprehensive assessment of economic corridor performance over time for investment and policy decisions requires data along three parameters: (i) the geographic location-bound availability of economic resources, including human resources, natural resources, capital and financial resources, and physical resources such as infrastructure; (ii) movements over time of people, including their services, and goods (mobility of resources) – these movements have a time and economic cost dimension; and (iii) the developing relationships of economic resources over time and through space, and the changing density of their interactions, interaction reliability, and quality.'[25] Once again, it appears that the concept of economic development corridors rests on the co-location of infrastructure and resources designed to facilitate

---

20. Mulenga, G, *Developing Economic Corridors in Africa: Rationale for the Participation of the African Development Bank*, AfDB Regional Integration Brief, NEPAD, Regional Integration and Trade Department (2013).
21. This involves enhancing the physical facilities needed for efficient and effective transportation and trade by establishing and revamping transport links; improving the quality of infrastructure, increasing carrying capacity, and dealing with related safety issues; upgrading infrastructure associated with priorities such as rural agriculture, agroindustry, and tourism; encouraging multimodal structures; and upgrading border areas.
22. The right logistics can harmonize corridor policies, regulations and institutions, moving people and goods more efficiently and facilitating storage, warehousing, trucking, insurance and freight management, and related services. Good logistics also involve implementing cross-border trade agreements; simplifying, standardizing and harmonizing immigration and quarantine procedures; promoting information and communication technologies; and establishing logistics centres. Mulenga, G, *Developing Economic Corridors in Africa: Rationale for the Participation of the African Development Bank*, AfDB Regional Integration Brief, NEPAD, Regional Integration and Trade Department (2013).
23. This stage promotes investments in areas such as agroindustry and manufacturing, natural resource-based enterprises, small-scale industries, trade (including planned roadside shops), tourism (rest houses and hotels), schooling, and health facilities, all located near the corridor. Other interventions might include the promotion of innovative trade techniques such as fair trade products and investment forums, again close to the corridor. The economic and social development stage might also market business opportunities in key industries; establish special economic zones where appropriate; publicize investment policies, rules and regulations; offer micro-financing; adopt special measures for approving business licences efficiently and effectively; and address other infrastructural deficiencies, such as inadequate water and power.
24. This stage addresses environmental and institutional capacity concerns and other social issues.
25. Brunner, H-P, *What Is Economic Corridor Development and What Can It Achieve in Asia's Subregions?* 117 Asian Developing Bank Working Paper Series on Regional Economic Integration 17 (2013).

the creation of a trans-border trade network within a geographical area. It is usual to link this infrastructure to high-speed rail lines, power plants, highways, pipelines, logistics centres, industrial parks, bridges, airports, power lines, social infrastructures, seaports and cross-border economic zones.

Figure 8.2 has illustrated how the physical dimension of B&RI combines SEZs, economic corridors, transit corridors and development mobility axes. The following table establishes a parity between these four different elements of mobility.

Table 8.1 Parity Between the Four Elements of Mobility

<table>
<tr><th>Designation</th><th colspan="2">Dominant Characteristics</th><th>Other Characteristics</th></tr>
<tr><td>Special economic zones, including its different categories (SEZ)</td><td>The policy solutions in relation to legal and economic aspects are unique and constitute an exceptional ad hoc regime in relation to the national systems. They are national arrangements in their nature with an international purpose.</td><td rowspan="2">Concentrate infrastructure, services and institutions while using them as economic mechanisms.
Both are composed of a co-located sets of mechanisms to facilitate interaction between economic agents within a defined geography.
Both are part of an integrated economic network.</td><td>Transportation infrastructure is generally speaking not part of the SEZ, but they must be collocated in its vicinity. SEZ function as an interface-gateway between national and international economic agents.</td></tr>
<tr><td>Economic Development Corridors (EDC)</td><td rowspan="2">The policy solutions in relation to legal and economic aspects represent a tailor-made solution within the national systems. They are based on international arrangements. They are infrastructural interfaces of economic flows</td><td>Transportation structures are part of the set of arrangements belonging to an EC within a certain geographic zone. Generally speaking, a transportation artery is the initial central element to boost further colocation of infrastructures, namely the SEZs. They are international connectors and development inducers.</td></tr>
<tr><td>Transportation corridors or fast transit routes (TC/FTR)</td><td>They are designed to provide physical complementary or additional connectivity between markets and production centres. They may connect two or more ECs or connect two or more geographic zones.</td><td>They do not provide a link between networks of economic agents. Rather, they provide physical support to material flows of people and goods. Therefore, they induce cooperation in other economic areas, apart from transit infrastructures. They are connectors in nature.</td></tr>
</table>

Designation	*Dominant Characteristics*		*Other Characteristics*
Development mobility axes (DMA)	Is a national arrangement in its nature, and represents a sort of priority of regional national investments, according to a central plan. They do not have special economic arrangements constituting ad hoc regimes.	They are designed to provide physical connectivity between national production centres, economic hubs and markets. They are inducers of co-location development structures.	They are driven by a rationale of transportation structures as facilitators of co-location of economic assets as they are the result of national regional integration plans. They are national connectors and development inducers.

Both SEZs and economic development corridors depend on the existence of 'transport infrastructure' and both provide effective links between economic agents within a defined geography. Both are composed of co-located sets of mechanisms to facilitate interaction between economic agents within a defined geography. Both are part of integrated economic networks. By their nature transportation corridors or FTR, and development mobility axes are connecting infrastructure, capable of indirectly inducing co-location of development assets. Economic development corridors are collocated elements of connectivity between economic agents, within the rationale of B&RI. They contribute to its global reach as an access strategy and they channel investments according to its perceived geo-economic value. However, the fast-transit routes seemed to be simple connectors, inducing cooperation between economic corridors.

§8.05 WHY DOES THE BBSP TRANSIT ROUTE MATTER?

Literature on economic corridors is easy to find, while research on transportation corridors (or fast-transit routes) is uncommon. From the strategic viewpoint of China, the positioning of the B&RI land and maritime corridors has vested three European areas with vital importance: Arctic corridor, Belarus-Poland and Greece-Serbia-Hungary. In light of this, we note the increased geopolitical importance of the Budapest-Belgrade-Skopje-Piraeus (BBSP) transit route (in Figure 8.4, the BBSP general location is encircled), because this route closes the loop formed by the New Eurasian Land Bridge (NELB), the China-Central West Asia Economic Corridor (CCWAEC), and the MSR. All three connect the centre of Europe with the Chinese heartland, and are in turn connected to each other by the BBSP. The geopolitical significance of the BBSP lies in its ability to bridge land and maritime economic corridors, to facilitate trade between the Euro-zone, Europe and China, and to increase flexibility between continental and maritime transportation flows (Figure 8.4).

The Budapest (Hungary)-Belgrade (Serbia)-Skopje (Macedonia)-Piraeus (Greece) transportation corridor[26] (BBSP) connects the NELB, running from Urumqi through

Figure 8.4 The NELB, the CCWAEC and the MSR

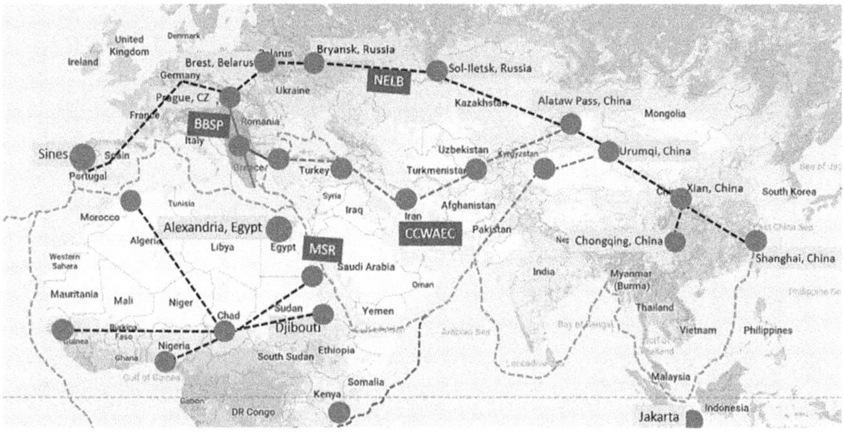

Source: Author based on Google Maps.

Eurasia in the direction of Brest (Belarus), and the MSR, running from China's southern coastal areas to the Red Sea and entering the Mediterranean Sea via the Suez Canal. Through either the Suez Canal or the Strait of Gibraltar, the SLOC are designed to reach major seaports in the Mediterranean Sea, such as Piraeus and Thessaloniki (Greece), Marseille (France), Benghazi (Libya), Tunis (Tunisia), Livorno and Venice (Italy) and Barcelona (Spain). The BBSP closes off the loop formed by the NELB, CCWAEC and MSR, connecting the Chinese heartland to central Europe by land and sea, and facilitating land access to one of the most productive regions in Europe.

The idea of the BBSP corridor is to create a land-sea express passage composed of a high-speed rail line along with special arrangements concluded through customs clearance treaties, trade and investment facilitation settlements, free trade agreements and FDIs (Figure 8.5).

26. Defining a trade axis in both directions: South of Germany, Prague (CZ), Bratislava (SK), Budapest (HU), Belgrade (RS), Prĭstina (XK), Skopje (MK), Thessalonica or Piraeus (GR).

Figure 8.5 The BBSP

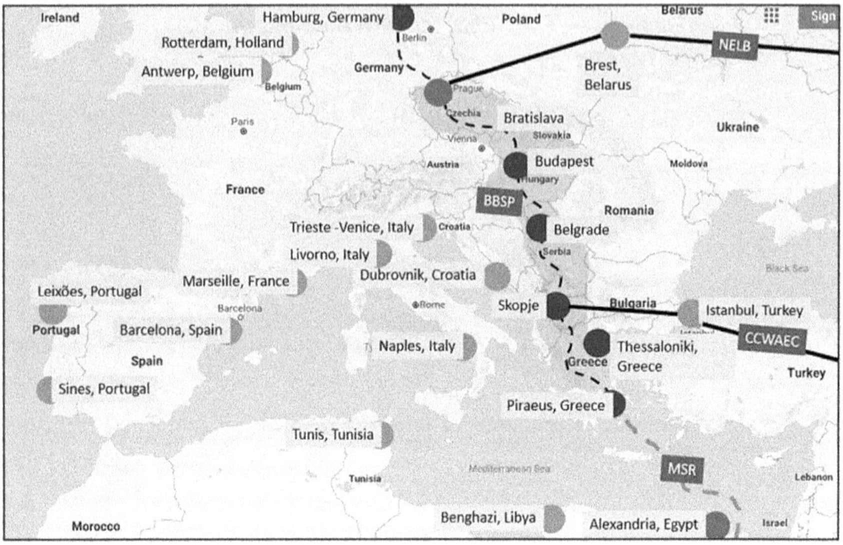

Source: Author based on Google Maps.

This corresponds to the idea of a transportation corridor or fast transit route designed to provide additional transport connectivity. At this moment this project neither includes other collocated development elements, nor any special economic or legal measures to facilitate the economic integration of local agents. However, as we shall see, due to ongoing partnerships between Hungary and Serbia, other development projects are being executed, though they are not directly related to the BBSP. The BBSP has the potential to further develop trade flows between China and the EU, taking into account the fact that China is already the EU's largest trading partner. In addition, the BBSP would advance the development of the so-called Central and Eastern European Countries (CEEC)[27] at the regional logistics level, to link the Mediterranean Sea and the Danube River, and to take advantage of the benefits of any future enlargement of the Suez Canal. Apart from the Volga, the Danube is the longest river in Europe, and flows eastwards across ten countries for 2,850 km. Access to the Danube River facilitates access to Germany, Austria, Hungry, Slovakia, Serbia, Croatia, Romania, Bulgaria, Ukraine and Moldova, and represents a complementary shipping route to the Black Sea as an alternative to the SLOC crossing the Dardanelles Strait, the Sea of Marmara and the Bosporus Strait.

27. OECD Glossary of Statistical Terms (2001): 'Central and Eastern European Countries (CEECs) is an OECD term for the group of countries comprising Albania, Bulgaria, Croatia, the Czech Republic, Hungary, Poland, Romania, the Slovak Republic, Slovenia, and the three Baltic States: Estonia, Latvia and Lithuania – Directorate, OECD Statistics'.

However, the importance of access to the Danube River has further implications. Germany completed the Rhine-Main-Danube Canal in Bavaria in 1992, and its 171 km connect the Main and Rhine rivers. The Main River is the longest right tributary of the Rhine River, so the Rhine-Main-Danube Canal makes it possible to navigate from Rotterdam (in the Netherlands) to the Danube Delta in south-eastern Romania and south-western Ukraine (or Constanța (Romania), through the Danube-Black Sea Canal). In fact, the Rhine-Main-Danube Canal and the BBSP corridor together connect not only the North Sea and Atlantic Ocean to the Black Sea, but they also connect the major European cities. For B&RI, this represents simple and easy access to the major European markets and production centres. Put simply, the BBSP combined with access to the Danube and Rhine is probably one of the spearheads of the access strategy which makes possible the B&RI corridors connecting the Xinjiang autonomous province in China and the Chinese coastal zones to the very centre of Europe. The BBSP completes the sea-land access between the Chinese production-consumption centre of gravity, to the European production-consumption centre of gravity. The BBSP is the currently missing link between two of the most important production-consumption centres of gravity in the world.

The BBSP further complements the Bratislava-Belgrade-Skopje-Sofia-Istanbul-Ankara corridor that runs into Turkey as an extension of the CCWAEC (Figure 8.6). The CCWAEC, which links China and the Arabian Peninsula, could be extended to Europe by the BBSP. The CCWAEC runs from Xinjiang (Urumqi) across Central Asia before reaching the Persian Gulf, Arabian Peninsula and Mediterranean Sea. It crosses Central Asian countries such as Kazakhstan, Kyrgyzstan, Tajikistan, Uzbekistan and Turkmenistan, and countries and regions in West Asia, including Iran, Saudi Arab, Syria and Turkey. In Turkey, the CCWAEC also connects to maritime sea routes across the Black Sea to Odessa (Ukraine), Constanța (Romania), and Varna and Burgas (Bulgaria). In Iran the CCWAEC also connects to maritime sea routes across the Caspian Sea. This region is also a pivotal area in the CCWAEC, and therefore vital to OBOR, which envisions a route connecting Asia, Europe and the rest of the world. Iran is also important because of its geopolitical link in the CCWAEC to the Persian Gulf and the river Shatt al-Arab. From this perspective, BBSP is a link that makes sense of an entire network of economic corridors.

Figure 8.6 The China-Central and West Asia Economic Corridor

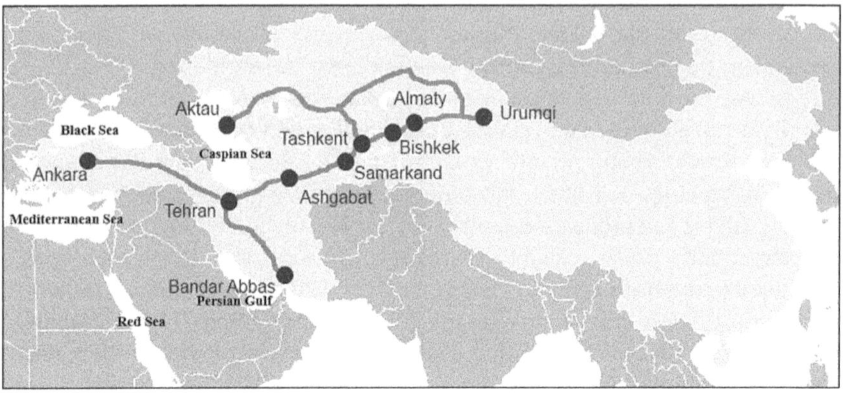

Source: http://www.oborerope.com/en/beltandroad/one-belt/.

The BBSP is designed to link the supply and demand sides of markets, decrease the travel time between the Serbian and Hungarian capitals from eight to three hours, and facilitate the movement of goods from the Greek port of Piraeus into the heart of Europe. Generally speaking, waterways are the cheapest means of transportation. Both railway and road (land transportation) are four times more expensive than waterways, and air freight is four times more expensive than land transportation. 'Simply put, air freight comes with a hefty price tag. Comparing air and ocean freight, a medium size 2,000 lbs box from Shenzhen, China, to New York, USA, can cost $1,200 by ocean but a whopping $4,000 by air.'[28] This matters for any sort of access strategy, and therefore to B&RI which relies mainly in shipping and rail freight. However, the BBSP should not be mistaken for just another economic corridor, similar to NELB, in which the co-location of infrastructures and resources is designed to facilitate the creation of a trade trans-border network within a particular geographical area. Normally speaking, in an economic corridor, the physical network, with a central transport artery, is complemented by a number of different arrangements, including customs clearance treaties, promotion of two-way investments, trade and investment facilitation settlements, free trade agreements and FDIs, bilateral visa agreements, transportation agreements and standardized technical memorandums, SEZs, tax exemptions, special tax regimes, dispute settlement mechanisms, and technical handling agreements. In the case of the BBSP fast transit route, we are talking about a land-sea express passage composed of a high-speed railway line (the central infrastructure) but not, at least for the time being, a geographically co-located set of mechanisms to facilitate the interaction between economic agents as part of a cross-border network. It would be difficult

28. https://www.freightos.com/portfolio-items/air-freight-rates-cost-prices/ (accessed 27 January 2018). Leandro, F J, *Steps of Greatness: Geopolitics of OBOR*, (Postdoctoral report, University of Saint Macau 2018).

to facilitate a land-sea express passage since Greece and Hungary are EU Member States, but Serbia and Macedonia[29] are not.

Sea-land connectivity requires deep water seaports, so the importance of Piraeus has grown in the context of B&RI. The Hong Kong Chinese Ocean Shipping Company (COSCO) purchased a thirty-five-year concession to upgrade and run two container cargo piers and transform Piraeus into a regional hub for sea trade with Europe. The poor performance of the Greek economy has made Greece a valuable partner for China. The importance of the Greek commercial fleet and the opportunities offered by the Chinese shipyards, especially the state-owned company Fujian Shipbuilding Trade Company, are also worth mentioning.

§8.06 WHICH ARE THE LEADING BBSP ACTORS?

The Chinese corporation COSCO has been operating the Greek container port at Piraeus since 2008, and in 2017 it acquired 67% of the port's shares. Piraeus is no longer a sleepy and unproductive port; it has been transformed into a promising investment whose success also very much depends on its land connectivity. The acquisition of the Port of Piraeus is an important step within the B&R strategy, but it is not a single-move strategy. Piraeus needs the BBSP as much as the BBSP needs Piraeus. Indeed, the objective is to transform the Port of Piraeus into the largest port of the Mediterranean region by 2020, using the synergies which will result from the Chinese development of other seaports along the MSR, namely in Sri Lanka (Hambantota), Pakistan (Gwadar), Myanmar (Sittwe and Kyaukphyu), Djibouti (Doraleh), Bangladesh (Chittagong), Kenya (Mombasa), Tanzania (Mtwara) and Mozambique (Beira).

29. Macedonia has been a candidate for accession to the European Union since 2005 but has not yet entered into accession negotiations.

Figure 8.7 The BBSP and the Rhine and Danube Rivers

The Rhine-Main-Danube Canal as a crucial axis of the European Productive Triangle

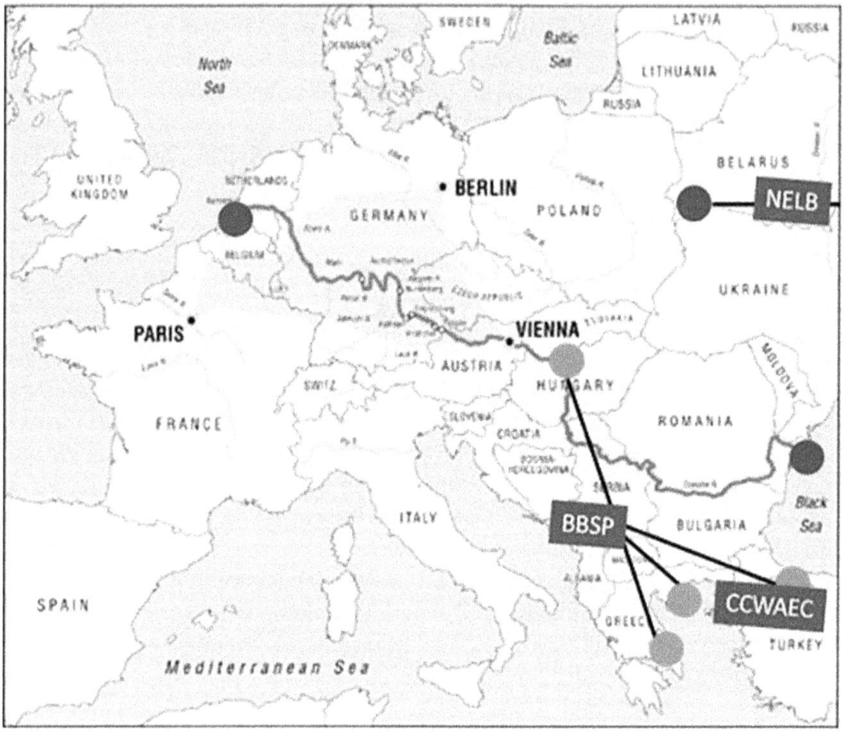

Source: http://www.schillerinstitute.org/economy/maps/maps3.html.

The great quantity of world trade carried by the shipping industry explains why the port of Piraeus, and perhaps also Thessaloniki, fits into this system of maritime and land corridors. This is extremely important, because Piraeus-Thessaloniki makes sense of the BBSP, allowing it to connect the maritime and continental sections of the Silk Road.

The geopolitical features of landlocked European states, such as Hungary and Serbia, are particularly interesting. These two countries are located between the Black Sea and Adriatic Sea, between the Carpathian Mountains and the Dinaric Alps. Their functional advantage lies in the fact that they are both rotational platforms for goods transported either by railway or waterway. In Belgrade, two important international rivers (the Danube-Tisza and the Sava) facilitate the regional exchange of goods and services, combining their potential with a high-speed rail line, Belgrade-Budapest and Belgrade-Skopje. According to Dimitrijević, 'China is a very good economic partner of

Serbia in Asia and one of the major pillars of Serbia's foreign policy.'[30] Dimitrijević further adds that 'Serbia is one of China's key partners in the region of Southern and Eastern Europe. China primarily sees Southern and Eastern Europe in terms of economic integration with the EU as a common market of high purchasing power and therefore an ideal space for the placement of its own products. In this regard, it is important to note that China supports Serbia's aspirations for full accession to the EU, without prejudice to its vital national interests.' The Sino-Serbian strategic partnership, established in 2009 and reinforced in 2013 with a joint statement signed by the Serbian Head of State Tomislav Nikolić and Chinese President Xi Jinping, is the visible face of the joint interests shared by Serbia and China. Serbia also established a strategic partnership with the Russian Federation in 2013. It must be borne in mind that China has always expressed diplomatic proximity to the Serbian Government in relation to the Kosovo affair, and that fact facilitates the development of bilateral relations in different areas. Therefore, railways are not the only infrastructure at the centre of the Sino-Serbian relations, but all infrastructure are to a certain extent related to the access strategy. Extraordinary loans, new bridges, new highways,[31] airport cooperation, power plant restructuring, telecommunications and national power grid development are sound examples of this promising cooperation. According to Teokarevic, 'Serbia desperately needs China's capital and know-how to improve its infrastructure.[32] There are two main reasons for this: a very poor transport and energy infrastructure that has not been properly renovated for decades, and the lack of necessary investment in this area by its other main partners, the EU and Russia.' Serbia's three key partners appear to be the EU (trade partner), the Russian Federation (trade partner) and the People's Republic of China (political partner). Teokarevic also observed that 'the "special relations" with Russia and China have great importance for a small country like Serbia, which has managed, unlike its neighbours in the region, to become a strategic partner of two big and powerful countries.[33] In times of economic crisis, diversification of

30. China occupies an important place in Serbia's strategic foreign policy. The strategy is designed on four pillars of foreign policy. The first pillar is the European Union of which Serbia would like to become a member. The second pillar is Russia as a rising power in world politics and Serbia's historical partner. The third pillar is the United States, as a great power with whom Serbia has had fluctuating relations in the past, but whom Serbia has accepted as a reality in terms of its importance and influence in international relations. The fourth important pillar of Serbia's foreign policy strategy is China as a global economic power and the traditionally good friend of Serbia in international relations (Dimitrijević, D, *Chinese Investments in Serbia – A Joint Pledge for the Future of the New Silk Road*, 7(1) Baltic Journal of European Studies 328 (2017).
31. 'The Serbian infrastructure minister Zorana Mihajlovic signed in Beijing two memoranda of understanding (MoU) with China Road and Bridge Corporation (CRBC) for infrastructure works with a combined value of 2.5 billion euro. The contracts are for the construction of the Preljina-Pozega and Pozega-Boljare stretches of a motorway which will connect Belgrade to the border with Montenegro, and Fruskogorski Corridor, a 123 km-long road in Serbia's Vojvodina autonomous province' (June 2017) https://seenews.com/news/chinas-infrastructure-investments-in-serbia-reach-55-bln-euro-serbian-govt-572427 (accessed 10 May 2018).
32. Teokarevic, J, *Serbia: Perspectives on Eurasian Integration*, European Council on Foreign Relations (2016), http://www.ecfr.eu/article/essay_eurasian_integration_serbia (accessed 2 April 2018).
33. Teokarevic, J, *Serbia: Perspectives on Eurasian Integration*, European Council on Foreign Relations (2016), http://www.ecfr.eu/article/essay_eurasian_integration_serbia (accessed 2 May 2018).

economic cooperation is essential, and Serbia feels that its relationship with Russia and China is a move in the right direction.' Sino-Serbian bilateral ties are likely to develop even further in the next decade, expanding to other areas of cooperation, including defence and security.

Figure 8.8 The Serbian Platform

Source: https://depositphotos.com/83815153/stock-illustration-serbia-political-map.html.

Improving relations between China and Hungary have resulted in a significant increase in Hungarian trade sales to China. Hungary and China signed a memorandum of understanding over the B&RI in 2015. In 2017, both countries established a comprehensive strategic partnership. Moreover, Hungary was the first European country to establish the Belt and Road working group with China. Hungary has actively participated in the China-CEE Investment Cooperation Fund. Budapest is located not far from the heart of EU, the German markets and the industrial centres in Poland, and Hungary has land borders with seven countries: Austria, Slovakia, Romania, Ukraine, Serbia, Croatia and Slovenia. Moreover, the quadrilateral perspective comprising Budapest, Bratislava, Vienna and Zagreb offers a viable logistics platform, considering the challenges of their mountainous terrain. The Budapest-Belgrade plain is surrounded by the Alps, the Balkan Mountains and the Carpathian Mountains, which are the last obstacle to accessing the northern European plain were Germany and Poland are located. The 350 km high-speed rail line from Belgrade to Budapest (184 km on the Serbian side and 166 km on the Hungarian side) has no other route option because of the geography and the distribution of markets and production centres. This high-speed rail line is to be connected to the China-run Piraeus port in Greece, maximizing the full potential of the BBSP. The Hungarian plain is a natural access corridor from the Mediterranean Sea to northern Europe. Bearing in mind the landlocked position of Hungary (and Serbia), and recalling the words of Eszterhai that 'it is the interest of the CEE Region and Hungary that the OBOR [one belt one road] connects rather than separates the EU and China, in which the CEEC fulfil the role of some kind of a bridge', their geopolitical role in the context of B&RI is expected to be that of an articulated land platform for access to markets and production centres, working in both directions – in and out.[34]

Matolcsy[35] explained why Hungary is a key country in the context of B&RI: 'We are close to the heart of the EU, the German market and a Central European economic hub is really evolving, as Poland is considered one in the north. The Central Bank of Hungary has already taken the first steps on the Silk Road. We established effective cooperation with one of the largest financial institutions of the world, the Bank of China. After the United Kingdom, we were second to sign an agreement with the People's Bank of China – China's central bank – and since then we have been using a lot of creative, innovative instruments within this framework. We want to understand what steps they take and why, and we want to take part in this process.' In relation to Hungary, the success of the Hungarian section of the BBSP railway is vital, as it will be the first time that Chinese corporations have built a railway within EU territory. This could set a precedent in relation to future infrastructural developments with Chinese participation in the EU. According to Nikolić, the CEEC geographic position and market capacities represented important 'regional potential' for the implementation of the

34. Eszterhai, V, *The One Belt One Road from Germany's Perspective* (2017), http://www.geopolitika.hu/en/2017/08/15/the-one-belt-one-road-from-germanys-perspective/ (accessed 2 January 2017).
35. Governor, Central Bank of Hungary, http://www.geopolitika.hu/en/2017/03/20/hungary-a-key-state-on-the-silk-road/ (accessed 2 May 2018). Matolcsy, G, *Hungary – A Key State on the Silk Road* (Opening Presentation Delivered at the 54th Annual Meeting of Economists, 15 September 2016), http://www.geopolitika.hu/en/2017/03/20/hungary-a-key-state-on-the-silk-road/ (accessed 2 May 2018).

'One Belt, One Road' initiative.[36] These countries already enjoy good political relations with China, they enjoy mutual trust and practical cooperation.[37] The agreements signed in Bucharest in 2013 at the meeting between China and the CEEC (16 + 1) are the rational result of a geopolitical analysis. In spite of the concerns raised by the EU in relation to Hungary, in light of potential infringements of the EU's public tender requirements for large-scale infrastructure projects, we all recognize that the BBSP is vital for the Serbia-Hungary axis. Thus, we believe that participation in the BBSP requires a common strategy towards B&RI, since it is an unavoidable initiative for Hungary, Serbia and the EU.

§8.07 CONCLUSION

We believe it is time to pay more attention to all issues involving China. It is time to write more, debate more and study more all issues related to China. B&RI is becoming increasingly important at regional, interregional and global levels, and it deserves greater attention, especially in the areas involving European states. Sooner or later, if it has not already, B&RI will impact European economies. B&RI has the potential to connect not only Chinese and European markets and production centres, but also to bring together the EU, Central Eastern European Countries, China, the Association of southeast Asian Nations, the Eurasian Economic Union and perhaps other economic communities in Africa and South America.

B&RI, as a global access strategy, combines domestic SEZ 'differentials' with development and mobility axes which, when extended beyond national borders as economic land corridors, acquire a neighbourhood and an interregional dimension. From a geo-political perspective, SEZs are synergetic and exceptional 'interface-gateways' between economic agents, co-localized in different economic and legal orders, using economic and transit corridors to facilitate and promote flows of exchange. Economic land corridors combined with the maritime road extend the reach of B&RI even further to take on a global dimension. Economic development corridors, development mobility axes, fast transit corridors and SEZs are made more effective by a network of immaterial flows covering a wide range of areas such as air transportation, capital transfers, cyber and space infrastructure, and cultural domains. Economic corridors and development axes take on an economic function and fast transit corridors exercise a functional power, which depends on previously defined economic functions and certain key locations, as in the case of the BBSP. Both economic development corridors and fast transit corridors depend on comprehensive international solutions (economic and legal), bilaterally or multilaterally negotiated between China and economically integrated areas such as the EU.

36. Nikolić, M, *Central Eastern European Countries and Serbian Perspective and Position Towards Chinese One Belt One Road Initiative – A Geopolitical Overview* (2017), http://www.16plus1-thinktank.com/1/20170830/1496.html (accessed 2 February 2018).
37. Mechanism for China-CEEC cooperation (China + 16) was established in Warsaw (Poland) in 2012 as a framework to facilitate growing cooperation in the areas of energy infrastructure, agriculture, science, education, culture and tourism, as well as faster construction of 'Silk Road Economic Belt'.

The steps taken by Hungary and Serbia towards the BBSP are governed by the perceived best interests of both landlocked states, and they are deeply related to their geo-location. Chinese interest in the BBSP fast transport route is natural, based on careful geopolitical analysis. Moreover, the BBSP is one brick belonging to the greater wall of B&RI, which is a global access strategy aiming to establish a network of corridors connecting production centres and markets. The BBSP is definitely intended to interconnect the continental and MSRs within the rationale of B&RI, but it cannot, for the time being, be considered an additional economic corridor. The BBSP is the convergence segment between the NELB, the CCWAEC and the MSR, the platform that maximizes the true potential of B&RI in Western and Central Europe. The BBSP is particularly decisive for landlocked economies such as Hungary and Serbia. Interestingly, Serbia is located right in the heart of this geographic triangle. Both countries need a common strategy to deal with the opportunities offered by B&RI, though Hungary is an EU and NATO Member State, while Serbia is not. The BBSP is also important to the EU and to all its members' states, but EU must put forward a common strategy that seeks opportunities to maximize mutual benefits. The EU, and in particular the Central and Eastern European states, are geographically bound to be part of B&RI, since the Greek port of Piraeus is a vital location serving both European and Chinese interests. Hungarian and Serbian options depend very much on the cooperation between them, on EU support, and less on their ability to bilaterally negotiate advantageous asymmetric trade and infrastructural arrangements. The disputes between Serbia and Hungary over Vojvodina 'Hungarian-populated' areas, the territorial disputes between Hungary and Slovakia, the statute of Kosovo, and the differences between Hungary and the EU over the refugee crisis do not help. Hungarian minorities in Serbia and the status of Kosovo are vital conflicts preventing the realization of national interests such as the accession of Serbia and Kosovo to the EU. Such divisive matters increase the challenges for both sides, and could prevent further international investments. However, the geopolitical narrative is wider than Serbia and Hungary; the role of China in Central and Eastern Europe is at stake. For Hungary, the BBSP could provide an infrastructural anchor to complement EU membership and give the Hungarian people new hope in terms of economic welfare. For Serbia, the BBSP is one of the core strategic options tending towards a new proximity to the Eurasian Economic Union, the Shanghai Cooperation Organization and its strategic partner, China. The BBSP represents an opportunity to put Central and Eastern Europe back onto the geopolitical map advancing common instruments of free trade. The BBSP transit route also has the potential to exercise a functional power, bringing together Greece, Macedonia, Serbia and Hungary in a win-win solution for all. In the case of Hungary and Serbia, the BBSP has induced other forms of cooperation and so initiated other projects. Transit routes or transport corridors might not have the ability to induce economic gains 'tout court', unlike SEZs or economic corridors, but in the case of BBSP it has a particular strategic economic importance if one considers the geopolitical big picture and the B&RI economic infrastructural network. The BBSP is important for China, for the EU and for the CEEC.

B&RI is based on connectivity elements within a network of economic agents, such as SEZs (and similar arrangements), EDC, FTR, economic development axes, and

China's Special Administrative Regions. All these elements are worth of geopolitical or geo-economic value. These connectivity elements and their correspondent economic agents, are transnational in that their nature, as its basic function locates them in one legal-economic order and calls for a permanent contact with different legal and economic orders. Therefore, this fact displays a major challenge in terms of their effective regulation, as they are located across the globe in states with 'alien' economic and legal orders. Moreover, the elements of connectivity, despite of their general function as 'differential' or 'interface-gateways' they deliver different contributions (as the case of BBSP demonstrates), they are required to operate in an exceptional framework in relation to their domestic 'environment', and they are supposed to be synergetic domestically and internationally. In our view, B&RI challenges the global regulatory trend with a call for minimal and multiple levels of voluntary economic integration and recognized standards of legal compatibility, capable of advancing free trade.

B&RI is a global access strategy combining different elements of mobility- and interface-gateways to integrate economic flows, with some degree of institutionalization. According to the Chinese way of doing business, the best deal is the one that maximizes the benefits to both parties. As the Chinese saying goes, only when all contribute with firewood can they build up a strong fire (众人拾柴火焰高). The BBSP, the Chinese Balkans corridor, the B&RI for Western Balkans fills a geopolitical void, which has the potential to negatively impact Serbia's accession to the EU or to reinforce the EU periphery with stronger links. Along these lines, B&RI will likely expand to other areas of cooperation depending on the success of the BBSP implementation. Therefore, the construction of the BBSP may be an opportunity for China and the EU. One way or another, the BBSP will be a milestone Chinese project requiring a response from Brussels, the likely result of which will be a 'rapprochement' between two leading commercial blocs: the EU and People's Republic of China.

CHAPTER 9

Special Economic Zones and the Perpetual Pluralism of Global Trade and Labor Migration

*Stephen Kim Park**

§9.01 INTRODUCTION

The international movement of people has been marked, ironically, by its stasis. In comparison to cross-border flows of goods, services, and capital, global migration is relatively small. Since World War II, the average annual growth rate in the trade of goods by volume has exceeded 5%, while the average annual growth rate of immigrants worldwide has been less than 2%, effectively equal to the corresponding growth rate of the world's population.[1] Countries are reluctant to create international legal institutions because of deeply rooted concerns about the impact of migration on national identity,[2] burdens on the social welfare

* This chapter is a revised and updated version of an article initially published by the author as Stephen Kim Park, *Special Economic Zones and the Perpetual Pluralism of Global Trade and Labor Migration*, 47 Georgetown J. Intl. L. 1379 (2016).

1. *See* Michael Trebilcock, Robert Howse & Antonia Eliason, *The Regulation of International Trade* 611 (3d ed. Routledge, 2005); UN, Dept. Econ. & Soc. Affairs: Population Division, *International Migration Report 2013*, UN Doc. ST/ESA/SER.A/346 (2013), http://www.un.org/en/development/desa/population/publications/pdf/migration/migrationreport2013/Full_Document_final.pdf (noting the relatively small share of international migrants as compared to world population and the lack of growth in North-South migration in the past twenty-five years).
2. *See* Jennifer Gordon, *People Are Not Bananas: How Immigration Differs from Trade*, 14 Nw. U. L. Rev. 1109, 1132–33 (2010). As Jennifer Gordon observes, migrants "put down roots, meet partners, have children, send for family members left behind, and create networks that change recruitment patterns for the jobs where they work". *Ibid.*, at 1132; *see also* Jagdeep S. Bhandari, *International Migration and Trade: A Multi-Disciplinary Synthesis*, 6 Rich. J. Global L. & Bus. 113, 174 (2006) (noting the wide-ranging implications of migration for cultural, linguistic, spatial, and socio-political assimilation).

state,[3] the so-called brain drain resulting from the emigration of highly skilled professionals from developing countries to wealthier developed countries,[4] and national security.[5] Perhaps most importantly, distrust and opposition to migration stem from protectionist sentiments in domestic labor markets and fears of foreign competition from migrants, whether permanent residents or temporary labor.[6]

As a result, international treaties and international organizations devoted to migration are largely ineffectual.[7] This global institutional vacuum comes at a significant cost. As the European migration crisis shows, countries may be increasingly ill-equipped to deal with migrant flows that threaten to overwhelm border controls and domestic political systems.[8] Less obviously, but just as importantly, the status quo fails to leverage the ability of international economic law to govern labor migration—i.e., the movement of people who leave their home country and re-locate to another country for employment and related economic reasons. Goods and services—along with the companies that build, provide, and sell them—move across national borders at a speed and magnitude never seen before in history. This free movement is enabled by a web of international legal rules and institutions, including the World Trade Organization (WTO), that comprise the global trade regime.[9] However, despite evidence that trade and labor migration directly affect each other,[10] international law largely treats them as

3. *See* Alan O. Sykes, *International Cooperation on Migration: Theory and Practice*, 80 U. Chi. L. Rev. 315, 319 (2013) (referring to negative externalities associated with welfare migration).
4. *See* Peter Stalker, *Workers Without Frontiers: The Impact of Globalization on International Migration* 107–08 (Lynne Rienner 2000); *see generally* Fernando R. Tesón, *Brain Drain*, 45 San Diego L. Rev. 899 (2008).
5. *See*, e.g., Rick Lyman & Alison Smale, *Attacks Change Europe's Migrant Focus From Compassion to Security*, N.Y. Times, Nov. 15, 2015, at A11 (describing tightening border controls in the EU following the Paris terrorist attacks in November 2015).
6. *See* Trebilcock, Howse & Eliason, *supra* note 1, at 614–16 (summarizing empirical research on the effects of immigration on native workers); Gordon, *supra* note 2, at 1110–11 (noting that most of the economic benefits from migration go to source countries and migrants themselves); Lori G. Kletzer, *Trade and Immigration: Implications for the U.S. Labor Market*, in *A Future of Good Jobs? America's Challenge in the Global Economy* 123–25, 132–38 (Timothy J. Bartik & Susan N. Houseman eds., Upjohn Inst. For Empl. Research 2008) (critiquing the impact of immigration on higher-skilled native workers).
7. *See* Martin Ruhs, *The Price of Rights: Regulating International Labor Migration* 22–23 (Princeton U. Press 2015) (noting the low levels of ratification of the International Convention on the Protection of the Rights of All Migrant Workers and Members of Their Families and related international treaties); *see also ibid.*, at 194 (characterizing the International Organization for Migration as a "service agency"); Vincent Chetail, *The Transnational Movement of Persons under General International Law: Mapping the Customary Law Foundations of International Migration Law*, in *Research Handbook on International Law and Migration* 1, 2 (Vincent Chetail & Céline Bauloz eds., Edward Elgar Publishing Limited, 2014) (describing international migration law as "poorly conceptualized").
8. *See*, e.g., BBC News, *Migrant Crisis: EU at Grave Risk, Warns France PM Valls*, http://www.bbc.com/news/world-europe-35375303 (Jan. 22, 2016) (warning that European countries were at risk of being "totally destabilised").
9. *See* Final Act Embodying the Results of the Uruguay Round of Multilateral Trade Negotiations, Apr. 15, 1994, 1867 U.N.T.S. 14, 33 I.L.M. 1125, 1143 (1994) (establishing the WTO).
10. *See*, e.g., Stalker, *supra* note 4, at 47–51 (describing the impact of trade liberalization on immigration flows); Phillip Martin, *Migration and Development: Toward Sustainable Solutions*, 15 Willamette J. Intl. L. & Dis. Res. 182, 212–15 (2007) (describing how trade and migration can be complements due to factor productivity differences and other macroeconomic factors).

separate at best, and antagonistic at worst.[11] While firms benefit from cross-border freedoms as producers—and people as consumers enjoy the fruits of such freedoms in the form of lower prices and greater variety—the regulation of people as workers is generally confined within national borders.[12] National values, national strategic objectives, and national regulatory systems remain paramount in the governance of migration.[13] Control over migration remains the last bastion of the sovereign state, and governments are loathe to willingly cede this power.[14]

As a result, the legal and institutional levers of the global trade regime as a potential means to govern labor migration are under-used, thereby leaving the potential synergies between trade and labor essentially untapped.[15] Instead, the relationship between cross-border trade and labor migration is governed by various competing and overlapping sources of jurisdictional authority. The legal frameworks that constitute this global trade-labor migration nexus are ad hoc, decentralized, and pluralistic. Trade disciplines in the global trade-labor migration nexus include Mode 4 of the General Agreement on Trade in Services (GATS)[16] and temporary business visa systems incorporated in free trade agreements (FTAs) such as the North American Free Trade Agreement (NAFTA).[17] International coordination on migration that is partly in response to trade—most notably, bilateral migration agreements (BMAs)—also fall in this category.[18] All of these frameworks predominantly rely on temporary migration and are conditional on the achievement of national macroeconomic policy objectives, rather than broad-based liberalization of migration per se.

---

11. *See* Ian Goldin, Geoffrey Cameron & Meera Balarajan, *Exceptional People: How Migration Shaped Our World and Will Define Our Future* 215–18 (Princeton U. Press 2011) (contrasting the rules-based system for cross-border trade and calling migratory flows the "orphan of the international system").
12. *See* Howard F. Chang, *Migration as International Trade: The Economic Gains from the Liberalized Movement of Labor*, 3 UCLA J. Intl. L. & For. Affairs 371, 411–12 (1998) (equating trade protectionism and labor protectionism).
13. *See* Christopher W. Rudolph, *Globalization, Sovereignty and Migration: A Conceptual Framework*, 3 UCLA J. Intl. L. & For. Affairs 325, 354–55 (1998) (concluding that state sovereignty will continue to be a preeminent factor in migration governance, albeit subject to the countervailing forces of globalization).
14. *Ibid.*, at 327 (citing economist Nigel Harris); *see also* Chetail, *supra* note 7, at 27 (characterizing the right of states to regulate the entry of non-citizens as a "well-established principle" under public international law).
15. *See* The Economist, *Putting Up Barriers*, http://www.economist.com/news/briefing/21690065-permanent-reintroduction-border-controls-would-harm-trade-europe-putting-up-barriers (6 Feb. 2016) (explaining how the re-imposition of national border controls within Europe would reduce cross-border employment opportunities and harm European export-based businesses).
16. The WTO provides for limited global labor migration under Mode 4 of GATS. *See* General Agreement on Trade in Services, Marrakesh Agreement Establishing the World Trade Organization, Annex 1B, 1869 U.N.T.S. 183, *reprinted in* 33 I.L.M. 1167 (1994).
17. NAFTA includes commitments from the United States, Mexico, and Canada to permit the temporary migration of certain classes of business persons. *See* North American Free Trade Agreement, Art. 1608 (Dec. 17, 1992), 32 I.L.M. 289 (1993) [hereinafter NAFTA].
18. BMAs do not expressly link migration liberalization with trade liberalization per se. Instead, BMAs constitute efforts by source countries (i.e., developing countries with excess labor) and destination countries (i.e., developed countries experiencing labor shortages) to coordinate and optimize migratory flows between each other. *See* Marion Panizzon, *International Law of Economic Migration: A Ménage à Trois? GATS Mode 4, EPAs, and Bilateral Migration Agreements*, 44 J. World Trade 1207, 1230 (2010).

These frameworks do not reveal the entire picture of trade and labor migration, however. This chapter analyzes a new and emerging approach to global labor migration through special economic zones (SEZs). SEZs are geographical areas that are governed by a single administrator and provide special legal treatment to multinational corporations (MNCs) that physically locate within them in order to attract investment and facilitate export-based industries.[19] SEZs, which encompass a wide range of zones (such as free trade zones and export processing zones), have become an integral component of many countries' trade policies and economic competitiveness strategies. To address the need for high-skilled foreign labor, an increasing number of SEZs, particularly in emerging market developing countries, include labor migration "flexibilities" that premise the easing of restrictions on labor migration on the promotion of export-based trade and foreign direct investment. International trade law facilitates SEZs, and SEZ-based migration laws and policies are expressly and implicitly recognized in regional FTAs.[20]

SEZs tangibly display the tensions between the predominant consequentialist conceptions of the global economy based on national interest and competing cosmopolitan views based on globally defined communities.[21] SEZ-based labor migration regimes liberalize labor through geographically and legally defined conditions: foreigners may enter the host country's labor market solely through the SEZ's parallel and separate regulatory system, which effectively functions as a "country within a country." Further, SEZs perpetuate the growth of regionalism and privatization in international law. SEZs advance country-specific approaches to labor migration that favor temporary migrants from regional trading partners.[22] Host country governments have established a constellation of public-private legal frameworks to regulate SEZs in conjunction with foreign MNCs that invest in the zones. In comparison to GATS and FTAs, SEZs may be more responsive to labor preferences of MNCs. Drawing on field research conducted in Panama, this chapter analyzes an illustrative example of the relationship between SEZ-based trade and labor migration, the Panamá Pacífico SEZ at the intersection of the Panama Canal and the Pacific Ocean.

This chapter shows how international trade law serves as a mechanism for limited labor migration either directly, such as through GATS or FTAs, or indirectly, through BMAs and SEZs. Individual countries can take advantage of the fragmented nature of this liberalization. By selecting from numerous legal frameworks in the global trade-labor migration nexus, governments compete for foreign investment and foreign workers by tailoring their immigration and labor rules to the needs of MNCs. While the global trade-labor migration nexus enables individual countries to partially liberalize to the extent necessary to attract foreign capital, the status quo impedes the broad-based opening of national borders to foreign workers.

---

19. *See* Sumeet Jain, *"You Say Nano, We Say No-No:" Getting a "Yes" Instead for Special Economic Zones in India*, 32 Nw. J. Intl. L. & Bus. 1, 2-3 (2011) (defining an SEZ as "an area where economic incentives are offered to investors with the objective of attracting investment").
20. *See* discussion section §9.05 [B], *infra*.
21. *See* discussion section §9.06, *infra*.
22. *See* Hiroshi Motomura, *Designing Temporary Worker Programs*, 80 U. Chi. L. Rev. 263, 279 (2013).

This chapter proceeds in four sections. In section §9.02, I explain how changes in the global economy have spurred newfound attention on the relationship between trade and labor migration, and briefly summarize the competing theoretical views on this relationship. Section §9.03 describes the closely related concepts of pluralism and fragmentation in international law and their impact on governance of international trade, thereby putting into context ongoing debates regarding trade and labor migration. Section §9.04 examines the growing use of SEZs as a means for states to exploit the synergies between trade policy, foreign direct investment, and labor migration. I examine the Panama Pacífico SEZ as an example of a new generation SEZ that integrates these synergies. Finally, in section §9.05, I explore the broader implications of the global trade-labor migration nexus, focusing on the bias toward higher-skilled labor and changes in the exercise of sovereign authority under international law.

§9.02 THE RELATIONSHIP BETWEEN INTERNATIONAL TRADE AND LABOR MIGRATION

What is the relationship between trade and labor migration, and why is this relationship important? The following discussion describes the economic forces and legal developments that have increasingly motivated governments and MNCs to address this relationship and examines theoretical challenges to the status quo.

[A] Labor Migration and the Global Competition for Competitive Labor

In spite of widespread political opposition in the United States (US) and other destination countries, global labor migration is likely to significantly grow in the future. Two factors explain its growing importance: growing disparities in labor market demographics and the various intertwined effects of globalization. First, the dramatic growth of the world's population (particularly in developing countries) coupled with persistent economic inequality between rich and poor countries enhance the global supply of migrant labor.[23] Declining working-age populations in many developed countries have led to growing concerns about the need to address labor shortages.[24] Developed country governments, facing chronic labor shortages due to aging populations and low birthrates, have resorted to various unilateral measures with uneven results.[25]

23. *See* Goldin, Cameron & Balarajan, *supra* note 11, at 220–24; Lant Pritchett, *Let Their People Come: Breaking the Gridlock on Global Labor Mobility* 22–26 (Ctr. Global Dev. 2006), http://www.cgdev.org/sites/default/files/9781933286105-Pritchett-let-their-people-come.pdf; Martin, *supra* note 10, at 187–91.
24. *See* Goldin, Cameron & Balarajan, *supra* note 11, at 249–50 (noting that technological change may create new types of jobs as well as substitute for workers).
25. Among the most notable responses was Japan's guest worker program, implemented in the 1990s, which granted long-term resident status (but not citizenship) to foreigners of Japanese descent. *See* Sumi Shin, *Global Migration: The Impact of "Newcomers" on Japanese Immigration and Labor Systems*, 19 Berkeley J. Intl. L. 265, 268 (2001). The program targeted the descendants of Japanese citizens who had emigrated to South America (primarily Brazil and Peru) several

Second, globalization is another backdrop to labor migration. Revolutionary advances in communication and transportation have made it easier to migrate and for migrants to work in their new countries in theory, creating a self-perpetuating cycle of migration.[26] These dynamics have favored relatively wealthy and well-connected migrants who have the economic resources to take advantage of existing legal channels.[27] Cross-border commerce has also raised awareness of the importance of human capital to national economic competitiveness.[28] MNCs and other businesses are engaged in a global competition for competitive labor (i.e., attracting high-skilled foreign workers) through lobbying for favorable migration rules.[29] Governments, on behalf of home country MNCs and native industries, compete with each other to obtain the most economically valuable (and increasingly mobile) human capital.[30]

[B] Theoretical Challenges to the Limited Scope of Trade and Labor Migration

Various competing paradigms seek to define the relationship between trade and labor migration. The disjuncture between international trade and international labor migration has not been lost among legal scholars and social scientists.[31] Critiques of the status quo generally fall into two distinct yet overlapping categories: institutional design and individual freedom approaches.

Institutional design approaches focus on the parallels between trade and labor and call for a global migration regime to address collective action problems among

---

generations ago. *See* Claire Hur, Comment, *Returnees from South America: Japan's Model for Legal Multiculturalism?*, 11 Pac. Rim L. & Policy J. 643, 652–53 (2002); *see also* Norimitsu Onishi, *An Enclave of Brazilians Is Testing Insular Japan*, N.Y. Times, Nov. 1, 2008, at A8. Due to a decline in the manufacturing sectors where most guest workers were employed and dissatisfaction with the program generally, the Japanese government has provided incentives to these workers to leave Japan. *See* Hiroko Tabuchi, *Japan Pays Foreign Workers to Go Home*, N.Y. Times, Apr. 23, 2009, at B1.

26. *See* Martin, *supra* note 10, at 192 (describing the role of migration networks); The Economist, *Weaving the World Together*, http://www.economist.com/node/21538700 (Nov. 19, 2011) (describing the role of Chinese and Indian diaspora networks in assisting immigrant businesses).
27. *See*, e.g., Julie Satow, *The Green-Card Carrot*, N.Y. Times, May 17, 2015, at RE1 (describing the use of the federal government's EB-5 program, which grants legal residency to foreign investors, by Chinese nationals residing in New York City).
28. *See* Trebilcock, Howse & Eliason, *supra* note 1, at 620 (noting the positive externalities of skilled foreign workers in destination countries).
29. *See* Goldin, Cameron & Balarajan, *supra* note 11, at 254–56; *see also* Andrés Solimano, *International Migration in the Age of Crisis and Globalization* 157 (Cambridge U. Press 2010) (listing "technology entrepreneurs, information technology experts, first-rate scientists, bright graduate students, skilled physicians, and gifted writers and artists" as examples of high-skilled foreign labor with important economic value to firms and countries).
30. *See* Solimano, *supra* note 29, at 179–82 (describing how special immigration policies attract "high-value" migrants); Ayelet Shachar & Ran Hirschl, *Recruiting "Super Talent": The New World of Selective Migration Regimes*, 20 Ind. J. Global Leg. Stud. 71, 75–86 (2013) (describing the participation of governments in the global race for talent).
31. *See*, e.g., Ethan B. Kapstein, *Economic Justice in an Unfair World: Toward a Level Playing Field* 115 (Princeton U. Press 2006) (asking whether justice in migration should be "'free', like trade in goods and services' and arguing for migration liberalization as part of 'a system of mutual advantage" based on compensatory mechanisms).

states.[32] International trade law is based on the concept of non-discrimination among states.[33] Under classical macroeconomic theory, trade and migration are viewed as substitutes.[34] Trumpeting the success of legally mandated trade liberalization to enable countries to exploit comparative advantage, advocates of the institutional design approach argue that the willingness and ability of people to move across borders for work can similarly increase global wealth through enforcement of non-discrimination rules against foreign workers.[35] Institutional design advocates point to the success of the WTO as evidence that trade liberalization can be a driver for wealth accumulation and improvement of human welfare.[36]

However, there are conceptual and political difficulties with applying rules of trade liberalization to labor migration. For one thing, empirical evidence is unclear regarding the substitutability of trade and labor.[37] Further, the core concept of most favored nation (MFN), which requires equal treatment of equivalent goods irrespective of national origin, disregards the legal, political, and moral distinctions among individuals made by all countries based on national origin.[38]

Individual freedom approaches address the relationship between trade and labor from a rights-based normative perspective. Advocates of these approaches characterize global labor migration as a fundamental right that prioritizes individual equality in the

32. *See* Howard F. Chang, *Liberalized Immigration as Free Trade: Economic Welfare and the Optimal Immigration Policy*, 145 U. Pa. L. Rev. 1147 (1997) (comparing trade barriers to immigration barriers and concluding that the removal of the latter would likewise lead to a net increase in global economic welfare); Richard A. Epstein, *Free Trade and Free Immigration: Why Domestic Competitive Injury Should Never Influence Government Policy*, 80 U. Chi. L. Rev. 201 (2013) (arguing for parallel regimes for free trade and free immigration).
33. Non-discrimination consists of two principles under WTO law: MFN, which prohibits discrimination against imports from different foreign countries, and national treatment, which prohibits discrimination against foreign imports *vis-à-vis* equivalent domestic goods. *See* John H. Jackson, *The World Trading System: Law and Policy of International Economic Relations* 157–58 (2d ed. MIT Press 1997).
34. *See* International Labor Organization (ILO), *International Labour Migration: A Rights-Based Approach* 55, http://migration.itcilo.org/en/resources/papers/international-labour-migration-a-right-based-approach (2010) (observing that due to the use of labor inputs in traded goods, economists look at trade as a substitute for migration); Howard F. Chang, *The Immigration Paradox: Poverty, Distributive Justice, and Liberal Egalitarianism*, 52 DePaul L. Rev. 759, 764 (2003) (stating that "[l]abor migration represents a form of international trade in which the source country exports labor to the host country").
35. *See* Trebilcock, Howse & Eliason, *supra* note 1, at 611; Dani Rodrik, *The Globalization Paradox* 266–72 (Norton 2011) (justifying temporary migration visas on economic gains to the world economy generally as well as to migrating workers in developing countries).
36. *See* Pascal Lamy, Dir.-Gen., WTO, *Humanising Globalization* (Jan. 30, 2006), http://www.wto.org/english/news_e/sppl_e/sppl16_e.html (describing trade as a "very visible" dimension of globalization and the WTO as being "at the heart of global governance"); *see also* Stephen Kim Park, *Bridging the Global Governance Gap: Reforming the Law of Trade Adjustment*, 43 Geo. J. Intl. L. 797, 800–01 (2012) (citing the former WTO Director-General's call for a "Geneva Consensus").
37. *See* James F. Hollifield & Thomas Osang, *Trade and Migration in North America: The Role of NAFTA*, 11 L. & Bus. Rev. Ams. 327, 336–38 (2005) (concluding that NAFTA has no discernible effect on migration trends between the United States, Mexico, and Canada).
38. Pritchett, *supra* note 23, at 116.

global economy.[39] They go beyond existing international labor law standards, which generally respect the sovereign right of states to control their borders,[40] and stand in direct contrast to predominant policy approaches to labor migration based on consequentialism, which premise liberalization on the fulfillment of political and economic national objectives.[41] Instead, they argue against territoriality based on national borders as the moral basis for excluding foreign workers.[42] Territorial presence as a prerequisite to a right to work and live in a country is characterized as arbitrary, insofar as it privileges the "fortuities of birthplace and parentage."[43] Instead, labor migration policies should be shaped by a universal right to free movement enjoyed by all individuals, regardless of citizenship.[44] This approach presupposes a global polity in which restrictions on the ability to migrate constitute a violation of liberal principles of individual equality.[45] This line of reasoning closely hews to theories of cosmopolitanism that cite the emergence of non-state communities as a new form of legal order that is superseding state-centric notions of sovereignty, national identity, and citizenship.[46] Under this view, the question of how to manage migration flows does not start with the presumption of territorial sovereignty.[47] Instead, cosmopolitanism asks how and to whom jurisdictional authority should be allocated in order to fulfill certain normative objectives.[48]

39. *See* Joel P. Trachtman, *Legal Aspects of a Poverty Agenda at the WTO: Trade Law and "Global Apartheid"*, 6 J. Intl. Econ. L. 3, 14 (2003) (comparing the current global system of restricted migration to the internal passport system under apartheid).
40. *See* ILO, *ILO Multilateral Framework on Labour Migration: Non-Binding Principles and Guidelines for a Rights-Based Approach to Labour Migration*, Art. 4, http://www.ilo.org/wcmsp5/groups/public/---asia/---ro-bangkok/documents/publication/wcms_146243.pdf (Nov. 2005) (stating that "[a]ll States have the sovereign right to develop their own policies to manage labour migration").
41. *See* Martin Ruhs & Ha-Joon Chang, *The Ethics of Labor Immigration Policy*, 58 Intl. Org. 69, 85–87 (2004).
42. *See* Joel P. Trachtman, *The International Law of Economic Migration* 96–111 (W.E. Upjohn Inst. For Empl. Research 2009); *see also* John A. Scanlan, *A View from the United States: Social, Economic, and Legal Change, the Persistence of the State, and Immigration Policy in the Coming Century*, 2 Ind. J. Global Leg. Stud. 79, 141 (1994) (describing the status quo of border controls as the persistence of state sovereignty "in all its selfish glory").
43. Linda Bosniak, *Being Here: Ethical Territoriality and the Rights of Immigrants*, 8 Theoretical Inquiries L. 389, 399 (2007).
44. Ruhs & Chang, *supra* note 41, at 84 (defining ethical cosmopolitanism).
45. *See* Howard F. Chang, *The Economics of International Labor Migration and the Case for Global Distributive Justice*, 41 Cornell Intl. L.J. 1, 11–12 (2008) (analogizing immigration restrictions to employment discrimination and residential segregation).
46. *See, e.g.*, Charles R. Beitz, *Political Theory and International Relations* (Princeton U. Press 1979) (developing a global cosmopolitan approach to international politics); Peter J. Spiro, *A New International Law of Citizenship*, 105 Am. J. Intl. L. 694 (2011) (observing emerging norms of rights of access to citizenship).
47. *See* Heike Brabandt & Steffen Mau, *Liberal Cosmopolitanism and Cross-Border Mobility*, 27 Global Socy. 53, 56 (2013) (taking note of the "fundamental tension between ... universal cosmopolitan rights such as the right to move across borders ... and the exercise of sovereignty by individual states").
48. Joel P. Trachtman, *Welcome to Cosmopolis, World of Boundless Opportunity*, 39 Cornell Intl. L.J. 477, 496 (2006).

§9.03 THE PLURALISTIC GLOBAL TRADE-LABOR MIGRATION NEXUS

International trade law in respect of migration is far from coherent and unified. The theoretical underpinnings of this fragmentation lie in the concept of legal pluralism.[49] Pluralism is defined as co-existing or overlapping legal norms and legal systems that regulate any given activity or actor.[50] These diverse legal orders may make competing claims of authority and impose conflicting demands or norms.[51] These legal orders invariably interact with each other, and pluralism addresses the dynamic, changing relationships between them.[52] In the context of international law, pluralism explicitly recognizes that the state does not enjoy a monopoly on lawmaking.[53] Instead, legal norms and systems are generated by a multiplicity of legal orders that lie above the state or outside of the state, such as multilateral institutions, non-governmental organizations, and transnational regulatory bodies.[54] In international business regulation, pluralistic relationships are evident in the regulation of activities by different regulators—either within a single national jurisdiction or across national jurisdictions—acting under their respective bodies of law and enforcement mechanisms.[55]

The closely related concept of fragmentation is defined as "conflicts between rules or rule-systems, deviating institutional practices and, possibly, the loss of an overall perspective on the law."[56] Fragmentation arises when pluralistic conflict or uncertainty perpetuates the fracturing of a purportedly unitary legal system, such as international law.[57] Conceptually, fragmentation appears in three general forms:

49. *Fragmentation of International Law: Difficulties Arising from the Diversification and Expansion of International Law: Report of the Study Group of the International Law Commission*, UN Intl. Law Comm'n,58th Session, U.N. Doc. A/CN.4/L.682 (Apr. 13, 2006), as corrected U.N. Doc. A/CN.4/L.682/Corr.1 (Aug. 11, 2006) [hereinafter ILC Fragmentation Report], at 11 n.13.

50. *See* Paul Schiff Berman, *Global Legal Pluralism: A Jurisprudence of Law Beyond Borders* 3–4 (Cambridge U. Press 2012).

51. Brian Z. Tamanaha, *Understanding Legal Pluralism: Past to Present, Local to Global*, 30 Sydney L. Rev. 375, 375 (2008).

52. Sally Engle Merry, *Legal Pluralism*, 22 L. & Socy. Rev. 869, 879 (1988).

53. *See* Paul Schiff Berman, *A Pluralist Approach to International Law*, 32 Yale J. Intl. L. 301, 311–15 (2007).

54. *See* Michael A. Helfand, *Introduction*, in *Negotiating State and Non-State Law: The Challenge of Global and Local Legal Pluralism* 5 (Michael A. Helfand, ed., Cambridge U. Press 2015).

55. *See* Marisa Anne Pagnattaro & Stephen Kim Park, *The Long Arm of Section 337: International Trade Law as a Global Business Remedy*, 52 Am. Bus. L.J. 621, 649 (2015) (defining regulatory pluralism).

56. ILC Fragmentation Report, *supra* note 49, at 11.

57. *See* Tomer Broude, *Principles of Normative Integration and the Allocation of International Authority: The WTO, the Vienna Convention on the Law of Treaties, and the Rio Declaration*, 6 Loy. U. Chi. Intl. L. Rev. 173, 177–78 (2008) (defining fragmentation as uncertainty about which institutions have ultimate authority to make or decide international law); *see also* Sean D. Murphy, *Deconstructing Fragmentation: Koskenniemi's 2006 ILC Project*, 27 Temp. Intl. & Comp. L.J. 293, 294 (2013) (observing that the ILC Fragmentation Report does not condemn fragmentation per se, but rather seeks to address frequent clashes between rules that destabilize the unity of international law).

different legal rules (substantive), different legal institutions (institutional), and different methods of legal interpretation (methodological).[58] State and non-state actors generate specialized rules and institutions to address autonomous spheres of social action, often without being aware of how such rules and institutions interact with other specialized areas of law.[59]

Spurred by the proliferation of distinct international legal rules and institutions in the past several decades, fragmentation in international law has been scrutinized in a number of different contexts.[60] Much of this scholarship has addressed "horizontal" fragmentation—i.e., interactions between different, autonomous branches of international law.[61] The global trade regime has been a focal point of scholarly scrutiny of horizontal fragmentation.[62] This is in part due to the WTO's relatively robust adjudicatory authority on so-called trade and … issues,[63] as well as the harmonization of domestic regulatory regimes through WTO-mandated harmonization.[64]

There is another form of fragmentation that is arguably underestimated by many public international law scholars due to its rapid and recent growth: fragmentation within international trade law itself. This alternate fragmentation is evident in the rise of regionalism in international trade law.[65] Regional trade agreements seek to address a wide range of non-trade policy objectives, including labor and migration.[66] Virtually

58. *See* Mads Andenas, *Reassertion and Transformation: From Fragmentation to Convergence in International Law*, 46 Geo. J. Intl. L. 685, 694–700 (2015).
59. *See* ILC Fragmentation Report, *supra* note 49, at 11.
60. *See ibid.*, at 12 n.14; Harlan Grant Cohen, *Finding International Law, Part II: Our Fragmenting Legal Community*, 44 N.Y.U. J. Intl. L. & Pol. 1049, 1050–52 (2012) (describing and citing contributions by various legal scholars).
61. *See* Ralf Michaels & Joost Pauwelyn, *Conflict of Norms or Conflict of Laws?: Different Techniques in the Fragmentation of Public International Law*, 22 Duke J. Comp. & Intl. L. 349, 366–71 (2012); *see also* Panagiotis Delimatsis, *The Fragmentation of International Trade Law*, 45 J. World Trade 87, 97 (2011) (describing "horizontal collisions or overlaps among regimes of sometimes equal force in terms of membership" as a form of fragmentation).
62. *See*, e.g., Chantal Thomas, *Convergences and Divergences in International Legal Norms on Migrant Labor*, 32 Comp. Lab. L. & Policy J. 405, 408–33 (2011) (examining doctrinal divergences between international trade law and other bodies of international law on human rights, labor, and crime).
63. *See* Robert Howse, *From Politics to Technocracy—And Back Again: The Fate of the Multilateral Trading Regime*, 96 Am. J. Intl. L. 94, 108–12 (2002) (describing the WTO Appellate Body's rulings on domestic environmental regulation); *see also* Joel P. Trachtman, *Trade and … Problems, Cost-Benefit Analysis and Subsidiarity*, 9 Eur. J. Intl. L. 32, 33 (1998) (defining conflicts between trade values and other social values, such as environmental protection and labor rights, as the "trade and … problem").
64. *See* Daphne Barak-Erez & Oren Perez, *Whose Administrative Law Is It Anyway? How Global Norms Reshape the Administrative State*, 46 Cornell Intl. L.J. 455, 483–84 (2013) (noting the WTO's dominant role in administrative law-based norm production through mandates under the WTO agreements on Technical Barriers to Trade and Application of Sanitary and Phytosanitary Measures).
65. Pagnattaro & Park, *supra* note 55, at 649–50.
66. *See* Rafael Leal-Arcas, *The Fragmentation of International Trade Law: Is Now the Time for Variable Geometry?*, 12 J. World Inv. & Trade 145, 154–55 (2011) (citing EU development-oriented trade agreements).

all regional FTAs include dispute settlement mechanisms with adjudicative functions.[67] Due to the non-hierarchical nature of the international trading system, the overlapping legal authority of the WTO and regional FTAs leads to potential substantive, institutional, and methodological forms of horizontal fragmentation.[68] Indeed, this intra-branch fragmentation may be facilitated by the inherent nature of the WTO. The WTO's incomplete remedies—which rely on the willingness of powerful states to enforce temporary breaches of WTO rules—have opened the door for opportunistic action outside of the global trade regime by China, Russia, and other countries.[69] The WTO's authority is also challenged by the halting process of WTO-based multilateral liberalization during the largely unsuccessful Doha Round,[70] which has led many countries to pursue regional and bilateral integration instead.[71] In addition to horizontal fragmentation between the WTO and its regional counterparts, there is also the possibility of conflict between individual regional and bilateral FTA regimes, which further exacerbates the potential costs of fragmentation.[72]

Another source of fragmentation in international trade law is driven by the multiple roles of MNCs. Under certain WTO agreements and numerous regional FTAs, MNCs have a private right of action against governments, either within domestic legal systems or in international legal fora.[73] In particular, the decisions of foreign

67. *See* Jennifer Hillman, *Conflicts Between Dispute Settlement Mechanisms in Regional Trade Agreements and the WTO: What Should the WTO Do?*, 42 Cornell Intl. L.J. 193, 195-96 (2009) (noting most regional FTAs permit the complaining party to bring a claim either under the regional FTA's dispute settlement rules or the WTO); *see also* Marc L. Busch, *Overlapping Institutions, Forum Shopping, and Dispute Settlement in International Trade*, 61 Intl. Org. 735, 753-57 (2007) (analyzing forum shopping behavior by NAFTA member countries).
68. *See* Joel P. Trachtman, *Fragmentation, Coherence and Synergy in International Law*, 2 Transnat'l. Leg. Theory 505, 507 (2011) (referencing WTO cases that also fell under the jurisdiction of other tribunals).
69. *See* Mark Wu, *Rethinking the Temporary Breach Puzzle: A Window on the Future of International Trade Conflicts*, 40 Yale J. Intl. L. 95, 143-50 (2015).
70. *See* Sungjoon Cho, *The Demise of Development in the Doha Round Negotiations*, 45 Tex. Intl. L.J. 573, 587-89 (2010) (analyzing the collapse of the Doha Round and its implications for the legitimacy of the WTO); Stephen Kim Park, *Talking the Talk and Walking the Walk: Reviving Global Trade and Development after Doha*, 53 Va. J. Intl. L. 365, 378-84 (2013) (attributing the collapse of the Doha Round to intractable discursive conflicts between the WTO's developed and developing Member States).
71. *See* Leal-Arcas, *supra* note 66, at 189-93 (describing the EU's turn toward FTAs following the suspension of the Doha Round in 2006); C. O'Neal Taylor, *Of Free Trade Agreements and Model*, 19 Ind. Intl. & Comp. L. Rev. 569, 576 (2009) (attributing the United States' shift to regionalism—which started with the enactment of NAFTA in 1994 and accelerated in the 2000s—to the sluggish Doha Round negotiations).
72. Chris Brummer describes conflicts between regional and bilateral arrangements as "structural inconsistency." *See* Chris Brummer, *The Ties That Bind? Regionalism, Commercial Treaties, and the Future of Global Economic Integration*, 60 Vand. L. Rev. 1349, 1362-71 (2007) (describing the incidence and effects of incongruity between bilateral treaties and regional integration arrangements).
73. *See* Joel P. Trachtman & Philip M. Moremen, *Costs and Benefits of Private Participation in WTO Dispute Settlement: Whose Right Is It Anyway?*, 44 Harv. Intl. L.J. 221, 222 (2003); *see also* United Nations Conference on Trade and Development, *Investor-State Dispute Settlement: A Sequel 18* (UNCTAD Series on Issues in International Investment Agreements, 2013), http://unctad.org/

investment tribunals acting under the authority of FTAs have established legal standards that vary from country to country.[74]

Limited private rights of action are not the only means by which MNCs may perpetuate fragmentation. MNCs indirectly shape international trade law through their interactions with domestic regulatory regimes. Many advocate for domestic regulations that may constitute de facto non-tariff barriers.[75] The lobbying power of MNCs has become more diffuse and fragmented due to the changing nature of global supply chains in which the same MNCs may be on both ends.[76] In addition, corporate self-regulation and other forms of private governance by MNCs in areas such as supply chain management, labor practices, and environmental sustainability exert an influence on cross-border trade flows.[77] In their most robust and sophisticated form, private transnational regulatory regimes consisting of multiple MNCs seek to fill governance deficits in the international economy.[78] Relying on soft law, codes of conduct, certification, monitoring, and other voluntary instruments, private transnational regulatory regimes stand in counterpoint to public regulation.[79] These private regimes increasingly interact with the public regulatory frameworks of individual governments either through destructive, competitive, or complementary relationships.[80] The nature of these interactions determines how a government implements domestic regulatory standards.[81]

---

en/PublicationsLibrary/diaeia2013d2_en.pdf (referring to nearly 3,200 agreements on foreign investment, including as chapters of trade agreements, the vast majority of which provide for investor-state arbitration). Investor-state relationships, in particular, arguably give rise to the capacity of MNCs to create international law by entering into contracts with states that are legally recognized and enforceable under FTAs and bilateral investment treaties. *See generally* Julian Arato, *Corporations as Lawmakers*, 56 Harv. Intl. L.J. 301 (2015).

74. Markus Wagner, *Regulatory Space in International Trade Law and International Investment Law*, 36 U. Pa. J. Intl. L. 1, 69–70 (2015). *See also* Trachtman, *supra* note 68, at 507 (noting the possibility of conflicting judgments arising from multiple litigations).
75. *See* Jackson, *supra* note 33, at 222 (referring to the "gerrymander[ing]" of product standards to protect domestic manufacturers vis-à-vis foreign competitors).
76. *See* Sungjoon Cho & Claire R. Kelly, *Are World Trading Rules Passe?*, 53 Va. J. Intl. L. 623, 642 (2013) (noting that more than half of global exported goods are in fact inputs for unfinished goods).
77. *See*, e.g., Larry Catá Backer, *Economic Globalization and the Rise of Efficient Systems of Global Private Law Making: Wal-Mart as Global Legislator*, 39 Conn. L. Rev. 1739, 1778–79 (2007) (positing that Wal-Mart's global supplier contracts constitute an autonomous, self-sustaining private regulatory system).
78. *See* Kenneth W. Abbott & Duncan Snidal, *Strengthening International Regulation Through Transnational New Governance: Overcoming the Orchestration Deficit*, 42 Vand. J. Transnat'l. L. 501, 509–10 (2009).
79. *See* Burkard Eberlein et al., *Transnational Business Governance Interactions: Conceptualization and Framework for Analysis*, 8 Reg. & Governance 1, 3 (2014) (defining transnational business governance as "systemic efforts to regulate business conduct that involve a significant degree of non-state authority in the performance of regulatory functions across national borders").
80. *See* Kevin Kolben, *Dialogic Labor Regulation in the Global Supply Chain*, 37 Mich. J. Intl. L. 425, 442–44 (2015).
81. *See* Tim Bartley, *Transnational Governance as the Layering of Rules: Intersections of Public and Private Standards*, 12 Theoretical Inquiries L. 517, 526–41 (2011).

§9.04 SEZs AND GLOBAL LABOR MIGRATION

SEZs are an emerging part of the global trade-labor migration nexus. The following discussion describes the scope and purpose of SEZs, the use of labor migration to support foreign direct investment and export-based trade by SEZs, and their incorporation into FTAs. The experience of Panama, which is broadly indicative of SEZ-based migration strategies to date, is analyzed as an illustrative example.

[A] SEZs in the Global Economy

The term SEZ, encompasses various types of zones that fall under this umbrella definition, including free trade zones and export processing zones.[82] Historical predecessors to SEZs date back to citywide zones located on international trade routes, including Gibraltar, Singapore, Hong Kong, Hamburg, and Copenhagen.[83] Modern SEZs emerged in the 1970s, starting in China and then expanding to other parts of East Asia, Southeast Asia, and Eastern Europe over the following two decades.[84] SEZs have proliferated throughout the world to 135 countries, which collectively manage approximately 3,000 SEZs.[85] In the US, the most prominent examples of SEZs are foreign trade zones within the country governed by the US Foreign Trade Zones Act[86] and the *maquiladora* export processing zones in Mexico along the US-Mexican border, which were primarily established following the implementation of NAFTA.[87]

The existence of SEZs reflects the widespread belief among governments that they must provide tailored and special regulatory treatment to MNCs in order to compete for globally mobile capital.[88] In addition to attracting foreign direct investment and promoting export growth, governments use SEZs as a means to increase foreign

82. Other names for various kinds of SEZs and variants of SEZs include free ports, transit zones, free perimeters, hybrid and single export processing zones, enterprise zones, empowerment zones, urban free zones. Susan Tiefenbrum, *US Foreign Trade Zones, Tax-Free Trade Zones of the World, and Their Impact on the US Economy*, 12 J. Intl. Bus. & L. 149, 153, 158–59 (2013) (listing variants of SEZs).
83. Gokhan Akinci & James Crittle, *Special Economic Zones: Performance, Lessons Learned, and Implication for Zone Development* 9, http://documents.worldbank.org/curated/en/2008/04/9915888/special-economic-zone-performance-lessons-learned-implication-zone-development (World Bank, Foreign Investment Advisory Service, Occasional Paper, Apr. 2008).
84. *See* Thomas J. Sigler, *Panama's Special Economic Zones: Balancing Growth and Development*, 33 Bulletin of Latin American Research 2 (2013).
85. Akinci & Crittle, *supra* note 83, at 7 (noting that SEZs account for over 68 million direct jobs and over USD 500 billion of direct trade-related value added worldwide). *See also* Tiefenbrum, *supra* note 82, at 174–80 (briefly describing specific SEZs in various countries throughout the world).
86. *See* United States Foreign Trade Zones Act, 19 U.S.C. §§ 81a-81u (1934). Each individual US foreign trade zone is operated by a corporation granted authority by the US Foreign Trade Zones Board and indirectly under the supervision of Customs and Border Protection of the U.S. Department of Homeland Security. Tiefenbrum, *supra* note 82, at 160–61. There are 174 active foreign trade zones in the United States. Mary Jane Bolle & Brock R. Williams, *U.S. Foreign Trade Zones: Background and Issues for Congress* Cong. Research Serv., RL 426867 (Nov. 12, 2013).
87. *See* Michael Engman, Osamu Onodera & Enrico Pinali, *Export Processing Zones Past and Future Role in Trade and Development* 37–38 (OECD Trade Policy Paper No. 53, May 2007) (describing the evolution and growth of the Mexican *maquila* system).
88. Engman, et al., *supra* note 87, at 32.

exchange earnings, generate domestic employment, promote technology transfer and information exchange with foreign MNCs, and raise government revenue through taxes and fees.[89]

Reflecting their bespoke nature, SEZs greatly vary in size, economic development purposes, physical characteristics, and government incentives.[90] The basic defining characteristics of all SEZs include a geographically delimited area, single management/administration, eligibility of firms for benefits based on their physical location in the SEZ, and a separate customs area with streamlined procedures.[91] Some SEZs, such as foreign trade zones in the US, are largely limited to production and transport.[92] For many developing countries, however, these kinds of SEZs are often inadequate due to the limited economic upside from decreasing returns on capital.[93]

This chapter focuses on another specific sub-set of SEZs in developing countries, which, as part of a broad-based national economic competitiveness strategy, focus on targeted human capital formation and infrastructure building to develop domestic economic capacity for higher value-added manufacturing and services industries.[94] Under this approach, the host country uses its SEZs to develop capacity to produce higher value-added goods, upgrade the skills of its workforce continually, and encourage domestic consumption of SEZ-produced goods.[95] The emergence of these new generation SEZs has been accompanied by two regulatory techniques: expanded economic incentives and public-private governance. A distinct customs regime, which permits imported goods to enter and exit SEZs at lower and zero tariff rates, legally demarcates the SEZ from the rest of the country.[96] Among the other fiscal, regulatory, and infrastructural incentives offered to foreign MNCs are favorable tax and regulatory treatment, property concessions, superior internal and transportation infrastructure, and streamlined administrative oversight.[97]

Traditionally, governments developed, managed, and regulated SEZs.[98] Recent years have seen increasing private participation. While autonomous government entities regulate SEZs, many host governments have divested development and

89. *See ibid.*, at 23–34.
90. *See* Bolle & Williams, *supra* note 86, at 2.
91. Akinci & Crittle, *supra* note 83, at 9 (referencing Annex D of the Revised Kyoto Convention of the World Customs Organization).
92. Bolle & Williams, *supra* note 86, at 2.
93. *See* Engman, et al., *supra* note 87, at 33–34 (noting the lack of success of many developing countries to develop "backward" linkages from foreign MNCs in SEZs and domestic companies).
94. *See* Akinci & Crittle, *supra* note 83, at 12 (listing four general policy rationales for SEZs: (1) as supporting a wider economic reform strategy, (2) by serving as "pressure valves" to alleviate unemployment, (3) as laboratories for regulatory experimentation, and (4) for attracting foreign direct investment).
95. Bolle & Williams, *supra* note 86, at 21.
96. *See* Jose Daniel Amado, *Free Industrial Zones: Law and Industrial Development in the New International Division of Labor*, 11 U. Pa. J. Intl. Bus. L. 81, 86 (1989) (defining SEZs as "basically customs-free industrial states" established "through a legal fiction").
97. *See* Andrew Lang, *Trade Agreements, Business and Human Rights: The Case of Export Processing Zones* 12 (Corporate Social Responsibility Initiative, John F. Kennedy Sch. of Govt., Harvard U., Working Paper No. 57, 2010).
98. Akinci & Crittle, *supra* note 83, at 20.

management of SEZs to the private sector.[99] In certain countries, SEZ regulators have themselves become privatized to varying extents, either becoming corporations and/or including private sector representatives on their board of directors.[100] According to the World Bank, private SEZs are both less costly to develop and operate, and perform better economically, particularly for "higher end" activities.[101] Public-private governance reinforces the extraterritorial nature of SEZs vis-à-vis their host countries. Although physically located within or adjacent to the rest of the country, SEZs are generally exempted from the laws and regulations in force in the rest of the country.[102]

[B] SEZs and the Global Trade-Labor Migration Nexus

The very existence of SEZs, particularly in developing countries that seek to use them as a springboard for higher value-added production, facilitate the integration of the country into the international trading system by serving as "beachheads of liberalization" that are shielded from the political pressures and economic demands of the country proper.[103] International trade law facilitates these liberalization-based policy goals in two ways.

First, international trade law may limit the kinds of economic incentives that countries can provide to foreign MNCs that locate in SEZs.[104] The WTO Agreement on Subsidies and Countervailing Measures (SCM Agreement)[105] applies to subsidies that constitute a financial contribution, are provided by a government, and confer a benefit to specific enterprises.[106] The SCM Agreement prohibits export subsidies[107] and local content subsidies,[108] with certain exceptions for developing countries.[109] Therefore,

99. *Ibid.*, at 20–21.
100. *Ibid.*, at 21 (noting the use of this approach by several Latin American countries and Thailand); Lang, *supra* note 97, at 17 (noting that over one-half of SEZs worldwide are privately owned and operated).
101. Akinci & Crittle, *supra* note 83, at 45–46. *But see* Konstantinos I. Hazakis, *The Rationale of Special Economic Zones (SEZs): An Institutional Approach*, 6 Regl. Sci. Polocy & Prac. 85, 93 (2014) (noting studies indicating that "public or private management does not lead per se to efficiency").
102. Amado, *supra* note 96, at 121.
103. Lang, *supra* note 97, at 15; *see also* Engman, et al., *supra* note 87, at 37 (characterizing SEZs as a "spearhead for [regulatory] reform").
104. Lang, *supra* note 97, at 15.
105. Agreement on Subsidies and Countervailing Measures, Apr. 15, 1994, Marrakesh Agreement Establishing the World Trade Organization, Annex 1A, 1869 U.N.T.S. 154, 33 I.L.M. 1125 [hereinafter SCM Agreement].
106. *Ibid.*, Art. 1.
107. Export subsidies are subsidies contingent, either in law or in fact, on export performance. *Ibid.*, Art. 3.1(a); *see also* Stephen Creskoff & Peter Walkenhorst, *Implications of WTO Disciplines for Special Economic Zones in Developing Countries* 14–15, http://documents.worldbank.org/curated/en/2011/01/14813550/special-economic-zones-progress-emerging-challenges-future-directions. (World Bank, Policy Research Working Paper No. 4892, April 2009).
108. Local content subsidies are subsidies that condition the provision of subsidies on the use of domestic over imported goods. SCM Agreement, *supra* note 105, Art. 3.1(b); *see also* Creskoff & Walkenhorst, *supra* note 107, at 15.
109. *See* SCM Agreement, *supra* note 105, Art. 27; *see also* Creskoff & Walkenhorst, *supra* note 107, at 17–25.

SEZs that restrict the amount of goods that can be exported to the host country effectively transform the applicable economic incentives received by foreign MNCs in the zone (such as direct subsidies or tax exemptions) into WTO-illegal export subsidies.[110] Any WTO member country may be subject to WTO dispute settlement proceedings and potentially countermeasures from other WTO members.[111]

Second, international trade law may be used to integrate trade liberalization and the policy goals of the SEZ. In particular, bilateral and regional FTAs increasingly expressly recognize the distinct legal status of SEZs vis-à-vis their host countries. Countries with SEZs that enter into FTAs must be concerned about trade triangulation, whereby a non-FTA product is able to enter an FTA member country's market duty-free via the SEZ, which would nullify the preferential duty benefits that the FTA accords to its member countries.[112] To address this concern, many FTAs include a provision stipulating that SEZ-processed products may not benefit from their status as an originating product of the host country.[113] In essence, this provision recognizes and reinforces the SEZ's unique status as a "country within a country."[114]

The issue of labor migration in SEZs largely follows the same pattern. In the package of regulatory incentives that SEZs offer foreign MNCs are special visas for foreign workers or other labor migration rules that constitute "flexibilities" or exceptions to the host country's immigration laws. SEZs permit governments to open their borders to labor migrants while effectively quarantining the economic, political, and social effects of liberalized labor. The scope and degree of migration liberalization is made contingent on its capacity to promote trade liberalization. However, unlike GATS Mode 4, bilateral and regional FTAs, and BMAs, SEZs are defined as much in spatial terms as in temporal terms. Instead of defining labor migration based on the amount of time that foreign workers work domestically, SEZs re-define "domestic" labor to include work by foreigners within the SEZ's host country but under SEZ-specific laws.

Traditionally, low-skilled migrant workers—both from other parts of the host country as well as adjacent countries—have filled substantial gaps left by a shortfall of local labor.[115] One of the primary goals of SEZs is job creation, both within the SEZ and in the host country proper.[116] However, in many developing countries, suitably qualified local talent is inadequate to meet the managerial and technical needs of

110. *See* Raúl A. Torres, *Free Zones and the World Trade Organization Agreement on Subsidies and Countervailing Measures*, 2 Global Trade & Customs J. 217, 219 (2007).
111. *See ibid.*
112. Thomas Farole & Gokhan Akinci, *Special Economic Zones: Progress, Emerging Challenges, and Future Directions* 136, http://documents.worldbank.org/curated/en/2011/01/14813550/special-economic-zones-progress-emerging-challenges-future-directions (World Bank, Policy Note No. 1, August 2011).
113. *Ibid*,. at 138. NAFTA went a step further by establishing a strict prohibition on the entry of goods processed in SEZs within a seven-year transitional period from 1994 to 2000. *Ibid.*, at 141.
114. *See* Amado, *supra* note 96, at 121.
115. Lang, *supra* note 97, at 14.
116. *See* Dorsati Madani, *A Review of the Role and Impact of Export Processing Zones* 35 (World Bank, Working Paper Series No. 2238, Nov. 1999).

foreign MNCs.[117] SEZ guest worker programs serve as a buffer between low supply and high demand for labor, with the extraterritorial nature of SEZs facilitating the departure of foreign workers once demand decreases.[118] Another class of workers is the beneficiary of new generation SEZs. These SEZs focus on regulatory incentives specifically targeted to corporate managers and white-collar professional service providers. While the application of labor standards to lower-skilled domestic labor in SEZs has been addressed by a number of legal scholars,[119] legal issues associated with higher-skilled foreign labor in SEZs have received relatively scant attention. Foreign corporate managers and professionals serve as a form of skills transfer through the expertise that they bring to the host country that complements the capital investments made by their foreign MNC employers located in SEZs.[120] This class of foreign labor fulfills one of the core objectives of new generation SEZs by "upskilling" the domestic workforce.[121]

[C] Case Study: Panama's SEZs and Labor Migration

The Panama Pacifico Special Economic Area (Panamá Pacífico) is an illuminating example of global labor migration in new generation SEZs. The case of Panama shows how governments use SEZs to work around the often-discordant relationship between trade liberalization and migration liberalization.

Panama's approach to SEZs reflects a set of legal mandates and policy decisions that seek to leverage the country's unique status in the global economy. Panama lies at the crossroads of the Western and Eastern Hemispheres, with narrowly separated borders on both the Atlantic and Pacific oceans. Panama's role in the global economy as a hemispheric intermediary is strongly tied with the Panama Canal.[122] Panama's

117. *See* Kurt Dassel & Kim Eckermann, *Economic Security and Competitiveness: Using Special Economic Zones to Drive Job Creation in MENA* 12 (2013), https://www2.deloitte.com/content/dam/Deloitte/tr/Documents/public-sector/EN_Economic%20Security%20and%20Competitiveness_16072014.pdf (referring to local employment challenges faced by SEZs); *see also* Ann Fenwick, *Evaluating China's Special Economic Zones*, 2 Intl. Tax & Bus. L. 376, 391–93 (1984) (describing the Chinese government's early efforts to address unskilled, under-productive local labor in its SEZs).

118. *See* Zai Liang, *Foreign Investment, Economic Growth, and Temporary Migration: The Case of Shenzhen Special Economic Zone, China*, 28 Dev. & Soc. 115, 128 (1999) (describing the "buffer theory" of temporary migration).

119. *See* Lang, *supra* note 97, at 17–23; Kevin Kolben, *Integrative Linkage: Combining Public and Private Regulatory Approaches in the Design of Trade and Labor Regimes*, 48 Harv. Intl. L.J. 203 (2007); Sherrie L. Russell-Brown, *Labor Rights as Human Rights: The Situation of Women Workers in Jamaica's Export Free Zones*, 24 Berkeley J. Empl. & Lab. L. 179 (2003).

120. *See* Engman et al., *supra* note 87, at 34.

121. Lang, *supra* note 97, at 14 (describing how domestic employees of foreign MNCs learn new skills relating to production techniques or managerial entrepreneurialism); Hazakis, *supra* note 101, at 93–94 (noting the use of SEZs for training and knowledge acquisition to enhance regional comparative advantages).

122. Thomas J. Sigler, *Panama as Palimpsest: The Reformulation of the "Transit Corridor" in a Global Economy*, 38 Intl. J. Urb. & Reg'l Research. 886, 890 (2014). The Panama Canal was built by the newly-independent Republic of Panama and opened in 1914. *See* Ruth Gordon, *Panama and the Specter of Climate Change*, 41 U. Miami Inter-Am. L. Rev. 129, 174 (2010). The United States controlled the Panama Canal until 1999 when sovereignty was transferred to Panama pursuant to the Torrijos-Carter Treaties. *Ibid.*, at 175–76.

operation of the canal directly accounts for approximately 6% of the country's GDP.[123] Trade routes between the east coast of the US and East Asia account for the largest amount of volume through the Panama Canal.[124] The canal's indirect economic impact is far greater, with exports of goods and services representing 81% of the country's GDP.[125] In particular, Panama's economy is heavily focused on maritime services and related intermediary services, including logistics, banking, tourism, and transhipment.[126]

Throughout the decades of US control of the Panama Canal, the outsize influence of the US in Panama was manifested by its control and ownership of the Panama Canal Zone, a ten mile strip of land on either side of the canal.[127] The Panama Canal Zone, both in legal and social terms, constituted an American enclave.[128] This territory has been the basis for Panama's SEZ strategy. Panamá Pacífico lies at the Pacific Ocean entrance to the Panama Canal on the former Howard US Air Force base outside of Panama City, the country's capital. Panama has sought to transform a substantial portion of this 2,500-hectare site, which includes various private assets left by the US government upon the transfer of control,[129] into a commercial, residential, logistics, and corporate hub. Whereas Panama's other SEZ, the Colón Free Zone, relies on transhipment, Panamá Pacífico focuses on cultivating high value-added business activities in order to expand the country's competitive advantages in the global economy.[130]

The legal framework, governance structure, and regulatory incentives of Panamá Pacífico reflect Panama's desire to use this new generation SEZ as a springboard for transforming the national economy. Panamá Pacífico was established by Law No. 41 of 2004 (Law No. 41).[131] Law No. 41 is complemented by several other statutes, which establish other rights and obligations for foreign MNCs in Panama, including Law

123. J. F. Hornbeck, Cong. Research Serv., RL 32540, The U.S.-Panama Free Trade Agreement 6 (Nov. 8, 2012).
124. *Ibid.*
125. Sigler, *supra* note 122, at 893.
126. *Ibid.*, at 894. Transhipment is a process that involves the shipment of goods or containers through an intermediate port in order to re-package and re-distribute bulk freight or take advantage of favorable tax treatment. *Ibid.*
127. Gordon, *supra* note 122, at 174. *See also* Hay-Buneau-Varilla Treaty art. II (1903) (granting to the United States "in perpetuity the use, occupation, and control" of the Panama Canal Zone).
128. Sigler, *supra* note 84, at 5 (noting that Panamanians were not allowed in the zone without written authorization from the US government). In 1937, the US federal government enacted a law granting citizenship to children of US citizens born in the Panama Canal Zone. *See* Act of Aug. 4, 1937, § 1, 50 Stat. 558 Ch. 563, *codified at* 8 U.S.C. § 1403(a).
129. Among such assets included housing and office buildings, a hospital, transportation infrastructure, a fiber optic cable network, an 8,500-foot runway, and four hangar facilities. Hornbeck, *supra* note 123, at 7.
130. *See* Sigler, *supra* note 84, at 9.
131. *See* Ley No. 41, Jul. 20, 2004, Que crea un régimen especial para el establecimiento y Operación del Área Económica Especial Panamá-Pacífico, y una entidad autónoma del Estado, denominada Agencia del Área Económica Especial Panamá-Pacífico, tit. 25103-A, Gaceta Oficial (Jul. 20, 2004) (Pan.) [hereinafter Law No. 41]. (An unofficial English translation of Law No. 41 is available at http://www.app.gob.pa/pdf/41_en.pdf).

No. 32 of 2011 (the free zones law),[132] Law No. 41 of 2007 (the multinational headquarters incentives law),[133] and Law No. 54 of 1998 (the investment stability law).[134] Pursuant to Law No. 41, Panamá Pacífico is governed by a semi-autonomous state-owned corporation, the Panama-Pacific Special Economic Area Agency (Agencia Panamá Pacífico, or APP).[135] APP has its own legal personality and is solely responsible for managing its assets.[136] It is subject to the policies and guidelines of the executive branch of the Panamanian government,[137] but is governed by its own board of directors.[138] The public-private governance of Panamá Pacífico is evident in the composition of APP's board, which includes two government appointees, two representatives of foreign MNCs located in the zone, and directors representing Panamanian businesses, labor unions, and the Colón Free Zone.[139]

Panamá Pacífico's hybrid governance is also evident in its mode of operation. Pursuant to Law No. 41, APP has the authority to select external firms to develop, promote, and operate all or any part of the zone.[140] In 2007, London & Regional Properties, a global private real estate development firm, won the bid for a forty-year concession.[141] The International Finance Corporation (IFC), the private sector investment arm of the World Bank Group, advised and assisted the Panamanian government at all stages of this process.[142] London & Regional Panama (LRP), as master developer, is the sole and exclusive developer and operator of all parts of Panamá Pacífico.[143] LRP manages Panamá Pacífico based on a master plan developed by LRP and approved by APP, which includes developing and building residences and related commercial

---

132. *See* Ley No. 32, Apr. 5, 2011, Que establece un régimen especial, integral y simplificado para el establecimiento y operación de zonas francas y dicta otras disposiciones, tit. 26757-B, Gaceta Oficial (Apr. 5, 2011) (Pan.). (An unofficial English translation of Law No. 32 of 2011 is available at http://www.app.gob.pa/pdf/32_en.pdf).
133. *See* Ley No. 41, Aug. 24, 2007, Que crea el Régimen Especial para el Establecimiento y la Operación de Sedes de Empresas Multinacionales y la Comisión de Licencias de Sedes de Empresas Multinacionales y dicta otras disposiciones, tit. 25864, Gaceta Oficial (Aug. 24, 2007) (Pan.). (An unofficial English translation of Law No. 41 of 2007 is available at http://sem.mici.gob.pa/doc/Law 41.pdf.) *See also* Sigler, *supra* note 84, at 9 (noting the tax and labor incentives offered to foreign MNCs that relocate to Panama).
134. *See* Ley No. 54, Jul. 22, 1998, Por la cual se Dictan Medidas para la Estabilidad Jurídica de las Inversiones, tit. 23593, Gaceta Oficial (Jul. 24, 1998) (Pan.).
135. *See* Law No. 41 *supra* note 131 Art. 1.
136. *Ibid.*, Art. 4.
137. *See ibid.*, Art. 11.
138. *See ibid.*, Art. 26.
139. *See ibid.*, Art. 18.
140. *Ibid.* Art. 41.
141. *See* Intl. Fin. Corp *Public-Private Partnership Impact Stories, Panama: Panama Pacifico SEZ,* http://www.ifc.org/wps/wcm/connect/b889f900498390bf82e4d2336b93d75f/PPPImpactStories_Panama_PanamaPacificoSEZ.pdf?MOD=AJPERES. (Aug. 2013).
142. *See ibid.*, at 2 (noting IFC's role in developing the project concept, drafting laws creating the SEZ, designing the master development agreement, and managing the developer selection process).
143. LRP was formed by a joint venture between London & Regional Properties and Southstone Investment. *See Master Plan*, Panama Pacifico, http://www.panamapacifico.com/master-developer (Nov. 13, 2018).

facilities, and attracting and managing foreign MNCs in the SEZ.[144] Panamá Pacífico includes a wide range of domestic and foreign companies in various commercial, industrial, and retail sectors, including back-office operations, multimodal and logistics services, high tech product and process manufacturing, offshore services and call centers, transhipment, and digital and data transmission.[145] Over 200 companies—including eight companies listed on the Fortune 500—operate in Panamá Pacífico.[146] Among them include global US-based MNCs such as 3M, Caterpillar, Dell, and KPMG, as well as Panamanian companies and local subsidiaries and affiliates of foreign MNCs. In the past two years, Panama Pacífico has grown by approximately 1,000 workers and thirty companies annually, with a long-term target of 40,000 total employees.[147] A substantial portion of the businesses operating in Panama Pacífico provide services to workers and their families residing in the zone.[148]

Like new generation SEZs in other parts of the world, Panamá Pacífico's development strategy hinges on various regulatory incentives. Law No. 41 provides for various fiscal incentives to foreign MNCs in the SEZ. Companies are exempted from all indirect taxes levied by the national government.[149] Companies in specific targeted industries are also exempted from income, corporate dividend, and transfer and withholding taxes.[150] Panamá Pacífico's "One Stop Shop" consolidates eleven regulatory agencies onsite in the zone in order to expedite government procedures and permits for companies, including the Ministry of Labor (responsible for granting worker permits) and the Directorate of Migration (responsible for issuing worker visas to foreign nationals).[151]

---

144. *See* Law No. 41 *supra* note 131 Art. 3(8); Panama Pacifico, *Master Plan*, http://www.panamapacifico.com/master-plan (Nov. 13, 2018).
145. Ga. Inst. of Tech Logistics Innovation and Res. Ctr., *Panama Pacifico: On-Site Companies*, http://logistics.gatech.pa/en/assets/special-economic-zones/panama-pacifico/companies (Nov. 13, 2018).
146. *See*, Panama Pacifico, *Press Release Global Investments Secure Panama Pacifico's Position as International Business Hub*, http://www.panamapacifico.com/global-investments (Mar. 11, 2015).
147. Unofficial data provided by APP (data on file with author). *See also Master Plan*, APP, http://www.app.gob.pa/index.php (Nov. 13, 2018).
148. *See* Panama Pacifico *Business, Retail*, http://www.panamapacifico.com/retail (Nov. 13, 2018) (noting consumer-facing business opportunities in the International Business Park and Town Center of Panamá Pacífico).
149. *See* Law No. 41, *supra* note 131, Art. 58; *see also* Panama Pacifico, *Panama Pacifico Special Economic Area Incentives*, http://cloud.panamapacifico.com/libraries/pdfs/spanish/Law-41.pdf (Nov. 13, 2018). These exemptions do not apply to employees of such companies. *See* Law No. 41, *supra* note 131, Art. 59.
150. *Ibid.*, Art. 60(4). Among the targeted industries to which this incentive is granted are back office operations, aviation, the film industry, distribution centers, and MNCs headquartered in Panamá Pacífico. *Ibid.*, Art. 60.
151. *See* Ga. Inst. of Tech. Logistics Innovation and Res. Ctr. Panama, *Panama Pacifico Services*, http://logistics.gatech.pa/en/assets/special-economic-zones/panama-pacifico/services (Nov. 13, 2018). The concept of a one stop shop located in the SEZ for all government administrative services reflects global best practices. *See* Tom Farole & Josaphat Kweka, *Institutional Best Practices for Special Economic Zones: An Application to Tanzania* 9 (World Bank, Africa Trade Policy Note No. 25, August 2011), http://siteresources.worldbank.org/INTAFRREGTOPTRADE/Resources/SEZ_Tanzania_Policy_note_Final.pdf.

A key aspect of Panama's development strategy is various immigration and labor benefits granted to foreign MNCs that invest in the country. Panamá Pacífico's migration "flexibilities" are similar in scope and purpose to bilateral FTAs following the NAFTA approach. Foreign nationals employed by companies in the zone are eligible for special work visas. Work visas to SEZ company employees range from three to five years and include special categories for foreign workers working in technical areas or management.[152] The percentage of workers granted visas is capped at 10–15% of the company's employees in the SEZ.[153] Foreign investors are also eligible for special resident visas of five years.[154] The general terms of these temporary worker visas are supplemented by visas to the immediate relatives of foreign workers[155] and duty-free importation of personal and domestic possessions.[156] In addition, foreign workers granted a Panamá Pacífico temporary residency visa have the right to apply for permanent residency in Panama after two years.[157] These special migration rules complement unique labor flexibilities, which compartmentalize Panamá Pacífico's labor regime from the rest of the country for domestic and foreign workers alike.[158]

The US-Panama FTA, which entered into force in 2012, does not expressly create new temporary work visas.[159] However, it indirectly addresses Panama's SEZ-based temporary migration framework. The status of Panamá Pacífico is clarified by side letters agreeing to modify the rules of origin provisions of the FTA.[160] Similar to other new generation SEZs, the side letters clarify that the "wholesale purchase or sale of a good" in Panama's SEZs does not constitute "subsequent production or any other operation" for purposes of determining whether it qualifies as an "originating good"

152. *See* Law No. 41, *supra* note 131, Arts 91 (limiting foreign employees to 10% of a company's total number of employees in Panamá Pacífico, or 15% if the company also employs technical and managerial staff) and 100(1)-(3) (establishing the number of special work visas that may be issued pursuant to these limits).
153. *Ibid.*
154. *Ibid.*, Art. 101. Eligible investors must invest at least B/250,000 (equivalent to USD 250,000) in venture capital. *Ibid.*
155. *Ibid.*, Art. 102.
156. *Ibid.*, Art. 104.
157. Ley No. 3, Feb. 10, 2015, Que modifica y adiciona disposiciones a la Ley 41 de 2004 que crea la Agencia Panamá: Pacífico [Law No. 3] tit. 27719-A, Gaceta Oficial (Feb. 11, 2015) (Pan.), Art. 6 (amending Art. 100 of Law. No. 41), http://gacetas.procuraduria-admon.gob.pa/27719-A_2015.pdf.
158. For example, labor disputes involving employees of companies located in Panamá Pacífico are governed by the Labor, Immigration and Social Security Matters Directorate (*Dirección de Asuntos de Trabajo, Migración y Seguridad Social*) within APP, which has primary jurisdiction to mediate disputes extrajudicially. *See* Law No. 41, *supra* note 131, Art. 95.
159. *See* US Trade Representative, *U.S.-Panama Trade Promotion Agreement*, https://ustr.gov/trade-agreements/free-trade-agreements/panama-tpa (Oct. 31, 2012) (Nov. 13, 2018). The FTA was signed in 2007 and enacted into US law in 2011. *See* Hornbeck, *supra* note 123, at 29–30 (chronology of US-Panama FTA).
160. *See* US Trade Representative, *Side Letter on Panama Free Zone* (September/October 2013), https://ustr.gov/sites/default/files/uploads/agreements/fta/panama/asset_upload_file203_10511.pdf [hereinafter US-Panama Side Letter]. This agreement superseded prior letters exchanged between the US and Panamanian government in 2007. *See* Org. American States Foreign Trade Information System (SICE) *Side Letter on Panama Free Zone* (June 2007), http://www.sice.oas.org/Trade/PAN_USA_TPA_Text0607_e/l_Panama_freezones.pdf.

under any other US FTA.[161] Expressly excluding goods that pass through Panama's SEZs from the scope of the FTA demarcates Panamá Pacífico from Panama's home market.[162]

Panamá Pacífico's regulatory framework, including its migration flexibilities, expressly seeks to promote the country's long-term economic development.[163] The objective to attract foreign investment is coupled with the objective to facilitate human capital formation.[164] For example, Law No. 41 expressly provides that companies that exercise the "worker training" exception to the 15% cap on foreign technical and managerial employees must assign one or more Panamanian workers to each foreign employee in order to comply with the aims of the specified training. Further, the special work visas for such foreign employees are subject to the approval of a full training program by the Panamanian government.[165]

Table 9.1 shows the number of visas and permits granted by the Panamanian government to foreign workers eligible to work in Panamá Pacífico.

Table 9.1 Annual Migration into Panamá Pacífico for the Period 2012–2015[166]

Visas/Permits	*2012*	*2013*	*2014*	*2015*[(a)]	*Total*
Multiple Entry Visa (Visa Múltiple)	144	67	199	121	531
Temporary Residency Card (Carnet de Trámite)	215	94	265	177	751
Definitive Residency Permit (Permiso Definitivo)	2	81	235	263	581
Investor Permit (Permiso de Inversionistas)	0	0	0	0	0

161. *See US-Panama Side Letter, supra* note 160, at 1.
162. This demarcation ensures that the SEZ does not facilitate trade triangulation through illegal transhipment. *See supra* text accompanying n. 112. The side letters also prohibit Panama from using its SEZs to leverage revenue from differences in preferential duty rates between the US-Panama FTA and other US FTAs. In other words, Panama cannot profit from permitting SEZ-based intermediaries to buy goods wholesale and then sell them to US-based importers as an originating good entitled to lower tariffs.
163. *See* Law No. 41, *supra* note 131, Art. 1 (describing Panamá Pacífico as "a special legal, tax, customs, labor, immigration and business regime ... designed to encourage and ensure the free flow and movement of goods, services and funds ... to make the Republic of Panama more competitive within the global economy").
164. *See* Press Release, Panama Pacifico, *Panama's National Assembly Strengthens Panama Pacifico's Incentive Offerings*, http://www.panamapacifico.com/pp-incentive (4 Mar. 2015) (characterizing Panamá Pacífico's immigration rules as a key driver of job creation within Panama Pacifico in high value-added industries such as manufacturing and processing, logistics, and research and development).
165. *See* Law No. 41, *supra* note 131, Art. 91.
166. Derived from unpublished data provided by the National Migration Service of the Government of Panama (data on file with author).

Visas/Permits	*2012*	*2013*	*2014*	*2015*[(a)]	*Total*
Visa/Permit in Processing[(b)] (Estatus Migratorio)	229	67	254	158	708
TOTAL	590	309	953	719	2,571

(a) Through 31 Aug. 2015.
(b) For visas and permits that have been provisionally granted and are under review for consideration under one of the four above categories.

The data in Table 9.1 show the scope and limits of Panama's SEZ-based migration strategy. Foreign workers constitute a small portion of the nearly 8,000 employees in Panamá Pacífico.[167] Notably, zero investor visas have been issued in the past three years, which underscores the difficulty of spurring foreign investment through temporary residency.[168] The relatively low number of foreign worker visas and permits undervalues the role of migration flexibilities, however. Temporary labor migration is viewed as a means to generate spillover effects in local firms through formal skills training and the transfer of foreign technical and managerial expertise.[169] Under Law No. 41, the Panamanian government has the authority to grant additional work visas to foreign workers for the purpose of training domestic workers employed by a company or due to a lack of qualified domestic workers in a specific area.[170] Further towards this end, APP manages a Center for Higher Education in Panamá Pacífico, which is dedicated to training domestic employees to work for SEZ-based companies and industries.[171] Several academic institutions are located in Panamá Pacífico, including two universities.[172]

In recognition of the competitive global landscape for professional worker visas, the Panamanian government continues to refine and expand Panamá Pacífico's

167. Less than 10% of employees are foreign-born. *See* unpublished data provided by APP (data on file with author). *See also* Ga. Inst. of Tech. Logistics Innovation and Res. Ctr., *Panama Pacifico-Facts and Figures*, http://logistics.gatech.pa/en/assets/special-economic-zones/panama-pacifico (Nov. 13, 2018).
168. *See* The Economist, *Indecorous Leave to Remain*, http://www.economist.com/news/finance-and-economics/21664150-schemes-offer-residence-permits-big-investors-usually-disappoint-indecorous (Sep. 12, 2015) (noting the widespread use of investor visas by the United States, Canada, and many European countries and the lack of substantial impact on investment). In addition to other countries, Panama Pacífico competes with the rest of Panama for foreign investors. In 2012, the Panamanian government enacted a fast track to permanent residency for investors from twenty-two designated countries that "maintain friendly, professional, economic, and investment relationships" with Panama. *See* Decreto Ejecutivo No. 343, May 16, 2012, Gaceta Oficial, May 21, 2012 (Pan.) (amending Decreto Ley No. 3, Feb. 22, 2008, Que crea el Servicio Nacional de Migración, la Carrera Migratoria y dicta otras disposiciones, tit. 25986, Gaceta Oficial (Feb. 26, 2008) (Pan.)), https://www.gacetaoficial.gob.pa/pdfTemp/27038/37901.pdf.
169. *See* Sigler, *supra* note 84, at 9 (noting Panamá Pacífico's nascent capacity building programs).
170. *See* Law No. 41, *supra* note 131 41, Art. 91.
171. *See ibid.*, Art. 97; *see also* Agencia Panamá-Pacífico *Training*, http://www.app.gob.pa/index.php?p=capacitacion (in Spanish) (Nov. 13, 2018) (describing capacity building in Panamá Pacífico in coordination with the National Institute of Professional Training for the Human Development (INADEH)).
172. *See* Panama Pacifico, *Education*, http://www.panamapacifico.com/education (Nov. 13, 2018).

migration flexibilities. Most recently, Law No. 3, enacted in February 2015, amended Law No. 41 by easing entry requirements for foreign workers.[173] The duration of temporary visas is shortened, and eligibility for permanent residency in the country is expanded.[174] Further, foreigners may now work in Panamá Pacífico either under visas granted under the Panamá Pacífico regulatory framework or any other Panamanian visa program.[175]

As evident with Panamá Pacífico's regulatory framework, new generation SEZs tend to favor the granting of short-term visas to business managers, technicians, and investors. Like other approaches to migration liberalization, SEZs migration flexibilities have a comparatively small impact on aggregate migration in host countries, in part due to their emphasis on temporary migration for high-skilled foreign workers. However, SEZs may arguably differ from GATS Mode 4 and FTAs in one important respect. Due to their bespoke legal structure and the predominance of public-private governance regimes, SEZs may be more responsive to labor preferences of MNCs than other approaches, which insulate government lawmakers and regulators from investor demands.

§9.05 IMPLICATIONS OF THE GLOBAL TRADE-LABOR MIGRATION NEXUS

The global trade-labor migration nexus enables governments to opportunistically compete for the most economically productive labor through customized regulatory frameworks.[176] Rather than being required to open their domestic labor markets broadly or comprehensively, countries are able to carve out "regulatory space" to define the parameters of global labor migration on their own terms through ad hoc arrangements.[177] Competing in the global marketplace to attract human capital, governments can pick and choose from a variety of strategies—such as SEZ-based migration flexibilities—to maximize their return on investment while minimizing the economic dislocation to domestic workers caused by foreign labor. In short, the economic pressures imposed by foreign trade competition and trade liberalization motivate countries to open their markets to MNCs while international trade law grants these countries the discretion to open their borders to foreign workers only as much as

173. *See* Ley No. 3, Feb. 10, 2015, Que modifica y adiciona disposiciones a la Ley 41 de 2004 que crea la Agencia Panamá: Pacífico [Law No. 3] tit. 27719-A, Gaceta Oficial (Feb. 11, 2015) (Pan.), https://www.gacetaoficial.gob.pa/pdfTemp/27719_A/GacetaNo_27719a_20150211.pdf.

174. *Ibid.*, Art. 6.

175. *Ibid. See also* Ernst & Young, *Panama amends Panama-Pacific Agency Law, assembly and processing activities are now eligible for certain tax exemptions*, http://www.ey.com/GL/en/Services/Tax/International-Tax/Alert--Panama-amends-Panama-Pacific-Agency-Law--assembly-and-processing-activities-are-now-eligible-for-certain-tax-exemptions. (Mar. 13, 2015).

176. *See* Tamanaha, *supra* note 51, at 375 (noting how individuals and groups can opportunistically advance their aims by selecting from co-existing legal orders).

177. *See* Wagner, *supra* note 74, at 5 (describing how international trade law and international investment law helps create regulatory space for member country governments).

necessary to attract foreign capital and know-how. Regionalism and privatization facilitate this regulatory flexibility.

The pluralistic nature of the global trade-labor migration nexus raises important fundamental issues in international law. Not only do these issues implicate the inter-relationships between trade, foreign investment, and migration, but they also highlight potential spillover effects of fragmentation on international law generally. The following discussion analyzes these broader implications, focusing on the issues raised by SEZs.

[A] Labor Migration and "Behind the Border" Treatment of Migrants

While the so-called behind the border treatment of foreign workers is distinct from rights of entry, these policy decisions are inextricably linked.[178] Disparate treatment of foreign workers vis-à-vis their domestic counterparts may deter or encourage migration.[179] There is no consensus regarding this relationship in the global trade-labor migration nexus. Under certain countries' schedules, GATS Mode 4 requires wage parity (i.e., equal pay to service-providing foreign workers vis-à-vis similar domestic workers), which arguably deters its adoption by other WTO member countries.[180] Starting with NAFTA, US FTAs have included increasingly robust labor rights provisions, which serve to define, codify, and enforce core labor standards.[181] However, neither FTAs nor BMAs address the specific labor rights at risk with temporary migrants.[182]

A similar dynamic is evident in SEZ-based migration governance. In the absence of binding international legal commitments, host countries, operating in conjunction with private SEZ administrators, exert a degree of de facto control over the geographic territory of the SEZ, which serves to fortify the power of host countries to control who migrates, for what reason, and for how long.[183] Compared to other global labor migration strategies, the inherent geographic boundaries of SEZs inhibit permanent residency through overstayed temporary visas and other legally gray actions, which has been an unintended but frequent consequence of traditional guest worker programs.[184]

---

178. *See* Ruhs, *supra* note 7, at 111–20 (analyzing trade-offs between migrant rights and openness to migration).
179. *See* Tomer Broude, *A Minimal Liberal Defense of (Some) Discrimination in Migration Regulation*, 36 Fordham Intl. L.J. 575, 593–96 (2013) (presenting examples of migration-encouraging and migration-deterring discrimination of migrants).
180. *See* Ruhs, *supra* note 7, at 150–52.
181. *See* Marisa Anne Pagnattaro, *U.S. Trade Policy: Increased Emphasis on Worker Rights*, 40 Ga. J. Intl. & Comp. L. 663, 680–87, 692–709 (2012) (analyzing labor provisions in the Dominican Republic-Central America-United States Free Trade Agreement (DR-CAFTA) and bilateral FTAs with South Korea, Colombia, and Panama).
182. *See* Marion Panizzon, *Migration and Trade: Prospects for Bilateralism in the Face of Skill-Selective Mobility Laws*, 12 Melb. J. Intl. L. 95, 141 (2011).
183. *See* Lang, *supra* note 97, at 22.
184. *See* Motomura, *supra* note 22, at 285 (noting the emphasis on criminal enforcement and coercive deterrence measures to discourage temporary migrants from overstaying); *see also*

Both entry of foreign workers into SEZs, as well as their legal rights and entitlements once they migrate into SEZs, are largely left unaddressed in bilateral and regional FTAs.[185] New generation SEZs, such as Panamá Pacífico, apply domestic labor laws to employees in the zone.[186] However, this may not necessarily result in fair and equitable of treatment of SEZ-based workers in other countries, particularly low-skilled foreigners without corporate sponsorship.[187] Even the US-Jordan FTA, with full incorporation of labor provisions in the agreement itself and dispute settlement available for any violations of labor rights, has failed to ensure the fair treatment of migrant workers in Jordan's SEZs.[188]

From a normative perspective, fragmentation highlights the need to clarify the objectives of the global trade regime with respect to migration.[189] Should the global trade-labor migration nexus use the institutional mechanisms of international trade law to increase the number of labor migrants or improve the conditions of a relatively smaller number of migrants?[190] This question has been characterized as a "numbers versus rights" dilemma.[191] Arguably, the currently predominant dynamic of states competing with each other for foreign investment and human capital through a constellation of customized regulatory frameworks makes it easier for countries to avoid reaching a global consensus on this question.[192]

This is particularly evident in the absence of meaningful dialog on how to address, if at all, the general bias of the global trade-labor migration nexus towards

---

Ruhs & Chang, *supra* note 41, at 98 (suggesting that limiting the duration and renewal of temporary visas may be socially beneficial).

185. *See* Bolle & Williams, *supra* note 86, at 22.
186. *See* Law No. 41, *supra* note 131, Art. 79 (providing that "the rules of the [Panamanian] Labor Code and other legal provisions in force on labor matters shall be applicable to the labor provisions within [Panamá Pacífico]").
187. Lang, *supra* note 97, at 18–21 (noting considerable variation in labor rights records in SEZs and summarizing concerns with freedom of association, gender discrimination, and health and safety, among other issues). For a contrary view, *see* Daniel W. Drezner, *Globalization and Policy Convergence*, 3 Intl. Stud. Rev. 53, 67–68 (2001) (finding scant evidence of a race to the bottom with respect to labor standards in export processing zones).
188. *See* Kevin Kolben, *Trade, Development, and Migrant Garment Workers in Jordan*, 5 Middle E. L. & Governance 195, 219 (2013) (noting the limits of FTA-based labor rights enforcement). Jordan's SEZs at issue are known as qualified industrial zones, which are designated areas in Egypt and Jordan from which a manufactured product may be sent duty-free to the United States if the product contains inputs from Israel. *See ibid.*, at 199–200.
189. *See* Barak-Erez & Perez, *supra* note 64, at 483 (noting the global trade regime's ideological bias towards neo-liberal, capitalist norms).
190. Ruhs, *supra* note 7, at 4. This question echoes the fundamental orientation clash between individualist and non-individualist cultural norms identified by Brian Tamanaha as one of several normative fault lines in legal pluralism. *See* Tamanaha, *supra* note 51, at 407–08.
191. *See* Philip Martin, *Managing Labor Migration: Temporary Worker Programs for the 21st Century*, UN/POP/MIG/SYMP/2006/07 39–40 (Jun. 21, 2006), http://www.un.org/esa/population/migration/turin/Symposium_Turin_files/P07_Martin.pdf (anonymously quoting a common saying in emigration areas, "What is worse than being 'exploited' abroad? Not being 'exploited' abroad").
192. *See* Ruhs, *supra* note 7, at 87–90 (finding a positive relationship between openness and rights for high-skilled migrants and an inverse relationship for low-skilled migrants).

higher-skilled foreign labor and the exclusion of low-skilled foreigners.[193] The traditional paradigm of wealthy developed countries as destination countries and relatively poor developing countries as source countries is now more complex. As source countries become wealthier, they may become themselves destinations for migrants (especially unskilled labor from comparatively poorer countries), thus muddling the advocacy of their governments.[194] In addition, as cross-border economic integration deepens through trade and foreign investment, global corporate elites in source countries may increasingly identify with their counterparts in destination countries and thus advocate for elite-based migration.[195]

From the perspective of MNCs and destination countries, highly specialized human capital has higher returns on investment, and therefore higher-skilled workers are the focus of joint and coordinated recruitment efforts.[196] Ayelet Shachar describes "a bifurcated market" for global labor that heavily restricts admission of low-skilled workers to desired destination countries (both in terms of numbers and a right to stay) while aggressively competing for the highly skilled and gifted by offering citizenship and permanent residency.[197] In the context of the international trading system, there is the possibility of conflict between blocs of countries bound to each other through FTAs that compete for this high-demand labor. While this may lead to a "race to the top",[198] it may also lead to underinvestment by governments in their own citizens and less highly sought migrants.[199] Taken to its logical extreme, the ratcheting up of the global competition for competitive labor may lead to citizenship being viewed as a strategic and instrumental exercise of state power.[200]

193. *See* Chantal Thomas, *Undocumented Migrant Workers in a Fragmented Legal Order*, 25 Md. J. Intl. L. 187, 207 (2010) (concluding that "[t]he practical effect of the trade regime is to confer the privileges of liberalization only to high-skilled workers").
194. *See* Jaya Ramji-Nogales, *Undocumented Migrants and the Failures of Universal Individualism*, 47 Vand. J. Transnat'l. L. 699, 757–58 (2014) (noting the difficulty of protecting migrants through coalitions of source country governments due to competing interests among them).
195. *See* David B. Wilkins & Mihaela Papa, *The Rise of the Corporate Legal Elite in the BRICS: Implications for Global Governance*, 54 B.C. Intl. & Comp. L. Rev 1149, 1161 (2013) (noting the role of corporate lawyers as "partners with power" and further analyzing the role of corporate lawyers in emerging market countries); *see also* Solimano, *supra* note 29, at 185–86 (noting that global talent is disproportionately concentrated in the wealthiest countries as well as China, India, and other emerging market economies).
196. Trebilcock, Howse & Eliason, *supra* note 1, at 631.
197. *See* Ayelet Shachar, *Picking Winners: Olympic Citizenship and the Global Race for Talent*, 120 Yale L.J. 2088, 2101 (2011).
198. *See* David S. Law, *Globalization and the Future of Constitutional Rights*, 102 Nw. U. L. Rev. 1277, 1321 (2008) (arguing that greater human rights attract elite workers in the global competition for human capital).
199. Indirectly addressing this concern, Panamá Pacífico's migration framework grants visas to foreign managers on the condition that they train domestic employees of zone-based MNCs. *See supra* text accompanying n. 170.
200. Shachar & Hirschl, *supra* note 30, at 104–05.

[B] Labor Migration and the Changing Roles of the Nation-State

The global trade-labor migration nexus operates in the shadows of the exclusive territorial authority of national governments. As Chantal Thomas declares, "the notion of a *right* to enter the territory of a sovereign state appears nonsensical, so deeply entrenched is the principle of territoriality as a feature of sovereignty."[201] The nature of sovereign authority over the cross-border movement of people is not static and unchanging, however. Rather, new regulatory developments show how governments modify how they exercise power over migration to account for changing economic conditions and policy objectives. The following discussion specifically examines four ways that sovereign authority over migration is evolving and broadening: regional integration, subnational devolution, private governance, and extraterritorial delegation of jurisdiction.

[1] Regional Integration

The European Union (EU) is the most advanced form of regional integration to date.[202] The EU's single market constitutes the most liberalized cross-border labor migration regime in the world.[203] Under the EU's right of free movement, EU citizens have the legal right to move freely between EU member countries for employment.[204] Most EU member countries have acceded to the twenty-six member Schengen Agreements, which facilitate free movement by establishing common border control and visa arrangements, thus diminishing the power of governments to unilaterally control their respective national borders.[205] Even the EU's liberalization is structurally limited, however. EU member countries retain complete control over regulation of the admission of migrants from the outside the EU.[206] Citizens of non-EU member countries do not enjoy freedom to enter the EU for employment.[207] Under current EU policies and rules, third country nationals are subject to special scrutiny at the national level, and EU member countries have terminated bilateral visa agreements previously in force with various developing countries.[208] The current European migration crisis has led to disputes between EU member countries regarding the EU's right to free movement and has highlighted the need for EU-level coordination on admission of refugees by

201. Thomas, *supra* note 62, at 411–12 (emphasis in original).
202. *See* Scanlan, *supra* note 42, at 131–32 (characterizing the EU as a "proto-federal State").
203. *See* Sykes, *supra* note 3, at 315–16 (contrasting the EU to other migration frameworks).
204. *See* Treaty Establishing the European Economic Community Art. 39 (Mar. 25, 1957), 298 U.N.T.S. 3 (granting free movement to workers to nationals of EU member countries); *see also* Trachtman, *supra* note 42, at 185–89 (summarizing the EU legal framework governing the free movement of workers).
205. Trachtman, *supra* note 42, at 185, 195–96.
206. Ruhs, *supra* note 7, at 36.
207. Trachtman, *supra* note 42, at 197.
208. Brabandt & Mau, *supra* note 47, at 67–68 (describing Austria and Finland's actions upon accession to the EU/Schengen regime).

individual EU member countries.[209] Even the future of the Schengen regime itself is threatened by the growing desire of many of its Member States to suspend or fundamentally restructure it.[210]

Regional FTAs with labor migration provisions, such as NAFTA, define the scope of sovereign authority over migration that its member countries may exercise vis-à-vis other members of the FTA. However, the ability of members to enforce these arrangements is constrained by the limited transfer of formal sovereign authority over migration from their respective member countries to supranational bodies. The US FTAs based on the NAFTA approach are indicative of the non-binding, consultative nature of supranational governance, which grants limited dispute settlement rights[211] and establishes coordinators or committees with limited powers.[212]

For FTAs generally, the benefits of liberalizing labor are dampened due to prevalence of regional trading blocs. Because these FTAs provide benefits to specific member countries, they may lead to "migration diversion"—i.e., the most efficient source of foreign labor may be foregone in favor of workers from an FTA member country.[213] Migration diversion can be avoided by applying MFN obligations on international migration cooperation—or, in other words, by requiring countries to grant equivalent rights of entry to non-FTA member countries.[214] This is not standard practice, however, which may lead to a web of regional and bilateral labor migration arrangements that grant preferred status to a limited number of FTA member countries and discriminate against other countries outside of the trade bloc.[215]

[2] Subnational Devolution

Another example of legal change is the devolution of territorial authority to localities and other subnational governments. The regional visa concept, like SEZs, delineates

209. *See*, e.g., Andrew Higgins, *European Leaders Agree to Strengthen Border Controls Over Migrant Crisis*, N.Y. Times (Oct. 16, 2015), at A12 (reporting on the European Council's decision to bolster the EU border agency and provide additional funding for national border services); *see also* Alison Smale & Melissa Eddy, *Crisis Tests European Core Value: Open Borders*, N.Y. Times (Sep. 1, 2015), at A1 (noting disagreement within the EU regarding freedom of movement).
210. *See* Ian Traynor & Helena Smith, *EU Border Controls: Schengen Scheme on the Brink After Amsterdam Talks*, The Guardian, http://www.theguardian.com/world/2016/jan/25/refugee-crisis-schengen-area-scheme-brink-amsterdam-talks (Jan. 26, 2016, 2:17 PM).
211. *See* Free Trade Agreement Chile-US, Art. 14.6 (Jan. 1, 2004); Free Trade Agreement, Singapore-U.S. Art. 11.8 (May 6, 2003).
212. *See* Free Trade Agreement Chile-US, Art. 14.5 (Jan. 1, 2004) (establishing a Committee on Temporary Entry); Free Trade Agreement, Singapore-US, Art. 11.7 (May 6, 2003) (establishing Temporary Entry Coordinators for each member country).
213. *See* Sykes, *supra* note 3, at 330–32.
214. *Ibid.*, at 331. The special treatment of service workers from Canada, Mexico, Chile, and Singapore under NAFTA and NAFTA-approach US FTAs with Chile and Singapore may violate the MFN principle in GATS. *See* William Thomas Worster, *Conflicts Between United States Immigration Law and the General Agreement on Trade in Services: Most-Favored-Nation Obligation*, 42 Tex. Intl. L.J. 55, 94–95, 109 (2010).
215. Economist Jagdish Bhagwati has famously likened these crisscrossing preferential arrangements emanating from each country to a metaphorical spaghetti bowl. *See* Jagdish Bhagwati, *Termites in the Trading System: How Preferential Agreements Undermine Free Trade* 63 (2008) (describing the genesis of the spaghetti bowl metaphor).

the right to migrate in spatial, as well as temporal, terms. Regional visa programs calibrate labor migration to the specific needs of local communities that, among other strategic priorities, are attempting to respond to foreign trade competition. In contrast to employment-based visas that tie a foreign worker to a specific firm, such as the H-1B, regional visas are tied to a specific locality.[216] Regional visas are sponsored by states or municipalities based on their economic needs, and make the issuance and validity of an employment visa conditional on residing and working for a company in the region.[217]

Canada and Australia have implemented programs following this approach.[218] The regional visa concept is evident in Canada's Provincial Nomination Program (PNP), which permits Canadian provinces to nominate individuals for visas every year,[219] and Australia's Regional Sponsored Migration Scheme, which provides a permanent residence visa for skilled foreign workers that wish to work in less populated parts of the country.[220] In the US, there has been serious policy debate but no implementation of regional visas to date. In 2014, Governor Rick Snyder of Michigan proposed the issuance of regional visas for 50,000 skilled foreign workers as part of a broad-based effort to revitalize the city of Detroit.[221] Under Michigan's proposed plan, Detroit regional visas would be issued under the federal EB-2 visa program, which grants permanent residency to foreigners with advanced degrees or exceptional abilities in the sciences, arts, or business.[222] In each of these cases, while the national government retains the ultimate legal authority to grant visas, economic criteria for granting them are based on regional public policy considerations.

[3] Private Governance

A third source of legal change is the growing influence of private and hybrid public-private governance regimes. In domestic immigration law, private companies

216. *See* Brandon Fuller & Sean Rust, *State-Based Visas: A Federalist Approach to Reforming U.S. Immigration Policy* (Cato Institute, Policy Analysis No. 748, Apr. 23, 2014), http://object.cato.org/sites/cato.org/files/pubs/pdf/pa748_web_1.pdf.
217. *See* Brandon Fuller & Sean Rust, *The Insanely Clear-Cut Case for Region-Based Immigration Visas*, Atlantic Cities, http://theatlanticcities.com/politics/2013/05/insanely-clear-cut-case-region-based-immigration-visas/5475 (May 2013).
218. The Economist, *See Going Where They Are Wanted: How Canada and Australia Let Regions Sponsor Immigrants*, 28, http://www.economist.com/news/united-states/21642229-how-canada-and-australia-let-regions-sponsor-immigrants-going-where-they-are-wanted (Feb. 17, 2015) (noting that 40% of economic migrants in Australia and 25% of economic migrants in Canada are admitted under regional visas).
219. *See* Canada visa *Provincial Nomination Program (PNP)*, http://www.canadavisa.com/provincial-nomination-program.html (Nov. 13, 2018).
220. *See* Austl. Govt., Dept. Immigration & Border Protection, *Regional Sponsored Migration Scheme visa (subclass 187)*, https://immi.homeaffairs.gov.au/visas/getting-a-visa/visa-listing/regional-sponsor-migration-scheme-187 (Nov. 13, 2018).
221. *See* Monica Davey, *Immigrants Seen as Way to Refill Detroit Ranks*, N.Y. Times, at A12 (Jan. 23, 2014).
222. *See* 8 U.S.C. § 1153(b)(2); *see also* US Dept. Homeland Security, *Employment-Based Immigration: Second Preference EB-2*, https://www.uscis.gov/working-united-states/permanent-workers/employment-based-immigration-second-preference-eb-2 (Nov. 13, 2018).

and associations have a substantial role in ensuring compliance.[223] The immigration laws of many countries restrict freedom of movement of migrants by binding their right of entry to a specific employer.[224] In the US, for example, H-1B visa holders are not permitted to work as independent contractors and their new employers are subject to the conditions attached to the original H-1B visa.[225]

Beyond domestic immigration law lies a broad range of hybrid governance approaches that delegate sovereign authority to private actors to varying degrees. BMAs have delegated significant public rule-making power to unions, industry associations, and private security firms.[226] The proliferation of localized approaches, such as regional visas, reinforces the practice of making entry contingent on the fulfillment of a specific employment obligation.[227] With respect to labor migration, SEZ public-private governance regimes affirm the potential efficiency gains from transferring operational control to privatized entities and away from the national government.[228] Public-private governance regimes whose express mandate is to maximize foreign investment in high value-added industries exacerbate the global trade-labor migration nexus' bias towards high-skilled labor. The prevalence of public-private governance regimes in new generation SEZs raises normative questions concerning their capacity to determine who is deemed to belong in the polity or who can, should, or must be excluded.[229] This poses a threat to the nation-state to the extent that private managers exercise the authority to change the SEZ's policies and practices.[230]

In the case of Panamá Pacífico, Law No. 41 expressly provides for a governance structure that delegates substantial operational autonomy to private managers but

223. In US law, one example of private governance is the affirmative duty of employers to ensure compliance with entry requirements. *See* Eleanor Marie Lawrence Brown, *Outsourcing Immigration Compliance*, 77 Fordham L. Rev. 2475, 2489 (2009) (referring to employer sanctions against employers that fail to screen aliens for work permits and report non-compliant persons).
224. *See* Matthew Lister, *Justice and Temporary Labor Migration*, 29 Geo. Immig. L.J. 95, 116–17 (2014) (arguing for visa portability in order to reduce the chance of exploitation of foreign workers).
225. *See* Epstein, *supra* note 32, at 221. Epstein suggests that the H-1B visa program further effectively restricts freedom of movement through requirements that mandate wage parity, equal benefits, good faith recruitment, and hiring of similarly qualified domestic workers. *See ibid.*, at 217–19.
226. Panizzon, *supra* note 182, at 128.
227. Canada's employer-led PNP program, which expressly gives priority to foreigners with job offers or a nomination from a province, reflects this phenomenon. *See* The Economist, *No Country for Old Men*, http://www.economist.com/news/americas/21638191-canada-used-prize-immigrants-who-would-make-good-citizens-now-people-job-offers-have (Jan. 10, 2015) (characterizing Canada's Express Entry as "a privatisation of immigration policy").
228. *See* Trebilcock, Howse & Eliason, *supra* note 1, at 626 (noting the "compelling case" for devolving and decentralizing power over immigration decision making).
229. *See* Peter J. Spiro, *The Boundaries of Cosmopolitan Pluralism*, 51 Wayne L. Rev. 1261, 1268–69 (2005) (arguing that the rise of non-governmental forms of association warrants looking more closely at the condition of rights within them).
230. *See* Robert Wai, *Transnational Liftoff and Juridical Touchdown: The Regulatory Function of Private International Law in an Era of Globalization*, 40 Colum. J. Transnatl. L. 209, 267 (2002) (describing the relationship between transnational private governance and national laws as "a dialectical one" in which neither is clearly dominant).

limited independent rulemaking powers. APP, Panamá Pacífico's public/private administrator, has governing authority to determine which MNCs may invest and operate in the zone and to whom temporary visas are granted.[231] However, APP's rulemaking authority is not independent insofar as the executive branch of the Panamanian government retains sole authority to establish visa requirements.[232] Furthermore, any decisions to grant or deny a visa may be appealed to the National Directorate of Immigration and Naturalization of the Panamanian government.[233] The institutional framework of Panamá Pacífico creates efficiency gains by devolving regulatory authority to APP and minimizing central government control. However, this largely precludes the possibility of complementary policy learning through parallel public and private regulation by de-linking Panamá Pacífico's regulatory regime from the rest of the country.[234]

Private governance may be helpful in addressing the distributional impact of immigration on domestic workers, which poses a substantial barrier to expanded migration. Trade adjustment assistance, known as TAA in the US, provides compensation to workers (through wage insurance, health care, and monetary support for occupational re-training, job search, relocation, and related expenses) who lose their jobs due to trade liberalization.[235] There is no comparable compensation mechanism to address job displacement caused by migration liberalization.[236] To address this governance gap, scholars have suggested that governments and dislocated native-born workers could be compensated by domestic employers for losses incurred by the hiring of foreign workers.[237] One potentially promising approach proposed by Robert Hockett focuses on private financial intermediation through modified employee stock ownership plans (SOPs).[238] Hockett proposes the creation of "outsource" SOPs that transfer globalization-derived wealth gains from firms to trusts that hold assets on behalf of

231. *See* Law No. 41, *supra* note 131, Art. 33 (defining the powers of the Labor, Immigration and Social Security Matters Directorate).
232. Law No. 41, *supra* note 131, Art. 103.
233. *Ibid.*
234. *See* Kolben, *supra* note 80, at 444 (describing complementarity in labor regulation in respect of the Dominican Republic's SEZs); *see also* Matthew Amengual, *Complementary Labor Regulation: The Uncoordinated Combination of State and Private Regulators in the Dominican Republic*, 38 World Dev. 405, 408 (2010).
235. *See* 19 U.S.C. §§ 2271–2331 (2014) (Trade Adjustment Assistance for Workers program); Park, *supra* note 36, at 817–24 (examining economic, political, and ethical justifications for trade adjustment assistance).
236. Many developed countries have robust social welfare programs and progressive tax systems, which help cushion the impact of migration liberalization on displaced domestic workers. However, these policy measures are largely exogenous to the liberalization process. *See* Hollifield & Osang, *supra* note 37, at 343 (calling for "automatic stabilizers" to reduce social instability and political backlash resulting from expanded immigration).
237. *See* Michael J. Trebilcock, *The Law and Economics of Immigration Policy*, 5 Am. L. & Econ. Rev. 271, 298–313 (2003) (proposing a private insurance scheme that would require sponsor employers to maintain social program insurance for foreign workers); *see also* Anu Bradford, *Sharing the Risks and Rewards of Economic Migration*, 80 U. Chi. L. Rev. 29, 46–50 (2013) (proposing a Migration Fund that would pool funds deposited by immigrants or their employer sponsors to insure destination countries against fiscal losses and source countries against brain drain).
238. Robert Hockett, *Toward a Global Shareholder Society*, 30 U. Pa. J. Intl. L. 101 (2008).

workers adversely impacted by globalization.[239] These trade-dislocated workers would become, according to Hockett, global shareholders through their beneficial ownership of SOP shares.[240] Akin to other proposed compensation schemes, SOP structures can be expanded globally to compensate domestic workers that lose their jobs due to the opening of labor markets to foreign workers.[241]

[4] Extraterritorial Delegation

The exercise of territorial sovereignty is changing because of the transposition and disaggregation of sovereign functions through extraterritorial delegation. The gatekeeper function of the nation-state—that is, who to admit into the country and on what terms—is delegated to another government or group of governments. The most ambitious and controversial manifestation is the concept of charter cities, championed by economist Paul Romer.[242] Charter cities stem from the same conceptual framework as SEZs.[243] Much like new generation SEZs, Romer's charter city is a territorial enclave where developing countries can innovate and experiment through liberalization of trade and labor migration rules while evading nationalist opposition.[244]

Where the charter city differs from new generation SEZs are the degree and locus of governing authority. Countries participating in a charter city program may serve as the host country, the source country, or as the partner *qua* guarantor country.[245] The host provides the land, the source provides the residents, and the guarantor provides the governance structure through implementation and enforcement of the charter.[246] These roles can be held by a single government or by any combination of multiple governments—including a developing country government as host and source, and a foreign developed country government with strong legal institutions as a guarantor.[247] The guarantor role can be further disaggregated into specific governance functions.[248] Because the legal rights of charter city residents are defined by the charter, not by the bundle of rights granted to citizens of the guarantor country, their ultimate recourse is

239. *See ibid.*, at 152–56.
240. Hockett, *supra* note 238, at 180–81.
241. *See ibid.*, at 156–62 (describing "global citizen" SOPs).
242. *See* Paul Romer, *Technologies, Rules, and Progress: The Case for Charter Cities*, Ctr. for Global Dev., http://www.cgdev.org/content/publications/detail/1423916 (Mar. 2010).
243. Charter cities share four principles: (1) an undeveloped piece of land large enough to host a city equivalent in size to Hong Kong or Singapore, (2) a charter that specifies the city's rules, (3) freedom of movement for the city's residents, and (4) equality of treatment. Brandon Fuller & Paul Romer, *Success and the City: How Charter Cities Could Transform the Developing World* 7 (Macdonald-Laurier Institute, Apr. 2012), http://www.macdonaldlaurier.ca/files/pdf/How-charter-cities-could-transform-the-developing-world-April-2012.pdf.
244. Christopher Freiman, *Cosmopolitanism Within Borders: On Behalf of Charter Cities*, 30 J. Applied Phil. 40, 45, 49 (2013).
245. Fuller & Romer, *supra* note 243, at 7.
246. *Ibid.*
247. *See* Romer, *supra* note 242, at 9.
248. *See* Justin Sandefur & Milan Vaishnav, *Imagine There's No Country: Three Questions about a New Charter City in Honduras* 8, Ctr. for Global Dev., www.cgdev.org/content/publications/detail/1426274 (March 2010) (noting Mauritius' role as a partner in the Honduran charter city's justice system).

by "voting with their feet" and leaving the charter city.[249] Whereas SEZs serve as "countries within a country", charter cities may be viewed as "countries without a country."

Despite their deep theoretical implications, the real-world impact of charter cities remains highly speculative, underscoring the persistence of national politics in transnational governance schemes.[250] In 2011, the government of Honduras created a new legal entity, called a "Special Development Region" (*Region Especial de Desarrollo* or RED), based on Romer's concept.[251] However, the RED model has been beset by controversy and skepticism regarding governance structures, leading to the appointment of an unelected governor to rule the RED,[252] Romer's departure from the project due to disputes with the Honduran government,[253] and the overhaul and replacement of the RED model.[254] Under the current Honduran charter city law, Honduran citizens must comprise 90% of the workforce and receive 85% of wages, which undermines the scope and impact of migration liberalization envisioned by Romer.[255]

§9.06 CONCLUSION

Much like international trade, cross-border migration is controversial and often disruptive to societies and economies. However, they are treated very differently under international law. Looking towards the success of the global trade regime to facilitate trade liberalization, scholars advocating for institutional transformation have called for the creation of a new multilateral institution to govern labor migration.[256] If there is currently any normative consensus that guides the global trade-labor migration nexus, it is that goods and people are not equivalent and, therefore, should not be subject to the same legal treatment.[257] The global trade regime does not appear to be a viable

249. *See* Freiman, *supra* note 244, at 48 (defending charter cities as a second-best solution to global poverty); *see also* Sebastian Mallaby, *The Politically Incorrect Guide to Ending Poverty*, The Atlantic, http://www.theatlantic.com/magazine/archive/2010/07/the-politically-incorrect-guide-to-ending-poverty/308134 (July/August 2010).
250. *See* Sandefur & Vaishnav, *supra* note 248, at 5–7 (questioning the ability of charter cities to insulate themselves from the poor governance practices of host countries).
251. *See* The Economist, *Hong Kong in Honduras*, http://www.economist.com/node/21541392 (Dec. 10, 2011).
252. *See* Sandefur & Vaishnav, *supra* note 248, at 2.
253. *See* Elizabeth Malkin, *Plan for Charter City to Fight Honduras Poverty Loses Its Initiator*, N.Y. Times (Oct. 1, 2012), at A4.
254. *See* Maya Kroth, *Under New Management*, For. Policy (Sep. 1, 2014) (reporting on the enactment of Zones for Economic Development and Employment (ZEDEs) in 2013 to replace the RED law struck down by the Honduran Supreme Court).
255. *See ibid.*
256. *See*, e.g., Goldin, Cameron & Balarajan, *supra* note 11, at 281–85 (calling for a new international organization to promote the expansion of global migration through progressive realization to the right of free movement); Solimano, *supra* note 30, at 203–05 (advocating for the creation of a new international organization that integrates the roles of the International Organization for Migration, the United Nations, the World Bank, and other existing organizations); Trachtman, *supra* note 42, at 319–35 (outlining the structure and functions of a World Migration Organization, an international organization dedicated to international economic migration).
257. *See supra* text accompanying n. 2–6.

vehicle for comprehensively realizing the aspirations of individual freedom advocates for open borders. While not an example of fragmentation per se, the global trade-labor migration nexus demonstrates the challenges of broad-based institutional and legal change in the absence of unitary authority over migration in international law. Pluralism will continue to define the global trade-labor migration nexus for the foreseeable future.

Further reinforcing this point, the diversity of approaches in the global trade-labor migration nexus reflects an implicit cost-benefit analysis by individual countries.[258] Given the divergent interests of poor versus wealthy countries and the lack of consensus on a global institutional framework, the pluralistic status quo enables countries to make case-by-case decisions as their supply and demand for foreign human capital changes.[259] As an element of the global trade-labor migration nexus, SEZs enhance rather than diminish territorial sovereignty.[260] Host countries use SEZs to fulfill national economic policy objectives that they otherwise cannot politically.[261] Through their embrace of hybrid governance frameworks, SEZs reflect the desire of governments to work directly with MNCs to improve the social and firm-level rates of return from foreign labor. This phenomenon merits consideration as a more politically feasible means of moving towards freer labor in a free trade world.

258. Trachtman, *supra* note 42, at 276.

259. *See* Dani Rodrik, One Economics, *Many Recipes: Globalization, Institutions, and Economic Growth* 149 (Princeton U. Press 2007) (advocating for greater policy autonomy for developing countries in respect of compliance with global trade rules).

260. *See* José E. Alvarez, *The Return of the State*, 20 Minn. J. Intl. L. 223, 258 (2011) (observing that fragmentation enables states to serve their own interests by avoiding supranational regulation).

261. *See* Rudolph, *supra* note 13, at 333 (noting how the interests of MNCs and host countries diverge when access to foreign labor is limited due to restrictive domestic immigration laws).

CHAPTER 10

The Law and Policy of Refugee Cities: SEZs for Migrants*

Michael Castle-Miller

§10.01 INTRODUCTION

Migration is quickly becoming one of the most pressing issues of our time. Conflict, persecution, natural disasters, and economic inequality are driving people from their homes in record numbers.

Meanwhile, traditional responses to mass migration are becoming increasingly inadequate. Humanitarian assistance and border policing are ineffective and costly over the long term because they fail to address the root causes of migration. Barriers to the labour market, both legal and socio-economic, prevent migrants from contributing to the economic development of the countries hosting them and force them into dependency.

Recognizing this, some countries are exploring pragmatic pathways toward integrating migrants into economies. The special economic zone (SEZ) concept offers one potential path forward. SEZs are designated areas designed to promote development through a distinct policy and administrative framework. They can serve as vehicles for initiating beneficial policies when political obstacles stand in the way of nationwide reform.

Refugee cities would be a type of SEZ designed to facilitate migrant integration. They would be special-status jurisdictions in which displaced people - who would otherwise be barred from working - can be employed, start businesses, access finance, and rebuild their lives. Applying principles from SEZs, refugee cities could help

* This chapter entitled 'The Law and Policy of Refugee Cities: Special Economic Zones for Migrants' was originally published as journal article (Chapman Law Review, Vol. 21, No. 2, 2018 and ICG Policy Paper #4, November 2018, at https://instituteforcompgov.org/publications/), and is included in this book because of its enduring importance.

countries benefit from migrants' presence in a politically realistic manner. They could also deliver high-quality infrastructure, foreign direct investment, and improvements to the business environment.

Refugee cities would also serve as a pathway for countries to come into closer alignment with international law. Under the Convention and Protocol Relating to the Status of Refugees ('Refugee Convention' and '1967 Protocol', respectively), refugees are entitled to relatively strong rights regarding property, employment, and entrepreneurship.[1] However, most countries' domestic legislation falls well short of these rights.

This chapter explores these gaps to show how refugee cities could fill them by creating designated areas in which refugee rights are respected and the policy benefits of migrant integration are achieved. Part I provides the background of the global migration situation. Part II discusses the evolution and role of SEZs. Part III explains the refugee-cities concept and its policy benefits. Part IV analyses international and domestic law pertaining to refugees, including a special focus on Turkey.

§10.02 BACKGROUND OF GLOBAL FORCED DISPLACEMENT

Forced displacement is a growing major global concern. By the end of 2016, the United Nations High Commissioner for Refugees (UNHCR) reported 65.6 million people were forcibly displaced by persecution, conflict, violence, or human rights violations.[2] Included in that total are 22.5 million refugees,[3] 40.3 million internally displaced persons (IDPs),[4] and 2.8 million asylum seekers.[5] Moreover, 10.3 million people were forcibly displaced during 2016 alone, meaning that twenty people were forced to flee their homes every minute that year.[6]

1. *Protecting Refugees: questions and answers*, UNHCR (1 Feb. 2002), http://www.un hcr.org/afr/publications/brochures/3b779dfe2/protecting-refugees-questions-answers.html [http://perma.cc/XY46-Z396].
2. UNHCR, *Global Trends: Forced Displacement in 2016* 2 (2016), http://www.unhcr.org/5943e8a34.pdf [http://perma.cc/5CCH-HMCT]. Actual numbers of displaced persons, including refugees, are probably much higher than the numbers provided in this section due to the number of people who would qualify as refugees, but are undocumented and thus not counted in official tallies. *See* Roger Zetter & Héloïse Ruaudel, *Refugees' Right to Work and Access to Labor Markets – An Assessment, Part I: Synthesis* 11 (KNOMAD Study 2016) (noting, for instance, that the Iranian government estimates 1.4 million to 2 million undocumented Afghans are within its borders, beyond the 979,400 documented refugees, and that there are an estimated 175,000 undocumented refugees in Venezuela, compared with only 5,000 who are documented).
3. UNHCR, *supra* note 2, at 2. 'Refugees' generally includes people who have been forced to leave their country because of a well-founded fear of persecution and includes people who fall under the definition of refugee under international treaties, people granted complementary forms of protection and temporary protection, and people in 'refugee-like situations.' *Ibid.*, at 56.
4. *Ibid.*, at 2. 'IDPs' are people who have been forced to leave their homes but have not left their country. *Ibid.*, at 56.
5. *Ibid.*, at 2. 'Asylum seekers' are those who have applied for international protection in a country, but whose refugee status is yet to be determined. *Ibid.* at 39.
6. *Ibid.*, at 2.

Developing countries hosted a growing majority of the world's refugees.[7] The top ten refugee hosting countries at the end of 2016 were:

- Turkey - 2.9 million
- Pakistan - 1.4 million
- Lebanon - 1 million
- Iran - 979,400
- Uganda - 940,800
- Ethiopia - 791,600
- Jordan - 685,200
- Germany - 669,500
- Democratic Republic of the Congo - 452,000
- Kenya - 451,100.[8]

Lebanon hosted the highest number of refugees relative to its population, with one in every six people in the country being a refugee.[9] Jordan (one in eleven) and Turkey (one in twenty-eight) were the next two highest.[10]

55% of refugees came from three countries: Syria (5.5 million), Afghanistan (2.5 million), and South Sudan (1.4 million).[11] Syrians also made up the largest number of forcibly displaced persons (12 million, including 6.3 million IDPs).[12] 65% of the Syrian population were forcibly displaced as of the end of 2016, a higher proportion than any other nationality.[13]

The year 2017 saw a major surge in Rohingya refugees fleeing ethnic cleansing campaigns in Myanmar. Between 25 August and 30 September of that year, over 600,000 Rohingya were driven out by reported human rights atrocities.[14] Bangladesh hosted approximately 800,000 Rohingya refugees as of 4 October 2017 in refugee camps and makeshift settlements that were straining to provide basic services like water, healthcare, shelter, and sanitation.[15]

7. *Ibid.*, (observing that 84% of refugees under UNHCR's mandate (14.5 million out of 17.2 million) are hosted in developing countries and 28% are in less developed countries (4.9 million)).
8. *Ibid.*, at 14–16.
9. *Ibid.*, at 3.
10. *Ibid.*
11. *Ibid.*
12. *Ibid.*, at 6.
13. *See ibid.*
14. *Rohingya Refugee Crisis*, UN Office for the Coordination of Humanitarian Affairs, https://www.unocha.org/rohingya-refugee-crisis [http://perma.cc/ WKG7-YKNT] accessed 27 Nov. 2017; *see also* Jeffrey Gettleman, *Rohingya Recount Atrocities: 'They Threw My Baby Into a Fire'*, N.Y. Times (11 Oct. 2017), https://www.nytimes.com/ 2017/10/11/world/asia/rohingya-myanmar-atrocities.html (reporting stories of gang rape, murder, and home burnings from Rohingya survivors).
15. *Rohingya Refugee Crisis, supra* note 14.

[A] Responses to Refugees

The international response to refugee situations has evolved over the last several decades. After massive displacement caused by the Second World War, the newly created United Nations (UN) formed the UNHCR and adopted a treaty, the 1951 Refugee Convention, obligating Member States to respect certain minimum standards of treatment of refugees. Since then, the UNHCR's main objective has been to ensure the international protection of refugees and to seek permanent solutions to their problems.[16]

Traditionally, the UNHCR's focus was on providing short-term humanitarian aid through emergency shelters, food, water, and medical care.[17] Over time, the UNHCR increasingly shifted to emphasize 'durable solutions' for refugees.[18] The three durable solutions are: voluntary repatriation to the refugee's home country, resettlement to a third country, or integration into the host country.[19]

However, in recent years, the UNHCR has increasingly recognized that durable solutions are often only a remote possibility for refugees.[20] Conditions in their home country often do not improve for many years, making repatriation impossible in the near future. Only a small portion of the global refugee population are accepted for resettlement in third countries,[21] and few of the major refugee-hosting countries are willing to meaningfully integrate refugees into their societies.

As a result, most refugees remain displaced for many years, often in isolated refugee camps or informal settlements. As of the end of 2016, 11.6 million refugees (two-thirds of the total) were in 'protracted refugee situations', generally lasting five years or more.[22] Of that number, 4.1 million people were in refugee situations lasting twenty years or more.[23]

To address this reality, the UNHCR has been seeking to identify new approaches to refugee situations, including 'complementary pathways', which countries have implemented when durable solutions are not possible.[24] Examples of current complementary pathways include private sponsorship programmes, labour schemes, family reunification programmes, talent registers, and education programmes.[25]

---

16. Office of Internal Oversight Services, *Evaluation of the Office of the United Nations High Commissioner for Refugees* 3 (2015).
17. *Ibid.*
18. *Ibid.*, at 4.
19. *Ibid.*, at 5.
20. UNHCR, *supra* note 2, at 24.
21. In 2016, 189,300 refugees were resettled into thirty-seven countries. *Ibid.*, at 3. The US admitted the largest number at 96,900. *Ibid.*
22. *Ibid.*, at 22. 'Protracted refugee situations' is defined as situations where 25,000 or more refugees from the same nationality have been in exile for five consecutive years or more in a given asylum country. *Ibid.*
23. *Ibid.*
24. *Ibid.*, at 24, 29.
25. *Ibid.*, at 29.

[B] Refugees' Access to the Labour Market

The vast majority of refugees are prevented from working, both de jure and de facto.[26] In addition to legal restrictions, which are discussed in Part IV, refugees face restrictive policies and practices like forced encampment or bureaucratic and expensive processes for obtaining work permits.[27] They also face socio-economic barriers impacting the freedom to work and the ability to assimilate, such as xenophobia and discrimination, language difficulties, inadequate access to the courts, and lack of vocational training for refugees who need to develop new skills.[28] As a result, most refugees work in the informal sector and under relatively poor conditions where they have less of a positive impact on the economy than if they were allowed to work formally.[29]

These barriers exist despite evidence that allowing refugees, and other immigrants to work tends to bring significant net economic benefits to host countries. Over the medium-term to long-term, refugees tend to raise wages, create jobs, stimulate commerce, fill gaps in the labour market, and increase cross-border trade.[30] Refugees represent a major underutilized labour force that could make significant contributions to the economies hosting them if activated.[31] Additionally, work would enable them to develop skills and capital to facilitate their return to their home countries and would help advance the UN's 2030 Sustainable Development Goals to end poverty and fight inequality.[32]

§10.03 SEZs HISTORY AND POLICY FUNCTIONS

An SEZ can be generally understood as a designated geographic area designed to promote economic development through a policy and administrative framework that is somehow different from the typical policy and administrative frameworks surrounding it.[33] The legal and regulatory regime is the most central aspect to an SEZ; their

26. Asylum Access & the Refugee Work Rights Coalition, *Global Refugee Work Rights Report: Taking the Movement from Theory to Practice* 5 (2014) [hereinafter Asylum Access].
27. *Ibid.*, Zetter & Ruaudel, *supra* note 2, at 14–19.
28. Asylum Access, *supra* note 26, at 5; Zetter & Ruaudel, *supra* note 2, at 20.
29. Zetter & Ruaudel, *supra* note 2, at 26.
30. *See, e.g., ibid., see also* Asylum Access, *supra* note 26, at 8; OECD, *Is migration good for the economy?* (May 2014), https://www.oecd.org/migration/OECD%20Migration %20Policy%20 Debates%20Numero%202.pdf [http://perma.cc/345C-LQAL]; Alexander Betts et al., *Refugee Economies: Rethinking Popular Assumptions* (2014), https://www.rsc.ox.ac.uk/files/files-1/ refugee-economies-2014.pdf [http://perma.cc/E5EQ-UBVZ].
31. Zetter & Ruaudel, *supra* note 2, at 4.
32. *Ibid.*
33. *See* Gokhan Akinci & James Crittle, *Special Economic Zones: Performance, Lessons Learned, and Implications for Zone Development* 2–6, 9–22 (World Bank Foreign Investment Advisory Service, Working Paper No. 45869, 2008) (referring to SEZs as 'geographically delimited areas administered by a single body, offering certain incentives ... to businesses [within it]' and noting how they enhance competitiveness through special policy, regulatory frameworks, and administration); *see also* Claude Baissac, *Brief History of SEZs and Overview of Policy Debates*, in *Special Economic Zones in Africa: Comparing Performance and Learning from Global Experience* 23 (Thomas Farole ed., 2011) (defining SEZs as areas where the 'rules of business are different from those that prevail in the national territory,' generally with more liberal policies and more

geographic, administrative, and infrastructural characteristics are also important, but less so.[34] The SEZ concept can include a wide variety of special-status jurisdictions going by different names from ancient to modern times, including free-trade zones, export processing zones (EPZs), freeports, and even semi-autonomous city-states.[35]

In recent years, new attention is being placed on the role of SEZs as vehicles for policy and structural transformation, such as by helping catalyse growth in new industry sectors or overcoming political roadblocks to beneficial legal reforms.[36] SEZs often also serve as industrial parks by providing facilities, infrastructure, and services designed to cater to certain types of businesses.[37] However, an increasing number are mixed-use or urban, in character.[38]

[A] History of Development

Modern SEZs emerged out of several historical precedents. The island of Delos functioned as a free zone during the Greek and Roman empires by serving as a place where goods could be stored and exchanged free of local prohibitions and taxes.[39] Medieval and Renaissance-era city-states, such as those in the Hanseatic League, had almost complete autonomy from the ruling powers around them and provided spaces for free trade and commerce.[40] Colonial-era chartered territories and trading posts were independently administered by state-backed private companies.[41] Some of these trading posts emerged in the modern era as prosperous city-states and freeports, including Singapore, Hong Kong, and Macau.[42] These also could be characterized as a type of SEZ.[43]

In the early twentieth century, free-trade zones ('FTZs'), or 'free zones', existed near major international transit points, offering exemptions from tariffs for trade-related activities, including warehousing, packaging, sorting, exhibition, and sales.[44] In 1934, the United States adopted the Foreign Trade Zones Act,[45] which created these types of zones to mitigate the damaging impact of high tariffs under the protectionist trade policies prevailing just before and during the early Great Depression under laws

effective administration); Lotta Moberg, *The Political Economy of Special Economic Zones* (2015) (PhD dissertation, George Mason University) (defining SEZs as 'areas where a government allows for different rules to apply than the rest of the country').

34. Baissac, *supra* note 33, at 24–25 (2011) (observing how some SEZ programmes – as in the case of 'single-factory zone' programmes – do not even have a designated geographic area; instead companies can acquire SEZ status while being located anywhere in the country).
35. Akinci & Crittle, *supra* note 33, at 9–12.
36. *Ibid.*
37. *Ibid.*
38. *Ibid.*
39. Baissac, *supra* note 33, at 31–32.
40. *Ibid.*
41. *Ibid.*
42. *Ibid.*
43. *See* Akinci & Crittle, *supra* note 33, at 14–16 (identifying Hong Kong, Macau, and Singapore as city-wide freeport SEZs).
44. Baissac, *supra* note 33, at 32. Notably, however, the FTZ at the Port of Cadiz included substantial industrial production, even featuring one of the first Ford Motor Plants in Europe. *Ibid.*
45. Foreign Trade Zones Act, 19 U.S.C.A. § 81a (1934).

like the Smoot-Hawley Tariff Act.[46] FTZs were deemed outside the customs territory of the country, which meant businesses could import foreign products and sell them in foreign markets duty free, and only pay customs duties if and when products were sold in the domestic market.[47]

FTZs evolved in the mid-twentieth century by opening up more to manufacturing industries, instead of remaining restricted to trade activities.[48] The starkest early example was the Shannon Free Zone (1959) which applied the FTZ model to a wide area located next to a major airport and offered ready-built industrial infrastructure and facilities, dedicated administrative support, and investment incentives.[49]

The Shannon Free Zone model was copied and spread throughout developing countries under the name 'EPZ' from the 1960s to the 1990s.[50] For developing countries, EPZs were tools for stimulating export-led industrial development, which boosted employment and labour productivity, diversified the economy, generated foreign exchange, attracted foreign direct investment, and facilitated technology transfer.[51] EPZs also had an important function as policy incubators – they served as pilots for trade liberalization in the midst of protectionist import-substitution regimes, which generally prevailed in developing countries at the time.[52] Over time, EPZ programmes grew increasingly open to a wider range of business activities, to linkages with local businesses outside the EPZs, and to domestic sales, as opposed to an exclusive focus on exports.[53]

China took a monumental step in shaping the nature of SEZs in the early 1980s, when several local officials sought to boost economic growth in their jurisdictions by designating areas as free-market enclaves.[54] The idea was an outgrowth of the Open Door reforms, which began in the late 1970s as a controlled experiment of market-based reforms.[55] In 1980, the country designated four 'SEZs' (perhaps the first use of

---

46. Tariff Act of 1930 (Smoot-Hawley Tariff Act), 46 Stat. 590; *see also* Baissac, *supra* note 33, at 32.
47. Akinci & Crittle, *supra* note 33, at 9, 52; *see also*, e.g., World Customs Org., *Glossary of International Customs Terms* 17 (2013) (defining 'free zone' as 'a part of the territory of a Contracting Party where any goods introduced are generally regarded, insofar as import duties and taxes are concerned, as being outside the Customs Territory'); 19 U.S.C.A. § 81c (2003) (describing the US Customs territory as distinct from the FTZs).
48. Baissac, *supra* note 33, at 32.
49. *Ibid.* As another example of a growing openness of FTZs to manufacturing, In 1950, the United States amended the Foreign Trade Zones Act to allow for manufacturing activities. *Ibid.* However, this did not result in much manufacturing activity until a 12 Apr. 1980 ruling from the US Customs Service changed the formula for calculating the tariff applied to finished products sold from an FTZ to the domestic market so that domestic parts and labour were excluded from the value. *A Brief History of the U.S. Foreign-Trade Zones Program*, Foreign-Trade Zone Res. Ctr., http://www.foreign-trade-zone.com/history.htm [http://perma.cc/M8N8-SV89] accessed 3 Dec. 2017.
50. Baissac, *supra* note 33, at 33.
51. *See generally* Thomas Farole & Gokhan Akinci, *Special Economic Zones: Progress, Emerging Challenges, and Future Directions*, (Thomas Farole & Gokhan Akinci eds., 2011) (evaluating the performance of SEZs in various countries).
52. *Ibid.* (describing policy incubation as an important dynamic benefit of SEZs around the world).
53. Baissac, *supra* note 33, at 28.
54. Moberg, *supra* note 33, at 92–93.
55. Douglas Zhihua Zeng, *How Do Special Economic Zones and Industrial Clusters Drive China's Rapid Development?*, in *Building Engines for Growth and Competitiveness in China: Experience*

the term now used generically), which spanned large city-sized areas and granted a wide range of free market policies affecting finance, labour, foreign investment, and trade.[56] Many of these SEZs, especially Shenzhen, experienced explosive growth in investment, wages, population, and living standards.[57]

Beginning largely in the 1990s, zones in Latin America initiated another major shift in the nature of SEZs.[58] Whereas previous zones were primarily government-driven projects, SEZs began to increasingly rely on private-sector companies to finance, own, develop, and provide services to users.[59] This model has allowed the state to concentrate its resources on providing effective regulation, ideally through a dedicated SEZ regulatory authority that independently performs or coordinates many of the functions of government in a streamlined fashion.[60] In general, anecdotal evidence suggests that SEZs managed by private-sector companies or public-private partnerships have delivered higher-quality services and facilities, better social and environmental outcomes, and higher financial returns at a lower cost than government-run SEZs.[61]

[B] Function of SEZs

While SEZs can bring static benefits such as employment generation and foreign direct investment to an area, their greatest potential is in delivering dynamic benefits, especially long-term structural transformation, upgrades to domestic economy capacity, and changes to nationwide policy.[62] Examples of countries that have achieved these dynamic benefits in a very noticeable way include Mexico, Costa Rica, Dominican Republic, China, South Korea, Taiwan, and Mauritius.[63]

Many, if not most, SEZs have failed to achieve significant dynamic benefits; some may have even been counterproductive. For instance, rather than serving as catalysts

---

with Special Economic Zones and Industrial Clusters 1, 8–9 (Douglas Zhihua Zeng ed., 2010) (noting how Chinese Premier Deng Xiaping referred to the choice to only open certain segments of the economy to the market as 'crossing the river by touching the stones').

56. *Ibid.*

57. *Ibid.* As an example, Shenzhen's GDP grew by 58% per year between 1980 and 1984, and its GDP per capita grew from under USD 100 at formation to over USD 25,000 in 2016. *Shenzhen (Guangdong) City Information*, HKTDC Res. (30 Aug. 2017), http://china-trade-research.hktdc.com/business-news/article/Facts-and-Figures/Shenzhen-Guangdong-City-Information/ff/en/1/1X000000/1X09VT4H.htm [http://perma.cc/7BB3-KU5G]. It grew from a fishing village of 300,000 people to over fourteen million people today, many of them young people from rural areas in search of opportunities. *See* Da Wei David Wang, *Continuity and Change in the Urban Villages of Shenzhen*, 4 Int'l J. China Stud. 233, 233–56 (2013). Many of the original fishing villagers became landowners in the city, profiting from the city's success. *Ibid.*, at 246.

58. Baissac, *supra* note 33, at 37.

59. *Ibid.* (noting how this shift was driven by the need to limit government spending and to regenerate stagnate free zone programs).

60. Akinci & Crittle, *supra* note 33, at 5.

61. *Ibid.*, at 45–47.

62. *See ibid.*, at 32; *see also* Thomas Farole, *Special Economic Zones in Africa: Comparing Performance and Learning from Global Experience* 3–16 (2011).

63. *See* Thomas Farole & Gokhan Akinci, *Introduction*, in *Special Economic Zones: Progress, Emerging Challenges, and Future Directions*, *supra* note 51, at 1, 8; Akinci & Crittle, *supra* note 33, at 26, 36.

of good policy, some SEZs may have acted as 'pressure valves' that allow elites to avoid or delay nationwide reform by diverting social movements and isolating their impact to zones.[64] Many SEZs impose economic costs that exceed their benefits, primarily when SEZs rely heavily on the public sector for financing or operation or on massive tax breaks to attract investment.[65] Numerous reports have observed that many SEZs have not performed well at advancing beyond low-wage/low-skill jobs, stimulating local economic activity, or promoting labour and environmental performance.[66] SEZs have generally been successful at job creation and access to income for women, though there have been significant problems with pay equity, denying women access to attain higher paying positions, discriminatory working conditions, and sexual harassment.[67]

SEZs are becoming increasingly important vehicles for wide-ranging reforms.[68] Previously, their primary function was to reduce tariff barriers between countries.[69] Today, with overall effective tariff rates very low worldwide, their primary value is in easing other constraints in the investment climate through reducing unnecessary regulatory barriers, streamlining customs inspection and compliance procedures, facilitating human development (especially skills), easing access to investment approvals and business licenses, delivering reliable infrastructure, and improving access to work visas for foreign workers.[70] Generous tax incentives no longer offset disadvantages in these areas.[71]

§10.04 REFUGEE CITIES CONCEPT

The refugee cities concept is an evolution of the SEZ model. Whereas traditional zones have prioritized tax reductions, customs exemptions, business registration and licensing, and similar measures, refugee cities would prioritize migrant integration.[72] In refugee cities, migrants could legally work, operate their own businesses, access goods

64. Akinci & Crittle, *supra* note 33, at 4, 34, 42.
65. *Ibid.*, at 32–34, 39, 45–47.
66. *See*, e.g., Sheba Tejani, *The Gender Dimension of Special Economic Zones*, in *Special Economic Zones: Progress, Emerging Challenges, and Future Directions*, *supra* note 51, at 247, 262–72; Int'l Labour Office, *Report of the InFocus Initiative on Export Processing Zones (EPZs): Latest Trends and Policy Developments in EPZs*, at 3–9, ILO Doc. GB.301/ESP/5 (March 2008); Int'l Labour Office, *Labour and Social Issues Relating to Export Processing Zones: Report for Discussion at the Tripartite Meeting of Export Processing Zones–Operating Countries*, at 47, ILO Doc. TMEPZ (1998). However, SEZs may perform better, in relative terms, than non-zone businesses and performance appears stronger in privately managed and geographically demarcated SEZs, as opposed to publicly operated zones and 'single-factory' zones scattered throughout the country. Akinci & Crittle, *supra* note 33, at 17.
67. *See* Tejani, *supra* note 66, at 269–70; *see also* Int'l Labour Office, *Report of the InFocus Initiative on Export Processing Zones (EPZs): Latest Trends and Policy Developments in EPZs*, *supra* note 66, at 4–7.
68. Akinci & Crittle, *supra* note 33, at 6, 42–43.
69. *See ibid.*, at 13.
70. *See ibid.*, at 57–58.
71. *See ibid.*, at 49.
72. *See Refugee Cities*, Refugee Cities: Expanding Options for Displaced People through Special Economic Zones 4 (November 2016), https://refugeecities.files.word press.com/2016/11/refugee-cities-concept-paper-november-2016.pdf [http://perma.cc/9ZKR-2AKU].

and services, have property rights, and enjoy other rights and privileges ordinarily denied to them.[73] Ideally, refugee cities would also include aspects of well-performing SEZs, such as an effective and efficient regulatory system, private-sector investment, and trade facilitation.[74] However, they would also go beyond these elements, offering diverse, multi-use urban areas, support for entrepreneurs and small-sized and medium-sized enterprises, healthcare, trauma counseling, education, financial assistance, and other support in collaboration with international organizations and non-governmental organizations.[75]

[A] Benefits of Refugee Cities

[1] Host Countries

For countries hosting large numbers of refugees, refugee cities convert a perceived problem into an economic growth opportunity.[76] Since these countries cannot keep migrants outside their borders for both practical and political reasons, they must decide how they will handle migrants.[77] If they house migrants in typical camps without economic opportunities, the migrants will tend to drain public resources and possibly become more prone to radicalization and violence.[78] The migrants will also tend to find ways to leave or avoid the camps and instead work in the informal sector 'where they have less of a positive impact on the economy than if they were allowed to work legally'.[79] However, efforts to allow refugees to work anywhere in the country face overwhelming political resistance, especially due to the fear that they will take away employment opportunities from citizens.[80]

Refugee cities would help countries realize some of the potential benefits of refugees[81] by designating new spaces where refugees can work and start businesses, and where new foreign investment can be brought in, without competing for existing resources in existing spaces.[82] Host populations could also live and work in the new spaces and benefit from the opportunities and infrastructure developed there.[83]

---

73. *See ibid.*, at 6–7.
74. *See ibid.*
75. *See ibid.*, at 8.
76. *See ibid.*, at 6.
77. *See ibid.*
78. *See generally* Rebecca Horn, *Exploring the Impact of Displacement and Encampment on Domestic Violence in the Kakuma Refugee Camp*, 23 J. *Refugee Stud.* 356 (2010) (analysing the connection between refugee camp residents' structural conditions and domestic violence); *see also* Barbara Sude et al., Lessening the Risk of Refugee Radicalization 3 (2015), https://www.rand.org/content/dam/rand/pubs/ perspectives/PE100/PE166/RAND_PE166.pdf [http://perma.cc/9KWK-J6ZD] (discussing the connection between refugee camp conditions and radicalization).
79. Refugee cities, *supra* note 72, at 6; *see also*, e.g., Betts et al., *supra* note 30, at 5.
80. *See* Zetter & Ruaudel, *supra* note 2 (studying twenty countries hosting 70% of the world's refugees and observing a general reluctance to ease restrictions on refugees' ability to work).
81. *See* Betts et al., *supra* note 30, at 16–20 (covering the economic benefits of allowing refugees to enter the labour market).
82. *See* Refugee Cities, *supra* note 72, at 6–7.
83. *Ibid.*, at 4.

Refugee cities are better tools for accomplishing the goals of refugee camps. Host countries often use refugee camps to cluster refugees to facilitate aid distribution, avoid competition for jobs, and more easily locate and, eventually, repatriate them.[84] Camps often do not accomplish this goal well, however, since refugees often avoid them because of the few economic opportunities there.[85] Refugee cities can reverse this trend by attracting migrants rather than repelling them.[86]

[2] *International Community and Aid Agencies*

Refugee cities can also offer the international community a more cost-effective response to refugee crises than existing humanitarian methods. International organizations traditionally respond to mass migration with food aid, tents, water, basic security, and emergency medical care.[87] Refugee cities would offer these services, while also creating a platform for migrants to become self-supporting.[88] Private capital can be invested in real estate, businesses, and infrastructure and can generate returns from these productive assets.[89] Donor institutions can simply facilitate and abet this investment through technical support, investment guarantees, and monitoring and evaluation.[90]

For developed countries, such as in Europe, that are weary or fearful of migrants passing through refugee hosting countries and entering their territory, refugee cities could provide refugees with other attractive areas for settling.[91] Rather than attempting to find opportunities in an advanced economy, they can find opportunities in the countries hosting them.[92]

[3] *Benefits for Businesses and Investors*

Refugee cities can also open up new markets and underutilized talent pools for foreign and domestic investors.[93] Refugees and other migrants are perhaps often among the most motivated and enterprising workers,[94] and yet their abilities are normally withheld from the labour force.[95] Businesses in a refugee city could benefit from their

84. *See* Milica Z. Bookman, After Involuntary Migration: The Political Economy of Refugee Encampments 134–36 (2002).
85. *Ibid.*, at 98.
86. *See* Refugee Cities, *supra* note 72, at 6.
87. *See* UN Economic & Social Council, *Evaluation of the Office of the United Nations High Commissioner for Refugees* 4 (2015).
88. *See* Refugee Cities, *supra* note 72, at 3.
89. *See ibid.*, at 1, 4.
90. *See ibid.*, at 7.
91. *See ibid.*, at 6.
92. *See ibid.*, at 4.
93. *See ibid.*, at 7.
94. *See*, e.g., Personal Income of Migrants, Australia, 2009–10, Australian Bureau of Statistics (9 Jun. 2017, 11:30 AM), http://www.abs.gov.au/ausstats/abs@. nsf/mf/3418.0 [http://perma.cc/3C8X-VW8U] (analysing economic activities of humanitarian migrants in Australia and observing above-average rates of income and entrepreneurship).
95. *See* Zetter & Ruaudel, *supra* note 2, at 4.

abilities, as well as from other regulatory and business environment reforms introduced from the SEZ concept.[96]

[4] Benefits for Refugees

Most importantly, refugee cities allow migrants themselves an often-rare opportunity to benefit themselves and their families through their own work.[97] They can earn income, experience the psychological benefits of meaningful work, and, perhaps, help rebuild their home countries from a better position than if they had lived in a refugee camp.[98]

[B] Progress

Significant strides are being made toward developing migrant-inclusive SEZs or refugee cities. Several projects I have consulted on are, as of the date of publication, underway in Africa (primarily the transit countries of Northern Africa) with support from European governments desiring to provide alternatives for migrants who are otherwise seeking refuge and opportunity within Europe.

Jordan has also made significant strides toward developing migrant-inclusive SEZs. In 2016, Jordan formed a trade agreement with the European Union (EU) that intends to attract EU-oriented investors to Jordan's SEZs in order to employ both Syrians and Jordanians.[99] The agreement grants manufacturers in eighteen of Jordan's industrial zones concessionary access to the European common market if at least 15% of their employees are Syrian refugees.[100] The agreement covers fifty-two product groups and will last for ten years.[101]

Also, in 2016, the World Bank launched a USD 300 million Programme for Results Loan to improve Jordan's investment climate, attract investment, implement labour market reforms, and allow the Syrian labour force to further Jordan's economic growth.[102] There is a special focus on supporting trade facilitation, investment promotion, and Syrian entrepreneurship activities in existing SEZs.[103] Disbursements are

96. *See* Refugee Cities, *supra* note 72, at 4.
97. *See ibid.*, at 8.
98. *See ibid.*
99. *See* European Commission Press Release IP/16/2570, *EU-Jordan: Towards a Stronger Partnership* (July 20, 2016), http://europa.eu/rapid/press-release_IP-16-2570_en.htm [http://perma.cc/V778-NCKP].
100. *Ibid.* (stating that after three years, the threshold will rise to 25%, and the agreement modifies the rules of origin applicable to qualifying products so that they are eligible for the same benefits applied to least-developed countries under the Everything but Arms Agreement).
101. *Ibid.*
102. *See* The World Bank Group, *Jordan – Economic Opportunities for Jordanians and Syrian Refugees Program-for-Results Project*, at 1–3, Report No. 108201-JO (2 Sep. 2016), http://documents.worldbank.org/curated/en/802781476219833115/pdf/Jordan-PforR-PAD- P159522-FINAL-DISCLOSURE-10052016.pdf [http://perma.cc/6GQ3-DJZ5].
103. *Ibid.*, at 5.

linked to transparency requirements ensuring compliance with good labour practices.[104]

Jordan set a global target of bringing 200,000 Syrian refugees into the formal labour market and began issuing work permits free of charge to Syrians for a three-month period.[105] It also removed the requirement for holding a valid passport to obtain a work permit, a requirement that was impossible for many Syrians to fulfil.[106] Instead, Ministry of the Interior identification cards now serve as a substitute for a passport.[107]

The King Hussein Bin Talal Development Area (KHBTDA), one of Jordan's SEZs, has been identified as a strong option for allowing refugees access to the labour market.[108] KHBTDA is located nearby the Za'atari refugee camp in Mafraq, which houses roughly 80,000 Syrian refugees.[109]

§10.05 LAW APPLICABLE TO REFUGEES

The laws applicable to refugees depend on the countries in which they find themselves. International law pertaining to refugees is relatively well-developed; however, the strongest rights are conferred under treaties to which countries may or may not be a party. Even if they are parties, the countries may have made reservations regarding certain provisions, thereby limiting their applicability.

Domestic legislation varies greatly across countries. In most cases, it falls well short of international law, particularly in those countries hosting most of the world's refugees. Migrant-inclusive SEZs, or refugee cities, could help countries move significantly closer to alignment with the standards under international law in designated areas.

This Part analyses both international law and domestic law. Regarding domestic law, it provides a general overview of countries hosting large refugee populations and then takes a more specific look at the law pertaining to refugees in Turkey – the largest host of refugees.

[A] International Law

While certain standards are enshrined in customary international law and in general treaties regarding humanitarian law and human rights (such as the Geneva Conventions), the most specific and protective sources of international law pertaining to

104. *Ibid.*, at 82.
105. *Ibid.*, at 4.
106. *Ibid.*
107. *Ibid.*
108. Bethan Staton, *Jordan Experiment Spurs Jobs for Refugees*, News Deeply: Refugees Deeply (25 Jul. 2016), https://www.newsdeeply.com/refugees/articles/2016/ 07/25/jordan-experiment-spurs-jobs-for-refugees [http://perma.cc/7M7D-GBWW].
109. *Ibid.*

refugees is the Convention and Protocol Relating to the Status of Refugees.[110] States that are parties to the Refugee Convention are obligated to certain minimum standards of treatment toward refugees within their borders.[111] To qualify as a 'refugee' entitled to protection under the Convention, a person must be outside the country of his or her nationality and unable to avail him-or-herself of the protection of that country[112] because of a well-founded fear of persecution 'for reasons of race, religion, nationality, membership in a particular social group, or political opinion'.[113]

There are 145 states party to the Refugee Convention.[114] Among those members hosting the largest numbers of refugees as of the end of 2016 are Turkey (2.9 million),[115] Iran (979,400),[116] Uganda (940,800),[117] Ethiopia (791,600),[118] Germany (669,500),[119] Democratic Republic of Congo (452,000),[120] and Kenya (451,100).[121] Notable non-members of the 1967 Protocol with large refugee populations include: Pakistan (1.4 million),[122] Lebanon (1 million),[123] and Jordan (685,200).[124]

110. Convention Relating to the Status of Refugees, 28 Jul. 1951, 189 U.N.T.S. 150, http://hrlibrary.umn.edu/instree/v1crs.htm [http://perma.cc/KV3T-5BBF] [hereinafter 1951 Refugee Convention]; Protocol Relating to the Status of Refugees, 31 Jan. 1967, 606 U.N.T.S. 267, http://hrlibrary.umn.edu/instree/v2prsr.htm [http://perma.cc/8NXC-JDQG]. When the 1951 Refugee Convention was adopted, it only applied to people displaced by events occurring before 1 Jan. 1951 (i.e., because of World War II). 1951 Refugee Convention, Art. 1(A)(2). Furthermore, states had the option of either applying it only to people displaced from events in Europe or from anywhere in the world. *Ibid.* Article 1(B)(1). However, the 1967 Protocol amended the 1951 Convention by removing the date restriction. Protocol Relating to the Status of Refugees, Art. 1.
111. *See generally* 1951 Refugee Convention, *supra* note 110 (providing wide-ranging obligations regarding the treatment of refugees).
112. *Ibid.*, Art. 1(A)(2). Stateless persons are also protected. For them, 'country of his [or her] nationality' is effectively replaced with country of his or her place of habitual residence. *Ibid.*
113. *Ibid.* There are certain types of people explicitly excluded from protection under the Refugee Convention. This includes people who can now receive protection from the country of their nationality. *Ibid.*, Art 1(C)(5). It also includes people receiving assistance from agencies of the UN other than the UNHCR. *Ibid.*, Art 1(D). For example, Palestinian refugees who receive assistance from the United Nations Relief and Works Agency for Palestine Refugees in the Near East (UNRWA). UNHCR, *Revised Statement on Article 1D of the 1951 Convention* (October 2009), http://www.unhcr.org/4add88379.pdf [http://perma.cc/Q7UV-3Q9Z]. War criminals and others who have committed serious non-political crimes are also not protected. 1951 Refugee Convention, *supra* note 110, Art. 1(F).
114. 1951 Refugee Convention, *supra* note 110. There are 142 countries party to both the Refugee Convention and the 1967 Protocol. *Ibid.* The United States is a party to the 1967 Protocol only. *See* Protocol Relating to the Status of Refugees, *supra* note 110.
115. Protocol Relating to the Status of Refugees, *supra* note 110; *see also* UNHCR, *supra* note 2, at 14.
116. Protocol Relating to the Status of Refugees, *supra* note 110; *see also* UNHCR, *supra* note 2, at 15.
117. Protocol Relating to the Status of Refugees, *supra* note 110; *see also* UNHCR, *supra* note 2, at 15.
118. Protocol Relating to the Status of Refugees, *supra* note 110; *see also* UNHCR, *supra* note 2, at 15.
119. Protocol Relating to the Status of Refugees, *supra* note 110; *see also* UNHCR, *supra* note 2, at 15.
120. Protocol Relating to the Status of Refugees, *supra* note 110; *see also* UNHCR, *supra* note 2, at 16.
121. Protocol Relating to the Status of Refugees, *supra* note 110; *see also* UNHCR, *supra* note 2, at 16.
122. *See* Protocol Relating to the Status of Refugees, *supra* note 110 (not listing Pakistan as a state party); *see also* UNHCR, *supra* note 2, at 14.
123. *See* Protocol Relating to the Status of Refugees, *supra* note 110 (not listing Lebanon as a state party); *see also* UNHCR, *supra* note 2, at 15.
124. *See* Protocol Relating to the Status of Refugees, *supra* note 110 (not listing Jordan as a state party); *see also* UNHCR, *supra* note 2, at 15.

Additionally, Bangladesh, which began hosting a sudden influx of Rohingya refugees in the last half of 2017, is not a party to the Refugee Convention.[125]

The Refugee Convention contains several provisions that are relevant to the refugee cities concept, including rights to property, work, residency and movement, and administrative facilities. These are discussed below.

[1] Rights to Property

First, refugees have the right to property. Article 13 requires states to 'accord to a refugee treatment as favourable as possible and, in any event, not less favourable than that accorded to aliens generally in the same circumstances,[126] as regards the acquisition of movable and immovable property and other rights pertaining thereto, and to leases and other contracts relating to movable and immovable property'.[127] Consequently, if a country generally allows aliens within its borders to purchase land, own shares of stock in a company, or lease real estate, it must also allow refugees this same right.[128]

Treatment 'not less favourable than that accorded to aliens generally' does not include rights that are only given to aliens by legislative reciprocity,[129] nor treatment conferred because of special economic and customs agreements between nations.[130] Therefore, refugees can only enjoy those rights that are accorded to aliens in the absence of reciprocity requirements or special agreements.[131] However, many commentators consider the right to acquire movable and immovable property as now recognized by customary international law, which would make refugees entitled to the right even if the country's laws condition the right upon reciprocity.[132]

[2] Rights to Work

Second, refugees have the rights to work and to operate their own businesses. These rights are included in Articles 17, 18, 19, and 24 of the Refugee Convention.

Article 17 of the Refugee Convention covers wage-earning employment. It states in the first paragraph that '[t]he Contracting States shall accord to refugees lawfully staying in their territory the most favourable treatment accorded to nationals of a foreign country in the same circumstances,[133] as regards the right to engage in

125. *See* Protocol Relating to the Status of Refugees, *supra* note 110 (not listing Bangladesh as a state party).
126. For the meaning of 'in the same circumstances,' *see supra* note 136.
127. 1951 Refugee Convention, *supra* note 110, Art. 13.
128. Grahl-Madsen, *supra* note 128, Art. 13, https://www.unhcr.org/3d4ab5fb9.pdf. This article includes the right to receive compensation in the case of expropriation, which is now enshrined in customary international law as well. *Ibid.*
129. That is, rights conditioned on the alien's home state conferring similar rights. *Ibid.*
130. *Ibid.*
131. *Ibid.*
132. *Ibid.*
133. 'In the same circumstances' is understood as including any requirements (such as to length and conditions of residence) that aliens would have to fulfil to enjoy the right in question, except for

wage-earning employment'.[134] Commentators assert that 'wage-earning employment' includes all kinds of employment that are not self-employment or a 'liberal profession' (two categories treated in Articles 18 and 19, respectively), including work in factories, agriculture, offices, sales, domestic work, and virtually all other industrial or service sector occupations, including state employment.[135]

The standard of 'most favourable treatment accorded to nationals of a foreign country' goes beyond the standard expressed for property rights (at least as favourable as treatment 'accorded to aliens generally').[136] It requires states to give refugees the same rights regarding employment as are given to any other aliens, even if they are given in the context of a special relationship with another state or under international agreements.[137] The purpose of this requirement, as expressed by the French delegate to the Convention, was to not deprive refugees of the support that could have only been obtained by the work of their home government, since refugees, by their very nature, are denied such support.[138]

On its face, this paragraph would appear to give refugees the same rights to receive work permits or visas as any other alien. Refugees would be subject to the most lenient requirements and standards for such permits or visas as are imposed on foreign nationals from other countries.[139] This would include work visas that are otherwise only issued on the basis of reciprocity.[140] Refugees would benefit regardless of whether their own government issues such visas or permits.[141]

The second paragraph of Article 17 goes further by requiring states to exempt refugees from 'restrictive measures imposed on aliens or the employment of aliens for the protection of the national labour market' if they have completed three years' residency in the country or if they have a spouse or children who are nationals of the country.[142]

This paragraph has its origin in earlier conventions pertaining to refugees in 1933 and 1938, in which similar paragraphs were drafted, despite the economic depression at the time – a period in which lawmakers became especially concerned with protecting

those requirements that a refugee is incapable of fulfilling by virtue of being a refugee. 1951 Refugee Convention, *supra* note 110, Art. 6. So, requirements such as education, examinations, membership in associations, length of residency, financial solvency, etc., that are generally imposed on aliens would need to be fulfilled by refugees as well. Grahl-Madsen, *supra* note 128, Art. 6, cmt. 3. However, for requirements the refugee is incapable of fulfilling, such as, potentially, the inability to produce a certificate of nationality or to produce a certificate of graduation from a university in the home state, the state must provide other means of satisfying the requirements. *Ibid.*

134. 1951 Refugee Convention, *supra* note 110, Art. 17.
135. Grahl-Madsen, *supra* note 128, Art. 17, cmt. 4.
136. 1951 Refugee Convention, *supra* note 110, Art. 17.
137. Grahl-Madsen, *supra* note 128, Art. 17, cmt. 3.
138. UN Economic & Social Council, *Ad Hoc Committee on Statelessness and Related Problems, First Session: Summary Record of the Thirteenth Meeting*, Refworld (6 Feb. 1950), http://www.refworld.org/docid/40aa1cc34.html [http://perma.cc/4JNB-MXFK].
139. Grahl-Madsen, *supra* note 128, Art. 17.
140. *Ibid.*
141. *Ibid.*
142. 1951 Refugee Convention, *supra* note 110, Art. 17.

nations' jobs for their own nationals.[143] It was felt that such restrictions should not apply to refugees who had a special link to their country of refuge.[144] Based on his reading of the history of this paragraph, commentator Grahl-Madsen asserts that the requirement of three years' residency is to be interpreted as broadly as possible, even including individuals who have not had the status of refugees for the entire period of their residence, individuals whose presence has not been legal, and individuals who have spent short periods travelling or visiting other countries.[145]

The second paragraph only lifts restrictions that intend to prevent competition for domestic jobs.[146] Measures that restrict employment of foreign nationals for other purposes, such as national security, are not affected by this paragraph.[147]

The third paragraph of Article 17 requires states to 'give sympathetic consideration' to giving refugees the same right to wage-earning employment as nationals, especially refugees who came to the country as part of labour recruitment programmes or immigration schemes.[148] This provision obligates governments to undergo a good faith process in which they consider fully integrating refugees into the nation's labour market.[149] It does so with extra force if the country attracted the refugees under the promise of having the right to work.[150]

The effect of Article 17 is that states must place refugees on par with the most favourably treated foreign nationals when it comes to the right to employment - or better, if the refugees have lived in the country for three years or have a spouse or children who are nationals.[151] In this latter case, the refugees are not held back by restrictions imposed on the employment of foreign nationals for the purpose of preserving jobs for the country's own citizens.[152] States must also favourably consider fully assimilating refugees into their labour market, giving them national treatment.[153]

Article 18 extends similar, but slightly different, rights to self-employed refugees. It requires states to:

> [A]ccording to a refugee lawfully in their territory treatment as favourable as possible and, in any event, not less favourable than that accorded to aliens generally in the same circumstances,[154] as regards the right to engage on his own account in agriculture, industry, handicrafts, and commerce and to establish commercial and industrial companies.[155]

The range of activities covered under this provision is the broadest possible.[156]

143. Grahl-Madsen, *supra* note 128, Art. 17, cmts. 1, 5.
144. League of Nations Doc. G.A. C.2/1933 (1933).
145. Grahl-Madsen, *supra* note 128, Art. 17, cmt. 7.
146. *Ibid.*, Art. 17, cmt. 5.
147. *Ibid.*
148. 1951 Refugee Convention, *supra* note 110, Art. 17(3).
149. James Hathaway, *The Rights of Refugees Under International Law* 763 (2005).
150. Grahl-Madsen, *supra* note 128, Art. 17, cmt. 12.
151. *Ibid.*, Art. 17.
152. *Ibid.*
153. *Ibid.*
154. For the meaning of 'in the same circumstance,' *see supra* note 133.
155. 1951 Refugee Convention, *supra* note 110, Art. 18.
156. Grahl-Madsen, *supra* note 128, Art. 18, cmt. 4.

The term 'lawfully in their territory' does not include the 'staying' component that is in other articles using this phrase, such as was seen in Article 17.[157] This suggests that short-term visitors and persons merely travelling through the state are covered, provided they are refugees and their presence is legal.[158]

Additionally, the standard of treatment is potentially lower than the standard for wage-earning employment in Article 17. It is the same as was observed for the right to property: '[A]s favourable as possible ... [but] not less favourable than that accorded to aliens generally in the same circumstances'.[159] Therefore, if the country generally allows aliens to be self-employed in the absence of reciprocity or special arrangements with other states, the country must grant the same rights to refugees.

Article 19 provides similar rights to refugees in 'liberal professions'.[160] States must 'accord to refugees lawfully staying in their territory who hold diplomas recognized by the competent authorities of that State, and who are desirous of practicing a liberal profession, treatment as favourable as possible and, in any event, not less favourable than that accorded to aliens generally in the same circumstances'.[161]

According to Grahl-Madsen, the term 'diploma' is to be understood as 'any degree, examination, admission, authorization, completion of course which is required for the exercise of a profession', such as admission to the bar (for lawyers).[162] The term 'liberal profession' is intended to include persons who act on their own in an occupation that requires certain qualifications, such as an advanced degree or license.[163] Lawyers, doctors, dentists, engineers, architects, and probably scientists would be included.[164]

Finally, Article 24 requires states to extend to refugees many of the same labour and social security protections as nationals. This includes covering them under any laws or regulations dealing with remuneration, work hours, overtime, holidays, child labour, apprenticeship and training, work-related injury, maternity, sickness, disability, and unemployment.[165]

[3] Residency and Movement

Third, refugees have rights pertaining to residency and movement within the territory. Article 26 requires each state party to 'accord to refugees lawfully in its territory the right to choose their place of residence and to move freely within its territory, subject to any regulations applicable to aliens generally in the same circumstances'.[166]

157. *Ibid.*, Art. 18, cmt. 2.
158. *Ibid.*
159. Grahl-Madsen, *supra* note 128, Art. 13(II).
160. 1951 Refugee Convention, *supra* note 110, Art. 19(1).
161. *Ibid.*
162. Grahl-Madsen, *supra* note 128, Art. 19, cmt. 3.
163. *Ibid.*, Art. 19, cmt. 4.
164. *Ibid.*
165. 1951 Refugee Convention, *supra* note 110, Art. 24.
166. *Ibid.*, Art. 26.

The right to choose a residence and to move about freely is distinct from the right to employment in Articles 17–19. To the extent that the country limits rights to employment to certain areas, that would not technically affect the right of refugees to move throughout the country or settle outside those areas, even though it might do so in practice.[167] Conversely, if the country requires aliens generally to only reside or travel in certain areas, this would also apply to refugees, even if they have the technical right to be employed anywhere in the country in accordance with Article 17.[168]

[4] Administrative Facilities

Fourth, states are required to provide administrative assistance to refugees. Article 25 obligates states to arrange for administrative assistance to be provided to refugees when they would normally only be able to obtain that assistance from a foreign country.[169] This includes documents and certifications like birth, marriage, and death certificates, affidavits, and divorce judgements (or substitute instruments); it also includes broader forms of assistance, such as correspondence, investigations, and counselling.[170]

Relatedly, Articles 27 and 28 obligate states to allow access to identity papers[171] and travel documents,[172] respectively. Article 34 requires states to facilitate the assimilation of refugees, to expedite naturalization proceedings, and to reduce as far as possible the charges and costs of such proceedings.[173]

Refugee cities can be well-positioned to fulfil these requirements concerning administrative assistance by adopting mechanisms employed by SEZs, such as one-stop shops and special dedicated regulatory authorities. Such mechanisms can greatly streamline administrative approvals both onsite and online,[174] which would help overcome the procedural burdens and delays that currently face refugees.[175]

167. Grahl-Madsen, *supra* note 128, Art. 26, cmt. 5 (observing that 'in so far as there are restrictions on the freedom to seek whatever employment one might desire, the right to choose one's place of residence may be restricted in fact though not in law').
168. *Ibid.*, Art. 26, cmt. 6 (describing situations in which immigrants are only admitted on the condition that they remain in certain regions of the country and how such restrictions would apply to refugees as well).
169. 1951 Refugee Convention, *supra* note 110, Art. 25.
170. Grahl-Madsen, *supra* note 128, Art. 25, cmts. 1–2.
171. 1951 Refugee Convention, *supra* note 110, Art. 27 (giving the right to identity papers to any refugee 'who does not possess a valid travel document').
172. *Ibid.*, Art. 28 (requiring states to issue refugees documents for the purpose of travelling outside their territory, subject to certain specified exemptions and restrictions).
173. *Ibid.*, Art. 34.
174. *See supra* notes 60–62 and accompanying text.
175. *See supra* note 207–210 and accompanying text (discussing the bureaucratic hurdles, costs, and delays associated with refugee status determinations, work permit applications, and other procedures).

[5] *Additional and Blanket Rights*

Other relevant protections in the Refugee Convention include the right of association,[176] free access to the courts,[177] housing,[178] education,[179] and welfare.[180] Several of the protections for refugees are considered so fundamental and reaffirmed in other international instruments that they are considered customary international law.[181] These include the principle of non-refoulement,[182] non-penalization,[183] and non-discrimination.[184]

Finally, the Refugee Convention contains a requirement for states to 'accord to refugees the same treatment as is accorded to aliens generally', unless other articles require more favourable treatment.[185] This blanket requirement covers all those benefits that aliens generally might enjoy that are not mentioned in the Refugee Convention.[186] The phrase 'aliens generally' means that the requirement excludes benefits conferred under special arrangements with other countries or benefits granted on the basis of reciprocity.[187] This would naturally include all those rights provided under customary international law, such as the right to leave the territory of the state, protection from confiscation of property without compensation, and the right to not be expelled without cause.

---

176. 1951 Refugee Convention, *supra* note 110, Art. 15 (granting lawful refugees the most favourable treatment accorded to nationals of a foreign country regarding non-political and non-profit-making associations and trade unions).
177. *Ibid.*, Art. 16 (conferring free access to the courts of law to the same degree as nationals for refugees who are habitual residents (including legal assistance) and, for non-habitual residents, to the same degree as nationals of the country of habitual residence).
178. *Ibid.*, Art. 21 (according to lawful refugees 'treatment as favourable as possible and, in any event, not less favourable than that accorded to aliens generally in the same circumstances' as regards housing laws, regulations, or other public agency controls).
179. *Ibid.*, Art. 22 (providing refugees the same treatment as nationals as regards elementary education and 'treatment as favourable as possible and, in any event, not less favourable than that accorded to aliens generally in the same circumstances,' as regards non-elementary education).
180. *Ibid.*, Art. 23 (securing for lawful refugees the same treatment as nationals as regards 'public relief and assistance').
181. *See* UNHCR, *Introductory Note by the Office of the United Nations High Commissioner for Refugees*, in *Convention & Protocol Relating to the Status of Refugees* 3 (2010), http://www.unhcr.org/3b66c2aa10.pdf [http://perma.cc/9HW3-HDTZ].
182. 1951 Refugee Convention, *supra* note 110, Art. 33. 'Non-refoulement' is a prohibition on expelling or returning refugees against their will to any territories where they fear threats to life or freedom. UNHCR, *supra* note 181, at 3.
183. 1951 Refugee Convention, *supra* note 110, Art. 31.
184. *Ibid.*, Art. 3.
185. *Ibid.*, Art. 7(1).
186. Grahl-Madsen, *supra* note 128, Art. 7, cmt. 2.
187. *See supra* note 30 and accompanying text. Grahl-Madsen, however, notes that reciprocity requirements may not apply at all if the benefits are ones that a country is prepared to grant to any alien and any number of aliens (as opposed to ones conferred on the basis of a particularly close relationship), since these are effectively a form of retaliation against the refugee's home state, but transmitted through the refugee, who has no power to affect his home state's policies. Grahl-Madsen, *supra* note 128, Art. 7, cmt. 5.

Moreover, refugees enjoy any benefits to aliens that are conditioned on legislative reciprocity after three years' residence.[188] This means that benefits that are only conferred upon foreign nationals if those individuals' home states confer similar benefits on nationals of the other state, are available to refugees, notwithstanding the refugee's home state's policies.

[B] Domestic Laws Pertaining to Refugees

Domestic law is typically far more restrictive toward refugees than the Refugee Convention. Even though many of the countries hosting large numbers of the world's refugees are parties to the convention, few fully apply key rights, especially work rights. Common concerns supporting these restrictions are the fear that refugees will decrease the supply of jobs available to citizens, strain and distort an already weak labour market, reduce wages and working conditions, encourage refugees to claim citizenship, and pose security risks.[189]

Turkey is one example. The vast majority of forcibly displaced people within it do not meet the technical definition of 'refugee' and thus do not have access to the rights granted by the Refugee Convention. Nevertheless, Turkey has made progress since the beginning of the Syrian refugee crisis at modifying its legal framework to extend more rights to refugees.[190] The refugee cities approach could help advance these efforts.

[1] Overview of Domestic Law

The legal framework for refugees in many countries has weaknesses in terms of the ability to obtain formal status as refugees and, for those who do obtain refugee status, the protections conferred to them.[191] Inability to obtain formal status and protection as refugees leaves these individuals, such as Eritrean refugees in Sudan and Colombian refugees in Venezuela, vulnerable to roundups, detention, and refoulement.[192] Refugees who are not granted formal status as refugees are sometimes given other classifications, such as temporary protection.[193]

Only seventy-five of the 145 states that are party to the Refugee Convention formally grant refugees the right to work.[194] Half of the states have declared full or partial reservations to the rights to work conferred in Articles 17–19, usually imposing similar restrictions as states not party to the Refugee Convention.[195] Only a few countries have refugee and labour legislation that specifically refers to a refugee's right

188. 1951 Refugee Convention, *supra* note 110, Art. 7(2).
189. Zetter & Ruaudel, *supra* note 2, at viii, xi.
190. *See ibid.*, at 15, 33.
191. *Ibid.*, at 11.
192. *Ibid.* Also noting that failure to make refugee status determinations skews official counts of refugees because people who would otherwise receive refugee status are often left undocumented and thus uncounted. *Ibid.*
193. *Ibid.*, at 12.
194. *Ibid.*, at 4–5.
195. *Ibid.*

to work.[196] Others, such as Chad, Ecuador, and India, handle refugees under the same provisions applicable to foreigners generally.[197]

Many countries impose restrictions on the sectors refugees can work in. Prohibiting refugees from working in security and defence, as well as government employment generally, are fairly common.[198] Many countries go further, such as requiring that no qualified nationals be available to work in the particular sector.[199]

Other legal limitations supplement restrictions on the right to work, such as restrictions on owning property, mobility, accessing credit, opening a business, opening a bank account, and entering into contracts.[200] Many countries restrict refugees from employment-related rights and benefits, such as social security, unemployment and disability insurance, and general labour rights, as in the case of stateless Palestinians in Jordan.[201]

There are exceptions. Uganda's 2006 Refugee Act provides a legal framework for refugees that is strongly oriented toward social and economic integration.[202] The Act aligns with the Refugee Convention and provides freedoms to work, operate businesses, access courts, receive an education, move and reside freely throughout the country, and own property.[203] The United States is similar.[204]

Beyond legal hurdles, countries' policies and practices often impose major constraints on employment.[205] There is significant confusion over where paperwork must be filed and whether obtaining refugee status is sufficient to work or whether an additional work permit is required.[206]

The processes for refugee status determinations, processing paperwork, and issuing permits and licenses are often slow, complex, costly, and burdensome.[207] In many countries, refugees must first obtain a job offer from an employer before they can obtain a work permit, as in Lebanon and Zambia.[208] Some countries are removing or simplifying these hurdles.[209] In 2016, for instance, Jordan provided a three-month

196. *Ibid.*, at 12 (noting the United States and Uganda as examples).
197. *Ibid.*
198. *Ibid.*, at 13.
199. *Ibid.*
200. *Ibid.*, at 13, 16. For example, Pakistan requires refugees to have a Pakistani partner in order to own real estate or a business. *Ibid.*, at 13. Ecuador and Turkey limit access to financial institutions. *Ibid.* Bangladesh prohibits refugees from accessing credit, engaging in trade, and owning property. *Ibid.* Refugees in India and Sudan are prohibited from purchasing land. *Ibid.*
201. *Ibid.*
202. *See* Uganda: The Refugees Act 2006 (24 May 2006), http://www.refworld.org/ docid/4b7baba 52.html [http://perma.cc/56G6-UYDF].
203. *Ibid.*, at 29; Refugee Law Project, *Critique of the Refugees Act* 3 (2006), https://www.refugeelawproject.org/files/legal_resources/RefugeesActRLPCritique.pdf [http://perma.cc/LJ 4M-KZXX]; *see also* World Bank Group, *An Assessment of Uganda's Progressive Approach to Refugee Management* (2016) (describing and assessing the impact of the law and policy affecting refugees in Uganda).
204. *See* Zetter & Ruaudel, *supra* note 2, at 12–13.
205. *See ibid.*, at 15.
206. *Ibid.*, at 12, 15 (observing that in the UK and US a work permit is not necessary if a person has been determined to be a refugee, but noting how many countries are different).
207. *Ibid.*, at 15.
208. *Ibid.*
209. *Ibid.*

period in which it would waive fees for twelve-month work permits for Syrian refugees, and Turkey permitted Syrian refugees to apply for work permits if they were in possession of temporary identity cards and resided in Turkey for six months.[210]

[2] Turkey

Turkey currently hosts the world's largest refugee population at approximately 3.7 million as of 2017, and is a primary route for Syrians and Iraqis to reach Europe.[211] The EU has been providing substantial assistance to Turkey to stop illegal or informal entry of these migrants into Europe.[212]

Turkey is a party to the Refugee Convention, yet counterintuitively, few, if any, of its refugees are actually protected by the Convention.[213] This unusual situation arose from the fact that the primary impetus and focus of the Refugee Convention was the large number of displaced people in Europe after World War II.[214] Therefore, when the Refugee Convention was adopted, its Member States had the option of limiting its scope to only people displaced by events in Europe or extending coverage to refugees from anywhere in the world.[215] Turkey was one of a few states that limited its scope to Europe, and expressly continued this limitation when it adopted the 1967 Protocol.[216] As a result, the only people technically under the protection of the Refugee Convention in Turkey are those who have fled European nations. [217] Nearly all of Turkey's refugee population is from non-European countries, especially Syria and Iraq.[218]

Nevertheless, Turkey has substantially adjusted its domestic legislation to protect refugees in recent years and collaborates with UNHCR.[219] The 2013 Law on Foreigners

210. *See ibid.*, at 15. *But see* Wendy Zeldin, *Turkey*, in *Refugee Law and Policy in Selected Countries* 256, 273 (The Law Library of Congress, Global Legal Research Center, March 2016) (noting that, in practice, less than 3% of Syrian refugees have been issued work permits under this policy because they have been deemed 'unqualified').
211. European Commission, *European Civil Protection and Humanitarian Aid Operations: Turkey*, http://ec.europa.eu/echo/files/aid/countries/factsheets/turkey_syrian_ crisis_en.pdf [http://perma.cc/RPN7-TZWA] (last updated 10 Jan. 2018).
212. *Ibid.*; *see also*, e.g., *EU-Turkey Joint Action Plan: Implementation Report* (Feb. 10, 2016), https://ec.europa.eu/home-affairs/sites/homeaffairs/files/what-we-do/policies/european-agenda-migration/background-information/docs/managing_the_refugee_crisis_-_eu-turkey_join_action_plan_implementation_report_20160210_en.pdf [http://perma.cc/56MS-XJQ3] (pledging EUR 3 million in assistance for measures aimed at curbing irregular migration); Council of the EU Press Release 144/16, EU-Turkey Statement (18 Mar. 2016) (arranging that for every Syrian returned to Turkey from the Greek islands, one Syrian will be resettled from Turkey to the EU).
213. Zeldin, *supra* note 210, at 256.
214. UNHCR, *supra* note 181, at 2.
215. *See ibid.*, Art. 1B(1) (providing states the option of interpreting the scope of Art. 1 as applying only to persons displaced by events in Europe or in any nation).
216. *See* UNHCR, States Parties to the 1951 Convention relating to the Status of Refugees and the 1967 Protocol 5 (April 2015) (observing that Turkey expressly maintained its declaration of geographic limitation).
217. Zeldin, *supra* note 210, at 261.
218. *Ibid.*
219. *Ibid.*

and International Protection (LFIP)[220] extended protections to categories of forcibly displaced people not meeting the strict Eurocentric definition of 'refugee', including 'conditional refugees' and persons covered under 'subsidiary protection' and 'temporary protection'.[221] UNHCR works with the Ministry of the Interior to conduct status determinations and attempts to resettle refugees into third countries.[222] Generally speaking, the legal framework is geared to prevent integration of refugees and toward a temporary status, with eventual resettlement in a third country or repatriation as the goal.[223]

The LFIP created several classifications into which asylum seekers can fall. First it created the following classifications of persons entitled to 'international protection status':

(1) Refugees, which are foreigners who, 'as a result of events *occurring in European countries*', cannot avail themselves of the protection of the country of their nationality or of former residence because of a well-founded fear of persecution for reasons of race, religion, nationality, membership of a particular social group, or political opinion.[224]
(2) Conditional Refugees, which are foreigners who, 'as a result of events occurring *outside European countries*', cannot avail themselves the protection of the country of their nationality or of former residence because of a well-founded fear of persecution for reasons of race, religion, nationality, membership of a particular social group, or political opinion.[225]
(3) Beneficiaries of '*subsidiary protection*', which are foreigners who cannot qualify as a refugee or conditional refugee, but if returned to their country of origin or former residence would face the death penalty, torture, inhuman or degrading treatment, or serious threat of indiscriminate violence from armed conflict.[226]

Persons who apply for and receive international protection status must undergo lengthy procedures and are entitled to several rights specified in the LFIP.

However, given the realities of mass migration, particularly of Syrians, and the attendant difficulties of satisfying the procedural requirements of international protection applications for each one, the LFIP added an additional category - *Temporary Protection*.[227] Temporary protection status is more immediate than the categories of

220. Law on Foreigners and International Protection (Law No. 6458) (4 Apr. 2013) (Republic of Turkey) (unofficial English translation), http://www.goc.gov.tr/files/files/eng_ minikanun_5 _son.pdf [http://perma.cc/KY8Y-H3RW] [hereinafter LFIP].
221. *Ibid.*, Art. 61-63.
222. Zeldin, *supra* note 210, at 261.
223. As an example, refugees, conditional refugees, and beneficiaries of subsidiary protection and temporary protection are explicitly exempted from receiving long-term residence permits. LFIP, *supra* note 220, Art. 42(2).
224. *Ibid.*, Art. 61 (emphasis added).
225. *Ibid.*, Art. 62 (emphasis added).
226. *Ibid.*, Art. 63 (emphasis added).
227. Zeldin, *supra* note 210, at 261-63.

international protection and does not involve the same procedures and rights as the international protection categories.[228] Beneficiaries of temporary protection are those 'foreigners who have been forced to leave their country, cannot return to the country that they have left, and have arrived at or crossed the borders of Turkey in *a mass influx situation* seeking immediate and temporary protection'.[229]

Syrians, who compose the vast majority of asylum seekers in Turkey, have been placed under temporary protection as a group, due to the large influx of them in recent years.[230] Non-Syrian asylum seekers are generally processed under one of the international protection categories by the UNHCR.[231]

The Temporary Protection status is further defined in the Temporary Protection Regulation.[232] Beneficiaries of temporary protection receive basic-needs assistance, including social services, translation services, IDs, travel documents, access to primary and secondary education, and the opportunity to receive work permits.[233]

People under temporary protection are typically required to live in designated reception and accommodation centres. These centres are managed by the Turkish Disaster and Emergency Management Authority and the Turkish Red Crescent, rather than by the UNHCR.[234] Camps reportedly have markets, reliable heating, religious services, communications infrastructure, psychosocial support, banking, and other services.[235] Residents are given three meals a day and electronic cards preloaded with funds for personal needs.[236] Residents are also covered under the country's social security and medical insurance programs.[237] Premium payments are at least partially covered by Turkey's Directorate General of Migration Management, though recipients are expected to contribute in full or in part in proportion to their financial means.[238]

Asylum seekers have limited access to the labour market. Persons who apply for international protection, as well as persons given conditional refugee status, may apply for a work permit six months after their international protection application was filed.[239] Persons who acquire refugee status or subsidiary protection status are automatically eligible to work, either in self-employment or regular employment, with their identity document substituting for a work permit.[240] However, such persons are subject to the general laws pertaining to foreign workers, which requires, among other things, for businesses to have at least five Turkish citizens as employees for every foreign worker.[241] Additionally, the LFIP states that refugees' and subsidiary protection

228. *Ibid.*
229. LFIP, *supra* note 220, Art. 91(1) (emphasis added).
230. Zeldin, *supra* note 210, at 261–63.
231. *Ibid.*
232. Temporary Protection Regulation (22 Oct. 2014) (unofficial English translation), http://www.goc.gov.tr/files/files/temptemp.pdf [http://perma.cc/9V29-HQZ5].
233. *Ibid.*, Art. 26–32.
234. Zeldin, *supra* note 210, at 270.
235. *Ibid.*
236. *Ibid.*
237. *Ibid.*
238. *Ibid.*
239. LFIP, *supra* note 220, Art. 89(4).
240. *Ibid.*
241. *Ibid.*

beneficiaries' access to the labour market may be restricted concerning certain sectors, professions, lines of business or geographical areas for a period when necessary because of 'the situation of the labor market', 'developments in the working life', and employment-related 'sectoral and economic conditions'.[242] However, no such restrictions apply to refugees and subsidiary protection beneficiaries who have resided in Turkey for three years or have a spouse or children with Turkish citizenship.[243]

Persons under temporary protection may similarly apply for a work permit six months after being registered.[244] In addition to the general requirements regarding the issuance of work permits, temporary protection workers cannot make up more than 10% of the Turkish citizens employed at a business, unless the employer can prove there is no qualified Turkish citizen in the province who can perform the job.[245] In practice, the government has deemed all but 3% of Syrian refugees as 'unqualified' for work permits because they 'do not have an identity card ... [and their] professions are unknown'.[246]

§10.06 CONCLUSION

Refugee cities provide a pathway for refugee integration and alignment with international norms in the face of political resistance to countrywide integration. They apply the most important feature of SEZs – their ability to overcome roadblocks to beneficial policy reforms – to address one of the most pressing global concerns and help countries benefit from, rather than be burdened by, migrants.

A refugee city would serve as a demonstration area where the benefits of extending international law pertaining to refugees would be tested. They would serve as a complementary pathway that helps achieve the UNHCR's objective of integrating refugees into host economies – one of its 'durable solutions' – in a designated geographic area. They would also help realize the policy benefits of integrating migrants into the formal economy.

Within refugee cities, countries could extend rights to property that fulfil Article 13 of the Refugee Convention. Residents of a refugee city could have formal rights to land, such as a lease, and rights to movable property. At the same time, countries could address reluctance to make refugees permanent by setting time limits and expiration dates on leases, business licenses, or work permits. When the expiration date occurs, the country will have enabled refugees to return home on a much better footing then they would have been on otherwise.

Countries could also extend rights to work and self-employment that match Articles 17–19 of the Refugee Convention. This would mean refugees would have the most favourable treatment accorded to foreign nationals, with restrictions designed to

242. *Ibid.*
243. *Ibid.* This exemption from labour market restrictions is analogous to Art. 17(2) of the Refugee Convention, which would apply anyway to refugees. The LFIP extends the exemption to subsidiary protection beneficiaries. *Ibid.*
244. Zeldin, *supra* note 210, at 272.
245. *Ibid.*, at 272–73.
246. *Ibid.*, at 273.

protect the domestic labour market removed for those who have lived in the country for three years or have a spouse or children who are nationals. Alternatively, refugees could be placed on par with nationals, fulfilling the aspirations of Article 17, paragraph 3.

Refugee cities could streamline regulatory functions through dedicated regulatory authorities and one-stop shops to enable a more efficient processing of residents' status determinations and applications for work permits. These mechanisms would overcome the current backlog in countries like Turkey and others facing large refugee influxes. Refugee cities could also fulfil the blanket obligation to treat refugees with at least the same treatment as is accorded to aliens generally in Article 7 of the Refugee Convention.

For the developing countries currently hosting the overwhelming share of migrants, refugee cities would transcend the traditional refugee camp model. They would be spaces in which international legal norms align with both political realities and good policy and drive economic and social progress.

CHAPTER 11

SEZs under the WTO's Scrutiny: Defining the Scope of Trade Issues

Sherzod Shadikhodjaev

§11.01 INTRODUCTION

The concept, classification, rationales and legal regimes of special economic zones (SEZs) vary from country to country. SEZs may be called differently as free trade zones (FTZs), export processing zones, free ports, enterprise zones, single-factory export processing zones or otherwise.[1] Despite their diversity, SEZs are common in creating a pleasant business climate not available in the rest of the SEZ-hosting country. In particular, governments apply business-friendlier policies and offer a more generous incentive package to investors working in SEZs.[2] These mostly include enhanced physical infrastructure, streamlined administrative services, fiscal benefits, relaxed regulations and export promotion services.[3] There may also be some peculiar 'incentives', such as, e.g., India's anti-dumping or countervailing duty exemptions for imports used in its SEZs for export production.[4]

SEZs are often used to test certain liberal policies that in case of success may later be applied to the entire country. For example, the China (Shanghai) Pilot FTZ was opened in 2013 to experiment with a new approach of regulating foreign direct investment (FDI) – potentially extendable to the other parts of China – that permits, in

1. *See* FIAS, *Special Economic Zones: Performance, Lessons Learned, and Implications for Zone Development* 10–11 (2008).
2. For an overview of SEZs as a specific industrial policy tool, *see* Sherzod Shadikhodjaev, *Industrial Policy and the World Trade Organization: Between Legal Constraints and Flexibilities* (Cambridge: Cambridge University Press, 2018) 115–119.
3. Michael Engman et al., *Export Processing Zones: Past and Future Role in Trade and Development*, OECD Trade Policy Working Paper No. 53, 17 (2007).
4. WTO, TPR Body – 2 and 4 June 2015 – TPR – India – Minutes of the Meeting – Addendum, WT/TPR/M/313/Add.1 (31 July 2015), 62–63, 163, 170.

principle, all investment projects not covered by a 'negative' list of restrictions.[5] The scope of the negative list in this and other pilot FTZs was reduced from about 190 items in 2013 to 122 in 2015 and 95 in 2017, with over 150 practices piloted in the zones being replicated in other regions or sectors of China.[6] Other widely accepted rationales for launching SEZs include generation of foreign exchange earnings, job creation, FDI inducement, encouragement of technological transfers and knowledge spillovers.[7]

The amended International Convention on the Simplification and Harmonization of Customs Procedures (also known as the 'Revised Kyoto Convention') – administered by the World Customs Organization – seems to be the only multilateral treaty that contains provisions specific to SEZs (or 'free zones') per se. Chapter 2 of Specific Annex D of the Revised Kyoto Convention is about free zones and associated customs issues like admission of goods, security, authorized operations, goods consumed inside zones, duration of stay of goods, transfer of ownership, removal of goods, assessment of duties and taxes and a zone's closure. There, the term 'free zone' is defined as 'a part of the territory of a Contracting Party where any goods introduced are generally regarded, insofar as import duties and taxes are concerned, as being outside the Customs territory'. Under this definition, free zones are considered to be an integral part of the national territory, and goods in the zone are deemed, for the fiscal purposes, to be outside the customs territory, i.e., 'the territory in which the [party's] Customs law … applies'.[8] In some countries, free zones as such, rather than goods, are excluded from the scope of their customs territory.[9] While being under a national jurisdiction, free zones are 'extraterritorial' in that goods moving between a free zone and the home market are treated as imports or exports, and in-zone goods enjoy certain preferences not available in the other parts of the country.[10] As of 19 September 2018, the Revised Kyoto Convention had 115 contracting parties, out which 106 were members of the World Trade Organization (WTO).[11] Chapter 2 of Specific Annex D above does not conflict with the existing WTO rules and can be applied in a mutually complimentary manner.[12]

Unlike the Revised Kyoto Convention, WTO agreements are silent on SEZs. But this fact does not mean the immunity of SEZs from trade disciplines, as WTO law is legally binding[13] and applies, unless otherwise specified, to the whole territory of each member, including SEZs.

5. *See* Daqing Yao & John Whalley, *The China (Shanghai) Pilot Free Trade Zone: Background, Developments and Preliminary Assessment of Initial Impacts*, 39 The World Economy 2 (2016).
6. State Council of the People's Republic of China, 'Pilot FTZs: Pioneers of China's Reform, Opening-up', 24 May 2018, http://english.gov.cn/policies/policy_watch/2018/05/24/content_281476159124926.htm (accessed 1 October 2018).
7. UNESCAP, *Free Trade Zone and Port Hinterland Development* 7 (2005).
8. Chapter 2, General Annex of the Revised Kyoto Convention.
9. *See*, e.g., WTO, TPRB – TPR – Report by the Secretariat – Panama – Revision, WT/TPR/S/186/Rev.1 (3 December 2007), 27.
10. Sherzod Shadikhodjaev, *International Regulation of Free Zones: An Analysis of Multilateral Customs and Trade Rules*, 10 World Trade Review 189 (2011), 192–193.
11. The lists of WTO members and signatories to the Revised Kyoto Conventions can be found at www.wto.org and www.wcoomd.org respectively.
12. Shadikhodjaev, *supra*, footnote 10, at 212–213.
13. *See* Arts II:2 and XVI:4 of the WTO Agreement.

In order to define the scope of SEZ-related issues scrutinized in the WTO, this paper particularly examines various WTO materials on accession, transparency and case law, among other things. Specifically, section §11.02 lists and discusses commitments of individual members on SEZs, followed by sections §11.03 and §11.04 that elaborate on trade issues raised in WTO transparency and dispute settlement procedures respectively.

§11.02 MEMBER-SPECIFIC COMMITMENTS ON SEZs

We reviewed accession documents of thirty-six members that joined the WTO between 1995 and 2018. All of these documents - working party reports - have a separate section on free zones and special economic areas where the acceding nations typically explained their SEZ policies, addressed questions and comments raised by existing members and specified their commitments (if any). Interestingly enough, while Estonia did not make any commitment on the grounds that there was no SEZ in operation,[14] a handful of other countries (e.g., Mongolia, Nepal and Georgia)[15] assumed future-oriented WTO commitments for a potential SEZ that could be opened after their entry into the WTO.

When existing members expressed their concerns about possible trade-restrictive aspects of SEZs, the acceding governments often responded by: (i) detailing the steps they had already taken to alleviate those concerns and/or (ii) undertaking legally binding commitments. As an illustrative example of the first type of response, Box 1 shows how Chinese Taipei elucidated why certain incentives in its zones would be deemed compliant with the Subsidies and Countervailing Measures (SCM) Agreement. But, of course, the acceder's position, even if reflected in the WTO records, does not necessarily determine the actual legal nature of such incentives and may not always be shared by other members.

Box 1. Excerpt from the WTO Working Party's Report on Chinese Taipei's Accession

> 94. Some members of the Working Party noted that some of the arrangements providing for fiscal incentives for businesses located or operating in the zones appeared to be in conflict with the provisions of the SCM Agreement and the Agreement on TRIMS. They requested further information on the fiscal incentives offered. In response, the representative of Chinese Taipei indicated that investments in the zones were exempted from customs duties and the commodity tax on imported machinery, raw materials, fuels, commodities, components and samples, and the deed tax on the new buildings purchased from or otherwise acquired from the zones' Administration. No business tax was charged on the

14. Working Party Report on WTO Accession: Estonia, WT/ACC/EST/28 (9 April 1999), para. 104.
15. Working Party Report on WTO Accession: Mongolia, WT/ACC/MNG/9 (27 June 1996), paras 50–51; Nepal, WT/ACC/NPL/16 (28 August 2003), para. 112; Georgia, WT/ACC/GEO/31 (31 August 1999), paras 112–113.

exported goods and their related services, nor was the business tax levied on purchases by those enterprises. These enterprises were also exempted from applying for tax exemption, guarantee, relevant bookkeeping, and paying provisional tax. He further stated that in Chinese Taipei's view those practices complied with the requirements of the WTO Agreement and did not constitute export subsidies. Their trade effect, if any, was minimal: 0.185 per cent of total exports.

95. Some members of the Working Party noted that import duty and tax exemptions on goods imported into the zones were provided for goods not directly incorporated into the exported product. Direct taxes on the profits from the exports of those enterprises were also exempted. In their view these practices appeared to be in conflict with the SCM Agreement. Those subsidies could also be countervailable. The representative of Chinese Taipei replied that the purpose of the zones was to create duty-free zones for the production of exports, in order to create an environment where exports manufactured from imported inputs need not obtain a refund of duties. This was consistent with the obligations contained in the WTO Agreement. The limitation on duty refunds/exemptions on inputs directly incorporated into exported products was applied by many developed economies, for the purpose of administrative expediency, rather than being based on the theory that refunds/exemptions of duties on imported inputs not directly incorporated into the exported products would unduly increase the exporters' competitiveness and should not be allowed. Because the products were primarily for export, it was therefore not necessary to limit exemptions or refunds to the extent of products directly incorporated into the products exported from the zones. In fact, in Annex II of the SCM Agreement, inputs consumed in the production process, for which drawback of import charges was allowed, were defined to cover energy, fuel and oil in the production process and catalysts which were consumed in the course of their use to obtain the exported product as well as the inputs physically incorporated. Because the exports from the zones did not receive 'undue' amounts of refund or exemption the relevant practices did not constitute a subsidy. The representative of Chinese Taipei added that the SCM Agreement Annex I 'Illustrative List of Export Subsidies' did not contain the requirement that the input be physically incorporated into the exported product. He stated that the exemption from corporate income tax for zones enterprises had been abolished together with the Statute for Encouragement of Investment at the end of 1990. The current tax exemption granted to zone's enterprises also applied to enterprises located outside the zones, whether or not they exported their products, provided that they met the requirements set forth in the Statute for Upgrading Industries. Consequently, the practice was neither a specific subsidy nor conditional upon export performance.

Source: Working Party Report on WTO Accession of Chinese Taipei, WT/MIN(01)/4 (11 November 2001).

As for the second type of response above, acceded members undertook specific commitments on SEZs as regards roughly four issues: (i) the scope of application of WTO law including the accession package, (ii) treatment of zone-located firms, (iii) withdrawal of fiscal preferences and exemptions for SEZ products sold to home markets and (iv) notifications. We group the issues in this way for the sake of convenience, with the caveats that the borderline between these categories is not always clear-cut, as some of the commitments may well be seated under more than one, and that the range and formulations of commitments vary from member to member.

In the first category on the application scope, members typically accept the applicability of WTO law to their SEZs and specify regulatory domains - mostly subsidies, trade-related investment measures (TRIMs) and trade-related aspects of intellectual property rights (TRIPS) - within which they undertake commitments. Arguably, such explicit references to particular areas of regulation merely exemplify most pertinent rules, but do not limit a committing member's WTO obligations on SEZs to those areas. Here, a relevant member recognizes SEZs as part of its territory and/or accepts the WTO-applicability/enforceability in SEZs[16] and commits itself to:

- implementing its tariff policy uniformly throughout its customs territory;[17]
- observing the SCM Agreement in providing incentives to SEZ firms;[18]
- ensuring enforceability of WTO law, including the TRIPS Agreement, within SEZs;[19]
- complying with WTO rules, including those on subsidies, TRIMs and TRIPS;[20]

16. Working Party Report on WTO Accession: Panama, WT/ACC/PAN/19 (20 September 1996), para. 77; Kyrgyz Republic, WT/ACC/KGZ/26 (31 July 1998), para. 115; Latvia, WT/ACC/LVA/32 (30 September 1998), para. 95; Jordan, WT/ACC/JOR/33, WT/MIN(99)/9 (3 December 1999), para. 164; Albania, WT/ACC/ALB/51 (13 July 2000), para. 118; Croatia, WT/ACC/HRV/59 (29 June 2000), para. 148; Moldova, WT/ACC/MOL/37 (11 January 2001), para. 145; FYROM, WT/ACC/807/27 (26 September 2002), para. 165; Cambodia, WT/ACC/KHM/21 (15 August 2003), para. 151; Nepal, WT/ACC/NPL/16 (28 August 2003), para. 112; Viet Nam, WT/ACC/VNM/48 (27 October 2006), para. 339; Tonga, WT/ACC/TON/17, WT/MIN(05)/4 (2 December 2005), para. 135; Cape Verde, WT/ACC/CPV/30 (6 December 2007), para. 187; Afghanistan, WT/ACC/AFG/36, WT/MIN(15)/6 (13 November 2015), para. 193; Kazakhstan, WT/ACC/KAZ/93 (23 June 2015), para. 933; Lao PDR, WT/ACC/LAO/45 (1 October 2012), para. 159; Russia, WT/ACC/RUS/70, WT/MIN(11)/2 (17 November 2011), para. 1124; Samoa, WT/ACC/SAM/30, WT/MIN(11)/1 (1 November 2011), para. 167; Tajikistan, WT/ACC/TJK/30 (6 November 2012), para. 239; Vanuatu, WT/ACC/VUT/17 (11 May 2011), para. 104; Yemen, WT/ACC/YEM/42 (4 October 2013), para. 188.
17. Working Party Report on WTO Accession: China, WT/ACC/CHN/49 (1 October 2001), para. 222.
18. Working Party Report on WTO Accession: Mongolia, WT/ACC/MNG/9 (27 June 1996), para. 51.
19. Working Party Report on WTO Accession: Panama, WT/ACC/PAN/19 (20 September 1996), para. 77; Jordan, WT/ACC/JOR/33, WT/MIN(99)/9 (3 December 1999), para. 164; Lithuania, WT/ACC/LTU/52 (7 November 2000), para. 138.
20. Working Party Report on WTO Accession: Georgia, WT/ACC/GEO/31 (31 August 1999), para. 113; Oman, WT/ACC/OMN/26 (28 September 2000), para. 116; Armenia, WT/ACC/ARM/23 (26 November 2002), para. 150; Saudi Arabia, WT/ACC/SAU/61 (1 November 2005), para. 228; Ukraine, WT/ACC/UKR/152 (25 January 2008), para. 345; Afghanistan, WT/ACC/AFG/36,

- complying with WTO rules, including those on subsidies and TRIMs;[21]
- applying WTO Agreements on, *inter alia*, TRIPS, sanitary and phytosanitary measures, technical barriers to trade, TRIMs, subsidies, and the General Agreement on Tariffs and Trade (GATT) 1994 in an SEZ.[22]

The second category of commitments works to forbid discriminatory treatment of SEZ firms and certain burdensome requirements to export or localize production. In particular, these are the obligations to:

- provide any preferential arrangements for foreign invested enterprises located within SEZs on a non-discriminatory basis;[23]
- extend preferential arrangements provided to SEZ enterprises to 'all enterprises whether domestic or foreign and maintained in a WTO consistent manner, in particular with regard to the principles of non-discrimination and national treatment';[24]
- eliminate all SEZ-related local content and export subsidies on or before accession; not reintroduce them and not introduce the new ones after accession;[25]
- not reintroduce export requirements or incentives in SEZs;[26]
- not subject SEZ firms to export performance, trade balancing or local content requirements.[27]

Two members confirmed that their local content and export performance requirements in SEZs were or would be deleted prior to accession.[28] It is noteworthy that while local content and trade balancing requirements are already banned by the provisions of

WT/MIN(15)/6 (13 November 2015), para. 193; Montenegro, WT/ACC/CGR/38, WT/MIN(11)/7 (5 December 2011), para. 177; Samoa, WT/ACC/SAM/30, WT/MIN(11)/1 (1 November 2011), para. 167.

21. Working Party Report on WTO Accession: Liberia, WT/ACC/LBR/23, WT/MIN(15)/2 (9 October 2015), para. 251; Tajikistan, WT/ACC/TJK/30 (6 November 2012), para. 239; Seychelles, WT/ACC/SYC/64 (5 November 2014), para. 314.
22. Working Party Report on WTO Accession: Seychelles, WT/ACC/SYC/64 (5 November 2014), para. 313.
23. Working Party Report on WTO Accession: China, WT/ACC/CHN/49 (1 October 2001), para. 228.
24. Working Party Report on WTO Accession: Chinese Taipei, WT/MIN(01)/4 (5 October 2001), para. 97.
25. Working Party Report on WTO Accession: Viet Nam, WT/ACC/VNM/48 (27 October 2006), para. 339.
26. Working Party Report on WTO Accession: Chinese Taipei, WT/MIN(01)/4 (5 October 2001), para. 97.
27. Working Party Report on WTO Accession: Ukraine, WT/ACC/UKR/152 (25 January 2008), para. 345; Afghanistan, WT/ACC/AFG/36, WT/MIN(15)/6 (13 November 2015), para. 193; Kazakhstan, WT/ACC/KAZ/93 (23 June 2015), para. 934; Liberia, WT/ACC/LBR/23, WT/MIN(15)/2 (9 October 2015), para. 251; Montenegro, WT/ACC/CGR/38, WT/MIN(11)/7 (5 December 2011), para. 177; Russia, WT/ACC/RUS/70, WTMIN(11)/2 (17 November 2011), para. 1124; Samoa, WT/ACC/SAM/30, WT/MIN(11)/1 (1 November 2011), para. 167; Seychelles, WT/ACC/SYC/64 (5 November 2014), para. 314; Tajikistan, WT/ACC/TJK/30 (6 November 2012), para. 239.
28. Working Party Report on WTO Accession: FYROM, WT/ACC/807/27 (26 September 2002), para. 165; Viet Nam, WT/ACC/VNM/48 (27 October 2006), para. 339.

the GATT and the TRIMs Agreement on national treatment and quantitative restrictions, the per se requirement to export - withdrawn under some members' commitments above - is not prohibited under 'common' WTO law. Unlike many investment treaties, WTO agreements, to our best knowledge, do not prevent members from requiring firms to export. This holds true, at least, for the GATT. Indeed, as the panel in *Canada – FIRA* found, 'there is no provision in the General Agreement which forbids requirements to sell goods in foreign markets in preference to the domestic market'.[29]

The third category comprises the most frequent commitment and calls for the discontinuation of preferential fiscal charges and exemptions for those subject goods that leave an SEZ for the domestic market. Specifically, a committing member pledged:

- to apply all relevant ordinary duties, taxes, charges, customs formalities and other import measures on goods moved from an SEZ to the rest of its territory;[30]
- to ensure uniform enforcement of taxes, tariffs and non-tariff measures on trade between a member's SEZ and the other parts of its territory.[31]

This commitment aims to prevent discrimination between zone-products and other like products competing in the domestic market outside of SEZs. By levelling the playing field, it protects the interests of not only foreign but also local companies operating out of the zone.[32]

29. GATT Panel Report, *Canada – Administration of the Foreign Investment Review Act*, L/5504, adopted 7 February 1984, BISD 30S/140, para. 5.18.
30. Working Party Report on WTO Accession: Ecuador, WT/L/77 (14 July 1995), para. 61; Mongolia, WT/ACC/MNG/9 (27 June 1996), para. 51; Panama, WT/ACC/PAN/19 (20 September 1996), para. 77; Kyrgyz Republic, WT/ACC/KGZ/26 (31 July 1998), para. 115; Latvia, WT/ACC/LVA/32 (30 September 1998), para. 95; Jordan, WT/ACC/JOR/33, WT/MIN(99)/9 (3 December 1999), para. 164; Georgia, WT/ACC/GEO/31 (31 August 1999), para. 113; Albania, WT/ACC/ALB/51 (13 July 2000), para. 118; Oman, WT/ACC/OMN/26 (28 September 2000), para. 116; Croatia, WT/ACC/HRV/59 (29 June 2000), para. 148; Lithuania, WT/ACC/LTU/52 (7 November 2000), para. 138; Moldova, WT/ACC/MOL/37 (11 January 2001), para. 145; China, WT/ACC/CHN/49 (1 October 2001), para. 222; Chinese Taipei, WT/MIN(01)/4 (5 October 2001), para. 97; Armenia, WT/ACC/ARM/23 (26 November 2002), para. 150; FYROM, WT/ACC/807/27 (26 September 2002), para. 165; Cambodia, WT/ACC/KHM/21 (15 August 2003), para. 151; Nepal, WT/ACC/NPL/16 (28 August 2003), para. 112; Saudi Arabia, WT/ACC/SAU/61 (1 November 2005), para. 228; Viet Nam, WT/ACC/VNM/48 (27 October 2006), para. 339; Tonga, WT/ACC/TON/17, WT/MIN(05)/4 (2 December 2005), para. 135; Ukraine, WT/ACC/UKR/152 (25 January 2008), para. 345; Cape Verde, WT/ACC/CPV/30 (6 December 2007), para. 187; Afghanistan, WT/ACC/AFG/36, WT/MIN(15)/6 (13 November 2015), para. 193; Kazakhstan, WT/ACC/KAZ/93 (23 June 2015), para. 934; Lao PDR, WT/ACC/LAO/45 (1 October 2012), para. 159; Liberia, WT/ACC/LBR/23, WT/MIN(15)/2 (9 October 2015), para. 251; Montenegro, WT/ACC/CGR/38, WT/MIN(11)/7 (5 December 2011), para. 177; Russia, WT/ACC/RUS/70, WT/MIN(11)/2 (17 November 2011), para. 1124; Samoa, WT/ACC/SAM/30, WT/MIN(11)/1 (1 November 2011), para. 167; Seychelles, WT/ACC/SYC/64 (5 November 2014), para. 314; Tajikistan, WT/ACC/TJK/30 (6 November 2012), para. 239; Vanuatu, WT/ACC/VUT/17 (11 May 2011), para. 104; Yemen, WT/ACC/YEM/42 (4 October 2013), para. 188.
31. Working Party Report on WTO Accession: China, WT/ACC/CHN/49 (1 October 2001), para. 225.
32. Shadikhodjaev, *supra*, footnote 10, at 200.

The fourth category confined to China consists in ensuring transparency of SEZs. Specifically, the Chinese government is committed to:

- maintaining, improving and regularly notifying statistics on trade between its SEZs and the rest of its territory;[33]
- providing information in notifications as to how the applied special trade, tariff and tax regulations are limited to the designated SEZs, including information concerning their enforcement.[34]

With respect to the timing of application, the SEZ commitments of virtually all acceders were effective as of the date of the WTO entry. On the other hand, Cape Verde managed to secure a nearly one and a half year grace period after its accession.[35] Russia's commitments were 'subject to the exceptions applied for the transition periods ... in respect of the goods of certain juridical persons and individual entrepreneurs of the Kaliningrad and Magadan SEZs'.[36] Kazakhstan also secured an SEZ-related transition period.[37]

Finally, member-specific commitments on SEZs can be found in national schedules on market openings as well. Unless there is an explicit reference to SEZs, all scheduled concessions and commitments apply to the committing member as a whole, including its SEZs. As Table 11.1 shows, Egypt and Jamaica – the original members of the WTO – have SEZ-specific entries in their schedules under the General Agreement on Trade in Services (GATS) that affect foreign firms and investors supplying listed services in their free zones. In addition, WTO-bound trade liberalization by individual members may be furthered within regional trade areas. For example, the Australia-China Free Trade Agreement (FTA) envisages improved GATS-plus market access for certain Australian service companies in the Shanghai FTZ.[38]

33. Working Party Report on WTO Accession: China, WT/ACC/CHN/49 (1 October 2001), para. 225.
34. *Ibid.*, para. 227.
35. Cape Verde (or Cabo Verde) has been a WTO member since 23 July 2008, but its commitment to enforce its WTO obligations in its free trade zones was effective as from 1 January 2010. *See* WTO, *Cabo Verde and the WTO*, https://www.wto.org/english/thewto_e/countries_e/cape_verde_e.htm (accessed 1 October 2018); Working Party Report on WTO Accession: Cape Verde, WT/ACC/CPV/30 (6 December 2007), para. 187.
36. Working Party Report on WTO Accession: Russia, WT/ACC/RUS/70, WT/MIN(11)/2 (17 November 2011), para. 1124.
37. Working Party Report on WTO Accession: Kazakhstan, WT/ACC/KAZ/93 (23 June 2015), paras 933–934.
38. WTO, Committee on Regional Trade Agreements – Factual Presentation – Free Trade Agreement between Australia and China (Goods and Services) – Report by the Secretariat – Revision, WT/REG369/1/Rev.1 (14 November 2016), 31, 32 (paras 4.48, 4.59).

Table 11.1 Services Commitments on SEZs

Modes of supply: (1) Cross-border supply (2) Consumption abroad (3) Commercial presence (4) Presence of natural persons

Country	*Sector or Subsector*	*Limitations on Market Access*	*Limitations on National Treatment*	*WTO Sources*
Egypt	HORIZONTAL COMMITMENTS		- Acquisition of land and/or real estate property in free zone areas is unbound.	GATS/SC/30 (15 April 1994)
	INSURANCE & INSURANCE RELATED SERVICES Life, health, personal accident	(3) Foreign and joint venture companies are allowed only to carry on business in free zones, provided that their activities shall be confined to the transactions carried out in convertible currencics. - No maximum limits required on the foreign shareholding in free zones.		GATS/SC/30/Suppl.2 (26 February 1998)

Country	*Sector or Subsector*	*Limitations on Market Access*	*Limitations on National Treatment*	*WTO Sources*
Jamaica	2. COMMUNICATION SERVICES C. Telecommunication Services International voice, data and video transmission services supplied to firms involved in information processing located within free zones	(1) None (2) None (3) Until Sept. 2013, interconnection with the local public switched network not permitted-.Service to unauthorized parties not permitted (4) Unbound except as indicated in the horizontal commitments	(1) None (2) None (3) None (4) Unbound except as indicated in the horizontal commitments	GATS/SC/45/Suppl.1 (11 April 1997)

Source: WTO documents as shown in the table.

§11.03 SEZs IN THE WTO TRANSPARENCY PROCESS

This section focuses on two areas in the WTO transparency process applicable to all members – notifications and trade policy reviews (TPRs) – involving SEZ issues. The Decision on Notification Procedures (1994) adopted during the Uruguay Round of multilateral trade negotiations contains an indicative list of notifiable measures, such as, *inter alia,* 'free-trade zones, including in-bond manufacturing'. According to footnote 1 of the Decision, this list 'does not alter existing notification requirements in the Multilateral Trade Agreements or ... the Plurilateral Trade Agreements' of the WTO. Accordingly, it does not substitute for the WTO requirement under Article 25 of the SCM Agreement to notify SEZ incentives that are considered as a specific subsidy. Subsidy notifications must be submitted by subsidizing members on a regular basis, or else other members may counter-notify instead. The process of notifying to the WTO requires sufficient skills of collecting, analysing and compiling related data – something that not all governments possess. In this regard, citing its 'limited capacity',

Myanmar even requested technical assistance from the WTO for the purpose of notifying its SEZ measures.[39]

Notifiability of an SEZ subsidy hinges upon whether there *is* a subsidy, and if so whether it is *specific* to a particular enterprise, industry or geographical area (region). Subsidies contingent upon the use of local content or export performance are deemed to be specific. As for the practice, responding to a question about the possibility to notify a subsidy, the United Arab Emirates merely said that incentives in its free zones were 'mainly related to tax regime and exemption from customs duties', and that 'there [were] no really any subsidies or countervailing offerings in the free zones'.[40] Members like Turkey, Korea and Panama refused to notify certain SEZ subsidies on the grounds of non-specificity, as these measures, they said, were not linked to exportation, import substitution or any particular industries.[41] It should, however, be stressed that many subsidies confined to SEZs as delimited territories would most likely be deemed regionally specific. In some countries (e.g., the United States (US) and the Dominican Republic) where free zone treatment is granted to companies rather than territorial sites as such,[42] the regional specificity test may indeed not work, but enterprise- or industry-specificity could still be pertinent.

As of 1 October 2018, the WTO database contained 165 SEZ-related notifications made under the SCM Agreement.[43] Such notifications typically specify an SEZ subsidy programme's title, purposes, form, contents, beneficiaries, duration and, etc. The notified information can later be reviewed in the SCM Committee – the WTO body which examines subsidy notifications as per Article 26 of the SCM Agreement. For instance, a US counter-notification of Chinese subsidies included a number of support programmes in China's SEZs, but in the SCM Committee's meeting China questioned the accuracy of the counter-notified contents pointing to the redundancy of certain items in the notification list and the absence of some listed SEZ subsidies.[44]

In addition to the SCM Committee's deliberations, SEZs are frequently discussed under the Trade Policy Review Mechanism (TPRM). Trade Policy Review (TPR)

39. WTO, TPR Body – 11 and 13 March 2014 – TPR – Myanmar – Minutes of the Meeting – Addendum, WT/TPR/M/293/Add.1 (11 June 2014), 28.
40. WTO, TPR Body – 1 and 3 June 2016 – TPR – United Arab Emirates – Minutes of the Meeting – Addendum, WT/TPR/M/338/Add.1 (5 August 2016), 95.
41. WTO, Committee on Subsidies and Countervailing Measures – Minutes of the Special Meeting – Held on 28 October 2010, G/SCM/M/74 (3 February 2011), paras 26–27; WTO, TPR Body – TPR – Report by the Secretariat – Republic of Korea – Revision, WT/TPR/S/204/Rev.1 (4 December 2008), 41, para. 22; WTO, Committee on SCM – Subsidies – Replies to Questions Posed by the EC Regarding the New and Full Notification of Panama – Revision, G/SCM/Q2/PAN/6/Rev.1 (13 April 1999), 2.
42. Raúl A. Torres, *Free Zones and the World Trade Organization Agreement on Subsidies and Countervailing Measures*, 5 Global Trade and Customs Journal 217 (2007), 218.
43. This number includes repetitive notifications – those that concern the same member's SEZs notified more than once over time. Search for document code: G/SCM/N/*; full text search criteria: 'free zone' at WTO, https://docs.wto.org/dol2fe/Pages/FE_Search/FE_S_S001.aspx (accessed 1 October 2018).
44. *See*, e.g., WTO, Committee on Subsidies and Countervailing Measures – Minutes of the Regular Meeting Held on 28 October 2014, G/SCM/M/91 (4 March 2015), sections 6–7; WTO, Committee on Subsidies and Countervailing Measures – Minutes of the Regular Meeting Held on 29 April 2014, G/SCM/M/89 (17 July 2014), section 10.

reports prepared by the WTO Secretariat and the reporting government often contain detailed information about a reporting member's SEZs. As a transparency tool, the TPRM does not serve as a basis for dispute settlement proceedings, nor does it impose new policy commitments on the member under review.[45] For this reason, the panels in *Canada – Aircraft* and *Chile – Price Band System* rejected the complainant's assertions that were based on the TPR reports on the respondent's trade policy.[46]

With respect to SEZs, many questions and comments in the TPRM have been posed for the purpose of clarification. Members have normally asked about, e.g., SEZ incentives, companies' eligibility terms or differences between various SEZ types or SEZs and other similar schemes in a reporting member.[47] While the TPRM typically scrutinizes a reporting member's own SEZs, during a 2017 review regarding Japan, Australia specifically inquired about Japan's actions of developing SEZs abroad. In the context of Japan's investment policy, Australia was curious about one SEZ in Myanmar which, Australia said, was owned 49% by the Japan International Cooperation Agency and Mitsubishi Corporation and housed approximately thirty-three Japanese companies. Japan replied that SEZs were a 'comprehensive development project' contributing to 'the improvement of living standards, job creation, and economic growth of partner countries'.[48]

A smaller number of enquiries under the TPRM have concerned the WTO-compliance of SEZs. Since this is a transparency process not judging the legality of the reviewed measures, it is not surprising that reporting members' answers have tended to be short and not always convincing enough. For example, to the question as to whether India could confirm if an SEZ scheme was consistent with WTO rules, India simply said that it was, without providing further explanation.[49] On another occasion, the European Union (EU) asked how Indonesia was going to ensure full compliance with WTO agreements with respect to tax exemptions in export-oriented production entrepôts. Since such zones were open to companies capable of exporting at least 75% of their production, the EU opined that the tax exemptions were an illegal export subsidy. But Indonesia denied, rather ambiguously, any violation of WTO rules on exports, because zone-products sold to the domestic market were subject to duties and the value-added tax just like any other imported like product, so there was no

45. Section A of Annex 3 ('Trade Policy Review Mechanism') to the WTO Agreement.
46. WTO Panel Report, *Canada – Measures Affecting the Export of Civilian Aircraft*, WT/DS70/R, adopted 20 August 1999, paras 8.14, 9.274; WTO Panel Report, *Chile – Price Band System and Safeguard Measures Relating to Certain Agricultural Products*, WT/DS207/R, adopted 23 October 2002, n 664 to para. 7.95.
47. *See*, e.g., WT/TPR/M/293/Add.1, *supra*, footnote 39, at 28, 46; WTO, TPR Body – 10 and 12 April 2013 – TPR – Indonesia – Minutes of Meeting – Addendum, WT/TPR/M/278/Add.1 (2 August 2013), 38, 82; WTO, TPR Body – 31 May and 2 June 2010 – TPR – China – Minutes of Meeting – Addendum, WT/TPR/M/230/Add.1 (22 February 2011), 28, 169; WT/TPR/M/338/Add.1, *supra*, footnote 40, at 6, 9, 69; WTO, TPR Body – 5 and 7 July 2017 – TPR – European Union – Minutes of the Meeting – Addendum, WT/TPR/M/357/Add.1 (6 November 2017), 18, 56, 397; WTO, TPR Body – 24 and 26 September 2014 – TPR – Mongolia – Minutes of the Meeting – Addendum, WT/TPR/M/297/Add.1 (13 January 2015), 18, 33.
48. WTO, TPR Body – 8 and 10 March 2017 – TPR – Japan – Minutes of the Meeting – Addendum, WT/TPR/M/351/Add.1 (27 April 2017), 19.
49. WT/TPR/M/313/Add.1, *supra*, footnote 4, at 42.

discrimination.[50] Further, to several questions on the consistency of local content measures in SEZs with the SCM Agreement, Malaysia replied that, from 1 January 2011, goods produced in its SEZ and sold to the domestic market could 'enjoy ASEAN or ATIGA duty rates if they complied with the origin criteria, i.e., local content or substantial transformation'.[51]

By contrast, the chairperson of a recent TPR meeting on the Jamaican policy noted that Jamaica 'was particularly praised for having adopted a new Special Economic Zones Act that meets its obligations under the WTO's Agreement on Subsidies and Countervailing Measures, as well as for its Omnibus Incentives Legislation 2014 which repealed the four incentive schemes that had been notified to the WTO as containing export subsidies'.[52]

The TPRM and other bodies with the monitoring functions lack an enforcement power and as such do not serve to secure the WTO-consistency of the reviewed measures, including SEZs. But these channels of member-to-member interactions contribute to greater transparency, better understanding and may thereby prevent trade disputes.

§11.04 SEZs IN WTO DISPUTE SETTLEMENT

In this section, we consider several WTO cases on governmental measures connected with SEZs. Among them, all adjudicated cases (*Brazil – Taxation, Colombia – Textiles, US – Carbon Steel (India)* and *Colombia – Ports of Entry*) do not have any parallel proceedings under the international investment regime, as there is no legal basis for investment dispute settlement between the parties concerned.[53] The following analysis is divided into three subsections based on the nature of the measure at issue.

[A] SEZ-Related Incentives

In *India – Export Related Measures*, the US, on 14 March 2018, requested consultations with India concerning certain export subsidies allegedly granted through five different schemes, including, *inter alia*, 'Electronics Hardware Technology Parks Scheme' and 'Special Economic Zones'. India is one of the WTO members listed in Annex VII of the SCM Agreement that exempts the covered members from the WTO prohibition on export subsidies. But the US submits that India has already graduated from Annex VII,

50. WT/TPR/M/278/Add.1, *supra*, footnote 47, at 81.
51. WTO, TPR Body – 3 and 5 March 2014 – TPR – Malaysia – Minutes of the Meeting – Addendum, WT/TPR/M/292/Add.1 (30 April 2014), 8–9, 164, 172, 178, 188.
52. WTO, TPR Body – 13 and 15 September 2017 – TPR – Jamaica – Minutes of the Meeting, WT/TPR/M/359 (31 October 2017), para. 6.5.
53. The covered measures are not necessarily justiciable under the investment legal system. Moreover, there is no operational legal instrument. Specifically, the Colombia–Panama FTA having provisions on investment dispute settlement was signed in 2013, but not put into force yet. Brazil's investment treaties with some EU members have not entered into force; the cooperation agreements between Brazil/MERCOSUR and the EU do not provide for investment dispute settlement. There is no investment agreement between the US and India. *See* UNCTAD's database, http://investmentpolicyhub.unctad.org/IIA (accessed 1 October 2018).

as it surpassed the eligibility thresholds set out in the SCM Agreement, such as gross national product per capita of USD 1,000 per annum and the economic benchmark of export competitiveness.[54] The US adds that despite the expiry of India's exemption, the Indian government has expanded subsidy programmes and increased exports tremendously:[55]

> In fact, India has increased the size and scope of these programs. For example, India introduced the Merchandise Exports from India Scheme in 2015, which has rapidly expanded to include more than 8,000 eligible products, nearly double the number of products covered at its inception.
>
> Exports from Special Economic Zones increased over 6,000 percent from 2000 to 2017, and in 2016, exports from Special Economic Zones accounted for over $82 billion in exports, or 30 percent of India's export volume. Exports from the Export Oriented Units Scheme and sector specific schemes, including Electronics Hardware Technology Parks Scheme, increased by over 160 percent from 2000 to 2016.

In two disputes against China, complainants challenged certain zone-related government preferences. Specifically, in *China – Measures Relating to the Production and Exportation of Apparel and Textile Products*, Mexico, on 15 October 2012, requested consultations regarding Chinese subsidies for producers and exporters of apparel and textile products, including tax incentives, preferential prices for land use rights, electricity price discounts for qualifying enterprises located in 'special economic zones' or 'economic development zones'.[56] But this dispute did not move to a panel proceeding. In *China – Demonstration Bases*, the US complained about China's export subsidies provided under the programme for 'Foreign Trade Transformation and Upgrading Demonstration Bases' and 'Common Service Platforms'. The US claimed that the Chinese government designated a cluster of enterprises in a particular industry (textiles, agriculture, light industry, medical products, chemical engineering, and, etc.) as a 'demonstration base' and offered export-contingent subsidies in the form of cash grants and price-discounted or free services by 'common service platforms'. Although this complaint does not seem to have targeted a Chinese SEZ as such, it questioned measures in an SEZ-like zone.[57] A panel was established, but on 14 April 2016, China and the US informed the WTO that they had reached an agreement under which China clarified, repealed and modified pertinent measures mentioned in the consultation request.[58]

---

54. WTO, *India – Export Related Measures* – Request for Consultations by the US, WT/DS541/1, G/SCM/D119/1 (19 March 2018); USTR, *United States Launches WTO Challenge to Indian Export Subsidy Programs* (2018), https://ustr.gov/about-us/policy-offices/press-office/press-releases/2018/march/united-states-launches-wto-challenge (accessed 1 October 2018).
55. USTR, *supra*, footnote 54.
56. WTO, *China – Measures Relating to the Production and Exportation of Apparel and Textile Products* – Request for Consultations by Mexico, WT/DS451/1, G/L/1004, G/SCM/D94/1, G/AG/GEN/103 (18 October 2012).
57. WTO, *China – Measures Related to Demonstration Bases and Common Service Platforms Programmes* – Request for Consultations by the US, WT/DS489/1, G/L/1105, G/SCM/D105/1 (19 February 2015).
58. WTO, *DS489: China – Measures Related to Demonstration Bases and Common Service Platforms Programmes*, https://www.wto.org/english/tratop_e/dispu_e/cases_e/ds489_e.htm (accessed

Two other disputes involving public favours associated with SEZs have been adjudicated as follows. First, in *Brazil – Taxation*, the EU took issue with, *inter alia*, the mandatory minimum level of R&D investments under the so-called 'Informatics programme' – a tax incentive scheme for the IT industry. Eligible companies had to invest in R&D the amount of a certain percentage of their domestic sales. But the government allowed them to deduct, from such sales, the value of their purchases of certain domestic products, including those made in Brazil's Manaus FTZ. This incentivized companies covered by the Informatics programme to increase those purchases in order to make lesser R&D investments. The panel concluded that the Informatics programme was inconsistent with Article III:4 of the GATT for promoting purchases of local products to the detriment of the imported like products.[59] The panel's ruling is currently under appeal.

Second, the panel in *Colombia – Textiles* found that the compound tariff on textiles, apparel and footwear exceeding the binding level violated Article II of the GATT. In defence, Colombia invoked Articles XX(a) and XX(d) of the GATT to assert that the compound tariff was directed against money laundering allegedly happening via importation at 'artificially low prices'. However, the panel was not persuaded that, in the context of those provisions, this measure was 'necessary' to protect public morals and to secure compliance with its criminal law.[60] Further, under the *chapeau* of Article XX, the panel's attention focused on the fact that goods imported to and remaining in Colombia's Special Customs Regime Zones were exempt from the compound tariff. Colombia justified the exemption by explaining that these were 'border zones with very low levels of development, or in a situation of isolation or economic integration with another state, which need to be managed differently from the rest of the national customs territory'.[61] But the panel concluded that such an inconsistent application of the compound tariff over Colombia's territory constituted 'a means of arbitrary or unjustifiable discrimination' and 'a disguised restriction on international trade' contrary to the *chapeau* requirements:[62]

> The ... exclusion [of the Special Customs Regime Zones] establishes a difference in treatment between products entering the Special Customs Regime Zones and products entering the rest of the Colombian customs territory. Therefore, there is discrimination in the application of the measure.

---

1 October 2018); WTO, *China – Measures Related to Demonstration Bases and Common Service Platforms Programmes* – Communication from China and the US, WT/DS489/7 (19 April 2016).

59. WTO Panel Reports, *Brazil – Certain Measures Concerning Taxation and Charges*, WT/DS472/R, circulated to WTO Members 30 August 2017 [appealed by Brazil 28 September 2017], paras 7.231–7.243.

60. WTO Panel Report, *Colombia – Measures Relating to the Importation of Textiles, Apparel and Footwear*, WT/DS461/R, adopted 22 June 2016, paras 7.189, 7.471, 7.536–537; WTO Appellate Body Report, *Colombia – Measures Relating to the Importation of Textiles, Apparel and Footwear*, WT/DS461/AB/R, adopted 22 June 2016, paras 5.117, 5.147–5.150.

61. WTO Panel Report, *Colombia – Measures Relating to the Importation of Textiles, Apparel and Footwear*, *supra*, footnote 60, para. 7.576.

62. *Ibid.*, paras 7.577–7.578 (footnotes omitted). *See also* WTO Appellate Body Report, *Colombia – Measures Relating to the Importation of Textiles, Apparel and Footwear*, *supra*, footnote 60, para. 5.153.

> Colombia tries to justify this discrimination by pointing out that imports into these zones are for local consumption, because they are border zones with a population living in conditions of extreme poverty, and that the goods would not be marketed in the rest of the national territory. However, Colombia has not shown that imports of textiles, apparel and footwear that enter these zones, and are consumed inside the zone, cannot be used for money laundering, nor that they pose a lower risk of being used for money laundering. Even if there is a different risk, Colombia has not explained what other measures it is taking in these zones to reduce the incentives for imports to be used for money laundering.

The panel's finding under the *chapeau* of Article XX – not reviewed by the Appellate Body for judicial economy reasons[63] – is remarkable for questioning the territorial limitation of a 'privilege' to an SEZ. Governments can avoid many possible challenges in the WTO if they at least ensure 'parallel' non-discrimination by according equal treatment to competitors in and out of the zone, with these inside and outside treatments not necessarily being the same. They can do so, *inter alia*, by providing all eligible companies with fair access to their zones and associated benefits and by revoking duty and tax incentives for the products that are removed from their zones for the home-market use.[64] But the *Colombia – Textiles* case seems to show some potential for contesting the non-extension of an in-zone benefit to the rest of the country, and hence 'zone v. non-zone' *discrimination* (as the panel said) within the same country. Yet, one should bear in mind that this issue arose in the context of a general exception of the GATT where the *chapeau* requires, in essence, a consistent application of a reasonable policy behind an illegal measure.

While we cannot, in principle, rule out a possibility of challenging an in-zone incentive for being 'discriminatory' on the grounds of its unavailability outside of the zone, any such challenge or a confirmative ruling under the WTO's general principles of most-favoured nation (MFN) or national treatment would arguably open up a Pandora's box. Indeed, this would deny the intrinsic attribute of any SEZ of being an 'extraterritorial' business site.

[B] Import Restrictions on SEZs

In *Colombia – Ports of Entry*, textiles, apparel and footwear from Panama and Panama's Colon Free Zone (CFZ) could be imported to Colombia only through two ports of entry despite the existence of a larger number of ports available to the same products coming from other countries. The panel found that such limited access to the Colombian ports amounted to a prohibited quantitative restriction on imports within the meaning of Article XI:1 of the GATT.[65] Under Article XX(d) of the GATT, Colombia however countered that its measure enabled a better control of goods' inflows and was hence

63. WTO Appellate Body Report, *Colombia – Measures Relating to the Importation of Textiles, Apparel and Footwear*, *supra*, footnote 60, para. 5.153.
64. *See* Shadikhodjaev, *supra*, footnote 10, at 198–202, as further developed in Shadikhodjaev, *supra*, footnote 2, at 128–132.
65. WTO Panel Report, *Colombia – Indicative Prices and Restrictions on Ports of Entry*, WT/DS366/R, adopted 20 May 2009, paras 7.209–7.275.

necessary to counteract illicit activities like under-invoicing, customs fraud, smuggling, money laundering and drug trafficking.[66] In this context, Colombia submitted that while the CFZ was 'an originating or transshipment point for some goods purchased with narcotics proceeds', the CFZ itself had 'limited resources to conduct supervisory programs and monitor for illegal activities'.[67] The panel acknowledged the importance to Colombia of the battle against CFZ-related wrongdoings.[68] But it eventually held that Colombia did not establish that the measure at issue was indeed 'necessary' to ensure compliance with national customs laws and regulations in the sense of Article XX(d), as Colombia could not elucidate how the ports-of-entry restriction at issue contributed to its goals without causing a significant negative impact on legitimate trade.[69] The panel's decision was not appealed.

As we observed elsewhere,[70] the *Colombia – Ports of Entry* case has certain implications on both sides of trade involving SEZs. For importing WTO members, it shows that restrictions imposed on even *SEZ* goods of other members are subject to WTO rules. In this connection, a government's decision (not) to restrict related imports may be influenced by the size of a foreign zone and trade involved, among other things. As the largest SEZ in the Americas and the second largest in the world,[71] the CFZ may indeed have threatened producers in Colombia, which is the biggest export destination of CFZ goods.[72] In addition, over 80% of Panamanian imports to Colombia arrived from the CFZ,[73] which explains why CFZ goods were of particular concern to Colombia. Although illicit activities associated with the CFZ may have occurred in relation to a wider range of products, Colombia targeted textiles, apparel and footwear products, i.e., the sector that constitutes an 'important national industry in Colombia'.[74]

As for members exporting from SEZs, the panel's findings above indicate that WTO benefits are available to their SEZs, regardless of the legal status of the zones under national legislation. The fact that the CFZ is not part of Panama's customs territory[75] did not prevent the panel from ruling against Colombia's restrictions on the CFZ exports.[76] It follows that unless SEZs are explicitly excluded from the WTO's regulatory domain (e.g., through accession instruments), SEZ exports will enjoy MFN-based market access abroad as guaranteed by WTO law.

66. *Ibid.*, paras 7.483–7.492.
67. *Ibid.*, n 892 to para. 7.554.
68. *Ibid.*, para. 7.612.
69. *Ibid.*, paras 7.482–7.620.
70. *See* Shadikhodjaev, *supra*, footnote 10, at 210–211.
71. WTO Panel Report, *Colombia – Indicative Prices and Restrictions on Ports of Entry*, *supra*, footnote 65, n 892 to para. 7.554; Wikipedia, *Colón Free Trade Zone*, http://en.wikipedia.org/wiki/Col%C3%B3n_Free_Trade_Zone (accessed 1 October 2018).
72. Wikipedia, *supra*, footnote 71.
73. WTO Panel Report, *Colombia – Indicative Prices and Restrictions on Ports of Entry*, *supra*, footnote 65, n 978 to para. 7.592.
74. *Ibid.*, para. 2.14.
75. WT/TPR/S/186/Rev.1, *supra*, footnote 9, at 27.
76. While 'extraterritoriality' of the CFZ was not the issue before the panel, we doubt that even if Colombia had raised this issue, the panel would have ruled otherwise.

[C] Countervailing Measures Involving SEZs

If SEZ incentives qualify as a specific subsidy, countries that import goods produced with the use of those incentives may impose countervailing duties subject to the SCM Agreement. But SEZ-hosting governments may then challenge these measures in the WTO dispute settlement proceedings. This is what happened in *US – Carbon Steel (India)*. There, India complained about countervailing duty determinations of the US Department of Commerce (DOC) concerning the following sub-programmes of India's SEZ Act:

> (i) duty free import/domestic procurement of goods and services for development, operation, and maintenance of SEZ Units Programme; (ii) exemption from excise duties on goods machinery and capital goods brought from the domestic tariff area for use by an enterprise in the SEZ; (iii) drawback on goods brought or services provided from the domestic tariff area into an SEZ, or services provided in an SEZ by services providers located outside India; (iv) 100 per cent exemption from income taxes on export income from the first 5 years of operation, 50 per cent for the next 5 years, and a further 50 per cent exemption on export income reinvested in India for an additional 5 years; (v) exemption from the central sales tax (CST); and (vi) exemption from the national service tax.[77]

At issue was an alleged inconsistency of the DOC's investigation with Article 12.7 of the SCM Agreement which allows an investigating authority to make determinations on the basis of 'the facts available' when a target member or party is not cooperative in providing necessary information. In an administrative review involving India's company Tata, the DOC found that Tata was subsidized through the sub-programmes above. For this, it relied on the facts available on the grounds that Tata did not cooperate, and that the Indian government's submission to the investigation did not provide supporting documentation showing that Tata did not benefit from those schemes. But a WTO panel's decision, in the part not reviewed by the Appellate Body, sided with India and concluded that, contrary to Article 12.7, the US had failed to identify any evidence on the record that would constitute a 'factual foundation' for the DOC's determination against Tata.[78]

§11.05 CONCLUSION

This analysis confirms full applicability of WTO law to SEZs despite their 'extraterritorial' features. Although SEZ-linked obligations were explicitly mentioned in accession documents of individual members rather than the text of the multilateral trade agreements, most of these obligations are arguably generic in nature and hence extendable to the rest of members in principle. For some time in the past, SEZs were largely outside of the WTO dispute settlement process, but recent noticeable movements on this front reveal vulnerability of SEZs to WTO challenges.

---

77. WTO Panel Report, *United States – Countervailing Measures on Certain Hot-Rolled Carbon Steel Flat Products from India*, WT/DS436/R, adopted 19 December 2014, n 803 to para. 7.474.
78. *Ibid.*, paras 7.474–7.475.

The issues raised in different WTO settings in relation to the SEZ policy of a host country have concerned predominantly incentives granted to SEZ enterprises. While many SEZ incentives may well cause trade-distorting effects and fall within the WTO definition of a specific or countervailable subsidy, the host government must, as a minimum, provide those incentives in a transparent and non-discriminatory way without conditioning them to localization, exportation or other overly burdensome requirements. Such a pre-emptive action will not necessarily ensure complete WTO-consistency, but it will at least reduce the probability of future frictions.

CHAPTER 12

China's Free Trade Zones in Its Post-WTO Accession ERA: A Case Study of Shanghai FTZ

Ting Han & Andrew D. Mitchell

§12.01 INTRODUCTION

The establishment of the China (Shanghai) Pilot Free Trade Zone (Shanghai FTZ) in 2013 marked a significant milestone for the country's economic reforms. Since the end of the 1970s China had established a number of Special Economic Zones (SEZs) to liberalize trade, encourage exports and attract foreign capital. The Shanghai FTZ signaled the beginning of the second stage in the use of zones with a much higher level of ambition for liberalization and a focus on rule innovation.[1] It also imposed unique challenges for the governance of the new FTZs in China. In this paper, with its focus on China, the term 'FTZ' is used to correspond precisely with the Chinese term 'Ziyou Maoyi Qu'[2] and differentiate this new class of zones from the SEZs established in China from the late 1970s.

Much has been written about China's SEZs, providing valuable insights about their history, operation and success, but the overwhelming majority of the literature deals with SEZs in the pre-WTO era[3] with only a few studies of China's SEZs after 2001

1. Yi Zhang, Tao Yue, Shaofei Wang and Bas Koene, *Excitement and Confusion: Shanghai (Pilot) Free Trade Zone* (RSM Case Development Centre 2017).
2. 'Ziyou Maoyi Qu' (Simplified Chinese: 自由贸易区) is the exact term used for 'Free Trade Zone' in Chinese, specifically referring to the areas approved by the State Council following the establishment of Shanghai FTZ in 2013.
3. Jao and Leung (1986), Oborne (1986), Falkenheim (1990), Jia (1994), Hannan (1995) and Cartier (2001) talk about the initial achievements of China's SEZs and their role in China's reform and opening up; Jung-Dong Park (1997) argues that the central government gave autonomy to the management council of each SEZ concerning economic affairs to allow the use of foreign capital

and their WTO consistency.[4] As for literature on China's FTZs, most focused on the background of their establishment and initial economic impact,[5] but rarely touched upon the new role of the FTZs in China's post-WTO context with a careful examination of their WTO compatibility.

This chapter undertakes a novel analysis of the WTO compatibility of China's Free Trade Zones (FTZs). In Part II, the paper briefly introduces the history of China's economic reform since the 1970s, the process of establishing FTZs and the main incentive policies adopted by the Shanghai FTZ. Part III makes a comprehensive analysis of the compatibility of the Shanghai FTZ under the Agreement on Subsidies and Countervailing Measures (SCM Agreement), Agreement on Trade-Related Investment Measures (TRIMs), General Agreement on Trade in Services (GATS), and WTO transparency obligations.

§12.02 CHINA'S FTZs

[A] China's SEZs

Beginning in the late 1970s, China initiated its far-reaching economic reform, best known for the policy of 'Reform and Opening-up'.[6] The establishment of SEZs in Shenzhen, Zhuhai and Shantou in Guangdong Province, Xiamen in Fujian Province in 1980 and the entire province of Hainan in 1988 marked a significant milestone for China's integration into the global economy. China used SEZs to pioneer new economic policies, provide modern infrastructure and attract investment for export-oriented industries.[7] The strong commitment to reform and pragmatism from top leadership, preferential policies and institutional autonomy encouraged significant Foreign Direct Investment (FDI) to these zones and expanded exports.[8]

---

and the adjustment of economic activities on the basis of market economy; Crane (1990), Litwack and Qian (1998) discuss more about the problems the SEZs faced and how they were not fulfilling their objectives; Roger C.K. Chan (1998) examines the establishment of the SEZs and their economic and spatial development against the objectives underlying the SEZ policy.

4. Ota (2003) and Zheng (2007, 2006a, 2006b) focus their work on the economic success of the SEZs; Lau (2001) and Brahm (2002) argue that the SEZs are losing their 'special' status since the central government has stopped giving them all the preferential policies that they enjoyed prior to WTO accession; the work of Creskoff and Walkenhorst (2009) provides an overview of the application of the WTO disciplines to incentive programmes, especially employed by developing countries.
5. Wan, Zhang, Wang and Chen (2014) presented a background of the Shanghai FTZ and some reflections on it; Yao and Whalley (2015) compared the differences between the Shanghai FTZ with other free trade areas, and evaluated the impact of the Shanghai FTZ.
6. 'Reform and Opening-up' (Simplified Chinese: 改革开放) refers to the programme of economic reforms termed 'Socialism with Chinese characteristics' in the People's Republic of China (PRC) that was started in December 1978 by reformists within the Communist Party of China, led by Deng Xiaoping.
7. Meng Guangwen, *The Theory and Practice of Free Economic Zones: A Case Study of Tianjin, People's Republic of China* (doctoral thesis, Ruprecht-Karls University of Heidelberg 2003); Edward Graham, *Do Export Processing Zones Attract FDI and Its Benefits? The Experience from China, International Economics and Economic Policy* (Springer-Verlag 2004).
8. Zeng Douglas Zhihua (ed.), *Building Engines for Growth and Competitiveness in China* 16–24 (The World Bank 2010).

China's economic reforms, characterized by gradualism and administrative decentralization, were extraordinarily successful in both political and economic terms.[9] From 1980 to 2017, China's GDP increased exponentially, from USD 191.15 billion to USD 12.24 trillion.[10] In 2010, China overtook Japan to became the world's second-largest economy.[11] As of 2017, according to the latest World Bank figures, China remained in the second place, following the United States (US), with 15.2% of the world GDP.[12] China's SEZs not only served as the engine for China's economic growth, but were also designed as the 'testing ground' for China's economic transition from a planned economy to a market-orientated one. The basic elements of a market economy were successfully introduced and adopted by the SEZs and replicated by the rest of the country. China's economic reform and growth since 1978 culminated in its accession to the WTO in 2001.

[B] China's Obligations upon WTO Accession

On 11 December 2001, after over fifteen years' negotiations, China became a member in the WTO. Following its accession to the WTO, China's foreign trade and investment have grown tremendously. From 1995 to 2015, foreign trade increased nearly fourteen-fold, more than 90% of which took place after the accession.[13] In 2017, China remained the second largest recipient of FDI in the world following the US, attracting USD 136 million in FDI.[14]

In pursuit of WTO membership, China has made comprehensive commitments set out in its accession agreement.[15] These provisions basically fall into two categories: market access and rule-based issues.[16] The decision of the Chinese leaders to accept the many onerous obligations of its WTO membership was motivated primarily by their desire to introduce external pressure to overcome internal obstacles to the reform process.[17]

In Article 2 of the Protocol, China promised to apply the provision of the WTO Agreement and the Protocol to 'the entire customs territory of China, including border

9. Susan L. Shirk, *Internationalization and China's Economic Reforms*, in *Internationalization and Domestic Politics* 196–205 (R. Keohane & H. Milner eds, 3rd edn, Cambridge University Press 1999).
10. The Word Bank, *Data*, https://data.worldbank.org/country/china (accessed 3 November 2018).
11. International Monetary Fund, *World Economic Outlook Database*, https://www.imf.org/external/pubs/ft/weo/2017/01/weodata/index.aspx (accessed 2 February 2018).
12. The World Bank, *Data*, https://data.worldbank.org/country/china (accessed 3 November 2018).
13. The total value of China's imports and exports was 280.9 billion USD in 1995, 509.7 billion USD in 2001, and USD 3,970 billion USD in 2017. Source: China National Bureau of Statistics.
14. United Nations Conference on Trade and Development, *World Investment Report 2018* 21.
15. The World Trade Organization, *Protocol on the Accession of the People's Republic of China (WT/L/432)*, which incorporates by reference selected paragraphs of *Report of the Working Party on the Accession of China (WT/MIN(01)/3)*. The texts of the Protocol and WPR are available at www.wto.org.
16. Nicholas R. Lardy, *Integrating China into Global Economy* 63–105 (Brookings Institution Press 2002).
17. *Ibid.*

trade regions and minority autonomous areas, SEZs, open coastal cities, economic and technical development zones and other areas where special regimes for tariffs, taxes and regulations are established (collectively referred to as 'special economic areas')'.[18] According to Article 2(B), China may sustain some preferential arrangements for its SEZs, but promised to comply with the transparency requirement prescribed in GATT Article 10.[19] Thus, in providing preferential arrangements for enterprises within the FTZs referred in this paper, WTO provisions on non-discrimination and national treatment shall be fully observed, except as otherwise provided for in this Protocol.

[C] China's FTZs

On 29 September 2013, the Shanghai FTZ was officially launched, consisting of the Waigaoqiao FTZ, Waigaoqiao Free Trade Logistics Park, Yangshan Free Trade Port Area and the Pudong Airport FTZ, with a total area of 28.78 square kilometers. In announcing the Shanghai FTZ the Chinese Government stated that it was expected to further liberalize trade, expand the provision of services, and upgrade the management level of FDI.[20] It is the first FTZ in mainland China and considered a comprehensive update of the SEZs (hence the new terminology). Since 21 April 2015, the territory of the Shanghai FTZ has expanded to incorporate the Lujiazui Financial Area, Jinqiao Export Processing Zone and the Zhejiang High Tech Park.[21] The State Council of China has also approved the establishment of the China (Guangzhou) Pilot Free Trade Zone, China (Tianjin) Pilot Free Trade Zone and the China (Fujian) Pilot Free Trade Zone. On 31 March 2017, seven more FTZs were created: the China (Liaoning) Pilot Free Trade Zone, China (Zhejiang) Pilot Free Trade Zone, China (Henan) Pilot Free Trade Zone, China (Hubei) Pilot Free Trade Zone, China (Chongqing) Pilot Free Trade Zone, China (Sichuan) Pilot Free Trade Zone and the China (Shanxi) Pilot Free Trade Zone. On 16 October 2018, China's southern island province of Hainan became the latest FTZ. Currently, China has twelve FTZs.

The establishment of FTZs is one of the Chinese government's most important domestic economic policies since the creation of SEZs more than three decades ago. The internal and external pressure China is facing calls for a deeper reform of China's legal and regulatory regime and a substantial upgrade of China's economic growth model. At home, China is gradually losing its comparative advantage in labour-intensive industrial production due to soaring wages and an aging workforce.[22] The rapid economic growth powered by foreign trade and investment has occurred at the

---

18. The World Trade Organization, *Protocol on the Accession of the People's Republic of China (WT/L/432)*, Article 2 (A) 2.
19. Wenger Vieli Belser, *Special Economic Areas of China and WTO – Will the Privileges Survive?* (WTO Beijing Office 2003).
20. State Council, *Framework Plan for the China (Shanghai) Pilot Free Trade Zone* ('Framework Plan'), http://en.pkulaw.cn/display.aspx?id = 15040&lib = law&SearchKeyword = pilot + free + trade + zone&SearchCKeyword = mc%2FrPBmvuUE%3D (accessed 15 March 2019).
21. *Ibid.*
22. Wei Shen, *A Tale of Three Zones – Promises and Pitfalls of Three Financial Experimental Zones in China*, 131 BLJ 399 (2014).

cost of severe environmental degradation and widening wealth disparity.[23] Abroad, China is being marginalized in the new round of regional trade negotiations, including the Comprehensive and Progressive Agreement for Trans-Pacific Partnership (CPTPP) and Transatlantic Trade and Investment Partnership. FTZs have taken on the role of the new vehicle to deeply integrate the country in the globalization of trade as well as, more broadly, put China in alignment with international standards of trade liberalization.

[D] Key Policies in the China (Shanghai) Free Trade Zone

According to the *Framework Plan*,[24] the key policies in the Shanghai FTZ include tax incentives, adoption of the negative list approach (only identifies sectors and businesses that are off-limits or restricted for investment), and further liberalization in service sectors.[25] We examine these key policies in turn. China expects a fairer, freer and more flexible investment landscape from these policies, so as to 'form a framework of fundamental rules compatible with generally accepted international rules for investment and trade'.[26]

[1] Tax Incentives

Several tax incentives are being offered in the Shanghai FTZ to promote investment and trade development, primarily set out in three Circulars.[27] Two of the major preferential tax policies are known as 'the policy on non-monetary asset investment' and 'the policy on stock right incentives'.

'The policy on non-monetary asset investment' is applied when computing corporate income tax (CIT). Investors investing nonmonetary assets as capital into the companies in the FTZ may apply for the 'deferred tax payment policy'. It allows the investors to evenly allocate the valuation gain from the asset appreciation of their nonmonetary assets capital contribution in the FTZ companies within a five-year

23. Qin Julia Ya, *The Impact of WTO Accession on China's Legal System: Trade, Investment and Beyond*, Wayne State University Law School Legal Studies Research Paper No. 07-15 (2007).
24. *'Framework Plan': Framework Plan for the China (Shanghai) Pilot Free Trade Zone*, issued by State Council on 16 August 2013, http://www.shanghaifreetradezone.org/en/framework.htm.
25. Liu, G., *Shanghai Pilot Free Trade Zone: Shaping of China's Future Foreign Investment Environment*, 40 ITJ 31 (2014).
26. State Council, *Framework Plan for the China (Shanghai) Pilot Free Trade Zone* ('Framework Plan'), http://en.pkulaw.cn/display.aspx?id = 15040&lib = law&SearchKeyword = pilot + free + trade + zone&SearchCKeyword = mc%2FrPBmvuUE%3D (accessed 2 February 2018).
27. Three Circulars refers to: *Circular on Corporate Income Tax Policies Concerning Asset Restructuring Activities Using Non-monetary Assets for Investment Purposes by Enterprises in the FTZ* (Cai Guan Shui [2013] No.91) jointly issued by China's Ministry of Finance and the State Administration of Taxation on 15 November 2013; *Circular on Relevant Import Tax Policies for the China (Shanghai) Pilot FTZ* (Cai Guan Shui [2013] No.75) issued by Ministry of Finance, General Administration of Customs and State Administration of Taxation on 15 October 2013; *Circular on the Framework Plan for the China (Shanghai) Pilot FTZ* (Guo Fa [2013] No.38) issued by the State Council on 19 September 2013.

period.[28] This would be particularly beneficial for the small and medium-sized enterprises (SMEs) within the FTZ to encourage capital reinvestment into the business.

Similarly, 'the policy on stock right incentives' is a tax instalment plan relating to individual income tax. For high-demand talent and professionals, the individual income tax payable, arising from share-based payments or stock ownership incentives granted by FTZ-registered companies, can be paid in instalments over a five-year period, subject to assessment by the appropriate tax authorities.[29] It is part of the preferential policies in Shanghai FTZ to attract talent and maintain entrepreneurship.

[2] Negative List Approach

The Shanghai FTZ also introduces, for the first time in mainland China, a Negative List Approach to the management of foreign investment. It identifies sectors for which restrictions on foreign investment will be retained. The previous approach, adopted in China nationwide, was a positive list approach (*2011 Catalogue of Industries for Guiding Foreign Investment*), where the Chinese Government had to explicitly ('positively') list the sectors and subsectors for which they took commitments in opening up for foreign investors.[30] In October 2013, the issuance of the '2013 Negative List'[31] symbolized the first step towards establishing the negative list. The 2013 Negative List included 190 restrictions, covering nearly all the restrictions outlined in the *2011 Catalogue of Industries for Guiding Foreign Investment.*[32] However, since then, the length of the negative list has been shortened over time, down from 190 restrictions in 2013, to 139 in 2014, then to 122 in 2015, to 95 in 2017, and now to 45 in 2018, though foreign investors in China's FTZs may still be subject to a National Security Review when participating in sensitive industries.[33]

Following the adoption of Negative List approach within the FTZs, on 2 October 2015, the State Council issued an *Opinion* that calls for the design of two negative lists - one for market access, applying to both domestic and foreign companies, and another for foreign investment.[34] On 28 June 2017, the *2017 Catalogue of Industries for Guiding Foreign Investment* ('2017 Catalogue'), governing the procedures for setting up a

28. Gladie Lui, *Shanghai Pilot Free Trade Zone: Shaping of China's Future Foreign Investment Environment*, 40 ITJ 31 (2014).
29. *Ibid.*
30. European Commission, *Services and investment in EU trade deals Using 'positive' and 'negative' lists*, http://trade.ec.europa.eu/doclib/docs/2016/april/tradoc_154427 (accessed 3 November 2018).
31. '2013 Negative List': *Bulletin of the Shanghai Municipal People's Government and Departments of Municipal People's Government on the Special Administrative Measures (Negative List) on Foreign Investment Access to the China (Shanghai) Pilot FTZ.*
32. Matthew Margulies, *Changes to Shanghai FTZ Negative List Fall Short of Expectation* 1 (The US-China Business Council 2014).
33. Dezan Shira & Associates, *The New Free Trade Zones Explained, Part II: The Negative List, China Briefing*, http://www.china-briefing.com/news/2015/04/30/new-free-trade-zones-explained-part-ii-negative-list.html (accessed 2 February 2018).
34. The State Council, *Opinions of the State Council on Implementing a Market Access Negative List System*, http://english.gov.cn/policies/latest_releases/2015/11/12/content_281475233639218.htm (accessed 2 February 2018).

foreign investment enterprise (FIE) outside the FTZ, which used to adopt the positive list approach, was restructured to include the negative list for the first time. On 28 June 2018, the National Development and Reform Commission and the Ministry of Commerce (MOFCOM) jointly released the new national negative list, *Special Administrative Measures on Access to Foreign Investment 2018 (Negative List) (2018 Version)*, which partly replaced the 2017 Catalogue and reduced the number of restrictive measures from 63 to 48.

[3] Opening-Up Service Sectors

One of the main goals for FTZs is to further liberalize the service sectors to meet international standards, such as the level of liberalization in Hong Kong and Singapore. In the Attachment of the *Framework Plan*, *Measures of the Service Industry*,[35] six service sectors are the main focus of the Shanghai FTZ: financial services, shipping services, commerce and trade services, professional services, cultural services, and social services.

Among the six sectors, reforms in the financial sector of the FTZs are the most highly anticipated and are considered barometers of the speed and determination of China's planned reform efforts.[36] Beginning in early 1997, the People's Bank of China ('PBC'), the country's central bank, licensed eight foreign banks to conduct business in Renminbi ('RMB')[37] in the Pudong district of Shanghai. However, due to four important restrictions, while there were a large number of foreign banks operating in China in the 1990s, their ability to expand business in domestic currency was extremely limited. Foreign banks have remained marginal players in RMB lending in the huge domestic market.[38] The most problematic area involves the ability of foreign banks to participate in the RMB business in China, a market segment that foreign banks are most eager to pursue, particularly with regard to Chinese individuals.[39]

On 2 December 2013, the PBC issued the *Opinions*,[40] providing various preferential policies to the Shanghai FTZ in terms of cross-border RMB usage, overseas financing and foreign exchange administration.[41] For instance, a new type of bank account, the Free Trade Account (FT Account), has been introduced to the Shanghai FTZ, available to both individuals and entities regardless of whether they are residents

35. '*Measures of the Service Industry*' refers to *Measures for the Expansion of Opening-up of the Service Industry in the China (Shanghai) Pilot Free Trade Zone.*
36. Gladie Lui, *Shanghai Pilot Free Trade Zone: Shaping of China's Future Foreign Investment Environment*, 40 ITJ 31 (2014).
37. Renminbi is the official currency of the People's Republic of China. The basic unit of renminbi is yuan.
38. Nicholas R. Lardy, *Integrating China into Global Economy* 70 (Brookings Institution Press 2002).
39. United States Trade Representative, *2017 Report to Congress On China's WTO Compliance*, https://ustr.gov/sites/default/files/files/Press/Reports/China%202017%20WTO%20Report.pdf 20 (accessed 3 November 2018).
40. '*Opinions*' refers to *Opinions on Leveraging the Role of Finance in Supporting the Creation of the FTZ.*
41. Gladie Lui, *Shanghai Pilot Free Trade Zone: Shaping of China's Future Foreign Investment Environment*, 40 ITJ 31 (2014).

or non-residents.[42] Setting up an FT Account, as introduced by China's central bank, enables cross-border transactions conducted in the Shanghai FTZ to be separated from onshore transactions, and funds can move freely between entities in the Shanghai FTZ and those offshore.[43] Till now, around 70,000 FT Accounts have been opened in Shanghai FTZ, attracting over CNY 1,100 billion[44] in total. As promised by the Mayor of Shanghai, the application scope of the FT Account will be further expanded this year and multiple functions will be added to the account.[45]

Regarding inbound investment, financial institutions and companies in the Shanghai FTZ can trade directly on the Shanghai Stock Exchange, without pre-verification by the China Securities Regulatory Commission (CSRC) as a Qualified Foreign Investment Institution.[46] In addition, Shanghai International Energy Exchange (INE) was set up in Shanghai FTZ by Shanghai Futures Exchange in November 2013. Approved by the CSRC in December 2014, China just launched its first yuan-denominated crude oil futures contract on 26 March 2018. The INE now allows foreign investors to trade the new oil contract, a first for China's commodities markets, and is a move by the Chinese government to bring in more foreign investors to its commodities exchanges and expand the country's influence in the global commodities market.[47]

However, after the fifth anniversary of Shanghai FTZ, foreign investor's expectations for market liberalization of the financial sector have not been met. The Shanghai FTZ has not led to the expected increase of foreign investment in the financial sector either in or outside the FTZs. In 2016, 6,991 foreign enterprises in financial sector were established nationwide, taking up only 0.81% of the foreign enterprises in total, with around 235 billion USD contractual capital involved, taking up 5.86% of the total foreign capital.[48] The 2017 United States Trade Representative (USTR) Report to Congress on China's WTO Compliance corresponds to the statistics shown above, pointing out that the US has inappropriately low market share in financial service sectors in mainland China.[49] With authorities now grappling with capital outflows, they appear reluctant to push ahead with measures that would enable even greater outflows.[50]

42. *Ibid.*
43. HSBC, News Release (21 January 2015), https://www.about.hsbc.com.hk/-/media/hong-kong/en/news-and-media/n13dec31e.cn/-/media/china/en/news-and-media/news20150121-en.pdf%3Fla%3Den-gb + &cd = 1&hl = zh-CN&ct = clnk&gl = au (accessed 2 February 2018).
44. 'Yuan' is the base unit of present-day Chinese currency.
45. *The Enlargement of the Application of Free Trade Account in Shanghai Free Trade Zone*, southeast Express, http://sports.163.com/18/0301/05/DBPOCC4Q0005227R.html (accessed 1 March 2018).
46. *Ibid.*
47. Caiping Liu & Denise Jia, *China's First Crude Oil Futures Contract to Debut on March 26*, Caixin, https://www.caixinglobal.com/2018-02-10/chinas-first-crude-oil-futures-contract-to-debut-on-march-26-101209988.html (accessed 10 February 2018).
48. Ministry of Commerce, People's Republic of China ('MOFCOM'), *Statistics on FDI in China* 21.
49. United States Trade Representative, *2017 Report to Congress On China's WTO Compliance*, https://ustr.gov/sites/default/files/files/Press/Reports/China%202017%20WTO%20Report.pdf.
50. Gabriel Wildau, *Shanghai Free-Trade Zone Struggles for Relevance*, Financial Times (London, 27 September 2015), https://www.ft.com/content/8cec0faa-6364-11e5-9846-de406ccb37f2 (accessed 2 February 2018).

As for the cultural service sector, further liberalization is also faced with severe challenges. The 2017 Negative List tightens control over some news, media and culture-related industries as well as research institutions in the humanities and social sciences,[51] and only one prohibition (prohibition on foreign investment in internet cafes) was eliminated in 2018 Negative List. This demonstrates China's continued efforts to maintain political stability, especially following the call of the Communist Party of China (CPC) for 'cultural confidence' since the 18th National Congress of the CPC in 2012. The introduction of western culture accompanied by increasing international communications, and the popularity of it among Chinese young generations owing to the huge influence of entertainment businesses and booming development of social media, have raised severe concerns by China's top leadership. Some sensitive concepts, such as 'democracy', 'human rights' and 'freedom of speech', which have been frequently avoided or carefully interpreted in China, are much more acceptable by educated young people. Thus, the western 'cultural invasion' and China's long-term pursuit of a unified ideology accelerated China's control over information inflow and its promotion of Chinese traditional culture.

In addition, China operates the largest internet censorship regime in the world, blocking access to thousands of websites including Google, YouTube, Facebook, Twitter and Instagram. But millions of Chinese citizens circumvent China's censorship system, known as the Great Firewall, by using Virtual Private Networks (VPNs), to access censored material and services.[52] In January 2017, the Ministry of Industry and Information Technology of the PRC published a circular on 'Cleaning up and Regulating the Internet Access Service Market',[53] which put new restrictions on VPNs and leased lines. The government has ordered China's three main internet providers, China Mobile, China Unicom and China Telecom, all of which are state-owned, to completely block access to VPNs by February 2018. It is an escalated level of internet control and will inevitably affect the cross-border trade in services in particular. The effect of the measure in disrupting, deterring or prohibiting cross-border transfers of information remains unknown but has raised international concerns.[54] The same set of rules was applied in the FTZs without exceptions, which makes the commitments of liberalization in cultural and social services difficult to be fulfilled. In response, the US notified the WTO in February 2018 of Chinese internet rules that it believes may create significant new restrictions for cross-border service suppliers.[55]

---

51. Ralph Koppitz & Cara Meng, *Opening the Market? China's 2017 Negative List for Foreign Investment* (TaylorWessing 30 June 2017), https://china.taylorwessing.com/en/from-july-28-2017-opening-the-market-china-s-2017-negative-list-for-foreign-investment (accessed on 2 February 2018).
52. Benjamin Haas, *China Moves to Block Internet VPNs from 2018*, The Guardian (London, 11 July 2017), https://www.theguardian.com/world/2017/jul/11/china-moves-to-block-internet-vpns-from-2018 (accessed 2 February 2018).
53. The Chinese version of the circular can be accessed through http://www.miit.gov.cn/n1146290/n4388791/c5471946/content.html.
54. Tom Miles, *United States Tells WTO of Concerns over China's New Web Access Rules*, Reuters (Paris, 23 February 2018), https://www.reuters.com/article/us-usa-china-cyber-trade/united-states-tells-wto-of-concerns-over-chinas-new-web-access-rules-idUSKCN1G7179 (accessed 23 February 2018).
55. *Ibid.*

Furthermore, a broader definition of 'national security' adopted during the foreign investment review and the enactment of *Cybersecurity Law*[56] *and National Security Law*[57] with several limitations taken for security concerns, represents a challenge for the opening-up process for almost all service sectors in China.

[4] Other Measures

Apart from the policies mentioned above, the Shanghai FTZ has come up with many other measures to liberalize and facilitate foreign investment into China. For example, provided the FIE business scope does not fall into the categories in the 'negative list', the foreign investors proceed through a simplified and efficient business registration process by a so-called 'recordation'. Recordation is not a pre-condition for issuance of a business license by the Administration for Industry and Commerce (AIC, equivalent of corporate registrar in China) in the FTZ and may occur before or after issuance of the business license of the FIE, in contrast to the traditional pre-approval system, in which FIE projects are subject to a substantial review process.[58] Specially, the Shanghai FTZ has established a unique one-stop application processing platform handled by the AIC to reduce the time taken to establish a company in the FTZ. All filing procedures are conducted via inter-departmental circulation, following which the required licenses and certificate (including the business license, enterprise code certificate and tax registration certificate) are issued together by the AIC.[59]

Furthermore, with the exception of specific sectors such as banking and insurance, there is no minimum capital requirement for registration in the FTZ, which encourages FDI.[60]

[E] Achievements

According to the statistics from the MOFCOM, around 90% of the industries in Shanghai FTZ have received pre-establishment national treatment, and over 90% of the FIEs were established through the recordation rather than pre-approval system.

In 2017, the Shanghai FTZ attracted approximately 6 billion USD of foreign capital, taking up 35.3% of that in Shanghai.[61] By April 2017, there had been 8,734

56. *Cybersecurity Law* was adopted by the National People's Congress (NPC) in November 2016 after a year of legislative proceedings, and came into effect on 1 June 2017.
57. *National Security Law* was adopted at the 15th session of the Standing Committee of the Twelfth National People's Republic of China on 1 July 2015 and came into force on the date of issuance.
58. Judy Deng & Jiaojiao Shi, *China's Ongoing Foreign Direct Investment Law Reform: A Major Move to Simplify Market Entry Matters* (Davis Wright Tremaine LLP, 22 September 2016), https://www.dwt.com/Chinas-Ongoing-Foreign-Direct-Investment-Law-Reform-A-Major-Move-to-Simplify-Market-Entry-Matters-09-22-2016/ (accessed 2 February 2018).
59. Gladie Lui, *Shanghai Pilot Free Trade Zone: Shaping of China's Future Foreign Investment Environment*, 40 ITJ 31 (2014).
60. *Ibid.*
61. Sohu Finance, *The 2017 Shanghai FDI report has come out, and the FDI in Shanghai Free Trade Zone has increased by 6.3%, taking up 35.3% of Shanghai in total*, http://www.sohu.com/a/219740205_815543 (accessed 22 March 2018).

foreign enterprises established in Shanghai FTZ attracting contractual foreign investment up to CNY 688 billion. There were 12,712 foreign enterprises in total founded in Guangdong FTZ, Fujian FTZ and Tianjin FTZ, attracting contractual foreign investment of CNY 1,135.7 billion.[62]

§12.03 THE SHANGHAI FTZ AND CHINA'S WTO COMMITMENTS

The WTO is the first international organization joined by China that is vested with the authority to police a wide range of domestic policies of its members and equipped with a mandatory dispute settlement mechanism with compulsory jurisdiction over all its members.[63] In this section, we test the main policies of the Shanghai FTZ against the SCM Agreement and TRIMs Agreement, as well as transparency obligations contained in its accession protocol and other WTO agreements to shed light on the new traits of the FTZs in China's post-WTO era.

[A] Agreement on Subsidies and Countervailing Duties Measures

Article 1 of the Agreement on Subsidies and Countervailing Duties Measures (the 'SCM Agreement') defines a subsidy as 'a financial contribution by a government or any public body within the territory of a Member'.[64] The subsidy needs to be of specific benefit to the industry to be subject to the SCM Agreement. Subsidies contingent upon export performance ('export subsidies') or the use of domestic goods ('local content subsidies') are prohibited. Other categories of subsidies, although not prohibited, may be challenged by other WTO members ('actionable subsidies').[65] In accordance with the SCM Agreement footnote 1, 'the exemption of an exported product from duties or taxes borne by the like product when destined for domestic consumption, ... shall not be deemed to be a subsidy'.[66] Thus, the most common SEZ incentive – the exemption of exported products from import duties or taxes assessed on like products shipped from the FTZ for domestic consumption – is excluded from the definition of subsidy.[67]

During the negotiations, China very reluctantly accepted not to use special and differential treatment (SDT) provisions under the SCM Agreement and accepted additional obligations in its accession protocol.[68] The SCM Agreement provides SDT for developing countries and transition rules for countries with formerly centrally planned

62. MOFCOM, *The Announcement of Negative List 2017*, NetEase Finance (Beijing, 17 June 2017), http://money.163.com/17/0617/08/CN4A14GK002580S6.html.
63. Qin Julia Ya, *The Impact of WTO Accession on China's Legal System: Trade, Investment and Beyond*, Wayne State University Law School Legal Studies Research Paper No. 07-15 (2007).
64. *Marrakesh Agreement*, Annex 1A, Agreement on Subsidies and Countervailing Measures ('*SCM Agreement*'), Article 1.
65. *SCM Agreement*, Part III Actionable Subsidies.
66. *SCM Agreement*, *supra* note 1.
67. Stephen Creskoof & Peter Walkenhorst, *Implications of WTO Disciplines for Special Economic Zones in Developing Countries*, World Bank Policy Research Working Paper 24 (2009), https://elibrary.worldbank.org/doi/abs/10.1596/1813-9450-4892 (accessed 2 February 2018).
68. *Protocol on the Accession of the People's Republic of China*.

economies.[69] However, because of its delayed WTO entry, China was not able to take advantage of this provision as a transition economy member.[70] China also agreed not to invoke several provisions of the SCM Agreement that are available to developing countries. Furthermore, in Article 20 of its Protocol, China agreed to the use of an 'alternative benchmark' by other WTO members when measuring the value of government-provided subsidies.[71] Analogous to the alternative nonmarket economy methodology used in antidumping cases, this provision facilitates action against Chinese industries that are charged with receiving soft loans or infusions of equity in countervailing duty cases.[72]

These commitments made by China on subsidies make it more likely that other WTO members will prevail in an investigation of subsidies not specifically related to exports and that Chinese exporters will face countervailing duties.[73] Therefore, China should carefully review the subsidies in FTZs to assure compliance with the SCM Agreement.

[1] Prohibited Subsidies

In its Protocol, China promised to eliminate all subsidy programmes falling within the scope of Article 3 of the SCM Agreement upon accession.[74] In 2007, a number of measures maintained by China, providing for refunds, deductions or exemptions from taxes, on the condition that enterprises purchased domestic over imported goods were challenged by the US. The dispute was settled after mutual consultation with China's withdrawal of the measures in question.[75] In 2008, when China imposed a higher customs duty on imported automobile parts if automobile manufacturers did not meet domestic content requirements, the WTO panel found it inconsistent with the prohibition on the use of domestic over imported goods provision.[76]

The subsidies offered in FTZs are particularly likely to cross the line as illegal measures under the WTO rules due to their geographical specificity. Given the tradition that many enterprises located within China's SEZs are export-orientated, if that is still the case in Shanghai FTZ, the 'general policy' granting subsidies in the FTZ could possibly be challenged as de facto, if not de jure export subsidies.[77]

---

69. Stephen Creskoof & Peter Walkenhorst, *Implications of WTO Disciplines for Special Economic Zones in Developing Countries*, World Bank Policy Research Working Paper 13 (2009), https://elibrary.worldbank.org/doi/abs/10.1596/1813-9450-4892 (accessed 2 February 2018).
70. *SCM Agreement*, Article 29.
71. Nicholas R. Lardy, *Integrating China into Global Economy* 89–93 (Brookings Institution Press 2002).
72. *Ibid.*
73. *Ibid.*
74. The World Trade Organization, *Report of the Working Party on the Accession of China (WT/ACC/CHN/49)* (1 October 2001).
75. *China – Certain Measures Granting Refunds, Reductions or Exemptions from Taxes and Other Payments*, WT/DS358/13 (13 July 2007).
76. *China – Measures Affecting Imports of Automobile Parts*, WT/DS339/R, WT/DS/340/R, WT/DS/342/R (18 July 2008).
77. *Canada – Aircraft*, WT/DS70/AB/R (2 August 1999).

[2] Subsidies in Shanghai FTZ

China's latest notification to the WTO Committee on Subsidies and Countervailing Measures (SCM) listed eighty-six programmes in force at the Central level between 2009 to 2014,[78] of which thirty had not been notified to the WTO previously, but no information was supplied to the Secretariat regarding support measures at the sub-central level.[79] A large part of these subsidies programmes involved income tax reductions and exemptions, based on the ownership of enterprises (particularly FIEs), their location, and their activities.[80] None of the preferential policies in Shanghai FTZ were included in the list, but the tax incentives and subsidies applied in the Shanghai FTZ are definitely worth examining under the SCM Agreement.

Tax Incentives

The two tax incentives mentioned above, 'the policy on non-monetary asset investment' and 'the policy on stock right incentives' are unlikely to be found WTO-inconsistent. According to SCM Article 2.2 second sentence, 'the setting or change of generally applicable tax rates by all levels of government entitled to do so shall not be deemed to be a specific subsidy for the purpose of this Agreement'.[81]

The Shanghai FTZ Sub-office of the SAT[82] and the Shanghai Sub-office of the Shanghai Municipal Bureau of Local Taxation[83] assume the functions of tax collection and administration within the scope of the Shanghai FTZ as an 'independent' government taxing authority. Thus, it excludes the tax incentives for all eligible enterprises and individuals within the FTZ from being 'specific'.[84] It is the high-level autonomy of the FTZs that qualifies them as ideal places for bold and flexible measures without being challenged under WTO rules.

De Facto Export Subsidies

Another controversial measure is the government subsidies to FTZ enterprises that export most of their production, which may constitute a de facto, if not de jure, export

78. *New and Full Notification Pursuant to Article XVI: 1 of the GATT 1994 and Article 25 of the Agreement on Subsidies and Countervailing Measures by China*, G/SCM/N/220/CHN, G/SCM/N/253/CHN, G/SCM/N/284/CHN, 30 October 2015.
79. *Trade Policy Review Report by the Secretariat China*, WT/TPR/S/342 (15 June 2016), 3.120-3.122.
80. Athziri Martha Moreno Romo, *China's Special Economic Zones: Are They Still 'Special' after China's Accession to the WTO?* (University of Technology, Sydney 2009).
81. *SCM Agreement* Article 2.2.
82. 'Shanghai FTZ Sub-office of the SAT' refers to Shanghai (China) Pilot Free Trade Zone Sub-office of the State Administration of Taxation.
83. 'Shanghai FTZ Sub-office of the Shanghai Municipal Bureau of Local Taxation' refers to Shanghai (China) Pilot Free Trade Zone Sub-office of the Shanghai Municipal Bureau of Local Taxation.
84. For details, *see* Official Reply of the Shanghai Municipal Office of the State Administration of Taxation and the Shanghai Municipal Bureau of Local Taxation on the Authorization of Institution Functions and Administrative Staffing Quotas of the Shanghai (China) Pilot Free Trade Zone Sub-office of the State Administration of Taxation and the Shanghai (China) Pilot Free Trade Zone Sub-office of the Shanghai Municipal Bureau of Local Taxation.

subsidy. Pursuant to Article 3.1(a) and footnote 4 of the SCM Agreement, an export subsidy exists 'when the facts demonstrate that the granting of a subsidy, without having been made legally contingent upon export performance, is in fact tied to actual or anticipated exportation or export earnings.'[85] In *Australia – Automobile Leather II*, the recipient was required to meet sales goals that exceeded the domestic market and 90% of the product was exported. [86] The Panel found that payments under a grant contract were prohibited subsidies because payments were in fact tied to export performance.

Assuming some preferential policy measures are considered 'specific' subsidies in Shanghai FTZ, they must also meet the 'contingent' requirement (either upon export or domestic content) to be 'prohibited subsidies'.[87] For the Shanghai FTZ, no such requirements can be found in any laws or regulations, which to some extent differentiate it from Chinese traditional SEZs. The FTZs are no longer safe harbours for those export-orientated domestic enterprises to promote international competitiveness by taking advantage of domestic protection policy. They serve more as platforms for both domestic and foreign enterprises, to immediately operate in a liberal economic environment, while the rest of the Chinese territory moves in that direction. According to the *2016 Statistical Bulletin of the Economic and Social Development of Shanghai*, the total value of exports within the Shanghai FTZ is around CNY 232 billion, representing 6.9% of total Chinese exports of approximately CNY 3.36 trillion.[88] Without other statistics such as the exact beneficiaries of a certain subsidy and their export activity, there is insufficient evidence of subsides 'contingent upon export performance'. For now, a majority of subsidies appear to be granted to projects or enterprises on the basis of innovation and entrepreneurship.[89]

Some scholars like Chen argue that the largest subsidy China confers to its exporters has been the artificially low value of the Renminbi. China has long been criticised for maintaining a significantly undervalued exchange rate peg to the USD as part of its strategy of export-led growth.[90] However, after suppressing its currency through 2014, China has turned to popping it up, and its trade surplus as a share of its economy has declined over the past decade.[91] Currently, RMB exchange rate is experiencing another round of depreciation since April 2018 amid the trade war risk. Meanwhile, internal consumption, rather than exports, has gradually become the new

85. *SCM Agreement* Article 3.1(a) and footnote 4.
86. *Australia – Subsidies Provided to Producers and Exporters of Automotive Leather*, WT/DS126/R (21 January 2000).
87. *SCM Agreement* Article 3.
88. 2016 Statistical Bulletin of Shanghai National Economy and Social Development, http://www.shanghai.gov.cn/nw2/nw2314/nw2318/nw26434/u21aw1210720.html (accessed 12 February 2018).
89. *See* the list of projects granted 'Special Development Fund' in FTZ by Pudong Administrative Agency, http://www.pudong.gov.cn/shpd/InfoOpen/InfoDetail.aspx?Id=862913 (accessed 3 November 2018).
90. Claus D. Zimmermann, *Congress Continues to Attack Currency Manipulations as China Defuses G-20 Pressure for Now: The International Law* (ASIL, 30 June 2010).
91. Eduardo Porter, *Trump Is Not Wrong on China Currency Manipulation, Just Late*, The New York Times (New York, 11 April 2017), https://www.nytimes.com/2017/04/11/business/economy/trump-china-currency-manipulation-trade.html (accessed 2 February 2018).

engine for Chinese economic growth. The Shanghai FTZ does not aim at harnessing cheap labour or currency to build an export-oriented manufacturing industry as the SEZs did, but to lead China up the value chain in global competition as part of China's strategy of massive and fundamental economic reform.

[B] Agreement on Trade-Related Investment Measures

The Agreement on TRIMs 'applies to investment measures related to trade in goods only.'[92] China agreed to full compliance with TRIMs on accession, which is somewhat faster than many countries committed to.[93] China also agreed that it would no longer enforce provisions of existing contracts with foreign firms that are inconsistent with its TRIMs commitments.[94]

China's WTO accession and the establishment of the Shanghai FTZ accelerated China's further reform of its legal regime, especially of its foreign investment law, a national priority to support China's economic progress. Traditionally, there are two parts of China's FDI laws: a long standing Foreign Investment Law framework providing for three model vehicles – Wholly Foreign-owned Enterprise, Equity Joint Venture (EJV) and Contractual Joint Venture, respectively governed by three corresponding laws;[95] and the Catalogue for the Guidance of Foreign Investment (Catalogue), acting as a guide for foreign investors.[96]

Though not directly prescribed in the TRIMs Agreement, China's long-time 'technology transfer' requirement contingent on the approval of investment has faced severe challenges, since China has made the promise of elimination and cessation of enforcement of trade and foreign exchange balancing requirements, local content and export performance offsets and technology transfer requirements made effective through laws, regulations or other measures in Annex 1A of the Protocol upon WTO accession. [97] The 2001 revision of the Laws of the PRC on Wholly Foreign-owned Enterprises ('WFOE') abolished TRIMs-inconsistent technology and export requirements that mandated that WFOE use advanced technology or export a minimum of 50% of their products each year. After the revision, the WFOE only requires the enterprises to 'benefit the Chinese national economy'.[98]

Currently, there is no law or regulation in China linking the admission of foreign capital to technology transfer. China states that foreign companies are free to base technology transfer decisions on business and market considerations and to independently negotiate and assign or license intellectual property rights to affiliated or

92. *TRIMs*, Article 1.
93. Nicholas R. Lardy, *Integrating China into Global Economy* (Brookings Institution Press 2002).
94. *Ibid.*
95. Three laws: *Laws of the PRC on Wholly Foreign-owned Enterprises ('WFOE')*, *Laws of the PRC on Chinese-foreign Equity Joint Ventures ('EJV')*, and *Laws of the PRC on Sino-Foreign Cooperative Enterprises ('SFCE')*.
96. Omar R. Gutierrez, *An Analysis of the People's Republic of China's Foreign Investment Law and Foreign Direct Investment in Shanghai's Free Trade Zone*, 29 FJIL 41 (2017).
97. The World Trade Organization, *China Trade Policy Review (WT/TPR/S/342)*.
98. *Ibid.*

unaffiliated enterprises. According to the *Notice of Recordation Administration*, issued by MOFCOM on 8 October 2016,[99] the procedures for establishment of a foreign enterprise are simplified to a great extent. The industries within the scope of the Negative List are no longer required to obtain pre-approval by the government. In the Shanghai FTZ administration, the establishment process has to be finished within five business days and can be done entirely online. This suggests that there is little space for any governmental 'forced technology transfer' against foreign investors. A reciprocal and market-orientated decision made by both Chinese and foreign enterprises to conduct technology transfer for common good is the commercial decision between market entities, not subject to the TRIMs. However, when State-Owned Enterprises and State-Invested Enterprises (SIEs) are involved, those 'business decisions' can blur with government directives, and raise questions under the TRIMs.

On 19 January 2015, the draft Foreign Investment Law ('Draft Law') was posted on the website of MOFCOM to solicit public opinion. The Draft Law intends to consolidate the existing three laws regulating foreign investments into one uniform statutory regime and unify the corporate legal requirements for both foreign and domestic investments in China. Though the legislative process of the unified Foreign Investment Law is still unclear, it shed light on the path for its future development and showed the improvement of rule of law in China following the establishment of the Shanghai FTZ.

§12.04 TRANSPARENCY

Transparency is one of the basic values of WTO system – open markets require transparent rules and procedures. China has accepted comprehensive transparency obligations upon its WTO accession, and some of them even go beyond the existing WTO rules.[100]

In its WTO accession protocol, China promised to 'establish or designate an official journal dedicated to the publication of all laws, regulations and other measures pertaining to or affecting trade in goods, services, TRIPs or the control of foreign exchange'.[101] China also committed to 'publish this journal on a regular basis and make copies of all issues of this journal readily available to individuals and enterprises'.[102]

Following its accession to the WTO, China did not establish or designate an official journal. Rather, China provided information and trade-related measures through multiple channels, including ministry websites, newspapers and a variety of journals, to provide information on trade-related measures.[103] The official website of MOFCOM serves as the main platform for publications of trade-related policies.

99. '*Notice of Recordation Administration*' refers to Notice of the Shanghai Municipal People's Government.
100. *Protocol of the Accession of the People's Republic of China*, Article 2 (C).
101. *Ibid.*
102. *Ibid.*
103. United States Trade Representative, *2017 Report to Congress On China's WTO Compliance*, https://ustr.gov/sites/default/files/files/Press/Reports/China%202017%20WTO%20Report.pdf 137 (accessed 3 November 2018).

In March 2006, the State Council issued a Notice, directing all central, provincial and local government entities to begin sending copies of all of their trade-related measures to MOFCOM for immediate publication in the *MOFCOM Gazette*. The *Gazette* is supposed to function as the 'fully compliant single official journal' and dedicated to the publication of all trade-related laws, regulations and other measures. However, the *Gazette* does not perform as well as it should have done. First, MOFCOM does not publish the *Gazette* on a regular basis. For example, all thirty-five issues of 2017 *Gazette* were released intensively from 25 March to 24 July 2017 and the first twenty issues of 2018 *Gazette* were released between 29 March and 3 May 2018.[104] Second, most issues of the *Gazette* listed only the titles of the measures with no text of the measure or other details. Only a few issues of the *Gazette* include hyperlinks to the full text, but even those do not provide any translation in one or more of the WTO languages (English, French and Spanish). This shows poor compliance with its translation commitment.

In 2006, China submitted its subsidy notification on SCM Committee for the first time, five years after the accession. The report includes more than seventy subsidy programmes, which was incomplete, as it failed to notify any subsidies provided by provincial and local government authorities or any subsidies provided by state-owned banks.[105] This is an obvious violation of its commitments under Article 2 and Article 10 of the Protocol.[106] The latest notification in 2015 included sub-central government subsidy programmes for the first time since its WTO accession. Unfortunately, the number and scope of sub-central government subsidy programmes covered represent a very small sample of the programmes administered at the sub-central levels of governments, without mentioning any subsidy in the FTZs.[107]

China has committed to apply the provisions of the WTO Agreement and its Protocol to the entire customs territory of China, including the areas where special regime for tariffs, taxes and regulations are established.[108]

As for the Shanghai FTZ specifically, its official website only posted the laws and regulations issued by the central government with English translation. The latest publication under 'Laws and Regulations' online is from 2014.[109] In particular, practical measures such as opinions, circulars, orders, directives and notices were rarely published or hardly accessible from its website. For now, the extremely opaque and elusive policies and procedures adopted within the FTZs are one of the main obstacles for foreign investors and government officials to have stable expectation about the future of the FTZs.

---

104. MOFCOM - Gazette, http://english.mofcom.gov.cn/article/policyrelease/gazette/ (accessed 19 March 2018).
105. United States Trade Representative, *2017 Report to Congress On China's WTO Compliance*, https://ustr.gov/sites/default/files/files/Press/Reports/China%202017%20WTO%20Report.pdf 137 (assessed 3 November 2018).
106. *Protocol* Article 2(3) and Article 10(2).
107. G/SCM/N/220/CHN, G/SCM/N/253/CHN, G/SCM/N/284/CHN, *China's Notification to the WTO Committee on Subsidies and Countervailing Measures*, 30 October 2015.
108. *Protocol* Article 2(A)(1).
109. China (Pilot) Shanghai Pilot Free Trade Zone, http://en.china-shftz.gov.cn/ (accessed 19 March 2018).

§12.05 CONCLUSION

China's establishment of the FTZs since 2013 is a milestone for its continued economic reform in the post-WTO era by promoting advanced governance of its economic zones, which demonstrates the determination and dedication of the Chinese government to further improve its domestic economy. The FTZs have showed an advanced model of development on the basis of modern service industries instead of traditional manufacturing. In this chapter, given the current, publicly available information, we have been unable to identify any WTO inconsistent aspects of the existing incentive policies within the Shanghai FTZ.

Despite the proclaimed ambition of the Chinese government to further liberalise its trade regime especially in its service sectors, the opening up process has progressed quite slowly in the past five years. The FTZs are not as 'free' as expected due to China's conservative approach to certain sectors, such as financial services. The internationalization of the RMB and free flow of the capital across the border have not achieved the level promised at the time of FTZs' establishments.

In conclusion, seventeen years after China's accession to the WTO, China has gradually eliminated laws and regulations ostensibly inconsistent with the WTO rules. However, China's transparency obligations have not been fully fulfilled, even after the establishments of twelve FTZs. Room remains for improvement.

CHAPTER 13

Recent Developments of Institutional Arbitration in China: Specialization, Digitalization and Internationalization*

*Jie (Jeanne) Huang***

§13.01 INTRODUCTION

Free trade zones (hereinafter 'FTZ') are a type of special economic zones and can be broadly defined as 'demarcated geographic areas contained within a country's national boundaries where the rules of business are different from those that prevail in the national territory'.[1] Since the establishment of China (Shanghai) Pilot FTZ in 2013,[2]

* In this Chapter, 'China' refers to Mainland China, excluding Hong Kong and Macao Special Administrative Regions and Taiwan. This paper is made possibly partly through the China National Social Science Fund (16BFX202).

** The author can be contacted at Jeanne.huang@sydney.edu.au. All comments are highly appreciated.

1. Farole, Thomas, *Special Economic Zones in Africa: Comparing Performance and Learning from Global Experiences*, World Bank 1 (2011) (indicating these differential rules principally deal with investment conditions, international trade and customs, taxation, and the regulatory environment; whereby the zone is given a business environment that is intended to be more liberal from a policy perspective and more effective from an administrative perspective than that of the national territory).
2. http://www.china-shftz.gov.cn/NewsDetail.aspx?NID=6a441b33-45d8-45e1-956f-f1df348cc85c&CID=fb463223-5bcd-4907-ad64-2c7e294c767f&MenuType=3&navType=0 (accessed 9 Jan. 2018).

China has established eleven FTZs.[3] These FTZs shoulder the historic mission as testing grounds to further open up China to outside world.[4]

Since the enactment of China Arbitration Law in 1994,[5] institutional arbitration has dominated China's arbitration market.[6] The recent developments of institutional arbitration in China is featured with three keywords: specialization, digitalization and internationalization. Many of important developments took place in FTZs and generated positive nationwide impacts. This chapter analyses the recent developments of institutional arbitration in China and asks whether these developments would bring more use of Chinese arbitration institutions in the 'One Belt, One Road' (hereinafter 'OBOR') contexts.

This chapter has five parts. The first three parts critically assess recent developments of Chinese arbitration institutions in specialization, digitalization and internationalization. The fourth part explores the question whether these developments would bring more use of Chinese arbitration institutions in the 'OBOR' context. The last part concludes the chapter.

§13.02 SPECIALIZATION

The first Chinese arbitration institution, China Foreign Trade Arbitration Commission, was established in 1956[7] and renamed as China International Economic and Trade Arbitration Commission (hereinafter 'CIETAC') in 1988.[8] It is not a specialized arbitration institution and accepts cases ranging from general business disputes to maritime disputes that requires expertise knowledge. As the first Chinese specialized

---

3. After establishing the Shanghai FTZ, China established the Fujian FTZ, the Guangdong FTZ and the Tianjin FTZ. *See* Decision of the 12th Session of the 12th Meeting of the Standing Committee of the National People's Congress on 28 Dec. 2014, http://news.china.com.cn/2014-12/29/content_34428633.htm (accessed 1 May 2018). In 2017, China further established additional seven new FTZs in Liaoning, Zhejiang, Henan, Hubei, Chongqing, Sichuan and Shaanxi provinces. Update 1-China Approves 7 New Free Trade Zones in Bid to Open Economy, https://www.reuters.com/article/china-trade-ftz/update-1-china-approves-7-new-free-trade-zones-in-bid-to-open-economy-idUSL3N1H83RM (accessed 29 Apr. 2018).
4. For China's FTZs, e.g., Jie Huang, *Challenges and Solutions for the China-US BIT Negotiations: Insights from the Recent Development of FTZs in China*, 18 Journal of International Economic Law 307 (2015). Shen, Wei, *A Tale of Three Zones – Promises and Pitfalls of Three Financial Experimental Zones in China*, 131 Banking Law Journal 399 (2014); *Introducing the Shanghai FTZ: What to Expect from the Chinese Government's Latest Foreign Investment and Trade Strategy (notes)*, 32 International Financial Law Review 38 (2013). Most of scholarship is in Chinese, e.g., He, Li, *On the Evolution of the Meaning of Trade and the Nature of China (Shanghai) Pilot FTZ*, Haiguan Yu Jingmao Yanjiu [Study of Customs and Trade] 69 (2014); Yang, Feng, *Reform and Improvement of Business Registration System in Shanghai FTZ*, Fa Xue [Law] 104 (2014); Xiaoyong, He, *Legal Safeguard for Financial Reforms in China (Shanghai) Pilot Free Trade Zone*, 12 Fa Xue [Law] 114 (2013); Ding Wei, *Exploration and Experiment of Legal Safeguard of China (Shanghai) Free Trade Zone*, 11 Fa Xue [Law] 107 (2013).
5. China Arbitration Law, promulgated on 31 Aug. 1994 and effective on 1 Sep, 1995.
6. In this Chapter, 'China' refers to Mainland China, excluding Hong Kong and Macao Special Administrative Regions and Taiwan.
7. Chinese Arbitration under Reform and Opening Up, http://szac.org/news/Info/d33a02e6912f4aa0b4bbaf897298bf8f (accessed 29 Apr. 2018).
8. Brief Introduction to CIETAC, http://www.cietac.org/index.php?m = Page&a = index&id = 2 (accessed 29 Apr. 2018).

arbitration institution, China Maritime Arbitration Commission, was established in 1959.[9] Since then, for a quite long period of time, there has been quite few specialized arbitration institutions established in China.

However, recent years have witnessed many specialized arbitration institutions burgeoning in China. Existing arbitration institutions also scrambled to launch centres focusing on certain types of disputes. A typical example is that many arbitration institutions have been established in China in the name of serving OBOR. For example, OBOR (China) Arbitration Institution was established in Wuhan City on 28 October 2016.[10] It mainly deals with disputes arising from OBOR construction, engineering and commercial projects between Chinese parties.[11] In 2017, it accepted five cases and the total monetary value of the subject matter is RMB 600,000,000.[12] The five cases are all contractual disputes between Chinese parties about subcontracting of overseas construction projects. Three projects are in Libya, and the other two are in Kuwait and Vietnam. On 8 September 2017, CIETAC Silk Road Arbitration Center was established in Xi'an FTZ.[13] It also aims to resolve dispute between Chinese parties in OBOR projects.[14] The roster of arbitrators includes the heads of legal departments of China Railway, the China State Construction Engineering Corporation, Power Construction Corporation of China, China Communications Construction Co., Ltd, and Sinohydro Corporation.[15] These companies are important state-owned corporate players in OBOR projects. Engaging these companies demonstrates that the SIETAC Silk Road Arbitration Center has gained wide support from major Chinese corporations, although the roster of arbitrators may make foreign investors dubious about the neutrality of the Centre. Moreover, under the OBOR contexts, in 2015, the China-Africa Joint Arbitration Centre and the BRICS Dispute Resolution Center were established in Shanghai. These two centres are featured with arbitrators from both China and African/BRICS countries and aim to resolve commercial disputes arising from economic exchange between China and these countries.

Besides the establishment of new specialized arbitration institutions, existing institutions also open various centres focusing on a certain type of disputes, such as disputes involving FTZs, Public Private Partnership, finance, air transport, intellectual property, and e-commerce. For example, almost all arbitration institutions in the major cities where an FTZ is established opened an arbitration centre for cases involving FTZs. In 2017, the CIETAC established the Public-Private-Partnership Arbitration Center, and the Wuhan OBOR (China) Arbitration Commission also founded its

9. Introduction to China Maritime Arbitration Commission, http://www.cmac.org.cn/index.php?m=Page&a=index&id=166 (accessed 29 Apr. 2018).
10. Establishment of the OBOR Arbitration Institution, http://legal.people.com.cn/n1/2016/1030/c42510-28819084.html (accessed 29 Apr. 2018).
11. *Ibid.*
12. Annual Review of the OBOR Arbitration Institution, http://new.qq.com/omn/20180119/20180119B0QNO3.html (accessed 29 Apr. 2018).
13. The Establishment of CIETAC Silk Road Arbitration Center in Xi'an, http://www.chinanews.com/cj/2017/09-08/8326252.shtml (accessed 29 Apr. 2018).
14. The Establishment of the OBOR Arbitration Institution, http://legal.people.com.cn/n1/2016/1030/c42510-28819084.html (accessed 29 Apr. 2018).
15. *Ibid.*

Public-Private-Partnership Arbitration Center.[16] Almost all arbitration institutions in Shanghai and Shenzhen established arbitration centres for financial and intellectual property disputes. The Shanghai International Arbitration Center (hereinafter 'SHIAC') and China Maritime Arbitration Commission each established an arbitration centre for air transport.[17] Hangzhou Arbitration Institution united with the other twelve arbitration institutions to form the Cross-border E-commerce CEZ Arbitration Union focusing on e-commerce disputes.

Several arbitration institutions began to provide ad hoc arbitration service. Zhuhai Arbitration Commission and Hengqin FTZ Management Authority jointly made Hengqin FTZ ad hoc Arbitration Rules in 2017.[18] Shenzhen Court of International Arbitration published Procedure Guide to UNCITRAL Arbitration Rules, which aims to facilitate ad hoc arbitration in Qianhai FTZ.[19]

In addition, the booming investment arbitration market also attracts Chinese arbitration institutions. Although thus far none Chinese arbitration institutions has ever conducted a single investment arbitration, this does not prevent them to prepare for digging into this market. In 2017, the CIETAC became the first Chinese arbitration institution publishing an Investment Arbitration Rules.[20] China's transition into a leading investment home country and the implementation of OBOR projects may possibly bring more investment disputes. Chinese arbitration institutions consider they should get ready and provide potential fora for these disputes.

China has more than 250 arbitration institutions. CIETAC used to be the largest arbitration institution in China; however, in 2012, it was split into three institutions: CIETAC, Shanghai International Arbitration Center and Shenzhen Court of International Arbitration.[21] Beijing, Shanghai and Shenzhen are the three major arbitration hubs in China. In Beijing, CIETAC headquarter competes with Beijing Arbitration Commission, and in Shenzhen, CIETAC Shenzhen Division competes with Shenzhen Court of International Arbitration. In Shanghai, there are three major arbitration institutions: CIETAC Shanghai Division, Shanghai International Arbitration Center and Shanghai Arbitration Commission. In the capital city of each province exists at least one local arbitration institution. All Chinese arbitration institutions can accept domestic and foreign-related cases. Essentially, all institutions compete with each other.

16. The Establishment of the OBOR (China) Arbitration Institution PPP Arbitration Center, http://www.xinhuanet.com/info/2017-12/13/c_136822155.htm (accessed 29 Apr. 2018).
17. For the SHIAC Shanghai International Aviation Court of Arbitration, *see* http://www.chinanews.com/sh/2014/08-28/6540284.shtml and http://www.shiac.org/Aviation/index.aspx (accessed 29 Apr. 2018). For the arbitration centre for air transport under the China Maritime Arbitration Commission, *see* http://www.gov.cn/xinwen/2017-12/16/content_5247745.htm (accessed 29 Apr. 2018).
18. Zhuai Hengqin, *Made the First Ad Hoc Arbitration Rule in China*, http://www.xinhuanet.com/legal/2017-03/23/c_1120684060.htm (accessed 29 Apr. 2018).
19. Procedure Guide to UNCITRAL Arbitration Rules, www.scia.com.cn/download/files/document/20161031184434.pdf and http://www.sccietac.org/web/news/detail/1646.html (accessed 29 Apr. 2018).
20. CIETAC Investment Arbitration Rules, http://www.cietac.org/index.php?m = Page&a = index&id = 390&l = en (accessed 29 Apr. 2018).
21. The Split of CIETAC, http://finance.sina.com.cn/china/20120504/011011981271.shtml (accessed 29 Apr. 2018).

Specialization becomes a strategy for Chinese arbitration institutions to excel in competition. Besides accepting general commercial cases, institutions want to show their expertise in certain types of disputes in order to attract more clients. Moreover, local governments consider launching OBOR- or FTZ-specialized new arbitration institutions demonstrates that they closely follow the central government's policy, so are politically correct and economically beneficial.

China's robust economy potentially leads to more commercial and investment disputes. China needs to develop few world-leading large arbitration institutions rather than maintain a large number of small institutions. In recent years, there are very positive moves in this direction. For example, in January 2018, Shenzhen Court of International Arbitration[22] acquired the Shenzhen Arbitration Commission.[23] Consequently, Shenzhen Court of International Arbitration is strengthened by avoiding local competition and enhancing national/international influence. This is the first merger and acquisition (M/A) between arbitration institutions in China. Merger and Acquisition helps to consolidate Chinese arbitration institutions in a competitive market. However, in China the legal status of arbitration institutions is *Shiye Danwei* (public institutions), which means organizations under the sponsorship of local governments. Therefore, a nationwide M/A between arbitration institutions without the support of the central government is unlikely. The legal status of arbitration institutions is a fundamental issue for amending Chinese Arbitration Law. The critical question is if Chinese arbitration institutions are not *Shiye Danwei*, what will they become? One possible solution is to reform them into non-governmental organizations. However, they may eventually become non-governmental organizations sponsored by the local governments, which is superficially different from *Shiye Danwei*. The central government has yet shown a clear plan to change the legal status of China's arbitration institutions.

Due to the unclear governmental support of M/A, arbitration institutions also form alliances and unions to share resources. For example, in April 2015, the China FTZ Arbitration Cooperation Alliance was established in Qianhai City.[24] This Alliance was initiated by the SHIAC, Shenzhen Court of International Arbitration, Tianjin Arbitration Commission, Zhuhai Arbitration Commission, Fuzhou Arbitration Commission, and China Nansha International Arbitration Center. It aims to enhance the rule of law in China's FTZs. In 2016, Guangzhou Arbitration Commission organized China Internet Arbitration Alliance.[25] In October 2017, Hangzhou Cross-border E-commerce Comprehensive Experimental Zone (hereinafter 'CEZ') led the other twelve E-commerce CEZs to form the Cross-border E-commerce CEZ Arbitration Union.[26] The

22. Shenzhen Court of International Arbitration is ranked No. 5 in China in terms of monetary value of caseloads.
23. Shenzhen Arbitration Commission is ranked No. 6 in China in terms of monetary value of caseloads.
24. Introduction to the China FTZ Arbitration Cooperation Alliance, http://www.shiac.org/Trade/introduction.aspx (accessed 29 Apr. 2018).
25. China Internet Arbitration Alliance will be discussed further in part 2 of this chapter.
26. The Establishment of the Cross-border E-commerce CEZ Arbitration Union, http://www.hangzhou.gov.cn/art/2017/10/28/art_812261_12158237.html (accessed 29 Apr. 2018).

Union includes Hangzhou Arbitration Institution and the other twelve arbitration institutions located in the twelve CEZ cities. It aims to make Hangzhou the centre of international Internet arbitration. Alliances and unions are a new development in China. However, the charters for current alliances and unions are unclear and the connections between members are still loose.

§13.03 DIGITALIZATION

Another feature of recent development of institutional arbitration in China is digitalization. Many Chinese arbitration institutions have actively explored online arbitrations in recent years. CIETAC Online Arbitration System is a pioneer in online arbitration.[27] Shenzhen Arbitration Commission developed *Yunshang Zhongcai* (Cloud Arbitration) online system, and Guangzhou Arbitration Commission launched the *Zhongcai Ren* (Arbitration professionals) mobile phone app. These platforms allow parties to submit their documents online, check the process of their cases, receive arbitration news, search case database, etc.

Thus far, the most innovative online system is developed by Guangzhou Arbitration Commission. It organized China Internet Arbitration Alliance and offered an Internet Arbitration Cloud Platform to conduct online ad hoc arbitration since October 2016.[28] It also published Rules for Bridging Ad Hoc Arbitration and Institutional Arbitration (hereinafter 'the Rules'), which came into effect on 19 September 2017.[29] The Rules applies to contractual or non-contractual property disputes and to parties who agree: (1) to submit their dispute to ad hoc arbitration or (2) to convert their ad hoc arbitration into institutional arbitration.[30] Both Chinese and foreign arbitration institutions can join the Alliance,[31] which creates the possibilities that arbitration institutions in the OBOR countries may become Alliance members. The Alliance runs the Internet Arbitration Cloud Platform providing online arbitration service including online case filing, online hearing and service of process, preparing arbitration documents based on artificial intelligence, and digital data service, etc.[32] The Alliance and the Platform may offer two main benefits for resolving OBOR related disputes.

First, online arbitration may make dispute resolution more time- and money-efficient. Parties involved in OBOR projects often come from different countries and have different places of establishment. It is unnecessary for parties and arbitrators to travel when arbitration can be conducted completely online. The Rules also allow

27. CIETAC Online Arbitration System, http://www.cietacodr.org/login.jsp (accessed 29 Apr. 2018).
28. Guangzhou Arbitration Commission, http://www.hrbac.org.cn/newsshow.php?cid = 69&id = 3 614. For the charter of the China Internet Arbitration Alliance, *see* http://zcy.gzac.org/info/ serviceProtocol.html (accessed 29 Apr. 2018).
29. Rule for Bridging Ad Hoc Arbitration and Institutional Arbitration, http://gd.qq.com/a/201709 27/063227.htm (accessed 29 Apr. 2018).
30. *Ibid.*, Art. 2.
31. *Ibid.*, Art. 3.
32. For more information about the Arbitration Cloud Platform, *see* https://www.gzyijian.com/site /index (accessed 29 Apr. 2018).

parties to conduct arbitration partly online and partly offline, or completely offline.[33] The data service offered by the Platform can simultaneously save all procedures and related documents in the Cloud and store them by technology such as timestamp and blockchain to ensure the authenticity of the data.[34] Although the arbitration can be conducted online, it stills has a seat. According to the Rules, parties can determine the seat of arbitration, and if they fail to reach an agreement, the arbitration tribunal can determine a seat.[35] If the tribunal does not choose a seat, the place where the award is rendered is the seat of arbitration.[36]

Second, enterprises registered either inside or outside of FTZs can all conduct ad hoc arbitration online. The Rules can bridge ad hoc arbitration conducted on the Platform with arbitration institutions that join the Alliance in two ways. (1) In any stage of ad hoc arbitration, parties or an arbitration tribunal can apply to the Alliance to convert ad hoc arbitration proceedings into institutional arbitration proceedings.[37] Except that parties agree otherwise, where an ad hoc arbitration is converted into institutional arbitration, the proceedings that are already conducted remain in force and the remaining proceedings will be conducted according to the arbitration rules of the selected arbitration institution.[38] (2) The Rules can also convert an arbitral award rendered in an ad hoc arbitration into an award issued by an arbitration institution in the Alliance.[39] The arbitration institution in charge of converting the award shall confirm whether the parties are eligible to arbitration, whether the arbitration procedure complies with the agreement of the parties and whether the contents of the arbitral awards violate the mandatory law and public order.[40] However, the confirmation shall not affect the independence of the ad hoc arbitration tribunal.[41] If an ad hoc arbitral award complies with the above requirements, the arbitration institution shall stamp the arbitral award with its official seal.[42] Consequently, this award will be converted into an award issued by the institution.

The parties to ad hoc arbitration can jointly choose an arbitration institution that can convert arbitration proceedings or an award.[43] If the parties fail to make a choice but they select the arbitration procedure of an institution, this institution can be the converting institution unless parties agree otherwise.[44] If neither of the above ways can determine a converting institution, parties or the arbitration tribunal can apply to the Alliance who will help determine a converting institution.[45]

33. Article 14 of the Rules.
34. *Ibid.*, Art. 19.
35. *Ibid.*, Art. 18.
36. *Ibid.*
37. *Ibid.*, Art. 22.
38. *Ibid.*
39. *Ibid.*, Art. 21.
40. *Ibid.*, Art. 23.
41. *Ibid.*
42. *Ibid.*
43. *Ibid.*, Art. 24.
44. *Ibid.*
45. *Ibid.*

The Rules is especially appealing to parties who have no complicated disputes and need to enforce their award in China. For example, a Hong Kong enterprise and a Singaporean enterprise conducted an ad hoc arbitration offline according to the Rules in a dispute about transferring shares of a port in Nansha District Guangzhou City.[46] They selected a sole arbitrator, designed their arbitration procedure, and had hearings in Nansha District.[47] The ad hoc arbitration award was converted into an institutional award by the Guangzhou Arbitration Commission according to the Rules and was enforced by a local court.[48] In another case, two companies had a dispute arising from an investment contract. They selected a sole arbitrator and conducted arbitration by using the administration service provided by the Platform. In order to ensure the enforcement of the final award, they converted the ad hoc arbitration award into an institutional award by the Guangzhou Arbitration Commission.[49]

However, the procedure for converting ad hoc arbitration proceedings or awards needs clarification. The current Rules does not provide whether the ad hoc arbitration tribunal can apply to the Alliance to convert the proceedings into an institutional arbitration without parties' agreement. It is also unclear whether the converting institution can review the merits of the award rendered in the ad hoc proceedings. The Rules has no provision for the time and procedure of the review. When parties and the ad hoc arbitration tribunal cannot determine a converting institution, the Alliance can help determine one. It is unclear the time, criteria and procedure for the Alliance to make such decision. Therefore, further amendments to the Rules are necessary to clarify its ambiguities.

Digitalization of arbitration can be divided into two types. The traditional online arbitration systems are limited to documents filing and service of process online. The recent trend of digitalization is featured with artificial intelligence, blockchain, big data and other technology to facilitate decision making in arbitration. It waits to be tested how these data technology can digitalize arbitration in China. For example, an important concern about ad hoc arbitration is that parties may use arbitration to 'resolve' their false disputes in order to achieve illegal purposes such as money laundering. The Platform aims to use timestamps and blockchain technology to address this concern. Technology may prevent illegal revising of the records of arbitration proceedings and contents of relevant documents. However, it cannot ensure that the parties have a real dispute and their purpose to arbitration is not illegal. The success of arbitration largely relies on a well-designed arbitration rule, experienced arbitrators, and supports from the law of the seat of arbitration. It still waits to be seen how artificial intelligence and big data analytical technology can facilitate or even replace experienced counsels and arbitrators.

46. *Ibid.*
47. *Ibid.*
48. *Ibid.*
49. The First *Ad Hoc* Arbitration Case, http://zcw.dl.gov.cn/info/69_85890.html (accessed 29 Apr. 2018).

§13.04 INTERNATIONALIZATION

In recent years, the Supreme People's Court (hereinafter 'SPC') has continuously made pro-arbitration judicial interpretations. Chinese Arbitration institutions also amended their arbitration rules to catch up with prominent arbitration institutions in the world. The development of arbitration laws and rules contribute to the internationalization of Chinese arbitration institutions.

[A] Arbitration Law

Internationalization is demonstrated by several judicial interpretations/opinions on arbitration published by the SPC. For example, in 2016, the SPC published its Opinions on Further Deepening the Reform of Diversified Dispute Resolution Mechanisms supports the reform of arbitrations system.[50] It requires the whole Chinese society to respect commercial arbitration law and procedural rules.[51] It also encourage courts to accept and process application of interim measures from arbitration institutions quickly, and decide the application to set aside or not to enforce arbitral awards according to law.[52]

Another significant development is to extend the reporting system for recognition and enforcement of foreign arbitral awards to awards issued by domestic arbitration institutions.

For more than one decade, China has established a reporting system for its refusals to recognize and enforce arbitral awards under the 1958 New York Convention: when a party applies to an Intermediate People's Court for recognition and enforcement of a foreign arbitral award, the Intermediate People's Court that decides to refuse the application should report its decision to the Higher People's Court in its jurisdictional area; if the Higher People's Court also decides to refuse the application, the Court should report to the SPC and receive approval.[53] The underlying policy of the arbitration reporting system is to create a unified national approach towards recognition and enforcement under the New York Convention.[54] In 2017, the SPC extended this system to setting aside or enforcement of arbitral awards rendered by domestic arbitration institutions in foreign-related or Hong Kong, Taiwan and Macao-related arbitration cases.[55] Regarding other arbitral awards rendered by domestic arbitration institutions, if an Intermediate People's Court decides to set aside or not to enforce the arbitral award, the court should seek the opinion of the Higher People's Court in its

50. Paragraph 10 of SPC's Opinions on Further Deepening the Reform of Diversified Dispute Resolution Mechanisms of http://gongbao.court.gov.cn/Details/2cfa52ab7897b70f8d9da10f212b38.html (accessed 29 Apr. 2018).
51. *Ibid.*
52. *Ibid.*
53. SPC Notice of the People's Court's Handling of Several Issues concerning the Foreign-related and Foreign Awards on 29 Aug. 1995.
54. Alyssa S King, *Procedural Perils: China's Supreme People's Court on the Enforcement of Awards in International Arbitration*, 17 Asian-Pacific Law & Policy Journal 1, 5–7 (2015).
55. Article 2 of Provisions of the SPC on Certain Issues Related to the Reporting System of Arbitral Cases (2017).

jurisdictional area and made a decision accordingly.[56] If the Higher People's Court agrees with the Intermediate People's Court to set aside or not to enforce the arbitral award, the Higher People's Court should report to the SPC in two circumstances. First is when the applicant is not from the province where the Intermediate People's Court is located, and the second is that public policy is the reason to set aside or refuse enforcement of the arbitral award.[57] Therefore, the awards rendered by the Chinese domestic arbitration institutions can benefit from the reporting system and be protected from local protectionism.

Moreover, the Chinese Civil Procedural Law does not indicate which court has jurisdiction on the validity of an arbitration agreement. Published in 2018, Provisions of the SPC on Certain Issues Related to the Execution of Arbitral Awards clarifies that the Intermediate People's Court in the place where the arbitral institution as stipulated in the arbitration agreement is located, or where the arbitration agreement is entered into, or in the place of domicile of the applicant or the respondent, shall have jurisdiction.[58] Moreover, the Chinese Civil Procedural Law only specifies courts that have jurisdiction to decide enforcement of arbitral award.[59] However, in practice the creditor may want to recognize the award without enforcing it. This is often the case where a foreign arbitral award is related to an arbitration heard by a Chinese arbitration institution. For example, an issue has been decided between Party A and Party B by a foreign arbitral award, but Party A brought a related or even the same issue against Party B in a related arbitration conducted by a Chinese domestic arbitration institution. Party B may want a Chinese court to recognize this award although Party A has neither domicile nor asset in China. The Intermediate People's Court in the place where the arbitral institution accepting the related case is located is often the most convenient court for Party B to recognize the foreign arbitral award. However, this court has no jurisdiction according to the Civil Procedural Law because it is not located in the place where the award debtor domiciles or has property. In order to fill in this gap, Article 3 of Provisions of the SPC on Certain Issues Related to the Execution of Arbitral Awards provides that where a foreign arbitral award is related to a case decided by a Chinese mainland-based arbitral institution, neither the place of the domicile of the respondent nor the place of the property of the respondent is located in China, and the applicant applies for recognition of the foreign arbitral award, the intermediate people's court in the place where the arbitral institution accepting the related case is located shall have jurisdiction.

Nevertheless, despite these positive developments, the current Chinese law and judicial interpretations have yet to grant competence-competence to arbitral tribunal to determine its own jurisdiction.[60] Outside of FTZs, arbitral tribunals have no power to

56. *Ibid.*
57. *Ibid.*, Art. 3.
58. Article 2 of Provisions of the SPC on Certain Issues Related to the Execution of Arbitral Awards (2018).
59. Article 273 of the CPL, which provides that if an award debtor fails to comply with the arbitral award, the creditor may apply for enforcement of the award to the Intermediate People's Court at the place where the debtor domiciles or has property.
60. Article 20 of the China Arbitration Law.

grant interim measures.[61] These profound issues to develop modern Chinese arbitration law are still unresolved.

[B] Institutional Arbitration Rules

The year of 2015 witnessed many major Chinese arbitration institutions amended their arbitration rules. The name list includes SHIAC Arbitration Center, China (Shanghai) FTZ (hereinafter 'SHFTZ') Arbitration Center, CIETAC, Beijing Arbitration Commission, Guangzhou Arbitration Commission, China Maritime Arbitration Commission, Zhuhai Arbitration Commission, etc.[62] Rules for multi-parties and multi-contract arbitration are a highlight for all the amendments.

For example, regarding consolidation, the CIETAC Arbitration Rules (2012) and the SHIAC Arbitration Rules (2013) are identical. Both provide that on the application of any party and with the consent of all other parties concerned, the arbitral tribunal may order the consolidation of two or more related arbitrations or arbitrations involving a similar subject matter.[63] The SHIAC Arbitration Rule (2014 and 2015), which replicates the SHFTZ Arbitration Rules (2014 and 2015), further provides that, unless otherwise agreed to by the parties, cases shall be consolidated into the case that has commenced first. Unless the parties otherwise jointly request for a single award, the tribunal shall render separate awards on the consolidated cases.[64]

Unlike the Shanghai International Arbitration Center (hereinafter 'SHIAC') Arbitration Rule (2012) that has no provision for joinder, SHIAC Arbitration Rule (2013) provides that a consenting third party may participate in the arbitration proceedings by a joint written application of the claimant and the respondent.[65] Whether to permit the application shall be granted by the arbitral tribunal or the SHIAC Secretariat.[66] This provision is an improvement compared with the 2012 Rules. However, it does not cover the situation that the joinder may be initiated by a third party. SHIAC Arbitration Rules (2014 and 2015) provides that a third party may also apply in writing to become a party in arbitration with the written consent of both parties.[67] The 2014 and 2015 Rules address joinder of third parties who has not concluded an arbitration agreement with the claimant and the respondent. However, they are not suitable for joining other parties who are under the same arbitration agreement with the claimant and the respondent. Since parties are already under the same arbitration agreement, a joint written submission for joinder is not necessary. Moreover, when other parties under the same arbitration agreement are joined, they may want to appoint arbitrators

61. SHFTZ Arbitration Rules (2014 and 2015) allows arbitration tribunals to grant preliminary measures while the Chinese Arbitration Act allows courts rather than tribunals to grant preliminary measures. *See* Arts 18–30 of the SHFTZ Arbitration Rules (2014 and 2015).
62. The list also includes Taiyuan Arbitration Commission and Fuzhou Arbitration Commission. Shenzhen Court of International Arbitration amended its rule in 2016.
63. Article 30 of the SHIAC Rule (2013).
64. Article 36.2 of the SHFTZ Arbitration Rule (2014, 2015).
65. Article 31 of SHIAC Rule (2013).
66. *Ibid.*
67. Article 38 of the SHIAC Arbitration Rule (2014 and 2015).

different from those appointed by the claimant and the respondent. The 2014 and 2015 Rules have no provision to deal with this issue. The SHFTZ Arbitration Rules (2014 and 2015) address these issues. It divides joinders into two circumstances: joinder of third parties[68] and joinder of other parties under the same arbitration agreement.[69] Article 37 of the SHFTZ Arbitration Rules (2014 and 2015) provide that where the claimant or the respondent requests another party under the same arbitration agreement to be joined into the arbitration proceedings, before the constitution of the tribunal, it shall submit a written application. The Secretariat shall make a decision on the application. In the case that the Secretariat has decided to permit the joinder, the multiple claimants and/or, as the case may be, the multiple respondents have failed to jointly appoint a respective arbitrator, the SHIAC Chairman shall appoint all the arbitrators regardless of whether the parties have previously appointed the arbitrators. The SHFTZ Arbitration Rule (2014 and 2015) also indicate where the tribunal has been constituted and any claimant or respondent requests another party under the same arbitration agreement to be joined into the arbitration proceedings as a respondent, the tribunal may decide whether to permit such application and such party has waived its right to re-appoint arbitrator and accepted the arbitration proceedings.[70] The following table summarizes the evolution of multi-party and multi-contract arbitration rules in SHIAC from 2012 to present.

Table 13.1 Evolution of Multi-Party and Multi-Contract Arbitration Rules in SHIAC

<table>
<tr><th>Arbitral Rules</th><th>Consolidation</th><th colspan="2">Joinder</th></tr>
<tr><td>SHIAC 2012</td><td rowspan="2">(1) Application
(2) Consent
(3) Related arbitration or arbitration involving a similar subject matter
(4) Constitutions of the arbitral tribunals</td><td colspan="2">N/A</td></tr>
<tr><td>SHIAC 2013</td><td colspan="2">(1) A Consenting third party
(2) A joint written application
(3) Decided by the arbitral tribunal or the Secretariat</td></tr>
<tr><td>SHIAC 2014/15</td><td rowspan="2">Including the above 4, and add:
(5) Cases shall be consolidated into the case that has commenced first</td><td colspan="2">Including the above 3, and add:
(4) A written application by the third party</td></tr>
<tr><td>SHFTZ* 2014/15</td><td>Joinder of other parties under same arbitration agreement</td><td>Joinder of third parties (Intervention)</td></tr>
</table>

* The SHFTZ Court of Arbitration was established by the SHIAC in 2013.

68. Article 38 of the SHFTZ Arbitration Rule (2014 and 2015).
69. *Ibid.*, Art. 37.
70. *Ibid.*

Multi-party and multi-contract arbitration help decrease inconsistent and conflicting decisions, alleviate problems related to preclusion, avoid duplicate proceedings, and enable arbitrators to get a more complete picture of parties' rights and obligations in complex commercial transactions.[71] The above development in China is very positive. The SHFTZ Arbitration Rules (2015) is among the most arbitration-friendly rules in China. However, if compared with Hong Kong International Arbitration Center (hereinafter 'HKIAC') Administered Arbitration Rules (2018), SHFTZ Arbitration Rules (2015) may be further improved from the following aspects.[72]

First, The SHFTZ Arbitration Rules (2015) does not address how to appoint arbitrators in case of consolidation because it has no rules for consolidation where the arbitrators of the tribunals are different.[73] In contrast, the HKIAC Rules (2018) applies to such situation. Where HKIAC decides to consolidate two or more arbitrations, the parties to all such arbitrations shall be deemed to have waived their right to designate an arbitrator, and HKIAC may revoke any confirmation or appointment of an arbitrator. HKIAC shall appoint the arbitral tribunal in respect of the consolidated proceedings with or without regard to any party's designation. [74]

Second, both the SHFTZ Arbitration Rules (2015) and the HKIAC Rules (2018) divide joinders into two types: joinder of other parties under same arbitration agreement and joinder of third parties.[75] However, the SHFTZ Arbitration Rules (2015) does not provide when the request for joinder shall be raised. The HKIAC Rules (2018) requires that the request shall be raised no later than in the Statement of Defence, except in exceptional circumstances.[76] The HKIAC Rules (2018) also provides detailed requirements in the joinder procedure, e.g., what information should be included in the request, when to submit an answer to the request, what information should be required in the answer, how to appoint an arbitrator when an additional party is joined, etc.[77]

Third, unlike the SHFTZ Arbitration Rules, the HKIAC Rules (2018) also provides rules for single arbitration under multiple contracts and concurrent proceedings. Claims arising out of or in connection with more than one contract may be made in a single arbitration, provided that: (a) a common question of law or fact arises under each arbitration agreement giving rise to the arbitration; (b) the rights to relief claimed are in respect of, or arise out of, the same transaction or series of transactions; and (c)

71. The multi-party and multi-contract arbitration has disadvantages such as loss of confidentiality, loss of the ability for parties to select their preferred arbitrator and being more time- and money-consuming. Klas Laitinen, 'Multi-Party and Multi-Contract Arbitratin Mechanisms in International Commercial Arbitration: A Study on Institutional Rule of Consolidation, Joinder, and Intervention from a Finnish Perspective' 6, https://helda.helsinki.fi/bitstream/handle/10138/44922/klaslaitinenprogradu.pdf?sequence=2 (accessed 29 Apr. 2018). Irene M. Ten Cate, *Multi-Party and Multi-Contract Arbitrations: Procedural Mechanisms and Interpretation of Arbitration Agreements Under US Law*, American Review of International Arbitration. 138 (2004).
72. HKIAC and SIAC are selected as comparative parameter because they are the biggest competitors to Chinese arbitration institutions.
73. Article 36.3 of the SHFTZ Arbitration Rules (2015).
74. Article 28.8 and 28.9 of the HKIAC Rules (2018).
75. Articles 38 and 39 the SHFTZ Arbitration Rules (2015) and Art. 27.1 of the HKIAC Rules (2018).
76. Article 27.3 of the HKIAC Rules (2018).
77. *Ibid.*, Art. 27.

the arbitration agreements under which those claims are made are compatible.[78] The arbitral tribunal may, after consulting with the parties, conduct two or more arbitrations under the HKIAC Rules (2018) at the same time, or one immediately after another, or suspend any of those arbitrations until after the determination of any other of them, where: (a) the same arbitral tribunal is constituted in each arbitration; and (b) a common question of law or fact arises in all the arbitrations.[79]

The following table is a summary of the differences between SHFTZ Rules (2015) and the HKIAC Rules (2018).

Table 13.2 Comparison Between SHFTZ Rules (2015) and the HKIAC Rules (2018)

Arbitration Rules	*Consolidation*	*Joinder/ Intervention*	*Multiple Contracts*	*Concurrent Proceedings*
SHFTZ 2015	1. Application 2. Consent 3. Related arbitration or arbitration involving a similar subject matter 4. Cases shall be consolidated into the case that has commenced first	1. Joinder of other parties under same arbitration agreement 2. Joinder of third parties	N/A	N/A
HKIAC 2018	Besides the above 4, also include: 5. Claims are made under the same arbitration agreement or 6. the claims are made under more than one arbitration agreement, a common question of law or fact arises, the rights to relief claimed are in respect of, or arise out of, the same transaction or series of transactions, and compatible 7. Appointment of arbitrators	Besides the above 2, also include: 3. Requirements for the Request for Joinder and the Answer to the Request 4. The procedure for the tribunal to decide whether to allow a joinder 5. Appointment of arbitrator	Claims arising out of or in connection with more than one contract may be made in a single arbitration	Conducting two or more arbitrations at the same time, or one immediately after another, or suspend any of those arbitrations until after the determination of any other of them

78. *Ibid.*, Art. 29.
79. *Ibid.*, Art. 30.

§13.05 CAN THE RECENT DEVELOPMENTS ENCOURAGE THE USE OF CHINESE ARBITRATION INSTITUTIONS COMPARED WITH FOREIGN INSTITUTIONS?

There is no easy answer to this question. The recent developments in specialization, digitalization and internationalization will help Chinese arbitration institutions to better compete with their foreign counterparts. However, at the same time, they will face more competition. SPC has allowed Chinese domestic companies in FTZs to arbitrate domestic disputes in foreign arbitration institutions.[80] This will open doors for more domestic companies to arbitrate disputes between them outside of China. In 2013, the SPC held that an arbitration clause providing for ICC arbitration in Shanghai was valid.[81] In 2015, the State Council's announcement that it would 'support the introduction of internationally renowned commercial dispute resolution institutions'.[82] In 2016 and 2017, HKIAC, SIAC and ICC all opened representative offices in SHFTZ.[83] Although initially the representative offices will not provide case management services, they help to promote HKIAC, SIAC and ICC in China. Considering the SPC and the State Council's pro-arbitration position, probably in the future, foreign arbitration institutions will be allowed to conduct arbitration in China. Moreover, SPC is considering to establish international commercial courts in Beijing, Xi'an and Shenzhen.[84] Foreign arbitration institutions and the proposed commercial courts may compete with Chinese arbitration institutions to attract clients.

In addition, companies registered in FTZs are allowed to conduct ad hoc arbitration.[85] After testing the water in the FTZs, if ad hoc arbitration functions well, Chinese government may extend it to all private parties. Nevertheless, ad hoc

80. Paragraph 1, Art. 9 of SPC Opinion on the Provision of Judicial Safeguards for the Construction of Pilot FTZ provides that if two wholly foreign owned enterprises that are registered within a pilot free trade zone enter into an agreement to submit disputes to arbitration seated outside mainland China, the courts should not hold such arbitration agreement as invalid merely on the ground that the dispute concerned is not foreign-related.
81. This is the famous *Longlide* case, *see* the Guide on the Trial of Foreign-related Commercial and Maritime Disputes on 25 Mar. 2013 published by the SPC.
82. Paragraph 11 of the State Council Plan to Further Reform SHFTZ, http://www.gov.cn/zhengce/content/2015-04/20/content_9631.htm (accessed 29 Apr. 2018).
83. For ICC, *see* http://shtb.mofcom.gov.cn/article/m/c/201606/20160601338188.shtml; for SIAC, *see* http://www.siac.org.sg/113-resources/press-releases/press-release-2016/467-opening-of-siac-office-in-shanghai; for HKIAC, *see* http://www.conventuslaw.com/report/hkiac-achieves-breakthrough-by-launching-office-in/ (accessed 29 Apr. 2018).
84. SPC will Study to Establish International Commercial Courts to Resolve Cross-border Disputes, http://m.news.cctv.com/2017/09/26/ARTIbToLfYr26N4c4jo0khbF170926.shtml (accessed 29 Apr. 2018).
85. Paragraph 3, Art. 9 of the SPC Opinion on the Provision of Judicial Safeguards for the Construction of Pilot FTZ provides that an arbitration agreement 'between two companies registered within the pilot free trade zones, which provides for arbitration in a specified location in mainland China pursuant to specified arbitration rules and by specified arbitrators' may be held valid.

arbitration is not directly competing with arbitration institutions, because the latter can provide administrative support and appointing service to the former.

Commercial arbitration and investment arbitration may also provide different answers to the question whether the recent developments would encourage more use of Chinese institutions opposed to foreign institutions. The venue of commercial arbitration generally depends on parties' bargaining powers. As the focal point of China's national strategy, OBOR Initiative encourages Chinese enterprises to invest in developing countries in middle, west and south Asia, and Africa.[86] Compared with their partners in these countries, Chinese enterprise may have more bargaining powers to impose CIETAC or other Chinese institutions for dispute resolution. Alternatively, Chinese enterprises may propose the China-Africa Joint Arbitration Centre and the BRICS Dispute Resolution Center, which are both located in China. However, if the Chinese enterprises' partners have equivalent or larger bargaining powers than them, they may end up arbitrating their disputes in HKIAC, SIAC or other non-Chinese arbitration institutions.

The venue for investment arbitration will depend on the relevant texts of the bilateral investment treaties (hereinafter 'BITs') and the investment chapters of free trade agreements (hereinafter 'FTAs') concluded by China.[87] China's FTAs and BITs can be divided into two groups: those concluded before 2000 and those after 2000. The Annex demonstrates that the majority of BITs in the first group restrict the venue of investment arbitration to ad hoc arbitration, few of them provide ICSID arbitration, and none allows arbitration in other institutions. The institutions to provide appointing service to ad hoc arbitration are limited to the Arbitration Institute of the Stockholm Chamber of Commerce (hereinafter 'SCC') or ICSID. Therefore, Chinese arbitration institutions have no chance to be selected if the investment disputes arise from BITs concluded before 2000.

However, after 2000, the BITs and the investment chapters in the FTAs concluded by China allow dispute resolution in arbitration institutions other than ICSID. The following table demonstrates the different arbitration venues in the China-Uzbekistan 1992 and 2011 BIT.[88]

86. The OBOR Initiative was written into the decision of the 3rd plenary session of CPC's 18th Central Committee and became a national strategy and priority since 2014.
87. For China's BIT list, *see* http://tfs.mofcom.gov.cn/article/Nocategory/201111/20111107819474.shtml and http://investmentpolicyhub.unctad.org/IIA/CountryOtherIias/42#iiaInnerMenu. For China's FTA list, *see* http://fta.mofcom.gov.cn/english/fta_qianshu.shtml and http://investmentpolicyhub.unctad.org/IIA/CountryBits/42#iiaInnerMenu (accessed 29 Apr. 2018).
88. The Agreement between the Government of the PRC and the Government of the Republic of Uzbekistan on the Reciprocal Promotion and Protection of Investments (hereinafter 'the 1992 China-Uzbekistan BIT') signed on 13 Mar. 1992 and effective on 12 Apr. 1994, and was replaced by a new BIT (hereinafter 'the 2011 China-Uzbekistan BIT') signed on 19 Apr. 2011 and effective on 1 Sep. 2011.

Table 13.3 Comparison of China-Uzbekistan 1992 and 2011 BIT

Article 9 of the 1992 BIT	*Article 12 of the 2011 BIT*
• Ad hoc arbitration • If within the period specified, the tribunal has not been constituted, either party to the dispute may invite the Chairman of the Arbitration Institute of the SCC to make the necessary appointments. • The tribunal shall determine its own procedure. However, the tribunal may, in the course of determination of procedure, take as guidance the Rules of the Arbitration Institute of the SCC.	• CSID; • An *ad hoc* arbitral tribunal to be established under UNCITRAL; or • Any other arbitration institutions or *ad-hoc* arbitral tribunals agreed by the disputing parties.

Article 12 of the China-Uzbekistan 2011 BIT is a typical investment arbitration clause that has been widely adopted in other recent BITs and FTAs concluded by China. In these BITs and FTAs, Chinese arbitration institutions may be selected to resolve investment disputes. However, since one disputing party is China or a Chinese enterprise, the other party may not agree to select Chinese arbitration institutions for dispute resolution because of lack of neutrality. Nevertheless, it is necessary first step to amend the pre-2000 BITs to give Chinese arbitration institutions the possibility to be selected.

§13.06 CONCLUSION

China's FTZs have fostered and promoted important and innovative reform related to institutional arbitration. The recent development of Chinese arbitration institutions can be summarized into three keywords: specialization, digitalization and internationalization. However, no development is perfect. There is no easy answer to the question whether these developments would bring more use of Chinese arbitration institutions in the 'OBOR' context. Chinese arbitration institutions will become more competitive but will be confronted with more competitions from foreign institutions, commercial courts and ad hoc arbitration. Regarding investment arbitrations, Chinese government should consider amend the BITs concluded before the year of 2000 to give Chinese arbitration institutions the potentiality to be selected.

Annex: Investor-State Dispute Resolution Clauses in the BITs Concluded Before 2000 Between China and Silk Road Economic Belt Countries

Area	*Country*	Ad hoc *Arbitration*	*ICSID Arbitration*	*Other Institutional Arbitration*
Europe	Norway	Yes. The Chairman of the International Arbitration Institute of the SCC[89] may appoint the presiding arbitrator. The arbitral tribunal shall determine its own arbitral procedure with reference to the ICSID Arbitration Rules.	No	No
	Italy	Yes. The Chairman of the SCC may appoint the presiding arbitrator. The arbitral tribunal shall determine its own arbitral procedure and may refer to the ICSID Arbitration Rules and SCC arbitral procedures.	No	No
	Denmark	Yes. The Chairman of the SCC may appoint the presiding arbitrator. The arbitral tribunal shall determine its own arbitral procedure with reference to the ICSID Arbitration Rules.	No	No
	Austria	No	No	No
	UK	Yes	No	No
	Poland	Yes. the president of the ICJ may appoint the presiding arbitrator.	No	No

89. Arbitration Institute of the Stockholm Chamber of Commerce (hereinafter 'SCC').

Area	*Country*	Ad hoc *Arbitration*	*ICSID Arbitration*	*Other Institutional Arbitration*
	Hungary	Yes. The Secretary General of the ICSID may appoint the presiding arbitrator. The arbitral tribunal shall determine its own arbitral procedure and may refer to the ICSID Arbitration Rules.	No	No
	Greece	Yes. The Secretary General of the ICSID may appoint the presiding arbitrator. The arbitral tribunal shall determine its own arbitral procedure by applying the UNCITRAL Arbitration Rules.	Yes	No
	Moldova	Yes. The Secretary General of the ICSID may appoint the presiding arbitrator. The arbitral tribunal shall determine its own arbitral procedure and may refer to the ICSID Arbitration Rules.	No	No
	Ukraine	Yes. The Chairman of the International Arbitration Institute of the SCC may appoint the presiding arbitrator. The arbitral tribunal shall determine its own arbitral procedure and may refer to the Arbitration Rules of the SCC.	No	No

Area	*Country*	Ad hoc *Arbitration*	*ICSID Arbitration*	*Other Institutional Arbitration*
	Belarus	Yes. The Chairman of the International Arbitration Institute of the SCC may appoint the presiding arbitrator. The arbitral tribunal shall determine its own arbitral procedure and may refer to the Arbitration Rules of the SCC.	No	No
	Albania	Yes. The Secretary General of the ICSID may appoint the presiding arbitrator. The arbitral tribunal shall determine its own arbitral procedure and may refer to the ICSID Arbitration Rules.	No	No
	Croatia	Yes. The Secretary General of the ICSID may appoint the presiding arbitrator. The arbitral tribunal shall determine its own arbitral procedure and may refer to the ICSID Arbitration Rules.	No	No
	Estonia	Yes. The Secretary General of the ICSID may appoint the presiding arbitrator. The arbitral tribunal shall determine its own arbitral procedure and may refer to the ICSID Arbitration Rules.	No	No

Area	*Country*	Ad hoc *Arbitration*	*ICSID Arbitration*	*Other Institutional Arbitration*
	Slovenia	Yes. The Secretary General of the ICSID may appoint the presiding arbitrator. The arbitral tribunal shall determine its own arbitral procedure and may refer to the ICSID Arbitration Rules.	No	No
	Lithuania	Yes. The Secretary General of the ICSID may appoint the presiding arbitrator. The arbitral tribunal shall determine its own arbitral procedure and may refer to the ICSID Arbitration Rules.	Yes	No
	Iceland	The amount of compensation for expropriation or other disputes agreed upon by parties can be submitted to ad hoc arbitration. The Secretary General of the ICSID may appoint the presiding arbitrator. The arbitral tribunal shall determine its own arbitral procedure and may refer to the ICSID Arbitration Rules.	The amount of compensation for expropriation can be submitted to the ICSID.	No
	Yugoslavia	Yes	Yes	No
	Macedonia	Yes	Yes	No

Area	*Country*	Ad hoc *Arbitration*	*ICSID Arbitration*	*Other Institutional Arbitration*
Asia	Mongolia	Yes	No	No
	Kyrgyzstan	Yes. The Chairman of the International Arbitration Institute of the SCC may appoint the presiding arbitrator. The arbitral tribunal shall determine its own arbitral procedure and may refer to the Arbitration Rules of the SCC.	No	No
	Armenia	Yes. The Chairman of the International Arbitration Institute of the SCC may appoint the presiding arbitrator. The arbitral tribunal shall determine its own arbitral procedure and may refer to the Arbitration Rules of the SCC.	No	No
	Kazakhstan	Yes. The Chairman of the International Arbitration Institute of the SCC may appoint the presiding arbitrator. The arbitral tribunal shall determine its own arbitral procedure and may refer to the Arbitration Rules of the SCC.	No	No
	Turkmenistan	No	No	No
	Tajikistan	Yes. The Chairman of the International Arbitration Institute of the SCC may appoint the presiding arbitrator. The arbitral tribunal shall determine its own arbitral procedure and may refer to the Arbitration Rules of the SCC.	No	No

Area	*Country*	Ad hoc *Arbitration*	*ICSID Arbitration*	*Other Institutional Arbitration*
	Georgia	Yes. The Secretary General of the ICSID may appoint the presiding arbitrator. The arbitral tribunal shall determine its own arbitral procedure and may refer to the ICSID Arbitration Rules.	No	No
	Azerbaijan	Yes. The Secretary General of the ICSID may appoint the presiding arbitrator. The arbitral tribunal shall determine its own arbitral procedure and may refer to the ICSID Arbitration Rules.	No	No
	Kuwait	Yes. The Chairman of the International Arbitration Institute of the SCC may appoint arbitrators. The arbitral tribunal may refer to the ICSID Convention or the UNCITRAL Arbitration Rules.	No	No
	Turkey	Yes. The arbitral tribunal may refer to the UNCITRAL Arbitration Rules.	Yes	No
	UAE	Yes. The Chairman of the International Arbitration Institute of the SCC may appoint the presiding arbitrator. The arbitral tribunal shall determine its own arbitral procedure in reference to the ICSID Arbitration Rules or the UNCITRAL Arbitration Rules.	No	No

Area	*Country*	Ad hoc *Arbitration*	*ICSID Arbitration*	*Other Institutional Arbitration*
	Oman	Yes. The Secretary General of the ICSID may appoint the presiding arbitrator. The arbitral tribunal shall determine its own arbitral procedure and may refer to the ICSID Arbitration Rules.	No	No
	Israel	No	Yes	No
	Lebanon	Yes. The arbitral tribunal shall be established according to the UNCITRAL Arbitration Rules.	No	No
	Syria	Yes. The Secretary General of the ICSID may appoint the presiding arbitrator. The arbitral tribunal shall determine its own arbitral procedure and may refer to the ICSID Arbitration Rules.	No	No
	Yemen	No	Yes	No
	Qatar	Yes. The Secretary General of the ICSID may appoint the presiding arbitrator. The tribunal with respect to its procedures shall apply the UNCITRAL rule. Venue of arbitration is the permanent Arbitration Tribunal in the Hague (Holland).	No	No
	Saudi Arabic	No	Yes	No

Area	*Country*	Ad hoc *Arbitration*	*ICSID Arbitration*	*Other Institutional Arbitration*
	Bahrain	Yes. The Secretary General of the ICSID may appoint the presiding arbitrator. The arbitral tribunal may determine its own arbitral procedure by referring to the ICSID Arbitration Rules.	Yes	No

CHAPTER 14

How the SPC Serves National Strategy and "Makes Law": The Pilot FTZ's Opinion and Its Implications

Susan Finder[*]

At the end of 2016, the Supreme People's Court (SPC) issued its "Opinion on Providing Judicial Guarantees for the Building of Pilot Free Trade Zones" (FTZ Opinion or Opinion)(最高人民法院关于为自由贸易试验区建设提供司法保障的意见).[1] In a November, 2018 conference, senior SPC leaders cited the FTZ Opinion as one of its accomplishments in the area of foreign-related commercial and maritime work in the last four years.[2] It is not the first time that the SPC has issued a document to provide judicial guarantees (*sifa baozhang*) to support the nation's major strategies (*fuwu guojia zhongda zhanlue*服务国家重大战略). Senior SPC leaders citing the FTZ Opinion as an accomplishment signals its importance. This article examines the FTZ Opinion, including its background and impact, drawing on local court data and analysis in specific areas of law.[3]

---

* The author wishes to express her appreciation to the persons who commented on earlier drafts of this article and to Wang Ru, STL class of 2018, for her research assistance, provided while she was working full time. Neither she nor the commentators are responsible for any of the views expressed in this article.

1. Zuigao Renmin Fayuan guanyu wei ziyou maoyi shiyan qu jianshe tigong sifa baozhang de yijian (Opinions of the Supreme People's Court on Providing Judicial Guarantee for the Building of Pilot Free Trade Zones), Supreme People's Court, Dec. 30, 2016, available at http://en.pkulaw.cn/display.aspx?cgid=288255.
2. Lu Bing, Diwu ce quanguo shewai shangshi haishi shenpan gongzuohuiyi zhaokai you xie yaodian ni zhidao (Do you know the important points of the convening of the fifth national foreign-related commercial and maritime trial work conference), Zhongguo Shenpan (China Trial), Nov. 8, 2018, https://mp.weixin.qq.com/s/6LoQFQnQN9mpxoCMJZsNpg.
3. *See*, for example, Tianjin Shi Binhai Xinqu Renmin Fayuan (Binhai New District People's Court, Tianjin Municipality), Quanguo fayuan sifa dashuju keti, quyu fazhan zhanlue beijing xia she zimaoqu anjian dashuju fenxi (National Court Judicial Big Data Project, Big Data Analysis of cases

The FTZ Opinion provides a window into multiple aspects of the operation of the Chinese judiciary and Chinese law generally, and also illustrates how the gaps in Chinese law, both substantive and procedural (among other issues), create obstacles to achieving the long-term goal set by the political leadership, of China becoming an international dispute resolution center. The FTZ Opinion provides insights into why and how the SPC fulfills its political and substantive roles, and how the SPC communicates and evolves judicial policy in the context of an important reform initiative to support changing Party and government policies, and its relationship with the concerns of the lower courts. Analyzing the FTZ Opinion requires an introduction to one of the SPC's responsibilities to the political leadership (also characterized as its political role), China's "national strategies," and SPC documents entitled "opinions."

§14.01 SOME BACKGROUND

The FTZ Opinion is an important example of how the SPC supports the Party and government by issuing documents to support important initiatives. As this one, these documents signal an evolution of judicial policy, establish new legal rules, and direct the lower courts. In recent years, SPC President Zhou Qiang has included a section of his report to the National People's Congress (NPC) on the SPC's accomplishments in fulfilling some of its responsibilities in supporting national economic policy goals.[4] Among the accomplishments that President Zhou Qiang mentioned was the services for the country's major development strategies provided by the SPC and lower courts. President Zhou Qiang's March, 2018 NPC report illustrates this clearly:

> Provided service for the country's major economic development strategies. Sixteen measures were issued to provide judicial support for our country's enterprises participating in offshore trade and investment, etc., serving "Belt & Road" construction. Established a coordination mechanism for the Beijing, Tianjin, Hebei courts, serving the coordinated development of Jing-Jin-Ji and the construction of Xiongan. The Liaoning, Jilin, and Heilongjiang courts provided judicial services focusing on the rejuvenation of the Northeast Old Industrial Base. **The Tianjin, Shanghai, Fujian, Guangdong and other courts focused on serving the construction of the FTZs, according to law fairly and efficiently tried related cases.**[5]

related to FTZs with the background of regional development strategy) May 28, 2018, http://bhxqfy.chinacourt.org/article/detail/2018/05/id/3319337.shtml.

4. On the concept of the political responsibilities of the SPC, *see*: Yu Zhong, Lun zuigao renminfayuan shiji chendang de zhengzhi gongneng--yi zuigao renminfayuan linian "gongzuo baogao" wei yiju (Discussion of the political function actually assumed by the Supreme People's Court—using the "Work Reports" of the Supreme People's Court as the basis), Qinghua Faxue) 7, 2005 of (Tsinghua Law Review), 7, 2005, republished at http://www.aisixiang.com/data/8366.html and Zhang Jiayu, Zuigaorenminfayuan jieru hengguan tiaokong shijian yu fans （The Involvement of the Supreme People's Court of China in Macro-Adjustment and Control: Practice and Reflection, Yanshan Daxue Xue Bao (Journal of Yanshan University, 3, 2017), 24, 27.
5. Zuigao renmin fayuan gongzuo baogao (quanwen) (Supreme People's Court Work Report (full text), Mar.25, 2018, available at http://www.court.gov.cn/zixun-xiangqing-87832.html.

As this author has commented elsewhere, President Zhou Qiang's March, 2018 report was intended to signal to the political leadership that the SPC's work (and that of the lower courts) in the next year is harmonized with the post-19th Communist Party Central Committee Congress (19th Party Congress) New Era and that the SPC is fulfilling its political responsibilities.[6]

For those unclear about what is meant by "national strategies," as mentioned by President Zhou Qiang, a Rand Corporation summarizes the views of an authoritative Chinese expert:

> China's national strategic objectives (*guojia zhanlue mubiao*) constitute those fundamental strategic principles, concepts, and priorities guiding not only foreign and defense policy but also critical domestic realms concerned with national construction and internal order. These objectives include the attainment of great power status in the economic, technological, social, and military realms ... and the development or maintenance of capabilities to defend against any internal or external threats to China's political stability, social order, national sovereignty, and territorial integrity.[7]

Expanding the role and operation of FTZs is a national strategy, linked to the 18th Party Congress and its Third Plenum Decision. President Xi Jinping affirmed the importance of and expansion of FTZ policy in his report to 19th National Congress of the Communist Party of China.[8] The report stated: "we will grant more powers to pilot free trade zones to conduct reform, and explore the opening of free trade ports."[9] For that reason, the SPC must continue to support the FTZs through its work and the FTZ Opinion continues to be important post 19th Party Congress.

In 2013, the first of China's FTZs was established in Shanghai, and as of 2018, twelve FTZs have now been established. The government uses the FTZs to test new policies to explore new development models and better integrate the Chinese economy with international practices.[10]

When establishing them, the Chinese government took account of the development of FTZs elsewhere in the world and the domestic situation:

---

6. Finder, Susan, Signals in Supreme People's Court President Zhou Qiang's 2018 report to the NPC (Part 1), May 10, 2018, https://supremepeoplescourtmonitor.com/2018/05/10/signals-in-supreme-peoples-court-president-zhou-qiangs-2018-report-to-npc-part-1/. Also *see supra* note 5.
7. Swaine, Michael, The Role of the Chinese Military in National Security Policymaking, 1998, https://www.rand.org/content/dam/rand/pubs/monograph_reports/MR782-1/MR782.1.chap2.pdf.
8. Guowuyuan guanyu jiakuai shishi ziyou maoyiqu zheanlue de ruogan yijian (Some Opinions of the State Council regarding accelerating the implementation of the Free Trade Zones (State Council FTZ Opinions), http://www.gov.cn/zhengce/content/2015-12/17/content_10424.htm; Guangdong zimaoqu, yongbao gaige xin jiu (Guangdong FTZ, embracing the new opportunity of reform, Apr. 20, 2015, http://www.scio.gov.cn/xwfbh/xwbfbh/wqfbh/2015/32766/xgzc32773/Document/1419136/1419136.htm.
9. Xi Jinping, Secure a Decisive Victory in Building a Moderately Prosperous Society in All Respects and Strive for the Great Success of Socialism with Chinese Characteristics for a New Era, Oct. 18, 2017, http://www.xinhuanet.com/english/download/Xi_Jinping's_report_at_19th_CPC_National_Congress.pdf at 31.
10. China to replicate FTZ practices nationwide, May 23, 2018, http://www.xinhuanet.com/english/2018-05/23/c_137201154.htm.

> the number of free trade zones around the world continues to increase, and the free trade zone negotiations cover the rapid expansion of issues and the level of liberalization has increased significantly. China's economic development has entered a new normal, and opportunities and challenges for foreign trade have coexisted. "Introducing" and "going out" are facing new developments. Accelerating the implementation of the free trade zone strategy is an objective requirement for China to adapt to the new trend of economic globalization, and is an inevitable choice for comprehensively deepening reforms and building a new open economy system.[11]

The FTZs are intended to pilot measures aimed both domestic economic policies as well as to attract foreign investment, promising easier access and better environment, to pilot a more open structure for foreign investment. Each FTZ is intended to pilot different industries and each has a slightly different focus.[12]

At the same time, part of current national policy is to expand the role of law in national strategies. This is particularly important in FTZ policy, because it relates to foreign investment and trade as well as commercial operations. Given the inadequacy of the Chinese legislative system in providing detailed legal rules to keep pace with domestic and international challenges, the SPC has an important substantive role in creating judicial policy, creating legal rules, and guiding the lower courts to implement that policy and rules.[13] Although all courts evolve their judicial policy to reflect evolving societal and national needs, the SPC uniquely uses documents in the form of opinions such as the FTZ to do so.

The SPC creates and transmits to the lower courts new judicial policy in the form of an "opinion" (*yijian*意见). The SPC classifies opinions as "judicial normative documents" (*sifa wenjian* 司法文件 or *sifa guifanxing wenjian* 司法规范性文件) and SPC judges and Chinese legal professionals describe them as "judicial policy documents" (*sifa zhengcexing wenjian* 司法政策性文件).[14] These documents are issued with the identifier "法发" (*fafa*), indicating that they have been approved by the judicial committee of the SPC or one or more senior SPC leaders.

Rules or policies included in SPC judicial policy documents may eventually be crystallized in SPC judicial interpretations and eventually codified in national law, but that process is slow and cannot meet the needs of the lower courts, which need to deal properly (politically and legally) with outstanding legal issues pending a more permanent stabilization. Lower courts implement these measures in various ways, including in their court judgments or rulings[15] and generally issue more specific guidance documents to further implement SPC judicial policy documents and deal with specific local issues. As is described below, this is true for the FTZ Opinion as well. Local courts

11. State Council FTZ Opinions, *supra* note 8.
12. Some of those policies are discussed at Current Landscape of Free Trade Zones (the "FTZs") in China, Aug 17, 2017, https://www.omm.com/resources/alerts-and-publications/publications/china-law-and-policy-august-2017/.
13. Finder, Susan, Supreme People's Court and Its Normative Documents, Aug. 28, 2015, https://supremepeoplescourtmonitor.com/2015/08/28/supreme-peoples-court-and-its-normative-documents/.
14. http://www.court.gov.cn/fabu.html; http://www.flfxglzk.org/arclist.php?sortid=26.; discussions with SPC judges.
15. This understanding confirmed in correspondence with the author.

have issued implementing guidance, as SPC policy is intended to be a framework under which local courts issue more specific measures.[16]

§14.02 FTZ OPINION

The SPC had to issue judicial policy based on research and analysis to understand the legal issues and greater environment in which the FTZs operate because operating FTZs require legal rules and that the SPC requires lower courts to pilot reform measures to support the FTZs, and adjust criteria for making judgments or rulings.[17] For this reason, the drafting of the FTZ Opinion followed a drafting process similar to judicial interpretations. The usual practice in drafting judicial interpretations is for the SPC to engage in extensive research and fieldwork, consult with related institutions within the SPC and external institutions when relevant.[18] The drafting team engaged in several years of field work, established an FTZ Research Base in Shanghai, held a Judicial Forum for the Pilot Free Trade Zones, solicited the views of experts and local courts, in the areas where FTZs are located. The SPC's Fourth Civil Division, in charge of foreign and cross-border related civil and commercial cases and related issues, took primary responsibility for drafting the opinion.[19] The reason that the #4 Civil Division took the lead was that much of the substantive parts of the FTZ Opinion relates to foreign trade, foreign investment, and cross-border arbitration issues. Moreover, earlier Shanghai local court guidance was incorporated into the FTZ Opinion.

Once the draft was relatively advanced, it was circulated to other relevant areas of the SPC for comments. As the team of judges who led the drafting focus on cross-border civil and commercial issues, they sought comments on related issues from the Research Office, likely one of the criminal divisions and the administrative division.[20] Consistent with general judicial practice (and SPC rules), the FTZ Opinion was not issued for public comment. The drafting of the FTZ Opinion reflects the quasi-administrative way in which the SPC operates.

The preamble and introduction to the FTZ Opinion set out its political background and purpose:

> For the purposes of giving full play to the trial functions and roles of the people's courts, and guaranteeing the building of China's FTZs, the following opinions on the trials of **FTZ-related cases** by the people's courts are offered: ... .

---

16. Correspondence on file with the author.
17. Jamie Horsley, Rule of Law, Incremental Progress, available at https://law.yale.edu/system/files/china-law-documents/2007_china_balance_sheet_publ_rol_paper_090212_05rule_of_law.pdf.
18. Correspondence with author.
19. "Zhang Yongjian, Liu Jingdong, Xi Xiangyang, and Yang Xingye, Guanyu wei ziyou maoyi shiyan qu jianshe tigong sifa baozhang de yijian" de lijie yu shiyong (Understanding and application of the "Opinion Concerning the Providing of Judicial Guarantees to the Construction of the Free Trade Zone Pilot Areas," Renmin Fayuan Bao, (People's Court Daily), Jan. 18, 2017, at 5, available at http://rmfyb.chinacourt.org/paper/html/2017-01/18/content_120979.htm?div=-1.
20. Correspondence with the author.

> Guarantee the systematic innovation in the construction of FTZs by law. The construction of FTZs undertakes the historic mission of exploring new ways and gaining new experience in China's comprehensively deepened reform and opening up, and is a positive attempt in making central decisions based on the lawfully recognized evidence in any major reform. People's courts at all levels shall explore reform measures to provide judicial safeguard for FTZs, which are required to be taken within the framework of the law. Timely adjust the trial criteria, actively support the transformation in government functions, respect contracting parties' autonomy, and guarantee transaction safety based on the accurate application of law.[21]

Although the preamble (and text) of the FTZ Opinion uses the phrase "FTZ-related cases" a dozen times, the text (and other related documents) lacks a definition of this term. The SPC Opinion on the Belt & Road similarly lacks a definition of "Belt & Road related cases." A Chinese scholar familiar with the FTZ Opinion explained that the definition should be implied into the FTZ Opinion would be one that draws on the Law on the Application of Law to Foreign-Related Civil Relations (and its judicial interpretation). In his view, an FTZ-related case was that had any of the following elements: one party is registered in an FTZ; the object in dispute in the case is located in an FTZ; the legal relationship, such as the contract or tort occurred in an FTZ.[22] The practice of local courts (as reflected in their white papers) confirms the scholar's view.[23]

It should be noted that the FTZ Opinion does not unify jurisdictional rules for FTZ-related cases. The same scholar mentioned above suggested that at the time some FTZ courts had not yet been established. Additionally, because the situation for each FTZ and its court is different, such as the piloting of specific judicial reforms, standardizing jurisdictional rules in the FTZ Opinion would not have been appropriate. For parties (and their lawyers) this means that they must to search for local court guidance to determine where their case will be heard. This article will use the term "FTZ courts" to refer to both courts located in FTZs, such as the Qianhai Court and local courts hearing FTZ-related cases.

SPC policy promoting the issuance of court white papers means that some statistics and analysis shed light on how the FTZ Opinion is operating in practice. The white papers provide insights into its relevance to issues that come before the local courts, the profile of cases coming before FTZ courts and specific innovations by the lower courts. The white papers use different criteria and analyze different time periods, so the statistics are most useful as an indication of general trends.

21. Emphasis added. *Supra* note 1.
22. Correspondence on file with the author.
23. *See*, for example, Statistics for the period ending Mar. 31, 2017.Guangdong Higher People's Court, Guangdong zimaoqu sifa baozhang baipishu (White Paper on Guangdong FTZ providing judicial guarantees), May 13, 2017, available at http://www.gdcourts.gov.cn/web/content/37184-?lmdm = 2001.

[A] Signals to the Lower Courts

The introductory section of the FTZ Opinion signals to the FTZ courts that they should play their part in advancing FTZ reforms and as part of that, engage in court innovations and reforms. The reason the SPC is doing so is to pilot specific judicial reforms and innovations within a limited scope in several more sophisticated courts. This policy is part of greater overall SPC policy.

In the FTZ Opinion, the SPC states that it encourages the FTZ courts to create a more impartial, open and transparent legal environment and a law-based and internationalized business environment., Encouraging FTZ courts to provide an internationalized business environment seems to imply the FTZ courts establishing English language websites.[24] Although SPC transparency policy means that the transparency in the Chinese courts is far greater than before,[25] one tiny illustration of the need for better disclosure rules is that the persistent researcher seeking to understand the legal framework under which one of the FTZ courts operates (the Qianhai Court) operates, for example, may have difficulty in locating the relevant SPC approval document.[26]

In other documents, the SPC has designated some of the FTZ Courts to engage in specific reforms. For example, the Qianhai Court has been designated as a comprehensive reform demonstration court, has established a flat management system, designated some Hong Kong citizens as people's assessors, and appointed some foreigners and Hong Kong residents as mediators for its court affiliated mediation center.[27]

[B] Caseload in the FTZ Courts

As further described below, most of the cases heard in the FTZ courts are civil and commercial cases (the maritime courts hear related maritime cases), with a tiny number of criminal cases. Minor offenses are punished outside the courts, and available data shows that most crimes punished by the FTZ courts were relatively minor. For reasons connected with the SPC's and the Party's concern with maintaining law and order and social stability, the FTZ Opinion placed issues of criminal law in a leading position.

[C] Criminal Law

Section 3 of the FTZ Opinion focuses on criminal law and practice. The principal audience for this section is the criminal divisions of FTZ courts and courts that have jurisdiction over criminal activity conducted in FTZs. The reason for this is that some FTZ courts, such as the Qianhai Court, lack a criminal division and so a local court with geographical jurisdiction over the FTZ hears criminal cases that arise in the FTZ. As

---

24. *See*, for example, http://www.ftzcourt.gov.cn/zmqweb/gweb/engpage/lg1.jsp; http://www.hlcourt.gov.cn/hlft/ywb/; http://en.szqhcourt.gov.cn/.
25. *See* this author's forthcoming article.
26. Mentioned here and in other reports, http://szqhcourt.gov.cn/fyjj/fygk.aspx?cls = 2.
27. http://en.szqhcourt.gov.cn/About/Index/7.html.

described below, criminal cases account for a tiny number of all cases that have come before the FTZ courts so far. Section 3 signals the SPC is concerned about certain types of criminal activity that have attracted interest from domestic and international authorities and that certain corporate acts have been decriminalized, so persons accused of these acts should be convicted only if current law so requires.

Criminal cases come before the courts only if they are prosecuted. Although the Supreme People's Procuratorate (SPP) guides the lower procuratorates in setting policy in prosecuting cases involving the FTZs, it has not yet issued a policy document in support of the FTZs. The SPP provided guidance to the FTZ procuratorates by convening a national conference for procurators involved in FTZ matters, a technique used by the SPC as well.[28] Similar to President Zhou Qiang, Cao Jianming, outgoing President of the SPP, showed that the SPP has fulfilled its political responsibilities by highlighting what the Procuratorate has done to support the FTZs in his 2018 report to the NPC.[29] Local procuratorates have issued more detailed guidance documents as well as established coordination mechanisms with administrative enforcement authorities such as Customs to deal with referring cases for criminal prosecution.[30]

The SPC called the attention of the lower courts to the following crimes: sabotaging FTZ construction (unclear which crime is meant); abusing special FTZ market regulation conditions; maintain social stability and market order. This section then lists: crimes related to infringement of intellectual property rights; smuggling; evasion of foreign exchange controls; illegal fund raising; and money laundering. Some of these crimes have international implications while others are domestic concerns. Counterfeiting and other intellectual property related crimes are top priority because the Chinese government is under pressure from international governmental organizations, foreign governments, and foreign business to reduce the trade of counterfeit goods through China's FTZs.

It appears likely that those involved with establishing the Shanghai FTZ would have been aware of the 2007 and 2010 Organization for Economic Co-operation and Development (OECD) and European Union Intellectual Property Organization (EUIPO) reports that link trade in counterfeit and pirated goods with FTZs. A 2016 report of the OECD and the EUIPO states that China appears as the largest producing economy of pirated and counterfeit goods, when relying on a detailed analysis of European Union (EU) data, while also showing that the IP rights of Chinese companies are frequently

28. Yan Zhonghua and Jiang Kui, Fuwu zimaoqu, jiachajiguan dang ruhe zuo [In serving the FTZs what should the Procuratorate do], Sep. 12, 2017, https://mp.weixin.qq.com/s/7tKmBAOoKo0Afb1KTjPaqw. On SPC practices, *see* Finder, Susan, Nov. 30, 2014, https://supremepeoplescourtmonitor.com/2014/11/30/what-you-should-know-about-foreign-related-cases-in-the-chinese-courts-a-heads-up/.
29. 2018 Zuigao jiancha gongzuo baogao quanwen [SPP Work Report (full text)], March 9, 2018, available at http://www.spp.gov.cn/tt/201803/t20180309_369886.shtml.
30. Nǔlì dāng hǐo zì mào shìyàn qū jiǎnchá gōngzuò "lǐngtóu yàn"—pǔdōng xīnq jiǎncháyuàn fúwù bǎozhàng zì mào jiǎnchá wǔ zhunián zhájì Work hard to be a good pilot in the Pilot Free Trade Zone—The 5th Anniversary of the FTZ Procuratorate, the Pudong New Area Procuratorate, September 11, 2018, Shanghai Fazhi Bao, Shanghai Legal System Daily, available at http://www.shzfzz.net/node2/zzb/shzfzz2013/tt/u1ai1356434.html.

infringed.[31] A 2018 OECD and EUIPO report, Trade in Counterfeit Goods & FTZs, showed that FTZs correlate with increased trade in counterfeit and pirated goods and that criminal elements worldwide make use of governance gaps in FTZs to engage in money laundering and smuggling.[32] As discussed below in the section on intellectual property law, problems with the Chinese evidentiary system prevent parties, particularly foreign parties, from liaising with the Chinese authorities to seek criminal prosecution of pirating and counterfeiting offenses.

Money laundering, evasion of foreign exchange controls, and illegal fundraising[33] are also concerns of the Chinese government, as the government is concerned that part of the business community will use the more flexible business environment of the FTZs to engage in conduct that is deemed illegal under Chinese criminal law. As mentioned above, Section 3 reminds criminal court judges that according to a legislative interpretation of the NPC Standing Committee, false declaration of registered capital, false capital contribution, withdrawing contributed capital, and engaging illegal business are no longer crimes, except for specified types of companies.[34] It is unclear whether any such cases have arisen.

Data from local courts shows that the profile of criminal convictions is different from those that attracted the SPC's concern. A recent study by the #1 Shanghai Intermediate People's Court (Shanghai Intermediate Court) found that of the small number of criminal cases involving the FTZ heard by the Pudong New Area People's Court and the Shanghai Intermediate Court, most involved credit card fraud.[35] The Shanghai Intermediate Court stated that the variety of crimes was increasing and included financial fraud, foreign exchange control evasion, and breach of personal information.[36] Data from the Guangdong High Court on criminal cases in the three Guangdong FTZ courts shows a small number of criminal cases (Figure 14.1).

31. *Trade in Counterfeit and Pirated Goods Mapping the Economic Impact*, https://read.oecd-ilibrary.org/governance/trade-in-counterfeit-and-pirated-goods_9789264252653-en#page13.
32. https://read.oecd-ilibrary.org/trade/trade-in-counterfeit-goods-and-free-trade-zon http://sjr.sh.gov.cn/ZhengWuDaTing/detail?informationid = 146724es_9789264289550-en#page75.
33. http://money.people.com.cn/bank/n1/2016/0406/c202331-28252955.html.
34. *See supra* note 19.
35. Shanghashi diyi zhongji renmin fayuan shanghai shi pudong xinqu renmin fayuan zimaoqu sifa baozhang baipishu (Shanghai Municipality #1 Intermediate People's Court, Shanghai Municpality Pudong New Area People's Court White Paper on Providing Judicial Guarantees to the FTZ), May 30, 2018, 17-18, available at http://www.hshfy.sh.cn/shfy/gweb2017/xxnr.jsp?COLLCC = 649976917&pa = aaWQ9MjAwNzg3NzQmeGg9MSZsbWRtPWxtMTcxz&zd = xwzx&vadipu = vb4bf.
36. *See supra* note 37.

Figure 14.1 Criminal Cases in the Three Guangdong FTZ Courts Red/Civil (4815), Grey/Maritime (470), Orange/Criminal (210)

Figure 14.1-A Yellow/Qianhai (2994), Green/Nansha (732), Blue/Hengqin (1089)

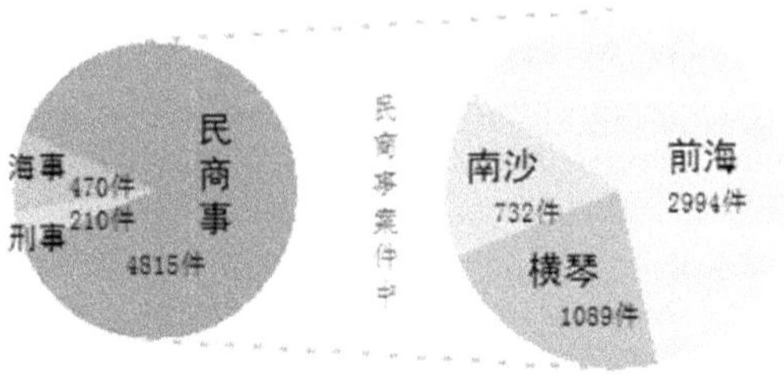

Source: Compiled by the author from various public sources (including https://www.shine.cn/news/metro/1810153452/ and https://hsfnotes.com/arbitration/2017/01/13/china-extends-access-to-offshore-arbitration/)

[D] Civil and Commercial Law

It appears likely that the SPC expected that the bulk of the FTZ cases would be civil and commercial cases, particularly cross-border cases because the #4 Civil Division took the lead in drafting the FTZ Opinion. Big data analysis shows this to be the case: Big data analysis of cases in the FTZ courts shows a rapid growth in case volume of the more established FTZ courts. Three of the four FTZs saw about 40% growth in cases, primarily commercial cases.[37] As Figure 14.2 indicates, each FTZ has its own rules on the jurisdiction of basic level courts in cross-border disputes based on the amount in dispute.

37. *See supra* note 3.

Figure 14.2 FTZ Rules on the Jurisdiction of Basic Level Courts in Cross-Border Disputes Based on the Amount in Dispute

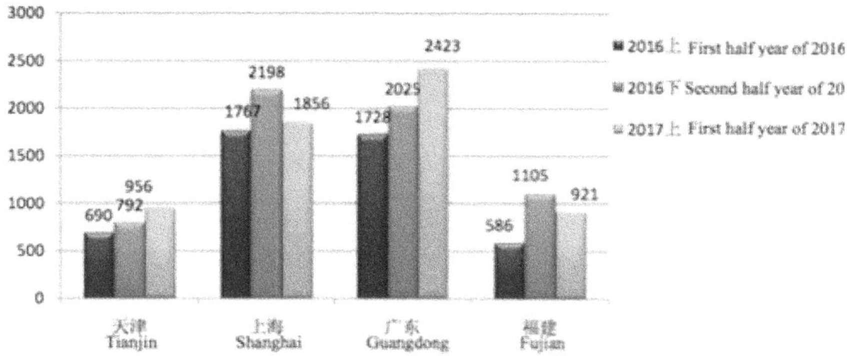

Source: compiled by the authors from public data.

Moreover, there is an important Hierarchical Jurisdiction over Foreign-Related Civil and Commercial Cases in Guandong FTZ (Figure 14.3) which also explains why the SPC expected that the bulk of the FTZ cases would be civil and commercial cases.

Figure 14.3 The Hierarchical Jurisdiction over Foreign-Related Civil and Commercial Cases in Guandong FTZ[38]

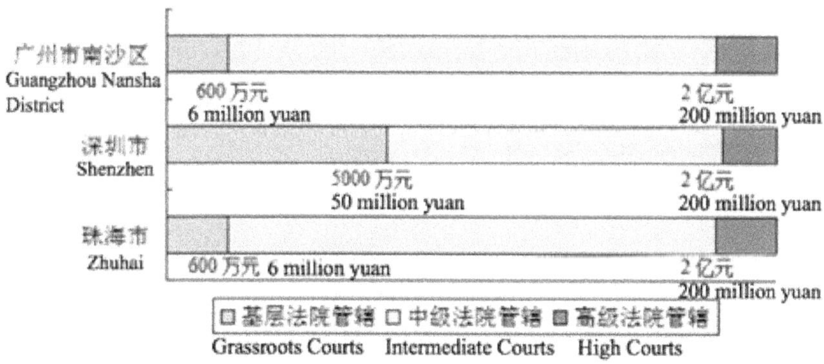

Source: compiled by the authors from public data.

As the FTZ Opinion signals evolving judicial policy to FTZ courts on civil and commercial law issues in several areas. For example, it states that courts should

38. Guangdong Gaoji Renmin Fayuan (Guangdong Higher People's Court), Guangdong Zimaoqu Sifa Baozhang Baipishu (White Paper on Judicial Guaranteets to Guangdong FTZs, May 13, 2017, http://www.gdcourts.gov.cn/web/content/37184-?lmdm=2002.

support FTZ finance leasing companies and should respect the agreement of cross-border parties regarding jurisdiction and governing law and a finance lease contract shall not be determined to be null and void because relevant procedures had not been performed. A report on Shanghai FTZ cases reveals that a relatively small number of finance leasing cases (97) have come before the courts in the period up to April, 2018.[39]

Another example of the SPC signaling evolving judicial policy through the FTZ Opinion is in the area of e-commerce. The FTZ Opinion sets out rules relating to e-commerce, directed at supporting the growth of e-commerce in China. It states that if an e-commerce enterprise imports in a large quantity and sells in batches, and a consumer claims that there established a sale contractual relationship between him and the e-commerce enterprise, the court should support its claim, and setting out special language on arbitration clauses with consumers. However, it appears that a relatively small number of e-commerce cases have come before the FTZ courts.

[E] Intellectual Property Law

The section of the FTZ Opinion on intellectual property rights reiterates general policies and is directed to the intellectual property section of FTZ courts or local courts with jurisdiction over intellectual property matters. It calls on the judicial protection of intellectual property rights in FTZs to be enhanced. It lists a number of government policies that should be encouraged or promoted or improved, such encouraging judicial protection of the processing trade, encouraging indigenous innovation and the balancing national trade policies and trademark owners' interests. It is unclear also whether the provision encouraging indigenous innovation is merely meant as a recital of one of the SPC's policies or is to be specifically implemented in the FTZ courts. From the language of the FTZ Opinion, it appears the latter. Further, although this section mentions promoting and encouraging various types of intellectual property related business activities favorable to the Chinese economy, it does not mention specific measures for dealing with these issues.

The profile of intellectual property cases in the four main FTZs is shown below, and is shown to be for the most part internet related rights and copyright issues:

Table 14[40]

案例類型 Case Type	量 Amount
信息網絡傳播權糾紛 Information Network Dissemination Right Disputes	233
版權相關爭議 Copyright Related Disputes	421

39. *See supra* note 38 at 21.
40. *See supra* note 3.

商標侵權 Trademark Infringement	40
關於聲音或視覺記錄製作者權利的爭議 Disputes on Sound or Visual Recording Producers' Rights	34
專利權糾紛 Patent Right Disputes	24
不公平競爭糾紛 Unfair Competition Disputes	137
投影權爭議 Projection Right Disputes	17
特許經營糾紛 Franchise Disputes	15
技術合同糾紛 Technology Contract Disputes	12
商業秘密糾紛 Trade Secret Disputes	7
商業誹謗糾紛 Commercial Defamation Disputes	3
實用新型專利糾紛 Utility Model Patent Disputes	3
網絡域名爭議 Network Domain Name Disputes	3
企業名稱糾紛 Enterprise Name Right Disputes	2

Source: compiled by the authors from public data

The underlying problems preventing litigants, both domestic and foreign from using the Chinese courts to protect their intellectual property rights are identified in white papers issued by Chinese courts (and one of the local procuratorate) and a report by prominent Chinese intellectual property specialists for the EU funded organization IPKey.

A 2018 white paper issued by the Chengdu Procuratorate stated that difficulties in obtaining evidence (取证难) are significant obstacles for the FTZ Procuratorate to prosecute intellectual property cases.[41] A 2018 nationally commissioned report by the Tianjin Binhai Court assessing data from the four principal FTZ courts also pointed out many difficulties for courts in determining the authenticity of various types of electronic evidence, and described the difficulties for litigants bringing intellectual property cases.[42]

41. Sichuan Sheng Chengdu Shi Renmin Jianchayuan (Sichuan Province Chengdu Municipality People's Procuratorate), at 9.
42. *See supra* note 3 at 80-82.

The IPKey report, while focused on intellectual property issues, had broader comments on obstacles for litigants and courts related to the inadequacy of China's civil litigation infrastructure. Among the problems that the authors listed was China does not have procedures analogous to either common law discovery procedures or civil law jurisdictions' information right provision, that enables one party to obtain evidence in the possession of the opposing party. Parties to Chinese civil proceedings have to collect and provide all the evidence supporting their arguments and there is no general obligation on a party to disclose evidence that go against its case. Although a procedure exists for a party to apply to a court if evidence is under the control of the opposite party; the applicant must pay the cost related to the production of document. One benefit of having parties better understand the opposite party's case is that parties can settle their dispute on a more informed basis. The data studies show that most of the FTZ commercial cases do not settle but go to trial, and are increasingly complex.

Other issues for litigants in a Chinese court is that rules relating to evidence preservation and analogous measures are too vague and make no distinction of pretrial and proceeding stage. According to existing laws, the only substantive examination standard of granting

evidence preservation order, either at pretrial stage or proceeding stage, is "the evidence might be destroyed or if it would be difficult to obtain the evidence later on." Issues related to cross-border litigants are further discussed below:

> [6. Maritime law
>
> In the area of maritime law, the SPC directed the maritime courts to focus on other new types of cases relating to the reform of the shipping registration system, the application of law, and rules related to jurisdiction in new types of maritime cases. The SPC called on the maritime courts in the areas with FTZs to use typical cases to publicize new legal rules that they evolve to industry. shipping, and the application of law and special jurisdiction issues in new-type maritime legal relationships shall be researched. Some local maritime courts have issued more detailed regulations to implement the FTZ Opinion.[43]

There is some data available on the maritime courts and FTZ cases. The first charts are from the Shanghai Maritime Court:

43. Xiamen Maritime Court: https://mp.weixin.qq.com/s/FYrTAPJoP8ueS3iYF38-9g.

Figure 14.4 Number of FZ-Related Cases Accepted and Concluded

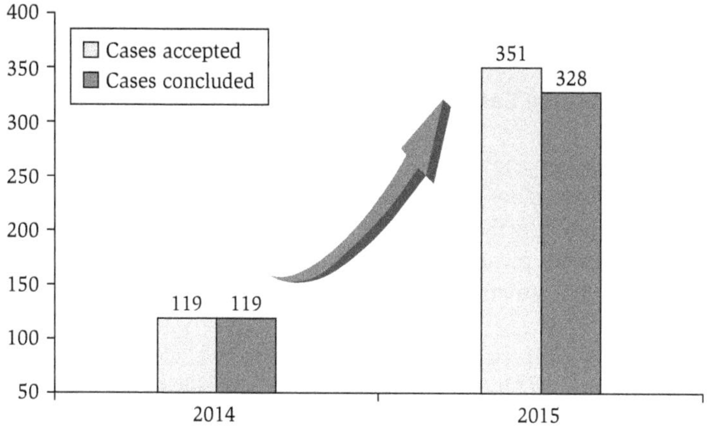

Source: compiled by the authors from public data

Figure 14.5 Types of FTX-Related Cases Accepter in 2015[44]

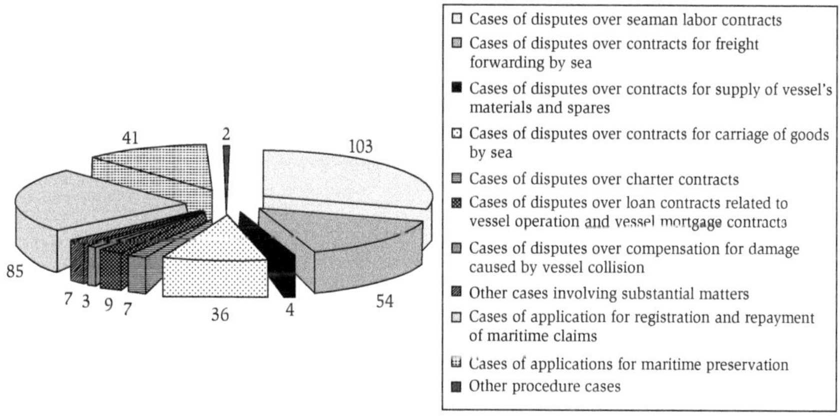

Source: compiled by the authors from public data.

As to the cases heard by the FTZ Maritime Courts in Guangdong, the various branches of the Guangzhou Maritime Court accepted 474 cases, primarily contract cases involving sea shipping, or a combination of sea and river transportation cases,

44. *Source: Compiled by the Authors from Public Data.*

primarily arising in Shekou, Shenzhen, with Guangzhou cases second, and Zhuhai disputes the fewest.[45]

Issues related to civil procedure law also affect the willingness of foreign parties in maritime cases to make use of the Chinese maritime courts.

[F] Administrative Cases

In the area of administrative law, the FTZ Opinion calls on the FTZ courts to forcefully hear cases against government authorities, and both support and monitor government actions, including promoting the disclosure of government information (within limits). The FTZ Opinion reminds local courts that they should provide judicial suggestions[46] to government bodies in situations in which administrative litigation reveals underlying legal problems.

According to the white papers issued thus far, relatively few administrative cases against FTZ authorities. In Shanghai, for example, up to the spring of 2018, nineteen cases were heard, most of them against the industry and commerce (business registration and regulation) authorities, as shown in Figure 14.6.[47]

Figure 14.6 Administrative Case Type in Pudong FTZ

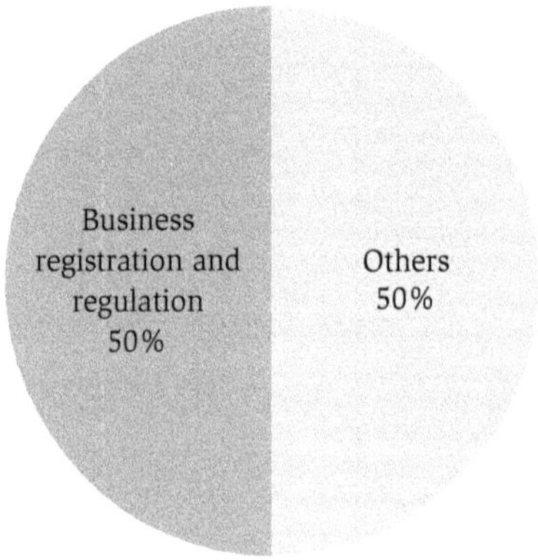

45. *See supra* note 39.
46. On the institution of judicial suggestions, *see* Liu Sixuan and Li Yougen, Why Does social management need judicial suggestions, Renmin Chinese L. Rev. 1-26 (2014) available at https://heinonline.org/HOL/LandingPage?handle = hein.journals/renmin2&div = 6&id = &page = .
47. See *supra* note 38 at 26.

[G] Arbitration Issues

Some of the most important content in the FTZ Opinion relates to arbitration issues and that has attracted the most attention from the professional community.[48] Those comments have focused on several important policy changes that indicate that the SPC is taking steps to liberalize and internationalize China's current arbitration regime within the confines of its authority. SPC policy and judicial interpretations may not contradict national law. This section will discuss an important aspect of the FTZ Opinion related to arbitration matters that has escaped the notice of most other commentators. That aspect relates to the centralization of the review of arbitration-related matters.

The provision that has attracted the most attention is Section 9 of the FTZ Opinion, which states that, if two wholly foreign owned enterprises (WFOEs) (which are Chinese legal persons) that are registered within a pilot FTZ enter into an agreement to submit disputes to arbitration seated outside China, the courts should not hold the arbitration agreement invalid because the dispute concerned is not foreign-related. Generally, only foreign-related disputes can be arbitrated with a seat outside mainland China and Chinese courts will usually hold arbitration clauses submitting "non-foreign related" disputes to arbitration outside China invalid. Normally disputes between two WFOEs would not be regarded as foreign-related, and could not be submitted to arbitration seated outside of China. The rule set out in the FTZ Opinion crystalizes the ruling of the Shanghai No.1 Intermediate People's court in November 2015 in the Golden Landmark case upholding the enforcement of a SIAC award although both parties were WFOEs registered in the Shanghai Pilot Free Trade.

Additionally, the second important innovation in the FTZ Opinion is the language in Section 9 permitting FTZ-registered enterprises (either domestic or foreign-invested) to select ad hoc arbitration (non-institutional arbitration), if their arbitration clause fulfills certain elements: The arbitration clause must designate a specific particular place in China; specific arbitrator(s), and specific arbitration rules.[49]

Section 9 of the FTZ Opinion is being read by the professional community as allowing arbitration administered by non-Chinese arbitration institutions in China, if all parties to the arbitration are companies registered within a pilot free trade zone. In the past, the generally accepted position has been that arbitrations seated in mainland China must be administered by domestic arbitration commissions. The FTZ Opinion "codifies" the SPC's determination in the 2013 Longlide case, where it upheld an arbitration agreement that provided for ICC arbitration with a "*place of jurisdiction*" in Shanghai.

On centralizing the review of arbitration-related matters with more specialized judges, in retrospect it is clear that the SPC used the Shanghai FTZ courts to pilot

48. *See*, for example, https://www.omm.com/resources/alerts-and-publications/publications/china-law-and-policy-august-2017/, https://hsfnotes.com/arbitration/2017/01/13/china-extends-access-to-offshore-arbitration/; http://arbitrationblog.kluwerarbitration.com/2017/05/14/enterprises-in-chinas-free-trade-zones-enter-2017-with-new-options-for-arbitration/.

49. Enterprises in China's Free Trade Zones Enter 2017 with New Options for Arbitration, Jan. 20, 2017, http://en.anjielaw.com/news_detail/newsId=462.html.

measures subsequently incorporated into SPC provisions applicable nationwide. In May, 2017, the SPC issued Notice Concerning Some Questions regarding the centralized handling of judicial review of arbitration cases, requiring lower courts to channel decisions related to the judicial review of arbitration to more specialized judges.[50] The SPC provisions were piloted in guidance that the #2 Shanghai Intermediate People's Court issued in 2014.[51] An official explanation of that court indicates that the SPC encouraged that court to pilot measures for the rest of the country.[52]

[H] Civil Procedure Law

Data analysis from the FTZ courts indicates that most cases are resolved by judgment. This relates to issues with Chinese civil procedure law discussed below (Figure 14.7).

Figure 14.7 FTZ Courts Dispute Settlement Mechanisms

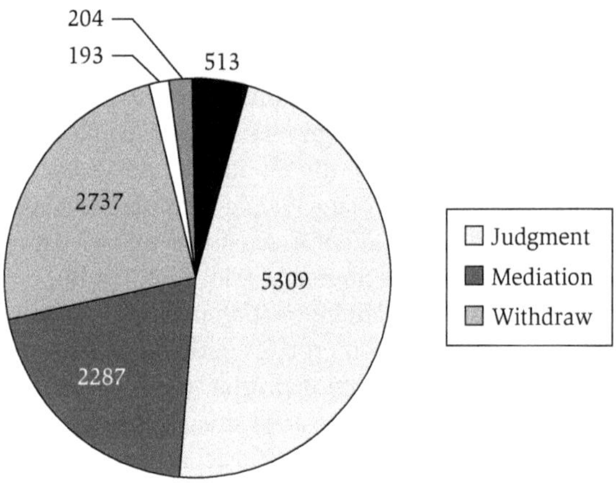

Statistics from the Shanghai maritime court are similar, as shown in Figure 14.8.

50. Finder, Susan, Supreme People's Court strengthens judicial review of arbitration, Nov. 9, 2017, https://supremepeoplescourtmonitor.com/2017/11/09/supreme-peoples-court-strengthens-judicial-review-of-arbitration/.
51. Shanghai No.2 Intermediate People's Court Opinions on Judicial Review and Enforcement of Arbitration Cases Applying China (Shanghai) Pilot Free Trade Zone Arbitration Rules, http://www.shiac.org/upload/day_140616/201406161008565800.pdf.
52. Shanghaishi dier zhongji renminfayuan guanyu shiyong "zimaoqu zhongcai guize" zhongcai anjian sifa shencha he zhixing de ruogan yijian de jiedu (Explanation of the Shanghai No.2 Intermediate People's Court Opinions on Judicial Review and Enforcement of "FTZ Arbitration Rules"), (http://www.shezfy.com/view.html?id=100117.

Figure 14.8 Methods of Settlement of FTZ-Related Cases Involving Substantial Matters in 2015

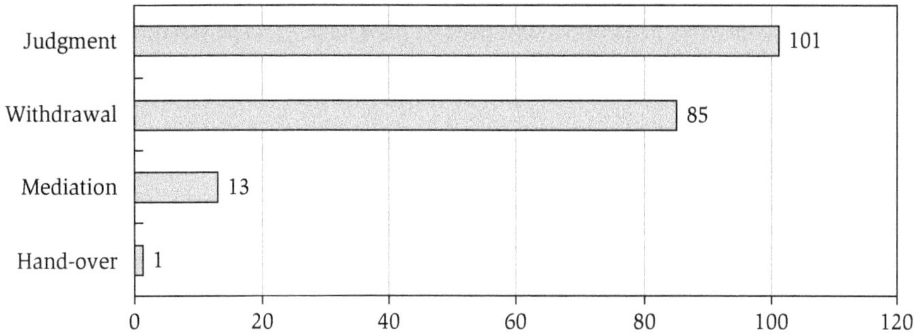

Source: Elaborated by the author from Public Statistics from the Shanghai maritime court (see http://shhsfy.gov.cn/hsfyywwx/hsfyywwx/index.html)

In the area of civil procedure law, the FTZ Opinion mentions issues related to service of process, so that companies that are "registered in an FTZ and operating out of FTZ" can be served and foreign parties can be served through their FTZ office or enterprise. Service of process reform continues to be a concern of the SPC and was included in the latest round of judicial reforms.

One of the critical issues for cross-border parties, not mentioned in the FTZ Opinion, because it relates to an issue beyond its control, is the formalistic requirements in most courts for a variety of documents fundamental to being a litigant to be notarized and consularized. The reason the Chinese courts impose these requirements is that China is not yet a party (except as applied to the Hong Kong Special Administrative Region) to the 1961 Hague Convention on Abolishing the Requirement of Legalization for Foreign Public Documents.[53] As explained below, these formalistic requirements create obstacles for many cross-border parties to use the Chinese courts to defend their rights.

These formalistic requirements start with the status and identity of the litigant, continues with the authorization of a foreign litigant of its lawyer or other representative in court. For a corporate litigant, it means that its evidence of corporate existence must be notarized and legalized, an expensive and time-consuming process. For parties registered in jurisdictions without a nearby Chinese embassy or consulate, it can mean that they are unable to enforce their rights when infringed in a Chinese court. This requirement also extends to a letter of authorization from a foreign litigant to its counsel.

Another set of formalistic requirements attaches to evidence from abroad. It also includes all sorts of evidence that may be required to provide a litigant's case.

53. *See* Convention of Oct. 5, 1961 Abolishing the Requirement of Legalisation for Foreign Public Documents (Entry into force: Jan. 24, 1965) available at https://assets.hcch.net/docs/b12ad529-5f75-411b-b523-8eebe86613c0.pdf.

Particular difficulties are posed by electronic evidence, such as telephone recordings, text messages, and content from the Internet, about which Chinese civil procedure law lacks settled rules, but pose particular problems when the evidence comes from abroad. Some Guangdong courts are taking a more flexible approach in relation to extraterritorial evidence, but this is determined on a case-by-case basis.[54]

Yet other obstacles are imposed on a litigant seeking to rely on foreign governing law, an issue addressed in the FTZ Opinion, expanding previous SPC guidance on this issue. Under Chinese law, foreign law may be applied by a Chinese court either by a court ascertaining foreign law or a party providing evidence of foreign law. The FTZ Opinion contains specific guidance on both. It repeats prior guidance allowing Chinese courts to default to Chinese law when parties have agreed upon foreign law governing law but fail to provide evidence of foreign law within a reasonable period. The SPC direct courts to ascertain foreign law within its powers when it is applicable, based on Chinese conflict of law rules. The practice is that many Chinese courts require proof of foreign law to be provided though a legal opinion that has been notarized and legalized. Although Judge Gao Xiaoli, now deputy head of the SPC's #4 Civil Division has written in a 2014 scholarly article that she disagrees with the practice, it remains prevalent.[55] The FTZ Opinion also permits an expert jointly designated by parties before the hearing of the Court of First Instance to testify. While this is a useful new rule, when parties are in hostile litigation, it may be difficult for them to agree upon an expert, whose testimony may affect the claim or defense of the parties. Although the FTZ Opinion permits a court to ascertain foreign law as permitted under Chinese civil procedure law, the extended period of time needed to ascertain foreign law and the pressure on judges and courts to close cases in a timely manner often means that judges find that foreign law cannot be ascertained. The issue of ascertainment of foreign law continues to be an ongoing one for the Chinese courts. Judge Shen Hongyu of the SPC has recently written and spoken on these issues, proposing better ways to ascertain foreign law.[56]

§14.03 CONCLUSION

The FTZ Opinion is an example of how the SPC "makes law" while supporting the Party and government in issuing judicial policy documents to support important government initiatives. It "makes law" by creating or shaping legal rules, rather than a formalistic sense under Chinese law. It does so by signaling an evolution of judicial policy, establishing new legal rules, and directing the lower courts. by filling in some of the

54. http://www.gdcourts.gov.cn/web/content/37184-?lmdm = 2001.
55. Meng Yu and Du Guodong, China's Supreme Court Judge Gao Xiaoli Talks About the Ascertainment of Foreign Law in Chinese Courts, https://www.chinajusticeobserver.com/insights/chinas-supreme-court-judge-gao-xiaoli-talks-about-the-ascertainment-of-foreign-law-in-chinese-courts.html.
56. Shen Hongyu, "Yidai yilu" beijingxia guoji shangshi susong yu yuwai fa chaming zhidu de xin fazhan (International commercial litigation with the background of the Belt & Road and new developments in the system of ascertaining extraterritorial law) Nov. 9, 2018, available at https://mp.weixin.qq.com/s/w0kxQyoPT5zGdjPHYnGInw.

gaps left by China's slow legislative process. Rules or policies included in SPC judicial policy documents such as the FTZ Opinion often eventually are crystallized in legal instruments recognized as having the force of law under Chinese law such as SPC judicial interpretations and national law, but the process of formulating both of those is slow and cannot meet the needs of the lower courts, which need to deal properly (politically and legally) with outstanding legal issues pending a more permanent stabilization of legal policy. For those unaware of the distinctive way in which case law is used in China, note that the SPC used the FTZ Opinion to "codify" earlier "case law" in the form of a lower court decision and its own determination. The drafting, content, and significance of the FTZ Opinion reflects the quasi-administrative way, professional yet politically attuned way in which the SPC operates.

The link between FTZ judicial policy and the larger Party and government goal to strengthen the international credibility of China's dispute resolution and rule of is revealed in SPC commentary incorporated into one of the Belt & Road Initiative typical cases:

> Pilot free trade zones are foundational platforms, important nodes, and strategic footholds for China's promotion of the "Belt and Road" construction. Aligning [China's practices] with common international practices, supporting the development of pilot free trade zones, and improving international arbitration and other non-litigation dispute resolution mechanisms will [all] help strengthen the international credibility and influence of China's rule of law.[57]

This analysis shows that the ability of the Chinese courts to have greater international credibility and influence is linked to having some basic legal infrastructure that better meets the expectations of international litigants (and its domestic ones as well). This legal infrastructure relates to both substantive and procedural rules. The highly knowledgeable members of the #4 Civil Division of the SPC are likely acutely aware of these issues. On the procedural side, those include a large number of formalistic requirements creating obstacles for a foreign litigant, lack of discovery procedures, difficulties for a Chinese court to apply the governing law selected by the parties, as well as an absence of institutions needed to make the concerns of litigants known. For these reasons, the newly established China International Commercial Law relaxes some of these formalistic requirements. The performance indicators driving decision making in Chinese courts often leads Chinese judges to ignore the express intent of contracting parties and declare that foreign law cannot be ascertained. A better method of requiring litigating parties to disclose evidence closer to international standards may apparently lead to fewer cases tried in the Chinese courts. A court system, particularly in the FTZs, that operates according to more international standards, particularly procedurally, would better strengthen the international credibility of the Chinese courts.

57. Siemens International Trading (Shanghai) Co., Ltd. and Shanghai Golden Landmark Company Limited, A Case of an Application for the Recognition and Enforcement of a Foreign Arbitral Award (Typical Case #12), https://cgc.law.stanford.edu/belt-and-road/b-and-r-cases/typical-case-12/.

Chapter 15
UNCITRAL: Investor-State Dispute Settlement Reform

Caroline Nicholas

§15.01 BACKGROUND TO UNCITRAL'S WORK ON INVESTOR-STATE DISPUTE SETTLEMENT REFORM

[A] UNCITRAL and Its Mandate

The United Nations Commission on International Trade Law (UNCITRAL) was established in 1966, with a mandate to further 'the promotion of the progressive harmonization and unification of the law of international trade'.[1] In establishing UNCITRAL, the United Nations General Assembly sought to address concerns that 'conflicts and divergences arising from the laws of different States in matters relating to international trade constitute an obstacle to the development of world trade'.[2]

The importance of the ability to enforce contractual obligations and commitments in an efficient and effective manner was a main area of focus in the General Assembly, which noted the 'recognised use of arbitration rather than domestic dispute settlement, with decisions capable of international enforcement' as a key method of settling disputes in international commercial relations, and as one that would both be amenable to and would facilitate such unification or harmonization.[3] States and commentators have regularly emphasized this area of UNCITRAL's work, especially in the context of developing countries in particular need of 'mechanisms to support

1. *See* General Assembly resolution 2205 (XXI) – *Establishment of the United Nations Commission on International Trade Law* (A/RES/2205(XXI)), https://undocs.org/en/A/RES/2205(XXI).
2. *Ibid.*
3. See *Progressive development of the law of international trade: report of the Secretary-General,21st Session*, 1966, A/6396 and Add.1 and 2, https://uncitral.un.org/en/commission/archivaldocs.

long-term and long-distance transactions'.[4] Indeed, UNCITRAL currently has two Working Groups (numbers II and III)[5] working on 'private' dispute settlement[6] and has issued six texts in this field since 2007.[7]

[B] UNCITRAL's Working Methods[8]

A former Legal Counsel of the United Nations, Hans Corell, in 2000, explained that UNCITRAL's success relied on 'two aspects of extraordinary cooperation ...: the cooperation among States participating in the work of the Commission and the cooperation with interested international organisations of the public and private sectors'. [9]

UNCITRAL's work in dispute settlement has long been characterized by cooperation in both these senses. As regards that with organizations, the UNCITRAL Arbitration Rules (1976) were developed after extensive consultation with arbitral institutions and centres of international commercial arbitration, as the General Assembly Resolution adopting them recorded.[10] In fact, the International Commission on Commercial Arbitration had facilitated consultation and discussion of an early draft of the Rules during its Fifth Congress in New Delhi in 1975.[11]

4. *See*, for example, Remarks of Jernej Sekolec, Former secretary of UNCITRAL, *Modern Law for Global Commerce: Proceedings of the Congress of the United Nations Commission on International Trade Law held on the Occasion of the Fortieth Session of the Commission* (Vienna 2007) 18. https://uncitral.un.org/sites/uncitral.un.org/files/media-documents/EN/Colloquia/09-83930_ebook.pdf.
5. UNCITRAL has established six working groups. Each of the working groups is composed of all Member States of the Commission. Working Group II's current topic of work is 'Dispute Settlement' and Working Group III's current topic is Investor-State Dispute Settlement Reform. For further details of the current topics of each Working Group, *see* https://uncitral.un.org/en/working_groups.
6. 'Private' in the sense of dispute settlement outside a national or supranational court structure.
7. UNCITRAL Working Group II developed the United Nations Convention on Transparency in Treaty-based Investor-State Arbitration (New York, 2014) (the 'Mauritius Convention on Transparency'); UNCITRAL Rules on Transparency in Treaty-based Investor-State Arbitration (effective date: 1 April 2014); UNCITRAL Secretariat Guide on the Convention on the Recognition and Enforcement of Foreign Arbitral Awards (2016); UNCITRAL Notes on Organizing Arbitral Proceedings (2016); and the Recommendations to assist arbitral institutions and other interested bodies with regard to arbitration under the UNCITRAL Arbitration Rules (as revised in 2010) (*see* https://uncitral.un.org/en/texts/arbitration). UNCITRAL Working Group III developed the Technical Notes on Online Dispute Resolution (2016, https://uncitral.un.org/en/texts/onlinedispute).
8. For UNCITRAL's rules of procedure, *see* UNCITRAL rules of procedure and methods of work (A/CN.9/638 and Adds. 1–6), and a description of UNCITRAL's working methods in Annex III to the Commission's 2010 report to the General Assembly (A/65/17), both available in https://uncitral.un.org/en/commission.
9. Opening Speech at UNCITRAL's 33rd session, H. Corell, http://www.un.org/law/counsel/uncitral.htm.
10. Adopted in General Assembly resolution 31/98 (1976), and https://uncitral.un.org/sites/uncitral.un.org/files/media-documents/uncitral/en/arb-rules.pdf.
11. ICCA, Resolution of the Fifth International Congress on Arbitration in New Delhi, January 10, 1975 https://www.arbitration-icca.org/media/0/12127372919000/new_delhi_combined.pdf.

Interstate cooperation is an integral part of the UNCITRAL process, to ensure both that UNCITRAL texts are 'widely acceptable as offering solutions appropriate to different legal traditions and to countries at different stages of economic development', considerations that are particularly important in the context of ISDS, in which developed countries bring most cases and the relative share of cases against developing countries remains relatively high.[12] UNCITRAL comprises sixty Member States, structured to ensure that the various geographic regions, different legal traditions and levels of economic development are represented, and thus to support the wide acceptability and suitability of UNCITRAL texts. The Member States are elected from among the UN Member States for terms of six years (the terms of half the members expire every three years).[13] The Commission, meaning the Member States of UNCITRAL meeting in an annual plenary session, sets UNCITRAL's programme of work, and adopts its legislative and other texts.[14]

In addition, all other United Nations Member States, as well as certain international and regional organizations with interest and expertise in the topics under discussion, are invited to attend all the Commission sessions as observers.[15]

The Commission usually assigns substantive preparatory work on topics on UNCITRAL's work programme to one of its Working Groups, which have the same membership structure and observer participants as the Commission. Working Groups generally meet twice per annum and report on their progress to the Commission.[16] The Commission considers and, if appropriate, adopts draft texts recommended by one of its Working Groups.[17] As further explained below,[18] the agreement on texts and their subsequent adoption is based on an intergovernmental process to build consensus among the Member States, meaning that interstate cooperation is indeed a critical element in UNCITRAL's success.

12. For example, in 2016, the relative share of cases against developed countries was 29%, down from 2017's 45%, and developed-country investors brought most of the sixty-two known cases in 2016. *See* UNCTAD, *Investor-State Dispute Settlement: Review of developments in 2016* (2017), http://unctad.org/en/PublicationsLibrary/diaepcb2017d1_en.pdf.
13. *See*, further, *Origin, Mandate and Composition of UNCITRAL*, https://uncitral.un.org/en/about/faq/mandate_composition.
14. UNCITRAL legislative texts include conventions, model laws, and legislative guides. UNCITRAL non-legislative texts, such as the UNCITRAL Arbitration Rules, can be used by parties to international trade contracts. *See*, further, *FAQ – UNCITRAL Texts*, https://uncitral.un.org/en/about/faq/texts.
15. *A Guide to UNCITRAL: Basic Facts about the United Nations Commission on International Trade Law (2013)*, para. 4, https://uncitral.un.org/sites/uncitral.un.org/files/media-documents/uncitral/en/12-57491-guide-to-uncitral-e.pdf. For a discussion of invited organizations in Working Group III, *see* section II.F below.
16. *See Official Records of the General Assembly, Thirty-third Session, Supplement No. 17* (A/33/17), para. 67, reproduced in UNCITRAL Yearbook, vol. IX: 1978, part one, Chapter II, section A, and *A Guide to UNCITRAL, ibid.*, p. 5.
17. *See A Guide to UNICTRAL: Basic facts about the United Nations Commission on International Trade Law* (2007), https://uncitral.un.org/sites/uncitral.un.org/files/media-documents/uncitral/en/12-57491-guide-to-uncitral-e.pdf.
18. *See* section II.E below.

[C] History of UNCITRAL Texts on Arbitration and Transparency in Investor-State Arbitration

The UNCITRAL Arbitration Rules were first adopted in 1976, and were revised in 2010.[19] They are 'used in a wide variety of circumstances covering a broad range of disputes, including disputes between private commercial parties, investor-State disputes, State-to-State disputes and commercial disputes administered by arbitral institutions, in all parts of the world'.[20] Their wide use for the settlement of treaty-based investor-State disputes is well-documented, but the Commission agreed it would not be desirable to include specific provisions on treaty-based arbitration in the UNCITRAL Arbitration Rules.[21]

Nonetheless, the Commission expressed the view that 'the issue of transparency as a desirable objective in investor-State arbitration' and that transparency in that field should be addressed in UNCITRAL's work.[22] The Commission, indeed, agreed expressly by consensus on the importance of ensuring transparency in investor-State dispute resolution, and decided that the topic should be dealt with as a matter of priority immediately after revision of the UNCITRAL Arbitration Rules (which was completed in 2010.)[23] Working Group II started work on transparency in treaty-based arbitration in 2010.

UNCITRAL adopted its Rules on Transparency in Treaty-based Investor-State Arbitration (the 'Rules on Transparency') in 2013, recognizing 'the need for provisions on transparency in the settlement of treaty-based investor-State disputes to take account of the public interest involved in such arbitrations'.[24] The Rules on Transparency make covered treaty-based investor-State arbitrations open and accessible to the public. They apply to investor-State arbitrations initiated pursuant to an investment treaty concluded on or after 1 April 2014, and make public case-related information and documents, provide public access to hearings, and provide for submissions by amici curiae and non-disputing State parties.[25] In adopting the Transparency Rules, the General Assembly expressed its belief 'that rules on transparency in treaty-based investor-State arbitration would contribute significantly to the establishment of a harmonized legal framework for a fair and efficient settlement of international investment disputes, increase transparency and accountability and promote good governance'. [26]

19. The texts of the various iterations of the Arbitration Rules are available at https://uncitral.un.org/en/texts/arbitration/contractualtexts/arbitration.
20. *See* General Assembly Resolution 65/22 (2010).
21. *See Official Records of the General Assembly, Sixty-third Session, Supplement No. 17* (A/63/17), para. 314.
22. *Ibid.*
23. *Ibid.*
24. *Official Records of the General Assembly, sixty-eighth Session, Supplement No. 17* (A/68/17), Annex I, at C.
25. For further details, *see* both the text of the Rules and a summary at https://uncitral.un.org/en/texts/arbitration/contractualtexts/transparency.
26. Sixth Recital, General Assembly Resolution 68/109.

UNCITRAL's commitment to transparency in investment treaty arbitration was further underscored by the adoption of the United Nations Convention on Transparency in Treaty-based Investor-State Arbitration (the 'Mauritius Convention on Transparency') on 10 December 2014.[27] The Mauritius Convention extended the scope of the Transparency Rules, by providing a mechanism for them to apply to arbitrations under investment treaties concluded before 1 April 2014. Under the Mauritius Convention, the Transparency Rules apply to earlier treaties where parties to the relevant treaty, or disputing parties, agree to their application.[28] They also apply to all disputes arising out of treaties concluded on or after 1 April 2014, using the UNCITRAL Arbitration Rules, unless the parties otherwise agree.

The Commission had agreed in 2010 that UNCITRAL Working Group II might bring additional issues arising in investment treaty arbitration to its attention.[29] In 2015, The Commission heard that investment treaty arbitration posed further challenges, and proposals for reform that were under discussion by a number of organizations were described.[30] After consideration of some ongoing reform efforts, possible reform options, and possible mechanisms for States to incorporate those options into their existing and future investment treaties in 2016,[31] and after further consultations with a broad range of stakeholders, the Commission gave a mandate to its Working Group III to work on ISDS reform in 2017.[32]

§15.02 MANDATE GIVEN TO UNCITRAL WORKING GROUP III TO WORK ON ISDS REFORM

The Commission's mandate to Working Group III is expressed in broad terms: to 'work on the possible reform of investor-State dispute settlement (ISDS)'. The work involves three stages: '(i) [to] identify and consider concerns regarding ISDS; (ii) [to] consider whether reform was desirable in light of any identified concerns; and (iii) if the Working Group were to conclude that reform was desirable, [to] develop any relevant

27. Text available at https://uncitral.un.org/en/texts/arbitration/conventions/transparency. The Convention entered into force on 18 October 2017. The Convention's provisions apply to investment treaty arbitration where the parties are States parties to the Convention, subject to reservations, and where claimants agree to the application of the Transparency Rules.
28. Explanation by the UNCITRAL Secretariat, https://uncitral.un.org/en/texts/arbitration/conventions/transparency.
29. A/65/17, *supra* note 8, para. 191.
30. *Official Records of the General Assembly, Seventieth Session, Supplement No. 17* (A/70/17), paras. 269–274.
31. Notably, including as that under the Mauritius Convention. *See* Commission Report 2016, *Official Records of the General Assembly, Seventy-first Session, Supplement No. 17* (A/71/17), paras. 187–194.
32. *Official Records of the General Assembly, Seventy-second Session, Supplement No. 17* (A/72/17), para. 264. *See*, also, Notes by the Secretariat on Possible future work in the field of dispute settlement: Concurrent proceedings in international arbitration (A/CN.9/915); on Possible future work in the field of dispute settlement: Ethics in international arbitration (A/CN.9/916); and on Possible future work in the field of dispute settlement: Reforms of investor-State dispute settlement (ISDS) (A/CN.9/917); and in Investor-State Dispute Settlement Framework – Compilation of comments (A/CN.9/918) and Addenda, https://uncitral.un.org/en/commission.

solutions to be recommended to the Commission.' The Commission agreed that broad discretion should be left to the Working Group in discharging its mandate.[33]

Reflecting both UNCITRAL's long-standing collaborative approach to legislative development, and the importance of the stakeholder perspective in investment treaty arbitration,[34] the Commission expressly added that 'any solutions devised would be designed taking into account the ongoing work of relevant international organizations and with a view of allowing each State the choice of whether and to what extent it wishes to adopt the relevant solution(s)'.[35]

The Commission emphasized the need for the work of Working Group III to include engagement with diverse stakeholders, including intergovernmental organs and organizations such as United Nations Conference on Trade and Development (UNCTAD), the World Trade Organization (WTO), the Organisation for Economic Co-operation and Development (OECD), International Centre for the Settlement of Investment Disputes (ICSID) and Permanent Court of Arbitration (PCA).[36] Finally, it required the Working Group, in line with the UNCITRAL process, to 'ensure that the deliberations, while benefiting from the widest possible breadth of available expertise from all stakeholders, would be government-led with high-level input from all governments, consensus-based and be fully transparent'.[37]

Before turning to the deliberations at the first two sessions of the Working Group on the questions before it, the next sections of this Chapter will consider the Commission's instructions on how the Working Group is to undertake its work in some detail and in the historical context of UNCITRAL.

[A] Broad Discretion Given to the Working Group in Discharging Its Mandate

The mandate of Working Group III was given after extensive discussion of issues that ISDS raised.[38] That discussion noted, among other things, that, 'discussion on ISDS reforms should be undertaken without prejudging the outcome and should not exclude any specific options. There was a general preference that work should cover the widest range of issues and possible solutions,'[39] and 'UNCITRAL should not rush to hasty conclusions about the need for reform or solutions for addressing issues'.[40] Consequently, the Working Group itself 'should determine the specific issues to be considered',[41] which the Commission noted might include concurrent proceedings and a code

33. A/72/17, *ibid.*, para. 264.
34. A/68/17, *supra* note 24, Annex I, at C.
35. A/72/17, *supra* note 32, para. 264.
36. *Ibid.*, para. 251.
37. *Ibid.*, para. 264.
38. *See*, both the discussion in the Commission session set out in A/72/17, *supra* note 32, paras. 240–246, and A/CN.9/918 and Addenda, *supra* note 32.
39. A/72/17, *supra* note 32, para. 252.1
40. *Ibid.*
41. *Ibid.*, para. 254.

of ethics, the consideration of the idea of a permanent multilateral investment court, an appellate mechanism, State-to-State dispute settlement mechanisms and any other means of investment dispute resolution, regional courts, appointment or selection of judges or arbitrators, the seat of arbitration, applicable law and fees, as well as overall cost of ISDS and the nature and enforcement of awards or judgment.[42]

[B] Allowing Each State the Choice of Whether and to What Extent It Wishes to Adopt the Relevant Solution(s)

UNCITRAL's Member States adopt texts upon recommendation from a Working Group (or, less commonly, following a Secretariat-led project)[43] at a Commission session. The Commission's decision is accompanied by a request to all States to use the text concerned. For example, when adopting the Transparency Rules, the Commission 'Recommend[ed] the use of the Rules on Transparency in Treaty-based Investor-State Arbitration and the UNCITRAL Arbitration Rules (with new Article 1, paragraph 4, as adopted in 2013) in relation to the settlement of investment disputes within the scope of their application as defined in article 1 of the Rules, and invites parties that include the UNCITRAL Rules on Transparency in Treaty-based Investor-State Arbitration in their investment treaties to advise the Commission accordingly.'[44]

This request underscores that UNCITRAL texts require enacting States to take steps to use and implement them (the accession process for a treaty, or the domestic enactment of a Model Law or of a law based on a Legislative Guide, and so on): the Commission has noted, '[t]he adoption of an instrument or a text by consensus [does] not give it any binding nature.'[45] Hence, for example, the Mauritius Convention entered into force on 8 October 2017, six months after the third State ratified it.[46]

When discussing the terms of the mandate to be given to Working Group III, the Commission noted the particular importance of flexibility in use of any outcome of the work of Working Group III. It emphasized, reflecting the divergent views that States had expressed on the question of ISDS reform, that future work 'should be without any prejudice to possible approaches States might wish to adopt in the future. States had different perspectives, and diversity in approaches should be fully respected. It was mentioned that participation of States in the process should not be construed as a commitment to the result of the work'.[47]

42. *Ibid.*, paras. 255–256.
43. *A Guide to UNCITRAL*, *supra* note 15, pp. 20–21.
44. Decision adopting the UNCITRAL Rules on Transparency in Treaty-based Investor-State Arbitration and the UNCITRAL Arbitration Rules (with a new Article 1, para. (4), as adopted in 2013), A/68/17, *supra* note 24, para. 128.
45. A/72/17, *supra* note 32, para. 259.
46. For the current status of the Convention, which has twenty-three signatories as at May 2018, *see* https://treaties.un.org/pages/ViewDetails.aspx?src=IND&mtdsg_no=XXII-3&chapter=22.
47. A/72/17, *supra* note 32, para. 253.

[C] Engagement with Diverse Stakeholders and Taking into Account Ongoing Work of Relevant International Organizations

The mandate to Working Group III emphasizes the need for its work to include engagement with diverse stakeholders, including intergovernmental organs and organizations such as the UNCTAD, WTO, OECD, the ICSID and the PCA.[48]

This engagement reflects UNCITRAL's overall mandate to 'establish(...) and maintain(...) a close collaboration with the United Nations Conference on Trade and Development' and to maintain 'liaison with other United Nations organs and specialized agencies concerned with international trade'.[49]

The Commission heard of reforms when considering the mandate to be given to Working Group III. ICSID reported on a process to reform its rules on ISDS.[50] UNCTAD reported to the Commission on its 2015 Road Map for IIA Reform (undertaken in the context of its Investment Policy Framework for Sustainable Development).[51] The OECD reported on its ongoing work on investment treaties, which had started in 2011.[52] The UNCITRAL Secretariat has therefore encouraged those organizations to provide materials for the Working Group to consider, and the resulting submissions are available on its website, both as written materials produced specifically for the Working Group and as links to published papers on reforms ongoing in other organizations. In addition, the European Union has submitted a paper describing concerns about ISDS in its current form to the Working Group (as, indeed, have certain Member States).[53]

As reported to the Commission, the Secretariat has participated in events organised by UNCTAD, the OECD, European Commission, International Chamber of Commerce, and a number of arbitral institutions and bodies,[54] with a view to raising awareness of UNCITRAL's work and the issues under consideration, and of encouraging participation and the provision of further materials for the Working Group.

There is considerable interest in UNCITRAL's work on ISDS reform in both academic circles and from practitioners. These groups of stakeholders are coming together with a view to providing contributions from their perspectives on the issues before the Working Group and have held a series of events on the margins of the sessions of the Working Group. While they are independent from the UNCITRAL Secretariat and UNCITRAL more generally, the Secretariat has encouraged these groups to include diverse membership and to take account of the comments of States at the Working Group sessions, so as to enhance the potential relevance of their work to that of the Working Group. The UNCITRAL website will provide links to information

48. *Ibid.*, para. 251.
49. A/RES/2205(XXI), *supra* note 1, sect. II, para. 8.
50. *See* A/CN.9/917, *supra* note 32, para. 67, and the information on the website of ICSID, at https://icsid.worldbank.org/en/.
51. A/CN.9/918/Add.7, *supra* note 32, section 2.
52. *Ibid.*, paras. 1-13.
53. *See* the Working Papers available on the webpage of Working Group III, https://uncitral.un.org/en/working_groups/3/investor-state, and the On-line resources https://uncitral.un.org/en/library/online_resources/investor-state_dispute.
54. *See* Note by the Secretariat, Coordination activities (A/CN.9/948), paras. 19–20, https://uncitral.un.org/en/commission.

on these groups and any materials they eventually publish, so that the Working Group can take them into account should it so wish.[55]

For discussions of participation in and manner of conducting the Working Group's deliberations, *see* Subsections D-F below.

[D] Government-Led Process

The Commission assigned the topic of ISDS reform to Working Group III, with the mandate as set out above including a requirement to ensure that the process be 'government-led'. This process requirement has particular resonance in the context of ISDS, which, unlike most UNCITRAL legislative development topics, raises complex issues of public international law.[56] When discussing the terms of the Working Group III mandate, the Commission noted the importance of such a process in which 'States would be able to openly discuss and consider a wide range of issues',[57] and stating that, in light of the policy issues involved, 'Governments should have a leading role in that process'.[58] UNCITRAL's working methods provide that while all participants can speak during the deliberations, only UNCITRAL Member States take decisions in Working Group (and, indeed, Commission) sessions. This approach enables States to lead the process and has long been reflected in UNCITRAL's description of its working methods.[59] Consequently, the role of invited observer organizations in participating in Working Group sessions is to provide information that States may take into account,[60] a point also recalled by the Commission in underscoring the need to engage with diverse stakeholders.[61]

Another aspect of participation in the Working Group III mandate is that 'high-level' input from governments is urged, reflecting the points made during discussions in the Commission, in light of the policy issues involved among other things, that governments should be represented in the process 'by officials with adequate expertise and experience in negotiating investment treaties or investment chapters in free trade agreements and with exposure to claims related to investor-State dispute settlement'.[62]

---

55. *See* https://uncitral.un.org/en/library/bibliography.
56. Report of Working Group III (Investor-State Dispute Settlement Reform) on the work of its thirty-fourth session – Part I (A/CN.9/930/Rev.1), para. 26, https://uncitral.un.org/en/working_groups/3/investor-state.
57. A/72/17, *supra* note 32, para. 250.
58. *Ibid.*
59. *See* A/65/17, *supra* note 8, Annex III, and UNCITRAL rules of procedure and methods of work: Note by the Secretariat (A/CN.9/639), para. 14(c). The approach was reaffirmed by the Commission in 2013: 'the development of UNCITRAL texts as a matter of course should be undertaken through the working group process. In that regard, the Commission recalled the link between that formal negotiation process and the universal applicability and hence acceptance of UNCITRAL texts, the importance of the transparency that that process conferred, and the need to continue the inclusive working methods of UNCITRAL.' *See*, further A/68/17, *supra* note 24, para. 300.
60. *A Guide to UNCITRAL*, *supra* note 15, p. 6.
61. A/72/17, *supra* note 32, para. 251.
62. *Ibid.*, para. 250.

[E] Consensus-Based Decision-Making

The Commission has resolved to reach decisions by consensus as far as possible.[63] As a general matter, consensus does not require unanimity, but is instead based on a flexible notion that is characterized by a strong majority of opinions and the absence of formal objection and vote,[64] a point that the Commission repeated when setting the mandate for Working Group III.[65]

The Sixth Committee of the General Assembly has emphasized that 'the consensus method [is] conducive to achieving a larger cooperation among countries having different legal, economic and social systems and [ensures] that the uniform rules derived from the work of the Commission [are] generally acceptable'.[66] It has also stressed the benefits of this approach to developing and (what would now be termed) transition States in particular,[67] an important consideration given that a significant motivation in establishing UNCITRAL was to offer developing countries a voice in the preparation of international trade law texts,[68] and as developing countries (along with smaller countries) are among the comparatively more active in adopting UNCITRAL texts.[69] These points of general application have particular resonance in the ISDS context: not only have developing countries been frequent respondents in ISDS cases, the comments provided to the Commission included the views of many about the challenges that ISDS cases posed,[70] and the Commission agreed on the need to take into account 'that States had different experiences and expectations with regard to the investor-State dispute settlement regime'.[71]

It is self-evident that the value of UNCITRAL's consensus would be undermined if it were based on an insufficiently diverse practice and experience. The General Assembly required UNCITRAL to 'bear in mind the interests of all peoples, and particularly those of developing countries, in the extensive development of international trade',[72] and the composition of UNCITRAL's Member States is therefore designed to ensure diversity. The Member States comprise fourteen African States,

63. A/65/17, *supra* note 8, Annex III, summary of conclusions, para. 2.
64. *See*, further, A/CN.9/638/Add.4, *supra* note 8 and *Official Records of the General Assembly, Sixty-fourth Session, Supplement No. 17* (A/64/17), para. 387.
65. A/72/17, *supra* note 32, para. 258.
66. A/CN.9/638/Add.4, *supra* note 8, para. 7. *See*, also, A/68/17, *supra* note 24, para. 300.
67. *Ibid.*, Para.7, and *See* A/CN.9/638/Add.4, *supra* note 8.
68. A/6396 and Add. 1 and 2, *supra* note 3, para. 210(b), in which it was stated that developing countries had 'had the opportunity to participate only to a small degree in the activities carried out up to now in the field of harmonization, unification, and modernization of the law of international trade. Yet those are the countries that especially need adequate and modern laws, which are indispensable to gaining equality in their international trade'.
69. *A strategic direction for UNCITRAL* (A/CN.9/752), para. 44, https://uncitral.un.org/en/commission.
70. A/CN.9/918 and Addenda, *supra* note 32.
71. A/72/17, *supra* note 32, para. 250.
72. A/RES/2205(XXI), *supra* note 1, para. 9.

fourteen Asian States, eight Eastern European States, ten Latin American and Caribbean States and fourteen Western European and other States.[73] Observer organizations are also invited to ensure diversity, as further explained in the following subsection.

[F] Inclusive Deliberations

The Commission also emphasized when issuing the mandate to Working Group III that the participation of intergovernmental organs and organizations with much experience in ISDS reform would be important. Relevant international organizations mentioned were UNCTAD, the WTO, OECD, ICSID and PCA.[74] The Commission, further, recognized the benefits of involving experts, investors, academia and practitioners, which reflects the importance that States in the discussion had placed on analysing available data and information of existing international investment agreements and ISDS mechanisms to build the basis for discussion.[75]

This approach to inclusiveness is a key attribute of UNCITRAL. Indeed, when setting the membership of UNCITRAL in 1966, and expanding it in 1973 and 2002,[76] the General assembly sought to encourage participation from all countries and regions, in its work so that the various geographic regions and the principal economic and legal systems of the world would be fairly represented.[77]

Securing sufficiently broad and informed participation in UNCITRAL's work has also long been recognized to involve challenges. At the second session of the Commission, in 1969, several representatives 'noted that the success of the Commission's work depended on the selection by Member States of skilled experts for the sessions of the Commission and the meetings of its working groups', and prior to the establishment of UNCITRAL, the General Assembly had observed that there could be a scarcity of qualified personnel within national administrations able 'to devote their limited amount of time to the preparation and adoption of laws approving international conventions'.[78]

A noted aspect of the challenge is the cost of participation in Working Group and Commission sessions, especially as the participants bear their own travel and related costs at UNCITRAL's sessions (which take place alternately in New York and Vienna). Recognizing this, the General Assembly established an UNCITRAL Trust Fund for Travel Assistance to assist delegates from developing countries to attend UNCITRAL sessions in Vienna in 1993.[79] Nonetheless, States have still queried whether participation is sufficiently broad and representative. For example, in 2007, a Member State expressed concerns about a 'perception that the working methods of the Commission and its working groups might not sufficiently encourage effective participation in the

73. UNCITRAL maintains a list of current Member States at https://uncitral.un.org/en/about/faq/mandate_composition.
74. *Ibid.*
75. *Ibid.*, paras. 249 and 251.
76. *A Guide to UNCITRAL*, *supra* note 15, p. 2.
77. A/6396 and Add. 1 and 2, *supra* note 3, para. 212.
78. *See*, for example, A/6396/Add.1, *supra* note 3, para. 9.
79. General Assembly Resolution 48/32, 9 December 1993.

creation of UNCITRAL standards or the subsequent enactment of those standards by a broad range of States';[80] and, in 2008, another Member State regretted 'that during the last year several members of UNCITRAL were not represented at its sessions and working groups'.[81]

Working Group III has itself noted that 'active and wide participation by both developing and developed States was essential to ensure the effectiveness and legitimacy of the UNCITRAL process in implementing the mandate'.[82] This point echoed the view stated in the Commission that UNCITRAL provided a forum to discuss issues in an inclusive manner.[83] The European Union and the Swiss Agency for Development and cooperation have, thus far, provided contributions to the Trust Fund to allow participation of developing States in Working Group III.[84]

The UNCITRAL Secretariat has engaged in awareness-raising of UNCITRAL's work on ISDS reform through participation in the events referred to in its annual report to the Commission on coordination activities,[85] and through a series of briefings in New York, Geneva and Vienna, among other locations, to United Nations Member States.

A further resource consideration arises in that effective preparation for the Working Group sessions requires the within-government exchanges and consultations, and some States engage in consultations at the national and local levels (using surveys and other means, in both public and private sectors).[86] Additional efforts are under way to support developing countries from this perspective, too.

These awareness-raising and fund-raising activities have borne fruit: the thirty-fourth session of Working Group III (the first Working Group session to consider ISDS reform) was attended by some 300 persons, comprising eighty delegations representing States, and thirty-five non-State observers (including the European Union, two United Nations System observers (ICSID and UNCTAD), four intergovernmental organizations and twenty-eight invited non-governmental organizations (NGOs)). The thirty-fifth session was attended by some 400 persons, comprising eighty-five delegations representing States, the Holy See, the European Union, and fifty non-State observers (including two United Nations System observers (ICSID and UNIDO), five intergovernmental organizations and forty-three invited NGOs).

Taking account of the Commission's instructions to engage with diverse stakeholders and to take into account ongoing work of relevant international organizations, the UNCITRAL Secretariat has taken steps to ensure as broad and representative stakeholder participation in its work, without prejudice to the government-led process

80. *Official Records of the General Assembly, Sixty-second Session, Supplement No. 17* (A/62/17 (Part I)), para. 234.
81. Austria's delegate, speaking to the Sixth Committee (Legal) of the General Assembly, 2008; *see* http://www.un.org/press/en/2008/gal3346.doc.htm.
82. Report of Working Group III (Investor-State Dispute Settlement Reform) on the work of its thirty-fifth session (A/CN.9/935), para. 15, https://uncitral.un.org/en/commission.
83. A/72/17, *supra* note 32, para. 258.
84. A/CN.9/935, *supra* note 82, para. 16.
85. A/CN.9/948 *supra* note 54.
86. *See*, for example, *U.S. Participation in the International Unification of Private Law: The Making of the UNCITRAL Draft Carriage of Goods by Sea Convention, Mary Helen Carlson*, 31 Tul. Mar. L.J. 615 (2006).

and so far as logistical constraints will allow. Broad participation of international organizations and invited NGOs in UNCITRAL also reflects the Commission's long-standing view that UNCITRAL provides an inclusive forum in which the 'interests not only of States but also of other stakeholders could be considered'.[87]

UNCITRAL has set out criteria and procedures for inviting NGOs to its sessions on its website, which are designed to 'achieve in sum a balanced representation at the sessions of the major viewpoints or interests in the relevant fields in all areas and regions of the world, with the purpose of assisting UNCITRAL to formulate legal texts'.[88] The application of these criteria in the context of ISDS has allowed organizations representing a wide community of stakeholders to be represented: not only those involved in the arbitral process, but also NGOs representing the public, the environment, workers, the investors, among others.[89]

[G] Transparent Deliberations

The Commission recognized the importance of transparency in the Working Group's deliberations,[90] and this importance has been underscored by a statement of UNCITRAL's commitment to transparency recently published on its website, which is reproduced below:

> UNCITRAL operates in a highly transparent environment. The Secretariat provides written materials for the Commission and each working group to consider at their respective sessions, which are made available on the UNCITRAL website in all six official languages of the United Nations in advance of each session. A report of each session, reflecting the main points raised and decisions taken, is posted on the UNCITRAL website as soon as possible after the session concerned. In addition, the Secretariat issues summary records of Commission meetings relating to the formulation of normative texts, though not for meetings of working groups and other discussions at the Commission session. By contrast with verbatim records, summary records contain condensed statements. Finally, the Commission has decided that, as a general rule, digital recordings of both Commission and working group sessions should be made publicly available by posting on the UNCITRAL website.
>
> The reports and, where issued, summary records and the digital recordings of the sessions are made publicly available on the UNCITRAL website after the session concerned. They allow any organization or person to follow both the deliberations leading to the adoption of an UNCITRAL text and the reasons for the policy decisions and drafting reflected in each text. In order to create an environment that allows open and frank discussion on technical questions, it has been the practice in UNCITRAL not to allow live-streaming of UNCITRAL meetings relating

87. A/72/17, *supra* note 32, para. 258.
88. *See* Frequently Asked Question 'What are criteria and procedures for inviting non-governmental organizations (NGOs)?' at https://uncitral.un.org/en/about/faq/methods.
89. Part II of each Working Group Report lists the States and organizations that have taken part. *See* https://uncitral.un.org/en/working_groups.
90. A/72/17, *supra* note 32, para. 258.

to the preparation of normative texts (whether at Commission sessions or in meetings of working groups).[91]

Transparency is thus assured in that all the materials before the Working Group and the reasons for its policy deliberations are available both to participants at the sessions themselves, and also to external observers. Official UNCITRAL documents - UNCITRAL texts, reports to the Commission and Commission Reports, Working Papers submitted to Working Groups and those Groups' Reports - are available in all six official languages of the United Nations. This level of transparency should also serve so as to encourage and enhance the quality of debate on the issues before the Working Group more generally, to the benefit of all stakeholders.

§15.03 ISSUES CONSIDERED AT THE SESSIONS OF WORKING GROUP III

At the first two sessions of Working Group III on ISDS reform, the Working Group based its deliberations on a Note by the Secretariat,[92] and also had before it submissions from States and international organizations.[93]

[A] Thirty-Fourth Session

The Report of the Working Group's thirty-fourth session, which sets out the deliberations in some detail and is in two parts, is available on the Working Group webpage.[94] A short summary of those deliberations follows.

The Working Group agreed to consider the three stages of the mandate set out above in sequence and to undertake a thorough analysis of all relevant issues, with the objective of identifying the core concerns that might justify reform.

As regards the scope of its work, the Working Group considered:

(a) Whether to focus on ISDS under investment treaties, or should also take into account investment laws and contracts. The Working Group decided to focus on treaty-based ISDS, but agreed to reconsider whether it might address contract- and investment law-based ISDS at a later stage.
(b) That its work should focus on investment arbitration, though other types of ISDS mechanisms (negotiation, mediation) might subsequently be included its review.

---

91. *See* Frequently Asked Question 'How are UNCITRAL materials made publicly available?' at https://uncitral.un.org/en/about/faq/methods.
92. *Possible reform of investor-State dispute settlement (ISDS)* (A/CN.9/WG.III/WP.142), https://uncitral.un.org/en/working_groups/3/investor-state.
93. *See Possible reform of investor-State dispute settlement (ISDS) – Submissions from the Government of Thailand, from the European Union, and from International Intergovernmental Organizations*. The materials before the Working Group available *ibid.*
94. *See* A/CN.9/930/Rev.1, *supra* note 56, and *Report of Working Group III (Investor-State Dispute Settlement Reform) on the work of its thirty-fourth session – Part II* (A/CN.9/930/Add.1/Rev.1), available *ibid.*

(c) That it would focus on procedural aspects of investment treaty arbitration as opposed to substantive treaty standards.

The Working Group emphasized the need for a fact-based analysis, but agreed that perceptions on the issues under discussion should be taken into account, as they were relevant to States in policy-making. The particular concerns of developing States and the burden of scarce public funds, as well as the possible restriction of access for small- and medium-sized enterprises, were noted as contextual issues of some importance.

The Working Group also agreed that it would first complete its review of the issues raised by ISDS, and then proceed to analyse the extent to which the identified concerns merited reform and possible solutions if so, together with other related topics yet to be considered, in a holistic approach.

The Working Group analysed the following topics identified in the Secretariat's Note: costs and duration of ISDS proceedings, allocation of costs, security for costs, third-party funding, early dismissal mechanisms and counterclaims. The Working Group exchanged views on these topics in some detail. It also exchanged preliminary views on concerns regarding outcomes in ISDS and, in particular, those arising from some commentators' observations of a lack of consistency and coherence in those outcomes. The Working Group noted that these observations addressed varying aspects of inconsistency, that inconsistency should be distinguished from legitimate distinctions in outcomes, that consistency should not be equated with correctness, and agreed to address the question of ISDS outcomes at its thirty-fifth session.

[B] Thirty-Fifth Session

At the thirty-fifth session, the Working Group continued with its review of the issues raised by ISDS, again on the basis of the Secretariat's Note referred to above. Materials from the Government of Thailand, the European Union, ICSID and the PCA were also submitted to the Working Group.[95] The Working Group's report is available on the Working Group III webpage[96] and, again, a summary follows.

The Working Group acknowledged that some States had had more opportunity than others to consider the wide-ranging issues in ISDS, and that the process should allow all delegates to contribute meaningfully without undue delay in making progress with the discussion.

The Working Group continued the discussion on coherence and consistency in ISDS outcomes that it had started at the previous session. It recalled that there were two key questions for consideration: the desirable level of consistency in ISDS outcomes and the extent to which undesirable inconsistency was perceived to be a concern. The Working Group agreed on the benefits of consistency (including in enhancing legal certainty and the predictability of the investment framework for both the State and the

95. *See* the materials for the 35th session, 23–27 April, New York, at https://uncitral.un.org/en/working_groups/3/investor-state.
96. A/CN.9/935, *supra* note 82.

investor and in promoting efficiency). It took note of the difficulty of achieving consistency in interpreting investment treaties negotiated by different parties, with specific objectives, and on the other hand that investment standards were often similar. The importance of correctness in outcomes was also emphasized.

The Working Group also exchanged views on the impact of unjustified inconsistency, including on the credibility and negative public opinion of the ISDS mechanism. Other considerations included potential constraints on States' regulatory activity, and increased risks to investors and consequently possible inhibitions on investment.

The Working Group agreed that research to provide further information on the prevalence of inconsistency would be helpful. Noting the interdependence of many of the issues before it, the Working Group underlined that efficiency, flexibility and cost-effectiveness should guide possible reforms on these matters.

The Working Group also considered concerns arising out of the party-appointment mechanism for arbitrators, including the following aspects: lack of sufficient guarantees of independence and impartiality; the limited number of individuals repeatedly appointed as and lack of diversity among arbitrators in ISDS cases; absence of transparency in the appointment process; individuals acting as counsel and as arbitrators in different ISDS proceedings, raising the possibility of conflicts of interest; perceptions that arbitrators are less cognizant of public interest concerns than judges holding a public office, and third-party funding. The experience of some States and appointing authorities was shared, and the Working Group agreed that further information and data would assist its deliberations, including on the operation of other relevant appointment mechanisms.

While some possible solutions were outlined, the Working Group agreed that solutions would be considered at a later date.

The Working Group also heard from participants on the perceptions of States, investors and the public, including from invited international NGOs. These participants highlighted concerns about the impacts of ISDS, including some discussed above, and more broadly on environmental protection; labour rights; transparency; democracy and the role of the domestic courts; accountability of the investors; and impacts on non-parties and access to justice. The Working Group was encouraged to take a holistic view of ISDS and to bear in mind a range of contextual issues.

§15.04 CONCLUSION

At the end of the thirty-fifth session, the Working Group agreed that its future deliberations would be informed by a list of the concerns raised in the Working Group and suggestions for a framework for those deliberations, together with the additional information it had noted would be helpful during the session. The Working Group is scheduled to meet next in Vienna, from 27 October 2018 to 2 November 2018, at its thirty-sixth session, for that purpose. At the thirty-fifth session, the Working Group also welcomed proposals for intersessional meetings from two States to support progress in its work.

UNCITRAL's work on ISDS reform is therefore proceeding at a measured pace, for the reasons set out above. The Working Group has noted that the concerns identified for future consideration do not presuppose any conclusion on the desirability of reform to address those concerns, and that desirability will be considered as it continues its work. It has emphasized that the government-led approach mandated by the Commission had been supported by the provision of information by States and observer organizations alike.[97] The Commission will review the reports of the thirty-fourth and thirty-fifth sessions of the Working Group at the annual plenary session of the Commission from 25 June – 13 July 2018, in New York. It is anticipated, in light of the constructive manner in which the Working Group has proceeded, supported by awareness- and fund-raising efforts described above, that the Commission will agree that the Commission's instructions on how the Working Group is to undertake its work are being followed, and that the Working Group will contribute to establishing a 'harmonized legal framework for a fair and efficient settlement of international investment disputes, increase[d] transparency and accountability and ... good governance'.[98]

97. A/CN.9/935, *supra* note 82, paras. 98–100.
98. General Assembly Resolution 69/116, fourth Recital. *See also* its resolution adopting the Transparency Rules, 68/109, *supra* note 27.

CHAPTER 16

Goetz v. the Republic of Burundi I&II: How Foreign Investors Challenge 'Free-Zone Regimes'

Olaoye Kehinde

§16.01 INTRODUCTION

The Goetz v. Burundi I[1] and II[2] investment disputes lasted for fifteen years.[3] This timespan challenges the very fundamental notion that arbitration-based dispute settlement serves as a quick and efficient means for settling investor-state disputes.[4] However, political and economic events in Burundi's history provide a broader context for examining the factors responsible for this prolonged dispute over the grant of SEZ status. Since gaining independence from Belgium,[5] a chequered history of ethnic strife

1. *Antoine Goetz and Others v. The Republic of Burundi (I)*, ICSID Case No. ARB/95/3, Decision on Liability (2 September 1998) (hereinafter Goetz I). This award has been translated into English and is reported in James Crawford & Karen Lee (eds), *Goetz and Others v. Republic of Burundi (Case No. ARB/95/3) Decision on Liability dated 2 September 1998 and Award (Embodying the Parties' Settlement Agreement) dated 10 February 1999*, 6 ICSID Reports (2004 Cambridge University Press) 3.
2. *Antoine Goetz and Others v. The Republic of Burundi (II)*, ICSID Case No. ARB/01/2, Award (21 June 2012) (hereinafter Goetz II). The author's English translations are based on this award.
3. The first dispute was instituted in 1995 and an award was made in 1999. The second dispute commenced in 2001 but did not result in an award until 2012.
4. *See* Andrea K Bjorklund, *Improving the International Investment Law and Policy System Report of the Rapporteur*, in *The Evolving International Investment Regime: Expectations, Realities, Options* 213, 223 (Jose E Alvarez & Karl P Sauvant eds, Oxford University Press 2011).
5. *See* Felix Chuks Okoye & Felix N Okoye, *International Law and the New African States* 212 (Sweet and Maxwell 1972); Jan Hendrik Willem Verzijl, *International Law in Historical Perspective* 534 (Martinus Nijhoff Publishers 1973). Ruanda-Urundi were annexed by Germany in 1894. After the First World War, Ruanda-Urundi was a United Nations (UN) Trust territory under Belgium until 1962. The joint history of both states is described as 'false twins' in literature.

has continued to have an adverse effect on Burundi's economy and development.[6] This chapter uses the Goetz disputes as case studies for examining how investment arbitration is used by investors to challenge SEZs.

In 1986, the International Monetary Fund and the World Bank, introduced structural adjustment economic reforms in Burundi as a response to its poor business climate characterised majorly by heavy reliance on coffee exports and poor fiscal policies.[7] As part of this reform, export promotion through the establishment of a free-zone regime was established in 1992. [8] Incidentally, a few years after the World Bank's recommendations, its investor-state dispute mechanism, the International Centre for Settlement of Investment Disputes (ICSID), will become the administering institution for settling a major dispute arising from the functioning of this free-zone regime.[9]

In February 1993, AFFIMET, a mining company owned by the Belgian-based Goetz family was granted a free-zone certificate by Burundi's minister for industry and commerce.[10] This was one of the last executive orders carried out under Major Pierre Buyoya, Burundi's military ruler from September 1987 to July 1993. On 20 August 1993, exactly two months before the assassination of President Melchior Ndadaye (Burundi's first democratically elected and Hutu president) in an attempted *coup d'état*, AFFIMET was informed that its free-zone certificate had been withdrawn.[11] Two months following his assassination, AFFIMET's free-zone certificate was restored, albeit temporarily. A 29 May 1995 ministerial order will finally withdraw the certificate and all rights from AFFIMET.

Between 1993 and 2005, the immediate time span of this dispute, Burundi was embroiled in civil war and conflict.[12] These events rooted in tensions between the usually-dominant Tutsi minority and the Hutu majority, have had a long-lasting effect on economic development of Burundi and the Greater Lakes region.[13] Vacillation by

6. The African Development Bank, *East Africa Economic Outlook 2018: Macro Economic Developments Manufacturing's Comparative Advantage and Competitiveness* 6 (African Development Bank Publications 2018). In 2016, Burundi informed the International Criminal Court that it was withdrawing from the Rome Statute. This withdrawal which took effect in 2017, was in the wake of investigations for crimes against humanity following President Pierre Nkurunziza's successful bid for an 'unconstitutional' third term in office.
7. The World Bank, *Burundi - Third Structural Adjustment Program* 2 (World Bank 1992), http://documents.worldbank.org/curated/en/749801468020992561/Burundi-Third-Structural-Adjustment-Program (accessed 14 January 2018).
8. The World Bank, *Memorandum and Recommendation of the International Development Association to the Executive Directors on a Country Assistance Strategy of the World Bank Group for the Republic of Burundi*, Report No. 14442-BU 11 (1995), http://documents.worldbank.org/curated/en/939651468215697965/text/multi-page.txt (accessed 4 April 2018).
9. Convention on the Settlement of Investment Disputes between States and Nationals of Other States (opened for signature 18 March 1965, entered into force 14 October 1966) ('ICSID Convention').
10. Goetz I, *supra*, footnote 1 para. 5.
11. *Ibid.*, para. 10.
12. Mpazi Sinjela, *The United Nations and Internal Conflicts: A Documentary Survey*, in *IV African Year Book of International Law* 293, 316 (Abdulqawi A Yusuf ed, Martinus Nijhoff Publishers 1997).
13. President Ndadaye was Burundi's first Hutu democratically elected president. His assassination led to ethnic violence resulting in the death of 50,000 civilians. This ethnic conflict is believed to

Burundi officials loyal to these two ethnic groups in the grant of the Goetz consortium's special economic status was an important trigger for the disputes. A poor SEZ regulatory framework and other governance issues were also important causes.[14]

Goetz V Burundi I is notably the second investment treaty-based claim filed before ICSID.[15] Although largely overlooked in current literature, governance of SEZs is integral to international investment law.[16] The Goetz I dispute which is also the first publicly known SEZ related dispute resulting in a final award underscores this important relationship.[17] Also distinct for the Tribunal's flexibility and the length of the dispute,[18] it shows the importance of international investment law and arbitration in governing relationships between host states and investors operating in SEZs. For host states, withdrawal of SEZ status even on grounds of public policy may result in breach of internationally recognised standards of treatment and protection. Thus, expected advantages of attracting foreign direct investment (FDI) through 'favoured' and 'special' treatment may diminish when states are confronted with the costs of investment arbitration.[19] At the same time, the Tribunal's recognition of Burundi's right to file a counterclaim in Goetz II, shows that within legally recognised regulatory space, regulation of SEZs in public interest may serve as an effective defence. For foreign investors, investment-arbitration remains an important tool for challenging host states' unlawful interference with SEZ grants.

This chapter examines, key legal issues and principles which arose in the Goetz disputes. It argues that in accordance with economic evidence, SEZs are not miracle formulas and thus host states must fully understand obligations arising from investment treaties and contracts. This case note is divided into two main sections which in

have been a contributory factor to the Rwanda genocide. *See* Marc Bossut, *UN Human Rights Procedures Regarding Rwanda, Zaire and Burundi 1994–1997*, in *International Law: Theory and Practice: Essays in Honour of Eric Suy* 495 (Eric Suy & Karel Wellens eds, Martinus Nijhoff Publishers 1998); Susan Breau, *The Responsibility to Protect in International Law: An Emerging Paradigm Shift* 221(Routledge 2016).

14. *See* Daniel Behn et al., *Poor States or Poor Governance? Explaining Outcomes in Investment Treaty Arbitration*, PluriCourts Research Paper No. 17-05. SSRN: https://ssrn.com/abstract=2978546.
15. In its decision, the tribunal recognised that when ICSID was established it was envisaged as centre for settling contract-based disputes and not treaty-based disputes (Goetz I para. 67). *See also* Muthucumaraswamy Sornarajah, *Resistance and Change in the International Law on Foreign Investment* 2 (Cambridge University Press 2015).
16. Teresa Cheng, *SEZ: A Catalyst for International Trade and Investment in Unsettling Times*, 20 Journal of World Investment and Trade 32(2019); Farole, Thomas & Akinci, Gokhan, *Special economic zones: progress, emerging challenges, and future directions (English).* Directions in development; trade. (Washington, DC: World Bank 2011). http://documents.worldbank.org/curated/en/752011468203980987/Special-economic-zones-progress-emerging-challenges-and-future-directions 3.
17. The first publicly known investor-state dispute resulting from the grant of special economic status is *Manufacturers Hanover Trust Company v. Arab Republic of Egypt and General Authority for Investment and Free Zones*, ICSID Case No. ARB/89/1. In this dispute, a New York bank, Manufacturers Hanover Trust Company, had obtained a license to operate a branch in an Egyptian free zone in 1975. Parties chose to settle the dispute. *See* Charles N Brower et al., *Lessons Confirmed While Serving as Arbitrator and Counsel in Arbitrations Involving Africa*, 30 Emory International Law Review 5, 10–11 (2015).
18. Notably, SEZ related investor-state disputes have resulted in multiple disputes.
19. Alex J Easson, *Tax Incentives for Foreign Direct Investment* 173 (Kluwer Law International 2004).

turn examine the factual background and legal reasoning of the Tribunals in the two disputes. In the last section, conclusions are drawn on the broad importance of foreign investment law for balancing the interests of host states and investors in SEZs.

§16.02 FACTUAL BACKGROUND

In 1992, by Decree No. 1/30 dated 31 August 1992,[20] based on World Bank recommendations, the Republic of Burundi established a 'free-zone regime' granting certain companies tax and custom exemptions.[21] This status was to be granted to businesses in the 'non-traditional sector' conditional on the grant of a 'free-zone certificate' by the relevant Minister on the advice of a consultative commission. [22] Sequel to this, in December 1992, Affinage Des Metaux (AFFIMET) was formed under Burundi law with the objective of producing, fining and marketing precious metals. 99.9% of its share capital was owned by Mr Antoine Goetz (75%) and five other Belgians while one share was held by a Rwandan national. [23]

On 3 February 1993, AFFIMET was granted a free-zone certificate by Burundi's minister of industry and trade. However, five months later, on 9 July 1993, AFFIMET was informed that differences of opinion had arisen within the Burundian administration as to the proper scope of the free-zone regime.[24] AFFIMET was then notified that pending the outcome of investigations, the company could continue to benefit from the free-zone regime only if it deposited a sum equivalent to the duties that it would have to pay if the certificate was withdrawn.

Following the completion of investigations, on 20 August 1993 AFFIMET was told that its free-zone certificate had been suspended.[25] However, by a letter dated 10 January 1994, the minister advised AFFIMET that the certificate had come back into force.[26] Following the intervention of Burundi's prime minister and a further study by an international consultancy firm, AFFIMET was informed that, pursuant to Ministerial Order No. 750/184 of 29 May 1995 (which provided that the regime no longer applied to companies involved in the extraction and sale of ore) its certificate had been

20. Goetz I, *supra*, footnote 1, para. 1.
21. *See* 31 Juillet 2001. - LOI n° 1/015 - Révision du Décretloi n° 1/30 du 31 Août 1992 Portant Création d'un Regime de Zone Franche au Burundi available at, http://www.droit-afrique.com/upload/doc/burundi/Burundi-Loi-2001-zones-franches.pdf.
22. The main criteria for eligibility were: export of all production; creation of substantial added value; compliance with environmental, health and safety regulations; importation or re-export after further processing or packaging of imported products based on a list established by the Minister responsible for the free zones. Advantages of free-zone status are: exemption from taxes for ten years at the rate of 15%; minimum tax of 1% for business commercial free; tax reduction 0.8% for companies that have created more than thirty permanent jobs; dividends are exempt from taxation for an indefinite period; right to repatriate capital and income; permission to have foreign currency bank deposits; flexible labour regulations; exemptions from import duties and taxes. Businesses do not require import licenses.
23. Goetz I, *supra*, footnote 1, para. 3.
24. *Ibid.*, para. 7.
25. *Ibid.*, para. 10.
26. *Ibid.*, para. 11.

withdrawn.[27] This ministerial order will bring an end to twenty-two months of oscillating communication between Burundi officials and AFFIMET.

In November 1995, on the basis of the BLEU (Belgium-Luxembourg Economic Union) - Burundi BIT 1989,[28] the Claimants filed a dispute before ICSID requesting that the Tribunal annul the decision of 29 May 1995 withdrawing the free-zone certificate.[29] Alternatively, they requested for substantial damages. In 1998, following a decision on jurisdiction and merits, the tribunal delivered a final award which embodied the parties' amicable settlement. This included a Memorandum of Understanding on amicable solution of the dispute and a Special Convention on the Operation of AFFIMET.

Two years after the 1998 award, the parties were back to an ICSID Tribunal before an almost similar Tribunal composition.[30] The Claimants in the second dispute were the Goetz conglomerate which now composed: S.A. African Bank of Commerce ('ABC'), S.A. AFFIMET ('AFFIMET'), S.A. City Connexion Airlines ('CCA'), and S.A. CCA Maintenance ('CCA Maintenance').[31] The Claimants argued that following their enforcement of the Goetz I arbitral award, they had solicited and obtained an exequatur judgment from a Belgain court.[32] They pleaded that following this enforcement of judgment action, Burundi had taken various retaliatory measures against the Goetz companies in breach of the BLEU-Burundi BIT, MOU and Convention.[33] After several delays and failed attempts to settle the dispute, in 2012, the Tribunal gave a final decision in favour of the Claimants.

The two sections below shall examine closely the claims and decisions of the Tribunals in the two disputes.

§16.03 GOETZ I AWARD (EMBODYING THE PARTIES' SETTLEMENT AGREEMENT)

The arbitration Tribunal made up of Professor Jean-Denis Bredin, Professor Andreas Bucher, and Professor Prosper Weil ruled that it had jurisdiction to consider the legality of the free-zone certificate withdrawal.[34] Burundi appointed an arbitrator but failed to submit a counter-memorial and did not participate in the proceedings. In accordance with Article 42(4) of ICSID Arbitration Rules, the Tribunal independently examined its jurisdiction and gave a decision in default of appearance.[35] Although Burundi did not raise any preliminary objections to the Tribunal's jurisdiction, the Tribunal extensively considered its jurisdiction *ratione materiae* and *ratione personae* to hear the claim.

27. *Ibid.*, para. 15.
28. Agreement between the Belgium-Luxembourg Economic Union and the Republic of Burundi on the Promotion and Reciprocal Protection of Investments (signed 13 April 1989, entered into force 12 September 1993) (Belgium-Luxembourg Economic Union (BLEU)) – Burundi BIT (1989).
29. Goetz I, *supra*, footnote 1, para. 18.
30. In January 2010, Professor Prosper Weil resigned and was replaced by Judge Gilbert Gillaume.
31. Goetz II, *supra*, footnote 2, para. 1.
32. *Ibid.*, para. 77.
33. *Ibid.*, para. 77.
34. Goetz I, *supra*, footnote 1, para. 81.
35. *Ibid.*, para. 53.

Applying Article 25 of the ICSID Convention and Article 8 of the BLEU-Burundi BIT, the Tribunal held that there was a dispute related to an investment and that the Claimants were foreign nationals.[36] The Tribunal also considered that the Claimants who were majority shareholders in AFFIMET were qualified to institute a claim in their personal capacities.[37] Rejecting claims for reimbursement of taxes and convertible shares changed into Burundian Francs, the Tribunal held that its jurisdiction only covered withdrawal of the free-zone certificate and not legality of events which occurred before this withdrawal.

Notably, the Tribunal did not consider in detail, qualification of a free-zone certificate as a covered foreign investment. Notwithstanding, arbitral jurisprudence establishes that activities within free trade zones may qualify as foreign investments under investment treaties.[38] The Tribunal however held that grant of SEZ status could not be assimilated to a state contract in the circumstances because the offer and grant were clearly unilateral acts.[39] In effect, mere grant of SEZ status cannot be equated with an investor-state contract which creates legally binding obligations and duties. Despite this distinction between the existence of a state contract and administrative acts, the Claimants could seek some redress under the BLEU-Burundi BIT.

The Tribunal examined the substance of the Claimant's alleged breaches under Burundi law and international law discussed under sub-headings below.

[A] Breach of Administrative Law

In their memorial, the Claimants argued that Burundi's decision to withdraw the free-zone certificate violated the theory of withdrawal of administrative acts, under

---

36. *Ibid.*, para. 86.
37. *Ibid.*, para. 91.
38. Based on searches on *Italaw* and *Investment Arbitration Reporter*, there are more than twenty publicly-known SEZ investor-state disputes These are *Manufacturers Hanover Trust Company v. Arab Republic of Egypt and General Authority for Investment and Free Zones*, ICSID Case No. ARB/89/1; *EDF International S.A., SAUR International S.A. and León Participaciones Argentinas S.A. v. Argentine Republic*, ICSID Case No. ARB/03/23; *National Gas S.A.E. v. Arab Republic of Egypt*, ICSID Case No. ARB/11/7; *Ampal-American Israel Corporation and others v. Arab Republic of Egypt*, ICSID Case No. ARB/12/11; *Yosef Maiman, Merhav (Mnf) Ltd,Merhav Ampal Group Ltd, and Merhav Ampal Energy Holdings Limited Partnership v. the Arab Republic of Egypt*, PCA Case No. 2012-26; Ampal ICC Case No .18215/GZ/MHM (unpublished), Ampal CRCICA Case No. 829/2012 (unpublished). *Lee John Beck and Central Asian Development Corporation v. Kyrgyz Republic* (2013); *Álvarez y Marín Corporación S.A., Estudios Tributarios AP S.A., Stichting Administratiekantoor Anbadi, Bartus van Noordenne and Cornelis Willem van Noordenne v. Republic of Panama* (ICSID Case No. ARB/15/14); *Iurii Bogdanov, Agurdino-Invest Ltd and Agurdino-Chimia JSC v. Republic of Moldova I; Iurii Bogdanov, Agurdino-Invest Ltd. and Agurdino-Chimia JSC v. Republic of Moldova* (II); *Yury Bogdanov v. Republic of Moldova (III)* (SCC Case No. 114/2009); *Yuri Bogdanov and Yulia Bogdanova v. Republic of Moldova (IV)* (SCC Case No. 091/2012); *Mr Gennady Mykhailenko & United Pipe Export Company Trading Ag v. The Republic of Belarus; Link-Trading Joint Stock Company v. Department for Customs Control of the Republic of Moldova*, UNCITRAL; *Carissa Investments LLC v. India* (2017); *Albacora S.A. v. Republic of Ecuador* (PCA Case No. 2016-11) *Lao Holdings N.V. v. Lao People's Democratic Republic (I)* (ICSID Case No. ARB(AF)/12/6).
39. Goetz I, *supra*, footnote 1, para. 75 (Distinguishing it from *Amco Asia Corporation and others v. Republic of Indonesia*, ICSID Case No. ARB/81/1, Award (20 November 1984) para. 189).

Belgian and French administrative law. They argued that principles relating to the parallelism of forms and to the hierarchy between legislative acts and administrative acts were incorporated into Burundi law through reception of the Napoleonic Code.[40] The Tribunal held that French administrative law was inapplicable to the facts as the actions of the Burundi government were not retroactive.
Reviewing, French administrative case law, the Tribunal held that a state will not be liable for arbitrary administrative acts which are intrinsically discriminatory decisions, as with economic issues, which are a result of authorisations or certifications which inevitably favour those who benefit. Second, a state bears no liabilities when the injury invoked is due to a measure taken in the pre-eminent public interest to protect the national economy and public finances. In conclusion, the Tribunal stated that even if Burundi law allowed for the strict liability within the same conditions as French administrative law, the Ministerial Order of 29 May 1995 would come within recognised exceptions. The Tribunal thus decided that it will be futile to examine Burundi law on strict liability.[41] The Claimant's attempt to base its arguments on breach of domestic administrative law are important for examining state regulation of SEZs. Executive regulatory actions in relation with SEZs are often administrative acts which interact with international investment law as a transnational legal order.[42] Tribunals have thus applied tests of proportionality developed from municipal administrative laws, in determining if measures achieve legitimate policy objectives.[43]

[B] Illegality of Ministerial Order No. 750/184 of 29 May 1995

The Tribunal rejected the Claimants' arguments that declaring activities relating to minerals ineligible for the free-zone regime was an illegal regulatory attack on rights acquired by virtue of a legislative decision.[44] In its analysis, the Tribunal established that illegality of the certificate withdrawal had not been established as a strict liability violation.[45]

Importantly, the Tribunal stated that '... there is no legal right to the maintenance of a regulation that the regulatory authority cannot at any time modify or abrogate a previous regulatory provision.'[46] Additionally, it stated that '... it would be contrary to all principle that a certification entailing certain benefits for its recipient, in particular in the area of duties and taxes, could carry an irreversible and absolute character.'[47]

---

40. Goetz I, *supra*, footnote 1, para. 101.
41. *Ibid.*, para. 102.
42. Rudolf Dolzer, *The Impact of International Investment Treaties on Domestic Administrative Law*, 37 New York University Journal of International Law and Politics 953 (2005). In particular part V titled: Administrative Sovereignty, Legal Stability and Good Governance: Towards A Transnational Regime for Foreign Investments.
43. *Electrabel S.A. v. Republic of Hungary*, ICSID Case No. ARB/07/19, Award (25 November 2015) para. 179.
44. Goetz I, *supra*, footnote 1, para. 106.
45. *Ibid.*, para. 119.
46. *Ibid.*, para. 107.
47. *Ibid.*, para. 112. Contrast with *Ampal-American Israel Corporation and others v. Arab Republic of Egypt*, ICSID Case No. ARB/12/11, Decision on Liability and Heads of Loss, (21 February 2017

Although tax benefits in SEZs may attract FDI and make host states more competitive, these have 'real and budgetary costs'.[48] The Tribunal's reasoning is generally in line with arbitral jurisprudence which recognises, the right of states to, make legislative changes in the absence of stabilisation clauses. [49] In contracting with states investors recognise the inherent risk that successive governments will make policy changes.[50] Additionally, the Tribunal dismissed the Claimants' arguments that the certificate withdrawal was an individual decision disguised as a regulatory measure. This was based on facts which showed that similar measures had an effect on Ejumeau, a tin mining company.[51]

International investment law has had a chequered history with relation to the effects of stabilisation clauses, legitimate expectations and changes in host state regulations. SEZs are long-term economic projects and when a new government does not recognise commitments of previous governments, this is often a trigger for disputes.[52] In the tribunal's opinion:

> from the moment when, in the judgment of the relevant State authorities, the common good for which this last was responsible no longer justified such a stimulus for a given product or activity, it was in their power to modify the texts governing the free-zone regime and to put an end – for the future, and without retroactive effect – to previously accorded certifications.[53]

As the Tribunal in *SA Total v. Argentina* held:

> The balance between competing requirements and hence the limits of the proper invocation of 'legitimate expectations' in the face of legislative or regulatory changes (assuming that they are not contrary to a contractual, bilateral or similar undertaking, binding in its own right) has been based on a weighing of various elements pointing in opposite directions.[54]

In Goetz I, the Tribunal's approach to finding this balance was largely based on a consideration of public interest. On a technical note, the Tribunal held that application of a provision concerning minerals to AFFIMET, whose activities related to gold was not illegal.[55]

---

para. 186) where the Tribunal held that the Respondent's decision to remove EMG's tax-free status took away a defined and valuable interest that had been validly conferred according to Egyptian law at the time that the investment was made and that had been guaranteed by the State for a defined period. It was not to be subject to the vicissitudes of changes in State tax policy over that time period. For this reason, the taking is tantamount to expropriation.

48. Easson, *Tax Incentives, supra,* footnote 19, at p. 194.
49. *EDF (Services) Limited v. Romania,* ICSID Case No. ARB/05/13, Award (8 October 2009) para. 217; *Ioan Micula and others v. Romania,* ICSID Case No. ARB/05/20, Award (11 December 2013) para. 529.
50. *Vigotop Limited v. Hungary,* ICSID Case No. ARB/11/22, Award (1 October 2014) para. 625.
51. Goetz I, *supra,* footnote 1, para. 108.
52. Douglas Zhihua Zeng, *Global Experiences with Special Economic Zones With a Focus on China and Africa* 10 (World Bank Publications 2015).
53. Goetz I, *supra,* footnote 1, para. 112.
54. *Total S A v. Argentine Republic,* ICSID Case No. ARB/04/01, Decision on Liability (27 December 2010) para. 121.
55. Goetz I, *supra,* footnote 1, para. 114.

[C] Indirect Expropriation

The Tribunal held that revocation of the free-zone certificate forced AFFIMET to halt all its activities depriving it of benefits which it could have expected from its investments. This decision was to be regarded as a 'measure having similar effect' to a measure depriving of or restricting property within the meaning of Article 4 of the BLEU-Burundi BIT. Next, the Tribunal determined if this indirect expropriation was lawfully carried out in accordance with Article 4 of the BIT. Based on the dossier and international expert studies, it established that exclusion of gold from the free-zone regime was done in national interest, lawfully and without discrimination.[56] However, in an interesting analysis and in recognition of the Burundi's prerogative, the Tribunal determined that until a compensation was paid, the legality of the decision of 29 May 1995 under international law remained in abeyance.[57] Thus, instead of determining the outright unlawfulness of expropriation without compensation, the Tribunal gave Burundi an option to pay an adequate compensation within a reasonable time.[58] Burundi could thus reinstate the free-zone certificate without bearing any liabilities for damages as the withdrawal was not illegal under Burundi law.
In its decision, the Tribunal gave Burundi a four-month period to either pay an indemnity to the Claimants or reinstate the free-zone certificate.[59]

The reasoning above is an illustration of a Tribunal's wide discretion which may be exercised in balancing the interests of host states and investors. Thomas Walde would thus argue in favour of this approach which he described as an exercise of a 'rarely used power of flexible sequencing of remedies'.[60] In foreign investment law scholarship, this decision has generally been described as an exceptional use of specific performance.[61] However, as Christoph Schreuer argues, Goetz I cannot be regarded as a specific performance because in the true sense of the word, the Tribunal offered Burundi the opportunity to avoid responsibility in the first place.[62] Tribunals are reluctant to grant non-pecuniary compensation like this because of the practical difficulties of restoring claimants back to their original positions.[63] Willingness of the

56. *Ibid.*, para. 126.
57. *Ibid.*, para. 131.
58. In the infamous *Texaco v. Libya* decision, Rend-Jean Dupuy giving effect to the deed of concession signed between parties, gave Texaco a period of six months to comply with the award. *See* Award on the Merits in Dispute between Texaco Overseas Petroleum Company/California Asiatic Oil Company and the Government of the Libyan Arab Republic (Compensation for Nationalized Property) [decisions] (1978) 17 International Legal Materials1, para. 113. *See also*, Sergey Ripinsky & Kevin Williams, *Damages in International Investment Law* 52 (BIICL 2008).
59. Goetz I, *supra*, footnote 1, para. 135.
60. Thomas W Wälde, *Remedies and Compensation in International Investment Law*, First Draft ILA Committee on International Law of Foreign Investment 26 (2005).
61. Meg Kinnear, *Damages in Investment Treaty Arbitration*, in *Arbitration Under International Investment Agreements: A Guide to the Key Issues* 551, 560 (Katia Yannaca-Small ed, Oxford University Press 2010).
62. Christoph Schreuer, *Non-Pecuniary Remedies in ICSID Arbitration*, 20 Arbitration International 325, 330 (2004).
63. Eric De Brabandere, *Investment Treaty Arbitration as Public International Law* 187 (Cambridge University Press 2014).

Tribunal to adopt a flexible approach may be explained by three main factors. First, the Tribunal considered party attempts at negotiations as indicative of willingness to settle.[64] Second, the Tribunal must have considered the political and financial difficulties of Burundi. Third, revocation of a free-zone certificate is relatively easy to reinstate.

Three and a half months after the award on merits, parties entered into a settlement under which Burundi agreed to reinstate the free-zone certificate and reimburse a USD 2,989,636 tax bond paid by AFFIMET.[65] Additionally, the parties entered into an agreement for the functioning of AFFIMET as a free-zone company. This agreement restored the free-zone status of AFFIMENT and imposed certain obligations.[66] Notably, the Agreement included a guarantee that any future legislation in Burundi which contradicts SEZ rights granted will be not applicable to AFFIMET.[67] Under the Agreement, AFFIMET made commitments to create 100 permanent jobs in two years and give priority to the employment of Burundi nationals.[68] Together these were adopted as the final award of the Tribunal.

§16.04 GOETZ II AWARD

On the basis of the BLEU-Burundi BIT, the MOU for settlement and the Agreement for Special Convention on the operation of AFFIMET S.A., the Claimants instituted the second dispute.[69] They alleged that Burundi breached these agreements by ordering the cessation of commercial activities and forcing the Claimants to close the four companies.

Burundi initially challenged the Tribunal's jurisdiction on the ground that the matter had previously being settled in Goetz I on the pre-condition that the Claimants withdraw the ICSID claim.[70] However seeking to bring an end to the dispute, the respondent abandoned this objection.[71] Notwithstanding, the tribunal examined in detail the basis of its jurisdiction to admit the claims. The Tribunal held that there existed a prior and irrevocable consent that any dispute of this nature be submitted to ICSID. Pursuant to Article 53 (1) of the Washington Convention, the Goetz I settlement award was binding. On this basis, the Tribunal held that it was competent to rule on the claims of the Goetz consorts.[72] Additionally, it held that an MOU concluded in 2004 between the parties for amicable solution could not be considered as Burundi's admission of liability.[73]

64. *See* Special Convention Regarding the Functioning of the Affimet Company, preamble, para. 521.
65. Protocol of Agreement in Relation to the Amicable Settlement of the Case of 'Antoine Goetz and Partners Versus the Republic of Burundi' Award (Embodying the Parties' Settlement Agreement) dated 10 February 1999.
66. Special Convention, *supra*, footnote 64.
67. *Ibid.*, Art. 4.
68. *Ibid.*, Art. 5.
69. Goetz II, *supra*, footnote 2, para. 1.
70. *Ibid.*, para. 78.
71. *Ibid.*, para. 136.
72. *Ibid.*, para. 143.
73. *Ibid.*, para. 166.

The Tribunal considered in turn the claims of the Goetz conglomerates and Burundi's counterclaim. In its decision of costs, it awarded USD 1,200,000 in favour of the Claimants. The Tribunal's fiindings establish that non-compliance with SEZ requirements is not suficient basis for unlawful expropriaiton or unfair treatment. These findings are examined seriatim below.

[A] Affinage Des Metaux (AFFIMET)

The Claimants averred that as a result of expropriatory measures, AFFIMET was forced to close business in 2002. It alleged that these measures were in breach of the BIT treatment standards and contractual obligations under the Special Convention. These alleged retaliatory measures included: a twenty-four-hour closure in connection with investigation of ABC bank; delays in custom clearance; requests that AFFIMET produce certificates issued by the Geology and Mines Department for Gold Exports from March to August 2001; and suspension of duty exemptions and export taxes for two months. The Claimants thus urged the tribunal to hold Burundi liable for damages resulting from breach of its obligations.[74]

In its defence, Burundi argued that AFFIMET had not kept its commitments under the Convention, to create 100 permanent jobs by the end of 2000.[75] According to Burundi, checks carried out in accordance with the mining legislation and Article 10 of the Special Convention to verify the gold content of the materials exported by AFFIMET only affected the company's export activities (and not its refining and processing activities). It argued that measures were only carried out for short periods and therefore had no impact on AFFIMET's profits. The Tribunal held that based on financial documents produced by AFFIMET, the company continued its activities between 2000 and 2002. Thus, although exports of material were suspended three times over a three-year period, AFFIMET had not shown that these suspensions led to a loss of control of the company or an impossibility of using the investment. The tribunal thus dismissed the claim of indirect expropriation.[76] Although conflicting arbitral jurisprudence has resulted in lack of clarity on the limits of indirect expropriation, the Tribunal's decision is in conformity with control and effect tests adopted by tribunals.[77]

In its defence, Burundi argued that license certificates, were necessary to ascertain the gold content of the exported metals, as provided for in the free-zone certificate. The Tribunal noted that according to Article 10 of the Special Convention, AFFIMET could freely export refined metals without being subjected to any qualitative inspection. These exports were therefore not subject to pre-grants by the Geology and

74. *Ibid.*, para. 105.
75. *Ibid.*, para. 115.
76. *Ibid.*, para. 196.
77. *Cervin Investissements S.A. and Rhone Investissements S.A. v. Republic of Costa Rica*, ICSID Case No. ARB/13/2, Decision on Jurisdiction (15 December 2014) para. 333; *Tenaris S.A. and Talta - Trading e Marketing Sociedade Unipessoal Lda. v. Bolivarian Republic of Venezuela* [II], ICSID Case No. ARB/12/23, Award, (12 December 2016) para. 320. *See* Andrew Paul Newcombe & Lluís Paradell, *Law and Practice of Investment Treaties: Standards of Treatment* 341 (Kluwer Law International 2009).

Mining Department attesting compliance with mining legislation or the gold content of metals exported.[78] The tribunal thus held that by requiring these certificates, Burundi had breached its contractual obligations under Articles 4 (5) and 10 of the Special Convention. Additionally, the tribunal held that breach of these obligations by Burundi was not justified by its defence that AFFIMET had failed to create 100 permanent jobs.[79] The Tribunal also held that export suspensions against AFFIMET were carried out without justification and in violation of Article 10 of the Special Convention.[80]

The tribunal thus held that all the measures taken against AFFIMET were a clear violation of Article 3 (1) of the Belgium-Burundi BIT which guaranteed foreign investors' fair and equitable treatment. According to the Tribunal, these measures were contrary to the legitimate expectations of the Claimants who had relied on compliance with the Special Convention.[81] Additionally, these measures were carried out without valid justification creating obstacles to the functioning of AFFIMET. As a result, the tribunal found that these measures were a breach of constant security and protection under the BIT.[82] In effect, in contrast to the facts leading to Goetz I, the Special Convention was a state contract which created sufficient basis for protecting the Claimant's legitimate expectations.

[B] ABC Company

On 25 July 1994, Burundi's minister of trade and industry issued a free-zone certificate to S.A. African Bank of Commerce (ABC), to offer banking services exclusively to non-residents and free-zone companies established in Burundi.[83] Prior to this grant, the Burundi Free-Zone Advisory Committee had however recommended that the certificate only cover bank services to free-zone companies.[84] Banking regulations laid down by Burundi's central Bank, Bank of the Republic of Burundi (BRB) had not been included in the certificate. They were however included in a letter dated 23 March 1995 in which the BRB recommended that before commencing operations appropriate legislation should be passed.[85] Notwithstanding, ABC began operations on the strength of its free-zone certificate. Between 1998 and 2000, different positions arose between the BRB and the Ministry of Trade and commerce. The BRB insisted that ABC could only provide services to free-zone companies while the ministry supported ABC's service provision to foreign residents.[86] These events were the main catalyst for the second Goetz dispute. While SEZs are aimed at improving economies through foreign exchange earnings, poor fiscal policies can result in financial losses. The central bank's

78. Goetz II, *supra*, footnote 2, para. 205.
79. *Ibid.*, para. 206.
80. *Ibid.*, para. 207.
81. *Ibid.*, para. 209.
82. *Ibid.*
83. *Ibid.*, para. 212.
84. *Ibid.*, para. 213.
85. *Ibid.*, para. 217.
86. *Ibid.*, para. 227.

attempts to regulate the operations of ABC Bank show the fiscal offsets that could occur as a result of very liberal SEZs.

Following several inspections, communication letters and cabinet changes, the Ministry of Trade and Commerce finally withdrew ABC's free-zone certificate.[87] On 14 October 1999, the Minister of Commerce suspended the free-zone certificate and on 25 January 2000, the Minister of Commerce asked the Chief General Staff of the gendarmerie to proceed with the immediate closure of ABC. Based on suspicions that ABC continued to carry out banking operations, on 14 February 2000, the Ministry of Commerce, instructed the gendarmerie to close the building housing the companies for investigative purposes. [88]

The Claimants argued that the different measures were expropriatory and in breach of Articles 3 and 4 of the BIT. In its defence, Burundi alleged that although ABC Company held a free-zone certificate, it had not been approved as a bank under the Banking Act. It also alleged that ABC violated the regulations under which it could provide services to only non-residents and free-zone companies.

The Tribunal held that suspension of ABC's free-zone certificate on 14 October 1999, and closure of its office by the government amounted to an indirect expropriation. These measures forced ABC to stop operations and robbed the Claimants of the benefits they could expect from their investments.[89] The Tribunal determined that ABC actually conducted some of its banking activities in ignorance of the exchange regulations fixed by Burundi's central bank. Assessing ABC's contributory fault, the Tribunal held that although there were misunderstandings of the regulations and inconsistent instructions from Burundi officials, ABC opened unauthorised bank accounts. In conclusion, the Tribunal held that although ABC could be blamed for continuing to operate outside a defined legislative regime, this was not a sufficient ground for Burundi to put an end to ABC's activities without compensation. Based on ABC's contributory fault, the tribunal held that the Claimants will be entitled to only two-thirds of compensation for the damages suffered.[90] With respect to breach of FET and FPS standards, the Tribunal chose not to consider these measures as they related to the same measures.[91]

[C] CCA Airline and CCA Maintenance

In 1998, the Goetz companies established S.A. City Connexion Airlines ('CCA') and an aircraft maintenance company called S.A. City Connexion Airlines Maintenance ('CCA

87. On 31 July 1999, President Buyoya appointed Darius Nahayo as head of the Ministry of Trade, Industry and Tourism replacing Nestor Nyabenda, who was implicated in scandals of speculation on essential commodities and in the granting of a license for the tax-free zone (zone franche) contrary to the advice of the consultative commission on the tax-free zone regime. On 12 January 2000, Darius Nahayo was replaced. *See* Filip Reyntjens, *Small States in an Unstable Region – Rwanda and Burundi, 1999–2000*, 23 Current African Issues 3, 10 (2000).
88. Goetz II, *supra*, footnote 2, para. 233.
89. *Ibid.*, para. 243.
90. *Ibid.*, para. 258.
91. *Ibid.*, para. 259.

Maintenance') to help with their gold mining business.[92] Like AFFIMET and ABC, CCA Maintenance was a free-zone company under Burundi law. At the time when the claim was instituted, CCA's free-zone certificate was about to be granted.[93]

The Claimants alleged that various measures by Burundi in breach of Articles 3 and 4 of the BLEU-Burundi BIT forced the two companies to stop operating in 2000. In particular, these measures were closure of its office for twenty-four hours in February 2000, flight cancellations due to aircraft embargos and prevention of spare part importation.

In its defence, Burundi argued that seizure of aircraft spare parts imported by CCA Maintenance, lasted for only two and a half months and that this was justified by a customs fraud investigation. Additionally, it alleged that CCA Maintenance had not been authorised to import spare parts for re-export.[94]

The Tribunal held that the Claimants had not established that measures taken by Burundi forced CCA and CCA Maintenance to cease operations.[95] However, the Tribunal held that the various measures were in breach of fair and equitable treatment guaranteed under Articles 3 (1) and 3 (2) of the BIT. The Goetz consorts were therefore entitled to compensation for the damages suffered.[96]

[D] Burundi's Counterclaim

Unlike during the Goetz I dispute, in Goetz II, Burundi participated in proceedings and even filed a counterclaim. It made a claim for a compensation of USD 1,000,000 damages for ABC's alleged failure to comply with operating conditions of the free-zone certificate and the BRB's letter of 7 July 1994. It argued that by illegally opening bank accounts for residents, ABC had created unfair competition resulting in loss of profits. The Claimants challenged the Tribunal's jurisdiction to hear the counterclaim arguing that the applicable investment treaty did not establish Burundi's right to file counterclaims. Additionally, they argued that ABC was not a party to the BLEU-Burundi BIT, so its obligations could not be transformed into obligations under the BIT.

Contrary to the Claimant's arguments, the Tribunal held that under Article 46 of the ICSID Convention and Article 40 of the ICSID Rules of arbitration, an arbitral tribunal can hear a counterclaim when: (a) the request falls within the competence of the Centre and is covered by the consent of the parties; and (b) it relates directly to the subject of the dispute and jurisdiction of the tribunal.[97] The Tribunal held that the counterclaim filed by Burundi met all these conditions as it was related to ABC's breach of the free-zone certificate and to a covered investment as defined by the BIT.[98] Therefore by accepting the offer contained in the BIT, the Goetz consorts had in turn

92. *Ibid.*, para. 260.
93. *Ibid.*, para. 80.
94. *Ibid.*, para. 120.
95. *Ibid.*, para. 266.
96. *Ibid.*
97. *Ibid.*, para. 275.
98. *Ibid.*, para. 277.

accepted the Tribunal's jurisdiction to hear related counterclaims. Referencing Professor Reisman's Declaration in *Spyridon Roussalis v. Romania*, the Tribunal held that refusing to accept counterclaims will be against the letter and spirit of the Washington Convention. According to the Tribunal rejecting counterclaims, will be to complicate the settlement of disputes investment policy, which is aimed at facilitating the interests of both States and investors.[99] After recognising its jurisdiction, the Tribunal however dismissed the counterclaim on the following grounds. First, Burundi failed to prove that the damage allegedly caused by ABC would have undermined competition and financial stability of the country. Second, the Tribunal held that alleged loss of earnings with regard to the collection of duties and taxes was caused by the ABC's misunderstanding of the obligations imposed on it by the free-zone certificate.

Generally, there are no clear conclusions on the rights of states to file counterclaims in investor-state disputes. Although Goetz II shows the latitude Tribunals have in interpreting investment treaties, doubt is still cast on successful use of counterclaims under BITs.[100] The *Goetz v. Burundi II* Tribunal's decision to recognise a counterclaim has been linked to the broad ISDS clause of the applicable BIT[101] which includes an applicable law reference.[102] Goetz II is notably one of the few cases where a Tribunal has accepted jurisdiction to hear counterclaims.[103] To create a balance between investor and state host rights, some recently signed international investment agreements expressly make reference to counterclaims. [104]

§16.05 GREAT EXPECTATIONS AND SPECIAL ECONOMIC ZONES

Like transnational economic activity and FDI driven proliferation of international investment agreements, while SEZs may go far beyond the expectations of foreign investors, for capital importing host states, many of these expectations may remain

99. *Spyridon Roussalis v. Romania*, ICSID Case No. ARB/06/1, Award Michael Reisman's Declaration (28 November 2011) para. 279.
100. *See* Jose Daniel Amado et al., *Arbitrating the Conduct of International Investors* 16 (Cambridge University Press 2018).
101. *See Oxus Gold Plc v. Republic of Uzbekistan*, UNCITRAL, Final Award (17 December 2015) para. 950.
102. Andrea K Bjorklund, The Role of Counterclaims in Rebalancing Investment Law, 17 Lewis & Clark Law Review 461, 474 (2013).
103. *See* Charles N Brower & Sadie Blanchard, *What's in a Meme – The Truth about Investor-State Arbitration: Why It Need Not, and Must Not, Be Repossessed by States*, 52 Columbia Journal of Transnational Law 689, 715 (2014). *Perenco Ecuador Ltd v. The Republic of Ecuador and Empresa Estatal Petróleos del Ecuador*, ICSID Case No. ARB/08/6, Interim Decision on the Environmental Counterclaim (11 August 2015) para. 34 'The tribunal agrees that if a legal relationship between an investor and the State permits the filing of a claim by the State for environmental damage caused by the investor's activities and such a claim is substantiated, the State is entitled to full reparation in accordance with the requirements of the applicable law.'
104. *See* for example, Comprehensive and Progressive Agreement for Trans-Pacific Partnership (opened for signature 8 March 2018) Art. 9.23(8); Agreement between Japan and the State of Israel for the Liberalization, Promotion and Protection of Investment (signed1 February 2017) Art. 24(12); Investment Agreement between the Government of the Hong Kong Special Administrative Region of the People's Republic of China and the Government of The Republic of Chile (signed 18 November 2016) Art. 26(7).

unmet.[105] The success of China's SEZs has led to an exportation of SEZs to the rest of Asia and the world.[106] The Goetz disputes however reiterate the importance of transparent and well formulated regulations for the success of SEZs.

> the commission declared itself as having 'strong worries that the law governing this regime was so liberal that the State of Burundi risked not being able to reap all the expected benefits'. In the specific case of affimet, it considered however that the shortfall due to fiscal and customs exemptions could be regarded as 'facilitative measures accepted by the government as attracting investors to the free zone regime'.[107]

Although international investment agreements make no express reference to SEZs, foreign investment norms including national investment codes are integral to SEZ governance. For instance, following the Goetz disputes, Burundi has incorporated the free-zone regime into its national investment code.[108] It is thus clear that although SEZ investment disputes involve distinct circumstances, they are not *lex specialis*. For foreign investors, investment arbitration remains an important mechanism for challenging arbitraty exercise of soverign power in SEZs. The Goetz disputes show the importance of investment agreements in protecting foreign investors.

The free-zone regime set up in Burundi in 1992 is unique because it has the singular distinction of being a legal regime with unlimited geographical area.[109] Traditionally, SEZ regimes have been defined as 'geographically delimited areas'.[110] Well-defined geographical areas equipped with one-stop investment facilitation incentives are aimed at attracting foreign investors. Indeed, it can be argued that lack of access to banking activities and other amenities often provided by central authorities in geographically defined areas led the Claimants to establish banking facilities.

Without using this as an excuse for poor governance, vacillation by Burundian authorities was largely due to political instability and frequent cabinet changes.[111] This case is thus an illustration of the dilemmas of regulating foreign investment further complicated by long-term SEZs which give investors extra incentives. Perceptions by successive governments that SEZs have been unfairly negotiated may result in SEZ cancellations. In both cases, the major trigger for withdrawal of the licenses was perceived low cost benefits in terms of benefits relative to the tax revenue forgone. It

105. Lucy Reed & Andrew Jacovides, *Great Expectations: Where Does the Proliferation of International Dispute Resolution Tribunals Leave International Law?*, 96 Proceedings of the Annual Meeting (American Society of International Law) 219 (2002).
106. *See* Deborah Bräutigam & Tang Xiaoyang, *African Shenzhen: China's Special Economic Zones in Africa*, 49 The Journal of Modern African Studies 27 (2011).
107. Goetz I, *supra*, footnote 1, para. 8.
108. Burundi Investment Code 2008, http://investmentpolicyhub.unctad.org/InvestmentLaws/laws/41 (accessed 14 May 2018). Article 16 provides that: 'The provisions of the Law No. 1/015 of 31 July 2001 on the revision of the decree-law No. 1/3 of 31 August 1992 on the creation of a free-zone regime in Burundi form an integral part of the present investment code.'
109. COMESA Regional Investment Agency, *Investors Guide to Burundi* 33 (2012).
110. Thomas Farole, *Special Economic Zones in Africa Comparing Performance and Learning from Global Experiences* 24 (World Bank Publications 2011).
111. Akin to what is described as roller coaster effect legislative changes. *See PSEG Global Inc. and Konya Ilgin Elektrik Üretim ve Ticaret Limited Sirketi v. Republic of Turkey*, ICSID Case No. ARB/02/5, Award (19 January 2007) para. 250.

is thus clear that host states seeking to attract FDI must create well-defined frameworks.[112]

A major challenge which is central to ongoing international investment law reforms is how to balance the rights of investors and host states in the interest of public policy. Growing interests in the governance of SEZs in Africa[113] and Asia must recognise both the risks and opportunities of SEZs. This requires a full understanding of the function played by transnational foreign investment norms in governing FDI. Investment arbitration's double-edged character is perhaps most evident in attempts to use counterclaims to hold investors liable for breaches of investment regulation. Thus, to build on the limited success of SEZs in the last decades, stakeholders must collectively create proper regulatory frameworks.[114]

The interpretation of the Belgium-Luxembourg Economic Union-Burundi BIT by the two Tribunals is in line with arbitral jurisprudence which has exploded in form and breadth since 1995.[115] Disputes have moved beyond expropriation compensation claims to broad application of investment treaties and customary international law. This is evident in the different approaches of the two Tribunals. Goetz V Burundi I&II will remain important juridsprudence to be applied by future arbitration tribunals considering the intricate relationship between international investment law and SEZs. Clearly, in the absence of a multilateral specialized SEZ treaty, investment treaties will continue to provide innovative mechanisms for governing SEZs.

112. OECD, *Southeast Asian Economic Outlook 2013 With Perspectives on China and India: With Perspectives on China and India* 97 (OECD Publishing 2013).
113. In November 2017, the Department of Trade and Industry of the African Union Commission organised the 1st African Union Symposium on Special Economic Zones (SEZs) and Industrial Development from 7 to 10 November 2017. https://au.int/en/pressreleases/20171107/african-union-commission-organized-1st-african-union-symposium-special (accessed 15 May 2018).
114. *See* UNCTAD, *ASEAN Investment Report 2017: Foreign Direct Investment and Economic Zones in ASEAN* (UNCTAD 2017).
115. While in 1995, Goetz was the second treaty-based dispute, by 2017 there are 855 publicly know treaty-based disputes. In 2012, when Goetz II was concluded, there were 520 known investment treaty-based disputes.

CHAPTER 17

Investment Protection in China's SEZs: Lee Jong Baek Case Study

Olga Boltenko

'The trap had a ghastly perfection'
- Stephen King, The Gunslinger

§17.01 INTRODUCTION

China's economic power has surpassed market expectations in the past decades. The World Bank shows China's GDP growth from USD 1.2 trillion in 2000, to USD 13.2 trillion in 2017,[1] amongst other indices of the country's economic development.

The World Bank deems 2% GDP per capita growth rate to be outstanding. China's annual GDP per capita growth rate has been steady since Deng Xiaoping's 1978 economic reforms, at around 9%.[2] In other words, an underdeveloped country suffering from widespread famine that took the lives of tens of millions in 1959 to 1961, China has become an economic superpower in less than sixty years.

In 2017, the top five investor nations in China in terms of the actual input of foreign capital were Hong Kong (USD 52.57 billion), Taiwan (USD 3.26 billion), Singapore (USD 2.81 billion), Japan (USD 1.84 billion), and USA (USD 1.78 billion).[3]

A large part of these foreign direct investment (FDI) inflows are directed through China's special economic zones (SEZs). SEZs offer significant tax flexibility along with other incentives to foreign investors. According to the World Bank Group, SEZs are responsible for 22% of China's GDP, 45% of total national FDI, and 60% of exports. In

1. *See*, https://data.worldbank.org/country/china (last accessed at 4 July 2018).
2. *See*, Peter Pham, *Is There a Secret Growth Hormone Added to China's Economy?* (Forbes, March 2018), https://www.forbes.com/sites/peterpham/2018/03/06/is-there-a-secret-growth-hormone-added-to-chinas-economy/#656df0223f13 (last accessed at 5 July 2018).
3. *Ibid.*

the last decade, SEZs have created over 30 million jobs, increased the workers' income by 30%, and accelerated industrialization agricultural modernization, and urbanization.[4]

Despite the various investment incentives offered by SEZs, China is considered a relatively high sovereign risk destination for foreign investment due to the risks of adverse regulation, expropriation, nationalization, denial of justice, and other forms of undue government interference.[5] These risks are particularly high in China's SEZs, where the concentration of FDI is the highest. Are China's SEZs Stephen King's traps of 'ghastly perfection' for foreign investors?

§17.02 THE RISE OF CHINA'S SEZs

An overview of investment protection in Chinese SEZ's would be incomplete without a brief foray into the history of this economic phenomenon.

China's first SEZs were established in 1979–1980 at Hong Kong's doorstep – in what was then the sleepy provincial towns of Shenzhen, Zhuhai, and Shantou. That was followed by an SEZ in Xiamen in Fujian Province, and an SEZ on the Hainan island.

The hallmark of these first SEZs was that in these areas, the local governments were allowed to offer tax incentives to foreign investors without Beijing's authorization.[6] As a result, these cities have become the epicentres of economic growth for China in the decades that followed.

Shenzhen's population alone grew from 30,000 in 1979 to over 12,000,000 in 2018.[7] These first SEZs will later lay the foundation for China's latest economic initiative – the Greater Bay Area megalopolis that will merge nine major South Chinese cities – including Shenzhen, Zhuhai, and Guangzhou, with China's Special Administrative Regions (SARs) Hong Kong and Macau – into a major regional manufacturing, scientific and technology, legal and financial hub.[8]

The first SEZs were established in July 1979 on the basis of a directive by the State Council and the Central Committee of the Chinese Communist Party. The text of the directive was made public in August 1979, in a speech by Xi Zhongxun (then First Party Secretary of Guandong Province):

> The central instructions state: Guangdong and Fujian provinces are close to Hong Kong and Macao. There are many overseas Chinese there and their resources are relatively abundant. They possess many favourable conditions for speeding up economic development. The central authorities have decided to adopt a special

---

4. *See*, Experience Gained in the Development of China's Special Economic Zones, China Development Bank, https://www.worldbank.org/content/dam/Worldbank/Event/Africa/Investing%20in%20Africa%20Forum/2015/investing-in-africa-forum-chinas-special-economic-zone.pdf (last accessed at 5 July 2018).
5. *See*, (https://www.credendo.com/country-risk/china (accessed at 7 July 2018).
6. *See*, https://www.britannica.com/topic/special-economic-zone.
7. *See*, https://en.wikipedia.org/wiki/Shenzhen (last accessed at 5 July 2018).
8. *See*, for example, http://www.hkicpa.org.hk/en/china-and-international/mainland-china-links-and-reference/greaterbayarea/ (last accessed at 5 July 2018).

> policy and flexible measures with regard to the external economic activities of these two provinces, and to give the local authorities greater initiative so that they can bring their superior conditions into play, take advantage of the present favourable international situation and go a step ahead of the others in order to promote the economy as rapidly as possible. This is an important policy decision with major significance for speeding up China's Four Modernizations.[9]

By mid-1980s, only a few years into their existence, the first SEZs accounted for more than 59% of FDI in China.[10]

Chinese SEZs vary in scope, function, operational and technical characteristics. The SEZs enjoy significant legislative autonomy in experimenting with new laws suitable for the particularities in the zones.[11]

Each SEZ has its own legislative basis that reflects the Government's vision for the economic development of particular areas. For example, the Shenzhen SEZ operates on the basis of multiple regulations that cover a number of vital aspects of SEZ's investment activities – the Regulations of the Shenzhen SEZ and Land Management,[12] Provisional Rules of the Shenzhen SEZ on the Resident Offices of Foreign Enterprises, on the Promotion of Financial Development, on the Cooperative Stock Companies, on Venture Capital, on the Encouragement of Overseas Chinese, Compatriots of Hong Kong, Macao, and Taiwan to Make Contributions to the Promotion of Education, and many others.[13]

In 2014, there were 6 SEZs in China, 14 open coastal cities, 4 pilot free trade areas, 5 financial reform pilot areas, 31 bonded areas, 114 national high-tech development parks, 164 national agriculture technology parks, 85 national eco-industrial parks, 55 national ecological civilization demonstration areas, and 283 national modern agriculture demonstration areas.[14]

Since the early 1990s, China has been the second largest foreign capital recipient in the world.[15] Of the total amount of FDI that China has received since 1989, the SEZs share has been over 90%.[16]

9. *See*, Ann Fenwick, *Evaluating China's Special Economic Zones*, 2(2) Berkley Journal of International Law (1984).
10. Madeleine Martinek, *Special Economic Zones in China and WTO: Bleak or Bright Future?* (2014).
11. *Ibid.*, at p. 47.
12. Available in English at http://english.mofcom.gov.cn/article/lawsdata/chineselaw/200211/20021100050581.shtml (last accessed at 5 July 2018).
13. Available in English at http://www.szqh.com.cn/Home/LAW_AND_REGULATIONS/ (last accessed at 5 July 2018).
14. *See*, https://www.worldbank.org/content/dam/Worldbank/Event/Africa/Investing%20in%20Africa%20Forum/2015/investing-in-africa-forum-chinas-special-economic-zone.pdf (last accessed at 5 July 2018).
15. *See*, Owen C.H. Ho, *Determinants of Foreign Direct Investment in China: A Sectoral Analysis, Economics Program*, School of Economics and Commerce, University of Western Australia. [K: Requires full reference].
16. *See*, Harry G. Broadman & Xiaolun Sun, *The Distribution of Foreign Direct Investment in China* (2002), https://onlinelibrary.wiley.com/doi/pdf/10.1111/1467-9701.00073 (last accessed at 5 July 2018).

§17.03 INVESTMENT PROTECTION IN CHINESE SEZs

Contemporary FDI is particularly vulnerable to the risks of adverse legislation, environmental regulations by the host States that might make investment less economical, and other forms of undue government interference that do not constitute outright taking or direct expropriation.[17]

These risks alter the risk profiles of foreign investment projects in the SEZs, raising the costs of foreign investment. Is this public perception of China's SEZs as high risk investment destinations justified?

The risk profiles of investing in China's SEZ would depend, to a certain extent, on whether foreign investment in SEZs benefits from international law protection that is typically available to foreign investors elsewhere in China under bilateral or multilateral investment treaties or under China's free trade agreements.

Investment protection is accorded to foreign investors on the basis of either bilateral or multilateral investment treaties between the country of origin of the investor and the host State, or under domestic legislation of the host state. Certain investment protections are at times included in investment agreements.

Investment protection typically provides for protection against expropriation, nationalization, and other forms of undue interference with the foreign investor and its investment by the host State. Investment protection mechanisms typically guarantee fair and equitable treatment of foreign investment, full protection and security, expatriation of investment returns, and a number of other substantive protections.

Investment protection mechanism allows a foreign investor to bring its dispute with the host State out of the domestic courts of the host State and before an international investment tribunal, and claim compensation for the lost investment before a neutral quasi-judicial forum.

These protections, and specifically, an ability to claim compensation before an international tribunal, significantly decrease sovereign risks and thus make foreign investment in volatile jurisdictions cheaper and more predictable.[18]

[A] Three and a Half Generations of Chinese BITs

China maintains a network of over 140 bilateral investment treaties and 23 multilateral treaties with inbuilt investment protection provisions. China is also a party to 21 investment-related instruments.[19]

China's bilateral numerous investment treaties (BITs) were negotiated at difference stages of China's economic development, and are thus reflective of China's investment patterns.

17. *See*, generally https://en.wikipedia.org/wiki/Country_risk (last accessed at 9 July 2018).
18. For example, Multilateral Investment Guarantee Agency (MIGA) takes into account the availability of Bilateral Investment Treaties or Multilateral Treaties with investment protection mechanisms when assessing the risk profile of a project that is seeking MIGA's insurance.
19. UNCTAD statistics, http://investmentpolicyhub.unctad.org/IIA/CountryIris/42#iiaInnerMenu (last accessed at 5 July 2018).

The first generation Chinese BITs was concluded in 1982–1989. At that stage of its economic development, China was predominantly a capital importing state. Its main interest in investment treaties was to attract foreign investment while shielding China as a host State from potential investment disputes. For that reason, China's first generation BITs are limited in scope. They allow investment arbitration only with respect to disputes 'concerning the amount of compensation for expropriation'. They do not guarantee fair and equitable treatment, full protection and security, or any other typical investment protections that are often found in contemporary investment treaties.

The second generation of China's BITs offer ICSID as a dispute resolution forum, but the scope of the BIT's dispute resolution provisions is still limited to disputes concerning the amount of compensation for expropriation. These BITs offer limited protection to foreign investors, for the same reason.[20]

The third generation of China's BITs (1998 – present) no longer contains 'the amount of compensation for expropriation' wording, and as such, allows for much stronger protection. This generation of Chinese treaties is reflective of the fact that China has become a 'hybrid state' – both capital-importing and capital-exporting. This means that China's treaty making practice has become more balanced as well, trying to shield China from treaty claims while also ensuring that Chinese investors overseas benefit from international law protection.

China is in the process of negotiating a treaty that is likely to open the fourth generation of China's BITs. This is China's BIT with the EU. Unfortunately, the treaty negotiations are kept strictly confidential, so predicting the content of this forthcoming mega BIT would be a guess work at this stage.[21]

[B] The First Obstacle: Do China's Treaties Apply to SEZs?

China's investment treaties remain silent on whether they apply to China's SARs – and incidentally, to China's SEZs.

The applicability of China's BITs to SARs had to be argued before an investment tribunal and later in Singapore courts, in dispute between Sanum (a Macanese investor) and Laos in 2013–2018.[22]

Laos argued that the China-Laos BIT does not extend to Macau, and that for this reason, a Macanese investor is not entitled to engage the treaty's investment protection mechanisms. The Singapore Court of Appeal, who had supervisory powers over that arbitration, ultimately decided that the treaty applies to Macao.[23]

20. *See*, J Chaisse & L Nottage, *International Investment Treaties and Arbitration Across Asia* 556 (2018).
21. Olga Boltenko, *The Rise of the RCEP: Regional Multilateralism and Its Impact on the EU-China BIT*, The Hong Kong Lawyer (2018).
22. *See*, *Sanum Investments Limited v. Lao People's Democratic Republic*, UNCITRAL, PCA Case No. 2013-13.
23. *See*, http://arbitrationblog.kluwerarbitration.com/2016/11/11/sanum-v-laos-the-singapore-court-of-appeal-affirms-tribunals-jurisdiction-under-the-prc-laos-bit-part-ii/ (last accessed at 5 July 2018).

At a press conference in October 2016, China's Foreign Ministry Spokesperson openly disagreed with the decision of the Singapore Court of Appeal. She said:

> [] as a principle, the investment agreements between the central government and foreign countries do not apply to SARs, unless otherwise decided by the central government after seeking the views of the SAR governments and consulting with the other contracting parties of the agreement.[24]

While the applicability of Chinese treaties to China's SARs had to be argued before an international tribunal, there has been no indication that the treaties might not apply to SEZs.

Indeed, China's SARs have high degree of autonomy, including by concluding their own investment treaties, while SEZ's autonomy is limited to adopting local targeted legislation that allows for investment incentives.

SEZ do not have the autonomy or the authorization of the Central Government to enter into investment treaties with foreign states. Finally, there is no doubt that SEZs are the 'territory of China' within the meaning of China's investment treaties.[25]

It is highly unlikely that China would argue – should a SEZ-related dispute arise – that SEZs are not covered by China's treaties.

[C] The Second Obstacle: Limited Scope of BITs' Dispute Resolution Provisions

Statistically, the largest importers of FDI to China are Hong Kong (USD 52.57 billion), Taiwan (USD 3.26 billion), Singapore (USD 2.81 billion), Japan (USD 1.84 billion), USA (USD 1.78 billion), R.O.K.(USD 1.75 billion), Netherlands (USD 1.36 billion), Germany (USD 1.24 billion), UK (USD 890 million), and Denmark (USD 610 million).[26]

The most pertinent treaties in this regard therefore would be China's treaties with these FDI importers.

Hong Kong

Hong Kong – China's biggest investor – maintains a close economic partnership arrangement with the Mainland (CEPA). In 2017, Hong Kong and China signed an Investment Agreement within the CEPA framework that lists the substantive investment protections that are available to Hong Kong investors in China and to Chinese investors in Hong Kong.[27]

These substantive protections include guarantees of fair and equitable treatment, full protection and security, prohibition of denial of justice, guarantees of treatment not

24. Available online at http://www.fmprc.gov.cn/mfa_eng/xwfw_665399/s2510_665401/2511_665403/t1407743.shtml (last accessed at 5 July 2018).
25. For example, the Australia-China BIT defines territory as 'Territory in relation to a Contracting Party includes the territorial sea, maritime zone or continental shelf where that Contracting Party exercises its sovereignty, sovereign rights or jurisdiction'.
26. *Ibid.*
27. Available online at http://investmentpolicyhub.unctad.org/Download/TreatyFile/5580 (last accessed at 9 July 2018).

less favourable than that accorded to domestic investors, most-favoured nation treatment, and protection against expropriation.[28]

Interestingly, the Hong Kong-China investment agreement specifically excludes protection of investors' legitimate expectations from the scope of investment protections available under the treaty:

> For greater certainty, the mere fact that one side takes or fails to take an action that may be inconsistent with an investor's expectations does not constitute a breach of this Article, regardless of whether there is loss or damage to the covered investment as a result.[29]

This exclusion significantly narrows the scope of the treaty's guarantee of fair and equitable treatment. In other words, under the CEPA Investment Agreement, investors from Hong Kong will be prevented from bringing a claim against the Government for breach of their legitimate expectations if the SEZ administration adopts adverse legislation that make the investment uneconomical, for example.

Finally, the CEPA Investment Agreement does not provide for international arbitration as means to resolve investment disputes. Instead Articles 19 and 20 of the Investment Agreement offer a range of options - from mediation to litigation in domestic courts.

China-Singapore BIT

The China-Singapore BIT was negotiated and signed in 1985. It belongs to the first generation of Chinese BITs. It does provide for certain protections against expropriation, but its dispute resolution clause is limited to 'disputes involving the amount of compensation resulting from expropriation'. Under Article 13 of the BIT, it falls onto the 'competent court of the Contracting Party accepting the investment' to determine whether expropriation has indeed taken place.[30] Needless to say, this treaty offers limited investment protections, be it in SEZs or elsewhere in China.

China-Japan BIT

The China-Japan BIT was negotiated and signed in 1988. It belongs to the second generation of Chinese BITs. It provides for ICSID as a venue for the resolution of investment disputes, but it limits the disputes that may be submitted to arbitration to disputes 'concerning the amount of compensation'.[31] Again, this treaty is somewhat limited when it comes to investment protection.

28. *Ibid.*, Chapter 2.
29. *Ibid.*, Chapter 2, Article 4.4.
30. Available at http://investmentpolicyhub.unctad.org/Download/TreatyFile/5377 (last accessed at 9 July 2018).
31. Available at http://investmentpolicyhub.unctad.org/Download/TreatyFile/747 (last accessed at 9 July 2018).

Crucial Questions

However limited investment protections under the first generation treaties, China does maintain a number of treaties that are more investor-friendly.

China's third generation of BITs contain guarantees of fair and equitable treatment, and offer international arbitration for 'any investment disputes' without limiting the treaty's jurisdiction to the 'amounts of compensation for expropriation'.

With the Belt & Road initiative, China has become an active capital exporting state. That means – in terms of China's treaty-making practice – that Chinese treaties will be more investor-friendly and responsive to China's efforts to protect its own investors overseas.

For example, China's treaties with most African states, where the Chinese capital has become increasingly present, are third generation treaties. China's treaties with Djibouti, Cote d'Ivoire, Congo, Chad, Botswana, Benin, Kenya, Namibia, Sierra Leone, Uganda, Zambia, while not yet in force, are predominantly investor-friendly.[32] They provide for a full range of substantive investment protections, including fair and equitable treatment, full protection and security, expropriation, and they allow for investment arbitration in case of disputes.

China's latest free trade agreements and multilateral treaties are equally investor-friendly. For example, the ASEAN-China Investment Agreement contains guarantees of fair and equitable treatment, full protection and security, along with protection against expropriation and access to international arbitration.[33]

For investments in Chinese SEZs under China's latest treaties, the question is whether foreign investors can bring claims against China for breach of their legitimate expectations, given the various incentives and investment assurances that the local SEZ governments give to foreigners in order to encourage investment activities.

Another important question that might affect the price of FDI in China's SEZ is whether measures such as, for example, adverse legislation, revocation of licences and concessions, and other undue government interference may constitute compensable taking under China's treaties.

Finally, for the risks and benefits analysis in the context of determining the price of investment, foreign investors will need to know whether acts of the SEZ administration may engage the international law liability of China as a State, such that they can claim compensation for the lost investment from China directly.

§17.04 LEE BACK AT ALV. KYRGYZSTAN: ARE SEZ INVESTORS PROTECTION FROM BREACH OF LEGITIMATE EXPECTATIONS?

In large majority of investment disputes, foreign investors allege breaches of expropriation provisions, as well as breaches of fair and equitable treatment standards.

32. Available at http://investmentpolicyhub.unctad.org/IIA/CountryBits/42 (last accessed at 9 July 2018).
33. Available at http://investmentpolicyhub.unctad.org/Download/TreatyFile/2596 (last accessed at 9 July 2018).

Protection Against Expropriation

The prohibition of expropriation is one of the oldest investment protection standards. It is present in most treaties.

Expropriation exists in two forms: direct expropriation, where the host State confiscates the investor's property, often with the property title being removed from the investor; and indirect expropriation, where a measure or a series of measures by the host State effectively deprives foreign investment of its benefits, without necessarily taking the property title.

The treaties' guarantees against expropriation operate to compensate foreign investors for both direct and indirect acts of expropriation, unless the expropriation is lawful. Most treaties describe lawful expropriation as the taking that is done: (i) for a public purpose, (ii) in accordance with due process of law, (iii) non-discriminatory, and (iv) accompanied by 'prompt, adequate, and effective' compensation.

Most Chinese treaties contain guarantees against both direct and indirect expropriation:

> China-Singapore BIT:
>
> '*Article 6. Expropriation*
>
> *Neither Contracting Party shall take any measure of expropriation. nationalization or other measures having effect equivalent to nationalization or expropriation against the investment of nationals or companies of the other Contracting Party unless the measures are taken for any purpose authorised by law, on a non-discriminatory basis, in accordance with its laws and against compensation which stall be effectively realisable and shall be made without unreasonable delay.*'[34]
>
> *The fair and equitable treatment standard.*

The fair and equitable treatment standard in an investment treaty operates to offer foreign investors protection from undue government interference that is not covered by protection from expropriation.[35]

Most third generation of Chinese treaties contain the fair and equitable treatment standard. The typical wording would be:

> China-Kore BIT:
>
> '*Articlc 2*
>
> *2. Each Contracting Party shall accord to investments in its territory of investors of the other Contracting Party fair and equitable treatment and full and constant protection and security.*'[36]

While the meaning of expropriation is relatively straightforward, investment treaties, including China's treaties, rarely describe the content of the fair and equitable

34. Available at http://investmentpolicyhub.unctad.org/Download/TreatyFile/5377 (last accessed at 9 July 2018).
35. R. Dolzer & C. Schreuer, *Principles of International Investment Law* 122 (Oxford University Press, 2008).
36. Available at http://investmentpolicyhub.unctad.org/Download/TreatyFile/3338 (last accessed at 7 July 2018).

treatment standard. The standard is thus open to interpretation, that is typically undertaken by a treaty tribunal on the interpretative rules of the Vienna Convention on the Law of Treaties.

The fair and equitable treatment standard has become so broadly interpreted in the last decade that – unless it is specifically limited in a treaty – it is likely to include a prohibition of denial of justice inn local courts, a prohibition of discriminatory, arbitrary acts by the State and its organs, a prohibition of inconsistent treatment, a prohibition of treatment of foreign investors that is not transparent, fair, and just, and a prohibition of treatment that frustrates the investor's legitimate expectations.[37]

Legitimate Expectations

The latest state of investment law on the government's breaches of the investors' legitimate expectations dictates that for the investor to prevail, the investor must demonstrate that his expectations were premised upon specific representations by the Government, and that those representations were the reason for the investor to decide in favour of undertaking the investment.[38]

In that regard, SEZ investments are peculiar because they are made on the basis of often generic local government's call for investments, but also often on the basis of the SEZs' local administration specific representations to foreign investors.[39]

Against the backdrop of such abundance of representations and public investment incentives, would foreign investors in China's SEZ be entitled to treaty protection if those representations turn out to be nothing but a commercial puff?

Treaty tribunals have not yet tested the SEZs' legitimate expectations resistance. However, there are cases that might inform future tribunals on how to interpret the various investment representations offered by SEZs.

Lee Jong Baekv. Kyrgyzstan

In *Lee Jong Baek v. Kyrgyzstan*, an investor from South Korea – Mr Lee Jong Baek – and his investment vehicle Central Asia FEZ Development Corporation – launched an investment claim against the Republic of Kyrgyzstan under the CIS Convention on the protection of investor's rights of 28 March 1997 (the Moscow Convention).

The dispute arose out of Mr Lee's investment in one of Kyrgyzstan SEZs – the Bishkek SEZ. The investment was made allegedly on the basis of a decree by the President of Kyrgyzstan on 9 December 1994 'On foreign investment zone in Bishkek'. Mr Lee started investing in the Bishkek SEZ in 1997, on the basis of the SEZ legislation and under other statutory investment assurances.

37. R. Dolzer & C Schreuer, *Principles of International Investment Law* 142 (Oxford University Press, 2008).
38. In *Isolux v. Spain*, the tribunal finds that an investor may derive legitimate expectations either from specific commitments addressed to it personally, or from rules that are put in place with a specific aim to induce foreign investments on which the foreign investor relied in making his investment.
39. *See*, for example, http://www.cadz.org.cn (last accessed at 9 July 2018).

His investment project began to sour in 2006 – the Bishkek administration revoked the lease agreement on which Mr Lee's investment was premised and terminated other associated investment arrangements with Mr Lee.

In treaty arbitration, Mr Lee alleged that through a series of measures, Kyrgyzstan effectively expropriated his investment, and that the expropriation was unlawful. He claimed over USD 20 million in compensation for his lost project in the Kyrgyzstan SEZ.

The tribunal constituted to hear the dispute noted that at the time the investment was made, the SEZ legislation offered significant incentive to foreign investors. From 1999 to 2001, however, the legislation changed for the worse, eventually breaching Mr Lee's legitimate expectations and making Mr Lee's investment uneconomical.[40] Specifically, the tribunal found that the SEZ's administration removal of certain land plots from Mr Lee's lease arrangements, cancellation of tax benefits and other incentives, and termination of investment arrangements with Mr Lee, constitute breaches of the Moscow Convention and are otherwise contrary to international investment law.[41]

The tribunal also found that the acts of the Bishkek SEZ administration qualify as acts of an organ of the Government under the draft ILC Articles on State Responsibility.[42] More specifically, the tribunal found that Article 4 of the draft ILC articles is customary international law, and relied on it to find that acts and omissions to act by the SEZ administration are attributable to Kyrgyzstan as a state.[43]

In essence, the Lee Jong Baek award gives hope to foreign investors in Chinese SEZ and in SEZs around the globe in that adverse regulation that changes significantly from the time the investment was made, may engage international law liability of the host State.

§17.05 CONCLUSION

China's economic miracle in the last several decades is premised to a large extent on the establishment and operation of multiple SEZs.

With that level of concentration of FDI in SEZs, the scope of international law protection afforded to foreign investors in SEZ becomes of crucial importance, in particular when it comes to investor risk analysis and the associated costs of foreign investment.

China's multiple investment protection treaties and free trade agreement afford varying levels of investment protection to foreign investors. These treaties apply to SEZs as well.

The latest investor-State case law suggests that SEZs public solicitation of foreign investment and open investor incentives may serve as basis for investors' claims against China if the foreign investment in SEZ is expropriated or if the SEZs'

40. *See, Lee Jong Baek et al v. Kyrgyzstan*, Award dated 13 November 2013, p. 11 and p. 38 (available in Russian).
41. *See, Ibid.*, at p. 37.
42. *See, Ibid.*, 38–39.
43. *See, Ibid.*, at p. 38.

administration breach the investors' legitimate expectations through adverse regulation or other measures. It is likely that the acts of SEZs' administration that negatively impact foreign investors may engage China's international law liability.

On the Lee Jong Baek authority, foreign investors are not defenceless in China's SEZs. If anything, foreign investors have easier access to international investment protection in SEZs, in particular against breaches of their legitimate expectation and indirect expropriation, because the investment incentives offered by SEZs tend to be public and specific.

In other words, while there is no risk-free investment, SEZs are no more a 'trap' than any other territory or economic unit in China.

CHAPTER 18

Free-Zone Company, Investment Standards and the Arab Spring: A Case Study of *Ampal-American and Others v. Egypt*

Prabhash Ranjan[*]

§18.01 INTRODUCTION

Countries often endeavour to develop special economic zones (SEZs) in their territories expecting that SEZs shall contribute to economic development.[1] An SEZ offers a liberalized environment for manufacturers and companies such as through tax exemptions, low tariff rules, relaxed labour standards, etc. While SEZs have been successful in some countries, they have failed in some others in making a significant contribution to economic development.[2]

Regulation of these SEZs may have implications for that country's obligations under the international economic law regime. For instance, if a state changes laws applicable to an SEZ, the foreign investors could bring claims against the state under a bilateral investment treaty (BIT). The purpose of this chapter is to study one such case that a foreign investor brought against Egypt challenging the sovereign regulatory measure of Egypt pertaining to investment made in a SEZ, which in case of Egypt are known as Free Zones.

* The author is extremely grateful to Tania Singla for her very proficient research assistance in writing this paper.

1. *See* Aggarwal, A. (2005), 'Performance of Export Processing Zones: A Comparative Analysis of India, Sri Lanka, and Bangladesh', Indian Council for Research on International Economic Relations Working Paper No. 155, http://icrier.org/pdf/wp155.pdf.
2. *See* Lotta Moberg, The Political Economy of Special Economic Zones, 11(1) Journal of Institutional Economics, 2014, 167–190.

In 1997, in order to incentivize investment, Egypt promulgated a law on investment guarantees and incentives.[3] Article 29 of this law provides for the creation of free zones in Egypt. The vision behind establishing these free zones in Egypt is to make the Egyptian free zones as business destinations to attract foreign direct investments.[4] The goals behind establishing these free zones is that boosting foreign investment inflows will help in raising Egypt's national income, generate employment opportunities, bring in new technology, etc.[5]

Article 29 of the 1997 law provides for two kinds of free zones in Egypt – public free zones and private free zones. Article 29 further provides that a public free zone shall be established by decree of the cabinet ministers based on the proposal of a competent administrative authority.[6] A private free zone can be established by a decree of a competent administrative authority.[7] Such private free zones shall be limited to a single project, if the nature of such projects so necessitates.[8]

In this chapter we study the case of *Ampal-American Israel Corporation v. Arab Republic of Egypt*.[9] This case involved a foreign investor challenging certain Egyptian regulatory measures pertaining to a company called the East Mediterranean Gas (EMG). EMG was established in 2000 and was granted a free zone company status by the Egyptian authorities under Law 8/1997 entitled '*Promulgating Law on Investment Guarantees and Incentives*'.[10] From a period of 2008 to 2012, Egypt adopted certain regulatory measures such as withdrawing the concessions that EMG enjoyed by virtue of being a free zone company under Egyptian law. These regulatory measures and other acts and omissions attributable to the state of Egypt were challenged before an investor state dispute settlement (ISDS) tribunal under the United States-Egypt BIT.[11]

To study this case, in §18.02 we examine briefly the facts of the case. In §18.03 we examine the legal issues that were raised in the case. Section §18.04 of the paper analyses the reasoning and the decision of the tribunal on the various issues that arose in the case. Section §18.05 provides the conclusion by observing how regulatory measures pertaining to SEZs can trigger claims of violation of international investment law.

3. Law 8/1997 Promulgating Law on Investment Guarantees and Incentives, http://www.egypt-law.com/Investments_law.pdf
4. General Authority for Investment and Free Zones, Investment Regimes, Free Zones, http://www.gafi.gov.eg/English/StartaBusiness/InvestmentZones/Pages/FreeZones.aspx
5. *Ibid.*
6. Article 29, Law 8/1997 http://www.egypt-law.com/Investments_law.pdf.
7. *Ibid.*
8. *Ibid.*
9. *Ampal-American Israel Corporation v. Arab Republic of Egypt*, ICSID Case No. ARB/12/11, Decision on Liability and Heads of Loss 21 February 2017.
10. Paragraph 153.
11. Treaty Between the United States of America and the Arab Republic of Egypt Concerning the Reciprocal Encouragement and Protection of Investments, Signed 11 March 1986, Entered into force, 27 June 1992 http://investmentpolicyhub.unctad.org/Download/TreatyFile/1123.

§18.02 FACTS OF THE CASE

The claimants are companies incorporated in the United States of America (USA),[12] and they own directly and indirectly EMG – an Egyptian company. The primary purpose behind creating EMG was to purchase natural gas from Egypt and to export it to Israel through a pipeline between Al-Arish in Egypt and Ashkelon in Israel.[13] As mentioned before, EMG enjoyed the status of a free-zone company and thus possessed a special status under Egyptian law.

EMG approached the Egyptian General Petroleum Corporation (EGPC) to purchase gas at source and commenced negotiations for a long-term upstream supply contract. EMG and EGPC concluded a preliminary agreement in 2000, which was subsequently confirmed by the Prime Minister of Egypt.[14] In 2001, Egypt established the State-owned Egyptian Natural Gas Holding Corporation (EGAS) to implement its gas sector policies.[15] In 2004, the Egyptian government authorized the EGPC and the EGAS to act as representatives of the Egyptian Ministry of Petroleum for the execution of a Source gas supply agreement (GSPA) and a tripartite agreement with EMG.[16] The Source GSPA and the tripartite agreement were concluded in 2005.[17]

Under law 8/1997, Egypt granted exemptions to free zone companies such as EMG from taxation on their revenue derived from commercial and industrial activities for a period of twenty years.[18] In 2005, Egypt promulgated tax Law 91/2005 which cancelled certain tax exemptions under Law 8/1997 for companies that were not subject to the free zones system and instituted a new corporate tax of 20%.[19] However, the Egyptian government through a decree in 2006 confirmed that the 91/2005 law had no effect on EMG and that EMG was authorized to operate as a free-zone company for a renewable term of one year i.e., till 2007.[20] In 2007, through another decree, the Egyptian government extended EMG's tax-free status for an additional period of eighteen years, until 18 April 2025.[21]

However, on 5 May 2008, Egypt promulgated law 114/2008, whereby it revoked the free-zone licenses of companies in certain industries including transportation of natural gas.[22] Consequently, EMG was now subjected to new taxes, including a corporate income tax of 20%, which was later increased to 25%.[23]

Based on these and other regulatory measures taken from 2008 to 2012 that had an impact on claimant's investment, the following allegations were levelled against Egypt:

12. ¶ 1, Decision on Jurisdiction.
13. ¶ 30.
14. ¶ 35.
15. ¶ 27.
16. ¶ 39.
17. ¶ 40.
18. ¶ 153.
19. Paragraph 154.
20. Paragraph 155.
21. ¶ 155.
22. ¶ 156.
23. *Ibid.*

First, the Egyptian government revoked EMG's free-zone status and its concomitant tax exemptions, leading to an increased incidence of taxation from 1% to 20% on its revenues, which had an adverse impact on claimant's investment.[24] Due to the revocation EMG was also obliged to pay customs duties and duties on equipment and machinery.[25]

Second, Egypt demanded renegotiation of the Source GSPA and forced the claimants into signing an amendment to the Source GSPA (first amendment) making significant concessions by withholding gas from EMG during the negotiations.[26] *Third*, Egypt consistently failed to meet its supply obligations under the Source GSPA, which in turn severely impacted EMG's ability to supply full contractual volumes to its customers.[27] *Fourth*, Egypt failed to provide protection and security to the EMG pipeline during attacks in the wake of the Arab Spring despite complaints by EMG regarding lack of security.[28] Over the course of fourteen months from February 2011 to April 2012, the pipeline was attacked thirteen times.[29] Additionally, Egypt failed to ensure that its authorities repaired the resulting damage within a reasonable period of time.[30] *Fifth*, EGPC/EGAS unlawfully terminated the Source GSPA citing alleged non-performance by EMG.[31] However, the claimants claimed that this termination was politically motivated.[32] The investors argued that they had suffered due to Egyptian state policy to cease gas exports to Israel due to worsening diplomatic relations.[33]

The claimants submitted that these measures destroyed their investment and therefore, constituted violations of many provisions of the US-Egypt BIT.

§18.03 LEGAL ISSUES

In wake of the allegations made by the claimants, the Tribunal identified seven legal issues for determination:[34]

I. *Attribution*: to what extent are the actions of EGPC or EGAS attributable to the State of Egypt under international law?
II. *Revocation of tax exemption to 2025*: whether the revocation of the tax exemption granted to EMG as a free-zone company until 2025 amounted to expropriation under Article III of the BIT?
III. *Revocation of tax exemption after 2025*: whether the revocation gave rise to a claim for breach of Article III i.e. the provision on expropriation beyond the expiry of the term of the licence for tax exemption in 2025?

24. Paragraph 44.
25. *Ibid.*
26. ¶¶ 49–52.
27. ¶ 54.
28. Paragraph 55.
29. ¶ 59.
30. Paragraphs 55 to 66 and para. 67 (iv).
31. ¶ 66.
32. Paragraph 65.
33. ¶ 65.
34. ¶ 70.

IV. *Execution of the first amendment*: whether the execution of the first amendment signed by EMG was forcible obtained that could be capable of giving rise to a separate treaty claim?

V. *Delivery shortfall until 2011*: whether the alleged shortfall in supply of gas from July 2009 to January 2011 breached the investor's rights under the US-Egypt BIT?

VI. *Protection of pipeline February 2011-May 2012*: whether the Respondent breached the full protection and security obligation contained in Article II(4) of the US-Egypt BIT by failing to exercise due diligence and protection of investor's investment?

VII. *Termination of the GSPA*: Whether the termination of the Source GSPA by EGPC/EGAS amounted to an expropriation of the Claimants' investment in EMG?

§18.04 ANALYSIS AND REASONING OF THE TRIBUNAL

[A] Attribution of the Acts of EGPC/EGAS to the Respondent

To demonstrate that the conduct of EGPC/EGAS was attributable to the Egyptian state, the claimants relied upon Articles 4, 5, 8 and 11 of the ILC Articles on State Responsibility.[35] The claimants argued that despite the separate legal personalities of EGPC/EGAS, these companies are the organs of the Egyptian state exercising sovereign authority.[36] Egypt disputed this position; it argued that EGPC/EGAS were not organs of the state because they possessed separate legal personality and acted like any private party to a contract.[37]

Before undertaking an analysis of the ILC Articles on State Responsibility, the tribunal made two preliminary observations.[38] *First*, the question of attribution was directly relevant only for the claim of expropriation arising from the termination of the GSPA and the resulting failure to supply the gas (Issue number 7 as identified in section II).[39] *Second*, the tribunal accepted the Egypt's submission[40] that the rules of attribution only apply to the determination of breaches of international law;[41] and that they do not apply for breaches of contractual obligations.[42]

35. Paragraph 83.
36. Paragraphs 83–117.
37. ¶¶ 118–131.
38. Paragraph 79.
39. ¶ 80.
40. Egypt had cited the following cases in support of its submission: *EDF(Services) Limited v. Romania*, ICSID Case No. ARB/05/13, Award, 8 October 2009, *Compañiá de Aguas del Aconquija S.A. and Vivendi Universal v. Argentine Republic*, ICSID Case No. ARB/97/3, Decision on Annulment, 3 July 2002, para. 96; *Impregilo S.p.A. v. Islamic Republic of Pakistan*, ICSID Case No. ARB/03/3, Decision on Jurisdiction, 22 April 2005, para. 216; *Gustav F W Hamester GmbH & Co KG v. Republic of Ghana*, ICSID Case No. ARB/07/24, Award, 18 June 2010, para. 347; *William Nagel v. Czech Republic*, SCC No. 049/2002, Final Award, 9 September 2003, para. 321; *Limited Liability Company Amto v. Ukraine*, SCC Case No. 080/2005 (ECT), Final Award, 26 March 2008, paras 110–112.
41. Paragraph 81.
42. *Ibid.*

From its subsequent analysis of the rules of attribution under international law, the tribunal found that the acts or omissions of the EGPC/EGAS with respect to the conclusion and termination of the Source GSPA were attributable to the state of Egypt.[43] The tribunal held that both EGPC and EGAS are corporate entities within the overall structure of the Egyptian ministry of petroleum.[44] According to the tribunal, the status of EGPC as a '*public authority*' under Egyptian law, controlled entirely by the Egyptian government with respect to its constitution and management was sufficient evidence to conclude that is a state organ under Article 4 of the ILC Articles.[45]

Likewise, the tribunal found similar evidence in the case of EGAS to show that it was wholly owned by the EGPC.[46] The tribunal held that both the entities acted under the direction and control of the Egyptian state, thus satisfying the standard under Article 8 of the ILC Articles.[47] The Tribunal further held that the Egyptian state had subsequently ratified the termination of the GSPA and thus acknowledged their acts as its own, which satisfied the requirements of Article 11 of the ILC Articles.[48]

Therefore, the Tribunal concluded that any acts of EGPC/EGAS constituting breach of the BIT are attributable to the Respondent under international law.

[B] Revocation of the Tax Exemption (Until 2025)

Since Egypt's taxation related regulatory measures were challenged before the ISDS tribunal, Article XI of the US-Egypt BIT became important. Article XI provides as follows:

> With respect to its tax policies, each Party should strive to accord fairness and equity in the treatment of investments of nationals or companies of the other Party. Nevertheless, all matters relating to the taxation of nationals or companies of a Party, or their investments in the territories of the other Party or a subdivision thereof shall be excluded from this Treaty, except with regard to measures covered by Article III and the specific provisions of Article V.

In other words, according to Article XI taxation measures are outside the ambit of the BIT except those taxation measures that were tantamount to an unlawful expropriation under Article III of the BIT.[49] In light of this provision, the tribunal held that taxation measures were not outside the ambit of the expropriation provision and thus it had the jurisdiction to decide whether the revocation of EMG's tax exemption was tantamount to expropriation.[50]

---

43. ¶ 135.
44. Paragraph 137.
45. ¶ 138.
46. Paragraph 139.
47. ¶ 140.
48. *Ibid.* Also *see* paras 146–147.
49. ¶ 151.
50. *Ibid.* Also *see* para. 152. On the issue of jurisdiction of the ISDS tribunal also *see Ampal-American Israel Corp v. Arab Republic of Egypt*, ICSID Case No. ARB/12/11, Decision on Jurisdiction, 1 February 2016.

The tribunal dealt with this issue in the following sequence. It first discussed whether the tax licenses were an investment within the BIT and second whether the revocation of the tax licenses amounted to expropriation.

B.1 The License as an 'Investment' under the BIT: Before investigating the claims of expropriation, the tribunal analysed whether the claimants' tax licenses were an 'investment' under Article 1(c) of the US-Egypt BIT.[51] Article 1(c) of the US-Egypt BIT provides that 'investment' means every kind of asset owned or controlled that includes licenses and permits issued pursuant to law.[52] The tribunal held that by virtue of law 8/1997 and other decrees, the Egyptian government conferred on EMG 'a right to the benefits of a free zone company'.[53] The tribunal further held that this right was vested in EMG 'in virtue of the license' the Egyptian government granted it.[54] The tribunal held that since the treaty defined investment to mean 'every kind of asset', and that since the licenses that were granted to EMG were issued pursuant to law; these licenses were protected investments under the BIT.[55]

B.2 The Revocation of the License as Expropriation: Next, the tribunal dealt with whether the revocation of the licenses amounted to expropriation. The foreign investors submitted that since the license was a protected investment in and of itself, the act of revocation constituted a direct and total taking by Egypt.[56] The Tribunal agreed with the claimants.[57] The tribunal found that Egypt i.e., the host state had taken away a '***defined*** *and* ***valuable*** *interest that had been* ***validly conferred*** *according to Egyptian law*' at the time of making the investment and had been '*guaranteed by the State for a* ***defined*** *period*' (emphasis supplied).[58] Further, the tribunal found that the tax-free status of EMG was an integral component of the economic structure of the investor's investment.[59] The host state, Egypt, had accepted and had confirmed by the issuance of the specific licenses to EMG allowing it to operate as a free-zone company until 2025.[60]

The Tribunal agreed with Egypt that the law revoking the licenses was enacted for a *bonafide* public purpose.[61] The tribunal also agreed that the law revoking the license did not specifically discriminate against EMG.[62] However, the tribunal, referring to Article III (1) of the US-Egypt BIT held that an investment is protected from

51. Paragraphs 160–174.
52. *See* Article 1(c) (v) of US-Egypt BIT.
53. Paragraph 172.
54. *Ibid.*
55. Paragraphs 172–174. The Tribunal cited the following decision in support of its conclusion: *Middle East Cement Shipping and Handling Co. S.A. v. Arab Republic of Egypt*, ICSID Case No. ARB/99/6, where the tribunal held that a free zone license granted by Egypt to Middle East Cement was a '[concession] conferred by law' and therefore met the definition of investment in Article 1 of the Egypt-Greece BIT. Award, 12 April 2002, paras 100–101.
56. Paragraph 179.
57. The Tribunal cited *Gami Investment Inc. v. The Government of the United Mexican States* (UNCITRAL, Final Award, 15 November 2004, paras 126–127) as an authority to support its position.
58. ¶ 183.
59. Paragraph 182.
60. *Ibid.*
61. Paragraph 184.
62. *Ibid.*

expropriation unless 'prompt and adequate compensation' is paid.[63] Further, the tribunal, referring to Article III (1) held that such compensation 'shall be equivalent to the fair market value of the expropriated investment on the date of expropriation'.[64] Thus, the tribunal held that Egypt was under an international obligation to pay compensation for having expropriated foreign investment.[65] The tribunal held that it had the power to calculate the compensation to be paid in the event of the host state failing to make the payment.[66]

Therefore, the Tribunal concluded that the revocation of the license was tantamount to an expropriation under Article III of the BIT.

After this finding, surprisingly, the tribunal said that it was not required to 'find that the expropriation in question was unlawful, as may be the case in the event that the taking was not done for a public purpose or was discriminatory'.[67] It is not clear what the tribunal meant here. If the tribunal meant that an expropriation can be unlawful only if it is not done for a public purpose or if it is discriminatory, then this finding is not consistent with Article III (1) of the US-Egypt BIT. Article III (1) provides that expropriation is permitted i.e., it is lawful if the host state follows certain conditions such as done for public purpose; is non-discriminatory; is accomplished under due process of law; does not violate any specific contractual engagement; and is accompanied by prompt and adequate compensation. In other words, failure to meet any of these conditions, including payment of prompt and adequate compensation, shall make the expropriation unlawful. Thus, failure to pay compensation for an expropriation even if it is done for public purpose and is non-discriminatory can still be unlawful.

[C] Revocation of the Tax Exemption (Post 2025)

The claimants also argued that EMG would have retained its free-zone status post the expiry of the license in 2025 and was thus entitled to claim damages on the basis of that legitimate expectation.[68] However, the tribunal rejected this claim summarily as entirely speculative and therefore, it stated that the damages owed by Egypt would only be calculated up to 2025 and not beyond.[69]

[D] Alleged Coercion in the Execution of the First Amendment

The claimants alleged that Egyptian authorities forced them into renegotiating and signing the first amendment to the Source GSPA, and that this coercion amounted to a breach of the FET, full protection and security standards, the umbrella clause and

63. Paragraph 185.
64. *Ibid.*
65. Paragraph 186.
66. *Ibid.*
67. *Ibid.*
68. Paragraphs 188, 190.
69. ¶¶ 192–193.

constituted an element of creeping expropriation.[70] However, the tribunal found that the claimants had failed to discharge their burden of proof to demonstrate coercion.[71] Further, the tribunal, after carefully evaluating all the records and documents, found contrary evidence suggesting that the claimants were open and responsive to the amendments.[72] In assessing coercion, the tribunal also analysed whether the amendments had adversely affected the claimants.[73] The tribunal concluded that the amendments had no such adverse effect on the claimant's investment.[74] Therefore, the tribunal dismissed this claim.

[E] Delivery Shortfall until 2011 (Between July 2009–January 2011)

The claimants alleged that in the period between the conclusion of the first amendment and the attacks on the pipeline, EGPC/EGAS failed to meet their supply obligations under the GSPA, which led to lost profits.[75] However, the tribunal was not persuaded that the alleged delivery failures gave rise to an international delict that would involve a breach of the Respondent's obligations under the BIT, including the commitments under the umbrella clause.[76] The Tribunal further noted that alleged delays by the EGPC/EGAS were anticipated in the GSPA itself, as amended by the first amendment.[77] It also observed that the GSPA provided for its own contractual procedure for compensation, which had already been considered in detail by the ICC Tribunal that decided the contractual dispute under the GSPA.[78]

Therefore, the Tribunal dismissed this claim.

[F] Protection of the Pipeline (Between February 2011–May 2012)

A major charge levelled against the state of Egypt by the foreign investors was that it failed to provide full protection and security to their investment. In the period between February 2011 and May 2012, in the wake of Arab Spring Revolution, EMG's gas pipeline was attacked thirteen times.[79] According to the claimants, the host state i.e., Egypt failed to take reasonable preventive and remedial measures to safeguard the gas pipeline from the attacks caused by third parties and hence, breached the full protection and security obligation under the US-Egypt BIT.[80]

70. ¶ 194.
71. ¶ 196.
72. ¶ 210.
73. *See* paras 207, 211.
74. ¶ 207, ¶ 211.
75. ¶ 226.
76. ¶¶ 228–229.
77. ¶ 231.
78. ¶¶ 231–232.
79. ¶ 237.
80. ¶¶ 235–236.

Egypt did not deny that the gas pipeline was indeed attacked thirteen times.[81] However, Egypt submitted that these events were a series of force majeure events.[82]

To deal with this issue, the tribunal first determined the applicable treaty standard to judge the alleged violation of the full protection and security obligation.

F.1 The Applicable Standard: The tribunal referred to Article II(4) of the US-Egypt BIT, which provides as follows: '*[t]he treatment, protection and security of investments shall never be less than that required by international law and national legislation*'.[83] In interpreting this provision, the tribunal held that Article II(4) did not impose a standard of strict liability on the host state.[84] Instead, according to the tribunal, under Article II (4) the state is '*obliged to exert due diligence in order to protect a claimant's investment – a standard that must be assessed according to the particular circumstances in which the damage occurs*'.[85]

The Tribunal also stated the operation of the standard does not depend on whether the acts have been committed by agents of the State or by third parties.[86] Instead, according to the tribunal, the focus is 'on the acts or omissions of the State in addressing the unrest that gives rise to the damage'.[87]

F.2 Res Judicata *Effect of the ICC Award*: After establishing the treaty standard applicable in the present case to determine whether the state breached the protection and security obligation, the tribunal said that it would next deal with the extent to which the ICC award in respect of attacks on the pipeline are *res judicata* between the parties to the current dispute.[88] While the current claim arose out of the BIT signed between US and Egypt, an ICC tribunal had already dealt with a contractual dispute between the parties under the GSPA.

Thus, the tribunal considered the effect of the ICC Award that had already given detailed consideration to issues of fact surrounding the nature of the terrorist attacks and the response of Egypt.[89] According to the tribunal, where an arbitral tribunal exercising jurisdiction over contractual disputes had decided the issue between the parties, the investment treaty tribunal was '*entitled to refer to and rely upon the findings of the contract tribunal provided that it finds the resulting award to be binding*

81. Paragraph 237.
82. *Ibid.*
83. Paragraph 240.
84. Paragraph 241.
85. *Ibid.* The Tribunal cited the following awards in support of its position: *Case Concerning Elettronica Sicula S.p.A. (ELSI) (United States of America v. Italy)* ICJ Rep. 15, Judgment, 20 July 1989, para. 108; *Asian Agricultural Products Limited v. Democratic Socialist Republic of Sri Lanka*, ICSID Case No. ARB/87/3, Award, 27 June 1990; *Tecnicas Medioambientales, Tecmed S.A. v. United Mexican States*, ICSID Case No. ARB(AF)/00/2, Award, 29 May 2003, para. 177; *Saluka Investments BV (The Netherlands) v. Czech Republic*, 15 ICSID Rep. 274, Partial Award, UNCITRAL, 2006, para. 484; *Pantechniki S.A. Contractors & Engineers v. Republic of Albania*, ICSID Case No. ARB/07/21, Award, 30 July 2009, para. 77.
86. ¶ 245. The Tribunal cited the following awards in support of its position: *American Manufacturing and Trading Inc v. Republic of Zaire*, ICSID Case No. ARB/93/1, Award, 21 February 1997; *Wena Hotels Limited v. Arab Republic of Egypt*, ICSID Case No. ARB/98/4, Award, 8 December 2000, upheld on annulment, 6 ICSID Rep 129, 114 fn 198.
87. Paragraph 246.
88. Paragraph 247.
89. ¶¶ 254–256.

upon the parties'.[90] The Tribunal further stated that the *res judicata* effect of the ICC Award bound not only the companies that were parties to the dispute but also to their shareholders.[91] Therefore, the tribunal concluded that the findings of the ICC tribunal that were relevant to the claim had a *res judicata* effect between the parties to the BIT proceedings.[92]

F.3 The Breach of the Full Protection and Security Obligation: After examining the issues related to *res judicata* effect of the ICC Award, the tribunal went on to examine whether Egypt acted diligently in preventing attacks on the gas pipeline.[93]At the outset, tribunal acknowledged Egypt's difficult position in the background of the Arab Spring Revolution.[94] Thus, the tribunal held that Egypt could not have prevented the first attack on 5 February 2011.[95] Thus, according to the tribunal, the first attack could not have amounted to a breach of the full protection and security standard in and of itself.[96] However, in order to determine whether Egypt breached the treaty standard, the tribunal considered the thirteen attacks as a whole.[97] On the basis of available evidence, the tribunal found that the first four attacks on the gas pipeline were sufficient to warn Egypt, who was then under an obligation to take reasonable steps to prevent further attacks on the gas pipeline[98] Therefore, the tribunal found that from the fifth to the thirteenth attack, Egyptian authorities had failed to exercise due diligence for ensuring full protection and security of the claimants' investment.[99]

[G] Termination of the GSPA

The tribunal first reiterated that the question of validity of the termination of the GSPA was an incidental question in its determination of whether the Respondent had breached the substantive obligations under the BIT.[100] In its analysis, the tribunal relied upon the findings of the ICC Tribunal, which had held that the termination of the GSPA by EGAS on 18 April 2012 was unlawful.[101] The tribunal reaffirmed the conclusion of the ICC Tribunal and proceeded to discuss whether the termination of the GSPA was tantamount to expropriation.

As a preliminary point, the tribunal found that the contractual rights conferred by the GSPA constituted a protected investment under the definition of 'investment'

90. ¶ 259. The Tribunal cited *Malicorp Limited v. Arab Republic of Egypt*, ICSID Case No. ARB/08/18, Decision on Annulment, 3 July 2013, paras 156–160, in support of its position.
91. ¶ 260–261. The Tribunal relied on *RSM Production and Others v. Grenada*, ICSID Case No. ARB/10/6, Award, 10 December 2010 and *Apotex Holdings Inc. v. United States of America*, ICSID Case No. ARB(AF)/12/1, Award, 25 August 2014 to support its position.
92. ¶ 270.
93. Paragraph 283.
94. Paragraph 284.
95. Paragraph 285.
96. ¶¶ 284–286.
97. Paragraph 286.
98. Paragraphs 288–290.
99. ¶ 290.
100. ¶ 292.
101. ¶ 329.

within the BIT.[102] The Tribunal further stated that the unlawful termination of the GSPA by the EGPC (attributable to Egypt) was tantamount to expropriation of the Claimants' investment. Since the expropriation was not in accordance with Article III of the BIT – public purpose, non-discrimination, due process and compensation – the Tribunal concluded that the Respondent had disproportionately and unlawfully expropriated the property rights in the GSPA through the unlawful termination of the GSPA.[103]

§18.05 CONCLUSION

The tribunal unanimously decided that Egypt had breached Article III (1) i.e., on expropriation; Article II (4) i.e., on providing protection and security and that the actions of EGPC and EGAS were attributable to the state of Egypt.

From the point of view of linkages between regulatory measures pertaining to SEZs and state's international economic law obligations under a BIT are concerned, this case study shows a direct link between the two. Revoking licenses or amending the terms at which licenses may be granted or changing the status of companies operating under an SEZ or a free zone, as they exist in Egypt, could trigger BIT claims against the state. While the issue of providing protection and security may not be relevant only to companies or foreign investments that may operate in a free zone, Egypt should have been careful in adopting taxation related regulatory measures that affected the working of a company that legally enjoyed the status of free zone. This case study shows that if countries wish to avoid liability under international economic law (in this case a BIT), then they need to carefully adopt and amend their regulations relating to a SEZ keeping in mind their international economic law obligations.

102. ¶ 339.
103. ¶ 342, ¶ 344.

Index

1. Emmanuel T. Laryea, *Paperless Trade: Opportunities, Challenges and Solutions,* 2002 (ISBN 90-411-9897-0).
2. Xiang Gao, *The Fraud Rule in the Law of Letters of Credit: A Comparative Study,* 2002 (ISBN 90-411-9898-9).
3. Yuwa Wei, *Comparative Corporate Governance: A Chinese Perspective,* 2003 (ISBN 90-411-9908-X).
4. Ross P. Buckley (ed.), *The WTO and the Doha Round: The Changing Face of World Trade,* 2003 (ISBN 90-411-9947-0).
5. Bradley J. Condon, Joyce C. Sadka & Tapen Sinha (eds), *Insurance Regulation in North America: Integrating American, Canadian and Mexican Markets,* 2003 (ISBN 90-411-2301-6).
6. Jan Hoogmartens, *EC Trade Law Following China's Accession to the WTO,* 2004 (ISBN 90-411-2301-6).
7. Yang Guohua, Bryan Mercurio & Li Yongjie, *WTO Dispute Settlement Understanding: A Detailed Interpretation,* 2005 (ISBN 90-411-2361-X).
8. Jan Job de Vries Robbé, Paul U. Ali, *Securitisation of Derivatives and Alternative Asset Classes, Yearbook,* 2005 (ISBN 90-411-2375-X).
9. Markus W. Gehring, Marie-Claire Cordonier Segger, *Sustainable Development in World Trade Law,* 2005 (ISBN 90-411-2366-0).
10. Yann Aubin & Arnaud Idiart, *Export Control Law and Regulations Handbook: A Practical Guide to Military and Dual-Use Goods Trade Restrictions and Compliance,* 2007 (ISBN 90-411-2601-5).
11. Henry Kibet Mutai, *Compliance with International Trade Obligations: The Common Market for Eastern and Southern Africa,* 2007 (ISBN 978-90-411- 2664-1).
12. Yong-Shik Lee, *Economic Development through World Trade: A Developing World Perspective,* 2007 (ISBN 978-90-411-2681-8).
13. Yanning Yu, *Circumvention and Anti-Circumvention Measures: The Impact on Anti-Dumping Practice in International Trade,* 2007 (ISBN 978-90-411- 2686-3).
14. Ross Buckley, Vai Io Lo & Laurence Boulle, *Challenges to Multilateral Trade: The Impact of Bilateral, Preferential and Regional Agreements,* 2008 (ISBN 978-90-411-2711-2).
15. K.D. Raju, *World Trade Organization Agreement on Anti-dumping: A GATT/ WTO and Indian Jurisprudence,* 2008 (ISBN 978-90-411-2780-8).
16. Xiaochen Wu, *Anti-dumping Law and Practice in China,* 2008 (ISBN 978-90-411-2790-7).
17. Amin Alavi, *Legalization of Development in the WTO: Between Law and Politics,* 2008 (ISBN 978-90-411-2795-2).
18. Henrik Andersen, *EU Dumping Determinations and WTO Law,* 2009 (ISBN 978-90-411-2827-0).

19. Sherzod Shadikhodjaev, *Retaliation in the WTO Dispute Settlement System,* 2009 (ISBN 978-90-411-2811-9).
20. Yi Shin Tang, *The International Trade Policy for Technology Transfers: Legal and Economic Dilemmas on Multilateralism versus Bilateralism,* 2009 (ISBN 978-90-411-2825-6).
21. Reem Anwar Ahmed Raslan, *Antidumping: A Developing Country Perspective,* 2009 (ISBN 978-90-411-3128-7).
22. Pietro Poretti, *The Regulation of Subsidies within the General Agreement on Trade in Services of the WTO: Problems and Prospects,* 2009 (ISBN 978-90- 411-3162-1).
23. Esther Lam, *China and the WTO: A Long March towards the Rule of Law,* 2009 (ISBN 978-90-411-3144-7).
24. Jorge Alberto Huerta-Goldman, *Mexico in the WTO and NAFTA: Litigating International Trade Disputes,* 2009 (ISBN 978-90-411-3169-0).
25. Laurence Boulle, *The Law of Globalization: An Introduction,* 2009 (ISBN 978-90-411-2828-7).
26. Daniel Lovric, *Deference to the Legislature in WTO Challenges to Legislation,* 2010 (ISBN 978-90-411-3145-4).
27. Gregory W. Bowman, Nick Covelli, David A. Gantz & Ihn Ho Uhm, *Trade Remedies in North America,* 2010 (ISBN 978-90-411-2840-9).
28. Madalina Diaconu, *International Trade in Gambling Services,* 2010 (ISBN 978-90-411-3248-2).
29. Mohamed Ramadan Hassanien, *United States Bilateral Free Trade Agreements: Consistencies or Conflicts with Norms in the Middle East?,* 2010 (ISBN 978-90-411-3281-9).
30. Marie-Claire Cordonier Segger, Markus W Gehring & Andrew Newcombe, *Sustainable Development in World Investment Law,* 2011 (ISBN 978-90- 411-3166-9).
31. Nellie Munin, *Legal Guide to GATS,* 2010 (ISBN 978-90-411-2824-9).
32. Thomas G. Kelch, *Globalization and Animal Law: Comparative Law, International Law and International Trade,* 2011 (ISBN 978-90-411-3338-0).
33. Yann Aubin & Arnaud Idiart (eds), *Export Control Law and Regulations Handbook: A Practical Guide to Military and Dual-Use Goods Trade Restrictions and Compliance*, Third Edition, 2016 (ISBN 978-90-411-5443-9).
34. Yulia Selivanova (ed.), *Regulation of Energy in International Trade Law: WTO, NAFTA and Energy Charter,* 2011 (ISBN 978-90-411-3264-2).
35. Germano Franceschin & Francesco Misuraca, *India: Commercial Law, Customs and Taxation,* 2011 (ISBN 978-90-411-2836-2).
36. Humberto Zúñiga Schroder, *Harmonization, Equivalence and Mutual Recognition of Standards in WTO Law,* 2011 (ISBN 978-90-411-3657-2).

37. Kati Kulovesi, *The WTO Dispute Settlement System: Challenges of the Environment, Legitimacy and Fragmentation*, 2011 (ISBN 978-90-411- 3406-6).
38. Martín Molinuevo, *Protecting Investment in Services: Investor-State Arbitration versus WTO Dispute Settlement*, 2012 (ISBN 978-90-411-3827-9).
39. Joachim Åhman, *Trade, Health, and the Burden of Proof in WTO Law*, 2012 (ISBN 978-90-411-3825-5).
40. Umair Hafeez Ghori, *Global Textiles and Clothing Trade: Trade Policy Perspectives*, 2012 (ISBN 978-90-411-3875-0).
41. Yenkong Ngangjoh Hodu, *Theories and Practices of Compliance with WTO Law*, 2012 (ISBN 978-90-411-3228-4).
42. Dan Wei & Fernando M. Furlan, *Brazil in World Trade: Contingent Protection Measures*, 2012 (ISBN 978-90-411-3335-9).
43. Jorge A. Huerta-Goldman, Antoine Romanetti & Franz X. Stirnimann (eds), *WTO Litigation, Investment Arbitration, and Commercial Arbitration*, 2013 (ISBN 978-90-411-4686-1).
44. Gilles Muller, *Liberalization of Trade in Legal Services*, 2013 (ISBN 978-90-411-4853-7).
45. Christian Struck, *Product Regulations and Standards in WTO Law*, 2014 (ISBN 978-90-411-4950-3).
46. Gonzalo Villalta Puig, *Economic Relations between Australia and the European Union: Law and Policy*, 2014 (ISBN 978-90-411-3405-9).
47. Maurizio Gambardella, Davide Rovetta & Simon van Cutsem, *Remission and Repayment of Customs Duties in the EU*, 2014 (ISBN 978-90-411-4764-6).
48. Lisa Spagnolo, *CISG Exclusion and Legal Efficiency*, 2014 (ISBN 978-90-411-5407-1).
49. Dennis Ndonga, *Single Windows and Trade Facilitation: A Tool for Development*, 2015 (ISBN 978-90-411-5834-5).
50. Malebakeng Agnes Forere, *The Relationship of WTO Law and Regional Trade Agreements in Dispute Settlement: From Fragmentation to Coherence*, 2015 (ISBN 978-90-411-6274-8).
51. Julien Chaisse & Jiaxiang Hu (eds), *International Economic Law and the Challenges of the Free Zones*, 2019 (ISBN 978-94-035-0893-1).

www.ingramcontent.com/pod-product-compliance
Ingram Content Group UK Ltd.
Pitfield, Milton Keynes, MK11 3LW, UK
UKHW020231290920
15470UKWH00002B/484

9 789403 508931